gift of Mary Barnes, 1965

THE CHRISTIAN CENTURIES

A New History of the
Catholic Church

THE CHRISTIAN CENTURIES

A New History of the Catholic Church

EDITORIAL COMMITTEE

LOUIS J. ROGIER (Chairman)
Professor of Modern History in the University of Nijmegen

ROGER AUBERT
Professor of Ecclesiastical History in the University of Louvain

M. DAVID KNOWLES
lately Regius Professor of History in the University of Cambridge

A. G. WEILER (Secretary)
Department of Medieval History in the University of Nijmegen

Consultant for the Western Hemisphere
JOHN TRACY ELLIS
Professor of Ecclesiastical History in the Catholic
University of America, Washington, D.C.

THE CHRISTIAN CENTURIES

Volume One

THE FIRST
SIX HUNDRED YEARS

by

JEAN DANIÉLOU and HENRI MARROU

Translated by

VINCENT CRONIN

with illustrations

selected and annotated by

PETER LUDLOW

DARTON, LONGMAN AND TODD

LONDON

DARTON, LONGMAN & TODD LTD
64 Chiswick High Road
London W 4

First edition 1964
©
Verlagsanstalt Benziger & Co. A. G., Einsiedeln
Uitgeverij Paul Brand N. V., Hilversum
Darton, Longman & Todd Ltd., London
McGraw-Hill Inc., New York
Les Éditions du Seuil S. A., Paris
1964

Text and illustrations printed in Belgium by Desclée & Cie, Tourn ai
Bound in Great Britain by W. & J. Mackay
& Co. Ltd, Chatham

GENERAL INTRODUCTION

The series of volumes, of which this is the first, will endeavour to present the history of the Church in a form, and on a scale, suited to the needs of the interested reader of to-day. There exist in several languages, though not in English, excellent multi-volumed church histories, of which the French series, still familiarly known as ' Fliche et Martin ', is the latest and in many ways the best. There exist also many short histories of the text-book family. The present enterprise aims at providing an account which will survey without undue compression the whole course of church history without exceeding either in length or in price the capacity of the general reader. It does not aim at becoming a universal text-book for examinations, nor at being a work of reference in which all notable names and significant dates may be found. It hopes rather to show the achievements, the developments, the crises of Christianity, to mark the character of the different epochs, and to display the riches of Christian life and culture — the art, the literature, the theology, the thought, the spirituality and the institutions — as fully, if not more fully, than the events and personages of external, political history. It is an international history, written by scholars of six countries, Belgium, England, Holland, France, Germany and Russia, drawn from the universities of Cambridge, Louvain, Munich, Nijmegen, Oxford and Paris, and it will at first be published in four languages, Dutch, English, French and German, both in Europe and in the United States of America, and to that extent the diversity of background and outlook will reflect the diversity of Christendom, while the fundamental agreement will mark the unity of the Catholic faith.

Historians of the Church labour under difficulties peculiar to their field of work. In the first place, they lack a manageable central theme such as is available for historians of a nation, an empire or a culture. Christendom was at first a group of cells, which soon grew into a group of organized churches differing from one another in language, liturgy, institutions and fortunes, and when Christendom at last became co-extensive with the known world its history lacked any central or overriding theme or purpose that could subsume all the manifold trends and varieties of Christian life. The succession of Roman pontiffs, which some writers of the past have taken as the backbone of their work, is even less helpful than the succession of Roman emperors or English kings. Not till half the course of the Church's history is accomplished does the Apostolic See stand out clearly as the effective head and centre of the Church's administrative life, and even after that date the Eastern church, though not acknowledging Roman supremacy, was regarded in the West as a part of the Church, schismatic but not formally heretical, which might well be reunited and which was in fact, so far as words went, twice received back into communion. Moreover, throughout its history the papal see has suffered from short pontificates—the average length over the whole series is a little over eight years—and while the number of able or eminent popes is large, the great changes of thought and sentiment and the shifts in the balance of European religious life have rarely taken place in the Curia. All to seek as we are for a central theme, a backbone to our story, it is in fact impossible, on whatever scale we choose, to write a history of the universal Church in all periods and do justice to all its component parts.

A similar difficulty meets us when we come to define or delimit our task. What do we mean by the Church? For five or six centuries we may agree that there was a single recognizable body of orthodox Christianity, with a shifting penumbra of ' heretical ' bodies. Then for five hundred years more there were eastern and western churches in uneasy double harness, and even after the eleventh century it is possible to treat the history of the Orthodox Church as running parallel to that of Roman Catholicism, as indeed we have tried to do in these volumes. But when once the sixteenth century is reached the dykes burst at every point. To write within a single frame the history of all, or even of the chief, bodies calling themselves Christian, or even to find any common factor or characteristic in their story, would be utterly impossible. From the days of Luther onwards we have regretfully confined our attention to the Roman and Orthodox Churches — regretfully, because as Christians we recognize our brotherhood with those who share our inheritance by baptism and a part, at least, of our creed by their faith, while as historians we realize that the Roman Church and the Reformed Churches have deeply influenced each other's character both positively and negatively, by mutual attractions and repulsions.

Finally, what limits in breadth are we to put to our history? If, as theologians hold, all the rational acts of a Christian may enter into his service of God, and if, as Lord Acton held, all history is religious history, where in politics, in culture or in social life are we to draw the line where church history ceases? We can but do as best we may to keep within reasonable limits, taking perhaps as our touchstone the word church rather than the word religion.

It is often said that for any committed Christian, and in particular for a Roman Catholic, the writing of history presents acute difficulties beyond those that face all historians in their endeavour to attain to truth. It is said that our subscription to a belief, whether in the divinity of Christ, or the truth of the gospels or the divine mission of the Church, commits us beforehand to a particular interpretation of history, and to a particular, authoritative interpretation of many historical happenings. This criticism has a certain validity. A Catholic historian may certainly in practice find himself, like Sigor the Aristotelian in Dante, marketing unpalatable truths, and in the past many have found this a painful experience. Until very recent times the methods and resources of critical history did not exist, and theologians and those concerned with the protection of the faith tended to regard candid criticism as potential heresy. Historians, for their part, unable to dispose of compelling evidence, often drew upon their opinions, their guesses, their prejudices or their party spirit to help themselves out. Now, however, far more frequently than before, the critical resources of an historian enable him to attain certainty in many areas and, if he is honest, to distinguish between those spheres in which he commands cogent evidence and certain conclusions, and those where he cannot do so. History, in consequence, in the last half-century has come to be recognized as autonomous in its own sphere and under certain conditions, and it is agreed that Catholic historians have the same basic rights as others. They may, and must, follow the evidence wherever it may lead. As believers they know that truth is one and that the truth in this discipline or that cannot contradict the truth on a higher level. Indeed, within the past century history, together with archaeology, anthropology, philology and other disciplines, has gradually won for itself an autonomy in its own sphere similar to that secured by philosophy in the thirteenth century and by astronomy and other sciences, not without dust and toil, in the eighteenth and nineteenth. History cannot be the mistress or judge of theology, but it may on occasion warn or assist theologians just as these in their turn may precede or confirm historical discovery. Just as anthropology and philology have in recent years antiquated some venerable opinions of biblical commentators and pointed the way to a more genial and elastic definition of biblical inspiration, so the established findings of historians may be taken into account by theologians attempting (for example) to give precision to the definition of papal infallibility.

In the last resort a proper appreciation of historical truth and above all of truth in ecclesiastical history depends as much upon the ear of the hearer as upon the word of the speaker. The hearer, or the reader, must constantly keep himself aware of the historical process. Christians of to-day, and perhaps Catholics more than others, must be distrustful of a closed mind. They must be prepared to find that matters on which neither they nor their instructors have ever had a doubt remained unsettled for a thousand years of the Church's life, and were doubted or even denied by popes. An example is the doctrine that holy orders imparted by schismatics, simoniacs and heretics are valid *positis ponendis*. They must accept the fact that even the most primitive ordinances, such as the eucharistic fast, have been changed and that the most central sacramental discipline, that on the frequency of Holy Communion, has varied from century to century and from place to place, and the most sacred laws, such as that prohibiting divorce, were interpreted differently for centuries by East and West without explicit condemnation from Rome. They must be prepared to find that exercises of lay intervention and control condemned in modern times and regarded by Catholics to-day as characteristic of revolt from the papacy were for centuries taken for granted without resistance by popes and saints. Examples may be seen in the so-called Caesaro-papism of Justinian and the control of all religious interests by Charlemagne.

A still more difficult exercise, perhaps, is the abandonment of what may be considered as an ' evolutionary ' or ' providential ' interpretation of church history : the attitude of mind, that is, that regards the past centuries as seeing a gradual progress from a rudimentary and imperfect understanding of dogma to a supposedly developed and ameliorated present. Slightly altered, this becomes an attitude that regards all past history as a providential and beneficent disposition in which everything has happened for the best. No doubt it is true that the unfolding scroll of history displays the pageant of life as God has seen it from all eternity, and that when all temporal actions are seen in the light of eternity all manner of things, in Dame Julian's phrase, will be well. But this is not to say that every event as it happens should be accepted by the Christian as the best possible in its visible effects for all men. The Black Death, the assassination of Abraham Lincoln, or the outbreak of war in 1914 will, when seen *sub specie aeternitatis*, be seen as occurring by the permission of God as incidents in the divine governance of the world and reflecting in this way or that the divine wisdom and love, but to the spectator and to the historian the spectacle of the maimed, the diseased, the suffering and the dead in a great war, the loss by the world of its noblest leader or its finest citizens, are all visible ills that can become boons only by a meta-historical judgment. So the historian, marking the consummation of the schism between East and West and the fragmentation of Christendom in the sixteenth century, can but note the events and their consequences, immediate and remote. He must not say, or think, that these happenings are in any historical sense predetermined or beneficial simply because they happened. It is not even for him to declare that these events as such were necessary for the development of the Church, but tragical for those outside its fold. He must remember that, humanly speaking, things might well have fallen out otherwise. The papacy might have established its paramount rights of teaching and ruling without the harshness, the occasional extravagance and the violence of the contest of empire and papacy or the establishment of the Inquisition. He may rightly point out that if the Orthodox Church lost its flexibility of spirit and the Reformed Churches the strength of dogmatic authority through the severance of the links with Rome, the Western Church for its part lost for long much of the depth and richness of the Greek patristic theology and spirituality, and that Catholicism in modern times is the poorer for the loss over many centuries of the peculiar genius and the national characteristics of the northern and Germanic peoples.

The historian is not and must not be an apologist or a controversialist. His service to the Church as a private person is of a different kind. In so far as he is successful in presenting historical truth, he will inevitably strip the image of the Church of all that is accidental and sordid and display the character of Christianity as it has been and as it is, in its essential beauty and nobility. It is a noteworthy and encouraging fact that during the past century critical historians of every persuasion have come ever nearer to agreement in their presentation and judgment of many of the epochs of church history that previously had divided their schools. The sub-apostolic Church, the Constantinian settlement, the achievements of Gregory the Great and of St Boniface, the contest between empire and papacy, the reign of Henry VIII in England, the history of Jansenism in France are some of the topics on which a striking degree of unanimity of judgment has been reached among scholars of every nation and confession. It is a step, if only a step which surmounts an obstacle, towards the deeper union of faith for which every historian of the Church must pray.

Peterhouse,   M. D. KNOWLES
Cambridge,
June 1963.

CONTENTS

PART ONE

THE ORIGINS TO THE END OF THE THIRD CENTURY
by Jean Daniélou, S. J.

PART TWO

THE GREAT PERSECUTION TO THE EMERGENCE OF MEDIEVAL CHRISTIANITY

by Henri Marrou

I : THE FOURTH CENTURY

II : The Fifth and Sixth Centuries

A. *The Countries of the East*

xvi

LIST OF MAPS

PART ONE

PART TWO

A NOTE ON THE ILLUSTRATIONS

The plates in this book are not only illustrations of the text, and examples of the variety of life in the Early Church, but form a series with a unity of its own : the pictures have been chosen to illuminate each other, by contrast or by similarity. There are broad chronological divisions, but inside any division the pictures are brought together not because they make a chronological series but because they illustrate or exemplify different aspects of one theme. The themes will be found in the List of Illustrations and the notes printed with the plates relate the pictures to each other.

The principal aim of the notes, however, is to explain the significance of each building, statue, mosaic or picture in the life of the community in which it was created, used or seen. For this reason, there are several references to contemporary literary sources; these, however, cannot possibly exhaust the complexity of relationships between the plates and the literary sources, for the pictures comprise a visual background and commentary to some of the most intricate and profound theological problems which were debated in the literature of the period. For instance, the different portraits of Christ must be related to the christological writings of the fourth and fifth centuries : this is explicitly done in one case (Plate 22), but it could also be done in every other — Plates 18, 21, 22, 23, 36, 40, 44 and 45. The pictures, therefore, are illustrations not only of the chapters dealing with the physical expansion and development of the Church, but also of those which describe controversies and councils and theological development.

The selection of the plates and the composition of the notes owe much to the advice and work of many different scholars, especially to the authors of the book itself. I would particularly like to record my thanks to Fr Gervase Mathew, whose book, *Byzantine Aesthetics* (London 1963), not only provided the basis of the notes on St Vitale (Plates 27-30) but also helped greatly in defining the general aims of the illustrations and notes; and to Mr Peter Brown in Oxford and Dr W. H. C. Frend in Cambridge who gave detailed advice on so many points that without their help the list of plates and the notes would have been very different.

PETER LUDLOW

LIST OF ILLUSTRATIONS

CHRONOLOGY OF PRINCIPAL EVENTS

Political		*Religious*
Death of Augustus. Tiberius emperor (Julio-Claudian dynasty, 14-68). Pilate procurator of Judea.	14	
	27-9	Preaching of John the Baptist
	c. 30	Death and resurrection of Christ
Pontius Pilate leaves Judea	36	
	36-7	Martyrdom of Stephen
Death of Tiberius. Gaius (Caligula) emperor	37	
	c. 38	Conversion of Paul
Claudius emperor	41	
Conquest of Britain	43-4	Martyrdom of James, brother of John
	49	Council of Jerusalem
The Jews expelled from Rome	50	
	51-2	Paul at Corinth
Death of Claudius. Nero emperor	54	
	58	Arrest of Paul at Jerusalem
	62	Stoning of James, the ' brother of the Lord '
Burning of Rome	64	First persecution
Revolt of Judea	66	
Suicide of Nero. Emperors : Galba, Otho, Vitellius	68	
Vespasian emperor (Flavian dynasty, 69-96)	69	
Titus captures Jerusalem	70	
Eruption of Vesuvius. Titus emperor	79	
Death of Titus. Domitian emperor	81	
Death of Domitian. Nerva emperor (Dynasty of the Antonines, 96-192)	*c.* 95	The letter of Clement of Rome to the Corinthians
Trajan emperor	98	
	c. 100	Death of John
Pliny the Younger, legate in Bithynia	111	
Campaign of Trajan against Chosroés	116	
Death of Trajan. Hadrian emperor	117	
Revolt of the Jews	132	
Death of Hadrian. Antoninus Pius emperor	138	
Revolt of the Jews	155	
Marcus-Aurelius emperor. Parthian invasion	161	

Political		Religious
		Religious
Political	161/9	Martyrdom of Polycarp of Smyrna
	163/7	Martyrdom of Justin at Rome
	c. 170	Appearance of Montanism
	175/7	The martyrs of Lyons. Irenaeus becomes bishop of Lyons
Consulship of Commodius, who is named Augustus	177	
	179	Abgar IX, king of Edessa, first Christian ruler (?)
Death of Marcus-Aurelius Commodius sole emperor	180	
	185	Birth of Origen
	189-190	Controversy (' quartodeciman ') over date of Easter, under Pope Victor
Assassination of Commodius	193	Clement teaching at Alexandria
Septimus-Severus sole emperor. (Dynasty of the Severi, 193-235, except for Elagabalus)	194	
	197	Tertullian : *Apologeticum*
	197	Edict of Severus forbidding Jewish and Christian proselytism
	203	Hippolytus : *Commentary on Daniel*
	207-8	Tertullian adopts Montanism
Caracalla emperor	212	
	217-222	Calixtus pope. Reform of penance. Condemnation of Sabellius. Schism of Hippolytus
Elagabalus emperor	218	
Alexander Severus emperor	222	
Sassanid dynasty in the Iranian empire (226-652)	226	
	231	Origen ordained priest
Assassination of Alexander Severus. Maximinus emperor	235	Pope Pontian and the antipope Hippolytus deported to Sardinia
Gordian III emperor	238	
Shapur King of Kings	241	
	242	Mani begins his preaching
Plotinus at Rome	244	
	247-8	Dionysius bishop of Alexandria
Decius proclaimed emperor	248	
Philip the Arabian defeated and killed by the Persians	249	Cyprian bishop of Carthage

Political		Religious
	249-250	Decius' edict of persecution. Martyrdom of Pope Fabian
Gothic invasion	250	
	251	Cornelius pope. Synod of Rome against the schism of Novatian
	252	Death of Origen
Valerian emperor	253	
Persians capture Antioch	256	Synod of Carthage
	257-258	Persecution. Martyrdom of Pope Sixtus II, of deacon Laurence, of Cyprian of Carthage
Shapur takes the emperor Valerian prisoner	259	
Gallienus sole emperor	260	Synod of Rome. Gallienus' edict of tolerance
The Goths at Ephesus and in Greece	264-5	Death of Dionysius of Alexandria
Emperor Claudius II halts the Goths. (Emperors from Illyricum, 268-284)	268	Synod of Antioch. Condemnation of Paul of Samosata
Death of Plotinus	269	
Emperor Aurelian halts the Alemanni	270	
Aurelian captures Palmyra	272	
Aurelian murdered	275	
Barbarian invasions	276-7	
	280	Conversion of Tiridates, king of Armenia
Diocletian emperor	284	
Maximian made Augustus	285-6	
Constantius and Galerius made Caesars in West and East respectively	293	
	297	Edict against the Manichaeans
	303-4	Diocletian's four edicts of persecution
Diocletian abdicates : second tetrarchy	305	
Constantine, proclaimed emperor in Britain. (Constantinian dynasty 306-363).	306	
Shapur II king of Persia	309	
	311	Galerius' edict of tolerance
Battle of Milvian Bridge : Constantine master of the West	312	Beginning of Donatist schism
Battle of Tzirallum : Licinius master of the East	313	
	314	Synod of Arles
	318	Interdict on private pagan sacrifices

Political		Religious
Political		*Religious*
	323	Synod of Alexandria : condemnation of Arius : foundation of Tabennisi by Pachomius
Battle of Adrianople : Constantine sole emperor	324	
	325	First ecumenical Council (Nicaea)
	328	Athanasius bishop of Alexandria
Foundation of Constantinople	330	Macarius at Scete
	335	Violence at Tyre-Jerusalem. Deposition of Athanasius. Death of Arius
Death of Constantine. The empire divided among his three sons	337	
	339	Persecution of Christians in Sassanid empire
Constans defeats Constantine and is supreme in the West	340	
	341	Council *in encaeniis* (Antioch). Wulfila bishop (Arian) of the Goths
	342	Imperial synod of Sardica (Sofia)
	346	Death of Pachomius
	347	Persecution of the Donatists by Constans
Magnentius liquidates Constans. The Salian Franks in Toxandria	350	Hilary bishop of Poitiers
Constantius sole emperor	351	
Invasion of the Franks, Alemanni, Saxons	355	
	356	Death of Anthony. Athanasius exiled
	357-9	Synods of Sirmium
Julian emperor in the West	360	Homoean Council of Constantinople. Martin at Ligué
Julian the Apostate sole emperor	361	General amnesty
	362	Synod of Confessors (Alexandria)
Julian killed in battle against the Persians	363	
Valentinian emperor in the West, Valens emperor in the East	364	
The Alemanni in Gaul and in Raetia	365	First National Council of Armenia
The Alemanni thrown back	366	Damasus I pope
	367	Death of Hilary of Poitiers
	370	Martin bishop of Tours, Basil bishop of Caesarea in Cappadocia
	371	Gregory of Nyssa bishop. Death of Lucifer of Cagliari

Political		Religious
Political		*Religious*
Campaigns of Valens in Armenia	372	Gregory of Nazianzus bishop
	373	Death of Athanasius of Alexandria and of Marcellus Ancyra
	374	Creation of the see of Pharan (Sinai). Ambrose bishop of Milan. Synod of Valence in Gaul
Gratian emperor in the West	375	Jerome in the desert. Beginnings of Priscillianism
The Ostrogoths cross the Danube	376	Death of Photinus of Sirmium Gratian suppresses Donatism
	377	Synod of Rome : condemnation of Apollinarius
Battle of Adrianople. Death of Valens	378	
Theodosius emperor in the East. Death of Shapur II	379	Death of Basil. Synod of Antioch
	380	Edict of Theodosius against Arianism Synod of Saragossa against Priscillanism
	381	Second ecumenical Council (Constantinople)
	382	Evagrius the Pontic at Scete
Valentinian II emperor in the West	383	Death of Wulfila missionary to the Goths
	386	Death of Pope Damasus. Siricius succeeds him. Conversion of Augustine. Synod of Rome
Campaigns of Theodosius in the West	388	
	389	Jerome at Bethlehem
	390	Death of Gregory of Nazianzus
	391	Legislation of Theodosius against paganism
Assassination of Valentinian by Arbogast	392	Theodore of Mopsuestia bishop
Theodosius, sole emperor, forecasts a new division	394	Death of Gregory of Nyssa
Death of Theodosius. The empire finally split	395	Augustine bishop of Hippo
The Huns in the East, the Goths in Greece	396	
	397	Synod of Carthage. Death of Ambrose and Martin
	398	John Chrysostom bishop of Constantinople
Yezdegerd I king of Persia	399	Toleration for the Christians in Persia. Death of Evagrius the Pontic
The Huns at the Elbe. Eudoxia empress in the East	400	Honoratus founds the monastery of Lérins. Augustine : *Confessions*

xxviii

Political		Religious
Political		*Religious*
Deposition of the last emperor in the West	476	
	478	Persecution of Catholic Christians by the Vandals
Clovis succeeds Childeric	482	Edict of union by the emperor Zeno the Isaurian
	484	Death of Sidonius Apollinarius. Schism of Acacius
Clovis defeats Syagrius at Soissons	486	Council of Seleucia : the Persian church becomes officially nestorian
	490	Avitus bishop of Vienne
Anastasius emperor in the East	491	The Armenian church adopts monophysitism
Theodoric (king of the Ostrogoths) becomes king of the Romans	493	
Battle of Tolbiac	(?) 496	
	498	Symmachus pope. Laurentius antipope
	c. 500	Baptism of Clovis
The Code of Gundobad	501	
	503	Caesarius bishop of Arles
Breviary of Alaric	506	
Battle of Vouille	507	
Death of Clovis	511	
Death of Gundobad king of the Burgundians	516	Conversion of the Burgundians to Catholic Christianity
Justin I emperor in the East	518	Severus of Antioch deposed by Justin Death of Avitus of Vienne
	519	End of the Acacian schism
The Franks defeat the Burgundians	523	
	524	Death of Boethius
Death of Theodoric the Great	526	Pope John I dies in prison
Justinian emperor in the East	527	Council of Toledo
	529	Second Council of Orange. Benedict at Monte Cassino
Conquest of Thuringia by the Franks	531	
Chosroes king of Persia	532	Severus of Antioch at Constantinople
Beginnings of Justinian's reconquest of Africa	533	Death of Fulgentius of Ruspae
The Code of Justinian	534	
Beginnings of Justinian's reconquest of Italy	535	Agapetus I pope. Success of monophysite mission in Nubia
	537	Vigilius pope. Dedication of the St Sophia basilica, Constantinople

Political		Religious
		Religious
	538	Birth of Gregory of Tours. Death of Severus of Antioch
	540	Benedict issues his Rule
	542	Death of Caesarius
	544	Justinian's edict of the 'Three Chapters,
Capture of Rome by Totila	546	
Belisarius recaptures Rome	547	Justinian removes Pope Vigilius
	553	Fifth ecumenical Council (Constantinople II)
End of the reconquest of Italy	555	Pelagius I pope
	556	Carraric king of the Suevi abandons Arianism
Clotaire king of the Franks	558	
Death of Justinian. Justin II emperor in the East	565	
The Lombards invade Italy	568	Leovigild, king of the Visigoths, persecutes Christians
Yemen conquered by the Persians	570	Monophysite infiltration in the Yemen. Birth of Mohammed
Childebert II king of Austrasia	575	
	576	Death of Germanus bishop of Paris
	577	Monte Cassino destroyed by the Lombards
Tiberius II emperor in the East	578	
	580	Death of Cassiodorus
Slav invasion in the East	587	Reccared king of the Visigoths abandons Arianism
	589	Third Council of Toledo
	590	Gregory the Great pope. Columbanus arrives in Gaul
Campaign of Childebert II against the Bavarians	595	
Death of Fredegund	597	Gregory sends a misson to the English
	598	Conversion of Ethelbert of Kent
Campaign of Childebert against the Gascons	602	Death of Fortunatus
Capture of Cremona and Mantua by the Lombards	603	
	604	Death of Gregory the Great

PART ONE

THE ORIGINS
TO THE END OF THE THIRD CENTURY

BY

JEAN DANIÉLOU

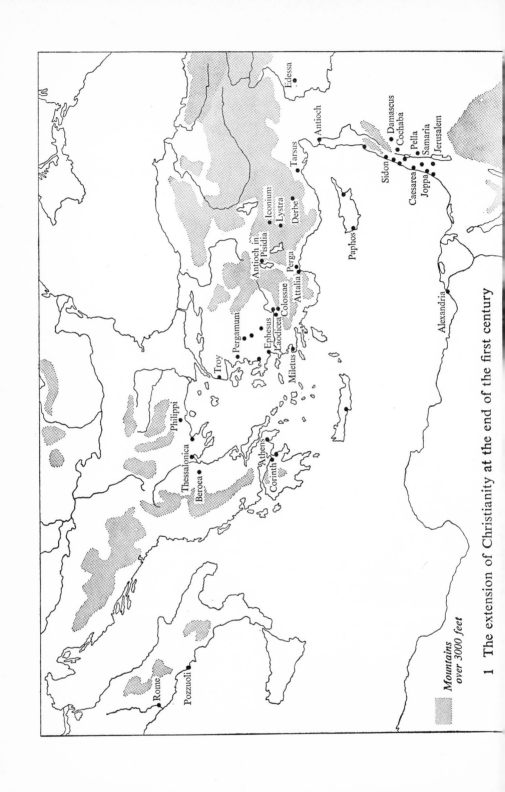

1 The extension of Christianity at the end of the first century

Edessa

Antioch

Damascus
Cochaba
Pella
Samaria
Jerusalem

Sidon
Caesarea
Joppa

Tarsus

Paphos

Iconium
Lystra
Derbe

Antioch in
Pisidia
Perga
Attalia

Pergamum
Ephesus
Laodicea
Colossae

Troy
Miletus

Philippi

Thessalonica
Beroea
Athens
Corinth

Alexandria

Rome
Pozzuoli

*Mountains
over 3000 feet*

PREFACE TO PART ONE

The problem of origins is always difficult for a historian. In order to ascertain events with scientific accuracy he requires official documents and archaeological remains. Now these exist only when a movement has emerged into public life. Moreover, pioneers are more concerned with making history than with writing it. That is true of Christianity as of every other historical subject and presents the main difficulty in the first chapters of this book. The documents available have to be handled prudently. Often their date is uncertain, their authenticity questioned, their interpretation ambiguous.

One solution would be to limit the narrative to absolutely certain facts. Such a history of the first decades of Christianity has been written many times. The *Acts of the Apostles* and the *Epistles* of Paul, references in Latin historians, and the documents collected by Eusebius of Caesarea allow one to make a number of statements of fact which no one can possibly question. But they give a picture of the early Christian centuries that is false because extremely one-sided. The *Acts* and the *Epistles* are interested only in the work of Paul; the Latin historians mention Christians only in connection with the Empire; Eusebius uses documents concerned almost exclusively with Asia, Syria and Egypt.

In order to present a more complete and therefore a truer picture, a different method must be used. Material does in fact exist which may lack precision but permits if not a detailed picture at least a general view. This method is scientifically exact provided that it does not go further than the evidence warrants. Now, although there are no documents giving precise historical information, we do possess an astonishingly varied literature belonging to the first Christian centuries.

In the past it was difficult to know how to use this literature in order to write a history of the Church. Critics are divided on the date and place of origin of the *Didache* and the *Odes of Solomon*, on Mandaeism and Gnosticism. Landmarks are lacking. But in the last twenty years the complex Jewish background to early Christianity has been discovered, and this, combined with a better understanding of the Greek and Roman world into which Christianity later emerged, makes it possible to place the texts more accurately and so to make use of them in a history.

True, a margin of uncertainty exists which will narrow only little by little. But at least the method has been found. Suddenly it becomes possible to give a more vivid and truer picture of the first beginnings of Christianity. Sketches are necessary before all the features can be determined with certainty. Often we can claim to do no more than sketch. But although a number of details can and must be made more precise, the main elements can now be put in place and this makes it possible to provide a general picture.

CHAPTER I

THE PRIMITIVE CHURCH

UNTIL recently the chief documentary evidence for the first decades of the Church was the *Acts of the Apostles*. The historical value of this canonical text is indisputable and in its second part, dealing with the mission of St Paul, it is based on direct evidence. But the fact remains that its account covers only part of the history of primitive Christianity. The man who wrote it was a Greek writing for Greeks; he took little interest in the Christianity of Aramaic-speaking people and he was hostile to Judaeo-Christianity. It is quite clear, however, that the very earliest Christianity used the Aramaic language and that the primitive Church for long remained deeply immersed in Jewish society.

Today a number of discoveries make it possible to add to the picture of this first period of Christianity. The Dead Sea Scrolls reveal in greater detail a part of the Jewish framework in which Christianity arose and permit us to distinguish more specifically Jewish elements in the surviving Christian documents. The discoveries of Nag Hammadi, particularly that of the *Gospel of Thomas*, perhaps put us in touch with an Aramaean tradition of the *logia* of Jesus. The Judaeo-Christian writings, the *Didache*, *Ascension of Isaias* and *Tradition of the Presbyters*, help us to rediscover, prior to or contemporary with the writings of the New Testament, an oral tradition which is the direct echo of the Judaeo-Christian community. The Judaeo-Christian inscriptions found by Frs Bagatti and Testa on the ossuaries of Jerusalem and Nazareth show us the symbols of the original Judaeo-Christian *milieu*.

So today it is possible to form a more complete picture of the very earliest origins of the Church. That does not imply any devaluation of the canonical documents, and their irreplaceable importance for an exact understanding of the history of the Church will presently be made clear. But the new elements now available allow any partiality in the *Acts'* account of events to be corrected. In reading the *Acts* there is a danger that we may fail to appreciate how important it was for early Christianity to belong to an extremely lively, varied and effervescent Jewish social *milieu*. In fact, the Judaeo-Christian Church of Jerusalem played a decisive role until the fall of Jerusalem in 70, and this historical truth, which is marked by the official documents, needs to be re-established.

1. Pentecost

It is as impossible to write the history of the Church without starting from the descent of the Holy Spirit at Pentecost in the year 30, as to write the history of Christ without starting from the incarnation of the Word on the day of the Annunciation. In both cases we are dealing with events concerning the story of man's salvation as well as with historical facts, and to envisage only their second aspect would be to misrepresent them completely. Rudolf Bultmann has clearly shown the intolerable flatness of biographies of Jesus. The same is true of histories of the Church which try to remove the divine dimension.

On this point the evidence of the *Acts of the Apostles* is crucial. They show the creation of the Church as an event in sacred history[1] and there is no reason to doubt this evidence. It corresponds, moreover, to the unanimous tradition of primitive Christianity. It can be treated as suspect only in the name of rationalist prejudices which *a priori* reject the existence of supernatural events. The essential facts of the event are these: on the one hand, a mission of the Spirit (Ac 2: 4), the creator and sanctifier; on the other hand, the object of this mission as related to the community established by Christ during his public life: it was on the Twelve gathered together (Ac 2: 1) that the Spirit descended; and finally, the Twelve were invested by the Spirit with an authority and power which made them preachers and dispensers of the riches of the risen Christ.

The event itself unquestionably took place, but Luke's presentation of it calls for comment. That it took place on the last day of the feast of Weeks in the year 30 and at Jerusalem is historically possible. The Twelve, even if they dispersed after the Sunday following the Pasch, could have returned to Jerusalem for the pilgrimage of Pentecost[2]. Moreover, the existence of a phenomenon of glossolalia (speaking with strange tongues) seems probable. It is, in fact, found on other occasions in the life of the early community (Ac 10: 47; 11: 15; I Cor 14: 23), and it gave rise to scoffing (Ac 2: 13; I Cor 14: 23). Luke would have had no reason to invent it; on the contrary, as will be seen, he tried to hide it.

1. See H. Conzelmann, *Die Mitte der Zeit*, Tübingen 1954, p. 183-186.
2. 'The Postresurrection Appearances in the Festival Pilgrimage', *NTS*, 4 (1957-1958), p. 58-61.

Peter's speech (Ac 2 : 14-36) represents a primitive kerygmatic (preaching) plan[3]; the ' list of peoples ' recalls that in Gn 10. Above all, several features described by Luke emphasise the parallel between the revelation of Sinai and that of Pentecost. Thus, the allusion to the violent wind and the tongues of fire recalls the description which Philo gives of the theophany on Sinai (*Dec.* 9 & 11. See also Ex 19 : 16-19; Heb 12 : 18 & 22)[4]. The miracle of tongues can be linked to a rabbinical tradition concerning the revelation on Sinai. Contrary to Trocmé's view, it seems probable that it is Luke who interprets the glossolalia as a miracle of tongues.

After Pentecost the Gospel began to be proclaimed by the Apostles, notably by Peter, who spoke in their midst and in their name. Chosen by Jesus during his public life, invested by him with an official mandate, they had received full powers to bear witness to the saving event of the resurrection and to discuss in God's name the conditions under which men could receive its effects. But it was only after Pentecost that, filled with the Holy Spirit, they began to exercise these powers. The circumstances of the announcement stressed the official character of their mission. Exegetes have noted the solemn character of the introduction to Peter's first speech (2 : 14); the second took place in the Temple (3 : 11), the third before the lawfully constituted assembly of the leaders of the people of Israel.

The theme of the Kerygma was the resurrection of Jesus (2 : 24; 2 : 39; 3 :15; 4 :10). This event was an act of God : ' God raised him up ' (2 : 24). This unheard-of statement the Apostles justified in three ways. First, by their own evidence (2 : 32; 3 :15); they took full responsibility for it. In essence, their evidence was that they had seen the risen Christ. The appearances of the risen Christ between Easter and the Ascension here take on their full meaning; their purpose was to establish the Apostles' faith. St Paul was later to show that they were one of the essential points in the tradition he received from the Apostles (I Cor 15 : 5-8). To have witnessed the risen Christ was the condition for being an Apostle (1 : 22) and as the last to whom the risen Christ had appeared, Paul belonged with the Twelve (I Cor 15 : 9). It is this evidence of the Apostles which the Church will transmit : the tradition is ' Apostolic tradition '.

The second proof of the resurrection of Christ was the works of power accomplished by the Apostles : ' so many were the wonders and signs performed by the Apostles ' (2 : 43). The *Acts* specify the case

3. See E. Trocmé, *Le livre des Actes et l'histoire*, Paris 1957, p. 207-209.
4. *Ibid.*, p. 202-203.

of a paralytic. These works of power threw the people into amazement and terror, that is to say the Jews recognised in them the hand of God (3 : 10); they were performed in the name of Jesus (3 : 16) and by faith in him the paralytic was cured (3 : 16). The miracles thus appear not merely as wonderful actions performed to support a statement, but also as the very efficacy of the resurrection, which was beginning to manifest itself. They bore witness to the presence in the Apostles of a divine power, and in the persons of the Apostles or at their hands this virtue produced divine works whereby men could recognise the presence of God and pay him glory.

Finally, there remained a last proof directed particularly at the Jews : the accomplishment of the prophecies. In the case of the Jews the problem of conversion to Christ raised a special difficulty. They did not require conversion to God : they already believed in him; they did not even need to be convinced that God would come among men, they already expected that; the only step demanded of them was to recognise in the Christ the realisation of this hope, to admit that in him the prophecies concerning the end of time were accomplished. That explains the considerable importance of this argument in the speeches of the *Acts*. It was an attempt to make the Jews recognise in the resurrection of Jesus the eschatological event announced by the prophets. Moreover, this is the meaning Peter intended, for at the beginning of his first speech he showed that Pentecost was the pouring out of the Spirit announced by the prophets for the ' last days ' (2 : 17), and this expression must be taken literally.

The purpose of the Kerygma was to make the Jews recognise that what had been accomplished in Jesus was God's work. This demanded first a total reversal of their attitude towards Jesus, a conversion. With this call to conversion Peter ended his speeches (2 : 38; 3 : 19). The Jews must recognise that they are mistaken : they have misunderstood the divine character of Christ and condemned him as a blasphemer because he claimed that divine dignity, and by so acting they have turned from God as their ancestors did in persecuting the prophets. To recognise the divinity of Jesus is therefore to turn back to God (3 : 19); the resurrection has shown that what was accomplished in Jesus was divine, and belief in the resurrection, on the evidence of the Apostles, is at the same time recognition of the wrong committed in crucifying him.

2. The Jewish Sects

It is important to see the primitive Christian community in the general context of the complicated structure of contemporary Judaism.

Certain groups within this structure had been hostile to it, first and fore-most the high priests and Sadducees, as the *Acts of the Apostles* attest (4 : 1-3). These two groups must not be confused. The high priests, since 6 A.D., belonged to the house of Sethi; in 30, the head of the family was Annas, and the high priest in office Caiaphas. They were primarily puppets in the hands of the Romans. The Sadducees were a political and religious party, devoted to the ideal of the priestly state centred on the Temple[5]. The high priests were especially jealous of their influence on the people (Ac 5 : 17), the Sadducees more hostile to religious innovations (Ac 4 : 2). In practice their interests were basically the same.

The *Acts* describe three successive outbreaks of hostility on their part towards the Christian community. In the first episode Peter and John, while preaching in the Temple (Ac 4 : 1-2) were surprised by the priests, the Sadducees and the superintendent of the Temple, who was head of the Jewish militia used by the high priest to keep order there (see Lk 22 : 52). Peter and John were arrested, accused before the Sanhedrin, then released (4 : 3; 6 : 23). On the second occasion all the Apostles were again arrested by the Temple superintendent on the orders of the high priests (5 : 17, 24) and again released after the Sanhedrin had met. These two liberations proved that the hatred shown by the high priests and the Sadducees to the Christians was not shared by the other parties represented on the Sanhedrin.

This is also confirmed by the *Acts* themselves : during the second session of the Sanhedrin, in fact, the Pharisee Gamaliel intervened on behalf of the Apostles, and later, before the Sanhedrin, Paul was to profit by this opposition of the Sadducees and Pharisees (Ac 23 : 6, 8). Gamaliel's speech was evidently the work of Luke, and it contains a clear historical error in that it alludes to the uprising of Theodas (Ac 5 : 36) which took place ten years afterwards. But it does show clearly what the Pharisees' position was. They admitted Messianism and had no reason to condemn *a priori* a movement stemming from Jesus. The Sadducees, on the other hand, were hostile to any Messianism, for doctrinal reasons. The high priests were even more hostile, for they saw in it a threat to their personal power, and that would seem to be the source of the hatred with which the house of Annas unceasingly persecuted first Jesus and later the community[6].

A third persecution probably originated from the hostility of the house of Annas. Before Easter 41 it had claimed a victim in one of the Apostles, James the brother of John, and caused Peter to be arrested.

5. See A. Meyer, Article Σαδδουκαῖος *TWNT*, VII, p. 32-54.
6. See P. Gaechter, *Petrus und seine Zeit*, Innsbruck 1957, p. 99, 104.

The same men were aimed at and the same origin may be inferred. According to Ac 12 : 1 the initiative came from Herod Agrippa I who, after playing an important role in the accession of the Emperor Claudius in 41, had been granted the restoration of the Kingdom of Israel as a reward. We know moreover that he was linked with Alexander the Alabarch, brother of Philo the philosopher. On coming to the throne he had removed from office the high priest Theophilus, a son of Annas, and replaced him by Simon ben Kanthera who belonged to the house of Boethos, a house which his grandfather Herod the Great had favoured. But in 42 he had replaced Simon by Jonathan, and Jonathan again in 43 by his brother Mathias, both sons of Annas.

This change evidently reflected a desire on Agrippa's part to gain the support of the powerful house of Annas, so that the return of this house to the functions of high priest and the persecution of the Christians represent a relationship of cause and effect : Agrippa sacrificed James to the hatred of the house of Annas. As for Peter's arrest, the *Acts* say that the motive was Agrippa's desire to ' please the Jews ' (12 : 3); moreover, it is likely that he had little personal sympathy for the ' Hebrews ', and he probably felt closer to the ' Hellenists '. It should be added that the latter incident has a special interest over and above that already discussed : it is the first that we can date with complete certainty. In fact it happened in the year before Agrippa's death at Caesarea, which the *Acts* record (12 : 20-23). The incident is also recorded by Josephus, and its dating in 44 is secure. So the date of 43 for the martyrdom of James is absolutely certain.

If the high priests and particularly the house of Annas were unswervingly hostile towards the Christians, the Pharisees' position was more complex. We have seen Gamaliel defending the Twelve. On the other hand during the persecution of the Hellenists and Stephen (September 36), it was they who played the chief role (Ac 6 : 12) and it was the Pharisee Saul who approved the stoning (7 : 59). This difference is significant. The Pharisees were favourable to the ' Hebrews ' and hostile to the ' Hellenists '. It was the difference of political attitude which in their eyes was all-important. The reproach they made to the Hellenists was their detached attitude towards Jewish independence, to the Temple which was its symbol and the legal structure of Israel (Ac 6 : 13-14). On the other hand the ' Hebrews ', though there might be converted Pharisees among them, were generally Christians attached to the Jewish fatherland, faithful to the cult of the Temple, and strict observers of Mosaic practices. It was doubtless they who formed the most important group in the first community. They won the sympathy of the Pharisees by their zeal for the Law.

It was to this group that the Twelve belonged. We find them loyal to the cult of the Temple, but their mission obliged them to be above all parties. The head of the group was James 'the brother of the Lord' (Gal 1 : 19), not to be confused with the two Apostles of that name; but it is noteworthy that the *Acts* scarcely mention him. It seems that *Luke* used traditions coming from converted Sadocites on the one hand and Hellenists on the other, and that he left in the background what was in reality the most important part of the primitive Church of Jerusalem. *Luke* presents Paul's point of view, and James's party was the one with which Paul was in continual conflict (Gal 2 :12); moreover, since it finally disappeared after 70, the memory of it was obliterated. This obliteration falsifies the history of Christian origins, for it was James's party and the Judaeo-Christian Church of Jerusalem which exercised the dominant influence during the first decades of the Church.

Some traces of this are discernible. As regards James himself, the *Epistle to the Galatians* makes clear his importance and attitude. And later non-canonical documents from Judaeo-Christian circles throw further light. First, there is the important position which James occupies in these documents. This in itself is significant. For example, in the *Gospel of the Hebrews*, which appears to be linked with a Judaeo-Christian community in Egypt at the beginning of the second century, it is to James that the risen Christ first appears[7]. In the *Gospel of Thomas*, found at Nag Hammadi, James the Just is said to be the one to whom the Apostles must go after the Ascension. Clement, in the *Hypotyposes*, mentions him with John and Peter as having received the gnosis of the risen Christ. The three *Apocalypses* of James found at Nag Hammadi, which are Gnostic, bear witness to the Judaeo-Christian sources of Gnosticism. In the Pseudo-Clementine writings which use Ebionite Judaeo-Christian sources, James is presented as the most important person in the Church (*Hom. Clem.* I, 1).

Hegesippus, who according to Eusebius (*HE*, IV, 22, 8) was a converted Jew[8], shows us James drinking neither wine nor intoxicating drinks, never shaving and spending his life in the Temple in intercessory prayer for the people (*HE*, II, 23, 4). He adds that he had the confidence of the Scribes and Pharisees (II, 23, 10). This confirms the links between James and rabbinical Judaism, which also appear in the *Epistle* that is traditionally attributed to him. Around James clustered a number of relations of the Lord, the desposynes, who had an important place among the 'Hebrews'. Stauffer has called them the Caliphate, and

---

7. See E. Hennecke, *Neutestamentliche Apokryphen*, 3rd impression, Tübingen 1959, I, p. 107.
8. But see W. Telfer, 'Was Hegesippus a Jew?', *HTR*, 53 (1960), p. 143-155.

they formed the kernel of a powerful party. Evidently they tended to
' corner ' the Church, if we are to believe the Hellenists' protests (Ac 6 : 1).
And after the dispersal of the latter, they were masters of the Church
of Jerusalem.

Traces of this rabbinical Christianity occur in the New Testament
writings, although the latter come from another *milieu* and tend to
minimise its importance. It is doubtless to this source that a whole
Targumic literature must be attributed, of which traces are found in
St Paul[9] and fragments in the *Epistle of Clement*, the *Epistle of Barnabas*
and other later works. In fact the targum is a characteristic *genre* of the
Pharisaic scribes, and parts of the *Targum of Jerusalem* certainly go back
to the pre-Christian era. The converted scribes practised the same
literary *genre* but gave it a Christian orientation. Again, many moral
regulations and liturgical formulas, of which echoes can be seen in the
Gospels, belong to the later stages of rabbinical Judaism.

Finally, there remains the question of the Essenes. The facts
about them are very odd. On the one hand Christian documents show
indisputable similarities between certain aspects of the Christian
community of Jerusalem, and characteristics of this group shown in the
manuscripts of the Dead Sea and references in Philo and Josephus[10].
Some of these similarities are striking, but they do not imply that the
first community was an extension of the Sadocite community. For one
thing, because of lack of evidence, we do not know whether similar
practices, which are attested only for Qumran, did not also exist in
Judaism. Certainly there existed *chaburah* or confraternities, where the
sharing of property and communal meals may well have taken place,
and this seems the most probable explanation of the similarities[11].

Moreover, it is beyond dispute that the Christian community shared
the eschatological hopes found in the Apocalyptic writings which come
from Sadocite circles. But it does not follow that the Christian
community recruited its members among the Sadocites. We know from
Philo that the Essenes were a small group like the Pharisees and
Sadducees. Most of the Jewish people did not belong to these groups,
but they felt their influence. In this respect it is certain that the Sadocite
influence extended far beyond the small number of its members, all the
more since their literary production was intensive. Their influence
certainly prepared people's minds to accept the Christ, and it is probable

9. R. Le Déant, ' Traditions targumiques dans le Corpus paulinien ', *Bibl.*, 42 (1961),
p. 28-48.

10. See especially *The Scrolls and the New Testament*, edited by K. Stendahl,
London 1958.

11. See P. Benoit, ' Qumran et le Nouveau Testament ', *NTS*, 7 (1961), p. 276-297.

that it was in circles influenced by them, where eschatological hopes were highest, that many were converted to Jesus.

It remains quite possible that there were some Essenes, in the strict sense, among the first converts to Christianity. Perhaps the Essene traits noticeable in the picture of the first community in *Acts* come from Luke's use of a document belonging to a Christian group of Sadocite origin. In some respects this picture recalls the one given of the Essene community by Philo a little earlier. The resemblance is so striking that Eusebius of Caesarea thought that Philo's description referred to the primitive Christian community. This may also explain other features of the first chapters of *Acts*. For example, the way Pentecost is described : we have seen that Luke was concerned to suggest a parallel with the revelation on Sinai, but we also know that, for the Sadocites, the Feast of Weeks, or Pentecost, was the feast of the revelation and the covenant (the *Book of the Jubilees* in particular bears this out), and that the last Sunday of the feast of the theophany of Sinai was especially commemorated[12]. It has also been pointed out that by their choice of quotations (Deut 10 : 16; 18 : 15-19; Am 5 : 25-27; 9 : 11) and in their method of exegesis, the speeches in the first chapters of *Luke* show a special connection with the manuscripts of Qumran[13]. These speeches belonged to the document used by Luke, and so doubtless reflect a catechesis of Sadocite complexion.

Then there is the further question of whether in the text of the *Acts* there are more precise allusions to converts from Essenism in the first community. This problem is a strange one; on the one hand, the first Christians seem to present the greatest affinity with the Essenes, yet at the same time the Essenes are the only one of the three great historic sects not to be mentioned in the New Testament. O. Cullmann has suggested that the Hellenists mentioned in chapter 6 of *Acts* may be Essenes[14]. It must be admitted that these Hellenists are difficult to identify. H. J. Schoeps sees in them the projection by Luke into the Church of Jerusalem of a situation which only existed later than 70[15]. Gaechter[16] and F. Trocmé[17] identify them as Palestinian Jews speaking

12. See J. van Goudoever, *Biblical Calendars*, Leiden 1959, p. 138-144; 228-235.

13. See S. C. Johnson, ' The Dead Sea Manual of Discipline and the Jerusalem Church in Acts ' in *The Scrolls and the Testament*, p. 131-132.

14. ' The Significance of the Qumran Texts for Research into the Beginning of Christianity ', *JBL*, 74 (1955), p. 220-224. See likewise M. Brände, ' Ein unklares Kapital der Apostelgeschichte im Lichte von Qumran ', *Orientierung*, 22 (1958), p. 251-254; 23 (1959), p. 16-121; P. Geoltrain, 'Esséniens et Hellénistes', *TZ*, 15 (1959), p. 241-254.

15. *Theologie und Geschichte des Judenchristentums*, Tübingen 1949, p. 440-441.

16. *Op. cit.*, p. 130-131.

17. *Op. cit.*, p. 189.

Greek, M. Simon as Jews of the Diaspora[18].   In reality, the group seems to have been composite.   According to *Acts*, its members were partly Palestinian Jews, like Stephen or Philip, whose Greek names show that they were hellenised, or they could belong to the circle of the Herods, like Manathen, foster-brother of Herod the tetrarch (Ac 13 : 1); some could come from the Diaspora, like Barnabas, a native of Cyprus (Ac 4 : 36); then there were also proselytes, that is to say, pagans converted to Judaism, like those in Ac 2 : 11, and Nicholas, a proselyte of Antioch, expressly mentioned as a Hellenist (Ac 6 : 5).   It is not impossible that some Essenes who were separated by their secession from official Judaism belonged to this group, for they would be drawn to it by their hostility to official Jewish circles and their contacts with Hellenism.

3.   The Life of the Community

While describing the environment in which the Jerusalem community developed, the *Acts* reveal something of its life.   The first Christians continued to share in the religious life of their people : ' thousands of the Jews have learned to believe, and they are all zealous supporters of the law ' (Ac 21 : 20).   This means that the children were circumcised, rules of ritual purification observed, and the Sabbath kept as a day of rest. In particular, the Christians of Jerusalem took part in the prayers which were recited daily in the Temple (Ac 2 : 46); Peter and John went there for morning prayer (5 : 21) and for prayer at the ninth hour (3 : 1). So Christians appeared to others as specially fervent Jews, whom the blessing of God accompanied (Ac 5 : 13).   They did, however, all go together to the Temple (Ac 2 : 46), and so they formed a special group within the body of Israel.

The Christians themselves were well aware that they constituted a special community.   The *Acts* already refer to them as *ecclesia*, which in Greek means an official assembly.   But it would seem that its meaning in *Acts* refers back to its use in the Greek translation of the Bible, where it means the people of God assembled in the desert (Ac 7 : 38). Henceforth the word signifies that the Christians considered themselves not only as one community among others, but as the new people of God. The word ἐκκλησία was first applied to the Church of Jerusalem.   Later it was applied to the various local Churches which were founded on the model of the mother Church; for example, Paul gathered together the Church of Antioch (14 : 27) and greeted the Church of Caesarea (18 : 22). The concrete character of the Church clearly appears in these passages.

18. *Les premiers chrétiens*, Paris 1952, p. 44.

But Christians were also aware that it was one and the same Church which was present in the different places, and the word took on the meaning of universal Church.

At the same time as they shared in the life of their people, the Christians had their own life. They met together. These meetings took place in private houses, as in the Upper Room, where the very first community gathered. Later there were many such meeting places and the *Acts* say that the Christians ' broke bread in their houses ' (2 : 45). One of these houses is known to be that of Mary, mother of John Mark, where quite a numerous group gathered and prayed while Peter was in prison (12 : 12). Again, we find that Paul exhorted the brethren in the house of Lydia in Philippi (16 : 40) and celebrated the Eucharist on the third floor of a private house in Troas (20 : 9). The Upper Room, usually larger and not lived in, was well suited to these lay meetings, and families gave their support to the Church in this way by placing their houses at the disposal of the community. Paul speaks of Aquila and Priscilla and of ' the church which is in their house ' (I Cor 16 : 19).

These Christian gatherings were frequent. The *Acts* tell of daily meetings including the breaking of bread, a meal and prayers of praise (2 : 46), and some of them were held at night, as when Paul found a large gathering at prayer in the house of Mary, mother of John Mark (12 : 12). One thing seems certain : that a meeting was held on Saturday night, as recorded in the *Acts* (20 : 7). On the Sabbath, the Christians took part in communal prayers and gathered together afterwards, and it would seem that this custom led to calling Sunday the eighth day, for this expression, which is found as early as the *Epistle* of the Pseudo-Barnabas, can only be explained in terms of the seventh day of the Jewish week; the usual expression was Kyriake (Lord's Day) which corresponds to our Sunday. It is not certain, however, that Christian meetings were always held at night, and it is quite possible that they were also held at other times. That was so notably when the Eucharist accompanied a meal, as described in the *First Epistle to the Corinthians* (11 : 17-33).

From what the *Acts* tell us it is possible to form a picture of these meetings. They included instruction, breaking of bread and prayers. Although the *Acts* provide plentiful examples of preaching to unbelievers (Kerygma), they are silent about the teaching given to the community; but we can form some idea from the expressions used to describe it. Sometimes there is instruction in the strict sense (*didache*); but that word is used primarily of the catechesis before baptism, and at ordinary meetings there were usually exhortations *(paraklesis)* in order to strengthen faith and charity (14 : 22; 15 : 32) or homilies (Ac 20; 11) and discourses of a more intimate kind. The *Epistles* of Paul and the other canonical *Epistles* give an idea of these discourses and exhortations which they themselves largely echo.

Instruction was followed by the ' breaking of bread '. That is the archaic phrase used in the *Acts* to describe the Eucharist (2 : 42; 20 : 7). It recalls Christ's gesture when sharing the bread after having pronounced the words of consecration over it. Christ had instituted the Eucharist during a Paschal meal : the blessing of the bread is that of the azymes (unleavened elements) before the meal; the blessing of the wine corresponds to the cup which followed the meal. These are the two rites which the Christians kept, separating them, however, from the Paschal meal and performing them either at the end of a meal or without any meal. The person who presided over the Eucharist, having given thanks, blessed the bread and wine by stretching his hands over them, and pronounced the words of Jesus at the Last Supper. The prayer of blessing and the outspread hands corresponded to what is found in the Jewish *berakah* of the manuscripts of Qumran.

The Eucharist was followed by prayers, according to the *Acts* (2 : 42; 12 : 5), and these prayers were said principally by the Apostles or the Elders who presided over the meeting (6 : 4; 13 : 3); but members of the meeting who had received the appropriate grace could also say prayers, as for example the prophets of the community of Antioch (13 : 3) and the prophet Agabus (11 : 28). In his *First Letter to the Corinthians* St Paul speaks of these prophets (12 : 28). As for women, they were excluded from instruction but were allowed to take part in the thanksgiving, and St Paul says that they must have their heads veiled (I Cor 11 : 7); the deacon Philip had four daughters who prophesied (21 : 9). It is noteworthy that the outpouring of the Holy Spirit took place chiefly during the Christian meeting (4 : 31), which was the New Temple where God dwelt (I Pet 2 : 5) and which rendered the Old Temple useless, although it was still in existence.

Another feature of life in the Jerusalem community — the one on which the *Acts* lay most stress — was its economic organisation. The *Acts* speak of the brethren pooling all they possessed : ' They sold their possessions and their means of livelihood, so as to distribute to all, as each had need ' (2 : 44; see also 4 : 34). The *Acts* mention in particular the case of Barnabas who, possessing a field, sold it and gave the proceeds to the Apostles (4 : 36-37). On the other hand, Ananias and Sapphira, having sold a field, kept back part of the proceeds and deceived the Apostles (5 : 1-2). The passage states that this pooling of resources was not obligatory : Sapphira's sin was that she lied to the community.

It is difficult to know exactly what this pooling of resources amounted to. It may have been a common cash-box to help the needy, like the one in the Synagogue; we know that Christian widows administered such relief daily (6 : 1). But Luke seems to mean something more than that, a true pooling of resources. This seems less astonishing today, now that it has been discovered that this custom existed among the Sadocites. The Essene flavour of Luke's narrative has already been mentioned, and its description may possibly have been influenced by practices in the community of Qumran. But the episode of Ananias and Sapphira recalls the discipline of Qumran so closely that it would seem to be an example of an effective influence of Essene practices on the Jerusalem community.

These problems of economic organisation are treated in the *Acts* in relation to another matter as well. The *Acts* record that as a result of protests from the Hellenists, who complained that their widows were neglected, the Apostles chose from among them seven persons, who included Stephen. We have seen that the Christians had already instituted relief for the poor, modelled on that in the synagogue; this had been in the charge of the Apostles who now handed it over to the Seven. But the Seven were not intended solely to take charge of poor relief; they also preached and baptised. In fact the Apostles took advantage of this opportunity to provide themselves with fellow-workers; they communicated part of their powers to them, and this was done by ordination (Ac 6 : 6).

The question then arises : did this institution apply only to the Hellenists? When the Apostles felt the need of fellow-workers, ought they not to have done likewise for the Hebrews, as Gaechter says[19]? Luke's silence may be explained by the lack of interest he shows in the Hebrews. Colson seems nearer the truth when he sees in the Seven an institution special to the Hellenists[20]. The Hebrews already had presbyters or elders and James the Just was certainly one of them; the *Acts* show us how the Christians of Antioch entrusted offerings for the poor to the elders *(presbuteroi)* of Jerusalem (11 : 30). Among the ' Hebrews ' these elders performed the functions which the Seven performed among the Hellenists.

Another important point is the pre-eminent position which James the Just held among the presbyters; he seems to be credited with a fuller share in the apostolic powers. When Paul came to Jerusalem in 41

19. *Op. cit.*, p. 133.
20. *La fonction diaconale aux origines de l'Église*, Paris 1961, p. 43-46. Note that Clement of Rome, describing the Church hierarchy, seems to liken the presbyters to the Jewish priests and the deacons to the Levites (*Epist.* XL, 5).

(Gal 1 : 18), he met Peter and this same James, and at the Council of Jerusalem James was the only one to speak with Peter. So James was then certainly head of the Jerusalem community. Moreover, he seems to have possessed powers like those of the Apostles. It is in this sense that Eusebius is to be understood when he writes that Peter, James and John did not reserve the direction of the local Church of Jerusalem for themselves, but chose James the Just as *episcopos* or bishop (*HE*, II, 1, 4). Henceforward he, not Peter and the Apostles, was responsible for the local Church of Jerusalem (Ac 12 : 17). He was both president of the local college of presbyters and heir to the apostolic powers.

In this way the Church of Jerusalem assumed its own special structure. The Apostles were the witnesses of the resurrection and the trustees of the fulness of power, and Peter appeared as their head. At the beginning, they directly presided over and administered the Church of Jerusalem. But they took associates to work with them. At first there were the presbyters who looked after the Hebrews; they formed a college with James as president, and James shared in the apostolic powers to a special degree. The Apostles also instituted a similar organisation for the Hellenists in which the Seven corresponded to the Hebrew presbyters though it is difficult to know whether Stephen was their equivalent of James. In any case the departure of the Hellenists was to make the college of presbyters the sole hierarchy in Jerusalem.

CHAPTER II

THE CHURCH
OUTSIDE JERUSALEM

So FAR we have focused our attention on the Church of Jerusalem and it is there that Christianity first appeared. But it is also almost exclusively of this Church that our chief source, the *Acts*, speaks in its first part. During the first fifteen years of their existence, Christians spread far and wide. Eusebius was doubtless exaggerating when he wrote that during the reign of Tiberius, that is before 37 when Caligula became Emperor, ' all the earth echoed to the voice of the Evangelists and the Apostles ' (*HE* II, 3, 1). But that is at least as true as what we are told in *Acts* where the expansion of Christianity in the Jewish world outside Jerusalem is barely mentioned. It is now possible to shed more light on certain areas.

The study of the primitive Church of Jerusalem has shown the complexity of the Jewish world in which the Church was growing, and the different elements which that framework introduced to it. We have mentioned the Pharisees, the Sadducees, the Essenes, the Hellenists, but there were also the Herodians and the Zealots, and Justin also names the ' Genists, the Merists, the Galileans, the Hellenians, the Baptists '[1]. The Samaritans are also mentioned. It is not easy to identify all these groups[2] for they represent so many different currents on the fringes of official Judaism. The Samaritans were one of them, the Jordanian Baptist sects were another[3]. There were also those disturbing persons, the ' Magi ', Simon and Thoudas — Jews influenced by Iranian dualism. We shall find these currents continuing in orthodox or heterodox Christianity.

Finally, if Christianity at first grew chiefly among Jews of Palestine and the Diaspora (Jews dispersed in other territories), from the very

1. *Dial.*, LXXX, 4.
2. See M. Simon, *Les sectes juives du temps de Jésus*, Paris 1960, p. 74-93.
3. See K. Rudolf, *Die Mandäer*, I, Göttingen 1960, p. 228-229.

beginning it also reached the pagans. But here again the documents, written in Greek for Greeks, are chiefly interested in the development of the Church in the western world. Now Christian missions also spread in the eastern world where Jewish missions had preceded them, and where the cultural language was Aramaic : Transjordan, Arabia, Phoenicia, Coelesyria, Adiabene and Osroene. Helen, Queen of the Adiabeneans, was converted from Zoroastrianism to Judaism about 30 A.D.[4]. This 'Syriac' Christianity played a very important part during the first two centuries. The *Acts* show that the mission was chiefly directed at the Hellenists, but there was also an Aramaean mission and Eusebius tells us that Thomas evangelised the Parthians (III, 1, 2). A whole cycle relating to Thomas — *Gospel of Thomas, Acts of Thomas, Psalms of Thomas* — echoes this mission.

Of this Judaeo-Christian complex certain components can be distinguished during the years 30 to 45. As regards Palestine, the question of the origin of the Church in Galilee remains an enigma[5]. The *Acts* show that it existed. Three facts should be remembered : E. Lohmeyer thinks he can distinguish in the sources of the Gospels a Galilean tradition as distinct from a Jerusalem tradition, the echo of Galilean catechesis. In the second place archaic Judaeo-Christian inscriptions discovered in Nazareth show that the Gospel reached there very early; in fact the links between Galilee and Judaea may explain why the *Acts* make no mention of it[6] and the family links of several Apostles with Galilee make it unlikely that it was not evangelised very early on. A final question remains : among the Jewish sects Justin and Hegesippus mention the Galileans and so do the documents of the Wadi Mouraba'at. This group must evidently be identified with the Zealots of Josephus; the Zealot movement had been founded in 6 A.D. by Judas the Galilean.

Did the first Christians have contacts with the Zealots? Cullmann has suggested that several Apostles, Simon the Zealot at any rate, came from this group[7]. In the eyes of the Jerusalem Jews, the Sadducees and Pharisees, the disciples of Jesus could have passed for such and the fact that they included Galileans could have contributed to this. Gamaliel likened Jesus's followers to those of Judas the Galilean. The works of Brandon and Reicke seem to show that if the Christian community was not linked to the movement, the elements coming from Zealotism were very active in it; they tried to drag the Christian community into the movement of revolt against Roman domination. One might

4. See Josephus, *Ant. Jud.*, XX, 101.
5. See L. F. Elliott-Binns, *Galilean Christianity*, Chicago 1956.
6. See L. Cerfaux in Robert-Feuillet, *Introduction à la Bible*, II, Paris 1959, p. 360.
7. *Dieu et César*, Paris 1956, p. 11-27.

well ask whether this Zealot Christianity was not composed of Galilean peasants and fishermen, speaking Aramaic, converts to Christianity, and whether its dependence on a world which was to disappear totally after the year 70 does not explain the silence of the New Testament writings about it.

The origins of the Church of Samaria are, on the other hand, described in the *Acts;* these are connected with the expulsion of the Hellenists from Jerusalem in 37.   One of the Seven, Philip, went down to Samaria (8 : 4), and as Cullmann has rightly pointed out[8], the Hellenists would have been welcomed by the Samaritans, with whom they shared a hostility towards the theocracy of the Temple and the Priesthood of Jerusalem.   But the Samaritan group had strange features which seem to have resulted in the failure of the mission, which is doubtless the meaning of the incident of Simon.   In the *Acts* Simon is shown practising magic, claiming to be ' the Great Power ' and exercising a very great influence (8 : 9-10). Justin, himself a Samaritan, was later to give other details (1 *Apol.* XVI, 1-3).   He shows Simon adored by almost all the Samaritans as the First God; and a woman, Helen, was associated with him in this cult as the First Thought.   He adds that Simon came to Rome.   Irenaeus says that Simon taught that the world was created by the angels, who governed it badly, and were dispossessed by the First Power (*Adv. Haer.*, I, 23, 3).

It is difficult to disentangle, in these traditions, Simon's own doctrine from that of his disciples, Simonians or Hellenians.   It seems that Grant was right in treating Simon as a representative of a Samaritan Messianism, like that of the ' prophet ' whose movement Pilate checked in 36[9].   Simon was himself a disciple of Dositheus, who applied to himself the passage in Deuteronomy 18 : 15 on the prophet announced by Moses.   Dositheus and Simon seem to represent an ascetical and eschatological current parallel to that of Qumran, with which they have points of contact[10]. But mixed with it were magic and syncretist elements, characteristic of a Jewish heterodoxy, a heterodoxy which was not yet Gnosticism.   But it was the *milieu* where Gnosticism was to appear after the year 70, reinterpreting it, as Grant well says in his discussion of Simon[11], in the direction of a more radical dualism, as a result of the setback to its eschatological hopes.   In this sense Simon was the father of Gnosticism, although not himself a Gnostic.

8. ' La Samaire et les origines de la mission chrétienne ', *Annuaire de l'École des Hautes Ét.* (1953-1954), p. 10.
9. See R. M. Grant, *Gnosticism and Early Christianity*, New York 1959, p. 76-97.
10. See Mcl. Wilson, ' Simon, Dositheus and the DSS ', *ZRGG*, 9 (1957), p. 21-40.
11. *Op. cit.*, p. 73.

Now Simon received baptism from Philip (Ac 8 : 13) and even tried to become associated with Peter in his power (8 : 18); he would thus have become a kind of bishop of the Samaritans, but Peter unmasked his insincerity and dismissed him. Simon nevertheless had some disciples; Justin tells us that they were numerous. It is possible that they composed a large part of the Christian community of Samaria. So there was here, very early on, a Christian heterodoxy which at first had eschatological features and which was later to become Gnosticism. This heterodoxy was henceforward to show signs of syncretism, characteristic of the Samaritan group. Dualism developed here only after the year 70. In fact it was at Caesarea that Philip settled (Ac 21 : 8), while Paul met communities in Samaria in 49 (Ac 15 : 8).

Among the religious groups on the verge of official Judaism another group must be mentioned. In the various references to the Jewish sects at the time of the Church's origins, Baptist sects are named. Besides the Essenes, Galileans, Samaritans, Sadducees and Pharisees, of whom we have spoken, Hegesippus mentions the Masbotheans (*HE* IV, 22, 7). Justin speaks of the Baptists[12] and Epiphanius of the Sabeans[13]; Sabeans and Masbotheans are synonyms for Baptists[14]. This group shared Noachic beliefs and practices with the Jews. Moreover, its essential rite was bathing in the Jordan, considered as a sacred river. It was composed of non-Jewish inhabitants of the Jordan, related to the Jews but not members of the Community of Israel; these were the ancestors of the Mandaeans.

The contacts between primitive Christianity and this group were complex. On the one hand, among the Jews of that period there was certainly some confusion of mind between the Christians and these Baptist sects, from the fact that baptism in the Jordan was adopted first by John the Baptist and later by the Christian Church. But, as Rudolf has shown, the only feature common to Sabeans and Christians was the importance given to the Jordan as a sacred river[15]. Another fact may have added to this confusion. The term Nazarene (Ναζωραῖος, nazoraios) is applied to Jesus in the Gospel (Mt 2 : 23). The same word appears as the earliest designation of the Mandaeans, moreover Epiphanius uses it under the form Νασαραῖος (nasaraios) to designate a Jewish sect. The disputes about the word are well known. It is certain that it means ' observing ', and it seems also to have been applied to the Baptists. Doubtless through a wilful confusion with the latter it was applied to

12. *Dial.*, LXX, 4.
13. *Panarion*, XI.
14. See K. Rudolf, *op. cit.*, p. 228-229.
15. *Op. cit.*, p. 76.

Christ and the Christians by the Jews (Ac 24 : 5), like the term Samaritan[16]. But by virtue of a pun familiar to the Semites, the term was taken as a claim to glory by the Christians and linked to *nezer*, scion, which is a Messianic title[17].

Curiously enough, there did exist a Christian sect of Nazaraeans, who lived in Transjordan, mentioned by Epiphanius[18]. They were Judaizing Christians and their centre was Pella in Gaulanitis. Some fragments of a *Gospel of the Nazaraeans* exist, written in Aramaic, which Jerome read in Transjordan. Epiphanius believed they were Judaeo-Christians driven from Palestine after the year 70, but these Judaeo-Christians probably joined an existing community, bearing the name of Nazaraeans, which it shared with the other Transjordanian groups and which was the generic name for the Baptist sects of this region. It had other characteristics. Archaeology has shown the importance in Transjordan of the sanctuaries consecrated to the non-Jewish saints, Lot, Job and Melchisedech. Moreover, this *milieu* was later to give rise to Ebionism, hostile to sacrifices, practising frequent baths of purification and attached to Noachic precepts.

Finally, without leaving Palestine, Christian missions were going to meet a last group, which raised new problems : Graeco-Roman paganism. Palestine in fact possessed Greek towns mostly inhabited by pagans which lay chiefly along the Mediterranean. The *Acts* tell us that the apostolate of the Hellenists also lay in this region and Philip is mentioned in Caesarea and Joppa. It was near Gaza that he baptised a Jewish proselyte of Ethiopian birth (8 : 27). In these various regions, first in Samaria, then in Caesarea, Gaza and Joppa, Philip was followed by Peter. This seems a proof of the control that the Twelve felt obliged to exercise over the Church as a whole. The universal character of the mission with which they had been charged concerned Peter in particular. Thus the role of arbiters which we have seen the Twelve play in Jerusalem was confirmed.

By spreading the Gospel on the coast, the Christian community was bound to come into contact with Greek and Roman paganism. The *Acts* tell us of the centurion Cornelius, of the Italian cohort (10 : 1). The incident is interesting, for it shows to what degree the Apostles felt incorporated in the Jewish religious community; in fact the passage points out that it was illegal for a Jew to have contact with a foreigner

16. On the parallel between the Nazarenes and the Samaritans, see M. Black, ' The Patriotic Account of Jewish Sectarianism ', *Bull. John Rhy. Library*, 41 (1959), p. 285-303.
17. See P. Gärtner, ' Die rätselhaften Termini Nazoräer und Iskariot ', *Horae Soederblomianae*, IV, Lund 1957, p. 5-36.
18. *Panarion*, XXIX.

(10 : 28), but nevertheless Peter recognised that he could not be refused baptism. Thus, from the beginning, the Apostles recognised that the Christian community was open to pagans. We shall see the problems that this was soon to raise, at a time when the Judaeo-Christians still felt tied by Jewish customs.

The sum-total of the early developments of the Church in Palestine outside Jerusalem amounted to very little. It seems that Galilee, Samaria and Transjordan were chiefly a centre of dissident groups : Simonians, Zealots or Ebionites, themselves reflections of marginal forms of Judaism. And this Jewish sensibility to heterodoxy was still one of the aspects of the close relations between primitive Christianity and the Jewish world. In fact the great centre of Christian expansion during the first fifteen years had been Syria, and the first Christian centre after Jerusalem was Antioch. But if Antioch is singled out for attention in the *Acts of the Apostles*, that is because the town belonged to the Hellenistic, not the Aramaean, world. There is also an Aramaean Syria which included Damascus in Phoenicia and Edessa in Osroene, and this played just as important a role, although the canonical documents barely mention it. Here again we must try to right the balance.

The first centre we meet is Damascus. The *Acts* give us two pieces of information. When Paul was converted in 38 there was already a Christian community in Damascus, since he went there to make arrests. Again, *Acts* 11 : 19 links the evangelisation of Phoenicia, of which Damascus is a part, to the Hellenists driven from Jerusalem. The first community of Damascus was therefore founded in 37. These Damascene Christians were Jews, otherwise they would not have fallen under the jurisdiction of the high priest of Jerusalem. Moreover it is stated that the word was announced to the Jews alone (11 : 19). The Christians were called ' the men of the way ', a strictly Jewish name for a sect, furthermore it is stated that Paul, after his conversion, preached in the synagogues (9 : 20). One of the Christians of Damascus, Ananias, is named (9 : 10) : he was a man devout ' according to the Law ' and esteemed by the Jews (Ac 22 : 12).

Can we be more specific about the Damascus community? First, it is important that it was founded by the Hellenists. The persecution of which St Paul was the instrument was directed against the Hellenists. So it was as Hellenists that Paul came to arrest the Damascus Christians[19]. That is a first indication. The Damascus community was at least partly composed of Hellenists. But there is a second point. There has come down to us the rule of a Jewish community related to that of Qumran,

19. See F. A. Shelling, ' Why did Paul go to Damascus? ' *ATR*, 16 (1934), p. 99-105.

which was established in Damascus. Now there are a certain number of resemblances between the first Christian community of Damascus and this Sadocite community. Stephen's speech, which represents the theology of the Hellenists, quotes a verse from *Amos* (5 : 25-27), which is found in the *Damascus Document: CDC* (IX, 11). Ananias's catechesis to St Paul, which is reproduced in *Acts* (22 : 14-16 and 26 : 16-18), shows remarkable links with the themes of the *Sadocite Document*[20]. So it is possible that the first Damascus community was composed of converted Sadocites[21].

Damascus was not the chief centre of the Sadocite community. The *Sadocite Document* speaks of the ' country of Damascus ' (VIII, 21; XX, 12), which seems to fit in better with the practices of the sect, for Philo tells us that it lived not in towns but in villages[22]. One scholar thinks that the village was Kokba, ten miles south-west of Damascus[23]. So it would seem that very early on there were Judaeo-Christians in Kokba[24]. Harnack recalls a tradition which says that Paul's conversion took place in Kokba[25]. The distances involved make this possible. But I see in this rather the survival of a relationship between Paul and Kokba which had another origin; it is said that in fleeing from Damascus, Paul took refuge in Arabia (Gal 1 : 17). At this period Arabia meant the Nabataean kingdom, which extended from Damascus to Petra. It is possible that the village of Arabia to which Paul withdrew was Kokba. It is noteworthy that *Acts* 9 : 23 does not suggest that Paul left the region of Damascus.

This would explain the Sadocite traces found in his thought[26]. The brief catechesis of Ananias before his baptism would be insufficient to explain them. Paul was a Pharisee and therefore, at the time of his conversion, hostile to Essenism. On the other hand everything is explained if Paul spent the three years between his conversion and journey to Jerusalem (38-41) among a group of converted Sadocites. We may add that Paul himself says that after his stay in Arabia he returned to Damascus (Gal 1 : 17), so he was not far from the town. Thus we are led to recognise the existence at Damascus and Kokba in 37 of a Christian

---

20. J. Daniélou, *Les manuscrits de la Mer Morte et les origines du christianisme*, Paris 1957, p. 98. See also W. Grundmann, ' Glaubensgerichtigkeit bei Paulus ', *Rev. Qum.*, 6 (1960), p. 250-251.
21. In 1933 Stefan Lösch suggested that Ananias was a member of the Sadocite community of Damascus converted to Christianity : *Deitas Jesu und Antike Apotheose*, Toltenburg 1933, p. 70-72.
22. *Prob.* 75.
23. See R. North in *VD*, 35 (1959), p. 49.
24. *Panarion*, XXX, 2, 8.
25. *Die Mission und Ausbreitung des Christentums*. II, 4th ed., Leipzig 1924, p. 636.
26. See W. D. Davies, *The Scrolls and the New Testament*, p. 157-183 : B. Reicke, *The Jewish Damascus Document and the New Testament*, Uppsala 1946.

community converted from Essenism. This group was doubtless the chief centre of Essenising Christianity; with it I am inclined to link the *Testaments of the Twelve Patriarchs*, the work of a Sadocite convert to Christianity[27]. The work shows remarkable links with the *Sadocite Document*[28]. It has been recast, but in its original form it was perhaps very old[29].

The second and chief centre of the Church's expansion in Syria was Antioch. Politically the town was very important; it was the legal centre of the Province of the East and an important centre of Greek culture. Its population, chiefly Syrian, was very cosmopolitan, with many Greeks and Jews. Its evangelisation, like that of Damascus, went back to the coming of the Hellenists in 37. The Gospel was first of all preached to the Jews, but the *Acts* say that some of these Hellenists, ' men from Cyprus and Cyrene ', coming from Jerusalem but speaking Greek, also spoke to the Greeks, that is to say, to the pagans (11 : 20). A great number were converted. So Antioch appears as the first centre of an important community of pagano-Christians. In 42, before the community had grown, the Apostles sent Barnabas there. This seems to have been a parallel to the sending of Peter to Samaria and shows that the Apostles were determined to ensure the unity of the communities under their joint direction.

At Antioch the name of ' Christians ' was given for the first time to the members of the community (11 : 26). As E. Peterson has shown, the word had a political ring[30]. It meant ' the supporters of Christos '. It shows us the Romans' image of the Christian community as a Messianic sect. It is the exact parallel of the first mention of Christianity by a pagan Latin writer : ' Judaei impulsore Chresto tumultuantes ', Suetonius was to say (Claudius, 25). The fact that the groups of Christians received an official name shows that the community was sufficiently large and united to emerge at the level of officialdom. This designation is therefore the first evidence of the existence of the Church in the eyes of the Roman Empire. It is also worth noting that the mention of the Christians of Antioch is dated by the author of *Acts* to the time of Claudius (41-54 AD), about the beginning of his reign. It is likewise during the reign of Claudius that Suetonius mentions the Christians.

The *Acts* tell us nothing further about the community of Antioch;

27. See J. Daniélou, *The Development of Christian Doctrine up to the Council of Nicaea*, Vol. I : *The Theology of Jewish Christianity*, London & Chicago 1964, p. 14-16.
28. See J. Daniélou, *Les symboles chrétiens primitifs*, Paris 1961, p. 109-119.
29. C. T. Fritsch has noted that Damascus and the surrounding country have always served as a refuge for various groups and individuals throughout the centuries. *The Qumran Community*, New York 1956, p. 21.
30. *Frühkirche, Judentum und Gnosis*, Vienna 1959, p. 64-88.

they were interested in Antioch only insofar as it was later to be the starting-point of the mission to Asia. But the *Epistle to the Galatians* discloses another of its aspects. We have said that the Church of Antioch was the first to reveal an important community of pagano-Christians, but *Galatians* 2 : 12 shows us that there was also a community of Judaeo-Christians. Antioch was the first town where this juxtaposition occurred. It is clear from the narrative of *Galatians* that the two communities were separate; converted to Christianity, the Jews remained subject to their customs, particularly to the law forbidding them to eat with non-Jews, that is to say with converted pagans as well. Since the Eucharist took place on the occasion of a meal, it was impossible for the Judaeo-Christians and pagano-Christians to celebrate it together. Later we shall see the problem that this raised for Peter; should he, a Jew, share the Eucharist with pagano-Christians? Or, being an Apostle, should he rise above these divisions and be present at both?

At a very early date, therefore, Antioch, as opposed to Jerusalem, was the centre of Christianity's expansion among Hellenistic pagans. It is from there that missionary work continued. It is also to Antioch that we must trace some of the oldest documents of Christianity, which have certain features in common. The *Gospel of Matthew*, if its final version is of later date, seems to be the echo of catechesis in Antiochene circles[31]. Peter's place in it supports such a hypothesis. It can be assigned to a *milieu* where relations between the Jewish community and the pagan community were close. The same is true of the *Didache*, which was very probably of Syrian origin. In its catechetical part it betrays a tradition parallel to that which we find echoed in *Matthew*, and the allusions to the prophets put us in a context similar to that which the *Acts* describe at Antioch. In its liturgical part we find an echo of the primitive Antiochene liturgy.

The evangelisation of Antioch must be linked to that of the neighbouring regions. In the *Epistle to the Galatians* Paul tells us that he preached in Syria and Cilicia, doubtless in 43-44, during the years he spent at Antioch with Barnabas. The Gospel was spread earlier in Cyprus; the *Acts* (11 :19) tell us that the Hellenists came there in 37, at the same time as to Antioch. When Paul and Barnabas went there in 45, they found communities already formed. Paul met the proconsul Sergius Paulus, whom we know from an inscription; he was under the influence of a Jewish prophet and magician, Barjesus. This is our first evidence of the competition between Jewish proselytism and the Christian

---

31. See L. Goppelt, *Christentum und Judentum im ersten und zweiten Jahrhundert*, Gütersloh 1954, p. 178-185.

apostolate, to which M. Simon has rightly drawn attention[32]. A little later at Antioch in Pisidia we shall meet Jews jealous of the conversions effected by Paul and training proselytes against him (Ac 13 : 50).

It remains true that of the regions evangelised there is most information about Asia, Macedonia and Achaea. Here two men played a decisive role : Paul and Barnabas. First we must consider the former. He is the figure in apostolic Christianity whom we know best, thanks to the *Acts*, which were written by one of his companions, and his own *Epistles*. A persecutor of the Hellenists in 36, converted in 38, he spent three years among a group of Christian Sadocites near Damascus. In 41 he went to Jerusalem, where he met Peter and James, the brother of the Lord (Gal 1 : 18; Ac 9 : 27). He clashed with the Jewish Hellenists (Ac 9 : 29) and returned to his native town, Tarsus (Ac 9 : 30). It was there that Barnabas came to look for him in 48. Barnabas had known him in Jerusalem in 41 and had introduced him to the Apostles; he took him to Antioch where they spent a year together (42-43).

Their position with regard to the Church of Antioch needs clarification. The *Acts* tell us that at this time there were in the Church of Antioch ' prophets and doctors ' (Ac 13 : 1). They are named : Barnabas, Simon called Niger, Lucius the Cyrenaean, Manahen, foster-brother of Herod the tetrarch, and Saul. This group seems not to have belonged to the local community of Antioch of which we have spoken, but to have comprised the Hellenist missionaries, which is true of Barnabas. Among the missionaries who came from Antioch, there were men from Cyrene (Ac 11 : 20); Lucius was a Cyrenaean and Manahen came from Herod's circle. This group included Saul. These missionaries worked at a higher level : Antioch was only their base. Their mission in fact continued that of the Twelve and they were in continual contact with the Twelve. Barnabas introduced Paul to them in 41, in 44 he again went to Jerusalem with Paul (Ac 11 : 30; 12 : 25); they brought back John Mark (Ac 12 : 25). Earlier the Apostles had sent them a group of prophets, including Agabus (Ac 11 : 27).

One has the impression that these men were directly associated with the work of the Twelve, and doubtless that was so. The *Acts* call them prophets and doctors (Ac 13 : 1); these two titles are found in I Cor 12 : 28, immediately after the Apostles. It seems impossible to see in these words solely the expression of charismatic gifts. Prophets and doctors later reappear in the *Didache* (XV, 1 & 2); they seem to have been ecclesiastical ministers. In contrast to the deacons and presbyters, who made up the local hierarchies, the words seem to suggest missionary ministers. The

32. *Verus Israël*, Paris 1948, p. 27-35.

Didache makes clear the parallel between the two (XV, 1). They had a universal character, like the Apostles, who delegated to them all or part of their power, as they did to local hierarchies. There was, moreover, movement from one group to the other. The Seven, at first members of the local hierarchy of Jerusalem, became missionaries when they were expelled.

It remains true that in this group of missionaries staying in Antioch, Barnabas and Paul were two special cases. Barnabas is named first; he took the part of leader. This seems to suggest that he had received from the Apostles a larger delegation of authority. He was to the other missionaries what James was to the presbyters of Jerusalem, and possessed all that could be communicated in the Apostolate. He corresponded to the ἄνδρες ἐλλόγιμοι (andres ellogimoi) later referred to in the *Epistle of Clement* (XLIV, 1-3), who had sole authority to establish ministers, that is, to confer ordination. Paul's case was different. He claimed to be an Apostle in the full sense of the word, namely to hold his powers directly from the Lord, in view of a special commission. This claim perhaps lay at the bottom of his later break with Barnabas.

It was from this group that in the spring of 45 a mission departed for Asia, to which the author of the *Acts* gives a special importance, because it marked the beginning of Paul's ministry. The *Acts* describe the circumstances of this departure. In the course of a eucharistic gathering, Barnabas and Paul were set apart and the others laid their hands on them. This cannot in fact have been an ordination because Barnabas and Paul were already invested with apostolic powers. It was, rather, a ceremony of farewell: Barnabas and Paul embarked at Seleucia, the port of Antioch. From then onwards Luke's narrative is based on documents that came to him from Paul and contains remarkable historical and geographical detail, as a result of which the spreading of the Gospel in Asia is much better known to us than that of any of the regions we have so far studied.

In fact, from a geographical standpoint, this mission was limited. The towns evangelised were Perga and Attalia in Pamphylia, Antioch in Pisidia, Iconium, Lystra and Derbe in Lycaonia. At first the apostolate of Paul and Barnabas took place among the Jews. They preached in the synagogues (Ac 13 : 4; 13 : 14; 14 : 1) on the Sabbath day and introduced themselves as belonging to a Jewish sect. But they also addressed the pagans; in Antioch in Pisidia the pagans came on the Sabbath day to listen to them in the synagogue (Ac 13 : 44) and the same happened in Iconium (14 : 1). At Lystra, Paul and Barnabas having performed a miracle, the people took them for Zeus and Hermes and wanted to sacrifice a garlanded ox to them (14 : 11-12).

In these two regions Paul and Barnabas made converts among Jews and proselytes (13 : 43; 14 : 1) and among the pagans (13 : 48; 14 : 1). They founded local communities, and to govern these they ordained ' elders ' by the laying on of hands (14 : 23), as at Jerusalem and Antioch. But everywhere they met violent hostility from Jewish circles (13 :45). The latter roused the pagan population against them; at Antioch in Pisidia it was the town authorities whom the Jews stirred up (13 : 50). At Iconium and Lystra it was the people (14 : 2; 14 : 19). In fact they received a friendlier welcome from the pagans than from the Jews. This was something new and of capital importance for Paul; it was at this juncture that he began to work out his theology of the rejection of the Jews and the conversion of the pagans (13 : 46-47). Moreover a new type of Kerygma emerges which no longer invokes the accomplishment of the prophecies but the covenant of Noah (14 : 15-17). So the significant aspect of the communities of Lycaonia of Pisidia is the importance of the pagano-Christians. Paul had not expected this; it was to raise grave problems for him.

Was Paul's the only mission to the West? The *Acts* tell us that in 43, after the death of James, Peter left Jerusalem ' for another place ' (Ac 12 : 17). He is lost from sight until 49, when we find him at the Council of Jerusalem. No canonical text has anything to say about his missionary activity during this time. But Eusebius writes that he came to Rome about 44, at the beginning of Claudius's reign (*HE* II, 14, 61). It seems certain that Rome was evangelised during the period from 43 to 49. Suetonius says that Claudius expelled the Jews in 50, because they were growing agitated ' at the prompting of Chrestos '. This shows that discussions between Jews and Judaeo-Christians were taking place, leading to conflicts which came to the ear of the emperor. In fact at Corinth in 51 Paul met some converted Jews driven from Rome by Claudius : Aquila and Priscilla. In 57 Paul addressed the community of Rome, already considered important. In 60 he found communities established in Puteoli[33] and in Rome.

33. See M. Adenolfi, ' San Paolo a Pozzioli, ' *Riv. Bibl.*, 8 (1960), p. 206-224.

CHAPTER III

THE CRISIS
OF JUDAEO-CHRISTIANITY

THE PERIOD from the years 40 to 70 was marked by two facts important for the Christian community. On the one hand, Jewish nationalism became more and more extreme[1], and the Judaeo-Christians came under strong pressure from it. On the other hand, the Fall of Jerusalem in 70 was a very serious blow to Judaism in general and to Judaeo-Christianity in particular. Moreover during this time, thanks chiefly to Paul's efforts, Christianity made progress among the pagans, and this led the Christians from these groups to break away from their Jewish context, though not without a difficult crisis. At the end there occurs a reversal of the earlier situation. Judaeo-Christianity, triumphant in 49, collapsed, while Pauline Christianity began its triumphant destiny[2]. At the threshold of this period the Council of Jerusalem took place and laid down lines to be followed; at the end came the Fall of Jerusalem, which decisively settled certain questions.

The year 49 was marked by two events which show that a crisis had arisen between Judaeo-Christians and Gentile Christians: the Council of Jerusalem and the Antioch episode. The chronological link between these two events is at present disputed[3]. The *Epistle to the Galatians*, the only one to mention the Antioch episode, places it second. The difficulties opposed to this order seem to be based on *a priori* grounds, so this order will be followed here. Paul returned to Antioch in 48 with Barnabas. He had described the results obtained among the pagans

---

1. Gaechter has collected from Josephus the list of Zealot uprisings from 44 to 52 (*op. cit.*, p. 223) under the first three procurators who succeeded to the Kingdom of Agrippa.
2. See S. G. F. Brandon, *The Fall of Jerusalem and the Christian Church;* B. Reicke, *Diakonie, Festfreude und Zelos.*
3. See J. Dupont, ' Pierre et Paul à Antioche et à Jérusalem, ' *RSR.*, 45 (1957), p. 42-60; 225-240.

of Asia (14 : 27) and the new prospects lying ahead. Gentile converts were not obliged to submit to Jewish practices, notably circumcision. This was the case of an Asiatic, Titus, whom he had brought with him.

And now in 49 ' men come down from Judaea ' disturbed the community of Antioch by teaching that circumcision was obligatory for all. Many scholars have seen in these men Judaeo-Christians holding James's point of view, opposed to Paul, who represents the Gentile Christians. Gregory Dix has rightly criticised this theory[4]. The Judaeo-Christians, who then comprised nearly all the Church, admitted from the start that converted pagans were not obliged to undergo circumcision, as Peter recalls (Ac 15 : 10). So the obligation to be circumcised must, on the contrary, be something new. To what must we link it? Evidently to the political situation of Judaism, which had come into open conflict with Rome. Christians were still considered to belong to the Jewish community; for them to admit non-circumcised members appeared an act of treason towards Judaism. So it was under the pressure of Jewish nationalists that certain Judaeo-Christians tried to uphold Christian membership of the Jewish community, of which circumcision was the seal.

What was at stake is quite clear. The danger was to link Christianity with the temporal destiny of Israel. Paul and Barnabas understood this clearly and strongly opposed these demands. By doing so they appeared as representatives of the Judaeo-Christian community itself, and not as innovators. Nevertheless, seeing the gravity of the dispute, the Antioch community wished it to be laid before the Apostles in Jerusalem (Ac 15 : 2). Paul and Barnabas were sent with Titus (Gal 2 : 1) and were received by the Apostles and the Elders. There the debate began again. Certain Christians of the sect of Pharisees defended the theory of circumcision of the Gentiles. Peter in the name of the Apostles, James in the name of the elders decided in Paul's favour, pointing out that the pagans were only obliged to carry out the Noachic precepts : abstinence from food sacrificed to idols, meat of strangled animals and fornication[5]. Paul and Barnabas, joined by Silas and Jude named Barsabbas, were sent to transmit the decision to Antioch. This important decision marked the break between Christianity and the Jewish community, which was to become accentuated in the next few years.

Important for the history of the relations of Christianity and Judaism, the Council of Jerusalem was also important for the development of the

---

4. *Jew and Greek*, p. 43.

5. The word πορνεία does not here mean fornication in the usual sense but refers to certain observances : perhaps an impediment of consanguinity or a law about sexual relations. See E. Molland, ' La circoncision, le baptême et l'autorité du décrit apostolique, ' *ST*, 9 1955), p. 37-38.

Christian community. The variety of the men taking part is noticeable. Peter and John represented the Twelve; Peter had left Jerusalem in 43, his presence in Jerusalem was accidental : either he came for the Council, or a period of relative calm on the part of the Jews allowed him to return. James, surrounded by the elders, represented the local community of Jerusalem. Silas and Jude named Barsabbas appear to have belonged to the elders; they are named ' higoumens ' (leaders); the word seems to be synonymous with presbyters. It is found in the *Epistle to the Hebrews* (13 : 7; 17 : 24) and the *Epistle of Clement* (1 :3)[6]. The Council also included Paul and Barnabas, who had the same rank as Peter and James. They were accompanied by Titus, who at the missionary level had the same rank as the elders.

In this picture we see the organisation of the hierarchy taking shape. The Twelve formed a rank apart, put in charge of the Church as a whole, now stationary, now moving about, with whom every Church had to be in communion. Peter had a special rank among them; Paul was assimilated to them. Beside them were two parallel hierarchies : on the one hand, the local hierarchy, composed of the Council of the elders, also called episcopes or higoumens. At their head was a president who was sometimes a man of the first rank, like James of Jerusalem, who possessed all the powers of the Apostles capable of being shared, and who alone had power to institute elders. On the other hand there was the missionary hierarchy (ἀπόστολοι, apostoloi), didascali or prophets. It also included men of the first rank, like Barnabas, who participated in the powers of the Apostles. The movement from one hierarchy to the other, as in the case of the Hellenist deacons, the higoumens of Jerusalem and the presbyters of the Didache, shows their equivalence.

The Council of Jerusalem had definitively settled the question of the circumcision of the Gentiles. But the nervousness of the Judaeo-Christians, stirred up by nationalist considerations, was not thereby calmed. We see this soon afterwards, at the end of 49, at the time of Peter's journey to Antioch. Peter was present at Jerusalem for the Council of 49, but the situation of the Jerusalem community was more and more difficult; the real work lay elsewhere. It was during his journey on a new mission that Peter stopped at Antioch. At the beginning he would have divided his time between the two communities, Judaeo-Christian and pagano-Christian, but on the arrival of people from James's circle he stopped eating with the pagano-Christians and Barnabas followed suit. Paul reproached them sharply for this. Some say that this was an act of cowardice on Peter's part. Gaechter seems to be nearer

6. See A. Büchsel, Art. ἡγοῦμαι in *TWNT*, II, p. 909-911. Note the equivalence higoumen = deacon in Lk 22 : 26.

the truth when he shows that Peter and Paul were concerned with opposite considerations[7].   For Paul, who thought of the pagano-Christians, it was essential to free Christianity from its Jewish links, whereas Peter feared the risk that the Judaeo-Christians, under the pressure of Jewish nationalism, might return to Judaism.   He wanted to keep them by showing that it was possible to be loyal both to the Christian faith and the Jewish Law.   It was doubtless in order to ask him for a gesture of this kind that James's men had come.

The two points of view were equally legitimate, but they were irreconcilable.   Paul at this moment gave up Judaeo-Christianity as lost and thought only of the Church's future among the Greeks.   We can understand the hostility of the Judaeo-Christians towards him which was later expressed in the Pseudo-Clementine writings.   Peter, on the other hand, despite the situation of the Church in Judaea, seems not yet to have lost hope of keeping a Judaeo-Christian community.   And perhaps he saw very far, just as far as St Paul.   But in fact our information about the events in Antioch comes only from the latter; his view is one-sided and amounts to special pleading.   Without accusing him of distorting the facts, we may well consider that he gives us only one aspect of them. In any case the incident gains its full meaning if placed in the framework of the double movement whereby Christianity is to spread among the Greeks, while the Jerusalem community is to dissolve in the rising tide of Jewish nationalism.

The first movement, the expansion of pagano-Christianity, was essentially the work of Paul and his colleagues.   For tracing its development there exists a remarkably rich documentation, historically the most exact of this period : the second part of the *Acts*, where Luke, who has become Paul's companion, uses the diary of his journey — and the *corpus* of the Pauline *Epistles*.   Here we shall only note the chief stages. At the beginning of 50 Paul set out on a new journey; he crossed Syria and Cilicia and doubtless passed by way of Tarsus, his native town. Then he visited the Christians of Derbe, Lystra, Iconium and Antioch of Pisidia.   From there he broke new ground : Galatia, northern Phrygia and Mysia.   He left with Silas, one of the higoumen prophets, who came to Antioch with him from Jerusalem, and joined Timothy in Lystra and Luke in Mysia.   The first two were to remain associated with Paul's missionary work and were to be his proxies[8].

But the striking event in this mission was Paul's journey to Europe, with the consequent foundation of the Churches of Macedonia and

7. *Op. cit.*, p. 234-239.
8. See Ac 17 : 14 & 15; 18 : 15; II Cor 1 : 19; I Ths 1 : 1; II Ths 1 : 1.

PLATE I

ISAIAH SCROLL FROM QUMRAN OPEN AT
ISAIAH 40

This scroll probably dates from the second century B.C., and was almost certainly used by the community at the time of Christ, and in the earliest period of the Church. It is made up of seventeen sheets of somewhat coarse parchment, sewn together and amounting in all to about 24 feet 6 inches in length. In this picture, the column which is completely visible contains in its second line the verse of Isaiah (40:3) quoted at the beginning of St Mark's Gospel: 'In the wilderness, prepare the way of the Lord'.

By permission of Yale University, New Haven.

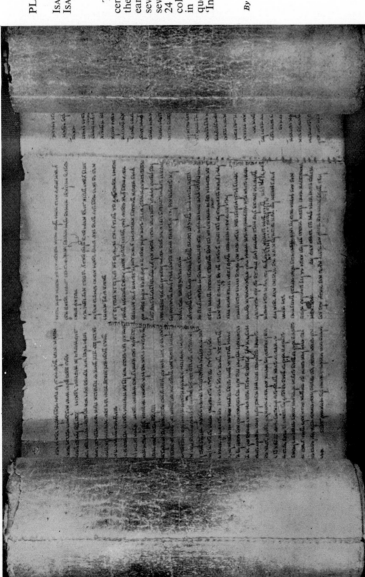

THE COMMUNITY IN THE WILDER-NESS

PLATE 2

GENERAL VIEW OF KHIRBET QUMRAN, LOOKING TOWARDS THE EAST

The ruins shown here are perched on a plateau surrounded on three sides by steep ravines, about a mile from the west coast of the Dead Sea. There are traces of an early Israelite settlement on the site, probably from about 8th century B.C., but most of the ruins belong to communities that lived here between the mid-2nd century B.C. and 68 A.D. Judging from the MSS discovered near the site, the community was a closely disciplined group which looked upon itself as the 'True Israel', called to be separate from the historic Israel and summoned to a life of work, prayer, and study of the Law in the wilderness,

Photo : A. Strobel, O.M.I.

Achaea (I Ths 7-8). In Macedonia he stopped at Philippi where he converted several pagans. Denounced and arrested by the Roman authorities, Paul made use of his title of Roman citizen (Ac 16 : 37; I Ths 2 : 3). At Thessalonica he spoke in the synagogue and converted the Jews, but he also converted some Greeks (17 : 4); the same thing happened in Berea. From there he went to Athens (Ac 7 : 16-34; I Ths 3 : 1) where he preached to the Areopagus in the presence of Stoics and Epicureans (17 :18). But he had little success there. Then he went to Corinth where he stayed for a year and a half (18 :11). This stay can be dated with certainty. On the one hand he met two Jews, Aquila and Priscilla, who had a weaving business and with whom he worked. Aquila and Priscilla had just been expelled from Rome by Claudius. Suetonius mentions this edict, which is dated 49. Moreover the proconsul of Achaea was Gallio (18 :12), who, according to an inscription at Delphi, exercised this office in 52. So the stay at Corinth ran from the beginning of 51 to the summer of 52. It was from there that Paul wrote the two *Epistles to the Thessalonians;* he then returned to Antioch by way of Ephesus and Jerusalem.

In spring 53 he left on a new journey. Again he crossed Galatia and Phrygia, but this time his goal was Ephesus. He preached not only in the synagogue but also in a school for the pagans (19 : 9). He stayed there nearly three years (54 to 57), and it was from there that he wrote the *Epistle to the Galatians* and the *First Epistle to the Corinthians.* His plan was to return to Jerusalem by way of Corinth and Rome (19 :21). In fact he stopped in Macedonia (I Cor 2 : 13) and arrived at Corinth at the end of 57 (20 : 2) after Titus had rejoined him (II Cor 7 : 6). During the winter 57-58 he wrote the *Epistle to the Romans.* He then went to Philippi, embarked for Troas and arrived at Tyre by ship, having touched at Miletus; he arrived in Jerusalem for Pentecost 58 (20 : 16).

So the balance sheet of Paul's missions shows a credit. Between 50 and 58 he founded the Churches of Macedonia (Philippi, Thessalonica) and of Achaea (Corinth). But what the *Acts* allow us to glimpse and what the *Epistles,* somewhat sadly, reveal is the growing opposition which he did not cease to meet from the Judaeo-Christians, aroused against him by Jewish nationalism : an opposition which led first to his arrest in Jerusalem in 58, then to his martyrdom in 67. As Brandon and Reicke have rightly shown, all the difficulties met by Paul stemmed from this one cause. They started at the beginning of the mission of 49. Barnabas and Mark refused to leave with him, and embarked for Cyprus (15 : 39). If we recall that, just before, Barnabas ' out of fear of the people of the circumcision ' had already loosened his ties with Paul (Gal 2 : 14), it is clear that the same motive led him to separate from him. At Lystra,

' because of the Jews ' (16 : 3), Paul circumcised Timothy, which was a concession. At Thessalonica the Jews, ' out of jealousy ', stirred up the people against him. But, worse still, the Church was disturbed by ' dissolute men ', who did not work and occupied themselves with frivolities (II Ths 3 : 11). They were members of the community and announced that the Day of the Lord was close at hand (II Ths 2 : 2). It is difficult not to see in this a political disturbance of a Messianic kind, which recalls what Josephus tells us about Jewish rebels at this time; it is against their influence that Paul wrote his two letters.

In Ephesus he was preceded by Apollo, an Alexandrian Jew who ' had instruction in the way of the Lord ', but ' he knew of no baptism except that of John ' (Ac 18 : 25). He had founded a community (Ac 18 : 26). He went to Achaea about 54 and we find him again in Corinth. He seems to have been at the bottom of difficulties mentioned by Paul (I Cor 1 : 12). What, then, did Apollo teach? He showed that Christ, was Wisdom (sophia) come down into the world and ignored by its rulers (I Cor 2 : 6-11). Paul did not condemn these speculations, but he reproached Apollo for making a gnosis out of Christianity. What did a Jew mean by gnosis at that time unless the apocalypse which reveals the heavenly secrets, the names of the angels? This gnosis was especially prevalent in Essene circles. But it was also found in Egypt among the Therapeutae, who were related to them. It was from this group that Apollo came[9]. Converted by Priscilla and Aquila, he retained in his Christianity this speculative turn of mind, which appears also in Judaeo-Christian writings like the *Ascension of Isaiah*.

This throws light on Asian Christianity. During his second journey the Holy Spirit had turned Paul aside into Asia (Ac 16 : 6). When he came there, from 54 to 57, he found Judaeo-Christians with the same tendency as Apollo and met sharp opposition from Judaising groups (Ac 19 : 33). Later he was to speak of his opponents there (I Cor 16 : 9). So it seems that Paul faced a very powerful Judaeo-Christian community, over against which he tried to found a Gentile community. Later he was delivered to wild animals (I Cor 15 : 32) as a result of the hostility shown to him by the Judaeo-Christians. In 51 he again clashed with the Judaeo-Christians of Ephesus (I Tim 1 : 3), then in 63 he complained that everyone in Asia had abandoned him (II Tim 1 : 15).

Simultaneously with disturbances among the Corinthians, and after those among the Ephesians, influenced by Apollo, disturbances took place in Galatia. Here the situation is even clearer. The Galatians returned to Jewish practices; having been freed by Christ, they returned to slavery

---

9. See C. Spicq, ' L'Épître aux Hébreux, Apollos, Jean-Baptiste, les Hellénistes et Qumrân ', *RQ*, 1 (1959), p. 365-391.

(Gal 5 : 1) and the obligatory observance of the Law even by the pagano-Christians (Gal 5 : 2). More particularly they attached importance ' to special days and months, special seasons and years ' (Gal 4 : 10). A study of Jewish Apocalyptic writings of the time shows the importance given to the calendar as an expression of the ordering of time by God[10]; this importance was linked to the expectation of the eschatological event. One could not have a clearer expression of the spirit underlying Jewish Zealotism. This contained two elements : fanatical attachment to legal observances and sharpening of eschatological hopes; it was these tendencies which stirred up the Galatians. What we witness is a Judaization of Christianity.

Paul found himself in the winter of 57 in a dramatic situation, supremely expressed in the *Epistle to the Romans*. A powerful current of revolt against Rome was shaking the Jewish world, and this also affected many Christians. Their conflict with Paul was not dogmatic; there was no question of two Christianities. It was a question of the Christians' situation with regard to the Jewish community, from which they came. To deny circumcision appeared political treason, not religious disloyalty, and to betray the Jewish community was to place Christians of Jewish origin in a difficult situation, expose them anew to Jewish persecution, drive them to despair and apostasy. The old problem raised at Antioch was still developing, but it had become sharper. Wise and outstanding men, Peter, Barnabas and others, thought that concessions would have to be made to safeguard a Judaeo-Christianity, which was still in the majority as regards numbers. Paul was afraid that even his companions would abandon him; the absence of Titus distressed him. Moreover he was also persecuted by the pagans at Philippi and Ephesus, mocked by the philosophers at Athens. He may well have wondered whether he was not mistaken and was ready to make concessions. He advised the Corinthians to avoid scandalising people by eating meat offered to pagan deities. But the certainty of the voice which had spoken to him prevented him from weakening.

In 58 this conflict gave rise to a dramatic crisis; in coming to Jerusalem Paul knew that he was courting danger (Ac 20 : 22). He was received by James and the elders, and the latter informed him of the charges the Jews were making against him : he was turning the Jews away from circumcision and their customs (21 : 21). They advised him to make a public act of loyalty as a Jew, so Paul went to the Temple. But some Jews from Asia recognised him and stirred up a riot against him. They accused him unjustly of having profaned the Temple by introducing

10. See M. Testuz, *Les idées religieuses du Livre des Jubilés*, Paris 1960, p. 121-165.

a pagan into it. He was arrested by the Roman soldiers, but having announced that he was a Roman citizen he escaped any ill treatment. A discussion took place before the Sanhedrin, followed by a new tumult, and a group of Jews planned to assassinate him. The tribune then sent him to Caesarea, to the procurator Felix, who was in office from 52 to 59. Felix realised that he was innocent but kept him in prison for two years; in 59 he was replaced by Festus (25 :27). The Jews demanded that Paul be brought back to Jerusalem, but Paul appealed to Caesar. Festus decided to send him to Rome. First, he was questioned by Agrippa II and his sister Berenice, who were convinced of his innocence.

Starting in this year 60, events succeeded one another rapidly. In Rome Paul remained on probation from 61 to 63. It was then that he wrote the *Epistles to the Colossians, to the Ephesians, to the Philippians.* The *Epistle to the Colossians* bears witness to Judaeo-Christian activity in Phrygia : questions about forbidden food and about the calendar were raised by them and disturbed the community (2 : 16). Paul did not condemn these usages as bad, but they belonged to an order of things which was obsolete. Elsewhere he puts the Colossians on their guard against speculations about angels, which were a feature of the Jewish Apocalypse (2 : 18). Christ on the cross has dispossessed principalities and powers (2 : 10). Paul also pointed out that what he was writing also concerned the neighbouring towns of Laodicea and Hierapolis — we shall see later that these towns were Judaeo-Christian fiefs. Paul announced that he was also sending a letter to the Laodiceans (4 : 16), but he probably never wrote it.

Freed in 63, Paul resumed his missionary work. Our information for this final period is contained in the *Epistles to Timothy* and the *Epistle to Titus.* The conflict with the Judaeo-Christians increased and Paul went to Crete. Shortly afterwards he wrote to Titus, whom he had left there in order to institute elders in each town (1 : 5), and put him on guard against the Judaeo-Christians (1 : 10). They lent an ear to Judaic fables (muthoi) — the technical term for millenarian dreams — and insisted on regulations about food (1 : 14-15). Paul advised Titus to leave aside disputes about genealogies, that is to say, speculations about the angels, and about the Law, that is to say Jewish observances (3 : 9).

The two *Epistles to Timothy* were directed at the situation in Ephesus where Paul had gone, doubtless after his journey to Crete. With him he had Timothy, to whom he entrusted the Church of Ephesus when he left for Macedonia, and it was from Macedonia that he sent him instructions. This is the first of the two Epistles. It was first of all a question of fighting those who taught fables and genealogies (1 : 4); they only created divisions. Timothy must guard what had been entrusted to him and avoid ' this quibbling knowledge that is knowledge only in name ' (pseudonumos) (6 :21) — this last word means Judaeo-Christian speculations and was later to be used by Irenaeus to designate Gnosticism, which was a branch of them. These Judaeo-Christians also forbade marriage and the use of certain foods (4 : 3). Timothy evidently let himself be influenced, for Paul recommended him to drink wine (5 : 3). Here a new feature of Judaeo-Christianity is in evidence : Encratism, which forbade marriage and wine. Encratism was chiefly a feature of Palestinian and Mesopo-tamian Judaeo-Christianity. It shows that Judaeo-Christian missionaries continued to be active in Ephesus.

Another feature of the *First Epistle to Timothy* is important. Paul gave instructions for the organisation of the community of Asia, similar to those he had given to Titus for Crete. There was a college of presbyters, with a president, who was one of its members. More specifically, he was given the title of bishop (episcopos) which suggests the function rather than the dignity[11]. There were also deacons, directly dependent on the bishop. There are thus two parallel hierarchies, the one more collegial, the other more monarchical, with the bishop as the link. These two hierarchies were often to come into conflict.

The emphasis placed by Paul in the pastoral *Epistles* on the institutional hierarchy has raised doubts as to their authenticity. Some have argued that the situation they describe is at variance with that found in the *Epistles to the Corinthians*, but the situation described seems in fact to correspond to the date in question[12]. We merely have the substitution of an ordinary local hierarchy for the missionary hierarchy. At this period in Syria the same development is found in the *Didache*.

Two years later, when Paul sent Timothy a second letter, the situation had grown still worse; Paul was gloomy. Men no longer heeded healthy teaching : they opened their ears to fables (muthoi) (4 : 3-4). The false apostles made their way into house after house, captivating women (3 : 6). The part played by women was a feature of the Judeao-Christian sects and was to reappear later in Gnosticism. They were like Jannes and Mambres, the opponents of Moses and Aaron in the Jewish tradition (3 : 8). In particular Hymenaeus and Philetas taught that the resurrection had already taken place (2 : 18). Later we find this claim in Cerinthus. It was a sign of the sharpening of Apocalyptic hopes. Everyone abandoned Paul in Asia (1 : 15). Judaeo-Christianity had never seemed so triumphant as at that time, but in fact it was on the eve of its defeat.

11. J. Dupont, *Le discours de Milet*, Paris 1962, p. 141.
12. See J. Jeremias, ' Zur Datierung der Pastoralbriefe ', *ZNTW*, 52 (1961), p. 101-104

At Rome during this time the drama broke out. July 64 was the date of the burning of Rome. Nero had been reigning since 54; he placed responsibility for the fire on the Christians. The accusation may have been aimed at the missionary disturbances of certain Judaeo-Christian groups, so it was still linked to the same atmosphere. Peter seems to have been one of the victims of the persecution; most historians today are agreed on this, and it is not impossible that it is his tomb which has been found on the Vatican Hill. It is possible that certain Judaeo-Christians denounced him, as a passage in *I Clement* (V, 2) seems to suggest[13], and still more the narrative of Tacitus, who speaks of a denunciation of their co-religionists[14] by the first Christians to be arrested. Paul was again a prisoner in Rome and everything suggests that the same conditions prevailed as on the first occasion. He then wrote the *Second Epistle to Timothy*. We can date his death at 67. Doubtless he too had been denounced by the Judaeo-Christians to the Roman authorities as a trouble-maker (II Tim 4 : 16; I Clem V, 4).

During this time the situation had deteriorated in Palestine. In 62 James, Bishop of Jerusalem, was stoned. The date is attested by Josephus, who records the event twice and its date as the year when the procurator Festus was replaced by Albinus[15]. This coincides with the accession to the high priesthood of a member of the family of Annas, Annas the younger[16]. Hegesippus gives a more detailed account than Eusebius (*HE*, II, 23, 1-25) of James's martyrdom; in this case it would seem to have been the Pharisees who feared the influence of James on the people. This would supply evidence of mounting anger against the Christians, doubtless because of their refusal, even among the Judaeo-Christians, to commit themselves to anti-Roman Messianism.

In 66 this nationalism reached its climax : the Jewish war began and the Christian community then withdrew to Pella, in Transjordan, which was equivalent to breaking its links with Israel's national destiny (*HE*, III, 5, 4). It was headed by Simon, Jesus's cousin, who had succeeded to James (*HE*, III, 2). This action, more than any other, marked the Church's definitive break with Judaism. The community of Jerusalem had tried right to the end to keep in touch with the Jews and work for their conversion to Christ despite persecution by them. Henceforth it would leave Israel to march to her destiny. In 70 Titus captured Jerusalem, massacred the Jewish population and razed the Temple.

13. O. Cullmann, *Saint Pierre*, Paris 1952, p. 93-96.
14. See H. Fuchs, ' Tacitus über die Christen ', *Vig. Christ.*, 4 (1950), p. 69-74; K. B. Bauer, ' Tacitus und die Christen, ' *Gymnasium*, 64 (1957), p. 495-503.
15. *Ant. Jud.*, XX, 197-203.
16. See P. Gaechter, *op. cit.*, p. 100-105.

CHAPTER IV

EPHESUS, EDESSA, ROME

THE Fall of Jerusalem, by putting an end to Jewish Messianism, freed Christianity from the pressure exerted on it by Judaism and released it sociologically from Judaism. Paul won a posthumous victory, but the Church had been too deeply engaged in the Jewish world to obtain release at a single stroke and find a new place in the Hellenistic world. In this sense the period between 70 and 140 constitutes a period of search; the Judaeo-Christian forms of thought survived, and Hellenistic Christianity had not yet produced the intellectual élite who would rethink them in the Greek tradition. It was also the period when, at the frontiers of Judaism and Christianity, ' Gnostic ' sects began to swarm, transferring disappointed Messianic hopes into a fantasy world and condemning man's present life. Finally the first clash with the Roman world was being prepared.

1. Asiatic Christianity

At the beginning of Book III of his *History of the Church*[1], after having described the Fall of Jerusalem, Eusebius says that ' the inhabited world ' was divided into zones of influence among the Apostles : Thomas in the region of the Parthians, John in Asia, Peter in Pontus and Rome, Andrew in Scythia. This statement contains a certain measure of historical truth, particularly for John, but it is difficult to verify for the others. One fact, however, gives support to it. The apocryphal writings of the New Testament are divided into cycles : the cycle of Peter, the cycle of Thomas, the cycle of Philip, the cycle of John. These cycles seem to refer to definite geographical areas, and it seems, in particular, that the Judaeo-Christian mission at the beginning of the second century took several different forms : the Mesopotamian, linked to James and Thomas; Asiatic Christianity, which depends on Philip

1. III, I, 1.

and John; the Petrine group comprising Phoenicia, Pontus, Achaea and Rome.

Asia Minor is the region where Christianity shows the most extraordinary vitality during our period.   It would seem to be divided into zones of influence; the eastern part, Lycaonia and Cilicia, is the one about which we have least information.   It retains the memory of Paul's preaching, later attested in the *Acts of Paul*.   On the other hand, Phrygia is better known to us, in fact we have a precious witness in Papias, who was Bishop of Hierapolis in this region.   Irenaeus tells us that he was a companion of Polycarp, and Irenaeus's evidence is excellent, for he himself knew Polycarp in his youth.   Irenaeus also declares that Papias was a disciple of the apostle John[2]; it is possible that it may be the apostle John whom Papias describes as the presbyter whose disciple he was (*HE* III, 39, 4)[3].

Papias had written some *Expositions of the Oracles of the Lord*, in which he had collected traditions about the Apostles from people who had known them, and he tells us, in particular, that he has heard the daughters of the apostle Philip speaking in Hierapolis; so we can believe as certain the information he gives us that the apostle Philip lived in Hierapolis.   Later the Montanist Proclus declared that it was not the apostle Philip but the deacon of the same name, the person described in the *Acts* as having stayed in Caesarea, whose four daughters remained virgins and uttered prophecies (*HE* III, 31, 4).   But Polycrates of Ephesus, at the end of the second century, confirms what Papias says, and it is certainly the apostle Philip who died at Hierapolis (*HE* III, 31, 3).   Two of his daughters had remained virgins and also died at Hierapolis; the others married (*HE* III, 29, 1) and one died at Ephesus (III, 31, 3).

Other facts seem to confirm this link between Philip and Phrygia. This region is close to that of the apostle John.   It is remarkable that Philip plays a specially important part in the *Gospel of John*, written at this time, the end of the first century[4].   Moreover a *Gospel of Philip* has been found at Nag Hammadi.   It is Gnostic in character and certainly of later date, but its contacts with the Asiatic theology of Irenaeus and the Asiatic Gnosticism of Mark the Magus are very remarkable.   There also exist apocryphal *Acts of Philip* which praise virginity.   Finally it should be noted that Hierapolis received no letter either from Paul or John, whereas the neighbouring cities of Colossae and Laodicea received letters; perhaps this is because Hierapolis was Philip's fief.

2. *Adv. Haer.*, V, 33, 4.
3. See P. Carrington, *The Early Christian Church*, I, Cambridge 1957, p. 194.
4. P. Carrington, *op. cit.*, p. 291.

At the end of the period we are studying, Hierapolis became the starting-point of Montanism. Papias (saying that they come from the presbyters) gives us traditions concerning Millenarian hopes markedly apocalyptic in character, and it is from him that Irenaeus inherited this doctrine. Apocalyptic enthusiasm seems to have been one of the features of the Asiatic *milieu*, and we find it again in the heretic Cerinthus; the *Apocalypse of John* also shows signs of it. Asiatic Judaeo-Christianity has a very special character, quite different from James's Palestinian Judaeo-Christianity or Peter's Syrian group. Hopes of an earthly Messiah have here survived the Fall of Jerusalem and have not degenerated into Gnosticism. It was doubtless also this enthusiasm which made Asia Minor at this period the area in which we find most martyrs, along with the regions which had relations with it, like Irenaeus's Gaul and Tertullian's Africa[5].

Under Domitian, Nerva and Trajan western Phrygia and the Asiatic coast appear to have been John's region. We have met John in Jerusalem, where with Peter he was one of the pillars of the Church (Gal 2 : 9). He was present at the Council of Jerusalem in 49, but later we lose trace of him until his exile in Patmos under Domitian (Ap I : 9). It is possible that he was already in Ephesus when he was exiled, and it is certain that he stayed there after his exile. We have a witness o, the front rank, St Irenaeus, himself a native of Asia who knew Polycarpf a disciple of John[6]. Irenaeus several times recalls the teaching of John in Ephesus[7]; he says that he lived there until the reign of Trajan[8]. Moreover, Clement of Alexandria records that he appointed bishops in the new Christian communities[9]. Polycarp and Papias were his disciples[10].

John was not the first to have spread the Gospel in this region, we have seen that Paul stayed in Ephesus, but neither was Paul the first to bring the Gospel there; he had found a Judaeo-Christian community in Ephesus, and we know what difficulties it had caused him. It is this Judaeo-Christian *milieu* which found in John its true direction, as Braun has noted : ' John belonged to the party intent on renouncing as little as possible of authentic Judaism[11] '. This attitude appears clearly in the *Apocalypse* (2 : 14 and 20), where he violently condemns the Christians

5. See W. H. C. Frend, ' The Gnostic Sects and the Roman Empire ', *JEH*, 6 (1954), p. 25-28.
6. *Adv. Haer.*, III, 3, 4.
7. *Adv. Haer.*, IV, 1, 1; IV, 3, 1.
8. *Adv. Haer.*, II, 22, 59.
9. *Quis dives*, 42.
10. *Adv. Haer.*, V, 33, 4. See E. Gutwenger, ' Papias, Eine chronologische Studie, ' *ZKT*, 69 (1947), p. 403-416.
11. *Jean le Théologien et son Évangile dans l'Église ancienne*, Paris 1959, p. 330.

who agree to eat idolothytes — meat offered to pagan deities. It is known that Paul took a less strict attitude on this point, and John seems much more in the line of Apollo. So Asia saw the growth of an original kind of Judaeo-Christianity, in which Millenarian hopes persisted; it was Asia that continued to celebrate the feast of Easter on the same day as the Jews. Literarily, the *Apocalypse* and the *Gospel of John* stem from this Judaeo-Christian *milieu*, where Essene influences are evident. The first of these works is stamped by the upheaval resulting from the profanation of the Temple in 70. The author sees in this the punishment of Israel but keeps his eyes fixed on Jerusalem. In the *Gospel*, the theme of the Temple remains dominant, but it is in the person of the Word made flesh that it becomes manifest.

The counterpart of John's evidence is to be found in the *Epistles* of Ignatius of Antioch; the latter crossed Asia at the end of Trajan's reign. The *Letters* he addressed to the Churches show the persistence of these Judaising tendencies, in fact they seek to curtail their excessive growth; these tendencies appeared in Ephesus[12]. In Magnesia they are more precisely described : ' the old fables '[13] referred to by Ignatius in the classic phrase used to describe Millenarian hopes[14]. The Christians do not observe the Sabbath, but the Lord's day[15]; it is absurd to speak of Jesus Christ and to Judaise[16]. These Jewish tendencies prevented the conversion of the Gentiles in Tralles[17]; the Judaisers taught that Christ was not really dead[18], a belief which stemmed from the Millenarian dream. In Philadelphia he had to be wary of those who interpreted Scripture according to Judaism[19]. We may note that this opposition to Judaeo-Christianity was accompanied in Ignatius by urgent calls to unity around the bishop. We may wonder whether, especially in Ephesus, there was not a kind of coexistence between two communities, a Judaeo-Christian and a pagano-Christian.

This Asiatic Judaeo-Christianity is expressed in Books V, VI and VII of the *Sibylline Oracles*. Book V has a very marked Jewish character, but a definite allusion to the birth of Christ shows that it is Christian[20].

12. *Eph.*, VII, 1; IX, 1.
13. *Magn.*, VIII, 1.
14. See Origen, *Contr. Cels.*, II, 4-6.
15. *Magn.*, IX, 1.
16. *Ibid.*, XI, 1.
17. *Tral.*, VIII, 2.
18. *Ibid.*, X, 1.
19. *Phil.*, VI, 3? See P. Meinhold, *Schweigende Bischofe*, Festgabe Lortz, II, Baden-Baden 1957, p. 457-490. E. Molland is mistaken in believing that these groups are Gnostics. ' The heretics combatted by Ignatius of Antioch ', *JEH*, 5 (1954), p. 1-6.
20. V. 256-269.

Geffcken dates it to the reign of Domitian. Allusions to Egypt might suggest this, but there is also an enumeration of the towns of Asia : Pergamum, Smyrna, Ephesus, Sardis, Tralles, Laodicea and Hierapolis[21], and the spirit is more Asiatic than Egyptian. Book VI is markedly Judaeo-Christian in character and shows affinities with the Millenarianism of Cerinthus; the same is true of Book VII. The former dates from the beginning of the second century, the latter a little later.

The *Apocalypse* and the *Letters* of Ignatius, Papias and Polycarp provide a glimpse of the various Christian centres of Asia. The first we meet is Ephesus, where John ended his life. To the Church there he was primarily speaking in the *Apocalypse* (2 : 1-8). He sets to its credit its past suffering (evidently an allusion to the persecution of Domitian, of which John himself was a victim) and adds that it detests the Nicolaitans, that is to say Judaeo-Christian heterodoxy which is turning into Gnosticism and entirely rejects the Old Testament, but he reproaches it with having lost its fervour. Thirty years later Ignatius still recognises in Ephesus the same supremacy[22]. He praises its purity from all heresy[23], and names its bishop, Onesimus[24]. About 190 the Bishop of Ephesus, Polycrates, says that seven members of his family have been bishops before him (*HE*, V, 24, 6). In 196, Apollonius attests the continuance of the Johannine traditions in Ephesus (*HE*, V, 18, 14).

The Church of Smyrna already existed when John was writing the *Apocalypse;* one of the letters is addressed to it. But at the beginning of the second century it became specially important because of the personality of its bishop, Polycarp. He was bishop in 110, since Ignatius was his guest at Smyrna on a journey to Rome[25], and he wrote him a letter from Troas. A little later Polycarp wrote to the Philippians when sending them the collection of Ignatius's letters[26]. From other sources we know Polycarp well, thanks to the writings of Irenaeus, who lived near him in Smyrna in his youth and speaks of him in his *Letter* to Florinus (*HE*, V, 20, 4-8). Polycarp was martyred in 155, under Antoninus. We possess the *Acts* of his martyrdom.

About the Churches of the interior there is less information. The *Apocalypse* mentions Pergamum, and it was said that Satan's throne was there. This may be an allusion to the fact that the town at this time was the centre of the imperial cult. A Christian, Antipas, had been martyred,

---

21. V, 119 122, 306; 276, 296, 307; 290; 318.
22. *Eph.*, I, 1.
23. *Ibid.*, VI, 2.
24. *Ibid.*, I, 3.
25. *Ibid.*, XXI, 1.
26. *Phil.*, XIII, 1-2.

moreover the Nicolaitans had followers there (Ap 2 : 12-16). The same was true of Thyatira, where a Nicolaitan prophetess, symbolically designated as Jezebel, performed her works (Ap 2 : 20). The Church at Sardis was more important. It was an old royal city and later, in the second half of the century, it was to have a famous bishop in Melito. Further inland was Philadelphia where the existence of a Church is attested by John and Ignatius. The former put the town on guard against those of the synagogue of Satan who usurped the title of Jews (Ap 3 : 9). It seems that this was a reference to the Gnostic rebellion. Ignatius on the other hand warned against the Judaisers who introduced discord. The last letter of John was addressed to Laodicea, near Hierapolis.

The *Letters* of Ignatius show us that in his day the Church developed south of Ephesus, in the Valley of Meander. There is a Church in Magnesia, with a bishop named Damasus[27], and another in Tralles under Bishop Polybius[28]. Again Ignatius warns the Magnesians against the Judaisers. It is noteworthy that the *Letters* of Ignatius make two points : on the one hand they insist on unity around the bishop, on the other hand they attack the Judaisers. It would seem to be one and the same problem. So in Asia at this time the Judaising tendency appears to have remained very strong, which tallies with what we have seen in the case of Papias.

2. The Palestine Mission

After the Fall of Jerusalem part of the Christian community, which withdrew to Pella in 67, returned to Palestine and doubtless to Jerusalem. Eusebius says that until the siege of the Jews under Hadrian, there were at Jerusalem fifteen successive bishops, all said to have been Hebrews of old family (*HE*, IV, 5, 2); all were circumcised. It is curious that there should have been a succession of so many bishops during such a short period. Carrington has suggested that Eusebius's list is that of the presbyters of Jerusalem, from whom the bishop was chosen[29]. The number given by Eusebius suggests that there were twelve of these presbyters; it is possible that the Church of Jerusalem was governed by a council of twelve presbyters, of whom one was pre-eminent : an archaic conception of the community. At Antioch Ignatius compares the presbyters to the ' Senate of the Apostles ', which suggests that they too were twelve in number[30].

27. *Magn.*, II, 1.
28. *Tral.*, I, 1.
29. See P. Carrington, *The Early Christian Church*, I, p. 419.
30. *Magn.*, VI, 1.

Eusebius notes that the community of Jerusalem was entirely made up of faithful Hebrews (*HE*, IV, 5, 2). It included members of Christ's family, especially some descendants of Jude (*HE*, III, 19 & 20), who lived until the reign of Trajan[31]. It is doubtless to this group that one must link the *Epistle of Jude*, markedly Judaeo-Christian in character. So the Church of Jerusalem emerges as the survival of the earliest Judaeo-Christian Church presided over by James. This group was marked by strict fidelity to Jewish practices. In the middle of the second century Justin tells us that Judaeo-Christians of this type still existed[32], but they do not seem to have found favour with the Jews, for Bar-coseba later persecuted them as bad Jews. According to Epiphanius, Akila, the translator of the bible, met some Christians from Jerusalem in about 120. Hegesippus, who provides all our information about this group, was himself a member of it by birth. The *Gospel of James*, with its ascetical tendencies, doubtless stemmed from this group, about 135.

With the Judaeo-Christian Church of Jerusalem is linked the origin of the Church in Egypt. It would be highly unlikely that Egypt did not have Christian missionaries. The reason we know nothing about them is doubtless that Egypt did not enter into Paul's sphere of activity, with which almost all of our documents are concerned, but depended on the Palestine mission[33]. The first missionaries were probably Hellenists. The *Epistle to the Hebrews*, which is almost certainly Egyptian, has points of contact with Stephen's speech. There are fragments of two apocryphal gospels from Egypt; Clement of Alexandria quotes the *Gospel of the Egyptians*, Clement and Origen the *Gospel of the Hebrews*. They would seem to be gospels of two Egyptian communities, one composed of Hebrew converts, the other of Egyptian converts[34].

The Judaeo-Christian characteristics of these two gospels are striking. The *Gospel of the Egyptians* in particular has ascetical features, like the condemnation of marriage, which is also to be found in other fields of the Jerusalem mission. The part played by certain women in the gospel, like Salome and Mary Magdalene, also seems linked with the Jerusalem *milieu*. It is noteworthy that the only mention of Alexandria in the New Testament concerns Apollo, whose baptism is of Palestinian origin[35]. It seems also that Pantaenus, the first Alexandrian Doctor,

---

31. See E. Stauffer, ' Zum Kalifat des Jakobus ', *ZAGG*, 4 (1952), p. 192-214.
32. *Dial.*, XLVII, 1.
33. See S. G. F. Brandon, *The Fall of Jerusalem and the Christian Church*, London 1951, p. 217-243.
34. E. Hennecke, *Neutestamentliche Apokryphen in deutscher Uebersetzung*, 3rd completely revised edition, Tübingen 1959.
35. See H. C. Snape, ' The Fourth Gospel, Ephesus and Alexandria ', *HTR*, 45 (1954), p. 1-5.

was a Judaeo-Christian linked to the Palestinian group. He knew Hebrew; doubtless through him Clement inherited Judaeo-Christian traditions concerning James and apocalyptic doctrines. At the end of the second century, at the time of the Paschal dispute, it was the Bishop of Jerusalem, Narcissus, who transmitted the Alexandrians' reply to Rome.

Another feature seems to link Egypt and the Judaeo-Christian mission : the structure of the hierarchy. Several fourth-century authors, particularly Jerome and Ambrosiaster, say that in Egypt the bishop was only the head of the community of presbyters, one among them and chosen by them. This is the Judaeo-Christian type of presbyterate, with the bishop presiding over the college. It is the organisation we have found in Jerusalem. In Asia Minor it was combined with the Hellenistic type, that of the bishop to whom are subordinated the deacons. The Egyptian organisation does not necessarily mean, as Jerome suggests, that the episcopacy is not of a different order from the rank of presbyter, nor does the designation of the bishop by the presbyters mean that he does not elsewhere receive consecration at the hand of other bishops[36].

Also from the Palestine mission stems the Christianity which was later to be the sole survivor among Aramaean Christian communities, that of Adiabene and Osroene[38]. As regards the former, Eusebius tells us, according to the *Chronicle of Addai*, that the King of Edessa, Abgar, wrote to Jesus and that Jesus sent him Thaddeus (*HE*, I, 13, 1-22). This legend anticipates events of a later century : it is Abgar IX, king from 179 to 186, who was the first Christian King of Edessa. But it seems reasonable to think that at the end of the first century some Aramaean Christians came from Palestine to Osroene and preached in the Jewish communities there[38]. There is a trace of this in the fact that it was the Jew Tobias who received Addai, the Judaeo-Christian missionary[39]. We may also note that the Christians of Osroene celebrated Easter like the Palestine Christians and not like those of Asia (*HE*, V, 25, 4).

It would seem, moreover, that there is something in Origen's statement, recorded by Eusebius (*HE*, III, 1, 1), according to which Thomas was the apostle of the Parthians, who at this period were masters of Eastern Syria[40]. The memory of Thomas remained linked to Edessa,

36. See W. Telfer, ' Episcopal Succession in Egypt ', *JEH*, 3 (1952), p. 1-13; E. W. Kemp, ' Bishops and Presbyters at Alexandria ', *JEH*, 6 (1955), p. 125-142.
37. See W. Bauer, *Rechtglaübigkeit und Ketzerei im ältesten Christentum*, Tübingen 1934, p. 6-48.
38. See Vööbus, *History of Asceticism*, p. 4.
39. *Doct. Add.*, 5; *HE*, I, 13, 11.
40. See P. Devos, ' Le miracle posthume de saint Thomas l'apôtre ', *An. Boll.*, 66 (1948), p. 249-254.

where his body was venerated in the fourth century. It is at Edessa that
the cycle of Thomas grew up, just as the cycle of Philip grew up in Eastern
Phrygia, and the cycle of John in Asia. This is true of the *Acts of Thomas*,
which date from the third century. The *Psalms of Thomas*, adopted later
by the Manichaeans, are partly (14 and following)[41] Judaeo-Christian
works linked with Edessa and written in the second century. The *Gospel
of Thomas*, found at Nag Hammadi, seems related to the Judaeo-Christian
group in Edessa[42]. We may note the important place given there to
James, which suggests that the Church of Edessa originated from
Jerusalem.

The *Gospel of Thomas* dates from the middle of the second century.
There exists another work which can probably be dated to the same
period and comes from Edessa; this is the *Odes of Solomon*. Their
Judaeo-Christian character is certain, and they seem to belong to the
end of the first century[43] and to have originated in Edessa[44]. The similarity
between these liturgical poems and the *Hodayoth* of Qumran is striking.
So these are certainly works that Judaeo-Christian missionaries coming
from Palestine — more precisely, Essene converts — could have written.
Another important work may be a product of the Edessene community
and date from a little later. The work called *Gospel of Truth*, which
some scholars consider a liturgical homily, has striking stylistic
resemblances with the *Odes*[45]. This too probably comes from Edessa[46];
it seems that it cannot be identified with the *Gospel of Truth* mentioned
by Irenaeus as a work of Valentinus. Also belonging to the same *milieu*
and period is the 'Song of the Pearl', preserved in the *Acts of
Thomas*[47].

It is likewise at the end of the first century that we find Christianity
spreading beyond the Tigris to Adiabene. Here there exists a document
which seems trustworthy, the *Chronicle of Arbela*, written in Syriac in the

41. *Die Psalmen des Thomas und das Perlenlied als Zeugnisse vorchristlicher Gnosis*,
Berlin 1959, p. 42.
42. *Un recueil inédit des paroles de Jésus*, Paris 1958, p. 41-47. See also A. F. J. Klijn,
' Das Thomas evangelium und das altchristliche Christentum ', *VC*, 15 (1961),
p. 146-159.
43. See J. Carmignac, ' Les affinités qumraniennes de la Onzième Ode de Salomon ',
RQ, 3 (1961), p. 101.
44. See J. de Zwaan, ' The Edessene Origin of the Odes of Solomon ', Quantulacumque
(Studies Presented to Kirsopp Lake), p. 285-302. See also F. M. Braun, ' L'énigme
des Odes de Salomon ', *RT*, 57 (1957), p. 624-625; A. Adam, ' Die ursprüngliche
Sprache der Salomon Oden ', *ZNTW*, 52 (1961), p. 141-156.
45. E. Segelberg, ' Evangelium Veritatis. A Confirmation Homily and its Relation
to the Odes of Solomon ', *Orientalia Suecana*, 8 (1959), p. 1-42.
46. M. Schenke, *Die Herkunft des Sogenannten Evangelium Veritatis*, Göttingen 1959.
p. 26-30.
47. See A. Adam, *Die Psalmen des Thomas und das Perlenlied*, p. 55-75.

sixth century by Mishiha Zkha[48]. The Gospel was spread in Adiabene at the end of the first century by Addai. Kahle thinks that only Adiabene was evangelised by him at this time and that the Gospel was spread later in Osroene, but Harnack may have been right in thinking that Addai baptised a certain Pekhidha, who was the first Bishop of Arbela. His episcopate lasted from 105 to 115, and it seems that it was followed by a break. This was the period of Trajan's campaign against Chosroes in 116. In 121 Samson was consecrated bishop; he was martyred in 123.

This evangelisation of Adiabene at such an early date need not surprise us if we recall that an important Jewish mission had gone to this region in the first century. The King of Adiabene, Izates, and his mother, Queen Helena, converted to Judaism, were buried at Jerusalem in a tomb still visible today. It was in this Jewish *milieu* that the Judaeo-Christian mission developed. It is noteworthy that the bishops of Adiabene in the second century all had Jewish names : Samson, Isaac, Abraham, Moses, Abel. The Bishop of Arbele, Noah, was visited by relations who came from Jerusalem, and it was from this region that Tatian came, at the end of the second century; he called himself an ' Assyrian '. The Christianity of Adiabene was very strongly affected by Judaeo-Christian tendencies[49].

Did the Judaeo-Christian mission spread as far as India? Eusebius says that Pantaenus undertook a mission to those parts and found there a *Gospel of Matthew* in Hebrew writing (*HE*, V, 10). May we suppose that Christianity penetrated as far as India by way of Judaeo-Christian missionaries in the first half of the second century? This is by no means impossible. Later tradition linked this evangelisation of India with Bartholomew, and it is possible that Bartholomew had Arabia as his missionary field and that as an extension of this mission the Gospel reached India. Pantaenus, moreover, was a Judaeo-Christian missionary who came from Egypt, and this confirms what we have said earlier about the essentially Palestinian character of the primitive community of Egypt.

3. The Petrine Mission

A third sphere in the Christianity of this period can be labelled Petrine. At first it comprised the Mediterranean coast of Palestine, Phoenicia, Syria and Cilicia, and the towns of Caesarea, Joppa, Tyre and Sidon were very closely connected with Peter's apostolate. The

48. A. von Harnack, *Die Mission und Ausbreitung des Christentums in ersten drei Jahrhunderten*, 2nd ed., Leipzig 1924, p. 683-694; P. Kahle, *The Cairo Geniza*, Oxford 1959, p. 274-276; A. Vööbus, *History of Asceticism in the Syrian Orient* (C.S.C.O. 184 & 197), Louvain 1958/60, p. 5-8.
49. See A. Vööbus, *History of Asceticism*, p. 5; Kahle, *The Cairo Geniza*, p. 270-273.

Kerygmas of Peter, incorporated in the Pseudo-Clementine writings of the third century, may be as early as the beginning of the second century; they are Ebionist in character. What they tell us about Peter's preaching in Caesarea, Tyre and Sidon has no historical value but shows at least that the memory of Peter lingered in this region.

The works of the cycle of Peter, in the strict sense, may also come from this part of the world. This is probably true of the *Second Epistle of Peter*[50], also of the *Gospel of Peter*. The oldest evidence for this work, that of Serapion of Antioch at the end of the second century, and of the *Didascalia* in the third, is Syrian. There we again find the themes, so dear to Syrian theology, of the descent into hell and the exaltation of Christ above the angels. The *Apocalypse of Peter* belongs to the same period and region, and is mentioned in the Muratorian Canon and quoted by Clement of Alexandria in the *Eclogae propheticae*. It is also to the beginning of the second century that the *Preaching of Peter*, quoted by Clement of Alexandria, must be dated. These last two works are quoted by Theophilus of Antioch, about 170, which confirms that they belong to Syro-Phoenicia[51]. The first part of the *Acts* of Peter is linked with this region. But the work known under this name and the Pseudo-Clementine writings that use it are later in date.

The position of Antioch was very special and appears unusually complex from the start. The Church there had been founded by the Hellenists, but very early on was made up partly of Christians holding James's views and partly of pagano-Christians converted by Paul. The works from this provenance during the period we are studying seem stamped with Hellenist influence, that is to say stem from a Judaeo-Christianity different both from that of Palestine and from that of Asia. The *Epistle of Barnabas* shows in its very name that it originated in Antioch. It belongs to the same family as the *Didache*, and in its doctrinal part it is dependent on a typically Judaeo-Christian exegesis. The same is true of the *Ascension of Isaiah*, which uses the theme of the *descensus* and *ascensus*, an extension of Jewish Apocalyptic imagery. The two works belong to the reign of Domitian and show resemblances with the *Apocryphon of James*, discovered at Nag Hammadi[52], and the *Epistle of the Twelve Apostles*, which is related to it[53].

50. See L. Goppelt, *op. cit.*, p. 177.
51. See G. Quispel & R. M. Grant, ' Note on the Petrine Apocrypha ', *Vig. Christ.*, 6 (1952), p. 31-32.
52. See W. C. van Unnik, ' The Origin of the Recently Discovered Apocryphon Jacobi ', *Vig. Christ.*, 10 (1956), p. 149-156.
53. See G. Kretschmer, *Studien zur frühchristlichen Trinitätstheologie*, Tübingen 1956, p. 49-61, for its Syrian origin, and H. Ch. Puech, in E. Henneckle, *Neutestamentliche Apokryphen in deutscher Uebersetzung*, 1, 3rd ed., Tübingen 1959, p. 249.

The same theological tendencies appear again in the *Letters* of Ignatius, Bishop of Antioch at the beginning of the second century. They too are related to the East Syrian works, the *Odes of Solomon* and the *Gospel of Truth*[54]. There was a flourishing Syrian theology at this period, moreover the *Letters* of Ignatius attest the importance in Antioch of the order of deacons, who are named with the presbyters in the hierarchy, but they also collaborated closely with Ignatius in his journey across Asia. Whereas the presbyters represented a collegial conception of the hierarchy, the deacons were the bishop's collaborators; this appears clearly in the case of Ignatius. The two groups had often been in opposition, which may be why Ignatius insisted on their union round a single bishop.

It remains true that if the Church of Antioch was not typically Petrine, it had many ties with Peter; we have seen that he had stayed there at a very early date. The Petrine apocryphal writings were popular in Antioch, as Theophilus and Serapion show. The *Ascension of Isaiah* is the first work to mention Peter's martyrdom. Antiochene Judaeo-Christianity thus appears as representing the Petrine position. We have also noticed its links with the Phoenician sector, which was specially dependent on Peter. The same links are to be found in the other regions which came under Peter's influence and which were in communication with Antioch.

Eusebius tells us that Pontus and the neighbouring regions of Bithynia, Cappadocia and Galatia were dependent on Peter; other facts confirm this. The *First Epistle of Peter* was addressed to the Christians of these regions. That may be the source of Eusebius's information, but this hypothesis is far from certain, since there is other evidence for the link. Pontus and Cappadocia are geographically an extension of North Syria and it was in that direction that Syria usually expanded. In a letter of Dionysius, Bishop of Corinth in the middle of the second century, we see the links between Corinth and Pontus. Now Corinth was in Peter's sphere of influence. In the Paschal controversy, the bishops of Pontus were in agreement with the Bishop of Rome and in disagreement with the Asiatic bishops.

For Christianity in Bithynia under Trajan there is an important source of information, a *Letter* of Pliny the Younger (X, 36). Christians were numerous in the towns, and also in the country, and belonged to all classes of society. One point deserves special attention. Pliny mentions two deaconesses *(ministrae);* the word is applied to Phoebe, a native of Cenchrae, near Corinth (Rom 16 : 1) and probably does not

---

54. See V. Corwin, *St Ignatius and Christianity in Antioch*, New Haven 1960, p. 220-227.

refer to a hierarchical function, as it was to do later, in the fourth century. But it makes clear the active participation of women in spreading the Gospel and probably also in certain liturgical rites, like the anointing of women before baptism, as Clement of Alexandria describes. It is interesting to note that, according to Tertullian, in the communities founded by Marcion, who came from Pontus, women taught, exorcised and baptised.

Greece was the great centre of Paul's apostolate. The Churches of Macedonia, Thessaly and Athens were dependent upon Paul. Athens, at the beginning of the second century, was a great centre of cultural revival: in philosophy with Taurus and Atticus, in rhetoric with Herod Atticus. It is there that Quadratus presented Hadrian with the first Apology, perhaps at the time of the Emperor's visit to the town in 124. Quadratus tells us that in his day people healed by Christ were still alive (*HE*, V, 5, 2), which suggests a rather early date. In Corinth the memory of Peter was closely associated with that of Paul by the bishop Dionysius. It is evident from the *Letter* that Clement of Rome wrote to the members of the Church at the beginning of the second century that there were links between Corinth and Rome, with which Peter and Paul were also associated. The *Letter* shows that the town was torn by discord, the presbyters against another party, perhaps that of the deacons.

For the Church of Rome, we have no information for the period following the persecution of Nero. It was probably then that Mark wrote down Peter's catechesis. The list of the bishops of Rome given by Irenaeus shows, at this period, Linus and Cletus, who are mere names to us. Things change about 88, when Clement took charge of the Church. We first come to know Clement in the *Epistle* he wrote to the Corinthians about 100, where he speaks in the name of the Church of Rome. He records the existence in this Church of presbyters or episcopes (XLII, 4-5; XLIV, 4-5) and mentions the deacons twice (XL, 5 : XLII, 5). So the structure of the Roman community appears very similar to that of the Church of Antioch. The bishop is both the first of the presbyters and the head of the deacons. Clement represents in Rome the same type of personality as Polycarp in Asia. Irenaeus tells us that he had known the Apostles; doubtless he is thinking chiefly of Peter and Paul. This seems to follow from what the Pseudo-Clementine writings tell us of these links with Peter, moreover the *Epistle* alludes to the martyrdom of Peter and Paul in Rome. Clement is heir to their tradition.

We may also note the Judaeo-Christian character of the *Epistle*[55]. It appears in the importance given to the figures of the Old Testament,

---

55. See E. Peterson, *Frühkirche, Judentum und Gnosis*, p. 129-157.

in the manner of the Jewish haggadah. Clement calls Christ ' the Well-Beloved ', as in the *Ascension of Isaiah;* and the Epistle uses the archaic Judaeo-Christian *midrashim.* These features recall Phoenician Judaeo-Christianity and seem to stem from the Petrine tradition, the two poles of which were the Mediterranean coast of Syria and Rome. We may also note that the words of Christ recorded in the *Epistle* seem to come not from the written *Gospels,* but from an oral tradition[56]. The same feature is found in the *Didache* and in the *Epistle of Barnabas.* This means not that the written *Gospels* were unknown to our authors, but that Christ's teaching was transmitted both in writing and in catechetical tradition.

Another outstanding figure in Rome is known to us at the same period, namely Hermas. He says that he wrote his first revelations at Clement's bidding, and lived in Rome until the time of Pope Pius, about 140, the period at which he published the definitive text of his revelation, according to the Muratorian Canon. Several points certainly bear on the state of the Roman community at the time of Clement. Hermas himself is a proof that there were prophets, a mark of an archaic community. The *Ascension of Isaiah* complained that prophets were disappearing in Syria. There are remarkable resemblances between the *Shepherd* and the doctrine of the Essenes : belief in the two spirits, pronounced asceticism, the importance of angelology[57]. Here we have a Roman *milieu* marked by Judaeo-Christian asceticism. The hostility of Hermas to the deacons should be noted, which is another piece of evidence in favour of this theory.

Little is known about events in the first two decades of the second century. Irenaeus's list records that Evaristus and Alexander were bishops at that time. It was under the latter, about 115, that Ignatius wrote to the Romans and extolled the dignity of their Church. Under the pontificate of Sixtus (115-125) discussions took place in Rome between Christians of Asiatic origin and the rest about the date of the celebration of Easter. Again the complexity of the Church in Rome at this date is evident. It is doubtless to this period that the work called *Second Epistle of Clement,* which is in fact a homily, must be dated. It presents a theology of the Church rather like that of Hermas, and probably belonged to the writings kept in the Roman Church with the *Epistle of Clement* — hence its name. Telesphorus replaced Sixtus in 125, and died a martyr in 136.

56. See H. Köster, *Synoptische Ueberlieferung bei den Apostolischen Vätern,* Berlin 1957, p. 57-75.
57. See J. P. Audet, ' Affinités littéraires et doctrinales du Manuel de Discipline ', *RB,* 60 (1953), p. 41-82.

Archaeological discoveries provide additional information about the Roman Church at this period. The excavations carried out under St Peter's on the Vatican Hill show that in about the year 120 the memory of the Apostle Peter was already venerated there. It is even possible that it may be Peter's tomb which has been discovered, but in any case it is certain that his memory was preserved there by a monument. The priest Gaius, at the end of the century, says he saw the trophies (τροπαῖα, tropaia) of the apostles Peter and Paul on the Vatican Hill and on the road to Ostia (*HE*, II, 25, 7). The fact that this monument is in a cemetery seems to confirm that it is indeed a memorial of Peter at Rome. The *graffitti* on the wall around the monument are also evidence that he was venerated there.

CHAPTER V

THE ORIGINS OF GNOSTICISM

THE years from 70 to 140, as well as being a period of expansion were also a period of internal crisis for Judaeo-Christianity. It was at this moment that there appeared in various forms a dualist current known as Gnosticism. This was something quite new, arising from a particular historical situation, and must be distinguished from Gnosis, which was, in a wider sense, the Jewish and Judaeo-Christian Apocalyptic current; Gnosticism was one of the forms in which it developed. Nor must it be identified with the dualist tendencies of certain Jewish movements, like that of Qumran, and which may betray Iranian influence. If it borrowed from these currents, it made of them something radically new : Gnosticism in the strict sense.

The *milieu* where it appeared was that of the marginal zones of Judaism and Judaeo-Christianity. The existence of these zones has already been mentioned. Before the year 70 they appeared as aberrations of the Messianic movement and Apocalyptic hopes, but we do not seem to find Gnosticism in the strict sense there. R. M. Grant has shown that Simon the Samaritan, held by heresiologists to be the father of Gnosis, was not a Gnostic, but that his disciples became Gnostics after 70. Asiatic Millenarianism was already active at the time when Paul wrote to Timothy, but it did not become a Gnostic heresy until the end of the first century, according to Cerinthus. H. J. Schoeps is doubtless correct in considering Ebionism as a very archaic Judaeo-Christian heterodoxy, in which Christ was the prophet announced by Moses, but not the Son of God. But O. Cullmann is also right in noting that, according to Epiphanius, it was after the year 70 that this group represented a heterodoxy[1].

Apparently it is in this sense that we must interpret a passage in Hegesippus on the origins of heresies (*HE*, V, 22, 5). Hegesippus writes

---

1. ' Die neuentdeckten Qumrantexte und das Judentum der Pseudo-Klementinen ', *Neutest. Stud. für R. Bultmann*, Berlin 1954, p. 35-51.

that it was under the episcopacy of Simon, after the death of James, that Thebutis introduced heresies, starting with the seven Jewish sects. He names as the originators of these heresies Simon, Cleobius, Dositheus, Gortheios and the Masbothaeans, and adds : ' From these come the Menandrians, the Marcionites, the Carpocratians, the Valentinians, the Basilitians, the Satornilians '. It is clear that this passage cannot be taken literally, but two ideas emerge from it. The first is the distinction of three stages in the movement that leads to Gnosticism. The original *milieu* was heterodox Judaism and it was there that the heterodox Christianity of Simon and the Nazaraeans developed. Finally this heterodox Christianity gave birth to Gnosticism in the strict sense. Hegesippus is right in dating the appearance of Gnosticism to the episcopacy of Simon, that is to say after the Fall of Jerusalem, but he is mistaken in dating Simon and the Masbothaeans to this period, for they belong to the third wave.

1. Ebionism

First we must note the existence after the year 70 of two heterodox Judaeo-Christian movements which were not strictly Gnostic. In his *Dialogue*, a little after 150, Justin distinguishes two categories of Judaeo-Christians : those who share the common faith but remain faithful to Jewish practices, and who are descendants of the community of James; and others ' who recognise Jesus as Christ, while maintaining that he was a man among men '.[2] Justin does not apply the name Ebionite to this group, but Irenaeus[3], Origen[4] and Eusebius[5] all consider this assertion that Christ is a man like any other, born of Joseph and Mary, to be the distinctive characteristic of Ebionism.

This acceptance of Jesus as the prophet announced by Moses, but not as the Son of God, was common to many heterodox Judaeo-Christian groups, and it is very probable that it existed well before the year 70; that much may be granted to H. J. Schoeps[6]. But it is possible to determine with greater precision the co-ordinates of the Ebionites in the strict sense. Epiphanius says that they originated after the capture of Jerusalem among the Judaeo-Christian refugees in Pella[7]. In this region he had their Gospel in his hands; and he preserved extracts from it. This

2. *Dial.*, XLVIII, 4.
3. *Adv. Haer.*, I, 26, 2.
4. *Contr. Cels.*, II, 17.
5. *HE*, II, 27, 1-2.
6. *Theologie und Geschichte des Judenchristentums*, p. 256.
7. *Pan.*, XXX, 1, 7.

Gospel represents a transformation of the *Gospel of the Nazaraeans* in a heterodox sense, and was written at the beginning of the second century, under Trajan[8]. Their baptismal customs also suggest a link with Transjordan[9].

Epiphanius includes among their holy books the *Itinerary of Peter*[10]. This work, which forms the basis of the *Homilies* and the *Clementine Recognitions*, itself rests on the *Kerygmas of Peter*, which belong to the first half of the second century[11]. Now these latter writings show remarkable resemblances with the doctrine of the Essenes, particularly the true Prophet, the two spirits, the rejection of bloody sacrifices. So it is on good grounds that Cullmann suggested that the Ebionites were a group of Essenes converted to Christ after the year 70 in Transjordan, either refugees from Qumran or belonging to the emigrants from Kokba, near Damascus[12]. They were probably Aramaic-speaking Christians, very attached to Jewish practices, but hostile to the Temple of Jerusalem and holding esoteric doctrines, like the transmigration of souls. Here we have a normal development of the Qumran group. The Ebionites shared the Essenes' conception of the opposition of the two principles, but Irenaeus expressly points out that they did not teach that the world was created by any other power but God[13]. So they were not Gnostics in the strict sense of the word.

2. Elkesaism

Another sect appeared in the reign of Trajan. Its founder, Elkesai, received a revelation through a book given him by an angel; the book proclaimed the remission of sins committed after baptism. Elkesai received his revelation in the country of the Parthians, in the third year of Trajan's reign, that is in the year 100[14]. Parthian rule then extended over Eastern Syria and Trajan was at war with the Parthians. The form of the revelation recalls ' The Song of the Pearl ' preserved in the *Acts of Thomas,* which belongs to the same period and shows some features of the Parthian mythology[15]. The Jewish characteristics are

---

8. See *Neutestamentliche Apokryphen*, I, Tübingen 1959, p. 102.
9. *Pan.*, XXX, 16.
10. *XXX*, 15, 1.
11. G. Strecker, *Das Judenchristentum in den Pseudo-Klementinen*, Berlin 1958, p. 214, suggests a later date, about 200.
12. ' Die neuentdeckten Qumrantexte und das Judenchristentum der Pseudo-Klementinen ', *Neutest. Stud. für R. Bultmann*, Berlin 1954, p. 35-51.
13. *Adv. Haer.*, I, 26, 2.
14. *Elench.*, IX, 6.
15. *Pan.*, XIX, V, 6.

also striking : Elkesai repeats that the faithful are obliged to be circumcised and to live according to the Law[16] and Elkesaites prayed facing Jerusalem[17]. Elkesai came from Judaism, ' thought like a Jew[18] ', and knew the teaching of Christ, but in many respects his Christianity recalls Ebionism. For him Christ is a prophet. The *Epistles of Paul* are rejected (*HE* VI, 36). So the Elkesaites were heterodox Judaeo-Christians[19], but they belonged also to heteredox Judaism. They rejected sacrifices[20] and retained only certain parts of the Old Testament (*HE* VI, 38); they also had baptist practices[21]. Peterson has shown that these were designed to drive out concupiscence, the bad yezer, considered as a devil[22]. Finally we may note the resemblance with Hermas, who also received a revelation by means of a book containing the announcement of a final remission of sins committed after baptism. Now Hermas was a Judaeo-Christian prophet, so we may conclude that Elkesaism was a heterodox Judaeo-Christian movement close to Ebionism, but belonging to East Syria.

3. The Nicolaitans

Those works of the New Testament which are later than the year 70 describe a movement which everywhere presents analogous features. The *Epistle of Jude* emanates from the Judaeo-Christians who came back to Jerusalem after 70. The author is full of Jewish Apocalyptic ideas. He denounces men who sully their flesh, scorn the heavenly powers and revile authority (11). They murmur and complain of their fate (16); they are scoffers, animal natures without the life of the Spirit (18). The same expressions appear in *II Peter*. The false teachers (2 : 1) scorn the heavenly powers and abandon themselves to defiling appetites (2 : 10). They scorn authority, follow the path of Balaam (2 : 15), and are mocking deceivers (3 : 3). They promise freedom, but they themselves are slaves of corruption.

The *Apocalypse of John* describes a group with similar tendencies in Asia Minor. At Pergamum and Thyateira he reproaches them for admitting ' followers of the school of Balaam, who eat what is sacrificed to idols and fall into fornication ' (2 : 14, 20) and claim 'to know ' the deep mysteries of Satan ' (2 : 25). If we collect the features common to

---

16. *Elench.*, IX, 4.
17. *Pan.*, XIX, 1, 5.
18. *Pan.*, LIII, 1, 8.
19. See J. Daniélou, *The Theology of Jewish Christianity*, p. 64-67.
20. *Pan.*, XIX, 3, 7.
21. See J. Thomas, *Le mouvement baptiste en Palestine et en Syrie*, Gembloux 1935, p. 140-156.
22. *Frühkirche, Judentum und Gnosis*, p. 227-228.

these passages, we note first of all a complete rejection of Noachic practices, which must have scandalised the Judaeo-Christians. But there is more than that; sovereign rule and authority are reviled, which certainly seems to mean a condemnation of the God of Creation and of the Old Testament. This doctrine is linked with Balaam, who, for contemporary Judaism, is the ancestor of the Magi and the father of dualism[23]. Here we have the basic features of the Gnostic revolt against the Old Testament God, considered as having failed to realise Apocalyptic expectations. This doctrine professes a complete freedom, which is a deceptive imitation of the spiritual freedom of the Pauline Churches.

The *Apocalypse* makes a distinction between this first group and that of the Nicolaitans. Ephesus is congratulated on hating them (2 : 6). On the other hand at Pergamum there are some who belong to them (2 : 15), and Irenaeus says that their teacher was a proselyte from Antioch, whom the *Acts* mention among the seven deacons[24]. This link appears suspicious to Eusebius (*HE* III, 29, 1). It may have resulted from the interpretation of an anecdote, told by Clement of Alexandria, according to which the deacon Nicolas offered his wife to other men[25]. So our information about the Nicolaitans amounts to very little. Nicolas was a Greek equivalent of Balaam[26]. This fact, when added to the link in the *Apocalypse* between the Nicolaitans and the earlier sect, suggests one and the same condemnation of the Old Testament God and of moral libertinism.

4. Cerinthus

These first Gnostic movements appeared in Judaeo-Christian circles in Palestine and Asia under Domitian. A second group was that of Cerinthus[27] who, so Irenaeus tells us, was a contemporary of John[28] and a Judaeo-Christian who clung to circumcision and the Sabbath[29]. After the resurrection, he awaited Christ's earthly Kingdom, very material in character, and the restoration of worship at Jerusalem (*HE*, IV, 28, 2-5). He taught that the world had not been created by God, but by a remotely distant power having no knowledge of God, who was above everything. Jesus was born of Joseph and Mary and was merely an outstanding man. Christ descended on him under the form of a dove at his baptism to

23. See H. J. Schoeps, *Aus frühchristlicher Zeit*, Tübingen 1950, p. 249-254.
24. *Adv. Haer.*, I, 26, 3.
25. *Strom.*, II, 118.
26. See H. J. Schoeps, *Aus frühchristlicher Zeit*, p. 245.
27. See G. Bardy, ' Cérinthe ', *RB*, 30 (1921), p. 344-373.
28. *Adv. Haer.*, III, 3, 4.
29. *Epiphanius, Pan.*, XXVIII, 5, 1.

announce the unknown Father.   He ascended to the Father, before the Passion[30].

If we analyse these beliefs, we find two main points.   On the one hand Cerinthus developed a heterodox Judaeo-Christian attitude, professing a very material kind of Messianism[31].   This Millenarianism was held in common with many Christians of Asia[32], but it denied the virgin birth of Jesus and his divine nature; Jesus was a great prophet on whom a divine power descended.   We are here dealing with heterodox Judaeo-Christianity, such as we find in Ebionism[33].   Epiphanius also links Cerinthus with the Ebionites[34].   Finally, Cerinthus considered that the world was not created by God, but by a demiurge who knew nothing of the true God.   There we have Gnosticism in the strict sense, for the first time precisely formulated.   It was in this respect, characteristic of the period of Trajan's rule, that Cerinthus modified an earlier Judaeo-Christian current, found in Jewish as well as in Christian heterodoxy[35].

5.   The Simonians

Hegesippus is surely mistaken in making Simon a disciple of Thebutis, after 70.   But what does seem true, as R. M. Grant has pointed out, is that the movement stemming from Simon, who had at first been a Samaritan Messianist, acquired new characteristics after the year 70[36]. It is possible to link this development either with Menander, who is discussed later, or with Cleobius, whom Hegesippus names as one of the heretics of Thebutis after 70, and who appears associated with Simon in several passages.[37]   Here can be seen a development similar to that of Asiatic Messianism, which, with Cerinthus, acquired more pronounced features after the year 70.   The first author to provide us with information on these developments of the Simonian movement is Justin, and as he himself was a native of Samaria, his evidence is trustworthy.   Irenaeus devotes a long notice to Simon.

Justin says that nearly all the Samaritans adore Simon as the first God and unite with him a certain Helen, who is his first thought (ἔννοια, ennoia)[38].   Here we find a considerable development compared with

30. *Adv. Haer.*, I, 28.
31. See H. Bientenhard, ' The Millenial Hope in the Early Church ', *SJT*, 6 (1953), p. 24-25.
32. See W. Bauer, ' Chiliasmus ', *RLAC*, II, col. 1076.
33. See A. Wurm, ' Cerinth ein Gnostiker oder Judaist? ', *TQ*, 86 (1904), p. 20-36.
34. *Pan.*, XXIX, 1, 3.
35. See G. Quispel, ' Christliche Gnosis und Jüdische Heterodoxie ', *ET*, 14 (1954), p. 2.
36. *Gnosticism and Early Christianity*, p. 70-97.
37. *Act. Paul.*, Vouaux, 408; *Didasc.*, VI, 8.
38. *Apol.*, I, 26.

what the *Acts* told us about Simon. Grant has pointed out that Simon appears as the first God, in opposition to the angels who have created the world and inspired the Old Testament; as Irenaeus states later on[39]. The first god came to free man from the angels who were ruling creation badly. Here we come face to face with Gnosticism, with the condemnation of the Old Testament God and of the creation which is his work. With good reason the Fathers of the Church considered Simonian teaching as the beginning of this movement. But the Gnostic dualism does not go back to Simon himself; it represents a development of his doctrine after the year 70, and it is at this moment that Gnosticism appears simultaneously in Asia and in Syria.

The association of the woman Helen with Simon may be connected with the cult of Helen in Samaria[40], or simply a concern for Hellenisation, as Grant thinks. In any case here at the beginning we meet an aspect of that syncretism which was to characterise Gnosticism. Justin also records the existence, at the period when he was writing (about 145), of a Simonian community in Rome, doubtless among the Samaritans. He dates the foundation of this community to a visit Simon paid to Rome under Claudius (before 54), at the same time as Peter. The Pseudo-Clementine writings, for their part, tell of controversies in Rome between Peter and Simon. Here we must see the legendary expression of the spread of Gnosticism during this period and of its conflicts with the Christian communities. Finally Justin records the presence of an altar consecrated to Simon in the Island of the Tiber; in fact, it was an altar consecrated to a Sabine fertility god, Semo Sancus and was rediscovered in 1574. But it is possible that Simon's disciples thought it belonged to the worship of their own founder and god.

6. Menander

Hegesippus mentions the Menandrians in the second wave of sects stemming from Jewish heterodoxy. Justin tells us that Menander was a Samaritan, like Simon, and a disciple of Simon[41], and adds that he came to Antioch. So it was through him that Gnosticism spread in western Syria, which was to become one of its chief centres. Justin first of all tells us that he practised magic, a feature common to the Samaritan Gnostics. Gnosticism was not only a theology, but also a theurgy. Eusebius notes that these magical practices helped to discredit the Christians in pagan circles, and in fact we find Lucian and Celsus in the second century saying that Christ himself was a magician.

39. *Adv. Haer.*, I, 23, 3.
40. See H. Vincent, ' Le Culte d'Hélène en Samaire ', *EB*, 45 (1936), p. 221-232.
41. *I Apol.*, XXVI, 4.

According to Justin, Menander taught that those who followed him would not die; here we probably have an allusion to Messianic hopes. Paul put the Thessalonians on guard against ' any spiritual utterance, any message or letter purporting to come from us, which suggests that the Day of the Lord is close at hand ' (II Ths 2 : 2). In Ephesus, Hymenaeus and Philetas taught that the resurrection had already taken place (II Tim 2 : 17). In Menander there is certainly a continuation of the Messianism of Simon and Cerinthus. Irenaeus tells us that Menander claimed to be the Saviour sent from on high, from the world of the invisible aeons, in order to save men[42]. By virtue of his baptism, a man became higher than the angels of creation. These doctrines are very close to those which Irenaeus attributes to Simon; it may be that it was Menander who gave Simon's Samaritan Messianism its Gnostic theology.

7. Saturninus

Menander was the hinge, as it were, between Simon's Samaritan Messianism and Gnosticism. He exercised his apostolate in Antioch between 70 and 100. His successor was, as Justin tells us, Saturninus, who was the first great figure in Gnosticism, active in Antioch between 100 and about 130. Ignatius, whose doctrine was a development of Menander's, was bishop during the first part of his career. He set the seven creator angels, the leader of whom is the God of the Jews, in opposition to the hidden God; these angels created man, but man crawled on the earth until the hidden God had given him a share in the light he emits[43]. Saturninus condemned marriage, which he said came from Satan[44] : some of his disciples abstained from meat.

Irenaeus notes that he was the first to have distinguished two races of men, those who share in the heavenly light and those who do not. It is this doctrine which goes to make up Gnostic dualism : what stems from the creation of the planetary angels is set radically apart from God. But we may also note that the framework of his thought remains largely Jewish — it depends on the account of creation in *Genesis :* one of the themes about which Jews at that time were speculating. His asceticism belongs to marginal Judaism; his doctrine of the seven archangels is that of the Jewish Apocalypse. But at the same time he makes Yahweh the prince of the angels responsible for creation. So here there is a crisis within Judaeo-Christianity, a rebellion against the God of Israel.

42. *Adv. Haer.*, I, 23, 8.
43. *Adv. Haer.*, I, 24, 2.
44. *Ibid.*, I, 24, 2.

8. The Barbelognostics

In Chapter XIX of Book I of his *Adversus Haereses*, Irenaeus sums up the doctrine of a sect whom he calls the Barbelognostics. We now possess the book, the first part of which he sums up; it is the *Apocryphon of John*, one copy of which is in Berlin and three copies of which have been found at Nag Hammadi. The large number of copies shows that is was an important work. It takes the form of a revelation made by the risen Christ to St John on the Mount of Olives. The first part contains a genealogy of the aeons of the pleroma, then, from 45 onwards, there is a kind of commentary on *Genesis*. The seven archons wish to make a man like God, a man incapable of moving. Wisdom, Sophia, gives him a power that makes him greater than the archons and arouses their jealousy, particularly of their leader Ialdabaot, the Jewish Yahweh.

The work is full of allusions to the Jewish apocrypha, and we are still in the same climate of thought. Its doctrine also resembles that developed in the *Epistle of Eugnostus*, found at Nag Hammadi. So it would seem to be the work of a disciple of Saturninus rather than of Saturninus himself; its Syrian origin seems clear. Here at last we have an original document of primitive Gnosticism, and H. C. Puech dates it to the first half of the second century[45]. All the Gnostic themes are already present, including the aeons of the pleroma and the role of Sophia. At the same time the unity of the Gnostic doctrine appears through its many different manifestations and currents.

9. The Sethians

In Chapter XXX of Book I Irenaeus follows up his account of the doctrine of the Barbelognostics with that of the Sethians. A comparison of this account with the second part of the *Apocryphon of John*, which Irenaeus had not summed up in the previous chapter, shows that here there is a development of the same gnosis, with a more pronounced Judaeo-Christian character. After the Father, the aeons of the pleroma are the Son and the Holy Spirit, then Christ and the Church. The aeons of the pleroma produce Sophia who, from her union with the lower waters, gives birth to seven sons: Ialdabaot, Iao, Sabaoth, Adonai, Elohim, Astaphain and Horaios (1, 30, 5). These angels make man in their image. Christ descends through the seven heavens, to the stupefaction of the powers, taking the shape of the angels of each heaven (1, 30, 11).

---

45. *Neutestamentliche Apokryphen*, 3rd ed., I, p. 243.

Here we have the same basic themes as in the *Apocryphon*, and it is noticeable that the seven angels have the different names of Yahweh in the Old Testament.   Once more the themes of Judaeo-Christian theology are evident, as found in the *Ascension of Isaiah*, the *Epistle of the Apostles* and the *Shepherd* of Hermas : the pre-existence of Christ and the Church, the hidden descent of Christ through the spheres of angels, the amazement of the powers.   Here is the most pronounced form of Judaeo-Christian Gnosticism, which is contemporary with Judaeo-Christian theology; its link with Antioch seems certain.   It is in this group that we must place several of the works found at Nag Hammadi, such as the *Book of the Great Seth*.

10.   Carpocrates

From Asia and Syria Judaeo-Christian Gnosticism spread to Egypt, where it made extraordinary progress.   It is known that Cerinthus came to Alexandria.   About 120 we find there a doctrine which appears to be a development of his, that of Carpocrates, who also taught that the world had been created by the angels, that Jesus was Joseph's son and that a power came down upon him[46].   Whoever partakes of this power is his equal and is able to scorn the archons who made the world and to accomplish the same miracles as Jesus.   This feature was absent from Cerinthus, but it may belong to Asiatic Gnosticism in its extreme form.

Carpocrates in fact shows no sign of Cerinthus's Messianic Millenarianism; the latter was confined to Asia and the western world.   On the other hand we do find in him the notion that man can be freed from the archons only after having been the slave of the vices over which they preside, otherwise he has to be reincarnated in order to pay his debt. The doctrine of the devils of the vices and that of reincarnation come from heterodox Judaism.   To them Carpocrates adds an amoralism which seems to stem from Gnostic rebellion not only against the Jewish God, but against the Law.   In this respect and in his scorn for the angels, he recalls the Nicolaitans and appears as an expression of pure Gnosticism in its violent rejection of creation.

11.   Basilides

Basilides too was an Alexandrian and a contemporary of Carpocrates, but Epiphanius says that he was a disciple of Menander.   It is clear that his Gnosticism was in the main line of Syrian Gnosticism.   But he was the first to organise and make a great synthesis of Simonian doctrines.

46. *Adv. Haer.*, I, 25, 1.

THE PROGRESS OF THE GOSPEL

PLATE 3

Left : THE 'CILICIAN GATES' THROUGH THE TAURUS MOUNTAINS

Below : THE VIA APPIA LEADING INTO ROME

In order to take the Gospel into Asia, Paul and his companions must have passed several times through this cleft in the Taurus mountains. References to 'dangers from robbers' (II Cor 11:26) may well refer to dangers encountered on journeys through this region. The Via Appia also must have seen many early Christian preachers and travellers. For Paul's entry into Rome as a prisoner, see Acts 28:13-15.

Left :
Photo : *Paul Popper Ltd, London.*

Below :
Photo : *Alinari.*

PLATE 4

THE GOSPEL OF THOMAS; CODEX FROM NAG HAM-
MADI

The Gospel of Thomas is one of 49 documents
found by some Egyptian farmers in a ruined tomb
near the village of Nag Hammadi, c. 1946. The
documents are contained in thirteen books, all in
codex form (cf. Plate 1).

LIFE AND BELIEFS OF THE 2ND AND 3RD CENTURY CHRISTIAN COMMUNITY :
I. Initiation

PLATE 5. CHRISTIAN SARCOPHAGUS; ROME, S. MARIA ANTIQUA, c. 270

This sarcophagus shows several of the main themes of early Christian art and catechesis. Pagan models were often used, and here the picture of Jonah recalls the sleeping figure of Endymion who was often depicted on pagan sarcophagi. See ch. 12, § 2 where it is suggested that the sarcophagus depicts the stages of initiation: Jonah, disgorged by the monster (faith), an orante (prayer), a philosopher (catechesis), the Shepherd (salvation), and finally baptism.

Photo : Hirmer Fotoarchiv, Munich.

LIFE AND BELIEFS OF THE 2ND AND 3RD CENTURY CHRISTIAN
COMMUNITY: II. Baptism

PLATE 6.   THE FONT IN THE BAPTISTRY OF THE HOUSE CHURCH AT DURA-
EUROPOS, SYRIA, BUILT C. 230

The font stands at the west end of the baptistry.   Over it is a
brilliantly painted aedicula on the inside or ceiling of which there
are paintings of stars.   On the back wall the figure of the Good
Shepherd standing near his flock occupies the higher and larger
portion of the painting, while below are Adam and Eve, the Tree
and the Serpent.   It is difficult to understand the significance
of the stars, but they may well represent the Kingdom of Heaven
in which the faithful will shine as stars.   The figure of the Good
Shepherd and the portrayal of Adam and Eve, draw together
ideas of sin and redemption, the Church and its Master,
particularly relevant to the candidate for baptism.
(For other illustrations from Dura-Europos, see Plates 7 and 25.)

In him we once again find the notion of angels creating the world and sharing its dominion; one of them is the God of the Jews, who tries to make the others submit to his power[47]. Basilides attached no importance to the fact of eating food sacrificed to the idols — John reproached the Nicolaitans with this in the *Apocalypse*. This total freedom from the Law was a feature of Gnosticism; it represented an exaggeration of teaching, at the opposite extreme from Johannine Judaeo-Christianity.

The interest of Basilides is that the Gnostic transposition of Jewish Apocalyptic ideas appears in him more than in any other teacher. R. M. Grant has noted how speculations about the sacred calendar, which were one of the expressions of the theology of history among the Jewish Apocalyptic writers, were transposed to a cosmological plane and provided a framework for the doctrine of the aeons. Thus, for Basilides, there are 365 heavens, to each of which corresponds an angelic order. Basilides, moreover, called himself an intermediary between Jews and Christians. It was also from Judaism that Basilides borrowed his doctrine of the vices as personal devils dwelling in the soul. This has also been found in Carpocrates.

The resemblance between these different movements can leave no doubt about their fundamental continuity. The basic element was the opposition between the hidden God, who became manifest in Christ, and the angels who create the world, to whom Yahweh belongs. The latter idea may have been based on the role which Jewish tradition accorded the angels in the creation of man and in the gift of the Law, but after the year 70 a certain number of Jews and Judaeo-Christians adopted it as the expression of their revolt against the God who had disappointed them in their eschatological hopes and against the creation which was his work. The Jewish and Judaeo-Christian origin of the movement clearly appears from the fact that all these elements — speculations about *Genesis*, the doctrine of the seven angels, the sacred calendar, angels of the vices and the descent through the spheres — derive from Apocalyptic thought.

The main historical course of the movement also appears. It was born simultaneously after the year 70 in Messianist Judaeo-Christian groups in Asia, with Cerinthus, and in Antioch, with Menander. The Asiatic current was more practical, and chiefly emphasised rebellion against the Law; it appeared as the exacerbation of certain Pauline tendencies, and was, in certain respects, amoral. The Antiochene current, on the other hand, was more speculative. With the *Apocryphon of John* it produced the first great Gnostic work known to us. The two currents

47. *Adv. Haer.*, I, 24, 4.

developed in Alexandria at the end of the period we are studying, but while the former was soon extinguished with the final blaze of Jewish Messianism, the latter was to find in Alexandria conditions that favoured remarkable growth.

CHAPTER VI

JUDAEO-CHRISTIAN
CUSTOMS AND IMAGES

DESPITE the varying forms they took, the Christian communities possessed certain features in common during the period from 70 to 140. These features were a kind of bridge between the original Christianity and its expression in a Graeco-Roman context. In fact they were still deeply tinged with Judaism. We can reconstruct them to some extent from certain books of the New Testament which reflect life in a Christian community, from Judaeo-Christian literature, the chief works of which we have already mentioned, and from archaeological remains — but these are still rare. Here we shall note the main facts. Certain heterodox books, like the Pseudo-Clementine works, Mandaean tracts and certain Gnostic works, also provide us with information.

1. Christian Initiation

About preparation for baptism there exists little information. A comparison with what we find in Jewish communities at that time, notably at Qumran, and later forms of Christian initiation, suggests that this preparation was formulated at a very early date. Justin gives us a glimpse of it in his *First Apology*; he explains that ' those who are convinced and believe the truths that have been announced and who promise to live in this way are taught to pray and, while fasting, to implore God to forgive their sins ' (LXI, 2). So there were two stages : during the first the person who wished to be converted received instruction and was taught how to lead a Christian life; then, when he knew the facts and had shown himself capable of leading a Christian life, he was admitted to a period of immediate preparation, liturgical in character.

The details of these two stages emerge from documents of the period, especially the *Didache* and the *Epistle of Barnabas*. The dogmatic catechesis varied for pagans and Jews. The former had to be taught about God the creator and the Resurrection; there is an echo of this instruction in Justin's *Apologies*. All had to be taught about Christ. We have this catechesis summed up in old formulas found in St Paul and other early writers in the Church : these are the earliest forms of the creed. Our Apostles' Creed is the development of the Roman creed of the second century, and so it is the echo of the oral tradition of faith, parallel to the written Gospels.

Instruction did not consist only in expounding the mysteries of Christ; it showed in them the fulfilment of the Old Testament prophecies, which was the aim of the *Epistle of Barnabas*. The same method is to be found a little later in *The Demonstration of the Apostolic Preaching* by St Irenaeus, who uses earlier material. The passages quoted in these documents were practically the same, and most of them are found in the New Testament, so it seems certain that the catechists already had at their disposal collections like that which we find in the third century in the writings of Cyprian, under the name of *Testimonia*. This is all the more probable since collections of this type already seem to have been in use among the Jews.

There is another proof of the existence of these collections of *Testimonia*. They are found in various authors with a certain number of characteristic modifications due to their adaptation to catechesis. In particular, it happens that we find combined quotations where several passages of the Old Testament are lumped together in a single quotation, which was already true in Judaism for *Deut* 6 : 5 and *Lev* 19 : 18. For example, the *First Epistle of Peter* combines three passages on the stone : *Is* 8 : 14; 28 : 16; *Ps* 117 : 22. Sometimes the quotations are intentionally modified : a word is changed or added. The most typical example is the addition of the words ἀπὸ ξύλου *(apo xulou)* and ἐπὶ ξύλου *(epi xulou)* to *Ps* 95 : 10 and *Deut* 28 : 66, which are also treated as references to the Cross.

Next we have a moral catechesis, remarkable examples of which are found in the *Didache* and the *Epistle of Barnabas*. The elements of this catechesis are the two commandments, to love God and our neighbour (*Deut* 6 : 5 and *Lev* 19 : 18), the Golden Rule, an explanation of the two ways, and finally certain regulations bearing particularly on the laws formulated by the Council of Jerusalem. All these come from Judaism. The catechesis of the two ways shows indisputable points of resemblance with the *Rule of the Community of Qumran*[1]. The words of Christ quoted in our catecheses are close to the New

1. *DSD*, III, 13–IV, 26.

Testament, but with notable variants. So it would seem that we have here an oral tradition, independent of the Gospels, preserved in catechetical instruction[2]. The doctrine of the two ways reappears in other works of the time, like the *Shepherd* of Hermas and the *Testaments*. There is, finally, a tradition of Sunday prayer [3].

A second group comprises the baptismal rites. Baptism is preceded by a fast undertaken by the catechumen and other persons[4]. This fast seems to have the same results as exorcism[5]; it is preceded by a renunciation *(apotaxis)* of Satan and an adherence to Christ *(suntaxis)*[6]. This action seems to be the culmination of the catechesis on the two ways and is found at the end of that catechesis in Qumran[7]. It would seem that Pliny's *Letter* to Trajan alludes to it, when it speaks of swearing to renounce certain crimes (X, 96, 7). Finally, besides the fasts, there was also doubtless a laying on of hands. This is mentioned by Clement of Alexandria[8]. Baptism itself, as a rite, was linked distantly with baptism in the Jordan, and immediately with John's baptism and its eschatological significance. Ultimately it was linked to Christ's baptism in the Jordan. It does not seem to have been connected with Jewish baptism of proselytes, for nothing justified such baptism in the case of converted Jews.

Baptism took place by immersion, as is shown by the *Didache* (VII, 1, 3) and the *Shepherd*[9], and usually in spring water. There was a triple immersion, corresponding to the invocation of the three Persons, which brought about remission of sins and the gift of the Spirit. This last point was stressed by many allusions to running water, which was connected with it[10] : running water (ὕδωρ ξῶν, *hudor zon*) means water that gives life. Its symbolism seems to depend on *Ez* 47 : 1-3, to which there are references in *Jn* 7 : 18, *Ap.* 22 : 2 and *Od. Solom.*, VII[11]. Probably that is also the origin of the baptismal symbol of the fish[12], which we find perhaps on a Judaeo-Christian ossuary of the *Dominus Flevit*[13]. We also find in Hermas the comparison of baptismal immersion with the

2. H. Köster, *Synoptische Ueberlieferung bei den Apostolischen Vätern*, Berlin 1957.
3. *Didache*, VIII, 2; *I Apol.*, XLXI, 2.
4. *Didache*, III, 3; *Rec. Clem.*, VII, 34; Justin, *I Apol.*, LXI, 2.
5. A. Benoit, *Le Baptême au Second Siècle*, Paris 1951, p. 11.
6. Hermas, *Praecept.*, VI, 2, 9.
7. *DSD*, V, 8-10. E. Peterson, *Frühkirche, Judentum und Gnosis*, p. 213.
8. *Excerpt.*, 84, 1 and in *Hom. Clem.*, III, 73.
9. *Sim.*, IX, 16, 6.
10. J. H. Bernard, *The Odes of Solomon*, Cambridge 1912, p. 114.
11. T. Klauser, *Taufet in lebendigen Wasser*, Pisciculi, Münster 1939, p. 157-165.
12. See J. Daniélou, *Les symboles chrétiens primitifs*, Paris 1961, p. 57-58.
13. See E. Testa, ' Fruttuose archeologiche ricerche palestinesi ', *Oss. Rom.*, 27-9, Sept 1960, p. 6.

descent into hell, which presupposes the symbolism of the waters of death[14].

Baptism seems to have been accompanied by several subsidiary rites. There was first an anointing with consecrated oil, which practice is attested by Theophilus of Antioch. The Coptic text of the *Didache* gives, after the Eucharist, a prayer for consecrating the oil (τὸ μύρον, *to muron*) (X, 7) which seems to be authentic[15]. The resemblance with the Valentinian liturgy suggests that this oil also served for Extreme Unction[16]. In the Valentinian liturgy, the anointing which follows baptism is the sign of the gift of the Spirit[17]. This notion, which reappears later in Tertullian, must be a vestige of Judaeo-Christian thinking, for whom baptism by water was John's baptism and brought only the remission of sins[18]. Some Judaeo-Christian groups seem to have been aware only of this baptism of repentance. This is true of the Ebionites and the Elkesaites. They were probably able to administer it more than once. We find the same notion held by Apollo, before he met Aquila and Priscilla, and perhaps by the Samaritans mentioned in the *Acts* (8 : 16). In the apostolic tradition anointing in conjunction with baptism make a single sacrament, in imitation of Christ's baptism and anointing in the Jordan.

With the anointing was closely linked the signing with the sign of the cross, the *sphragis*. The sign could have many uses, but it was primarily linked with the baptismal anointing. The rite is so important that in Hermas it actually means baptism by itself. It seems clear that the sign + originally means the Hebrew *tav*, symbol of the name of God; *Apocalypse* 7 : 2, looking back to *Ezekiel* 9 : 4, states that the elect have the mark on their brow. The *Damascus Document* seems to assume that the Essenes were marked with this sign (XIX, 4). The Judaeo-Christian inscriptions of Palestine show it.

That a white robe was put on seems implied by many passages which use the symbolism of donning and doffing clothes in connection with baptism; this is found in Paul, but it was Jewish in origin[19]; the *Odes of Solomon* often mention it[20]. The *Testament of Levi* speaks of a clothing[21] and the Pseudo-Clementine writings call baptism

14. See P. Lundberg, *La typologie baptismale dans l'ancienne Église*, Lund 1942.
15. ' Erwägungen zur Herkunft der Didache ', *ZKG*, 68 (1957), p. 8-11.
16. See A. Orbe, ' Los primeros hereses ante la persecucion ', *Estudios valentinianos*, V (Rome 1956), p. 134-137.
17. E. Segelberg, ' The Coptic-Gnostic Gospel according to Philip and its Sacramental System ', *Numen*, 7 (1960), p. 197.
18. This view was attacked by Clement of Alexandria. See A. Orbe, ' Teologia bautismal di Clemente Alessandrino ', *Gregorianum*, 36 (1955), p. 410-448.
19. See D. Daube, *op. cit.*, The *New Testament and Rabbinic Judaism*, London 1956, p. 126.
20. XI, 9-10; XXV, 8.
21. VII, 5.

' clothing ', (ἔνδυμα, *enduma*)[22]. Hermas speaks of a white robe in a baptismal context[23]. It would seem that a crown of leaves was also given, as is still the custom in Syria[24]. The practice is mentioned by Hermas[25], by the *Odes* (I, 1-2), by the *Ascension of Isaiah* (VII, 22) and by the *Testament of Levi* (VIII, 3, 9). Despite the view of E. Goodenough[26], it was of Jewish origin. It seems linked to the Feast of the Tabernacles and was part of the Mandaean ritual of baptism[27]. It is possible that the crown was given only to virgins[28]; in the celestial liturgy, it was given only to martyrs[29].

The rite of the crowning seems to belong chiefly to eastern Judaeo-Christianity or to affiliated communities, like that of Hermas in Rome. The same is true of another rite, that of drinking baptismal water. Hanssens has discovered that a cup of pure water was drunk with the neophytes' eucharistic communion in the ancient Syrian Church[30]. This rite was also part of Mandaean baptismal practices, which, according to Segelberg, originated at the period we are discussing[31], and he points out that this rite was purely baptismal. It may be that the numerous allusions in the New Testament and Judaeo-Christian literature to a drink of living water are linked to ritual usage, which would seem particularly to be the case in *Jn* 4 : 14 and *Odes of Solomon* VI, 10[32]. Finally it seems certain that baptism was followed by a manducation of milk and honey : this is suggested by *I Pet* 2 : 2, *Barn.*, VI, 8-17 and *Odes* IV, 10. The rite is attested among the Gnostics, and among the Marcionites, according to Tertullian[33]. Its Judaeo-Christian origin is shown by its presence among the Mandaeans, as Segelberg has pointed out[34]. It would seem that the rite immediately followed baptism, coming before the Paschal catechesis.

The whole group of baptismal rites seems to have been followed by a post-baptismal catechesis, which was the starting-point for the mystagogical catecheses of the fourth century. As baptism was prefer-

22. *Hom.*, VIII, 22; *Rec.*, IV, 35.
23. *Sim.*, VIII, 2, 3-4.
24. A. Vööbus, *History of Asceticism in the Syrian Orient*, I (1958), p. 91.
25. *Sim.*, VIII, 1, 1-4.
26. *Jewish Symbols*, II, p. 143-144. See Daniélou, *Les Symboles chrétiens primitifs*, p. 21-30.
27. E. Segelberg, *Masbuta*, Uppsala 1958, p. 61.
28. *Od. Salom.*, IX, 9.
29. *Sim.*, VIII, 3, 6.
30. *La liturgie d'Hippolyte*, Rome 1959, p. 484.
31. *Op. cit.*, p. 59-60.
32. See E. Peterson, *Frühkirche, Judentum und Gnosis*, p. 161.
33. *Adv. Marcion.*, I, 14.
34. *Masbuta*, p. 166-167.

ably administered on Easter night, this catechesis took the form of a Paschal homily. More exactly it replaced the *haggadah* on the liberation of the Jewish people at the time of the Exodus, which inaugurated the Jewish Paschal meal. There would appear to be a remarkable example of that in *I Peter*, which seems to be a baptismal catechesis and which in its first part compares the liberation of the Christian by baptism to the liberation of Exodus (1 : 13; 2 : 13)[35]. This is also true of the *Paschal Homily* of Melito of Sardis, which is a little later and which records the events of the departure from Egypt[36].

This homily was followed by a meal, which replaced the Jewish Paschal meal. The *Didache* gives three prayers of thanksgiving, the first for the wine, the second for the bread, the third at the end of the meal; all certainly refer to the initiation and make up the sequel to baptism. The eucharistic overtones of these prayers are unmistakable, nevertheless it is possible that they are merely blessings related to the *agape* that preceded the Eucharist[37]. This meal was probably a relic of the Jewish Paschal meal reduced to the second cup of wine and the unleavened bread, preceded and followed by a blessing. In a liturgical fragment by Melito we probably have the inaugural prayer of the meal that followed the Paschal homily and preceded the Eucharist[38]. The *Didache* would here exhibit a very archaic state in its juxtaposition of a Paschal rite and the Eucharist.

The celebration of the Eucharist ended the vigil. We do not possess any information about its celebration at this period apart from that provided by the New Testament. It would seem that it was instituted by Christ during a Paschal meal and so was inspired by the Jewish liturgy of this meal. The consecration of the bread was linked to the blessing of the unleavened bread, before the meal[39]. This blessing was a form complete in itself, and so could be separated from the meal. It was the ' breaking of bread '. On the other hand, the consecration of the wine doubtless corresponds to that of the third of the four cups, that immediately after the meal, before the singing of the Hallel. So the eucharistic prayer originally seems to have been the revival of these two blessings, and to have taken the form of the Jewish *berakah*[40] :

---

35. See F. M. Boismard, ' Une liturgie baptismale dans la Prima Petri ', *RB*, 65 (1958), p. 182-208; 66 (1957), p. 161-183; F. L. Cross, *I Peter : A Paschal Liturgy*, London 1954.
36. See F. L. Cross, *The Early Christian Fathers*, London 1960, p. 107-109.
37. A. Audet, *La Didache, Instruction des Apôtres*, p. 405; E. Peterson, *Frühkirche, Judentum und Gnosis*, p. 168-182.
38. E. Peter, *Ein Hymnus zur Ostervigil von Meliton*, Freiburg 1960, p. 62-67.
39. H. Kosmala, *Hebraër, Essener, Christen*, Leiden 1959, p. 178.
40. A. Audet, ' Esquisse du genre littéraire de la Bénédiction Juive et de l'Eucharistie Chrétienne ', *RB* (1958), p. 371-400.

All the same, it is possible that in the *Didache* we may have something which belongs to the eucharistic liturgy in the strict sense. The last of the three acts of thanksgiving, the one which follows the meal, ends with the words : ' Hosanna to the Son of David. If anyone is holy, let him come forward; if he is not, let him be converted. Marana tha! ' (IX, 6). The Hosanna verse is borrowed from Ps 117 : 25, which was one of the psalms of the Hallel sung after the meal, before the last cup of wine[41]. Kosmala points out that the object of this last part of the Paschal *haggadah* was to ask Yahweh to accomplish in future the same works of liberation that he had accomplished in the past and which were commemorated by the Paschal *haggadah* before the meal[42]. But, for the Christian, God fulfils this prayer at once, by coming in the Eucharist. So the *Marana tha* may be the initial prayer of the Eucharist in the strict sense. In this respect it is correct to see in it a trace of the Aramaean Eucharist. Its presence at the end of the *Apocalypse* has the same meaning[43].

2. The Liturgical Calendar

Besides the ceremonies of initiation, the best attested Christian institution during this period is the Sunday gathering. The New Testament refers to it several times. The *Didache* mentions it : ' Gather together on the Lord's Day to break bread and give thanks ' (XIV, 1). So too does the *Epistle of Barnabas* (XV, 9). Ignatius of Antioch condemns the observance of the Sabbath and champions that of Sunday[44]. Pliny's *Letter* speaks of meeting ' on a fixed day ' to sing hymns in turn to Christ ' before dawn ' *(antelucanum)*. We may note that the *Didache* speaks of a Confession before the Sunday synaxis[45]. This Confession was of a liturgical kind, it was collective and was an extension of a Jewish practice. There was evidently a normal liturgical Penance linked to the Sunday assembly, distinct from the reconciliation of sinners, of which Hermas's *Shepherd* speaks and which was reserved for exceptional cases. The formula of this Penance may have been the last petition of the Sunday Prayer[46].

The most complete details of the Sunday assembly are given by Justin, and his *Apology*, dating from 140, describes earlier practices.

41. H. Kosmala, *op. cit.*, p. 183.
42. *Ibid.*, p. 183.
43. O. Cullmann, *Le culte dans l'Église primitive*, Paris 1943, p. 17-18.
44. *Magn.*, IX, 1.
45. IV, 14. See also *I Clem.*, II, 4; *II Clem.*, VIII, 1-3; *Barn.*, XIX, 12.
46. K. Stendahl, ' Prayer and Forgiveness ', *Svensk Exegetisk Arboosk*, 22-23 (1957-1958), p. 75-86.

The assembly began with the reading of ' the memories of the apostles ', and ' writings of the prophets'[47]. The first expression seems to indicate that the *Gospels* were made up for liturgical reading[48]. The second seems to refer to works like the *Epistles* of Paul and Clement and the prophecies of Hermas. These readings were followed by a homily, then came prayers for the chief intentions of the Church[49], and the kiss of peace. Then the eucharistic prayer was said and the people answered *Amen*. The deacons distributed the consecrated bread and wine; alms were collected for the poor.

The various names given to Sunday provide us with hints as to its origin. The oldest is found in the *Didache :* Κυριακή *(Kyriake)*; the word first meant the christian Easter. In the *Apocalypse* (1 : 10), when Easter takes place on the 14 Nisan, the word does not perhaps mean Sunday, but that is the case everywhere else except in Asia. The *Epistle of Barnabas* speaks of the eighth day (XV, 9). The expression is found in a Judaeo-Christian context, where the faithful, after having celebrated the Jewish seventh day, prolonged it until dawn by their own celebration. It also shows that attention was paid to the peculiarities of the calendar in Jewish and Judaeo-Christian circles at that time. Finally Justin speaks of the ' first day ', linking it to the creation of the world[50]. In certain calendars, similar to that of Qumran, the first day of the Feast of Weeks was the Sunday after Easter. It was the day for offering the sheaf of corn or first fruits *(aparche)* and was linked with the theme of creation. We know the importance of the theme of the *aparche* in connection with the resurrection of Christ, in St Paul, and the designation of Sunday as the first day may belong to this line of thought. Since the resurrection was the first day *par excellence*, all the Sundays were, by extension, so called[51].

Apart from Sunday, the *Didache* shows that Wednesday and Friday were days of Christian fasting, in contrast to the days of Jewish fasting (VIII). It is noteworthy that these two days, Wednesday in particular, had a special importance in the calendar of Qumran and it is possible that we have here a trace of that calendar. Finally it should be noted that the keeping of the Sabbath as well as circumcision continued to be observed in many Judaeo-Christian communities. This is

47. *I Apol.*, LXVII, 2.
48. See H. Riesenfeld, *The Gospel Tradition and its Beginnings*, London 1957; P. Carrington, *The Primitive Christian Calendar*, Cambridge 1952.
49. *I Apol.*, LXV, 1.
50. *I Apol.*, LVIII.
51. See J. Van Goudoever, *Biblical Calendars*, Leiden 1959, p. 168, 169, 225-227; A. Jaubert, ' Jésus et le calendrier de Qumrân ', *NTS*, 7 (1960), p. 1-30; J. Daniélou, *The Bible and the Liturgy*, Notre Dame 1956 - London 1960, p. 320-327.

certainly true of the Ebionites, but also of the Judaeo-Christians attached to the Great Church mentioned by Justin and Epiphanius. Also, Ignatius's polemic against the observance of the Sabbath shows that at Antioch, at the beginning of the second century, certain Christians were continuing to observe it.

The question of the attitude of the early Christians to the observance of the feasts is more complex. In the first place it is certain that the Judaeo-Christian communities in the strict sense continued to observe Jewish feasts, but we know that in the Judaism of the period there was a great diversity of calendars, so the christian communities reflected these divergencies. It seems, moreover, that the majority of christian feasts were transformations of certain Jewish feasts. Was this so at the beginning of the second century? One thing is certain, the celebration of the 14 Nisan, the day of the Jewish Pasch, by the Christians of Asia. This observance extended to groups in Palestine, Syria and Rome. Those who kept it were called Quartodecimans. There were differences among them as to the exact day, like the differences among the Jews. In particular some of them, following the Essenes, fixed it on the fourteenth day of the seventh solar month, which still persists among the Montanists. The question was debated at Laodicea about 162 (*HE*, IV, 26, 3)[52].

We have evidence that a rival feast to that of the 14 Nisan was celebrated on the following Sunday. The feast of the Sunday after the 14 Nisan is linked to the historical remembrance of the resurrection, just as that of the 14 Nisan is linked to that of the Passion. But it also coincides, as we have seen, with the first day of the feast of Weeks; the presence of the theme of the *aparche* in St Paul shows this. That day was a Sunday in the nearby priestly circles of Qumran, which suggests that the feast first developed in Christian circles stemming from Essenism. A final feature seems to confirm this : we know that, in this Essene calendar, on the vigil of the inaugural Sunday of the feast of Weeks the crossing of the Red Sea was celebrated. Now that event remains the essential theme of the christian Easter vigil, in the Ambrosian *Exultet* for example[53]. It is this group which finally prevailed over that of the Quartodecimans.

Did the Christian liturgical year contain other feasts at the beginning of the second century? The Judaeo-Christians continued to celebrate the Jewish feasts, a custom which probably remained. So despite the Alexandrian tendency to interpret Jewish worship in an allegorical

52. See J. Van Goudoever, *op. cit.*, p. 155-163; B. Lohse, *Das Passafest der Quarto-decimaner*, Gütersloh 1953, p. 98-101; O. Perler, *Ein Hymnus zur Ostervigil von Meliton*, Fribourg 1960, p. 27-31.
53. J. Van Goudoever, *op. cit.*, p. 124-129.

sense, certain Jewish feasts reappeared with a Christian meaning. This is true of the celebration of the fiftieth day of the feast of Weeks, or Pentecost, in the third century; the keeping of the fortieth day, on which certain Jewish traditions fixed the Ascension of Moses on Sinai[54]; and the feast of the Tabernacles, which was to reappear in the fourth century under the form of the Feast of the Dedication. It seems clear that Luke connects the outpouring of the Holy Ghost and the fiftieth day of the Weeks[55], while John connects the Nativity with the Feast of the Tabernacles[56]. But that does not permit us to conclude that there was a liturgical celebration of these mysteries in the communities to which they belonged. Perhaps the observance of the fifty days of the feast of Weeks was kept as a festive usage in communities which celebrated the feast of the first Sunday[57].

3. The Doctrines

So far we have studied the basic structure of Judaeo-Christianity; now we must look at its more complex characteristics. First, those relating to knowledge. To this group belongs Christian gnosis, which derives largely from the culture of Low Judaism. On the one hand, it comprises exegesis of various passages of the Old Testament, in the manner of the Jewish *Targumim*. Fragments are extant referring to the Prophets, especially Jeremiah and Ezekiel. One of its most obvious features is the importance of speculations about the first three chapters of *Genesis*. An echo of these is to be found in Theophilus of Antioch and in the *Eclegae Propheticae* of Clement of Alexandria; according to Anastasius the Sinaite, Papias had interpreted all the *Hexameron* in terms of Christ and the Church.

The Judaeo-Christians also took certain Jewish works, in particular some of Aramaean origin, and partially rewrote or added to them. That is true notably of the *Testaments of the Twelve Patriarchs* and the *Ascension of Isaiah*, parts of which are Jewish, and other parts certainly Christian. It is true also of the *Prayer of Joseph*. Book V of the *Sibylline Writings* also seems to be a Jewish book revised by a Christian. It is possible that ' The Book of the Parables ' in *I Enoch*, referring to the Son of Man, is Christian; no trace of it has been found at Qumran, although important fragments of the other parts have been found. Again, *II Enoch* and *IV Esdras* contain parts that are probably Christian.

54. G. Kretschmar, ' Himmelfahrt und Pfingsten ', *ZKG*, 66 (1954), p. 211.
55. J. Van Goudoever, *op. cit.*, p. 138-144.
56. A. Guilding, *The Gospel of John and Jewish Worship*, London 1960, p. 98-104.
57. J. Van Goudoever, *op. cit.*, p. 183.

Besides these, the Judaeo-Christians wrote the *Apocalypses* which were directly inspired by contemporary Jewish apocalyptic ideas. Several take the form of revelations made by the risen Christ to the Apostles : for example, the *Apocalypse of Peter*, the *Letter of the Twelve Apostles*, the *Gospel of Truth*, the *Homily of Clement* and the *Apocryphon of James*. This kind of book was in use among the Gnostics. The *Apocalypse of John* and the *Shepherd* by Hermas are revelations of an apocalyptic nature. Ignatius of Antioch, Papias and the *Gospel of Peter* provide us with fragments of christian apocalyptic thought.

Whatever the literary form in which these works were cast, they all reveal the same intention, namely to establish the fact of revelation itself. The secrets of the heavenly world are unveiled, in the strict meaning of the word, by the opening of the firmament, which allows the seer to penetrate this upper world and to contemplate what is happening there or to receive a message that explains its realities to him. These secrets are the sacred cosmology, the dwellings of God, angels, devils and the dead; and sacred history, that is to say the periods fixed eternally by God in the heavenly books, which are communicated to the seer. The knowledge of these secrets constitutes Gnosis, *da'at*[58]. Gnosis means first of all apocalyptic knowledge. When the Apocalypse blazes with Gnosticism, the false Gnosis will be shown as the knowledge of the world pre-existing the aeons. This false Gnosis will be a deformation of the Apocalyptic Gnosis[59].

Let us now single out some of the favourite themes of Judaeo-Christian Gnosis. First of all, speculations about the Trinity starting from categories borrowed from angelology. The Son, who is usually called the Well-Beloved in the *Ascension of Isaiah*, is called the glorious Angel by Hermas[60]. He is the leader of the six archangels[61]. This appears already in Ez 9 : 2. He is substituted for Michael, as we see in Hermas[62], and as we may conclude from a comparison of *Ap.* 12 : 10 and the Essenian *Rule of War : DSW* (XVII, 8). The Holy Spirit is presented under the form of Gabriel in *As. Is.*, IX, 27, 36. Again, the two seraphim of *Is.* 6 are a representation of the Son and the Spirit, according to a tradition found in Irenaeus[63], and which Origen explicitly attributes to a Judaeo-Christian. This notion was again put forward in the fourth century by Jerome.

58. See J. Dupont, *Gnosis. La connaissance religieuse d'après les Épîtres de saint Paul*, Louvain 1949.
59. See R. M. Grant, *Gnosticism and Early Christianity*, New York-London 1959, p. 76-97.
60. *Sim.*, VIII, 1, 1.
61. *Sim.*, IX, 12, 7.
62. *Sim.*, VIII, 3, 3.
63. *Dem.*, 10.

The Word was designated by a certain number of expressions of Old Testament origin and more closely connected with the speculative interpretations of Judaism. The main ones are the Name, used specially in the *Gospel of Truth* (37, 37-41, 3); the Law, the Torah, as Hermas[64] and the *Kerygma of Peter* explicitly state[65]; the Alliance, a reference to *Is* 8 : 3, as Justin shows[66]; the Beginning, according to a Judaeo-Christian exegesis of the Bêreshîth (ἐν ἀρχη, *en arche*), or verse I of Genesis, interpreted as meaning ' in the first (-born) ' : this origin is given during our period in the *Dialogue of Jason and Papiscos*, quoted by St Jerome[67]; the Day, as Clement of Alexandria[68] and Justin[69] show, a reference to *Gn* 2 : 4; we may note in this connection the importance of such interpretations of the first part of *Genesis*.

Also with reference to angelology the mystery of Christ is presented as a descent of the Well-Beloved through the seven heavens inhabited by the angels and then as an ascent through the same heavens. The plan appears in *Eph* 4 : 9. It is developed in the *Ascension of Isaiah*. We may note that the descent of the Well-Beloved remains hidden from the angels[70] : this is the notion of the Son putting on the shape of the angels as he reaches each sphere. On the other hand, when he ascends in a blaze of glory, the angels adore him[71]. But we also find in Justin the idea that during the ascension the angels do not recognise the Son because of the human nature he has put on[72]. This second aspect clearly brings out the theological bearing of such representations : the mystery of the descent is that divinity is humbled to a condition lower than the angels; that of the ascension is that humanity is exalted above them. These themes are linked with Ps 24, as early as the *Apocalypse of Peter*.

Another form of expression of the mysteries of Christ in Judaeo-Christian theology is the symbolism given to the cross. It is considered a living reality, which accompanies Christ in his descent into hell and in the ascension, in the *Gospel of Peter* and in the *Sibylline Oracles* (VI, 26-28). It will go before him at the Parousia[73]. It is in fact the expression of Christ's irresistible power and divine efficacy : it is in this sense that we find it prefigured in various passages of the Old Testament, like Moses' prayer, arms held in the shape of a cross[74], or the horn of the unicorn[75]; one might add Judaeo-Christian symbols, mentioned by Justin, like the mast and the plough, which have been

64. *Sim.*, VIII, 3, 2.
65. *Strom.*, I, 29.
66. *Dial.*, LI, 3.
67. *Quaest. Heb. Gen.*, I, 1.
68. *Eclog.*, LIII, 1.
69. *Dial.*, C, 4.

70. *Asc. Is.*, XI, 16.
71. *Asc. Is.*, XI, 25-26.
72. *Dial.*, XXXVI, 5-6.
73. *Epistle of the Apostles* 27.
74. Justin, *Dial.*, XC, 5.
75. *Dial.*, XCI, 2.

found on Judaeo-Christian ossuaries. The wood of the cross, united to water, is a sign of the saving power communicated to the baptismal water[76]. Finally the four points of the cross symbolise the universality of the redemptive action, as Irenaeus shows[77], referring to the presbyters.

Again, among the main themes of Judaeo-Christian theology we may note that of the descent into hell. It seems first and foremost linked to the question of the salvation of the just in the Old Testament, as can be seen in an old Targum by Jeremiah, quoted by Justin[78]. Hermas adds the strange theme of the Apostles' descent into hell in order to baptise the dead[79]. More generally, the descent into hell is the expression of Christ's victory over death[80]; this aspect is especially developed in the *Odes of Solomon*[81]. This descent of Christ to the Kingdom of the Dead is not the same as his victory over the devil, whose prison is the firmament, according to the *Ascension of Isaiah*, or the air, according to Col 2 : 15.

The Church's theology includes the use of several symbols originating in contemporary Judaism : that of the plantation[82] stems from the Essenes[83]; that of the ship is found on ossuaries, an allusion to Noah; that of the building[84] occurs in Eph 8 : 20. But the most remarkable is that of the pre-existing Church. It is found in the *Shepherd* with the symbol of the woman who is old 'because she was created first, before all things'[85], with that of the tower built on water, which refers to speculations on the beginning of *Genesis*[86], and finally with that of the man and woman, inspired by an Apocalyptic exegesis of Gn 2 : 24, which is met in Eph 5 : 25-32 and also in *II Clem.*, XIV, 1-2.

A final aspect is concerned with eschatology, the waiting for Christ's return and the establishment of his Kingdom on earth. This eschatology has several components : the coming of Christ, which appears in all the authors; the resurrection of the just, or first resurrection (Ap 20 : 4; I Cor 15 : 23)[87]; the transfiguration of saints still alive (I Ths 4 : 17)[88]; and the Messianic reign (Ap 20 : 4)[89]. This reign, as before, is held to last a thousand years. The expression, which occurs in the *Apocalypse* (20 : 4), symbolises paradisal life, with man living a thousand years. This symbolism is found in Judaism (*Jub.*, XXIII, 27; IV, 29) and is taken over by Judaeo-Christians, for example by Papias. This reign is interpreted in a very materialistic way by heterodox doctrines like that of

76. *Barn.*, XI, 1.
77. *Adv. haer.*, IV, 17, 4.
78. *Dial.*, LXXII, 4.
79. *Sim.*, IX, 16, 5-7.
80. *Asc. Is.*, X, 8-14.
81. XVII, 8-11; XXII, 1-7.
82. *Asc. Is.*, IV, 3.

83. *DSH*, VI, 15-17.
84. *DSD*, IX, 6.
85. *Vis.*, II, 4, 1.
86. *Vis.*, III, 3, 3-4.
87. *Asc. Is.*, IV, 15.
88. *Zs. Is.*, IV, 16.
89. *Idem.*, IV, 17.

Cerinthus, but as an expression of the Parousia it is found in many authors, notably in Asia in John's sphere of influence and in Philip's.

CHAPTER VII

THE CHURCH AND THE EMPIRE

DURING the first decades of its history the Church did not loom large enough, from the sociological point of view, to raise problems for the Roman Empire. It was because of the Jewish question that certain Roman civil servants had had dealings with Christians; these first encounters have already been mentioned. The title of ' Christians ', bestowed in Antioch about 42 on the disciples of Christ, appears to have been a Roman nickname. In 45 Paul met the procurator Sergius Paulus in Cyprus, and Suetonius mentions the presence of Christians in the Jewish community of Rome in 70[1]. In 59 the procurator Festus sent Paul to Jerusalem with a report on his case. In all this no hostility appears towards the Christians on the part of the Roman civil servants. They intervened in the conflicts between Jews and Christians, and tended to protect the latter, whom they viewed as politically harmless.

1. The First Persecutions

It was during Nero's reign, in 64, that measures against the Christians first appear. Suetonius mentions them : ' Nero had the Christians tortured, a people addicted to a new and guilty superstition '[2]. Tacitus's account is more detailed :

To silence the rumours about the burning of Rome, Nero ordered the accusation of certain persons hated for their abominations, commonly called Christians. This name came to them from Chrestos who, under Tiberius, had been tortured by the procurator Pontius Pilate. For a time this hateful superstition was repressed, then broke out anew, not only in Judaea, cradle of the scourge, but in Rome, whither every known kind of atrocity or infamy flows from all over the world. Those who confessed their faith were arrested first; then,

1. Suetonius, *Lives of the Caesars*, Claudius, XXIX, 1.
2. *Lives of the Caesars*, Nero, XVI, 3.

on their directions, a crowd of others, not so much for having set fire to the town as for their hatred of the human race[3]. This passage calls for several comments. First of all, we again find the names ' Chrestos ' and ' chrestiani ', already used by Suetonius. They are warranted by the opposition of the name of Christian and the charge of abomination, which makes a pun on χριστός (christos) and χρήστος (chrestos), meaning good[4]. The allusion to Pontius Pilate is interesting from the standpoint of relations between the Empire and the Christians, but the most important point is the ground of the accusation. Besides the charge of sedition, linked to Messianism, we have that of *odium humani generis*. The phrase is equivalent to the Greek *misanthropia*. The charge had already been made against the Jews[5]. Essentially, it expressed the fact that a community was suspect by reason of its peculiar customs. It was an easy jump from the idea of different customs to that of inhuman customs, since the Graeco-Roman civilisation was considered as the norm of *philanthropia*, of humanism. Hence the charges, already made against the Jews and renewed against the Christians, of adoring a donkey, ritual murder[6] and incest. Here we have a first stage in the pagans' 'judgment on Christians'[7]. The Christians began to be distinguished from the Jews, but the charges against them were still based on those made against the Jews.

Under Galba, Otho and Vitellius, who succeeded one another in 68, there is no trace of any persecution, nor under Vespasian (68-79) or Titus (79-81). The attention of the Roman Government was focussed on the Jewish rebellion and the Christians appear to have been forgotten, but under Domitian (81-96), a persecution is recorded by Melito (*HE*, IV, 2, 6, 9. See also III, 17). It seems to refer to a number of rather scattered incidents. In Palestine, after the Fall of Jerusalem, some of the Judaeo-Christian refugees at Pella had doubtless returned to Jerusalem; Eusebius records that they gathered round the relations of the Lord (*HE*, III, 11). Simon, a cousin of Jesus, had succeeded to James. Hegesippus says that Domitian summoned before him the descendants of Jude, another cousin of the Lord, who had been denounced to him as descendants of David (*HE*, III, 20). A little earlier Eusebius recalls that Vespasian had ordered a search for all the descendants of David after the capture of Jerusalem (*HE*, III, 2). So this was repression of Jewish

---

3. *Ann.*, XV, 44.
4. ' Tacitus über die Christen ', *VC*, 4 (1950), p. 69-74.
5. Diodorus, *Hist.*, XXIV.
6. See Josephus, *Contr. Apion.*, 79.
7. On the passage in Tacitus, see J. B. Bauer, ' Tacitus und die Christen ', *Gymnasium*, 69 (1957), p. 495-503.

Messianism.   Christ's relations were involved because of his descent from David proclaimed in the Kerygma.

At Rome another problem arose.   Domitian ' pitilessly crushed all resistance in the aristocracy and among the intellectuals'[8].   Among the people he persecuted there may possibly have been Christians. One was probably Manius Acilius Glabrio, consul in 91, executed with two other noblemen as an ' atheist ' and ' innovator ' (*Domit.*, 10). Now one of the properties of the Acilii Glabriones was later used as a cemetery by the Christians[9].   Better attested is the tradition that Flavius Clemens, a cousin of Titus and Domitian, and especially his wife Flavia Domitilla, were Christians.   The former was condemned to death in 95 for atheism and ' Jewish practices ' (*Domit.*, 15), the latter was exiled to the isle of Pontia in 96 (*HE*, III, 18, 4).   The Cemetery of Domitilla may have been one of her estates which was used for the burial of Christians.   A reference by Clement in his *Epistle*, I, 1, to misfortunes suffered by the Church of Rome may allude to these persecutions.

These facts, however, are somewhat problematical[10].   On the other hand there does exist a region in which Domitian's persecution of the Christians is proved with certainty, namely Asia Minor.   Here there is a document of the first importance : the *Apocalypse*.   *The Apocalypse* gives us information about a group of Churches in Asia, Lydia and Phrygia; it seems certain that persecutions took place in these parts at that time.   John himself had been exiled from Ephesus to Patmos (1 : 9).   The Church of Ephesus had suffered ' for the Name ' of Christ (2 : 3). In Pergamum Antipas had been put to death (2 : 13) in connection with ' the throne of Satan ', which probably means the temple of Rome, and so indicates emperor-worship.   Tertullian records the martyrdom of Antipas in the reign of Domitian (*Scorpiacum*, 12).   John tells the Church of Smyrna that several of its members are going to be thrown into prison (2 : 10). We must remember that the literary form of the *Apocalypse* was a message of hope addressed to the faithful in their ordeal and so implied persecution.

But if the *Apocalypse* is important as evidence of the persecutions in Asia under Domitian, it is still more so as evidence for the change of attitude shown by Christians to the Empire.   The contrast with the *Epistles* of Paul is striking.   For Paul the danger was that the Church might be dragged into opposition with Rome by the Jews, and so he made repeated calls for obedience to the imperial power.   But now

8. See J. Moreau, *Lactance.   De la mort des persécuteurs*, II, Paris 1954, p. 206.
9. See H. Grégoire, *Les persécutions dans l'Empire romain*, Brussells 1951, p. 27.
10. See J. Moreau, *Les persécutions du christianisme dans l'Empire romain*, Paris 1956, p. 37-39.

the situation is reversed; the Empire since Nero was considered as persecuting Christians and John described it under the symbol of the beast
which comes up from the sea. The ten horns and seven heads represent
the line of emperors (13 : 1). The allusions to emperor-worship are
explicit (2 : 10; 3 : 10; 13 : 3-8), Rome is referred to as Babylon, symbol
of persecuting paganism (14 : 8). The same hostility to Rome is found
in Asia at the same period in the fifth book of the *Sibylline Oracles*.

This theme of the persecuting Empire crystallises chiefly around
the figure of Nero. It is probable that the number 666 refers to him
(13 : 18). Belief in his survival and future return had appeared in pagan
circles immediately after his death[11]; a belief taken up in the *Apocalypse*
(13 : 12-14; 17 : 8), but the *Apocalypse* is not the only Christian work
of Domitian's reign where the theme appears. The *Ascension of Isaiah*
belongs to the same period and is probably the work of the Christian
community of Syria. There too we find the theme of Nero's return
(IV, 2, 4); emperor-worship appears (IV, 11). The Church is called
' the plantation planted by the Twelve Apostles of the Well-Beloved ',
a typically Judaeo-Christian image, and suffers persecution (IV, 3).
One of the Twelve is put to death, certainly a reference to Peter's
martyrdom under Nero (IV, 3). Finally we may note that the same theme
appears in the Jewish Apocalypses of the time, the Fourth *Esdras* (V, 6)
and the fourth book of the *Sibylline Oracles* (119-120; 137-139), the
former being Palestinian, the latter Asiatic.

We may wonder what provoked this stiffening in the attitude of
the imperial government towards the Christians and of the Christians
towards Rome. On the Roman side it would seem to have been one
aspect of the conflict between the Empire and the Jews; it was because
they were more or less confused with the Jews that the Christians were
persecuted by the Flavians. It is noticeable that the members of the
Roman aristocracy were persecuted for Jewish practices, and the relatives
of Jesus were arrested in Palestine as descendants of David. That is
why the Churches of Asia bore the brunt of the persecution. Christianity
in this region had been stirred by Messianic currents, and it was there that
Millenarianism appeared : the awaiting of the establishment by Christ
of his universal kingdom centred on Jerusalem. Papias links this doctrine
with the presbyters of Asia, disciples of the Apostles (*HE*, III, 39, 12)
and John himself refers to this attitude in the *Apocalypse*, while Cerinthus
gives it a heterodox form (*HE*, IV, 28, 1-6).

It was natural that the Roman authorities should have confused
Asiatic Millenarianism with Jewish Zealotism. True, this confusion was

11. See Tacitus, *Hist.*, I, 2; II, 8.

groundless, but the fact is that the Johannine group remained deeply committed to Judaism. It is, therefore, understandable that Roman persecution aimed against the Jews should have assailed it and considered this group as forming part of the latter. In fact the reign of Domitian in Asia and in Palestine provides an astonishing parallel between Jewish literature and Christian literature. The Fourth *Esdras* and Book IV of the *Sibylline Oracles* on the one hand, and John's *Apocalypse* on the other, express an identical hostility to Rome.

2. The Church under the Antonines

The coming of the Antonines to the imperial throne inaugurated a period of calm, starting with the reign of Nerva. Eusebius tells us that John returned from Patmos to settle in Ephesus (*HE*, III, 21, 9; 23, 1); Clement of Alexandria states this earlier (*Quis dives*, 43). It was doubtless also under Nerva that the *Epistle* of Clement of Rome was written. In the name of the Church of Rome the author wrote to the Church of Corinth, where troubles had taken place. He states that he has not intervened earlier because of the incidents and misfortunes which have occurred (I, 1). These misfortunes certainly seem to be the Roman persecutions of the time of Domitian. Clement had profited from the respite resulting from Trajan's accession to perform this task. The Church of Rome seems to have been governed by a college of presbyters of whom Clement was the spokesman.

Trajan (98-117) succeeded Nerva. His reign provides a remarkable document which proves that the Christians were persecuted and also gives details of the technique : the *Letter* of Pliny the Younger. Pliny, governor of Bithynia, wrote to Trajan to ask for instructions on the occasion of the proceedings being brought against the Christians (X, 96). ' Is it the name, in the absence of any crime, or the crimes inseparable from the name that are to be punished? ' Pliny had taken the line that those who, after several interrogations, had refused to abjure, ought to be executed. He noted that ' it is impossible to force those who are really Christians '. He also said that the Christians were numerous. Trajan replied that Christians must not be sought out; that if they are denounced and refused to abjure they must be condemned; that Pliny must not allow anonymous denunciations, ' which are not in accord with the spirit of our times '.

This passage is highly important, for it certainly seems to have been the law during the whole century, and with it the apologists had to come to grips. We may note that there is no proscription of the Christians by the central government and therefore no general persecution. In the second place there are local attacks coming from the people; these are submitted to the local magistrate, as had already occurred in the case of the passion of Christ. In the third place, the basis of accusation is not the fact of having committed crimes, but simply the name of ' Christian '. Moreover, the inquiry made by Pliny seems to show that they are innocent of specific crimes, so the government does not seem to be taken in by the calumnies spread against them. Finally, however, the name Christian is in itself sufficient reason for passing sentence. That is the essential point and against it the apologists will direct their main arguments.

The question of the legal basis for passing sentence on such grounds is much disputed. It has often been suggested that it rested on a positive law proscribing Christianity dating back to Nero, the evidence for this suggestion being Tertullian's reference to an *institutum neronianum*. But as we have seen this interpretation appears unjustified. Nero was certainly the first to have taken steps against the Christians, but he based himself on common law in the case of criminal acts of which the Christians were accused. This, for Pliny, laid the Christians open to legal conviction, not because there was a law against them but because they belonged to a sect believed to indulge in practices contrary to morals *(flagitia)*. Even if they were found innocent they could be ordered to pay acts of worship and with these they were unable to comply, which justified a sentence for *pertinacia*[12]. We may add that Nero's decision and motives may have been taken as a precedent for later charges. It is this precedent that Tertullian rightly terms an *institutum*[13].

So the characteristic feature of the Christians' position during this period is precariousness; they continually live under the threat of informers. Now reasons for hostility on the part of the pagan masses were not lacking, and here one must modify the usual picture of the persecutions. Eusebius and Lactantius, apologists of Constantine, have made them the responsibility of the pagan Emperors, but on the whole the pagan Emperors were tolerant; hostility came from the people, whether pagan or Jewish. This situation was to last throughout the second century. The accession of the Severi was to raise new problems for the following century, where we shall meet legislative acts proceeding from the central government. It is important not to confuse the two periods.

Can a clear idea be formed of the extent of these convictions under Trajan? There is Pliny's evidence for Bithynia. In Palestine Simon, second Bishop of Jerusalem, son of Cleophas, was put to death

12. *Epist.*, XCVI, 2-3.
13. C. Saumagne, ' Tertullien et l'institutum Neronianum ', *TZ*, 17 (1961), p. 334-336.

(*HE*, III, 32), but the fact that he belonged to the race of David seems to have been one of the reasons. The most famous martyr of the period is Ignatius, Bishop of Antioch, martyred in Rome (*HE*, III, 36). The Greek writer Epictetus, banished from Rome in 89, who died in Nicopolis in 140, speaks of the fanaticism of the Galileans, which leads them to resist threats (IV, 7, 6).

The reign of Hadrian (117-138) seems to have been especially peaceful for the Christians. A precious document by Justin has been preserved (I *Apol.*, LXVIII, 6, 10), which makes an interesting comparison with Trajan's letter. Hadrian addressed it to Minucius Fundanus, proconsul of Asia; he confirms the previous ruling, saying that there must be no sentence based on mere accusation, and that proceedings must be taken against those who make false charges, and severe penalties inflicted. But this does not imply a change in legislation (as Justin, who quotes the passage, claims)[14].

Under Antoninus a progressive change took place in the relations between Christianity and the Graeco-Roman world. Formerly, Christianity had seemed linked to Judaism and the first persecutions were connected with the conflict between Judaism and the Empire at the end of the first century. It seems that the martyrdom of Telesphorus in Rome in 137 was an effect of the Jewish war. The Christians, for their part, were inspired by the Jewish Apocalypse. Rome seemed to them as if it were the city of Satan; they believed that God would soon intervene to put an end to its conflict with the city of God. This spirit continued throughout the second century; it is notably apparent in Montanism, and Celsus still considered Christianity a Jewish heresy. But gradually the Christians appeared to pagans in a different light. Their originality was recognised, but at the same time people did not know how to classify them.

The Christians appeared as curious beings, on the fringe of society. This is the picture obtained from the evidence available during the reigns of Antoninus and Marcus Aurelius. For the intellectuals of the time, the Christians belonged to the world of eastern mystagogues, disturbing because of their magical powers and despicable because of their questionable morals. The earliest evidence is that of Fronto, the tutor of Antoninus and Marcus Aurelius, consul in 143 under Hadrian. Minucius Felix tells of the charges he made against the Christians : adoration of a donkey's head, immolation and manducation of a child in the ceremonies of initiation, incestuous unions after a banquet on feast days[15].

14. See W. Schmid, ' The Christian Reinterpretation of the Rescript of Hadrian ', *Maia*, 7 (1955), p. 5-13.
15. *Octav.*, IX, 6; XXXI, 1-2.

Already, in the first *Apology*, about 155, Justin referred to these same charges. He was speaking of the Gnostics : ' Are they guilty of the horrible deeds with which the Christians are charged, such as putting out the light in order to commit acts of promiscuity and eat human flesh? That we do not know '[16]. Justin probably used the passage from Fronto, for his account exactly follows that of Minucius Felix, so Fronto's attack dates from the beginning of the reign of Antoninus. We may note that Justin suggests that the charges brought against the Christians were perhaps true of the Gnostics. It is certain that in pagan eyes Christians of the Great Church, Montanists and Gnostics of various kinds were confused. The same thing will be found in Celsus, and this muddle was doubtless very damaging to the Christians.

Further evidence is provided by Lucian. Born in 125, living in Athens in 165, he was active under Antoninus, Marcus Aurelius and Commodus. In his *Life of Peregrinus* he tells how this imaginary figure, whom he presents as a charlatan, is converted to Christianity in Palestine[17]. Having found the Church, he obtains important appointments, just as he had hoped; he is ' prophet ', ' thiasarch ', ' leader of the assembly ', ' he interprets the books ' and ' he writes books '. Here we have a picture of a Palestinian community in the middle of the second century described by a pagan. Peregrinus is prophet, presbyter and Didascalos. Arrested for his faith in Christ, thrown into prison and possessing the glorious aureole of a confessor, he receives visits from Christians who load him with presents; in this way he amasses a fortune, but on his release from prison he is excluded from the Christian community for having eaten the idolothytes; this last incident is appropriate in a Judaeo-Christian community. Peregrinus then continues his peregrinations. Lucian shows the Christians in a different light from Fronto : they are not criminals but naive people taken in by the first impostor[18].

During the reign of Antoninus, Crescens the cynic, who was in Rome about 152-153, spread ' infamous calumnies ' against the Christians — at least so Justin tells us — doubtless a renewal of Fronto's charges. Galen, who stayed in Rome between 162 and 166, is more moderate in his judgement. He admits that the Christians face death with courage and says they are capable of leading a philosophic life; on the other hand he reproaches them with credulity, a reproach already made by Lucian; it will recur in Celsus. Christianity appears to these men as innocent but fraught with baseless superstitions; it is still the same tone

16. *I Apol.*, XXVI, 7.
17. See H. D. Betz, *Lukian von Samosata und das Neue Testament*, Berlin 1961, p. 5-13.
18. See P. de Labriolle, *La réaction païenne*, Paris 1934, p. 106.

of scorn. Marcus Aurelius has only one word to say about them : their spirit of opposition whereby they offer themselves to death. The point is an interesting one and certainly characteristic of certain groups like the Montanists. Rusticus, prefect of Rome, who condemned Justin in 165, was a friend of Marcus Aurelius.

But this was a mere reference in passing. The first great indictment of Christianity was made by Celsus, where a new stage is reached : Christianity no longer appears as an unimportant fanatical belief or superstition, worthy at most of an anecdote. This stiffening of the pagan intellectuals under Marcus Aurelius means that there are now Christian intellectuals, and it is in fact possible that the *True Discourse* by Celsus may be a reply to Justin[19]. Celsus presents Christ, the Apostles and the Christians as vagrants who pride themselves on their own importance, moreover he considers their doctrines as mere ill-digested borrowings from traditional wisdom, and insidiously points out that their attitude presents a danger to the city.

Calumniated and scorned by public opinion, the Christians found themselves in a dangerous position. It was enough for one man like Crescens to show them malice for them to face death. There was one particularly grave threat. At certain solemn moments of the year the Romans were accustomed to put on shows for the people, and for combats in the circus victims were required. If we study martyrdom under Hadrian and Marcus Aurelius, we find that the most notable of these Christian martyrs suffered at pagan festivals. This is true of Polycarp, martyred in Smyrna on the occasion of the festival given by the Asiarch Philip, and of the martyrs of Lyons in 177, thrown to wild animals during the festival which every year brought delegates from the three Gauls together in Lyons.

Here, doubtless, the persecution of Christians takes on its deepest meaning. This was not only a question of ideological incompatibility. Surprise has sometimes been shown that under liberal, philosophical emperors like the Antonines there were martyrs, but the fact is that under the humanist veneer Graeco-Roman civilisation still had a core of cruelty[20]. It is this fact which rationalist historians fail to grasp when they try to explain the persecutions in terms of sociological problems. Justin and Tertullian are better historians because more faithful to the whole complex of facts. The whole of Justin's argument consists in showing the philosopher-emperors the contradiction in their behaviour when they persecuted Christians.

19. A. Andresen, *Nomos und Logos. Die Polemik des Kelsos wider das Christentum*, Berlin 1955.
20. See P. Carrington, *The Early Christian Church*, p. 243.

3. The Apologies

Faced with this situation, the Christians had to try to dispel the prejudices which made them misunderstood and to win their case before the authorities and also before public opinion. To this end a whole series of works appeared, and in every way their appearance marks something quite new in Christianity; they are Greek not only in their language, but in thought and expression, and they are concerned to show that Christianity conforms to the ideal of Hellenism — or, better, that it alone truly realises that ideal. Some of them take official measures to clear the name ' Christian ' of the charges made against it, but their main object is to show public opinion the true nature of Christianity, and thereby not only to obtain respect for it but to attract new members.

The first Apology dates from the reign of Hadrian[21]. According to Eusebius, it was given to him during his stay in Athens in 124-125 by Quadratus; only a fragment is extant. The second is by Aristides, and Eusebius dates it to the reign of Hadrian, and the Syriac translation to that of Antoninus. It is not absolutely certain that the text we have is the work by Aristides mentioned by Eusebius[22]. In fact, it is with Justin, under Antoninus, that we find the point of view just defined. Justin is a person of outstanding importance. Born in Samaria of a pagan Greek family, he has described in the *Dialogue with Trypho* how he looked for wisdom in the various schools of philosophy until the day when he was converted. We find him again in Ephesus, shortly after the Jewish War, holding discussions with the Jew Trypho, and he came to Rome under Antoninus, about 150, where he founded a school on the lines of those of the pagan philosophers. He had disputes with Crescens the cynic, and was martyred about 165. Justin represents a new type of Christian : he was a Greek philosopher who, after his conversion, retained his old manner of thinking and way of life.

Only a small part of his writings is extant. The list given by Eusebius, who may have known works now lost in the library of Caesarea, shows that they were mainly philosophical. There is a *Discourse to the Greeks*, in which he replies to the philosophers' questions and discusses the nature of spirits. Another work, addressed to the Greeks, is entitled *Refutation* (elenchos). A book *On the Monarchy of God* discusses the subject in terms of the bible and also of Greek writings. Another, *On the Soul*, recalls the opinions of the Greek philosophers. All these problems are found in philosophy of the period, in Plutarch, Albinus and

21. For the chronology of the Apologies, see R. M. Grant, ' The Chronology of the Greek Apologists ', *Vig. Christ.*, 9 (1955), p. 25-34.
22. See G. C. O'Ceallaigh, ' Marcianus Aristides on the Worship of God ', *HTR*, 51 (1960), p. 227-255.

Galen.   Andresen has shown that Justin belonged to the school of Middle Platonism[23].   We shall find signs of this in his philosophy.

Besides these philosophical books, there are controversial writings : the *Dialogue with Trypho,* which is a very important document for the interpretation of the bible in the second century, and Irenaeus quotes a work *Against Marcion,* now lost; he himself mentions his *Treatise* (syntagma) *against all the Heresies,* and finally we have the two *Apologies,* written some time between 150 and 165.   The first seems to be a reply to the calumnies of Fronto and is addressed to Antoninus.   The second was perhaps destined for Marcus Aurelius.   Justin appeals to the philosophical sentiments of the Emperors, to their piety and virtue.   His whole aim is to show first that the Christians represent true piety and that their doctrine tallies with that of the best Greeks, Socrates, Heraclitus and Plato.   Then he comes to the question of morals : he shows the Christians' virtues and stresses the fact that they obey the laws; he contrasts Christianity with paganism, whose theology he denounces and whose immorality he describes.   These themes will recur in all the literature that follows.

A new group of books is linked to the persecution of Marcus Aurelius between 176 and 180.   Melito addressed an apology to the Emperor. Perhaps he presented it to him in 176 when the Emperor travelled through Asia Minor.   He refers to new edicts against the Christians; we know nothing of these edicts, but they correspond to the renewal of hostilities towards the Christians which marked the end of the reign, and Eusebius has preserved some fragments of the *Apology.*   Melito explains that the Christian ' philosophy ', after having blossomed among the barbarians, has come to full flower in the Empire, and he shows that this flowering coincides with the development of Roman power, recalling that Antoninus has forbidden any changes in the treatment of Christians (*HE,* IV, 13, 6).

Eusebius links Melito's *Apology* with that of Apollinarius of Hierapolis.   The latter may have been presented to Marcus Aurelius at the same date and in the same circumstances.   Apollinarius, according to Eusebius, also wrote five books *To the Greeks* and two *On Truth.* About the same time, between 177 and 180, Athenagoras, in Athens, presented his *Apology* to Marcus Aurelius and to Commodus, whom the Emperor had just taken as a colleague and who was to succeed him later, in 180.   This work is extant and in spirit it is similar to Justin's works.   It was to the same Emperors that Miltiades, in Asia, addressed his *Apology,* no longer extant.   He had written tracts *Against the Jews* and *Against the Greeks* (*HE,* V, 17, 5).

23. *Op. cit.*

The works we have just listed are official documents, pleas addressed to the Emperors. In the same period we also meet works similar in spirit but addressed to private persons or to the Greeks in general. Theophilus, bishop of Antioch under Marcus Aurelius, intervened in the disputes of the day and wrote against Marcion and against Hermogenes; Eusebius saw works of catechesis from his pen. Here we may note his book *To Autolycus*. Theophilus is very different from Melito, an Asiatic, and Justin, a philosopher. Still very much steeped in Syrian Judaeo-Christianity, he tries to prove the truth of Christianity chiefly from history. This book shows the interest he took in historical questions; he refers the reader to a book *On Histories*, no longer extant. We hear nothing more of him after the death of Marcus Aurelius, so his book dates from about 180.

We must also mention Tatian, a disciple of Justin before becoming an Encratite. Tatian published a *Discourse to the Greeks*, which takes a different form from the pleas; its object is exclusively the refutation of Greek errors. That too was doubtless the theme of the books with the same title by Justin, Miltiades and Apollinarius, now lost. Tatian's tract is notable for the violence of his attacks on Greek philosophers, forms of worship and mysteries. Like Justin he identifies Christianity with the true philosophy[24], but, in contrast to Justin, he finds no trace of this philosophy among the Greeks and sees only their distortions. Finally, the *Epistle to Diognetus*, whose author is still unknown, is a remarkable presentation of Christianity confronted with the objections of a pagan intellectual[25].

From these examples we see that the aim of the *Apologies* was not simply to demand legal status for the Christians, their ambition was much greater than that; they aimed at nothing less than presenting Christians as the authentic heirs of Graeco-Roman civilisation. The Apologists chose to fight on their opponents' ground; the latter accused them of being unreasonable in their teaching and loose in their morals. They accepted this appeal to reason and morality, in fact their whole purpose was to show that it was their opponents who contravened reason and morality, and that they, the Christians, embodied these principles. Hence the dual nature of their work : on the one hand they denounced the various forms of paganism, mythology, the mysteries and emperor-worship, and made charges against pagan morals; on the other hand they expounded Christian doctrine, emphasising chiefly monotheism and the Resurrection, and describing Christian morals.

24. See M. Elze, *Tatian und seine Theologie*, Göttingen 1960.
25. See H. I. Marrou, *L'Épître à Diognète*, Paris 1951, p. 98-111.

This point of view implied a remarkable interpretation of the continuity between Christianity and Hellenism. The truth is one. First it has been communicated to the barbarians, that is to say, the Jews. Hence the importance for Tatian and Theophilus of arguments from history. This truth has been distorted by the Greeks under the influence of devils. The devils themselves became the object of adoration and instead of adoring the true God, they borrowed the mysteries proclaimed by the prophets and made of them the fables of mythology. In this sense Justin does not hesitate to compare the ascension of Perseus and that of Jesus, Danaë's conception and Mary's : the former, for him, are only the distortion of the latter. The Logos, moreover, was perpetually present in men : a Socrates or a Heraclitus were swayed by it and had condemned paganism. It is this Logos which in the person of Christ has shown itself in its plenitude, whereas until then men had only a partial knowledge of it[26].

It is a new approach that we find here. The Apologists do not merely demand tolerance; they proclaim the alliance of Christianity and philosophy, of the Church and the Empire. In all sincerity they accept the world in which they are living. The *Epistle to Diognetus* emphasises that the Christians are in no way different from other men either in habitat, dress or language; Justin shows that they are the best citizens and Melito stresses the fact that Christianity has made the Empire greater. This is not simply an argument against opponents. Justin, Athenagoras and the author of the *Epistle to Diognetus* belonged to Hellenism by birth, culture and way of life. They considered that by becoming Christians they had in no way renounced it, but had found its true meaning.

4. Rhetoric and Philosophy

This Christian Hellenism began to appear in the reigns of Hadrian and Marcus Aurelius. In the Hellenistic world the second century was the century of Rhetoric. Aelius Aristides, Dio of Prusa and Herod Atticus developed prose as an art under Antoninus; Maximus of Tyre was contemporary with Hadrian. The orators gave their brilliant improvisations in the lecture halls of the whole world, while the Cynics perfected the literary *genre* known as the diatribe. Lucian of Samosata was writing his biting dialogues, the schools of philosophy were flourishing, Aristotle's works formed the basis of training in dialectic, Stoic morality found one of its noblest exponents in Marcus Aurelius,

26. See J. Daniélou, *Message évangélique et culture hellénistique*, Paris 1961, p. 34-39 (E.T. in preparation as *The Gospel and Hellenic Christianity* = Vol. II of *The Development of Christian Doctrine up to the Council of Nicaea*).

but it was Platonism above all that regained its original impetus after the eclecticism of the New Academy : Gaius, Albinus, Atticus and Numenius applied themselves to the study of authentic Platonism and prepared the way for Neo-Platonism.

The Christian writers of the period were trained in Greek and Roman schools; their culture was that of their environment and age. Melito was doubtless the most artistic of the Christian writers of the time : Eusebius tells us that his brilliance was remarkable. We might be inclined to doubt this if we judged only on the basis of the fragments preserved by Eusebius or of the ' chains ', though the fragment of his *Apology* quoted by Eusebius ends with a splendid alliteration; another fragment describes baptism in terms of Homeric images[27]. But we now possess the text of his *Homily on the Passion* and a short fragment of paschal Liturgy which followed it. In the *Homily* there is a continual display of antitheses, a taste for pathetic descriptions of a highly skilful rhythm which make it a typical model of the Asiatic school of rhetoric[28]. Also from Asia, and belonging to the same period, is the epitaph of Abercius.

Theophilus of Antioch has curious points of resemblance with Aelius Aristides[29], and in him we also find the techniques of Asiatic rhetoric. Justin, on the other hand, is an Attic writer and finds inspiration in the classical authors. The beginning of his *Dialogue with Trypho* is clearly an imitation of the beginning of Plato's dialogues; his straightforward, spare style is admirably clear. Tatian is also an Attic writer but he is nearer Lucian than Plato. He has the taste of his century for curious anecdotes, and jeers at the gods of mythology and their adventures, rather like the cynics. He is interested in history and delights in giving dates. We find this trait in Hegesippus, the first historian of the Church, who, wherever he happens to be, notes the list of bishops and their dates of office. Theophilus likewise goes through the Greek historians in order to study what happened before the events recorded in Scripture. All of them — Athenagoras, Theophilus and Justin — adorn their Apologies with quotations from Homer and the tragic authors, probably drawn from scholarly collections.

More even than the literary form it is the thought itself which is steeped in Hellenism. And why not? Did not Justin declare that it was the Logos who spoke through Socrates and Plato? Tatian and

27. See R. M. Grant, ' Melito of Sardis on Baptism ', *Vig. Christ.*, 4 (1950), p. 33-36.
28. See A. Wifstrand, ' The Homily of Melito on the Passion ', *Vig. Christ.*, 2 (1948), p. 201-224.
29. See R. M. Grant, ' Scripture Rhetoric and Theology in Theophilus ', *Vig. Christ.*, 13 (1959), p. 33-45.

Athenagoras have been shown to be influenced by the early works of Aristotle[30], and the Apologists used parts of his psychology and logic which had entered into the course of instruction in schools; we even find them borrowing themes from the Stoics. Justin likens the ἐκπύρωσις (ekpurosis), the destruction of the world by fire, to the Last Judgment. In Justin and Athenagoras the vocabulary of the theory of knowledge is largely Stoic. Tatian draws inspiration from the psychology of the Stoa, while Athenagoras sees in nature the Stoic enchainment ἀκολουθία (acolouthia) of causes. The *Epistle to Diognetus* seems to allude to the doctrine of universal sympathy. Above all, the principles of Stoic morality are recognised by Justin as being true and the Christian is shown to fulfil the ideal of the Stoic sage[31].

But in fact the Stoic and Aristotelian elements found in the Apologists are almost exclusively those that belonged to the eclecticism of culture in the schools and had become a common language; the only philosophy that really influenced them is Middle Platonism. Justin tells us how disappointed he was by the other philosophies and how he adhered to Platonism before becoming a Christian. After his conversion he remained a philosopher and his school in Rome resembled those kept by representatives of the philosophical sects. His disciple Tatian was likewise a philosopher and very typical of Middle Platonism[32], and the same is true of Athenagoras[33]. Here we find a new type emerging : the Christian intellectual, who did not have any equivalent in Judaeo-Christianity; he represents the dynamic element in the Church at that time, in contrast to the great bishops, Melito, Irenaeus and Theophilus, who were primarily upholders of tradition.

30. See L. Alfonsi, ' Motivi tradizionali del giovane Aristotle in Clemente Alessandrino e in Atenagora ', *Vig. Christ.*, 7 (1953), p. 133-152.
31. See N. Smannent, *Le stoïcisme des Pères de l'Église de Clément de Rome à Clément d'Alexandrie*, Paris 1957.
32. M. Else, *Tatian und seine Theologie*, p. 23.
33. G. Andresen, *Justin und der mittlere Platonismus*, ZNTW, 44 (1952-1953), p. 157-195.

LIFE AND BELIEFS OF THE 2ND AND 3RD CENTURY CHRISTIAN COMMU-
NITY: III. Remission of sins

PLATE 7.   THE HEALING OF THE PARALYTIC; WALL PAINTING FROM THE BAPTISTRY
OF THE HOUSE CHURCH AT DURA-EUROPOS

On the right the paralytic lies on his bed. In the centre at the top of the picture, Christ speaks the words recorded in Mark 2:10-11. On the left of the picture we see the paralytic walking away, carrying his bed. The immediate significance of this picture in this context lies in the linking of the power to heal with the authority to forgive sins, in the words of Jesus. Baptism was understood as effecting the remission of sins (cf. ch. 6, § 1). The picture has additional significance in that it is the earliest known portrayal of Jesus. He is depicted here as a young man with short hair and no beard, dressed in tunic and pallium and wearing sandals on his feet. His face is that of a young aristocratic intellectual and it is clear that the community saw him as the Logos teacher. The double scene is unique in early Christian representations of the incident. As such it may well have been influenced by the narrative style or 'strip-cartoon' method popular with Syrian artists (cf. ch. 12, § 2).

LIFE AND BELIEFS OF THE 2ND AND 3RD CENTURY CHRISTIAN COMMUNITY: IV. The Eucharist

THE CELESTIAL BANQUET; FRESCO IN CATACOMB OF PETER AND MARCELLINUS, ROME, LATE 3RD OR EARLY 4TH CENTURY

The picture shows two men and a woman reclining at a meal. At the end of the semi-circular table 'Peace' and 'Love', personified as women, sit as hostesses. There is a fish on the tripod table in the centre and beside it a young servant holds a cup. The inscription reads: 'Peace, give warm water' (i.e. to mix with wine), 'Love mix [wine] for me'. The picture draws on the theme of the common meal so frequently portrayed on ancient funerary monuments, and uses the model to bring out the significance of the eucharist: the association of love and peace, the anticipation of the Celestial Banquet, etc. The fish had a double meaning: at one level it could be understood as representing the Christ, but it could also be understood derivatively as representing the baptised Christian, swimming in the waters of baptism (cf. Tertullian, *De Baptismo*, 1).

By permission of *Societa Amici delle Catacombe*, Rome.

Photo : British Museum, London (after Wilpert).

LIFE AND BELIEFS OF THE 2ND AND 3RD CENTURY CHRISTIAN COMMUNITY :
V. The Christian Hope

PLATE 9. THE HEAVENLY JERUSALEM AND PARADISE; WALL PAINTING FROM THE HYPO-
GAEUM OF THE AURELII, ROME, VIALE MANZONI, 3RD CENTURY

The scene on the left shows a large group of men and women dressed in white and listening to the central figure, the Lord, who expounds the Law. Note that the Master is much larger than the other people in the picture. He holds a rod in his right hand and seems to be seated on some sort of throne. The entrance to the City is guarded by a woman who is also superhumanly large. The group in the garden on the right is much smaller. A woman with her right hand raised is shown in the company of three men; the woman's gesture suggests that the group may be praying rather than talking together. In the front of the picture, outside the walled garden, a figure tries in vain to enter. The paintings in this catacomb (cf. Plate 13) were almost certainly produced by a group of heterodox probably Gnostic Christians, but even though one may detect Gnostic nuances in this picture, the imagery is drawn from the traditional imagery of the Christian Hope; as such the best commentary is the *Passio Perpetuae* (cf. e.g. ch. 4: 'then I saw an immense space, a garden, and in the middle thereof sat a man with grey hair a tall figure, dressed as a shepherd, milking his sheep. And around him stood many thousands of white-robed figures.')

Photo : Societa Amici delle Catacombe, Rome.

PLATE 10.   THE CRUCIFIED ASS; WALL DRAWING FROM THE DOMUS GELOTIANA, ROME,
PALATINE, 2ND CENTURY

This drawing from a 2nd century house, probably used as a school for imperial pages, is the earliest picture of the Crucifixion. Its intention is obviously derisory. The Greek inscription reads: 'Alexamenos [presumably the figure on the left] [adores] God.' The charge of onalotry made against the early Christians is mentioned several times in Christian writings, e.g., in Tertullian, *Apology* 16: 'You imagine the head of an ass to be our God...';   The origin of the charge appears to have been twofold.   In the first place, the Jews were accused of worshipping a *caput asinum* (Tacitus, *Hist.* 5, 3) and this God was later identified with Christ.   In the second place, the Jews themselves made this charge against the Christians as a derisory and incredulous comment on the belief in the Virgin Birth.   (The first evidence of this latter charge seems to be in the words of the late 1st century Rabbi, R. Jehoschuah'b Chananja, quoted in Strack-Billerbeck *KNT*, I, p. 236, Munich 1922).

Photo : Alinari.

CHAPTER VIII

HETERODOXY
AND ORTHODOXY

BETWEEN the years 70 and 140 Christianity grew in various regions and expressed itself in various ways. The Aramaean Churches, the Asiatic Churches, the Syrian and Roman Churches each had their own traditions. On the frontiers of Christianity, and not always easily distinguishable from it, heterodox groups abounded : Gnostics, Ebionites, and others. But this situation inevitably brought about clashes, and as these tendencies asserted themselves more vigorously, an open struggle was bound to occur; this is what we find in the middle of the second century. The clash took place between heterodoxy and orthodoxy, and also between the different orthodox traditions. In these struggles, Rome at this time played a decisive role.

1. Marcion

With Marcion we enter a world about which we have so far said little. He was the son of the Bishop of Sinope, in Pontus, according to Hippolytus. The practices of the Church of Sinope, which Marcion observed, were orthodox. For example, the baptismal rites included consignation, anointing with oil, the milk and honey[1]. Certain features are noteworthy : prayer facing the East, psalms and hymns composed by Christians[2]. There was a special method of calculating the date of Easter, which recalls the Samaritan calendar; the hierarchy was composed of bishops, deacons, presbyters and lectors, and there seem also to have been deaconesses. Tertullian reproached the Marcionites for allowing women to exorcise, to lay hands on the sick and to baptise[3].

1. *Adv. Marc.*, I, 14; III, 22.
2. *Murat. Canon*, 82-84.
3. *Praescript.*, 41.

Marcion considered continence obligatory, a feature betraying Judaeo-Christian influence.

But the most important aspect of Marcion's Christianity is his Paulinism. He reduces the canonical writings to the *Gospel of Luke* and the *Epistles of Paul*. It is possible that this may be primarily a mark of archaism and that the *Gospel* of Luke was that used by the Sinope community; it was the Gospel of Greece. We have already noted the contacts of Pontus with Corinth. It seems that at first, in Asia Minor, Marcion preached a rather extravagant Paulinism, rejecting the Old Testament, and he tried to get this accepted by the presbyters of Rome in about 144. It was doubtless on this occasion that he wrote his *Antitheses;* his standpoint was not approved. Marcion's doctrine then became more radical. Here we must doubtless bring in the influence of Cerdo, who according to Irenaeus[4], had come to Rome under Hyginus (136-140). Cerdo contrasted the ' just ' God of the Old Testament with the ' good ' God of the New. This was nothing less than Judaeo-Christian Gnosticism. Marcion adopted this theology, which confirmed his theories[5].

Marcion was not a great theologian, but he gave a simple, radical form to Pauline pessimism and at the same time he stripped the Gnostic rebellion of its Apocalyptic expression. This doctrine was to have an immense success, all the more so since Marcion was a remarkable organiser. His sect was a Church in the true sense. As early as 150, in his *First Apology*, Justin notes its existence[6]; he refutes it in a special tract[7]; Irenaeus gives it only a short notice in his *Adversus Haereses*[8], but elsewhere he attacks it. Dionysius of Corinth wrote a letter against Marcion to the Christians of Nicomedia (*HE*, IV, 23, 4) and Philip, Bishop of Gortyna in Crete wrote a book against him[9], as did Rhodo, Tatian's disciple (*HE*, V, 13, 1). Tertullian's tract *Adversus Marcionem* is extant and we know that the Marcionite Churches were powerful in Mesopotamia, where they paved the way for Manichaeism. Bardesanes attacked Marcion at the end of the second century[10].

2. Valentinus

Whereas Marcion was a founder of a Church, Valentinus was primarily a mystic. According to Epiphanius[11], he was born in Egypt and like

4. *Adv. Haer.*, III, 4, 3; I, 27, 1-2.
5. See E. C. Blackman, *Marcion and his Influence*, London 1948, p. 68-71.
6. *I Apol.*, XXVI, 5.
7. *Adv. Haer.*, IV, 6, 2.
8. *Ibid.*, I, 27, 2-4.
9. See P. Nautin, *Lettres et écrivains chrétiens des IIe et IIIe siècles*, Paris 1961, p. 22-24.
10. See A. Vööbus, *History of Asceticism*, p. 47-53.
11. *Pan.*, XXXI, 2, 5.

Cerdo, he came to Rome under Hyginus. According to Tertullian[12], he seems to have tried to obtain the post of Bishop of Rome by intrigue; doubtless this was on the death of Pius, in 140. Hippolytus says that he had a vision in which a new born child was revealed to him as the Logos[13]. This visionary character also appears in a fragment of a psalm[14]. Valentinus, in fact, shared the archaic Gnosticism of the Sethians. This is clear from a fragment quoted by Clement of Alexandria, in which we find the angels, after making Adam, ' struck with amazement because of the germ of the substance from on high '[15] which is in him. The Jewish elements of this doctrine are evident, and this Jewish origin is also evident in the notion of devils dwelling in the soul[16]. Valentinus also shows signs of Egyptian Judaeo-Christianity of Encratite tendency[17].

What exactly Valentinus taught is difficult to discover. The letter preserved by Epiphanius is probably not by him[18]. The Gospel of Truth found at Nag Hammadi seems not to be the work of that name which Irenaeus attributes to him, and it is not certain that Valentinus wrote it[19]. The references in Irenaeus to Valentinian Gnosis are chiefly based on the works of his disciples, Ptolemy and Heracleon on the one hand, Theodotus and Mark the Magus on the other. Nevertheless the doctrine of the Valentinian school is very coherent in its main lines and it is the genius of Valentinus that created it. Through him Sethian Gnosis, which was only one form of Judaeo-Christian Gnosticism, became a powerful synthesis. Its essential elements are as follows : the absolute transcendence of the invisible Father and his thought (ennoia), the generation of the pleroma of aeons to the number of thirty, the last being Sophia; a quest of the Father by Sophia; this desire becomes the principle of the terrestial world, where spiritual elements are imprisoned; the sending of the Lord who brings the Gnosis, thanks to which those who are spiritual are saved.

The tragic sense that the Apocalypse has failed to happen, which is the historical starting-point of Gnosticism, here for the first time found speculative expression and became a theology, a doctrine which

---

12. *Adv. Valentin.*, 4.
13. *Elench.*, VI, 42, 2.
14. *Ibid.*, VI, 37, 2.
15. *Strom.*, II, 36, 2.
16. *Ibid.*, II, 20, 114.
17. *Ibid.*, IV, 89, 3. See E. Peterson, ' Valentino ', *Enc. Catt.*, XII (1954), p. 979-980.
18. *Pan.*, XXXVII, 5, 1. See A. J. Visser, ' Der Lehrbrief der Valentinianer ', *VC*, 12 (1958), p. 27-37.
19. See H. M. Schenke, *Die Herkunft des sogenannten Evangeliums Veritatis*, Göttingen 1959, p. 15-24; H. C. Puech and G. Quispel, ' Les écrits gnostiques du Codex Jung ', *VC*, 8 (1954), p. 1-51.

proved profoundly attractive; Valentinus had his own school. We have extracts from his disciple Theodotus, in Alexandria, which have been preserved by Clement, who had profited from them. Irenaeus has described the strange numerological Gnosticism of Mark the Magus, in Asia; it was accompanied by theurgic practices which were not foreign to Valentinus. The western school in particular was later to give Valentinian Gnosticism a philosophical look. Heracleon wrote the first commentary on the Gospel of John and provoked in reply Origen's commentary. Ptolemy, above all, whose doctrine has been preserved by Irenaeus in a long passage at the beginning of the *Adversus Haereses*, was to give the system its most finished form. The discovery of the Gnostic manuscripts of Nag Hammadi has increased our knowledge of Valentinian Gnosis. Several tracts belong to this school, notably the *Tract of the Three Natures*[20] and the *Letter to Reghinos* on the Resurrection[21].

The school of Valentinus does not represent the whole of Gnosticism in the second half of the second century; the references in Hippolytus show that other branches continued to grow. For example, Justin's Gnosis, of which Hippolytus has summarised the *Book of Baruch*. The manuscripts of Nag Hammadi contain a number of works belonging to this period and to Sethian Gnosis, though not directly linked with Valentinus, for example the *Hypostasis of the Archons*[22]. Later, in the third century, the *Pistis Sophia* shows the vitality of Gnosticism; the hypogeum of Viale Manzoni reveals the existence of a sect of Sethians in Rome[23]. Porphyry lists among the Gnostic works known to and refuted by Plotinus, the *Apocalypse of Allogenes* and the *Apocalypse of Zostrian*, which have been rediscovered at Nag Hammadi. But it was the school of Valentinus that raised a problem for the Church : both by its high quality and its moderation it proved intellectually tempting.

3. Montanus

Marcion and Valentinus are examples not only of Gnostic doctrines but of the continuation of certain tendencies in the Church : Marcion the Paulinism of northern Asia Minor, Valentinus Egyptian Judaeo-

---

20. See H. C. Puech and G. Quispel, ' Le quatrième écrit du Codex Jung ', *VC*, 9 (1955), p. 65-103.
21. See G. Quispel, ' The Jung Codex and its significance ' in *The Jung Codex*, London 1955, p. 54-57.
22. See the translation by H. M. Schenke, *Koptischgnostische Schriften aus den Papyrus-Codices von Nag Hammadi*, Hamburg 1960, p. 69-78.
23. See J. Carcopino, *De Pythagore aux Apôtres*, Paris 1956, p. 85-224.

Christianity. This connection with local variations within the Church at the beginning of the second century is even more striking in the case of Montanus. Montanus was a Phrygian who, with two women, Maximilla and Priscilla, claimed to have received the charisma of prophecy. The date when his movement began is disputed; Eusebius, in his Chronicle, says 172, while Epiphanius associates Montanus with Marcion and Tatian in 156[24], but he gives 172 as the date when Thyatires joined the Montanists, which tallies with the date given by Eusebius. So it seems that we can place the origin of the movement in 156 and that 172 is the moment when it reaches its height in Asia[25]. In 177, the case was submitted to Rome. The confessors of Lyons adopted a moderate tone when they intervened with Eleutherius. It would seem that Maximilla died in 179. Thirteen years later (*HE*, V, 16, 19) the movement disturbed all Asia, notably Ancyra (*HE*, V, 16, 4; 17, 4) and Ephesus (*HE*, V, 18, 9 & 12).

Montanism was an explosion of prophesying. It was characterised first and foremost by the importance given to visions and revelations, and in this respect women played an important role. As for the content of these revelations it was essentially eschatological. The time of the Paraclete had begun with the coming of Montanus, the new Jerusalem was going to be inaugurated and last for a thousand years; to prepare for it men and women must live in continence. Montanism appeared first in Phrygia and spread there very quickly, but it encountered strong opposition, notably from Apollinarius, Bishop of Hierapolis from 171 (*HE*, V, 16, 1). About 193-196 its extension throughout Asia gave rise, to new refutations, chiefly from Apollinarius (*HE*, V, 18, 1-14). Eusebius has preserved an important fragment by an anonymous author addressed to Avircius Marcellus, perhaps Bishop of Hierapolis and successor to Apollinarius, whose epitaph has been discovered (*HE*, V, 16, 2-17). Montanism spread elsewhere; Serapion of Antioch attacked it (*HE*, V, 19, 1) and we shall meet it in Rome under Eleutherius, where it aroused violent opposition among the Romans. There was not only resistance to heresy but a conflict of attitudes, an opposition to the spirit of the Asiatic Church. It was in Rome that Tertullian later met and adopted Montanism.

It has been suggested that Montanism represents a revival within Christianity of the enthusiasm of the Phrygian cult of Cybele and Dionysius[26], but this view is surely mistaken. In reality Montanism

24. *Pan.*, XLVIII, 2.
25. See G. S. P. Freeman-Grenville, ' The Date of the Outbreak of Montanism ', *Journ. Eccl. Hist.*, 5 (1954), p. 7-15.
26. See W. Schepeler, *Der Montanismus und die phrygische Kulte*, Tübingen 1929.

BITHYNIA

MYSIA

GALATIA

Pergamum

•Thyatira

PHRYGIA

LYDIA

A S I A

Sardis

Pepuza Synnada

Smyrna

Philadelphia

Hieropolis

Ephesus

Tralles

Hierapolis

Magnesia

Laodicea

Apamea

PISIDIA

LYCAONIA

Miletus

Colossae

CARIA

PAMPHILIA

LYCIA

Mountains over 3000 feet

2 · Phrygia and Lydia at the time of the Montanist heresy

was a development of the spirit of Asiatic Christianity[27]. It was in Hierapolis that two of the daughters of Philip the Apostle lived at the beginning of the century, and they were prophetesses and virgins. Papias was Bishop of Hierapolis and it was there that he taught Millenarianism. Ammia, a woman from Philadelphia in Lydia, was considered a prophetess in the second century (*HE*, V, 7, 2-6). Millenarianism appears to have been a general characteristic of Phrygian and Asiatic theology; we find it in Cerinthus, and Irenaeus was later to take it to Gaul.

Prophecy and the exaltation of virginity were features common to the Montanists and to Melito. More exactly, we are here confronted with an exaggerated development of Johannine Christianity. It represents a branch of the quartodeciman observance, based on John's chronology of the passion. The name Paraclete given to the Holy Spirit is Asiatic and doubtless came to Montanus from the *Gospel of John;* the millennium is in the *Apocalypse*. The thirst for martyrdom which characterised the Montanists is in harmony with the *Apocalypse* and expresses the heroic vision of the conflict between Rome, the city of Satan, and Jerusalem. Praise of continence is found in the *Apocalypse* and the apocryphal *Acts of John*. It is also noteworthy that one of the Roman opponents of Montanism, the priest Gaius, rejected the *Gospel of John* and the *Apocalypse*. Inversely, the Martyrs of Lyons, who belong to the Asiatic tradition, used a moderate tone in intervening with Eleutherius.

Montanism raises no problem of doctrine, none of its enemief charged it with heresy, but it represented the continuance of archaic tendencies. It was a sign of communities living too separated from the main body of the Church. Finally, prophetism resulted in an arraignable illuminism. Maximilla had announced imminent wars and upheavals which had not happened. The anti-Roman violence and pursuit os martyrdom were dangerous to the peace of the Church, but these excesses must not blind us to the spirit of Asia preserved in large measure by Montanism during the great period of Papias and Polycarp — a spirit which succeeded in attracting a mind as far-ranging as Tertullian's.

4. Tatian

Tatian's character has so many different facets that it can be interpreted in diametrically opposite ways. The author of the *Discourse to the Greeks* and the author of the *Diatessaron* belonged to two different worlds. Martin Elze explains all his work in terms of Middle Platonism[28].

27. K. Aland, ' Der Montanismus und die Kleinasiatische Theologie ', *Zeitsch. Neut. Wiss.*, 46 (1955), p. 109-116.
28. *Tatian und seine Theologie*, Göttingen 1960.

R. M. Grant[29] and A. Orbe[30] see in him a Valentinian Gnostic, while
F. Bolgiani[31] treats him as a Judaeo-Christian. Nothing suggests that
he was a Gnostic. Irenaeus, who has a note about him, makes no
mention of Gnosticism, and the resemblances which have been found
between him and the Valentinians bear on points which are part of the
generally accepted theology of the day and are found in Theophilus and
Athenagoras. We will come back to them. But they are far from
explaining everything. In fact Irenaeus is right in considering him
primarily a representative of Encratism. This is the conclusion which
A. Voöbus has arrived at[32]. Here we are up against a special tradition.
Tatian was an Assyrian, that is, he came from Mesopotamia, doubtless
from Adiabene; we have seen that this region belonged to the Palestinian
mission and was characterised by ascetic tendencies. Tatian was born
a pagan and seems to have been converted during a journey to Rome,
and he was a disciple of Justin. It was then that he wrote his *Discourse
to the Greeks*. Irenaeus tells us that during this period he held no
disputable doctrine. It was after the martyrdom of Justin, in 165,
that he began to spread Encratism, by condemning marriage. That
is the basis of Irenaeus's charges against him. It is possible, as Voöbus
suggests, that at Rome he met some Syrians from the East; Pope Anicetus
(155-166) came from Emesa, and the Roman Church at that time was
largely composed of easterners. Tatian felt closer to eastern radicalism.
On his return home, he wrote the *Diatessaron*, in which his Encratist
tendencies clearly emerge.

The case of Tatian resembles that of Montanus. There is no question
of doctrinal heresy. Bolgiani has shown that the error with which
Irenaeus reproaches him, denial that Adam was saved, apart from the
fact that it cannot be found in the *Discourse* (which often mentions Adam)
was specially serious in the eyes of Irenaeus because of the consequences
it led to, but Tatian himself did not draw these conclusions. In fact
Tatian expressed a type of radical Christianity, which was popular
in eastern Syria, something of which has persisted in Monasticism, but
which was contrary to tendencies in Rome. The Syrian East did not
treat him as a heretic. Irenaeus says that Tatian gave rise to Encratism,
but we should note that Encratism appears throughout the Judaeo-
Christian mission. We have met it in Egypt with Valentinus. It is
possible that Marcion too came under Syrian influence on this point,

29. ' The Heresy of Tatian ', *JTS*, N. S. 5 (1954), p. 62-68.
30. ' Variaciones gnosticas sobre las alas del Alma ', *Gregorianum*, 35 (1954), p. 21-33.
31. ' La tradizione crescologica sull' encratismo ', *Att. della Academia delle scienze
de Torino*, 91 (1956-1957), p. 1-77.
32. *History of Asceticism*, I, p. 32-46.

for he granted baptism only to virgins or to married people if they agreed to live apart. In the correspondence of Dionysius of Corinth and Pinytus of Knossos we find the question being raised in Crete, and doubtless this Encratism shows a continuation of Jewish influence, apparent elsewhere in Tatian.

Tatian does not seem to have founded a school in the West. Severus is said to have been his disciple; Eusebius says that Severus interpreted scripture in his own fashion, doubtless in a somewhat Encratist sense, and that he rejected the *Epistles of Paul* and the *Acts of the Apostles*. This last point, diametrically opposed to Marcionism, confirms that Tatian's group belonged to a Judaeo-Christian *milieu* influenced by the Church of Jerusalem, which is exactly what we find among the Ebionites. It is remarkable that Tatian's day saw the beginning of the appearance of apocryphal *Acts*, where Encratist tendencies appear almost everywhere. Contacts between this literature and Tatian are possible, but not certain. It would seem rather that the *Acts* appeared in various regions : those of Thomas in Osroene, those of Peter in Phoenicia, those of John in Asia, those of Paul in Lycaonia, and show the importance at that period of the Encratist movement in eastern Christianity.

5. The Paschal Question

The conflicts that marked the second half of the second century did not occur only between extremist groups and the main body of the Church. Whole Churches stemming from various traditions clashed on the question of Easter[33]. The Asiatic Church on the whole followed the Johannine tradition, celebrating the Easter of the Saviour on the same day as the Jews, that is to say, the fourteenth day of the moon of the month of Nisan; that was the quartodeciman custom. It was observed in the Judaeo-Christian communities, especially those of Palestine and in the Palestinian mission, but the majority of Christians outside Asia celebrated the feast on the Sunday after the fourteenth day of the moon. As we have already mentioned, this was probably a continuation of the Jewish feast of the first fruits, which inaugurated the feast of Weeks. Paul's Paschal imagery seems to retain traces of this coincidence.

The problem of this diversity of practice arose very early on. Under Pope Sixtus, about 120, a conflict had broken out in the community of Rome between the Romans and the Asiatics, which was ended by an agreement granting mutual toleration. The same conflict was renewed

33. See B. Lohse, *Das Passafest der Quartodecimaner*, p. 113-138.

when Polycarp, Bishop of Smyrna, visited Rome under Anicetus (155-166). Irenaeus tells us this in a letter preserved by Eusebius, and he says that Anicetus could not persuade Polycarp not to observe the fourteenth day, since that was the custom ' of John and the other Apostles with whom he had lived '. Polycarp on his side ' could not get Anicetus to abandon the custom of the presbyters before him ' (*HE*, V, 24, 15). But they parted in peace. The question was often raised later. Irenaeus wrote to Victor : ' The presbyters before Soter who governed the Church that you govern today, that is to say Anicetus, Pius, Hyginus, Telesphorus and Sixtus did not observe the fourteenth day themselves, but did not forbid its observance by those who came from Christian communities in which it was observed ' (*HE*, V, 24, 14).

It would seem from Irenaeus's words that it was under Soter (166-174) that the question grew more acute. It was then that Blastus found himself in schism at Rome with Eleutherius over this matter. Under Victor (189-199) synods were held in various places to study the question, and they communicated their decision to the other Churches by letter. In the library of Caesarea, Eusebius was able to consult the letter of the bishops of Palestine, that of the Synod of Rome presided over by Victor, another from the Synod of the bishops of Pontus, presided over by Palmas, one from the Christian communities of Gaul, one from the bishops of Osroene and one from the bishop of Corinth (*HE*, V, 23, 3-4). The last is precious because it shows that the Churches of Palestinian origin took the same position as the West on this point. This was notably the case of Alexandria (*HE*, V, 25). All these Churches declared that Easter ought to be celebrated on Sunday.

But the bishops of Asia did not abandon their position. Polycrates of Ephesus wrote to Victor, recalling that the quartodeciman custom was followed by Philip and John, by Polycarp and Melito. Melito had written a tract about Easter; we also possess his *Homily on Easter*, which followed the quartodeciman custom. Victor, according to Eusebius, wrote to the bishops to declare the Churches of Asia excluded from communion, but this decision provoked a scandal among the bishops. Irenaeus intervened and, while declaring that he stood by the celebration of Easter on Sunday, he invited Victor to follow his predecessors and accept both customs.

6. The Roman Schools at the End of the Second Century

To the great fringe movements we have listed we must add other groups which appeared only at the end of the second century, but which also continued the Judaeo-Christian line of thought. We are here dealing with archaic theological tendencies whose heterodoxy only gradually became apparent. One of the most frequent at the beginning of the second century was the view which held that Christ was a man specially chosen by God. We find this in the Ebionites, in Cerinthus and in Carpocrates. It was proposed at the end of the second century by a Byzantine leather-dresser, Theodorus. He spread his doctrine in Rome, when he was excluded from the community by Victor, about 198; his disciples continued their propaganda in Rome.

More important is the Monarchian doctrine. It appeared as the continuation of Jewish monotheism, treating the Son and the Spirit merely as powers of the one God, in the Judaic sense of the word. So it was the unique divine person who was manifest in Jesus Christ. Certain archaic Judaeo-Christian works, like the *Testament of the Twelve Patriarchs*, contain expressions which could be understood in this sense. It is in Asia Minor that we meet believers in this doctrine and Tertullian attributes it to Praxeas, but that seems to be a mistake. Praxeas had suffered for the faith. He seems to have been one of a group violently opposed to Montanism, which provides evidence of the existence of divergent movements in Asia, though his trinitarian theology does not seem to have differed from Melito's. But it was based on an archaic formulation. Praxeas came to Rome, where he continued his struggle against Montanism and obtained its condemnation by Eleutherius. Then he went to Africa where his attitude to Montanism provoked violent opposition from Tertullian. It was in order to discredit him that Tertullian claimed that he was the father of Modalism.

Another Monarchian group is described by Hippolytus in his *Elenchos*, that of Noetus. Noetus was born in Smyrna. According to Hippolytus he was excluded from the Church there by the presbyters. His disciple Epigonus came to Rome under Victor. If we are to believe Hippolytus, he was received sympathetically by the Bishops of Rome, Victor first, then especially by Zephyrinus, after 199. In any case it seems certain that Monarchian theology found all the more favour with them in that it was radically opposed to Montanism. In this way the disputes between Asiatic communities were transferred to Rome. The Monarchian quarrel lasted far into the third century, and Hippolytus and Tertullian were deeply involved in it.

A remarkable fact becomes apparent at the end of our consideration of these various groups : the presence at Rome of representatives of all the different opinions[34]. We have seen Marcion come there and

---

34. See G. La Piana, ' The Roman Church at the End of the Second Century ', *Harv. Theol. Rev.*, 18 (1925), p. 201-277.

expound his teaching to the presbyters under Hyginus; Valentinus
was there at the same period; Cerdo met Marcion in Rome; Marcellinus
spread the doctrine of Carpocrates there, under Anicetus; Justin founded
his school there about 150, and among his disciples was the Assyrian Tatian.
Hegesippus came to Rome about 160; Praxeas, Epigonus and Theodotus
went there. At the end of the second century we have a swarm of schools
at Rome. In Justin's school the Asiatic, Rhodo, succeeded Tatian,
who had gone back to Assyria and broken with the Church. The
Marcionites were divided into three different groups : Apelles recognised
only one principle, Petitus and Basilicus two; Synetus three (*HE*, V,
13, 8)[35]. The Valentinians were represented by Ptolemy's opinion and
that of Heracleon. There were also Carpocratians, Basilidians and
Nassenians. The Montanists had two schools, that of Proclus and
that of Eschines. The author of the *Adversus Artemonem* indicates
four groups of Adoptionists (*HE*, V, 28, 16-19). Montanists and
Monarchianists vied with each other. The majority of these teachers
came from Asia, but their battlefield was Rome.

We may note that nearly all these men were foreigners. They came
from Asia, Syria, Egypt and Mesopotamia. That was the reflection,
at the ecclesiastical level, of Rome's extraordinary influence under the
Antonines. The city had changed since Augustus and Nero; it was
now a great cosmopolitan centre where all races and religions met.
Greek was spoken there as much as Latin. The Christians in particular
belonged to this cosmopolitan world. True, they already had close
links with leading Roman families. They buried their dead in estates
belonging to the Caecilii and Aurelii, but most of them were easterners.
Rome was the centre where Asiatics and Syrians of all opinions spoke
openly. This important role which Rome played in the life of the Church
marks the end of the second century. It was linked to the city's influence
as a civilising force; but it also bears witness to the eminent position of
the see of Rome in the whole body of Christianity.

7. The Bishops

In contrast to the multiplicity of schools typical of this period we
find the authority of the bishops. That again was a distinctive feature
of the end of the second century. In opposition to the varied new
doctrines they stood for the tradition of the common Faith and the
unity of that Faith. In this respect the fifty years from Hyginus to Victor
produced a number of remarkable men. Palestine now had gentile
bishops. Under Marcus Aurelius Jerusalem boasted a great bishop

35. See Epiphanius, *Pan.*, XLII, 3.

in Narcissus. Eusebius tells us that he miraculously changed water into oil on the eve of Easter. Much calumniated, he abandoned his see and hid in the desert. He was replaced by another bishop; then, having been found, took possession of his see again. In his old age his successor was appointed — Alexander, with whom he shared his duties.

At Antioch there was Theophilus, known chiefly as a writer and catechist. Eusebius says he was the sixth bishop of the town. After Maximinus, the next bishop was Serapion, who played an important role in the struggle against Montanism (*HE*, V, 19); he also intervened in the matter of the Petrine apocrypha (*HE*, VI, 12, 2). Asia was the most vital centre of the Church's life — it was there that the heresies sprang up. But it is also there that we meet the greatest bishops : at Hierapolis there was Apollinarius, whose many interventions we have noticed; he condemned Montanism and addressed an *Apology* to Marcus Aurelius; at Sardis Melito was the glory of the Church of Asia[36]; his *Apology* and his literary talent have already been mentioned, and Tertullian praised his gift of prophecy[37]. He was a fervent defender of quartodeciman usage. Polycrates of Ephesus appeared as the metropolitan of Asia; it was he who represented his colleagues in discussions with the Bishop of Rome.

In Greece Dionysius of Corinth exercised a widespread influence with his ' Catholic ' letters. He was in touch with the Churches of Crete and Pontus in particular and he gives us the names of several bishops of these regions : Philip, Bishop of Cortyna, who wrote against Marcion; Pinytos, Bishop of Knossos, with whom he discussed the question of continence and marriage; Palmas, Bishop of Amastris, who intervened in the name of the bishops of Pontus in the Paschal controversy[38]. In Alexandria Demetrius became bishop under Commodus. Finally, during this period we find at the head of the Church of Rome : Pius (140-155), Anicetus (155-166), Soter (166-174), Eleutherius (174-189), and Victor (189-199).

A bishop's influence was of course chiefly felt in the community he governed, but we may note that this influence took on a more general character. We find this happening in many ways. First, the bishops of one region gathered in local synods. We have an example of this in the Paschal dispute, when synods met in Palestine, Pontus and Asia. It seems that each region had a kind of patriarch : Polycrates in Ephesus, Victor in Rome, Serapion in Jerusalem, Palmas in Pontus, who could

---

36. See F. L. Cross, *The Early Christian Fathers*, London 1960, p. 103-109.
37. According to Jerome, *Vir.*, III, 24. See also *HE*, V, 24, 5.
38. On Dionysius's letters, see P. Nautin, *Lettres et écrivains chrétiens des II*^e^ *et III*^e^ *siècles*, p. 13-32.

act outside their ecclesiastical boundaries. Serapion of Antioch collected bishops' signatures against Montanism as far afield as Thrace (*HE*, IV, 25). Dionysius of Corinth wrote to the Churches of Crete, Pontus, Nicomedia and Athens (*HE*, V, 19, 3) but it would seem that the Churches in question had some special links[39].

One cannot help being struck by the difference between the behaviour of the founders of sects, which was personal and resembled that of the head of a school, and the bishops' behaviour, essentially collective, an attempt to bring out the common Faith. Irenaeus was only describing a historical fact when he wrote : ' The (heretics) are all later than the bishops, to whom the Apostles have transmitted the churches, and the manifestations of their doctrine are different and produce a veritable cacophony. But the path of those who belong to the Church, dwelling throughout the world and holding firm to the tradition of the Apostles, shows that all have one faith and one kind of organisation '[40].

Within this framework the Church of Rome possessed a special authority. Polycarp came there in 155 to discuss various questions with Anicetus. Dionysius of Corinth wrote to the Church of the Romans and to Soter, and it was to the Bishop of Rome that Polycrates of Ephesus addressed his defence of the quartodeciman usage in the name of the bishops of Asia. It is difficult to see in this group of facts nothing more than the political and individual importance of the capital of the Empire. At the ecclesiastical level, Rome does not appear merely as representative of one of the various traditions inherited from the Apostles. Or, rather, it represents one of these traditions, that of Peter, but that tradition appears to be invested with a special authority. This is what Irenaeus, an Asiatic by birth, Gaulish by adoption, admits in his *Adversus Haereses*.

8. Irenaeus

For this crucial period of the clash between the schools and the Church, there is a witness of the first importance, a man directly involved in these conflicts : St Irenaeus. His work provides us with both the most exact documentation and the most profound interpretation; he was at the centre of the Church's life. Born in Smyrna about 115, as a young man he knew Bishop Polycarp and inherited the Johannine tradition from him. He seems to have stayed in Rome. In 177 he was a priest of the Church of Lyons and accompanied the confessors who discussed the question of the Montanists with Eleutherius. It was

39. See H. Marot, ' Conciles anténicéens et Conciles œcuméniques ', in *Le Concile et les Conciles*, Paris 1960, p. 25.
40. *Adv. Haer.*, V, 20, 1.

during the reign of Eleutherius that he wrote a great work against the Gnostics, the *Adversus Haereses*, in which all the heterodox schools are studied. Appointed Bishop of Lyons, he wrote to Blastus about the Paschal dispute; he tried to win Florinus from Gnosticism. In the pontificate of Victor, he defended the position of the Quartodecimans before Victor. He summed up his catechetical teaching in the *Demonstration of the Apostolic Preaching*.

Irenaeus witnessed the conflict between the various schools and the bishops as a whole. He reflected on the nature of their opposition, and this led him to consider both the source and content of Christian truth. First, what Irenaeus disputes is the authority of the heads of schools; their doctrine has no other basis but their own imagination, and what they are preaching is their own selves. When they claim to be the witnesses of an esoteric tradition, this assertion is false. In fact, they do not represent a tradition — each is the origin of his own doctrine. The ideas they put forward may be attractive, but they do not thereby possess any divine authority; they are merely human doctrines, creations of the intelligence.

Over against the heretical teachers Irenaeus sets the bishops. The bishops do not draw their authority from their own personal merits. They have been instituted and invested with an office which is to transmit a doctrine older than they are, and if we ask to whom this doctrine goes back, we see that it is to the Apostles, who instituted the first bishops. Irenaeus establishes that the episcopal succession clearly went back to the Apostles. He does what Hegesippus had tried to do, but draws on his own experience. So he establishes the succession of the three Churches he knows well : that of Smyrna, which goes back to John by way of Polycarp, that of Ephesus which goes back to Paul, and finally that of Rome, which goes back to Peter and Paul, and for which alone he gives the complete list of succession.

What we find in these lists of bishops is the tradition of the Apostles *(traditio ab apostolis)*[41]. The Gnostics also claim a link with the Apostles, but their tradition is without authority because it does not rest on the legitimate institution and transmission of authority; on the contrary, the bishops are heirs of the Apostles' authority and have the same authority for transmitting as the Apostles for teaching. What we find here in Irenaeus is a theology of ecclesiastical institution. The transmission of the Apostles' teaching is not left to the initiative of private teachers; the Apostles themselves established the organs by which they intended their teaching to be transmitted. These organs instituted

41. See H. Holstein, 'La tradition des Apôtres chez saint Irénée', *RSR* (1949), p. 229-270.

by the Apostles are the only ones to possess the Apostles' authority; it is they alone who are the criteria of doctrines and guarantee their conformity with revelation.

Irenaeus sees confirmation of this in the unity of the bishops' teaching. Whereas the Gnostic schools are divided and contradict one another, the teaching of the bishops is one everywhere on earth. Here again Irenaeus's thought reflects the historical situation whose meaning it expresses. Nothing is more striking in the survey we have made than the swarm of sects, and doubtless for that reason our survey has been extensive and could be developed further. Facing them is the teaching of the bishops, the rule of faith contained in the Creed, in its simplicity and unity.

Irenaeus not only claims that this rule of faith exists, he develops its content. In contrast to the doctrines we have described, he unfolds the content of tradition. His work is essentially catechetical, whether it be the *Adversus Haereses* or the *Demonstration*[42]. He does not claim to be an original theologian but sets forth the generally held doctrine; his sources are chiefly catechetical tradition and scripture[43]. But he expresses this doctrine with a profundity that shows its spiritual riches and itself provides evidence of divine authenticity. It is not for nothing that Irenaeus came from Asia, the land of charismata. His teaching is animated by the Spirit.

One characteristic gives his work a striking coherence, whether in his unfolding of the faith or in his formal study of it : unity. Unity characterises the bishops' teaching over against that of the Gnostics; unity also characterises the content of this teaching. The Gnostics shatter unity : they set in opposition God the saviour and God the creator, the invisible world and the pleroma of the aeons, the Old Testament and the New Alliance, the man Jesus and the Christ of the pleroma, the flesh and the spirit in man. In contrast, Irenaeus describes God's unity of design. One and the same God modelled the first Adam by his Word and Spirit, then in the fulness of time came to win back this man who belongs to him, in order to lead him to the accomplishment of his destiny.

The centre of this theology is the ' recapitulation ' of all things in Christ. By this Irenaeus means first that man in his entirety is taken up by the Word and to man the Spirit communicates incorruptibility.

---

42. See A. Benoit, *Saint Irénée. Introduction à l'étude de la théologie*, Paris 1960.
43. But Irenaeus draws on Justin for his doctrine of the recapitulation (M. Widmann, ' Irenäus und seine theologische Väter ', *ZTK*, 54 (1957), 151-166) and on Melito for the progressive education of humanity (J. Daniélou, ' Bulletin d'histoire des origines chrétiennes ', *RSR*, 49 (1961), p. 583-585).

But it is not only human nature, it is historic man with all his past, who is restored by the action of the Word. The unity of Christianity is the unity of a single plan by God. He begins with creation; sin spoils it, without destroying it; the Old Testament prepares mankind for the gift of the Spirit; in Christ the Word of God leads man to his fulfilment; the Spirit given in baptism makes every believer participate in this divine life.

CHAPTER IX

THE CHRISTIAN COMMUNITY

THE Christian community continued to develop in a manner at once
original and many-sided. It can be studied from several standpoints.
First, it had a hierarchic structure and a laity; there were various
charismata, with corresponding special vocations; there was a contrast
between those who participated fully in the community and those who
shared in it only partially : catechumens and penitents; there were virgins
and ascetics who aimed at the perfection laid down in the gospel, and
there were married people who strove to realise the Christian ideal.
There were those who belonged to the *avant-garde* in bearing witness to
the Faith : confessors and martyrs. We will sketch first a general picture
of the community, then emphasise two questions that were specially
important at that moment, the question of marriage and virginity, and
the question of martyrdom.

Two passages from the *Shepherd* by Hermas can serve as an
introduction. The first is the Vision of the Tower. Hermas goes to
a field where an elderly woman, who is the Church, has told him to come
at the fifth hour. He sees an ivory bench, on which the woman is seated
with six young men. She dismisses them and makes Hermas sit on her
left. Then, raising a shining wand, she says to him : ' You see something
great? ' ' Madam ', I replied, ' I see nothing '. ' Come now ', she
continued, ' look carefully : don't you see in front of you a great tower
being built in the water with splendid hewn stones? ' (Ch. 24). The
woman explains the vision : the tower is the Church; the water baptism;
the six young people who build the tower are the angels. As for the
stones of various shapes, they correspond to the different categories
of Christians.

The first stones, ' squared and white ', are ' the Apostles, Bishops,.
Doctors and Deacons '. Here are four groups we have mentioned
already. ' The stones drawn from the bottom of the water to become
part of the building are those who have suffered for the name of the

Lord '; they are the martyrs. Then come ' the men whom God has tested for their faithfulness in walking on the straight path ', the faithful Christians. The new stones that are brought represent the men new in faith, the neophytes. The stones thrown aside are those who have sinned; if they repent, they can be used for the building; these are the penitents.

Beside these stones which serve for building, there are the rejected stones. Some, which are broken, are the hypocrites, who, under the appearance of faith, have not given up their evil ways. Other stones, crumbled, are those who have not persevered. The cracked stones are those who cling to malice in the bottom of their heart. The white, round stones which cannot be used for building are those who have not renounced wealth. The stones thrown round about, in inaccessible places, are those who have abandoned the way of truth. The stones that fall in the fire are those who have conclusively abandoned the living God. Finally, those who approach the water without reaching it are the souls who do not have the courage to become converted.

In the Ninth Similitude, which is the vision of the twelve mountains from which the twelve kinds of stone are taken, Hermas gives a rather similar classification, but this time he begins at the end. The believers who come from the first mountain are the apostates : for them all penitence is henceforth impossible; those from the second mountain are the hypocrites; those from the third, which is covered in thorns, are the wealthy and those steeped in the affairs of this world; those from the fourth mountain are the undecided, whose faith is not strong, and who prove traitors in time of persecution; the fifth mountain produces believers ' impenetrable in their doctrines, presumptuous, wanting to know everything and knowing nothing ' (22, 1) : these are the Gnostics; the sixth mountain, full of crevices, produces cracked stones, namely, men who harbour resentment.

Then come believers from a mountain covered with smiling greenery : ' those who, full of compassion for men, have helped their needy fellows by the sweat of their brow ' (24, 2). These are the Christians who practise material charity. The believers from the eighth mountain are ' the Apostles and Doctors who have preached throughout the world and taught the word of God '. The believers of the ninth mountain are the dishonest Deacons. ' They have robbed widows and orphans and grown rich in the posts given them in order to minister to the needs of others '. They are also the renegades and the ' rogues and slanderers '.

There remain the three last mountains. ' The believers who come from the tenth mountain, that on which grow trees as a shelter for flocks, are the bishops and hospitable men, who have always extended a frank, joyful hospitality to God's servants. These bishops have made of their ministry a continual shelter for the poor and for widows, and constantly led a holy life '. We may note that the bishops are chiefly praised for hospitality and care of the poor and of widows. This brings out one of the essential features of the role of the local hierarchy : the material welfare of the involuntary poor (the needy) and the voluntary poor (widows consecrated to prayer). This charity shows that the community was responsible for the material welfare of all its members, under the direction of its leaders. Polycarp recommends the presbyters to neglect neither widows nor orphans.

The believers of the eleventh mountain are ' the men who have suffered for the name of Christ '. These are the martyrs, to whom Hermas here allots a high place, since he puts them above the representatives of the hierarchy, deacons and Episcopi (bishops). Finally, the believers from the twelfth mountain, ' the white mountain ', resemble ' very small children who do not have the least idea of evil... They have in no way broken the Lord's commandments, but every day of their life have preserved the innocence of their first childhood ' (Chapter 29). ' They enjoy greater glory than all those we have met so far '. This praise of the spirit of childhood and innocence is also found at the beginning of Clement's *Pedagogy*.

In this complex picture let us first pick out what concerns the members of the hierarchy. Hermas distinguishes two different categories. On the one hand are the presbyters. Hermas calls them by different names, according to their function : Episcopi, Didascali, Missionaries. Beside the presbyters we find the deacons, quite a distinct category, chiefly concerned with the practical management of the Church. Hermas tells us nothing about the role of the bishop who presides over the community. For that we must turn to the *Letters* of Ignatius of Antioch, who describes the bishop's role incomparably well. This role is primarily to ensure the unity of the community. For example, in the *Epistle to the Magnesians :* ' Seek to do everything in a divine harmony, under the presidency of the bishop, who takes the place of God, of the presbyters, who take the place of the senate of the Apostles, and of the deacons, who are dear to me, to whom the service of Jesus Christ has been entrusted. So adopt God's principles : love one another in Jesus Christ ' (VI, 1).

It is the bishop, surrounded by the presbyterium, who presides at the Eucharist, which is the reunion of the community : ' Let this Eucharist alone be considered lawful : the one which takes place under the presidency of the bishop or of him whom the bishop has appointed. Where the bishop appears, there let the community be '[1]. The same

1. *Smyrn.*, VII, 2.

is true for the other reunions of the community : ' Only the bishop is allowed to baptise, and to hold the *agape* '[2]. In a general way, he had to watch over reunions of the community, whether liturgical or not : ' Let reunions take place often; invite all the brethren by name. Do not neglect the widows; after God, it is you who must concern yourself with them. Do not despise male and female slaves '[3]. Marriage also required his approval : ' It is also fitting for men and women who wed to contract their marriage with the bishop's advice ' (*Polyc.* V, 2). So nothing in the communal life of his flock must be foreign to him.

For that the bishop must show charity to all his people. Ignatius invites Polycarp to do this in admirable terms : ' Justify your episcopal dignity by complete solicitude for body and soul; concern yourself with union, than which there is nothing better. Bear patiently with all the brethren as Christ bears with you; support them all with charity, as in fact you do. Busy yourself ceaselessly with prayer : ask for greater wisdom... If you love the good disciples, you have no merit. It is chiefly the most infected whom you must subdue by gentleness... The present moment has need of you '[4].

Another important point is the existence of an order of widows. The *First Epistle to Timothy* mentions its existence : ' Give widows their due, if that name really belongs to them... The woman who is indeed a widow, bereft of all help, will put her trust in God, and spend her time, night and day, upon the prayers and petitions that belong to her state... If a woman is to be put on the list of widows (καταλέγειν), she must have reached, at least, the age of sixty, and have been faithful to one husband, have been hospitable, washed the feet of the saints, attached herself to every charitable cause ' (5 : 9-10). The stress is laid more on the ascetical and contemplative side of a widow's life than on her function in the community. But the interesting point is that they are listed in a register with the conditions that this implies; this shows that it is not a question of all the widows, but of certain among them who make up a group in the community.

The existence of this order of widows is confirmed by early ecclesiastical literature. Polycarp is the first to call them ' the altar of God '[5], an expression which recurs often and is an extension of Paul's phrase about their spiritual intercession. Ignatius, in a strange phrase, speaks of the ' Virgins called Widows '[6], which clearly shows that the

2. *Id.*, VIII, 3.
3. *Polyc.*, IV, 1-2.
4. *Id.*, II, 2.
5. *Phil.*, IV, 34.
6. *Smyrn.*, XIII, 1.

word ' widow ' has discarded its ordinary meaning and put on an ecclesiastical meaning. These brief references provide no information about
the ministry of widows. But Hermas tells us of a woman named Grapte,
ordered to make known the revelation he has received to the widows
and orphans, while he will read it in front of the presbyters[7]. Grapte
probably belongs to the order of widows. This suggests that their main
task was to teach women.

Besides these institutional ministries, we find spiritual charismata;
these had an important place in the communities which St Paul described.
The *Ascension of Isaiah* complained about the decreasing number of
prophets (III, 25), but the *Dialogue with Trypho* shows that charismata
continued to be found in the community. The women receive them as
well as the men. The chief charisma is that of prophecy. It mainly
concerns thanksgiving in the liturgical assemblies, not the presidency
or teaching. Hermas gives us the portrait of the prophet : ' When the
man who has in him the Spirit of God enters an assembly of just people,
inspired by faith in the divine Spirit, and this assembly begins to pray
to God, then the angel of the prophetic Spirit who helps this man takes
possession of him, and the man thus filled with the Holy Spirit speaks
to the crowd the words that God wishes '[8].

In contrast to the prophet, we meet the false prophet : ' Every man
who speaks possessed by a spirit is not a prophet ', says the *Didache*,
' but only if he sees things in the Lord's way. So the true prophet can
be distinguished from the false only by his behaviour '[9]. Hermas lays
down the same principles :

Lord — I asked — how distinguish the true from the false prophet?
Listen to the rules that I am going to give you for distinguishing
the true from the false prophet : it is by his life that you will recognise
the man who possesses the Spirit of God... The false prophet raises
himself up; he wants to have the first place; he takes payment for his
prophecies; without wages, he does not prophesy. Can a spirit coming
from God take payment for prophesying? If he enters an assembly
of just men, filled with the spirit of God, as soon as they begin to
pray, he finds himself empty; the earthly spirit, overcome with terror,
flees far away and our man remains silent, incapable of uttering a
word[10].

Another important aspect of Hermas's description relates to sinners.
Hermas, as we have seen, names several groups. There are first those

7. *Vis.*, II, 3.
8. *Prec.*, XI, 8-9.
9. *Id.*, 12.
10. *Id.*, 13.

who have heard the Gospel but refuse baptism, because this involves committing themselves, so they never belong, in the strict sense, to the Church; this is the group furthest outside. Then come those who, having been baptised, have conclusively cut themselves off from the living God : the hardened sinners. Then come the heretics who, after having embraced the Faith, have strayed from the path of truth. Next come the Christians who remain attached to the good things of this world : these are the round stones, unsuitable for building. When persecutions come, their wealth leads them to deny Christ. Then come the truncated stones, the cracked stones, the chipped stones, the broken stones.

What characterises all these groups is that those who compose them are outside salvation, but they can repent. ' Those who wish to repent are not thrown very far from the Tower because, if they repent, they may be used for building. Only it is now that they must be converted, because the Tower is still being built '[11]. This passage is important from the historical point of view and it gives us the key to Hermas's work. This message, the inspired word which, as a prophet, he has to proclaim is that the possibility of repenting is given by God only once.

What are the conditions of this repentance? It would seem first that it covers all sins. The only passage which appears to suggest unforgivable sins is *Sim.*, IX, 19, 1, the first mountain : ' These are the apostates who have blasphemed the Lord and betrayed God's servants. For those people, no repentance : their lot is death '. But this passage is contradicted by others, where Hermas shows that the concession granted by God may extend to all sins. The duration of it seems limited to the period when Hermas is preaching : ' When you have made these words known to them, they will obtain pardon for their past sins; if they sin again, there will be no salvation for them '[12]. We see from the letters of Dionysius of Corinth that these same questions were discussed throughout the Church.

The conditions of penance are severe. They include first and foremost conversion, that is to say, change of life. No word recurs more often in the book we are studying than *metanoia :* ' I repeat it to you, I, the angel of repentance, if you are converted to the Lord with all your heart, if you practise justice all the rest of your life, he will heal you of your past sins '[13]. But conversion is not enough; there must be expiation. As *Similitude VI* says : ' So you imagine that the sins of penitents are

11. *Vis.*, III, 5, 5.
12. *Vis.*, II, 2, 4.
13. *Prec.*, XII, 6, 2.

remitted at once. Not at all. The penitent must submit his soul to suffering, practise a profound humility in his behaviour and undergo all kinds of tribulations ' (VII, 4).

One question arises at this period in an acute form : the relationship between marriage and virginity. It had been discussed since the origin of the Church. St. Paul had written about it in the *First Epistle to the Corinthians* and the superiority of virginity to marriage had never been questioned. But during the first two centuries certain thinkers had gone much further than that; being a Christian seemed to them to imply virginity. Married persons who did not separate could be only imperfect members of the Church. In the heterodox sects this doctrine was the expression of a total condemnation of creation, but it seems clear that tendencies of this kind existed at the very heart of the Church.

This ' Encratist ' aspect of Judaeo-Christianity has been shown in the books of E. Peterson and A. Voöbus. It was not confined to heterodox sects like the Ebionites and Corinthians, but expressed a much more general movement. This movement is particularly evident in the sphere of Judaeo-Christianity belonging to the Palestinian mission, that is to say in Egypt with the *Gospels of the Hebrews* and *of the Egyptians*, in Palestine with the *Gospel of James*, in Edessa with the *Odes of Solomon* and the *Gospel of Thomas*, in Rome with the *Shepherd* by Hermas. We see in *I Corinthians* the controversies it aroused in other communities. In the second half of the second century it seems to have been more or less condemned in the western world, where it was associated with the Judaising sects, the Montanists, the Marcionites and the school of Tatian. But it continued among certain groups of virgins and ascetics, and in the fourth century overflowed into various marginal forms of eremitical and cenobitical life.

The most evident feature is the high value set on virginity, which appears in certain passages of the New Testament. In *I Cor* Paul, while refusing to make virginity obligatory, expresses his own opinion that virginity is the best condition for man to be in (7 : 25). The *Acts of the Apostles* mention four daughters of the deacon Philip who had remained virgins (21 : 9). Later Ignatius of Antioch addresses virgins called widows[14], which seems to indicate a canonical status; Justin, in the middle of the second century, lists as one of the features of Christianity that ' many men and women, aged fifty and sixty, instructed since childhood in the teaching of Christ, have kept their virginity '[15].

14. *Smyrn.*, XII, X.
15. *I Apol.*, XV.

This esteem for virginity is found throughout the Church, but in the groups most affected by Judaeo-Christianity it assumes a more striking aspect. On the one hand, exaltation of virginity appears as the aim of certain writings, such as the *Gospel of James* where the virginity of Mary is exalted, not as an expression of the miracle of the Incarnation, but as an ideal in itself. Inversely, we find polemic against marriage, which is particularly noticeable in the *Odes of Solomon;* marriage is the bitter grass of Paradise (XI, 18); the same in the *Gospel of the Egyptians,* where again we find marriage called ' bitter grass '[16]. Marriage belongs to the same order of things as mortality[17].

It would seem that in the regions influenced by Judaeo-Christianity there was a tendency to consider the fulness of Christianity as incompatible with marriage. The Marcionites admitted to baptism only virgins or married people who had taken a vow of chastity[18]. The Montanists taught that sexual abstinence was an obligation for all christians (*HE*, V, 18.2). Elsewhere the separation of married people was commended at least, for example in the *Acts of John* (63); but in the *Shepherd* the angel advises Hermas to live with his wife as with a sister[19]. The same ideal is expressed by *II Clement* (XIII, 2-4), with reference to the *Gospel of the Egyptians.*

Traces of this attitude are found later. Vööbus has shown that in the communities of Osroene, in the third century, the virgins were baptised before other people and had a prominent place in the community[20]. The important point here is the link between virginity and the structure of the Church[21]. In the *Acts of Thomas* the crown which refers to baptism is linked with virginity[22]; it is possible that the reference to the crown in the *Odes of Solomon* (IX, 9) takes up the same theme[23]. Perhaps the crown was given only to virgins, even when all were admitted to baptism. Complete adherence to the christian life appears to have been inseparable from abstinence from sexual life. We also find an echo of these views in the Millenarianist doctrine. For Justin, it is to Millenarianism that the word of Christ applies : ' They will take no wives, but they will live like angels '[24]. This same idea is found later in Methodius[25].

16. Clement, *Strom.*, III, 9.
17. *Idem.*
18. Tertullian, *Adv. Marc.*, IV.
19. *Vis.*, II, 2, 3.
20. *Celibacy : a requirement for Admission to Baptism in the Early Syrian Church,* Stockholm 1951, passim.
21. *History of Asceticism*, p. 89.
22. *Op. cit.*, p. 91.
23. *Ibid.*, p. 91.
24. *Dial.*, LXXXI, 3-4.
25. *Conv.*, IX, 1.

It is doubtless also in this context that we must understand the leading of a common life by an ascetic and a virgin. It is possible that Paul is referring to it in *I Cor* 7 : 36-38. *Didache* XI : 7 sees in these marriages of prophets a figure of the union of Christ and his Church[26]. The *Epistle on Virginity* by the Pseudo-Clement mentions this custom. It was still prevalent in the fourth century, but it appears to be very archaic. It was considered the only form of marriage compatible with the perfection of the christian life. Doubtless it was linked with the advice given to christian married people to live in chastity, and as a result this type of marriage showed an important development. It was to continue among the Gnostics[27].

These tendencies appear to have been linked with Judaeo-Christianity, in fact, they are first found in Palestinian communities. The portrait of James given by Hegesippus shows that he was an ascetic who abstained from wine and did not anoint himself with oil (*HE*, 23, 5). The same characteristics are found among the Ebionites, but on the other hand these tendencies were not in conformity with official Judaism. Once again we see the important part played in original Christianity by the side branches of Judaism[28]. In fact, asceticism was a characteristic of the Essenes; we know from Philo that they preserved their virginity. So this movement seems characteristic of Essenising Judaism, and it is therefore not surprising to find it particularly in Egypt and Edessa and in the writings of Hermas, exactly where we have seen the Essene influence at work.

It seems to derive, as Peterson has shown, from the Essenes, identification of the bad yezer, the spirit of evil, with the sexual instinct[29] : sexuality as such seems linked to an evil principle in man. Hence we can understand other aspects of Judaeo-Christian asceticism. The use of baths of purification, outside baptism, which we find among the Ebionites and Elkesaites, but which also seems to have been found elsewhere, stems from the same principle. It has influenced the theology of baptism in certain christian authors[30]. The passage on fornication in the Jerusalem decree may be aimed at certain sexual prohibitions, and in particular the obligation to take baths of purification[31].

26. A. Adam, ' Erwägungen zum Herkunft der Didache ', *ZKG*, 68 (1959), p. 20.
27. See the ceremonial of this marriage among the Marcosians ' in the image of the unions on high '. (*Adv. Haer.*, I, 21, 2.) See E. Segelberg, ' The Coptic-Gnostic Gospel According to Philip and its Sacramental System ', *Numen*, 7 (1960), p. 197-199; R. M. Grant, ' The Mystery of Marriage in the Gospel of Philip ', *Vig. Christ.*, 15 (1961), p. 129-141.
28. See H. J. Schoeps, *Theologie und Geschichte des Judenchristentums*, p. 195-196.
29. *Frühkirche, Judentum und Gnosis*, p. 225.
30. *Ibid.*, p. 235.
31. E. Molland, ' La circoncision, le baptême et l'autorité du décret apostolique ', *ST*, 9 (1955), p. 33.

These tendencies met with opposition in the second half of the century. Dionysius of Alexandria wrote to the Bishop of Knossos in Crete ' to exhort him not to impose on the faithful the heavy burden of continence as an obligation, but to take account of the weakness of the majority ' (*HE*, IV, 23, 7), but Pinytos replied advising him ' to give a more solid food to the undernourished people he directs ' (23, 8). Dionysius adopted the same attitude with the Bishop of Pontus, Palmas (*HE*, IV, 23, 6). Gradually the radical position was held only by heretical sects. Only eastern Syria clung to Judaeo-Christian Encratism. Clement of Alexandria showed that marriage was fully compatible with the christian life[32].

He devoted a whole book of the *Stromata*, the third, to defending marriage. There he criticised Encratism under its various forms, that of the Valentinians, that of Julius Cassian, that of Tatian. True, Christ did not marry, but Clement explains this with admirable profundity : ' Some people claim that marriage is fornication and has been communicated by the devil; they say that they are imitating the Lord, who did not marry. They are ignorant of his motive. First, he had his own wife, the Church; then again, he was not an ordinary man who needs a helpmeet according to the flesh; he did not need to have children (to perpetuate himself), living, as he does, eternally, and being the only Son of God '[33]. Virginity is holy when it springs from love of God, but it is not good if it stems from contempt for marriage. A man must love his wife with a charitable love, not with mere desire. The sexual life does not imply any impurity and Clement condemns the Jewish custom of purification after sexual intercourse.

Martyrdom appears as the outstanding form of Christian sanctity, according to the *Apocalypse*, which is wholly consecrated to the glory of ' those who have washed their robes white in the blood of the Lamb. And now they stand before God's throne, serving him day and night in the temple ' (7 : 14). This is shown by the veneration in which the martyr is held. If he dies, he is considered as entering paradise immediately, while the rest of the dead await the Parousia (7 : 9). His bones are venerated. For example, in the *Martyrdom of Polycarp:* ' We gathered his bones — more valuable than precious stones — in order to place them in a suitable spot. There, whenever possible, we shall gather in joy and happiness to celebrate, with the help of the Lord, the anniversary of the day when Polycarp was born to God by martyrdom ' (XVIII). Here we find the origin of the cult of martyrs; the Eucharist is sacrificed

32. *Strom.*, III, 6, 49, 1-4.
33. *Strom.*, III, 6, 59, 4.

on their tomb, and if they survive, they are specially venerated by the community.

Martyrdom in the first place is considered a supreme conflict with Satan; there is much evidence for this. Hermas writes : ' Those who have been crowned are those who have struggled against the devil and conquered him : it is they who have suffered death for the Law '[34]. So too in the *Martyrdom of Polycarp :* ' The devil used all his wiles against the martyrs, but he could conquer none of them ' (III, 1). The most remarkable evidence here is the *Martyrdom of Perpetua.* In a vision she sees herself led to the amphitheatre and set against ' an Egyptian of terrifying appearance, with his assistants. From another direction handsome young men, who are my assistants and supporters, come to me ' (X, 6-7). The combat is presided over by a man of extraordinary size, whose head rises above the amphitheatre, having a band of purple on his chest and holding in his hand a green branch with golden apples. And he says : ' If she triumphs, she will receive this branch ' (9). Then the struggle begins. Perpetua is raised into the air by the Egyptian, but she seizes his head : ' Then I stepped back and I understood that it was not against the wild beasts but against the devil that I had to fight ' (14).

Martyrdom, being a victory over Satan, is a conformation to the passion of Christ. But it is also a translation into God and a conformation to the Resurrection. This longing for martyrdom as the way to total transformation into Jesus Christ found its noblest expression in Ignatius of Antioch's *Epistle to the Romans.* In no other text does martyrdom appear more clearly as a mystical sharing in the death and resurrection of Christ and as the perfect realisation by the Christian of his essence : ' It is good for me to die in order to be united to Jesus Christ. It is he I am seeking, he who died for me; he I want, he who is risen for us. My hour of birth approaches. Let me receive the pure light; when I am there I shall be a man. Allow me to be an imitator of the Passion of my God. . . There is no longer any fire in me to make me love matter, but a living water which murmurs and says inside me : " Come with the Father " '[35]. We may note the expressions : ' My hour of birth approaches '; ' When I am there I shall be a man '. Elsewhere to be a martyr is ' to become a true disciple '[36].

Martyrdom was accompanied by mystical phenomena. We have seen the vision that Perpetua was granted; Polycarp likewise had a vision before his martyrdom (XII, 3). Felicity replied to her gaoler who was surprised to see her moaning in childbirth : ' Now it is I who suffer, but

34. *Sim.*, VIII, 3, 6.
35. *Rom.*, VI, 1–VII, 2.
36. *Ibid.*, IV, 2.

then another will be in me, who will suffer for me, because I too shall be suffering for him ' (XV, 6). Likewise Blandina ' was filled with strength to exhaust and wear out her executioners' (*HE*, V, 1, 18). Clement of Alexandria gives the Gnostic who has achieved ordinary union with God the name of martyr (*Strom.*, IV, 14, 96). In this lies the demonstrative value of martyrdom. The value is not in the martyrs' heroism — martyrdom does not prove the truth of Christianity by showing that Christianity is a cause powerful enough to inspire heroes; human causes could also give rise to heroes — but it proves the truth of Christianity by attesting the presence of the spirit who accomplishes what is beyond human power by making frail creatures who are not heroes face death with bravery.

A martyr does not merely edify the Church as a witness : he has a redemptive value. His is a work of fraternal charity. The martyr lays down his life for his people : ' Polycarp, like the Lord himself, patiently waited to be delivered, thus wishing to teach us by his example not to think only of our own interests but also of our neighbours '. For the sign of a true and solid charity is to seek not only one's own salvation, but that of one's brethren '. This last aspect of the theology of martyrdom is admirably expounded by Clement of Alexandria. For him, martyrdom is essentially the perfection of the *agape*, the fulness of charity : ' The Apostles, imitating the Lord, true and perfect Gnostics, gave their lives for the Churches they had founded. So the Gnostics who walk in the steps of the Apostles must be sinless and, because of their love of the Lord, love their neighbour so that should a crisis arise, bearing their ordeals without faltering they may drink the chalice for the Church '. Now this is the fulness of charity, which is perfection : ' We call martyrdom perfection *(teleiotes)*, not because it is the end *(telos)* of man's life, but because it shows the perfection of charity '.

CHAPTER X

ALEXANDRIA

AT the end of the second century Christian Hellenism came into bloom at Alexandria. As we have seen, the Church in Egypt had first taken root in Jewish circles, but very soon it had to direct its attention to the pagans. The *Gospel of the Egyptians* proves this. This pagan *milieu* had a dual character. On the one hand, there was the countryside with its peasant population. Despite the Hellenisation of Egypt, old demotic Egyptian continued to be spoken there. It was in the second century that the Coptic alphabet was probably created, using Greek characters to transcribe a non-Greek language. It is in this language that the Christian Gnostic writings found at Nag Hammadi are written. Some of them belong to the second century; they seem to have been written directly in Coptic which would imply that there was a Coptic Christianity, both orthodox and heterodox, in the second century, and it may have been the source of Coptic writing.

But at this period there are no documents bearing on Coptic Christianity, which in the fourth century was to show astonishing vitality; on the other hand, there was another group, the urban population of Alexandria, for which there exist rich sources of information. Here the Hellenisation of the old Egyptian paganism was complete. The old gods had taken Greek names : Horus had been identified with Apollo, Amon with Zeus, Ptah with Hephaestus, Thoth with Hermes, Osiris with Dionysius. Alexandria had become the main centre of Hellenistic culture. The papyrus industry and a famous library gave cultural life a solid economic foundation and incomparable intellectual equipment. Its geographical position, which made the town a crossroads of civilisations, promoted religious liberalism where propaganda and proselytism could flourish. Christianity found an exceptionally favourable climate.

Alexandria, therefore, is going to play an important part in the history of the Church at the end of the second century and the beginning of the third. It was there that Christianity, sprung from a Semitic people, completed its Greek education at the same time as Hellenism completed its Christian education. Alexandria was the pole of Christian culture, just as Rome was the doctrinal pole. This is true in two spheres; on the one hand, at the level of ordinary Christian life it is in Alexandria that we find Christian morals, inherited from the Christian Church, breaking free from their Jewish forms and putting on what was best in Hellenistic humanism. On the other hand, at the cultural level, it was in Alexandria that Christianity accepted the legacy of ancient Rhetoric and Philosophy; it was Alexandria that gave rise to Christian Hellenism, which was to become the miracle of human history.

We have an eminent witness of this Hellenised Christianity in Clement of Alexandria, but little is known about his life. The hypothesis that he was born in Athens rests only on a tradition of Epiphanius, who puts it forward as doubtful. His familiarity with Alexandrian currents of thought and ways of life makes it more probable that he was born in Alexandria. His name, Titus Flavius Clemens, is Latin, but at that time names of this sort are often found in the Greek East. He was born into a pagan family and converted, and we know from the beginning of the *Stromata* that he travelled in Magna Graecia, Greece, Syria and Palestine. On his return to Alexandria he became a disciple of Pantaenus and succeeded him as a teacher about 190. He was a presbyter of the Church of Alexandria. He left Alexandria for Jerusalem where we find him about 215, at the time of the installation of the bishop, Alexander, who sent him on a mission to the Church of Antioch. Two of his books, the *Paedagogus* and the *Stromata* are our chief sources for Alexandrian Christianity at this period.

1. The Heritage of Greece

The important point about the Alexandrian movement is the alliance of the gospel and Greek culture. This alliance had already been made for the Old Testament by the Jews of Alexandria, notably Philo. Clement was not the first to make use of the literature of Hellenistic Judaism; the Jewish pseudepigraphers are known to us from the Apologists and they quote the Orphic discourses or the *Sibylline Oracles*, pseudo-Euripides, pseudo-Sophocles and pseudo-Homer. But I do not think an unmistakable reference to Philo has been proved either in Irenaeus or in Justin, and the Philoism of the *Epistle to the Hebrews* is very doubtful, when we take into account how largely Philo echoes a whole literature, now lost. On the other hand Clement certainly draws on Philo, both in explicit quotations and the application of the same exegetical method.

PLATE 11.   THE THREE YOUNG MEN IN THE FIERY FURNACE; WALL PAINTING FROM CATACOMB,
ROME, VIA LATINA, LATE 3RD OR EARLY 4TH CENTURY

The story of the three young men in the fiery furnace belonged to that stock of Old Testament stories of deliverance so frequently cited by the early persecuted Church. There was a clear affinity between the situation of the Christian martyrs and that of the three young men described in Daniel 3. There may even be an allusion to the story in the vision of Perpetua during her martyrdom (*Passio Perpetuae*, 10, 6-7). She is set against 'an Egyptian, of terrifying appearance...' but 'handsome young men, my assistants and supporters, come to me'. Martyrdom is seen as a struggle against the devil, and derivatively the relation of the Church and the World is understood as one of conflict. The situation in this picture, which appears at first sight simply to use the traditional imagery, is, however, complicated by the dress of the three young men; they are in fact dressed as women.

The significance of this departure from the normal representation is to be understood against the background of this particular (recently discovered) catacomb. In the first place, it was clearly the property of rich people, since here, as distinct from other Christian catacombs, the whole catacomb is covered with wall paintings. Secondly, more specifically, there are scattered among the Christian paintings, pictures of mythological figures, including several 'Victories' whose dress is identical with that of the three young men here.

It seems probable therefore, that we find in this picture the reinterpretation, by a wealthy Christian family, of the traditional conflict imagery, in the light of pagan mythology. Such a juxtaposition of conflict and assimilation indicates the tensions appearing in the Church's attitude to the world in the 2nd and 3rd centuries. (Cf. chs. 7, § 2; 9; 10; 11).

Photo: Pontifical Institute of Christian Archaeology, Rome.

PLATE 12. OIL LAMP IN FORM OF SHIP, SHOWING (?) CHRIST AND PETER; FLORENCE, ARCHAEOLOGICAL MUSEUM, 4TH CENTURY

The situation illustrated by Plate 11 raises the question of how the Church thought of itself. This picture shows one way, where the Church is seen as a ship sailing through the waters of the world. It is not certain whom the figures in the ship are intended to represent. They may be Christ at the helm and Peter in the bow of the boat, or Peter and Paul, or, perhaps most likely, Christ and an orante. The inscription on the top of the mast reads: *Dominus legem dat Valerio Severio Eutropi vivas.* A passage which illuminates both the inscription and the form of the lamp is Clement of Alexandria, *Cohortatio ad Gentiles,* 12: 'If you wish to, you will overcome sin: bound to the saving wood, you will be delivered from all corruption. The Word of the Lord will be your pilot, and the Holy Spirit will direct you to the harbour of God...' (Cf. ch. 11, § 2)

The process of accommodation with the world of mythology is here carried to extremes. On the lower left hand section of the picture are three athletic young men, probably intended to represent Penelope's suitors; they are separated from Penelope by her loom. She is talking to a man seated on the far right, who has no sandals, wears a short tunic, whose hair is untidy and whose beard is unkempt. This figure is Ulysses, disguised as a beggar by the goddess Athena but seeking, despite his disguise, to make himself known to Penelope. The scene above, idealised with its strange selection of animals and its impressive buildings, is clearly Ithaca, Ulysses' fatherland, to which he is about to return. The germ of the religious interpretation of the Ulysses story lies in the *Odyssey*, Bk 5, 42: 'The destiny of Ulysses is to return to the land of his fathers, under his own roof, in his great house.' In both pagan and Christian writings, the return of Ulysses to Ithaca became a type of the passage of the individual soul to eternal life (cf. Plotinus, *Enneads* I, 6-8, and 16-23). Homer was particularly important to certain groups of Gnostics — 'Homer is their prophet' (Irenaeus, *Adv. Haer.* 4, 33, 3) — and it seems almost certain that this picture shows a Gnostic use of Homer. According to Hippolytus (*Philosophoumena* V, 7, 29ff.), the Naasene Gnostics in particular attached special significance to the Ulysses theme, and it is therefore probable that the group of Gnostics who were responsible for the pictures in this catacomb were Naasenes.

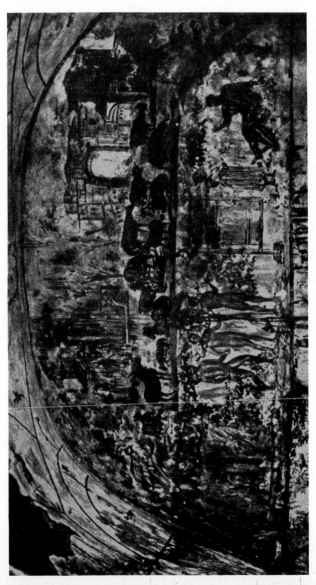

By permission of Amici delle Catacombe Romane, Rome.

HETERODOXY AND HELLENISM

PLATE 13

ITHACA, ULYSSES, PENELOPE AND THE SUITORS; WALL PAINTING FROM THE HYPOGAEUM OF THE AURELII, ROME, VIALE MANZONI, 3RD CENTURY

PLATE 14. LEAF FROM A PAPYRUS CODEX CONTAINING A COPTIC VERSION OF A MANICHAEAN PSALM-BOOK, 4TH CENTURY (FOLIO 206)

With Manichaeism, accommodation with other faiths develops into syncretism and the Gospel becomes one of several ingredients in a new faith (cf. ch. 13, § 2). This picture shows part of a psalm entitled 'Concerning the coming of the Soul' and attributed to Thomas, the disciple of Mani. The Psalm-Book from which it is taken was part of a library of Manichaean works translated into Coptic from lost originals, and found near Medinet Madi in the Faiyum in Egypt in 1930. For a translation cf. C.R.C. Allberry, *Manichaean Manuscripts in the Chester Beatty Collection*, Vol. II: *A Manichaean Psalm-Book, Part II*, (Stuttgart 1938).

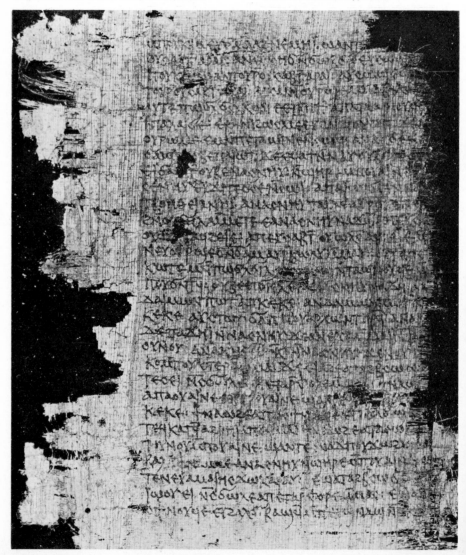

This is important from the point of view of the Alexandrian school. There is a continuity between Christianity and Alexandrian Judaism. At Alexandria Philo was born, preached and taught; his spirit is typically Alexandrian. Clement transferred this spirit to the christian tradition. Until the time of Clement christian exegesis followed the lines of exegesis in Palestinian Judaism. It was a prophetic, apocalyptic, typological exegesis which looked for correspondences between the realities of the Old Testament and those of the New Covenant. We find this exegesis in Justin's *Dialogue with Trypho*, in Irenaeus and in Melito. We find it continued in Hippolytus and Tertullian.

With Philo we find something quite different. The Hellenism of the time of Christ had worked out an exegesis of Homer and Hesiod which found a symbolic meaning in the stories of mythology[1]. It found in the stories of the gods forces of nature, or powers of the soul or mysteries of metaphysics. There is extant the *Theologia Graeca* by the Stoic Coruntus, belonging to the first century A.D. Maximus of Tyre used these allegories abundantly. Philo applied the same method to the texts of the *Pentateuch*, and for the same reasons : in order to remove the scandal of out-of-date legislation and unedifying or naive stories.

Clement used the method with discretion; in his writings the various sources are easy to disentangle. If he borrows from Philo an allegory about Sara and Abimelech, he first gives Philo's interpretation, then works out another, more christological. We may say that he draws on Philo as on one of the treasures of Alexandrian culture, but his exegesis is basically along typological or Gnostic lines, that is to say it follows the catechetical tradition or Gnostic tradition of Pantaenus. It is Origen who later makes use of Philo's allegorical method in his moralising exegesis of Scripture.

The influence of Philo on Clement was not confined to the use of allegory. Philo had tried to use the whole of secular culture, of the ἐγκύκλιος παιδεία *(encyclios paideia)* in order to understand the bible. In his *De Congressu eruditionis gratia*, he had weighed the principle of the need for profane culture as a preparation for understanding Scripture. And in fact he does use the various scholarly techniques of Hellenism for his exegesis; this begins with grammar and the importance given to etymology, then comes the use of rhetorical amplification, followed by dialectical reasoning, in order to make the thought clear. The various sciences, arithmetic, music, physics and astronomy, are often used, notably the symbolism of numbers.

---

1. See F. Buffière, *Les mythes d'Homére et la pensée grecque*, Paris 1956; J. Pepin, *Mythe et Allégorie. Les Origines grecques et les contestations judéo-chrétiennes*, Paris 1958.

Philo's work was continued by Clement, doubtless in the wake of Pantaenus. Origen was later to continue it in the *Didascalion*. True, we have seen that Justin opened a school, but he merely gave lectures, as philosophers were accustomed to do at that time. Clement's venture was much more far-reaching; it took the same lines as Philo's. It would be interesting to know whether Alexandrian Judaism in Clement's day had schools continuing Philo's work and to what extent Clement was influenced by them.

For Clement the most important discipline for understanding Scripture is philosophy, and he lists its different uses : it allows one to unmask the philosophers' errors; it helps to make the content of Faith more precise, but above all it helps one to pass from naive to scientific knowledge *(episteme)* which, at the philosophic level, amounts to research *(zetesis)*. Research starts with ordinary data, but by linking them to principles which are certain it permits the transformation of simple opinion into certainty *(gnosis);* this process is demonstration, in the strict sense. These principles are set forth by Clement in the eighth book of the *Stromateis*, a little treatise on philosophical method inspired by Antiochus of Ascalon.

These principles Clement applies to the christian Faith; his starting-point is the facts of Scripture. The first principles are the essential revealed truths. Research *(zetesis)* consists in linking to the fundamental truths the various facts of Scripture, which then become the object of theological knowledge; we thus pass from faith to Gnosis. This process is Scriptural demonstration *(apodeixis)*. These works by Clement are fundamental and we may say that he lays the foundation of theological method.

It is noteworthy that Clement gives the name Gnosis to the scientific knowledge resulting from demonstration. He also gives that name to knowledge of the secrets revealed by the Apocalypse. This parallel usage is very characteristic of the period; we may say that the main characteristic of the method is equivalence. Just as there is a parallel between Stoic allegorism and biblical typology, so there is a parallel between philosophical Gnosis and Apocalyptic Gnosis. As we shall see, Clement also established equivalences between episodes in the bible and the myths of Homer; he looked for equivalents both in their contents and in their method. The scientific advance of Judaeo-Christianity is found side by side in Clement with its Graeco-Latin equivalent; as yet there is no interchange.

2. The World of Images

Clement was not the first Christian to raise the question of the relations between philosophy and revelation; Justin had already done this. From Justin Clement took over some of these themes, *e.g.* the participation of the whole mind in reason, which is the Word itself, and the philosophers' borrowings from revelation, but he worked out a theory which he seems to have been the first to propound : namely, a divine inspiration given to certain privileged men among the pagans. The comparison is made several times by Clement. There was a preparation for the Gospel in the pagan world.

But who are these philosophers? Clement criticised his contemporaries. If he has to recount the history of the development of philosophy, he begins with Orpheus, Linus and the oldest poets. He mentions Homer and Pythagoras among those who are inspired; he goes further and declares that philosophy does not come from the Greeks; the earliest philosophers were born barbarians or studied under the barbarians, and it is among these that philosophy first flourished. It appeared among various races : those who originated it are ' the Prophets of Egypt, the Chaldaeans of Assyria, the Druids of Gaul, the Magi of Persia, the Gymnosophists of India '.

Here we have a remarkable theory of the history of thought[2] which is purely traditionalist and positivist. In the beginning, God sent the angels to communicate to each race, through the intermediary of an inspired man, a certain wisdom. This primitive wisdom has gradually become decayed; the history of philosophy shows not progress, but decadence. It is at the very beginning that we find truths in their pure state, as God gave them. Among these ' wisdoms ', Clement of course particularly stresses that of the Hebrews, but he recognises that the others are also valuable. It is this exegesis, this true philosophy that Christ came to restore.

Clement did not invent this theory; it corresponds to a whole intellectual movement of the day. After Aristotle the theory of progress in philosophy gave way to a feeling of decadence. These views were developed at the beginning of the first century B.C. by the Stoic Posidonius and the Platonist Antiochus of Ascalon, whose influence on Clement we have mentioned. The same views are found in the second century A.D. among philosophers whom Clement resembles, like Maximus of Tyre and Numenius of Apamea. We may note that all these philosophers are from Palestine or Syria. They represent a movement very different from Middle Platonism, more scholarly than Albinus or Atticus, with whom Justin has more affinities[3].

2. See J. Daniélou, *Message évangélique et culture hellénistique*, p. 41-72. (See n. 26, p. 93).
3. See C. Andresen, *Logos und Nomos*, p. 113-132; O. Gigon, *Die Erneuerung der Philosophie in der zeit Ciceron; Recherches sur la Tradition platonicienne, Entretiens sur l'Antiquité classique*, III, Vandœuvres-Geneva 1957, p. 57.

This theory of a revelation made to the wise men of other nations, parallel to that made to the Jews, joined to the theory of borrowing by the Greeks from the Jews, led Clement to stress much more than Justin the parallels between the bible and the Greek poets, especially Homer and Hesiod. These two, in fact, Clement considers holy men, inspired by God, who taught noble doctrines in the form of stories. There are endless examples : the description of the world on the shield of Achilles is parallel to the story of the creation of the world in *Genesis;* the history of Thetis and Ocean corresponds to the separation of the waters and the earth in Gn 1 : 79, the creation of Eve is paralleled by that of Pandora; the account of the deluge is likened to that of Deucalion, and the story of the Tower of Babel to that of the giants heaping up Pelion on Ossa. The fall of Phaeton is compared to the fall of the angels in Gn 6 : 1.

The comparison extends to the details of the two literatures. Jacob sleeping with his head on a stone is compared to Ulysses strengthening his bed with a stone; the daughters of Jethro near the well call to mind Nausicaa going to the wash-house; Lot's wife changed into a pillar of salt recalls Niobe changed into stone. Certain themes are specially emphasised, with the parallel between Minos, lawgiver of the Cretans and Zeus' confidant, and Moses, who gave the Jews their laws on Mount Sinai. David is likened to Orpheus, both performers on the harp, at the beginning of the *Protrepticus.* Here the picture widens, for Orpheus and David are, in their turn, figures of Christ. Thus there is an equivalence on three levels.

In these subtle equivalences Clement's artistic nature shows to good advantage. There are analogies of attitudes and forms. David appears under the appearance of Orpheus, Christ under that of Hercules. We become aware of the movement which at the same period gave rise to Jewish and christian works of art, the characters being represented under the appearance of mythological figures : for example, Jonah sleeping under the shrub like Endymion under the oak, the Good Shepherd like an Orpheus carrying the lambs, or David in the synagogue of Dura Europos, under the appearance of Orpheus.

But the interesting thing about Clement is that these transpositions are not merely adaptations; he justifies each one with very deep learning. It is the unique Word which has given out to each nation, through the angel set over it, the form of wisdom proper to it; this wisdom is one in principle but multiform in presentation. This same Word manifests itself anew in Christ, but the same pattern remains. The revelation of Christ takes the forms appropriate to the various cultures. If Christianity spreads in the Greek world, it must doff its Semitic form and put on a Hellenist form, it must speak the language of Plato and Homer and take the attitudes of Hermes and Ulysses.

This is true at the level of images and symbols and also at the level of customs. The Gospel spirit comes to improve the behaviour of the city of Alexandria. The spirit is that of the Gospel, but the forms of expression are no longer those of Palestine. It is Greek habits which are moulded by the Gospel at the same time as the Gospel becomes Hellenised, and there is no trace of syncretism — the Gospel remains the Gospel, but its modes of expression are no longer the same. It is permissible to wear jewels; but they must take a form susceptible of a christian interpretation : a ship, a fish, a dove. Baths are useful in moderation and sport is recommended for men; the moderate use of wine is praiseworthy.

This is a far cry from the Encratist tendencies of the primitive Palestinian *milieu*. Clement, moreover, was aware of that; he attacks Tatian and his severe attitude to marriage, he does not agree that wine should be condemned, he wants to create a type of Christian in touch with the Hellenistic ideal of man and has no sympathy with anything Jewish that the Gospel may happen to bear along on its tide. To change the simile, the Jewish elements must be abandoned, like old clothes. The process of sociological uprooting from Judaism, at first so difficult, and still far from finished, is being achieved in Alexandria. It is no longer even a matter of uprooting; the Jewish clothes fall away like dead skin, and a new christian appears, in all outward respects like any other Alexandrian, with the same dress, language and customs, as the *Epistle to Diognetus* admirably expresses it; but he is animated by a different spirit.

Clement sums this up in one word : christianity is the true philosophy, the true wisdom. It fulfils the ideal promised by the wise men of Greece. Clement knows them; he has read Epictetus and Musonius and knows the virtues of the sage : *apateia, parrhesia*. But it is the christian who embodies them. The ideal christian, as described in the *Stromateis*, conforms closely to the Gospel but he no longer in any way resembles a Palestinian prophet. Outwardly he resembles the Stoic sage, but there is in him quite a different spirit. It is not only in his outward attitude, but rather in his inward appearance that the Hellenised christian emerges for the first time in the Alexandrian's work.

3. Gnosticism and Hellenism

The transition from a Semitic to a Hellenistic form is not only found among representatives of the Church. It is a feature of the period we are studying and we find it just as clearly in the heterodox sects.

It was Christianity as a whole, with the single exception of eastern Syria, which adopted Greek culture. This is eminently true of Gnosticism which did not originally contain any Hellenism. Valentinus and Basilides inaugurated the use of philosophy at Alexandria. With the western disciples of Valentinus, Ptolemy and Heracleon, the transformation was completed and Gnosticism became a philosophical system. The transition was easy; Platonism offered a dualist system, emphasising the transcendence of God and setting the visible world over against him, while Gnosticism expressed its own dualism, of quite a different origin, in terms of these categories.

Here we have a general characteristic of the period. In cosmopolitan Alexandria the great religious trends of the ancient world met Greek culture. It was in the period when Hermetism appeared, a Hellenisation of the old Egyptian religion. The *Chaldean Oracles* were a similar phenomenon among the religions of Chaldaea. We may say with equal truth that the East invaded the Graeco-Roman world or that Graeco-Roman culture invaded the East. In reality the two statements are not on the same level. On the religious level, it was the eastern religions which triumphed; on the cultural level it was Hellenism. This is true of Gnosticism, which is no more a Hellenisation of christianity, as Harnack thought, than it is an orientalisation of Hellenism, as Reizenstein thought. It is a definite religious movement, born at the frontiers of Judaeo-Christianity, and it becomes Hellenised at the same time as Judaeo-Christianity[4].

The philosophical basis on which the Gnostics built was the same as that of the christian apologists and the Hermetic authors : Middle Platonism[5]. In earlier pages we have made this clear. Valentinus, Clement and the Pseudo-Hermes belonged to a single intellectual current, which is Platonic, but on certain points the Gnostics were precursors. Basilides, an early thinker, knew how to apply the Aristotelian distinction between privation and negation[6] and his son, Isidore, gave a more philosophical turn to the doctrine. Heracleon's use of Aristotelian categories has been noted[7]; they make his works remarkable for close

4. This point is missed by those who, like van Unnik, ' Die jüdische Komponente in der Entstehung der Gnosis ', VC, 15 (1951), p. 65-85, minimise the Judaeo-Christian origins of Gnosticism. These origins have been clearly shown by Burkitt, *Church and Gnosis*, Cambridge 1931.
5. See J. H. Waszink, ' Der Platonismus und die altchristliche Gedankenwelt '. *Recherches sur la Tradition platonicienne, Entretiens sur l'Antiquité classique*, III, Vandœuvres-Geneva 1957, p. 146-150.
6. See H. A. Wolfson, ' Negative Attributes in the Church Fathers and Gnostic Basilides ', *Harv. Theol. Rev.*, 50 (1957), p. 155-156.
7. See A. Orbe, *En los labores de la exeqesis johannea (Joh., 1, 3)* (Estudios valentinianos II), Rome 1955, p. 174-176; G. Quispel & H. C. Puech, ' Le quatrième écrit du Codex Jung ', *Vig. Christ.*, 7 (1955), p. 65-103.

reasoning. For a long time the christians remained suspicious of this ' technology '. It was the Arians who used it first at the beginning of the fourth century, and it came into general use only with the Aristotelian revival at the end of the fourth century.

In another matter the Gnostics preceded the christians : the use of Homer, as interpreted by the allegorical exegesis of the Neo-Pythagoreans and the Platonists. Irenaeus writes of the Valentinians that ' Homer is their prophet '[8]. Hippolytus accused the Simonians of taking their theories from the Greek poet[9]. In fact, they did give an important role to Helen, and were interested in the symbolism of the μολύ (moly) given by Homer to Ulysses, but the two incidents are commented upon in the same sense by Maximus of Tyre, and Helen appears in the stuccoes of the Pythagorean basilica of the Greater Port as a symbol of the soul delivered[10]. The same is true of the Valentinians. Irenaeus gives us the gist of Homeric verses written by them about Ulysses and Hercules. These two figures are similarly associated by Maximus of Tyre[11]. This use of Homer assumed important proportions among the Naossenes, the Perates and Justin the Gnostic.

An indirect proof of the effect of Greek philosophy on the Gnostics is provided by the heresiologists. Irenaeus and above all Hippolytus looked for the origins of the various branches of Gnosticism among the Greek schools of philosophy. It is interesting to find that Hegesippus linked them with the different Jewish sects; he would appear to be right. The argument of Irenaeus and Hippolytus, both rather unfavourable to philosophy, is intended to discredit the Gnostic sects, and is essentially polemical, but if it was to be effective, it had to look probable; so it indirectly indicates that the Gnostic sects named had borrowed from Greek schools of philosophy[12]. But under this coating Gnosticism remained unchanged; basically it was no more influenced by Hellenism than by christianity. Plotinus, who knew all about it, was perfectly right when he saw in Gnosticism a kind of thinking profoundly antipathetic to Hellenism.

This process of Hellenisation affected not only Gnosticism but also the other marginal sects of christianity. The prophetism of Montanus was succeeded by Proclus's literary talent, which Tertullian admired. The Marcionites argued as to whether there are one, two or three

8. *Adv. Haer.*, IV, 33, 3.
9. *Elench.*, V, 8, 1.
10. See J. Carcopino, *La Basilique pythagoricienne de la Porte Majeure*, Paris 1927, p. 331-350.
11. See J. Daniélou, *Message évangélique et culture hellénistique*, p. 81-84. (See n. 26, p. 93).
12. See H. Jonas, *Gnosis und spätantike Geist*, II, 1, Göttingen 1954, p. 163-168.

principles; they were opposed by the Didascaleans. Apelles, one of their leaders, wrote a book of *Syllogisms* which Origen later used (*HE*, V, 13, 3-4). The popular Monarchianism of Noetus assumes a more philosophical form in his disciples, and the same is true of the Adoptionism of Theodotus the Cobbler. The author of the *Adversus Artemonem*, quoted by Eusebius, accused his disciples Asclepiodotes and Theodotus the Money-changer of abandoning Scripture in order to discover syllogisms, of admiring Aristotle and Theophrastus, and abusing profane studies (*HE*, V, 18, 14-18). New types of heresies appeared, like that of Hermogenes in Antioch, which were philosophic in the strict sense[13].

* * *

So the half century from 150 to 200 was a turning point for christianity. The legal position of christians remained precarious; calumnies from the masses continued to harass them; persecutions were again to rage, but they had left the ghetto in which the world had meant to shut them up; there was no longer any question of treating them as a small eastern sect. According to Tertullian, they filled the forum, the baths, the markets, the schools. They had no reason to break with a civilisation which they loved, rejecting only its perversions. The violence of Judaeo-Christian Apocalyptic ideas and the exaggerations of Encratism were not completely dead; but already they seemed old-fashioned. A new type of christian was born who claimed to unite the values of Hellenism and the christian faith; he was going to produce the great men of the beginning of the third century.

13. See A. Orbe, *Hacia la primera teología de la procesión del Verbo*, (Estudios valentinianos I), Rome 1958, p. 270-280.

CHAPTER XI

THE WEST UNDER THE SEVERI

THE last of the Antonines, Commodus, was assassinated in 193 and left the empire in a state of fearful anarchy. An African, Septimus Severus, assumed power and the age of the philosopher-emperors returned. Severus was the administrator who re-established order in the empire. The relations between the empire and the Church were about to take a new turn. Severus did not share Marcus Aurelius's intellectual antipathy for the christians. His marriage with Julia Domna, daughter of the high priest of Ephesus, opened up the empire to eastern religions. There were christians in his court. But he had an authoritarian idea of the empire. Towards the end of the second century a large number of christians were still inspired by Messianic hopes. A conflict was going to ensue, which would mark a stage in the reciprocal limitation of the spheres of the Church and the empire[1].

1. The Edict of Severus

The last years of the second century and the beginning of the third show a surprising revival of Apocalyptic hopes in christianity. This was a new flare-up of the original Judaeo-Christian Messianism, with its hope of Christ's imminent return and its call to complete asceticism. These trends first appeared in Montanism. During the reign of Severus Montanist propaganda spread in Italy and Africa. Proclus, whom Tertullian venerated, exercised his apostolate in Rome during the pontificate of Zephyrinus (199-217). Eschinus represents another branch of the movement. In Africa, Tertullian was won over to Montanism about 207; Montanism appeared as the party of Martyrs and it is true that the movement did have some martyrs. The Montanists considered martyrdom the mark of the authenticity of their inspiration. Their opponents were themselves witnesses to this, since they tried to contest not the

1. See J. Moreau, *Les persécutions du christianisme dans l'Empire romain*, p. 75-78.

existence of these martyrs but their value as proofs. For example, the anonymous anti-Montanist quoted by Eusebius remarked that other heresies, such as Marcionism, had a great number of martyrs (*HE*, V, 15, 20). He added that when they were arrested with Montanists the Catholics refused to enter into communion with them, for example, in Apamea Meander (*HE*, V, 15, 21). Apollonius disputed the value of these martyrdoms : a certain Alexander, who passed himself off as a martyr, had in fact been condemned for theft by the proconsul of Ephesus, Aemilius Frontinus (*HE*, V, 18-19).

But this Apocalyptic movement was much wider than Montanism. The Asiatic movement had retained elements of Millenarianism[2]. In Africa, Tertullian, on his conversion to christianity and well before his conversion to Montanism, represents a somewhat fanatical kind of christianity[3]. This was just before the edict of Severus. In his treatise *Ad Martyres*, which a reference to the defeat of Clodius Albinus by Septimus Severus allows us to date with certainty to the year 197, he encourages some christian prisoners by showing them that they are taking part in a battle against devilish powers. And the *Apologia*, written at the same period, provides evidence of a christianity that refused all compromise.

We may note also that the end of the second century and the beginning of the third were the period when many apocryphal *Acts of the Apostles* appeared. The first evidence we have about the *Acts of Paul* comes from Tertullian; in his *Tract on Baptism* he says that they were recently written by a priest from Asia. Tertullian's work dates from about 200, so the *Acts of Paul* date from about 190. They glorify the combats of Thecla and Paul against their persecutors. The central idea is the conflict between the worship of Christ and Emperor-worship. As in Montanism we find women prophets and glorification of virginity.

The same themes reappear in the other Acts[4]. The *Acts of Peter* preach the separation of married people and end with the account of the martyrdom of Peter, preceded by the famous incident of the ' Quo Vadis? ' The Eucharist is celebrated with bread and water. These *Acts* must be of Phoenician origin. The *Acts of John* and the *Acts of Andrew* show the same trends : an account of martyrdoms, glorification of virginity and separation of married couples. All this literature is related to Montanism, but represents other groups too. In particular we find in it the probable influence of Syrian asceticism[5].

2. Nautin seems to consider that Irenaeus's relations with Asia were of little importance (*Lettres et écrivains chrétiens des IIe et IIIe siècles*, p. 100-103).
3. See H. Karpp, *Schrift und Geist bei Tertullien*, Gütersloh 1957, p. 15.
4. See E. Peterson, *Frühkirche, Judentum und Gnosis*, p. 183-220.
5. *Ibid.*, p. 218.

Another feature was the development of *Acts of the Martyrs*[6]. Some of these are the actual records of the trial, preserved and handed round by christians. This is true of the *Acts of St. Justin*, martyred in Rome in 165. We also possess the *Acts of the Martyrs of Scillium* in Africa; it is the earliest document for the African Church. Their martyrdom took place under Commodus, 17th July 180. Other acts of the martyrs are narratives partly based on eye-witness accounts. The glorification of martyrdom is even more in evidence; among them we find the *Martyrdom of Polycarp*. It is possible that our version may belong to the reign of Septimus Severus and echo discussions about Montanism[7]. The *Acts of the Martyrs of Lyon*, preserved by Eusebius, date from 178. While glorifying their martyrs, they react against Montanist tendencies and Encratism; they belong to the same context[8]. The *Acts* of Perpetua and Felicity, on the other hand, are the manifesto of Tertullian the Montanist.

This literature could not fail to affect christian sensibilities. Tertullian tells of christians going in crowds to the tribunal of the Proconsul of Asia, Annius Antoninus, and getting sent away by him; this took place in 184 or 185. The exaggerations resulting from this *mystique* led the Church to intervene. Disapproval was shown towards christians who tried to provoke the authorities.

This glorification of martyrdom was linked with belief in the imminence of the Parousia, which appeared in numerous places about 200. Eusebius mentions a writer of this period, Jude, who, he says, wrote about the seventy weeks of Daniel, making them terminate in the last year of the reign of Severus, that is to say, in 203. ' He thought ', adds Eusebius ' that the Parousia of the Anti-Christ, of which everyone was talking, was then approaching, to such a degree did the violence of persecution disturb most people ' (*HE*, VI, 7). In his *Commentary on Daniel* Hippolytus tells the recent story of a Syrian bishop going off to the desert with his community to meet the Lord, and another story about a bishop of Pontus proclaiming, as a result of visions, that the Last Judgment would take place the following year[9].

Several of Hippolytus's works belong to the same context, even if they do not run to such excesses. The *Commentary on Daniel* was written in 203 or 204, that is to say just after the edict of Severus. It

6. See E. Simonetti, ' Qualche osservazione a proposito dell'origine degli atti dei Martiri ', Mémorial Bardy, *Rev. Et.Aug.*, 1 (1956), p. 39-57.
7. See H. von Campenhausen, *Bearbeitungen und Interpolationen des Polykarp-martyriums*, Heidelberg 1957, and the review by H.-I. Marrou.
8. See Nautin, *op. cit.*, p. 32-61.
9. *Com. Dan.*, III, 18.

corresponds to the chronological speculations about the weeks of years which were linked to expectations of the Parousia[10]. The *Tract on the Anti-Christ*, which is a little earlier, about 200, also takes account of these preoccupations. Against those who made the coming of the Anti-Christ coincide with the persecution of Severus, he shows that Rome is not the fourth of the powers announced by Daniel and so the time of the Parousia has not yet come. Its context is eschatological.

Even Alexandria does not appear to have been free from this fever. It is to be found in the attitude of the young Origen, as described by Eusebius. Even when due allowance is made for a historian heightening his subject matter, and for the fact that it was during time of persecution that Origen showed his eagerness for martyrdom, the fact remains that his disposition tallies too well with the climate of opinion at that time to be an affectation. It is sufficient to recall the words of Eusebius : ' Such a passion for martyrdom possessed the soul of Origen, when still a youth, that he took pleasure in running risks, in leaping and throwing himself into the struggle ' (*HE*, VI, 2, 4). And we know how his mother hid his clothes to prevent his risking his life. Later, during the persecution of Maximinus, in 235, Origen glorified the ideal of martyrdom when writing to his friend Ambrose.

We may note that Clement, who lived in Alexandria, adopted quite another attitude. He left the town, like a number of others. Origen belonged to a different group, more influenced by eschatological trends. Other points bring out the difference. Eusebius tells us that for part of his life Origen did not drink wine; we know that love of continence drove him to self-emasculation. All that derives from a state of mind very akin to Montanism. Origen's attitude also recalls the severity of Tertullian and Hippolytus, and his attitude to the Empire was very like theirs. He later modified his point of view and became more moderate, but his youth was passed in the Apocalyptic climate of the years about 200.

We may note that a similar attitude is found at the same date in Africa, Asia, Rome and Alexandria. It is the same eschatological christianity expressing itself. Origen, Tertullian and Hippolytus showed the same indifference towards the destiny of the earthly city. What they hoped for was martyrdom, which would show the incompatibility of the earthly and heavenly cities. The earthly city seemed to them already condemned; it was useless to ensure continuance by engendering children or to defend it by enlisting in the army — all that belonged to a vanished world. The christian city, already present and soon to be made manifest,

---

10. See J. Daniélou, ' La typologie millénariste de la semaine dans le christianisme primitif ', *VC*, 2 (1948), p. 1-16.

called for angelic chastity and universal love; above all, no concessions must be made.

This christianity was not the only christianity at that period; in particular, it was not the kind professed by the bishops. On the contrary, they showed greater concern for the salvation of the majority, the shepherd's solicitude for his flock, the quest for a realistic christianity, the desire for agreement with the authorities. But Tertullian broke with the Church to found one more sect; Hippolytus violently attacked the Roman episcopate, Zephyrinus as well as Callistus, and reproached it for laxity and worldliness; Origen was exiled by the Bishop of Alexandria, Demetrius. Their motives may appear different, but the conflict was one and the same : that of the intellectuals who imagined an ideal church, against prelates aware of the conditions of the real Church.

It is here that the problem of relations with the Empire arose. The position of the christians in the last years of the Antonines had somewhat improved. Their legal status remained the same, but care was taken not to disturb them. The last persecution had occurred under Marcus Aurelius. Commodus, who succeeded him in 180, had some christians at his court : for example, his concubine Marcia who pleaded on behalf of Confessors condemned to the mines of Sardinia and obtained their release; senior civil servants like the Secretary to the Treasury, Prosenes, whose epitaph has been found, and Carpophorus, who employed Callistus as a slave. Only a few death penalties were inflicted in his reign : that of the Scillitan martyrs in 180, and that of Senator Apollonius between 183 and 185[11].

This situation seems to have continued at the beginning of the reign of Severus, who also had christians at his court. He was treated by the christian physician Proculus, and kept Prosenes in office. He knew that the christians had supported him in Asia in his struggle against Pescennius Niger; he did not hesitate to protect christians of senatorial families against the anger of the masses. In all this Severus appears to have been a realist, for the christians were now a power to be reckoned with; the administration must not deprive itself of valuable men because they happened to be christians. To the extent that christians served the state — which was his sole concern — he was ready to protect them.

In 202, however, Severus issued an edict forbidding christians to make proselytes, that is to say practically preventing the spread of Christianity, which was the first legislation to be directed against the

11. See J. Moreau, *La persécution du Christianisme dans l'Empire romain*, Paris 1956, p. 61-64.

christians.   Severus tried to find precedents for it; his legal expert,
Ulpian, collected previous decisions relating to the christians.   These
were primarily negative : they did not recognise Christianity's right to
legal existence, but they were not opposed to its existence and expansion.
Only particular circumstances could lead to the arrest of christians.
Here, on the other hand, we have a general measure ordering civil servants
to check the progress of Christianity.

It is difficult not to connect this with the Apocalyptic movement
we have been discussing, and we must admit that Severus had grounds
for anxiety; the movement worried even the leaders of the Church,
for it contained tendencies which went against his determination to
re-establish the Empire.   At the moment when Severus was reforming
the laws on marriage and trying to strengthen the family, these christians
condemned marriage and urged all their brethren to practise continence.
At the moment when the frontiers of the Empire were threatened by the
Parthians on the east, by the Scots on the north and when all available
forces had to be mobilised, the christians were urging one another to
refuse to serve in the army[12].

Even the location of persecutions proves that Severus was aiming
less at the Church as such than at certain extreme tendencies.   In fact
the groups affected were those who held Messianic views, among whom
were Catholics and also heretics; the Montanists were especially hard
hit, the Marcionites also, for their ascetical tendencies were well known,
and they seem to have been influenced at this period by Montanism.
Inversely, we find two categories, with quite opposite views, untouched
by persecution.   One group was the Gnostics, who were notoriously
anti-Millenarianist and projected their hopes to an after-life[13], and
another group was the bishops, who do not seem to have been disturbed
at this period.

Finally, we may note that the measures taken by Severus were
aimed at Jewish proselytism as well as at christian proselytism; they
were promulgated during a journey through Palestine.   We may wonder
whether the revival of christian Messianism did not coincide with
a movement of Jewish Messianism, especially in Palestine and Mesopotamia[14].   The Jews still submitted to the Roman yoke with impatience
and the campaigns of the Parthians during the second century aroused
their hopes of deliverance.   It was at the beginning of the third century

12. See H. Grégoire, Les persécutions dans l'Empire romain, Brussells 1951, p. 61-64.
13. W. H. C. Frend, ' The Gnostic Sects and the Roman Empire ', Journ. Eccles. Hist.,
    5 (1954), p. 25-36.
14. On the relations between Montanism and Judaism, see H. Grégoire, op. cit.,
    p. 107-108.

that the synagogue in Dura-Europos on the Euphrates was decorated with paintings, still in existence, which seem to express Messianic hopes[15].

The edict of Severus unleashed a persecution, but it was not very violent and soon calmed down. Severus's successors — Caracalla, Elagabalus and Alexander Severus — do not seem to have enforced the edict. In fact, the two centres about which there is information are Egypt and Africa. In Egypt, Eusebius tells us that in 202 christians were sent from all parts to Alexandria to be martyred. We know that Leonidas, Origen's father, was beheaded. Origen, despite his youth, was put in charge of catechesis because the others had left.

Persecutions continued during the following years, under the prefect of Egypt, Serbatianus Aquila. Eusebius shows us Origen helping the christians who had been arrested : in prison, before the tribunal and even at the place of martyrdom, rousing the fury of the pagans against him. Among those put to death after having been instructed by him, Eusebius names Plutarch, brother of Heracleon, who became bishop of Alexandria, Serenus, who was burned, Heraclides and Hero, the former a catechumen, the latter a neophyte; and another Serenus who was beheaded. Among the women, Herais, a catechumen, ' received baptism by fire ' (*HE*, VI, 3, 4). Eusebius writes at length about the martyrdom of Potamiene, who with her mother Marcella was burned in boiling pitch. A pagan, Basilides, who had been one of Origen's audience, was a companion of Potamiene; he declared himself a christian, was baptised by his brethren and beheaded (*HE*, VI, 4, 3).

We may note that the martyrs were chiefly neophytes and catechumens. This seems to be connected with the nature of Severus's decree, which forbade proselytism. The prohibited offence was to prepare oneself for baptism or to receive it. The measure was a clever one, for it did not strike at people already christian, and it made admission to the catechumenate a matter for great caution. So this explains the danger of being a catechist, which was a direct violation of the law. We understand why the majority avoided these duties; the zeal of a man like Origen was required to perform them.

The same situation appears in Carthage. Here Tertullian is our informant. A first persecution took place in 203, under the procurator Hilarianus. The victims were the catechist Satyrus; a neophyte, Perpetua, with her slave, Felicity; and four catechumens. The situation was very much like that in Alexandria, but here the catechist was also put to death. We possess the *Acts* of these martyrdoms, probably by

15. See R. Wischnitzer, *The Messianic Theme in the Paintings of the Dura Synagogue*, Chicago 1948.

Tertullian; they also betray a marked Montanist outlook.   We may note the part played by Perpetua's three visions in the *Acts*.   They are an incomparable document for christian imagery at that time.

In the reigns of Severus and his successors there are still some cases of martyrdom, but it is difficult to know whether they were connected with the edict or whether they were only a continuation of earlier legislation.   It is to this period that the martyrology dates the martyrdom of St. Irenaeus in Gaul.   In Cappadocia a bishop, Alexander, who was later to become Bishop of Jerusalem, was imprisoned, and in 211, while a prisoner, he learned of the election of Asclepiades to the see of Antioch[16]. In Rome Eusebius tells us the story of a certain Natalios whom the Adoptionists won over with bribes; but, because he had confessed his faith, Christ did not allow him to remain in heresy.   The episode seems to have taken place in 203; perhaps he was a neophyte and this was an application of the edict.   Finally Tertullian tells us that under Caracalla, the proconsul of Africa, Scapula, put to death certain christians who had been denounced.   This seems to be an example of the earlier procedure.

2. Hippolytus and Callistus

We have seen what the Church of Rome was like under Victor (189-199).   Two tendencies clashed, each trying to win over the Church authorities.   Montanism put out a lively propaganda there and won much sympathy; even among those who were not members of the group, it expressed the spirit of Asiatic Christianity.   The writings of John and the *Apocalypse* in particular kept alive a picture of tension between the imperial authorities and the Church; the end of the world was believed to be imminent.   The climate of persecution created by Septimus Severus strengthened this movement.

But the community as a whole was not favourable to Montanism or to Asiatic Millenarianism; even in Asia it met opposition from the bishops.   Praxeas seems to have been sent from Asia to Rome to warn against Montanist propaganda.   Eleutherius had heeded Praxeas's warning.   Victor's successor, Zephyrinus (199-217) seems to have been more definitely hostile to this movement; for deacon he had Callistus, his future successor (217-222).   The Roman priest Gaius even went as far as to reject the *Apocalypse*, considered, not without reason, as one of the sources of Montanism.   These circles were hostile not only to Montanism but to all speculation about the Word and clung to an

16. See Nautin, *op. cit.*, p. 112-114.

old theology, which we find also professed by Praxeas and Callistus. But this theology had been warped in a Modalist direction by Noetus. Epigonus had brought these ideas to Rome; Zephyrinus and Callistus did not fight sufficiently shy of Epigonus, and in this they gave their critics ground for complaint.

It was in this climate that Hippolytus appeared. The history of this great man has been complicated by a confusion between him and other men with the same name. We must first distinguish him from an eastern bishop whom Eusebius names (*HE*, VI, 20, 2) without giving his see[17]; then from a martyr of Antioch; thirdly from an officer who witnessed St. Lawrence's martyrdom, was martyred with him and buried at Ager Veranus. On the other hand, unlike Hanssens, I believe that he is the same person as Roman priest exiled with Pope Pontian to Sardinia in 235 and buried near the Via Tiburtina[18]. Finally, despite the grave objections put forward by Nautin in a series of articles[19], it seems likely that it is his statue which has been discovered near the Via Tiburtina. Nautin argues that the list of writings mentioned on this statue does not tally with the list of Hippolytus's works as we know them today. According to him, the statue depicts the Roman priest Josipus, also the author of the *Elenchos against all Heresies*. He claims that Hippolytus was of eastern origin.

But this theory does not seem to outweigh the arguments in favour of the identification. In the first place, it is not surprising that the majority of Hippolytus's works are not on the statue. In fact, the beginning of the list is missing from the statue; and the list ends with the works published about 224, the date when the statue was erected, soon after the paschal reckoning engraved thereon, which begins in 222. The *Elenchos*, in particular, which Nautin attributes with certainty to the person represented, does not appear there; this is indisputably true for the other works. So the list on the statue contains only Hippolytus's works between about 210 and 224, and is in chronological order.

In the second place, so many of the works mentioned on the statue tally with writings known to be by Hippolytus that they can hardly be the works of two different men : Nautin is obliged to explain this by Josipus's influence on Hippolytus. Certain titles are the same : *On the Charismata*, the *Apostolic Tradition*, the *Demonstration of the*

---

17. He is perhaps the same as Hippolytus of Bostra, who has left a work in Syriac. See L. M. Froidevaux, ' Hippolyte Évêque de Bostra ', *RSR*, 50 (1962), p. 63-64.
18. See J.-M. Hanssens, *La liturgie d'Hippolyte. Ses documents, son titulaire, ses origines et son caractère*, Rome 1959, p. 300-323.
19. This is disputed by P. Nautin, *Hippolyte et Josipe. Contribution à l'histoire de la littérature chrétienne au III*e *siècle*, Paris 1947. See also by the same author : *Lettres et écrivains chrétiens au II*e *et III*e *siècles*, p. 177-209.

Dates of Easter, the *Paschal Table*, the treatise *On the Apocalypse.* On the other hand there is an indisputable link between the *Chronicles*, mentioned on the statue, and the *Commentary on Daniel*, which is certainly by Hippolytus; between the *Elenchos*, which is certainly by the author represented by the statue, and the *Against Noetus*, which is certainly by Hippolytus. The greater precision of the *Chronicles and of the Elenchos* makes them more authoritative works, and this difference is better explained by the development of a single author than by the dissimilarity between two authors.

It is possible to reconstruct the life of Hippolytus. He was probably born about 170 and, as we have already mentioned, his first works, *On the Anti-Christ* and the *Commentary on Daniel*, date from the persecution of Severus. It was likewise at this period that he published a good part of the exegetical works mentioned by Eusebius and Jerome. He began his controversy with Callistus about 217 with his *Summary* (suntagma) *against the Heresies*, of which the section *Against Noetus* is the end. Then comes the period of the works on that part of the inscription which has been preserved. It includes two further works of exegesis, the continuation of the polemic against Callistus, as well as the defence of the *Apocalypse*, the *Apostolic Tradition*, the *Chronicle*, the tract *On the Universe*, the *Exhortation to Severiana.* This period coincides with the pontificate of Callistus (217-222). Hippolytus was then in conflict with the Pope.

But in 222 Urban succeeded Callistus. Hippolytus was ordered to work out a method for reckoning Easter. The statue was erected about 224, and it lists the latest works written by Hippolytus between the establishment of the method and the erection of the statue, that is to say, between 222 and 224. These are the *Demonstration of the Dates of Easter*, the *Odes*, a work *On the Resurrection* addressed to Julia Mammaea, mother of Alexander Severus, who had become Emperor in 222, and a work *On Good and the Origin of Evil.* Until his death in 235 Hippolytus continued to publish numerous works, but these of course are not mentioned on the statue. He continued his exegetical work and published his *Elenchos against the Heresies.* This book was aimed particularly at the expansion of Gnostic sects in Rome under Alexander Severus. These included the Nassenes, the existence of which is known to us through the hypogia in the Viale Manzoni. It ends with the Elkesaites, whose propaganda Origen notes at the same period. Hippolytus took advantage of the opportunity to square accounts with Callistus, whom he attacked violently *à propos* the heresy of Noetus. This attack was facilitated by the anti-Monarchian reaction under Pope Pontian (230-235). In 234 Hippolytus revised his *Chronicle*, a first

edition of which, before 222, is listed on the statue, taking account
of the calculations for his paschal reckoning and continuing it as far
as the thirteenth year of Alexander Severus.   In 235, after the
assassination of the Emperor, he was sent to the Sardinian mines with
his friend Pope Pontian. It was there that he died.

From his literary work we can glimpse his character. We have
spoken of his early writings, inspired by the persecution of Severus,
and he has also left a considerable exegetical work, a large part of which
has survived : the *Blessings of Isaac and Jacob*, the *Blessings of Moses,
David and Goliath*, the *Commentary on the Song of Songs*, and *Homilies
on Psalms 1 & 2*.   Hippolytus's exegesis is eminently traditional; there
is no trace in it of Alexandrian allegory.   It is first and foremost
an expression of the usual catechesis at Rome, and it also describes
the types of deliverance : Daniel in the midst of the lions, Jonah saved
from the monster, the three young men in the furnace, Joseph saved
from the well, Susanna and the elders — the same which begin to be
found in decorations of the Roman catacombs at this period[20].

The same is true of certain important symbols, which we also find
in Roman art of the period and which echo the catechesis. For example,
the spiritual vine, of which the vine shoots are the saints and the grapes
the martyrs; the harvesters are the angels, the wine-press the Church,
and the wine the power of the Spirit[21].   Another example is the ship,
a figure of the Church, which crosses the sea of the world, as Noah's
ark traversed the Flood; the oars are the churches, Christ is the pilot,
the mast is the cross.   The image had already appeared in Justin.   The
detail is found in the catechesis of the *Clementine Homilies*, which belong
to the same period.   Yet another example is the Paradise of the Church,
where the trees are the saints, and Christ the sun surrounded by the
Apostles as by the stars.

We may note the resemblances between these symbols and those
found in the *Clementine Homilies*. Now the latter are an echo of Petrine
catechesis.   We have, then, an exegetical tradition which was not at
all the same as that of Alexandria, nor as that of Asia; it seems to have
been typically Roman. Its Jewish origins are obvious; the types of
deliverance are the same as those in Jewish prayers of intercession[22].
The chief symbols are those of Palestinian and Syrian Judaeo-Christian
literature : the ship of the Church is in the *Testaments of the Twelve*

---

20. A.-G. Martimont, ' L'iconographie des catacombes et la catéchèse antique ',
Riv. Arch. Crist., 25 (1949), p. 105-114.
21. C. Leonardi, *Ampelos*, Rome 1947.
22. P. Lundberg, *La typologie baptismale dans l'Ancienne Église*, Uppsala 1942,
p. 33-63.

Patriarchs, the seven-branched candlestick was one of the favourite symbols of contemporary Judaism, along with the mystical vine.

This raises the question of the *Apostolic Tradition*. Hanssens suggests that it is an echo of the Alexandrian liturgy. Now Alexandria is the only place with which Hippolytus certainly had no contact. There is no reason for believing that it had Asiatic origins. Elsewhere in the work of Hippolytus the catechetical and liturgical elements appear to be typically Roman, and it would be surprising if the *Apostolic Tradition* were the one exception. If it be objected that it shows an affinity with the Syrian liturgy, the answer is that, all liturgies were imported from the east into the west. In fact this is rather an argument in the other direction, for the catechetical elements in Hippolytus are of Petrine origin, that is to say, in the last analysis, Syrian. Its affinities are with the *Clementine Homilies*, which is doubtless also true of the liturgy.

But at the same time Hippolytus had links with the Asiatic tradition. Photius says that he introduced himself as a disciple of Irenaeus in his *Summary against the Heresies*, already mentioned. We find in him a theology of the relations between the two Testaments which is completely Irenaean. In fact he expresses in Irenaeus's words the doctrine of the recapitulation of Adam by Christ[23]. Other characteristics remind us of Asia. The typology of Joseph is a feature of Melito and Irenaeus[24]. The *Homily on Easter* is inspired by that of Melito. Typical, too, is Hippolytus's esteem for the *Apocalypse :* he defended its Johannine authenticity, he shared the Millenarianism of the Asiatics and he believed in the imminence of the end of time. Finally we may note that his hostility to philosophy in the *Elenchos* and, insofar as he used it, his preference for Stoicism are in the spirit of Melito.

We now have a picture of Hippolytus. He belonged to the Roman tradition. His work is typical of catechesis, thereby confirming the tradition that he was a Roman presbyter. As regards the liturgy, he is a precious witness to the Roman rites. But the Church of Rome at this time was split between two tendencies. It was disturbed by an Apocalyptic movement, connected with the early character of the Church. It was at this time that the prophet Hermas preached. The martyrs Peter and Paul were being venerated. And these traditional tendencies were strengthened by Montanist propaganda. There was also another movement, likewise traditional, found chiefly in the hierarchy. It took a moderate view and chiefly sought to maintain contacts between the different groups of the community, showing itself rather indulgent and trying to be on good terms with the imperial government.

23. *Com. Dan.*, IV, 11.
24. See J. Daniélou, *Message évangélique et culture hellénique*, p. 241-242. (See n. 26, p. 93.)

It is against this background that we must read the pages in Hippolytus devoted to Zephyrinus and Callistus in the *Refutation* (elenchos) *of all Heresies;* they are extremely violent. He accuses Zephyrinus of having been bribed to favour the propaganda of Cleomenes and of having himself belonged to Monarchianism. Furthermore, he makes an indictment of Callistus. He claims that Callistus was a Christian slave of the pagan Marcus Aurelius Carpophorus, that he launched into finance and ended up in bankruptcy. Thrown into prison, released, then condemned to the mines of Sardinia, he obtained his freedom by putting his name on a list of Christian Confessors for whom Marcia, Commodus's concubine, had obtained pardon.

He won the confidence of Zephyrinus, a priest of the Roman Church, and when the latter succeeded Victor, Callistus was put in charge of the cemeteries. He entirely dominated the Pope and supported him in his Montanist tendencies, and on the death of Zephyrinus he succeeded him. Not only did he continue to profess Modalism, but he relaxed the Church's discipline. Hippolytus interprets Callistus's innovations regarding penance in this sense; he reproaches him with forgiving the sins of the flesh provided that the penitent adopts his ideas, with admitting bishops, priests and deacons married two or three times, with allowing priests to marry and with tolerating abortion.

The account which Hippolytus gives us is clearly a caricature. Violence was the usual tone at that time; we find it in Tertullian, but behind the caricature we can glimpse the group that Hippolytus was attacking. This group was first and foremost that of christians belonging to the ruling classes, whose position was delicate and who hated provocation; several of these high officials have been mentioned. We might add the lawyer Minucius Felix, whose *Octavius* describes a very courteous discussion with an important pagan on the sea wall at Ostia. It was in the Church's interests to conciliate such men, who could be very helpful in avoiding friction and smoothing out difficulties.

This group also included those in charge of the Church. The bishops' responsibility was largely administrative, and this was particularly true in Rome, where the duties were heavy. Hermas praised the bishops for their hospitality. Callistus, a good administrator, rendered Zephyrinus important services. The latter placed him in charge of the cemeteries belonging to the Church. It is possible that that was an innovation and that previously christians had been buried in estates belonging to private persons, as with the cemetery of Priscilla and that of Domitilla[25].

25. See A. Amore, ' Note di topomastica cimiteriali romana ', *Riv. Arch. Crist.* 32 (1956), p. 59-87.

This post was important; it meant dealing with the artists decorating the tombs. Callistus's name was given to the cemetery which he looked after. It was quite normal for this great administrator to succeed to Zephyrinus.

Zephyrinus and Callistus were not intellectuals but men of action; under their pontificate the Church made enormous progress. It won the sympathy of the imperial government, and grew considerably in numbers; this growth implied an adaptation of discipline to these new circumstances. Against all that Hippolytus protested; he dreamed of a Church which was a handful of saints in conflict with the world : poor, without property. But the pastors, who had charge of souls, could not accept this vision. For a christian people on the increase institutions were required.

The theological disputes, in this case, were mere pretexts. The so-called Monarchianism of Zephyrinus and Callistus rests only on the assertions of Hippolytus and Tertullian. Zephyrinus and Callistus were not theologians; faced with the Apocalyptic crisis, they looked for support to other groups in Rome, notably the Monarchians. In this reaction abuses occurred. Gaius went too far in rejecting the *Apocalypse*, but when the danger of Monarchianism became clear to Callistus, he condemned Sabellius, which greatly annoyed Hippolytus, who considered it merely a trick[26].

These details complete the picture of Hippolytus; a Roman priest, he was violently opposed to Zephyrinus and Callistus. In this he appears first and foremost as a representative of the old Roman presbyterate, whose catechetical tradition and liturgical usages he retains. He is hostile to the more monarchical notion of the episcopate put forward by Zephyrinus and Callistus, and to the role given to deacons. The hatred of the priest Hippolytus for the deacon Callistus stems from an old antagonism, which we have already mentioned; in Hermas we found the same hostility towards deacons. Hippolytus also remains loyal to the old idea of a Messianic Church, heroic and in conflict with the world.

Another trait which reveals his reactionary spirit is his loyalty to Greek. Few scholars ever believed that at this period Greek was the usual language of the Church of Rome, but Christine Mohrmann has shown that as early as the middle of the second century the christians of Rome began to speak Latin[27]. Latin christian expressions have been found in Hermas's *Shepherd*, written in Rome. It seems clear that the earliest Latin versions of the bible appeared in Rome at the same

26. *Elench.*, IX, 12.
27. See C. Mohrmann, ' Les origines de la latinité chrétienne à Rome ', *Vig. Christ.*, 3 (1949), p. 67-107; *Études sur le latin des chrétiens*, Rome 1958, p. 52-54.

time as in Africa. It was in Rome too, about this time, that certain Greek works specially important for the Romans were translated: certainly the *Epistle of Clement of Rome*, and probably Hermas's *Shepherd* and the *Didache*. The fragment of Muratori, whether it be a Latin original or a translation from the Greek, belongs to the end of the second century. So Hippolytus appears old fashioned by having written in Greek, while his contemporary Tertullian, who knew Greek, was using Latin in Africa.

Hippolytus was mistaken. He did not see that the growth of God's people implied new situations, that Christianity was not a sect of pure people, but a city expressive of its inhabitants. He mocked Callistus's admirable image of the Church as Noah's ark, containing animals of all kinds, who will be sorted out only at the Last Judgment, but there is no reason to make of him an anti-pope, or even a schismatic; his writings reveal the purest tradition. Much of his violence stems from the literary form he used. He was the representative of an Integrism which the hierarchy was right not to accept. But he was a great Doctor of the Church, and there is no reason not to venerate him as a saint, like his opponent Callistus, just as at a later date Cornelius and Cyprian were united in sanctity.

3. The Birth of Christian Africa

Septimus Severus was of African birth; he was born in Leptis Magna. His reign and that of his successors witnessed progress at all levels in Africa: roughly speaking, the territory which today forms Tunisia and Constante. It was at that time that the cities of Leptis, Tungad and Djemila were built; today their ruins are still inscribed with the names of the emperors. At the intellectual level Carthage was an important centre; the town was made famous by Fronto and Apuleius at the end of the second century. Open to the influence of Hellenism in all its forms, it was, however, less cosmopolitan than Rome and it was the most important centre of literature in the Latin language at that time. Its population of sailors, soldiers and businessmen was lively, turbulent and passionate, in contrast to Roman seriousness.

Christianity was probably planted in Carthage as early as the end of the first century, otherwise it is difficult to explain how the city had a large christian population at the time of Tertullian. ' We fill your squares, your markets, your amphitheatres ', he writes in the *Apologeticum*. The Council of Carthage, in 216, was attended by seventy-one African bishops, but we know nothing about the conditions in which the Gospel was spread. Probably the first converts came from the Jewish communities, numerous in Africa[28]. Christianity grew next among Greek-speaking groups and the first liturgies were in Greek but in the year 180 a Latin African work appeared, the *Acts of the Martyrs of Scillium*. These martyrs said that they had some *libri et epistulae Pauli*, which seems to imply the existence of a Latin translation of the New Testament. Tertullian tells us a little later that there was a complete translation of the bible into Latin.

So before Tertullian, African Christianity seems to have increased in numbers, but to have shown no sign of originality. The movements we find in Africa during his lifetime all came from elsewhere, chiefly from Asia, often by way of Rome. The heresies he fought were those we have met earlier elsewhere and which ended up belatedly in Africa. There exists a book by him against the Valentinians, and in the *De praescriptione haereticorum* he lists the other Gnostic sects we already know. He attacked Marcion; he is the only writer to name one of his disciples, Lucanus; he fought the Syrian, Hermogenes, who seems to have come to Africa; his most formidable opponents were the Monarchians, and he himself was converted to Montanism. Nothing here raises new problems.

The same is true of the Catholic authors on whom he depends. He had no African Christian literature on which to draw; it is noteworthy that he was bilingual. Some of his works were originally written in Greek : for example, the *De Spectaculis*, the *De Baptismo*, the *De Virginibus velandis*, the *De Extasi* and the *Apologeticum*. The models he chose were christian authors writing in Greek at an earlier date. Tertullian took Justin for his model in the *Adversus Marcionem*. His lists of heresies come from Irenaeus; he quotes Irenaeus, Miltiades and Justin in his work against the Valentinians. Doubtless he made use of Theophilas of Antioch's tract against Hermogenes; he followed Melito in his theology of history; his trinitarian vocabulary comes from Tatian. In this sense, as Stephan Otto has rightly pointed out[29], Tertullian is an important link between Greek Christianity and Latin Christianity. It is through him that a whole world of controversies worked out during the second century in Greek-speaking countries appeared for the first time in Latin-speaking countries. In this respect he offers a striking contrast to Hippolytus : the latter remained loyal to western Hellenism; Tertullian inaugurated African Latinism, thereby putting Africa in advance of Rome.

28. See M. Simon, ' Le judaïsme berbère dans l'Afrique ancienne ', *Rev. Hist. Phil. Relig.*, 26 (1948), p. 23.
29. S. Otto, *Natura und Dispositio. Untersuchung zur Naturbegriff und zur Denkform Tertullians*, Munich 1960, p. 218.

So Africa before Tertullian presents two characteristics : a christian people chiefly of Latin origin, numerous and full of vigour; and a culture still almost exclusively Greek. Tertullian's achievement was to give this Christianity its autochthonous form of expression. It is rare to find an example where the creative influence of a single man has played so clear a role. Tertullian endowed the African Church — and through it, the whole Latin Church — with a liturgical, theological and ascetical vocabulary. He did this not by transplanting artificially, as Cicero sometimes did in transplanting Greek philosophical terms, but by letting the ideas he had found elsewhere express themselves in language full of character.

Tertullian was born about 160. In 197 we glimpse him for the first time, in full maturity; he was the son of a centurion in the proconsular cohort; he studied law in Carthage, which was a training-ground for advocates, and made a reputation in Rome as a lawyer. It is possible that we should identify him with the author of the same name found in the Digest[30]. This stay probably coincided with the accession of Septimus Severus, which would have drawn young Africans to Rome. After some years of lax living, he was stirred by being present at martyrdoms, and became a christian about 195. He went back to Carthage where he was put in charge of the catechumenate and ordained priest. Several of his early works echo his teaching : the *De Testimonio animae*, the *De Oratione*, the *De Baptismo*, the *De Paenitentia*, the *Ad Uxorem*, and the *Adversus Judaeos*. These appeared from 200 to 207.

But chiefly he took part in all the christian disputes, showing extraordinary gifts as a controversialist. At first these disputes were between the christians and the Roman Empire. Tertullian glorified the courage of the martyrs *(Ad Martyres)*. In two works he defended Christianity against pagan accusations *(Ad Nationes, Apologeticum)*; at the same time he took the offensive and attacked pagan morals *(De Spectaculis, De Cultu Feminarum)*. Finally he held disputations with the heretic Hermogenes, who at that time was spreading propaganda in Carthage for an over-Platonist version of Christianity.

In 206-207 his sympathies with Montanism attracted notice; this was not something new. Tertullian had already met Montanism in Rome at the time of his conversion; his whole temperament was in tune with it. In the early days of his return to Carthage, he was welcomed by the Church as a great leader; he defended its tradition against heretics, he avenged pagan attacks, but there arrived a moment when he became aware of discord between himself and the bishops, like that which we

30. See A. Casamassa, *Scritti patristici*, II, Rome 1956, p. 109.

have seen in the case of Hippolytus. He favoured a militant Christianity which stands out against the pagan world and will have nothing to do with it, and pitilessly hurled outside the Church all who did not share his attitude. The episcopate, in Carthage as in Rome, was concerned for the flock and looked for ways of increasing it.

Tertullian then became aware of his sympathy with the Montanists; in his eyes they represented true Christianity. This sympathy appears in the works written between 207 and 211 : the *Adversus Marcionem*, the *Adversus Valentinianos*, the *De Resurrectione carnis*. One of his most curious works, the *De Pallio*, typically African in its truculent style and illnatured banter, shows his hostility to the city of Rome : as J. Moreau rightly points out, by doffing the toga and donning the *pallium* ' Tertullian hurls defiance at Rome : he intends to ridicule the orders of Imperial propaganda and issues a veritable manifesto against *Romanitas* '[31]. The *De Exhortatione castitatis* glorifies virginity as the expression of total Christianity; the *De Corona* invites christian soldiers to desert. All this went directly against government decrees, which were trying to restore the family and glorify patriotism.

We can well understand that the Church was endangered by these opinions, which had recently occasioned the edict of Severus. The bishops were trying to show that the christian faith was compatible with a just patriotism; Paul had done just that, so too had the bishops of Rome, particularly Zephyrinus, but Tertullian professed an Apocalyptic Christianity that opposed the Church to the Empire without distinction. This opposition was also found at the level of daily life. The christian must not share the life of the city : the *Apologeticum* rejected pagan culture as a whole; the *De Spectaculis* forbade christians to take part in the manifestations of collective life; the *De Cultu Feminarum* tried to prevent christian women from following the change in fashions; the *De Virginibus velandis* tried to make young women wear veils when they went out.

A conflict of attitude, like that between Tertullian and his friends in the hierarchy, has its place in the Church, where it is quite right that movements should meet and clash; the bishops' standpoint was defensible; so was Tertullian's. However, in 211 an unfortunate rupture occurred : Tertullian broke with the Church and joined the Montanist community. It was then that he published the *Acts of the Martyrs Perpetua and Felicity* in order to glorify the ideal of martyrdom; the *Scorpiacum*, where he refutes Gnostic arguments against the value of martyrdom and simultaneously discredits the episcopacy for adopting a similar

31. *La persécution du christianisme dans l'Empire romain*, p. 78.

position; the *De Fuga in persecutione* attacks christians who try not to expose themselves to martyrdom, an attitude approved by the bishops; the *Ad Scapulam* is a passionate pamphlet against the procurator Scapula during the arrest of christians in 212.

At the same time his moral doctrine became even more strict. The *De Idololatria* shows the incompatibility of Christianity and many activities, including that of teaching literature. We find a similar bent in Hippolytus[32], and we may wonder whether in the case of Hippolytus this was not also a piece of polemic. The *De Jejunio* tries to make fasting on Wednesday and Friday obligatory; the *De Monogamia* opposes remarriage. Finally his hostility was openly professed in the *De Paenitentia*. There Tertullian violently attacked the edict of Pope Callistus (217-222) admitting to penance all sins without exception; this was the same edict which Hippolytus had rejected in the *Elenchos*. Tertullian opposed it with his theory of unforgivable sins, like adultery, murder and apostasy. He accused the bishops of Rome and Carthage of making worldly christians and of compromising with evil. Tertullian shows that there was a conflict of attitudes in Africa as in Rome, but he is also of interest because with him African Christianity takes on a distinctive character. In the first place we find in him certain features typical of the Latin world which we have not yet seen in contact with Christianity. Tertullian is a Latin writer and so is an heir to Latin culture and literature. If the language he creates is original, it draws on the Latin classics. Reminiscences of Lucretius have been found in his writings, and he quotes Lucretius in the *De Anima;* Lucretius was in favour at that time, but Tertullian seems to have had a special interest in him, for we do not find this influence in Tertullian's contemporary, Minucius Felix[33].

In the second place, Tertullian was a lawyer; he emerges as a lawyer in his way of arguing in his controversial works : thus he introduces quite a new element, different from what we find in the Greek apologists and controversialists. In the *Apologeticum* he makes a more thorough analysis of the legal position of christians and of the illegal measures taken against them. Above all, in the *De Praescriptione haereticorum*, he attacks the Gnostics and heretics in general with a strictly legal kind of argument, that of prescription : the criterion of truth is the authority of the hierarchical Church, because it is to her that Christ entrusted his message, to her Scripture originally belongs, it is the Church who

32. *La liturgie d'Hippolyte*, p. 127-136.

33. J.-W.-Ph. Borleffs, 'Tertullian und Lucrez ', *Philologische Wochenschrift*, 52 (1932), p. 350-352; H. Hagendahl, *Latin Fathers and the Classics*, Göteberg 1958, p. 79-81.

is heir to the Apostles. This type of argument became a feature of the Latin world.

Tertullian introduced to theology a legal vocabulary, which remains a characteristic of western theology and creates a gulf between it and eastern theology[34]. For example he represents God, in his relations with man, as the legislator who makes the law and the judge who carries it out; sin is a violation of this law, *culpa* or *reatus;* inversely, virtuous action satisfies *(satisfacit)* the law and is meritorious *(promereri);* a distinction must be drawn in God's law between precepts and counsels. Here we see the origin of the categories which were later to be incorporated into western theology; these, it is often forgotten, are linked to Tertullian's legal training and were adopted by his successors because of the Latins' predilection for law.

As well as being a writer and lawyer, Tertullian was also a philosopher; he is less profound than Origen, but more logical. Now here again he introduced a new characteristic. As we have seen, the philosophy of the Greek Apologists was Middle Platonism; it is true that one also finds expressions borrowed from Stoicism, but these had been adopted by Middle Platonism of the day. Tertullian too had studied Middle Platonism : the influence of Albinus on his thought is well attested[35]. Plato formed part of his literary culture, as with all his contemporaries, but, in contrast to the Alexandrians, Tertullian's affinities were with Stoicism, by which he was more and more influenced[36]. He was radically opposed to Alexandrian circles; he was closer to the Asiatics, but the Asiatics were not philosophers. As his latest exponent has said, ' he adopts the Irenaean notion of economy, but he also tries to introduce contemporary Stoicism into the edifice of theology '[37].

There are many examples of this. In the *De Testimonio animae* Tertullian says that he is going to bring forward a new argument regarding all man's natural knowledge of God. He is clearly claiming to be different from the writers who preceded him, Justin and Clement of Alexandria. Now the argument he introduces is that conscience gives to man a sense that allows him to form an idea of God. This theory comes from Chrysippus; it came to Tertullian by way of Seneca, *Seneca noster,* as he calls him[38]. Tertullian's psychology, as expressed in the *De Anima,*

34. P. Vitton, *I concitti juridici nelle opere di Tertulliano,* Rome 1924.
35. J.-H. Waszink, *Tertulliani De Anima,* Amsterdam 1947, p. 41-44.
36. See N. Spanneut, *Le Stoïcisme des Pères de l'Église, de Clément de Rome à Clément d'Alexandrie,* Paris 1957, p. 425; H. Fine, *Die Terminologie der Jenseitsvorstellungen bei Tertullian,* Bonn 1958, p. 77-79.
37. S. Otto, *op. cit.,* p. 11.
38. C. Tibiletti, *De Testimonio animae : Introduzione, Testo e Commento,* Turin 1959, p. 31.

with its notion that the soul is corporeal, is borrowed from the Stoic Soranus, to whom he refers explicitly, and it is radically opposed to Platonism. In a more general way, we may say that the notion of *natura* is the key to his theology[39], a notion which dominates Stoic thinking.

But if he introduces a new tradition — Latin, legal and Stoic — into Christianity, Tertullian is not servile in his method, like Minucius Felix. In the matter of language he does not depend closely on classical models, although he remains loyal to the precepts of oratory. As Christine Mohrmann has clearly shown, ' he utilised the riches of the language as spoken in christian communities, thus becoming not the creator of the christian idiom but the great initiator who introduced the christians' idiom, so revolutionary and highly untraditional, into Latin literature '[40]. This again set the west and the east apart. Christian Latin was to remain a living language, in touch with the people's way of speaking; christian Greek was to remain fixed in its imitation of classical models.

The same is true of his thought. He draws on Stoicism, but does so freely, rejecting Stoic theories opposed to the Faith, more radically than Origen rejects Platonist theories. And so at the very beginning he gives Latin theology a firm foundation such as Origenism for long prevented Greek theology from achieving. His vocabulary is often legal, but his thought rarely so — it is his readers who were later to take his images too literally. He is concerned to express christian dogma with exactitude. For that he takes words where he finds them, from the Stoics and also from legal language and current usage.

39. S. Otto, *op. cit.*, p. 11.
40 C. Mohrmann, *Études sur le latin des chrétiens*, p. 146.

CHAPTER XII

CHRISTIAN SOCIETY
IN THE THIRD CENTURY

THE third century marks a definite step forward in the development of christian life. Freed from its Jewish context, Christianity was now expanding in the Graeco-Roman world; it was faced with a new situation, both as regards the obstacles it encountered and the values taken for granted. The Church also extended its sphere of influence considerably; it could now claim to be a great people. This expansion implied an organisation, which was not required in the early days, and the obligation to take account of the important social differences appearing in the christian community. We shall now study the chief characteristics of this change : the organisation of the catechumenate, the discipline of penance and the formation of Christian society.

1. The Organisation of the Community

The works of Clement of Alexandria, Tertullian, Origen and Hippolytus provide a collection of documents which give us a clear idea of the state of Church institutions at this date. The first characteristic is the importance of the catechumenate. In Justin's day those who wished to prepare for baptism found what instruction they could, either with individuals or by attending lectures, like those of Justin, or by reading. Things had changed by the beginning of the third century. Origen explains that after an initial testing period, future christians entered the catechumenate, during which they received instruction and practised the Christian life; then, when they had shown that they were sufficiently prepared, they took a second step and received direct preparation for baptism. This second step was considered part of baptismal initiation. Origen adds that certain christians examined those who presented themselves at the beginning of each stage[1].

1. *Contr. Cels.*, III, 51.

There are details of the same institution in the *Apostolic Tradition* by Hippolytus of Rome. The work exists in four different versions, but it is possible to make out the parts that are early; it reflects the discipline of Rome at the beginning of the third century. The candidate for the catechumenate is introduced by certain christians, who are his godparents, and he is examined by Doctors, that is to say by those responsible for the catechumens. He is questioned about the motives for his conversion, his legal status and his profession. Hippolytus gives an interesting list of professions which the candidate is obliged to renounce, such as soldiering or teaching literature. If the candidate passes this examination he is admitted to the catechumenate, which lasts three years, but can be shortened. During this time instruction is given by the catechist, either a layman or cleric; this ends with prayer, the kiss of peace which men give to other men, and women to other women, and the laying-on of hands by the catechist.

At the end of this time the catechumens, in Latin *audientes*, became those who are going to be enlightened (φωτιζόμενοι, photizomenoi) : the Latins called them *electi* or *competentes*. This was the immediate preparation for baptism; we do not know how long it lasted. It was inaugurated with an examination of how far each catechumen had led a christian life during the catechumenate. From now on there was a daily meeting with exorcism and laying-on of hands, and on the Friday and Saturday before baptism the candidates fasted. On the Saturday there was a solemn exorcism by the bishop, accompanied by an *exsufflatio* on the face and a *signatio* on the brow, ears and nose. In the evening there was a vigil, with reading and instruction, at the end of which baptism was administered.

If we compare this discipline with what we find in Judaeo-Christian books, we see that the important feature is the establishment of a rank of catechumens in the strict sense, that is to say an intermediary stage between the simple desire to become a christian and admission to direct preparation. This intermediary stage was a testing time, when the candidate's aptitude for leading the christian life was studied and his faith weighed up. Its long duration may surprise us, but if we read the works of Origen or Tertullian we see that a serious test was indispensable before admission to baptism; perhaps some people were admitted too quickly. The existence of the catechumenate is attested by Tertullian for Africa, and by the *Didascalia Apostolorum* and the Pseudo-Clementine writings for Syria. There the distinction made between catechumens and *electi* is not explicitly made, but Tertullian speaks on the one hand of the catechumenate and on the other of the

PLATE 15. CONSTANTINE I. FRAGMENT OF THE COLOSSAL STATUE FROM THE BASILICA ON THE FORUM; ROME, PALAZZO DEI CONSERVATORI

This portrait of Constantine and the two other Imperial portraits that follow it, tell as much about the imperial position and authority in the 'Christiana Tempora' as they do about the physical characteristics of the individual emperors. This Emperor with his fixed, frontal gaze, is remote and immovable. He has been removed from the world of ordinary mortals. The physical size of the statue alone must have helped to create this impression, since the bust shown here is itself 8 feet high, and the statue to which it belonged must have been over 30 feet.

Photo : Hirmer Fotoarchiv, Munich.

THE IMPERIAL IMAGE: II

PLATE 16.   THEODOSIUS I WITH HONORIUS AND ARCADIUS; SILVER MISSORIUM, 388, MADRID
ACADEMY

The process noted in the previous picture is even more apparent in this silver *missorium* made in 388 to celebrate the tenth anniversary of Theodosius' reign. The Emperor, enthroned in the centre, is by far the largest figure. The contrast between him and the little official to whom he hands a diptychal *codicillus* is especially clear. Again there is the fixed gaze, giving an impression of remoteness and superhuman strength, and this impression is enhanced by the addition of a halo, a sign not of sanctity but of royalty. This particular *missorium* gives perhaps the clearest insight into the understanding of the emperor's position as it developed in the 4th and 5th centuries. His gesture is that of a mediator, of one who hands his truth to ordinary mortals from his own vantage point at the juncture of two worlds. (Cf. Plates 18 and 33.)

Photo : Hirmer Fotoarchiv, Munich.

PLATE 17. JUSTINIAN I WITH BISHOP
MAXIMIANUS; DETAIL FROM MOSAIC ON
NORTH-EAST WALL OF APSE IN S. VITALE,
RAVENNA, 547

The church of S. Vitale was built some
time after 525 and was dedicated in 547
by Bishop Maximianus during the reign
of Justinian I. Here Justinian is shown
carrying a eucharistic offering in the
company of Maximianus and several cour-
tiers, of whom the one in this detail may
be Julianus Argentarius who financed the
building of S. Vitale. Note that the halo
is given to the Emperor and not to the
Bishop. The main significance of the
mosaic is its presence in the church at all;
by portraying the Emperor, the intention
was to seal his presence and his 'genius'
in the Church. The relevance of the portrait and of the understanding lying
behind it, to icons is clear (cf. plates 34, 40).
The Bishop too is given a prominent
place in this mosaic, since he alone has his
name inscribed above his head. (On the
importance of the bishop in the Byzantine
Empire, see ch 33.)

Photo : Hirmer Fotoarchiv, Munich.

PLATE 18

Christus Legem Dat; MOSAIC FROM APSE OF THE SOUTH AMBULATORIUM IN S. CONSTANZA, ROME, SECOND HALF OF 4TH CENTURY

Christ, enthroned on the globe, hands the Law to Peter with his right hand. Here is the same fixed, frontal gaze, the halo, and the general impression of remoteness and strength noted in the imperial portraits, and it is clear that the portrait of Christ is influenced by the late Roman understanding and portrayals of the emperor. Compare this mosaic with the central panel of the Junius Bassus sarcophagus (Plate 23) where the beardless Christ stands very close to Peter and Paul and has much more in common with his companions than the Christ in this mosaic has with the humble and submissive Peter in front of him.

Photo: Alinari.

immediate preparation for baptism[2]. What is not stated is the duration of these two periods.

The administration of baptism is on the whole similar to what we have found in the previous century. Baptism is given by a triple immersion accompanied by a triple profession of faith; it is surrounded by subsidiary rites : anointing, clothings, a meal of honey and milk, the drinking of water, but a number of details are given regarding the arrangement of the ceremony, which the brief indications in the earlier documents do not mention, or which have been added. The *Apostolic Tradition* is here our chief source, in its various versions. Children are baptised first; this is positive evidence of the baptism of children : we find it in Origen and it goes back to apostolic times. It is in the fourth century that the practice for a time becomes less frequent[3]. Only Tertullian has doubts about it, but Jeremias has shown that these doubts related only to children of pagan parents.

Women have to let down their hair and take off their jewels. Before baptism the bishop consecrates a kind of holy oil and pronounces an exorcism over another kind of oil, and two deacons carry these oils on each side of the priest. The first rite is the renunciation of Satan; there is a reference to this in Origen, Tertullian and Hippolytus; the candidate faces west; then comes the anointing with consecrated oil; the candidate then enters the church; the bishop lays his hand on the baptised person, pours the consecrated oil on his head and makes the sign of the cross on his brow. This rite, separate from baptism, is a sacrament in itself. The baptised person then prays for the first time with the faithful and receives the kiss of peace.

Then comes the presentation of the offerings to the bishop by the deacons; he consecrates the bread and wine; he also blesses the milk and honey mixed together, a symbol of Christ's flesh, and also the water, as a sign of purification. Then he distributes the consecrated bread, and the deacons offer the faithful the three cups of water, milk and wine, from which they drink. We find here the old Judaeo-Christian rite of milk and honey, and that of the cup of water. The priest or bishop accompanies these rites with an explanation, which is the homily we have mentioned. There is, however, no longer any sign of the meal, which survived in Judaeo-Christianity; there is no question, either, of crowns. The most interesting point is the sharp distinction between the post-baptismal chrismal anointing of the whole body and the sacramental anointing which is distinct from the baptismal rites.

2. *De Bapt.*, XX, 1.
3. See J. Jeremias, *Die Kindertaufe in den ersten drei Jahrhunderten*, Göttingen 1958.

Besides the initiation, in the third century we find the reconciliation assuming greater importance. Two different problems arise here : the first is that of the rites of reconciliation; the second is that of the cases where reconciliation must be allowed : this is the point on which advocates of strictness and advocates of moderation clash. Origen, Hippolytus and Tertullian are our chief sources. Reconciliation is not only a legal act but a sacrament in the true sense; every grave sin, public or private, is considered to come into its sphere; if it is private, it implies confession to the priest. Then comes public exclusion from the community, during which the guilty person belongs to the group of penitents; exclusion is more or less long according to the gravity of the sins, and it can be shortened if the penitent shows signs of a deeper conversion. Then there is a public readmission, which constitutes the sacrament, and which seems to include a laying-on of hands and perhaps an anointing with exorcised oil[4].

We may note that at this time the discipline of penance was considered as being parallel to that of the catechumenate and very similar to it[5]. In both cases there was a period of trial, before admission or re-admission. In the *De Poenitentia* Tertullian stresses the parallel between the two disciplines. Reconciliation probably took place at Easter, like admission to baptism. The requirements for reconciliation were of course more exacting, for the guilty person had shown that he was not capable of leading a christian life and assurances had to be given that his conversion was serious.

On the question of the conditions of reconciliation a great debate arose at the beginning of the third century in which Hippolytus, Tertullian, Origen and Callistus took part. The first question was that of the requirements for reconciliation; Tertullian gives an implacable description of what the penitent's state must be in order to merit reconciliation. Others were less severe without, however, laying themselves open to charges of laxity; the question was only one of degree. Much more important was whether penance could be administered more than once. Tertullian, Hippolytus and Origen were unanimous in saying that it could be administered only once, and this seems to have been the usual practice at that time. Finally, there was the problem of whether all sins could be remitted by the Church in the sacrament of penance or whether only some could be remitted : this was the main point at issue. Tertullian considered adultery, murder and apostasy as unforgiveable, whereas the majority of the bishops denied this. A dispute of this kind had

4. Origen, *Hom. Lev.*, VIII, 11.
5. See *Didasc.*, II, 41, 2.

already arisen at the end of the second century among the bishops of Pontus, and Dionysius of Corinth had decided it in favour of the more indulgent opinion[6].

The organisation of the hierarchy was now more uniform. Besides the *Apostolic Tradition* and the *Didascalia Apostolorum* we have an ordination ritual inserted in the Pseudo-Clementine writings. We find everywhere three chief ranks : the episcopate, the presbyterate and the diaconate. The bishop was chosen by the people, and he was ordained by those bishops who were present; the priests were ordained by the bishop, jointly with the other priests; the deacon was ordained by the bishop alone, because he was ordained to serve the bishop and not for the priesthood[7]. Besides these three, we find in nearly all the *ordines* the lector (anagnostes)[8]. In the liturgy of the Pseudo-Clementine writings he is not mentioned, but on the other hand there is an order of catechists. We may well wonder whether these were not the same group and whether the lector did not often fulfil the functions of a catechist. Usually the lector was not ordained by the laying-on of hands, but received the book, and everywhere we find ' healers ' or exorcists. Finally in 251 a letter of Pope Cornelius, quoted by Eusebius, proves the existence in Rome of doorkeepers (*HE*, VI, 43).

A special case is that of the confessors, that is to say christians who had been imprisoned for the Faith; they were a special order. According to Hippolytus, without requiring the laying-on of hands, they had attained the dignity of the priesthood; that was not true of someone who had only been ' made a mockery of '; he had to receive the laying-on of hands in order to attain the priesthood. Even in the first case it is probable, as Dom Botte has shown, that they received a dignity equal to that of the priests, but not priestly powers. In any case in Africa confessors made intercessions but did not exercise powers of absolution. In Rome, according to Pope Cornelius's letter, they did not belong to the hierarchy.

A final question is that of the orders of women. The oldest was that of widows. At the beginning of the third century it had an important place. The *Apostolic Tradition* mentions the widows immediately after the deacons; it says they are instituted, not ordained. Clement of Alexandria and Origen also place widows in the hierarchy[9]. Their function was to pray and visit the sick; widows belonged to the early

6. See P. Nautin, *Lettres et écrivains des IIe et IIIe siècles*, p. 24-26.
7. *Hom.*, III, 50-79; *Rec.*, III, 65-66; *Epist. Clem.*, 7. See G. Strecker, *Das Juden-christentum in den Pseudoklementinen*, Berlin 1958, p. 105-113.
8. See A. Quacquarelli, *Retorica e Liturgia antenicena*, Rome 1950, p. 37-57.
9. *Ped.*, III, 12, 97; *Orat.*, XXVIII, 4.

Judaeo-Christian structure. But at this period the order of virgins tended to assume greater importance; they are mentioned in all the versions of the *Apostolic Tradition*. The Pseudo-Clementine writings do not mention them, but in this respect they were old-fashioned. This promotion of the virgins was linked with the important place given to virginity and at the same time with the fact that it was a special vocation.

Finally, in the middle of the third century, we find deaconesses appearing; their beginnings stemmed back to apostolic times, but it was in the third century that this order became important and replaced that of widows; it was linked to the deacons, and through them to the bishop. The most notable evidence of this promotion of the deaconesses is the *Didascalia Apostolorum*. The deaconesses are a parallel order with the deacons; they replace the latter in ministering to women : visiting the sick, baptismal anointing. The deaconess must also look after women neophytes, instruct them and encourage them. There seems at this period to have been an ordination of deaconesses with a laying-on of hands.

The life of the community included a number of assemblies, the most important being the Eucharist, which seems to have been celebrated only on Sunday. The Eucharist was preceded by prayers, which were intercessions for the Church, and by the kiss of peace; the bread and wine were presented by the deacons to the bishop. There is no reference to an offering made by the faithful in the liturgy itself. The celebrant laid his hands on the offerings and inaugurated the consecratory prayer by the dialogue which is still used in the Roman liturgy today. The prayer preserved for us by Hippolytus includes the thanksgiving for the Incarnation, the words of institution, the commemoration of the Passion and the Resurrection, the invocation of the Holy Spirit that he may come down on the community, and the final doxology. The Eucharistic bread was distributed to the faithful, who received it in a jar and took it away. This seems to be attested by Origen also[10].

But as well as the Eucharistic assembly on Sunday, there were meetings for instruction, and these seem to have been daily. Hippolytus says that the deacons and priests must gather every day in the place designated by the bishop, instruct those assembled and pray. In Origen's *Homilies*, given in Caesarea, we have a precious document for these daily teaching conferences. First came the reading of a passage from Scripture; this reading was uninterrupted. Origen comments only on certain passages and tries to draw a moral from the text, hence misusing

10. *Hom. Ex.*, XIII, 3.

allegorism, but this misuse does not prevent the *Homilies* from being rich in spiritual teaching.   The audience was composed of men, women and children, baptised people and catechumens; they were more or less numerous, more or less attentive; Origen chides those who leave before the end and those who gossip in the corners[11].

The *Apostolic Tradition* also speaks of other assemblies.   There was the evening assembly, at the hour when lamps were lit, when the bishop, or the man taking his place, gave thanks for the day's gifts. There were meals presided over by the bishop — agapes — preceded by a blessing and followed by the singing of psalms and blessings of the cup[12]; we have already met this kind of meal among the Judaeo-Christians on Easter night; it had now disappeared from the Paschal vigil; it was entirely separated from the Eucharist, but it survived as an independent form.   There were also meals offered to the widows, where we again find traces of a very old custom, mentioned in the *Acts of the Apostles.*

With the growth of the Church the organisation of the community gave rise to problems.   In the middle of the century Origen echoes this development; he says that the number of christians has grown considerably but the standard has gone down : ' In truth, if we judge matters according to reality and not according to numbers, according to people's dispositions and not according to the crowds who gather, we shall see that we are not believers '[13].   Origen was an exact contemporary of this development; his youth corresponded to the period described by Tertullian and Hippolytus; he was involved in the persecutions under Septimus Severus; his manhood coincided with the expansion of the Church under the last of the Severi; he shows us christians immersed in worldly affairs and neglecting to attend services[14]; even when they attended church they busied themselves with other things[15]; they had the Faith, but their behaviour was pagan[16].   New converts received a poor welcome from traditionally christian groups.

2.   The Origins of Christian Art

We have described the structure of the christian community at the beginning of the third century; now we must say something about its framework.   At the beginning, christians met in a room put at their disposal by the owner of the house; this room may sometimes have

11. *Hom. Ex.*, XII, 3.
12. See also Tertullian, *Apol.*, XXXIX, 16-19.
13. *Hom. Lev.*, IV, 3.
14. *Hom. Gen.*, X, 1.
15. *Hom. Ex.*, III, 1.
16. *Hom. Jos.*, X, 1.

been set apart for worship; for more important gatherings a christian would offer his whole house. There is an example of this in a passage of the *Clementine Recognitions* (IV, 6), which belongs to the oldest part of the work and can therefore be treated as evidence for the situation at the end of the second century. A certain Paron puts his house *(aedes)* at the disposal of St Peter, as well as its inner garden, which could hold five hundred persons.

But the beginning of the third century was an important milestone : we begin to find references to buildings consecrated to worship. This change corresponds to the relatively peaceful period when Zephyrinus and Callistus were Popes; we know that at this time the Church possessed its own cemeteries, since Zephyrinus entrusted Callistus, then only a deacon, with the administration of a cemetery of this kind; probably the same was true of buildings for worship; there is a reference to this in the *Octavius* of Minucius Felix, where he speaks of *sacraria* (IX, 1); the word can only mean sacred place. Tertullian, for his part, writes in a puzzling passage : ' Our dove dwells in a simple house, always on a high place, openly and in full daylight '[17]. The dove symbolises the Church, the community, and the passage describes the place where it gathers. There are similar references in Clement of Alexandria[18], and Origen[19].

Are there any traces of these early ' churches '? One of them which can be dated with great certainty is the church of Dura Europos, built before 256; an interesting point is that it does not differ in structure from the dwelling houses which surround it, so it is a dwelling house transformed into a church. This is the kind of development we have found in other spheres. The building is constructed round a square courtyard; on the south side a large rectangular room was the place of worship, and on the north side a small rectangular room was transformed into a baptistery; frescoes have been found there which we will discuss later; the rest of the house probably served for ecclesiastical administration and for the bishop's lodgings. The basilica of Amwas (Emmaus, Nicopolis) was built during the reign of Constantine on the site of a Roman villa, the plan of which was partly followed, but extended on the long side; this Roman villa may have been turned into a church about 220[20]. The same is true of a large house of the Augustan period, rearranged at the beginning of the third century, when the building of

17. *Ad. Valent.*, 3.
18. *Strom.*, VII, 5, 29, 4.
19. *Orat.*, 31, 5.
20. See L. H. Vincent and F. M. Abel, *Emmaüs. Sa basilique et son histoire*, Paris 1932, p. 250-262.

the basilica of St Clement of Rome began. Again, at Aquileia, the basilica built under Constantine replaced a house adapted as a place of worship, where mosaics of the end of the third century have been found.

This evidence allows us to sketch the situation at the beginning of the third century. What characterises this period is the adaptation of private houses as places of worship, but it would not seem as though any buildings were erected for the express purpose of worship; the few texts which might suggest this are doubtful, and the archaeological data do not suggest that there were any basilicas at that date. The position changed in the second half of the third century; the building of churches then began, and they took a form different from private houses. So we cannot say that there was such a thing as christian architecture in the first half of the third century; on the other hand, it seems clear that at the end of the second century the christian communities owned houses set aside for worship and no longer gathered in private houses.

Parallel with the question of churches is that of christian cemeteries, inasmuch as these were used as meeting-places, especially during times of persecution. Here again we must follow the development closely, although it raises problems still in dispute. We will turn our attention chiefly to the Church in Rome, about which there is most information in this matter, and take account both of the archaeological data and literary sources. Of course we can only indicate the main points. The earliest period is that opened up by excavations on Vatican Hill; christian tombs are found side by side with pagan tombs in a cemetery on the surface. This is the situation at the end of the first century, and it is possible that the tomb of the Apostle Peter is among the christian tombs. There are no Christian cemeteries yet.

The second century shows innovations. On the one hand we find christian family hypogea or subterranean tombs, belonging to rich families; the fact is indisputable but the actual dating of these hypogea is a matter for discussion. In the Catacomb of Domitilla, the hypogeum of the Flavii goes back to the end of the second century, whereas Ferlini considers the crypt of Ampliatus one of the *nuclei* of the catacomb and dates it to the beginning of the second century[21], but that is probably too early. The same is true of the crypt of the Aurelii, which may belong to the end of the second century. The crypt of Lucina on the Appian Way, in the neighbourhood of the Catacomb of Callistus, belongs to the same period. The crypt of the popes is not earlier than 235, but it is the development of an earlier hypogeum, probably belonging to the beginning

21. ' La cripta di Ampliato nel cemeterio di Domitilla ', *Riv. Arch. Crist.*, 28 (1952), p. 77-117.

of the third century; the same would appear to be true of the *cappella greca* in the Catacomb of Priscilla.

Besides these hypogea, belonging to families, the second half of the second century witnesses the appearance of christian cemeteries; their origin is disputed. Were they private estates belonging to christian families, who put them at the Church's disposal? Did they belong to associations of freedmen, according to Rossi's theory, which has often been advanced since? Or were they the property of corporate funerary bodies, like pagan corporate funerary bodies, and hence raising no special legal problem? At what period did the Church directly take possession of the cemeteries and administer them? These hypotheses are not mutually exclusive; various arrangements may have existed side by side. All the same, it seems clear that at the end of the second century the Church had at its disposal cemeteries which directly belonged to it. The passage in Hippolytus saying that Zephyrinus put Callistus in charge of the cemeteries does not imply an innovation but seems to assume that cemeteries belonging to the Church were already in existence.

Another question concerns the topography of these cemeteries. Attention in the past has been almost exclusively centred on what is the best preserved form of cemetery, that is to say the subterranean galleries generically termed catacombs (although the word in the strict sense means only a fixed *area*, that situated ' *ad catacumbas* '), which corresponds to the site of the cemetery of Callistus, but it is possible that the earliest cemeteries in Rome were not of this kind. Excavations in the area of Priscilla have revealed a cemetery at surface level. Pope Zephyrinus, who died in 217, was buried in his own cemetery, in a tomb on the surface. This raises the problem : at what date did underground catacombs begin to develop? The answer would seem to be : under the pontificate of Zephyrinus; a sign of the growth of the christian community at that time. Callistus, in fact, may have been named by Zephyrinus to take charge of the great work involved.

If the end of the second century and the beginning of the third reveal little in the way of christian architecture, it is otherwise with the decoration of places of worship. At this period we discover frescoes, mosaics and christian sarcophagi. The *cappella greca*, in the Catacomb of Priscilla, and the crypt of Lucina, which is nearby, have their walls covered with frescoes, so does the baptistery of Dura at the beginning of the third century. The sarcophagi of the Via Salaria Nova and of Santa Maria Antica go back to the end of the second century. Here, even more than with architecture, it is difficult to fix dates, but we can be sure of certain terminal limits, and the period under consideration constitutes a remarkable whole.

Moreover there exist pagan works of the time which provide a useful comparison. The first christian works were not independent of the general artistic movement; their decorative elements were borrowed from it. We find everywhere in christian art a whole group of motifs : trellises, flowers, masks, dolphins, butterflies, cupids, birds and fish; they are found in the pagan tombs of the Vatican, in the synagogue of Dura and in the Catacombs of Domitilla. Even in the depiction of Gospel or Old Testament scenes christian artists were inspired by familiar images : the Good Shepherd was copied from the Greek Orpheus, Jonah under his ricinus was modelled on the sleeping Endymion, Christ teaching was inspired by the μουσικὸς ἀνήρ *(mousicos aner)*. The theme of the ship in the midst of the sirens and that of the fisherman casting his net were borrowed from pagan art and given a christian meaning. The variations in pagan art are found in christian art : the Alexandrian style, the Parthian art of eastern Syria and the Roman style — all are different. There are also changes in time : the style of the Antonine period differs from that of the Severi.

This early christian art expressed christian life at the time : the images that were specially familiar to it. A comparison between the decorations and the literary documents is absolutely decisive : we find in the paintings on the hypogea and the sculptures on sarcophagi the great themes proclaimed in catechesis. We have only to compare the *De Baptismo* by Tertullian, the *Demonstration* by Irenaeus and the *Paschal Homily* by Melito with our monuments, and we find the great figures of the Old Testament : Noah, Isaac, David, Daniel and Jonah; the most significant scenes of the New Testament : the adoration of the Magi, the baptism of Jesus, the woman of Samaria, the raising of Lazarus; and the great symbols of the Church : the ship, tree, garden and tower. It is sometimes more difficult to know what aspect of the christian mystery is signified : is it the life of Christ, the sacraments or the after-life? It is not surprising that in certain cases we should be doubtful, for the writings offer several interpretations, but in other cases, for example that of certain sacramental symbols, the meaning is certain.

The best approach, therefore, is to take the various themes and show their meaning in the light of contemporary writings. Let us start with the Old Testament. The theme of original sin appears in the baptistery of Dura Europos, at the beginning of the third century, with Adam and Eve beside the tree. We may note that the contrast between Adam's plight and the situation of a catechumen was a specific theme in later Syrian baptismal catechesis. We find it also on the vault of the vestibule of the catacombs of St. Januarius in Naples, at the end of the second century. But it is noteworthy that, generally speaking, we do not find scenes representing the first chapters of Genesis; this seems connected with the essentially prophetic and typological manner in which the Old Testament was used.

It is this typology that we usually find. Noah in the ark appears in the *cappella greca* : he is one of the great types of man's salvation; the scene may have either a baptismal or eschatological meaning. Its typological meaning appears in Rome in the time of Justin. Abraham's sacrifice is found in the *cappella greca* : as early as Melito it is used as a figure of Christ's sacrifice[22]. We may note that it is found at Dura, in the synagogue. In the Moses cycle, the crossing of the Red Sea, an ancient figure of baptism, is absent. On the other hand, the theme of water springing from the rock is one of the most common. We find it in the *cappella greca* and the chapels of the sacraments in the Catacomb of Callistus; it becomes more frequent during the third century and it is certain that it had a baptismal meaning. Its absence in the baptistery of Dura may be explained by the fact that the Syrian tradition, stemming from St Paul, gave to the incident a eucharistic, not a baptismal, meaning.

David is a figure of salvation in his battle with Goliath; this was the theme of a work by Hippolytus of Rome at the beginning of the third century. We are not surprised to find it in the baptistery of Dura, but it does not appear at Rome in the fourth century. Jonah, on the other hand, is one of the most popular figures; his meaning is fixed by the New Testament; he is the great type of the resurrection. He is found in the crypt of Lucina; in the chapels of the sacraments A1, A2 and A6; in the room of the Annunziata in the Cemetery of Priscilla; and on the sarcophagi of the second and third centuries. His meaning may be either baptismal or eschatological. Stuiber's theory, which denies that Jonah or any other miracles of deliverance can be taken in the latter sense[23], has been justly refuted by Bruyne[24]. We may well think that the artists' predilection for this theme, and for that of the shepherd, arises from the fact that with these themes could be incorporated traditions from pagan art, which was familiar with the ship, the sea monster and the figure sleeping under a tree.

One of the most important cycles is that of Daniel. First, it shows Daniel delivered from the lions, which belongs to the themes of deliverance already traditional in Judaism. We find it in the *cappella greca*, and in the crypt of Lucina, at the end of the second century, and in the catacomb

22. See D. Lerch, *Isaaks Opferung*, Tübingen 1950, p. 27-30.
23. *Refrigerium interim*, Bonn 1957, p. 138.
24. *Riv. Arch. Crist.*, 34 (1958), p. 87-119.

of Domitilla, in the third. The same is true of Susanna delivered from the elders; Hippolytus considers her a figure of baptism in his *Commentary on Daniel*. The theme may be either baptismal or eschatological; it is found in the *cappella greca*, and in an arcosolium (tomb) of the third century, in the Cemetery of Callistus. We may note that this is one of the oldest subjects, that later it almost totally disappears and that it is special to Rome; this gives a hint about the origins of the Roman community and its very marked Jewish character. Finally, a third theme is that of the three children in the furnace, a theme of deliverance that is also of Jewish origin. It is found in the *cappella greca* and on several third century carcophagi.

This first group corresponds to the Old Testament figures that generally appear in catechesis. Besides figures (τύποι, *tupoi*), catechesis made use of collections of prophecies drawn from the Pentateuch, the Psalms and the Prophets, grouped in *Testimonia*. Among the texts most often quoted we find Psalm 22, Ezekiel 47 and the prophecy of Balaam (Num 24 : 17). We find these texts illustrated by Judaeo-Christian art. The theme of the fish (Ez 47), of the star (Num 24 : 17), of the vine (Ps 79 : 9), of the heavenly chariot (Ez 3 : 4) and of the garden (Ps 22 : 2) appear both on Judaeo-Christian ossuaries in Palestine and in Judaeo-Christian writings[25]. So it is not surprising that we should find these themes developed in Hellenistic and early Roman christian art, but at the same time, as might be expected, they undergo a profound transformation. Whereas the Jewish *milieu* abhorred any representation of human beings, the Graeco-Roman *milieu* was drawn towards such representation. Nowhere else do we see so clearly the contrast of cultures in their treatment of the same themes.

Among the prophetic *Testimonia* there is the star of Jacob; the theme is reproduced in a fresco of the Catacomb of Priscilla, near the *cappella greca*, but the key representation in this sphere is that of the shepherd. It has several aspects, each with its source in the bible. In the baptistery of Dura, the shepherd is related to the fall of Adam and Eve; it is he who brings them back to Paradise. This comes from Psalm 22, which was part of the baptismal liturgy, and was to remain a common theme in the decoration of baptisteries. The picture of Paradise signifies the Church, a frequent piece of symbolism in the second and third centuries. Another theme is the shepherd carrying a lamb on his shoulders; it appears chiefly in funerary art; it may signify both the mystery of salvation in the general sense and the deliverance of the soul after death; it is found in the *cappella greca*, in Room 2 of the

25. See J. Daniélou, *Les symboles chrétiens primitifs*, Paris 1961.

Sacraments, in the oldest parts of the Catacomb of Domitilla, in the hypogeum of Lucina, in the vault of Clodius Hermes, and on a second-century sarcophagus from the Via Salaria. A final theme is that of the shepherd defending his flock against the wolf. This is found in a room of the *spelunca magna*, decorated at the beginning of the third century.

Another group is composed of New Testament representations. These, too, are depicted not for themselves but for the allusions to christian catechesis which they hold. For example, the adoration of the Magi in the *cappella greca*, which is the expression of conversion, a first step on the way to baptism. The healing of the paralytic, in the crypt of Lucina, Room A3 of the Sacraments, and the house-church of Dura, signifies the remission of sins. The woman of Samaria, in the baptistery of Dura, and Christ walking on the waters, in the same baptistery, are figures of baptism, according to the *De Baptismo* of Tertullian. The raising of Lazarus and the holy women at the tomb, in the *cappella greca*, express faith in the resurrection.

A last group of representations is also related to the stages of christian initiation, but these are direct, not symbolic. The sarcophagus from the Via Salaria, which depicts on one side a 'philosopher' with two disciples, and on the other a woman in the same attitude, seems to allude to catechesis and gives us a glimpse of the widows' role as teachers of women. Scenes of baptism are quite common. A sarcophagus of Santa Maria Antica seems to depict the stages of initiation : Jonah disgorged by the monster (faith), an orante (prayer), a philosopher (catechesis), the shepherd (salvation) and finally baptism. The crypt of Lucina and Room A2 of the Sacraments also have scenes of baptism. It is sometimes difficult to tell whether the philosopher is Christ or a catechist : for example in Room A3 of the Sacraments, where a well of living water, a figure of baptism, also appears.

The Eucharist is often depicted; sometimes there is only a basket of bread and a fish. The fish seems to show the festive and eschatological nature of the banquet, in keeping with its symbolism for Judaism. Hence too its sacramental symbolism, to show that the bread is a divine food : for example, in the crypt of Lucina. Sometimes the bread and fish are placed on a tripod and pointed out by someone : for example, in Chapel A3 of the Sacraments. We also find other scenes of a meal, with bread and fish; these are not pictures of the Eucharist, but have a symbolic meaning. It has been debated whether they show the heavenly banquet, the *refrigerium*, or a symbol of the sacramental Eucharist; it seems that in christian thought at that time the two were inseparable. A comparison with pagan works shows that the immediate symbolism is heavenly happiness, but the eucharistic connotation also seems certain.

3. The Christians and Pagan Society

Achievements at the beginning of the third century in the sphere of art are paralleled in the christians' way of life. Here again they take the practices of the Graeco-Roman world and penetrate them with a new spirit : we witness the first stages in the making of eastern and western christian civilisation, expressed in several famous passages. The oldest is the *Epistle to Diognetus*, which dates from the end of the second century. ' The christians ', writes the unknown author, ' do not set themselves apart from other men either by their vocabulary or their language or their clothes; they conform to local usage as regards food and way of life. . . They marry like everyone else, they have children, but they do not abandon their new-born babies ' (V, 1-6). We have here almost a catalogue of the various spheres in which the incarnation of Christianity is expressed in behaviour : language, dress, food, family life.

In the *Apologeticum* Tertullian develops this same idea. ' We live with you, we have the same food, the same clothes, the same way of life. We are not Brahmins or Gymnosophists from India. We frequent your forum, your market, your baths, your inns and your fairs. With you we take ship and serve as soldiers ' (XLII, 1-2). But at the same time the christians reject, in their social life, whatever is contaminated by idolatry, though in itself good : ' I do not go to the baths at dawn, during the Saturnalia, not to lose both my night and my day; instead, I take a bath at a suitable time. I do not sit down to table in the street on the feasts of Liber; yet wherever I dine, I am served food which comes from Thee ' (XLIII, 3-4). So the christian participates in family, economic and political life; but he intends to do so as a Christian.

In this sphere of the creation of christian patterns of behaviour, the beginning of the third century is of crucial importance. It was the period when christians ceased living in a small group and went out into society. The problem was to know which of society's habits they must keep and which reject; it was the task of the great christian moralists of the period, especially Clement and Tertullian, to help them to make the choice. True, their picture of pagan habits was perhaps sometimes exaggerated; it was heightened by literary devices borrowed from the Cynics' dialectic. Moreover, the ideal which they suggested to christians was somewhat unreal and certainly exceeded what the majority were capable of, but it remains true that in their books we find christian requirements at grips with the details of daily life.

Clement first of all condemns too much luxury : ' What shall we say of love of ornament, dyed materials, the vanity of colours, the luxury of jewels, goldwork, hair waved or curled, eyes mascaraed, eyebrows

plucked, rouge, ceruse, dyed hair and all these deceitful artifices[26]? '
His ideal is what is simple and natural; he is saying what the wisest
of the pagans say.   Certain points are interesting : as regards jewels,
Clement condemns their use altogether, but he allows a signet ring;
he says that men must not wear it on the second finger, which is where
women wear it, but on the little finger; the seal must depict a symbol
acceptable to christians; representations of idols, swords and bows,
and cups must be avoided; he allows a dove, fish, ship with swelling
sails, lyre, anchor and fisherman.   The same rules are found in Africa,
in the *De Cultu feminarum* of Tertullian, and in Asia about 196, in
Apollonius (*HE*, V, 18, 11).

Likewise with food, which must be simple and unaffected. ' The
devilish art of cooks ', who try to titillate one's sense of taste at the
expense of health, is condemned.   Clement denounces the various
kinds of greed; the question of wine is studied at length; the dangers
of drunkenness are denounced; examples are given, like that of Elpenor
in Homer, and of Noah in the Old Testament, but it is permissible for
wine to flow freely at banquets.   Meals raise the question of plate and
how luxurious it may be; the use of drinking cups, whether gold, silver
or encrusted with jewels, is not fitting, for it is not convenience but
vanity alone which inspires it.   Clement gives a list of the various kinds
of drinking cups.   Included in the chapter about meals are certain
amusements; drinking sessions must be avoided if they last long into the
night *(pannuchides)*, accompanied by harps, flutes, choruses, dances
and Egyptian castanets, but Clement allows the cither and lyre to be
played at christian gatherings.

Clement then gives instructions about good behaviour and deport-
ment : ' Let the christian be characterised by tranquillity, calm and
peace '.   Whistling and snapping fingers are all right for servants when
they call animals.   The question of the use of perfumes and crowns
is raised in Chapter VIII; both are forbidden.   Flowers are made to go
into bouquets or for their scent, not to be put on the head.   It is curious
that Tertullian says the same thing : ' I do not buy crowns of flowers
to adorn my head.   However, if I do buy flowers, what does it matter
how I use them?   If we use flowers made into crowns, it is our nose
that smells the scents of the crown '[27].   In this way the christian also
encourages trade.   It is only pagan practices contrary to nature that
he rejects.

Baths, spectacular shows and sports were essential parts of the pagan
world at that time; here the judgment of christian writers is more severe.

26. *Ped.*, II, 10, 104, 1.
27. *Apol.*, XLII, 6.

Apollonius proscribes them in Ephesus (*HE*, V, 18, 11). ' We frequent your baths ', writes Tertullian. But Clement points out their dangers. At the baths were found everything conducive to relaxation. Clement describes them like this : ' Well-designed, well-built buildings, crowded, covered with a curtain that allows the light to pass, with gold- and silver-fitted seats, and countless gold and silver utensils, some for the bar, others for the restaurant, others for the bath. There are also coal stoves. People go so far as to feast and get drunk while bathing '. Clement also denounces promiscuous behaviour at the baths and the fact that they were patronised by both sexes, but the bath in itself is excellent for cleanliness and health.

The rules regarding sport are interesting. A gymnasium is necessary for young people, even if there is a bath establishment adjoining. Sport is not only useful for health, but it excites eagerness and competition for physical well-being and moral health. But young girls should not take part in wrestling and running. For men there are wrestling, ball games in the open air and walking; gardening is not undignified; it is permissible also to draw water and fell trees; reading too is an exercise; as for wrestling, it must not be approached in a spirit of rivalry; fishing may be practised, as it was by St Peter, if study allows sufficient leisure, but the best kind of fishing is that taught by Jesus to his disciple : the fishing of men.

Shows give rise to more serious questions; Clement condemns their immorality. Tertullian goes even further in the *De Spectaculis :* shows are idolatrous in name, origin, accompanying rites and in the places where they are held (V, i-ix, 6). Besides idolatry they arouse passions : impurity at the theatre, cruelty at the circus (XIX, i, 5). The theatre is a parody of everything worthy of respect. ' How can the mouth which has answered Amen to God applaud the actor? How can it say εἰς αἰῶνας ἀπ' αἰῶνος *(eis aionas ap'aionos)* to anyone but Christ?' (XXV, 5). How can we linger at shows on the eve of that other show : the certain, glorious and triumphant coming of the Lord? And Tertullian describes all the pagan world, from kings to philosophers, from actors to charioteers, appearing in their misery before God's tribunal (XXX, 5).

So much for the outward framework of life. It was the very forms of social life, where Christianity encountered pagan morality, which had to be changed. First of all, the family. The christians, adopting the notion of Roman law, regarded consent as constituting marriage. They also kept the practices accompanying the pagan celebration of marriage : the importance of the veil, the reading of the contract and the joining of hands. They removed only what was specifically idolatrous : sacrifice and the reading of horoscopes. At the beginning of the third century the christians had no liturgical celebration of marriage, but they realised that they were being united before Christ, as we see in bas-reliefs where Christ is represented crowning the bride and joining the couple's hands. The bishop's blessing was often sought. Tertullian speaks of christian marriage like this : ' How can we describe the happiness of this marriage which the Church approves, which the oblation confirms, which the blessing seals, which the angels recognise, which the Father ratifies[28]? ' Here we find a whole christian liturgy being substituted for the idolatrous parts of the Roman matrimonial rites.

As regards the morality of marriage, christians were opposed to the conventional behaviour of the Roman world. Tertullian condemns divorce unreservedly, and appeals to Roman tradition ' where not one family gave notice of divorce '; now ' it has become such that women long for it '[29]. He also denounces polygamy. The point he is most insistent about is the condemnation of abortion; we also find this in Clement[30]. Clement has several pages about the dignity and respect which are the chief elements in christian love. Tertullian warns against marriages with pagans, showing the difficulties they lead to : the husband wants to organise a banquet on a day when christians fast; how will he allow his wife to leave him all night for the paschal celebrations? Or go round prisons, visiting the martyrs? What will he make of her liturgical gestures : the *signatio* of the body or the Eucharist received before a meal? What attitude will she take when her husband performs traditional rites towards the household gods[31]?

The education of children raised a very delicate problem. It was usually given by the *grammatistes*, and later by the *grammatici*, who were civil servants; but their teaching was linked with idolatry. Ad Tertullian explains in his *De Idololatria*, they taught mythology, the names and genealogies and gods. The school was decorated with a picture of the seven gods; the obol silver coin given to them by a new pupil was consecrated to Minerva, and the pagan festivals were celebrated there (X, 1-3). However, there was no question of christian children not attending school; Tertullian himself was definite on this point : ' How can we reject profane studies, without which religious studies are impossible? Without them how build up man's prudence, teach him to understand and to act, since literature is something we need all our lives? ' (X, 4). This was also the view of Clement of Alexandria, who defended the need for a literary education against its detractors.

28. *Uxor.*, II, 6.
29. *Apol.*, VI, 5-6.
30. *Ped.*, II, 10, 96, 1.
31. *Uxor.*, II, 4-6.

What course were christians to follow? Tertullian believes it impossible for a christian to teach literature, for then he was an accomplice in idolatry. The *Apostolic Tradition* prefers that anyone who has such a job should give it up, but does not force him to do so, if he has no alternative. Origen, born of christian parents, was later, at the age of eighteen, to become a teacher of literature in order to support his family, so there is a certain amount of tolerance regarding the teaching profession. As for the problem of children attending pagan schools, it was everywhere permitted; the sole proviso was that christian children should not take part in acts of idolatry, which naturally aroused many difficulties. But thereby christians gradually freed the school of idolatrous aspects and finally made it christian; the child received instruction in Christianity in his own family[32].

We have detailed information about the education of a christian child in what Eusebius tells us of Origen. He went through the usual course of studies; he went to the *grammatistes* who gave elementary lessons, then to the *grammatici*, who gave a course in humanities. Origen speaks of these studies from experience[33], but at the same time we know that Origen's father taught him Scripture from boyhood. ' Every day he made him recite and review certain passages ' (*HE*, VI, 2, 8). So a biblical education at home completed the secular education, given at school.

Economic life also raised many problems. Christians did not question the economic principles on which society was based at that time; they recognised the law of property, and admitted inequality of circumstances. Clement of Alexandria devoted a whole treatise, the *Quis dives salvetur*, to the problem of riches; he did not contest the legality of wealth, but he showed its dangers and stressed its duties. We find in Clement and Tertullian no condemnation of slavery, but only a reminder of the human and christian dignity of the slave. Christians shared in every way in the economic life of their day : ' With you we plough the land, we do business, we exchange the products of our toil. How can we be useless in your undertakings[34]? ' So manual work, trade and business were, in themselves, perfectly compatible with being a christian.

But in practice economic life as it existed at the beginning of the third century raised grave problems for the christian conscience. First of all, professional life was steeped in idolatry. Artisans were grouped

32. See H. I. Marrou, *Histoire de l'éducation dans l'antiquité*, Paris 1948, p. 425.
33. *Hom. Jud.*, VI, 2.
34. *Apol.*, XLII, 3.

in professional bodies under the patronage of a god, Hephaestus for the blacksmiths, Hermes for the merchants. Even apart from worship in the strict sense, certain professions cooperated in idolatry. This is a subject to which christian writers often return. First, there were the makers of idols — sculptors, engravers, painters :

The devil has raised up in the world makers of statues and images and all kinds of representations. In this way the art of making idols has become the source of idolatry. It matters little whether it is a sculptor who models it, a chiseller who makes it, a weaver who weaves it. It matters little what material the idol is made of : plaster, colours, stone, bronze, silver or thread. Likewise it matters little what is represented, for we must not think that idols are only shaped like human beings. Otherwise people would be less idolatrous in consecrating the image of a calf than that of a man[35].

The making of idols was not the only point in question. ' There are other trades which, although not directly connected with the making of idols, make objects without which the idols would be useless. It amounts to the same thing to build or decorate a temple, a house or a sanctuary, to roll sheets of gold or to manufacture emblems in a house ' (VIII, 1). We may note in these texts the details about making of idols and their constituent materials. But the commercial side of idolatry is more interesting; many professions had an interest in it. All the people engaged in selling pious objects in places of pilgrimage had a stake in idolatry, and we may suppose that they were concerned to preserve it. Tertullian has to explain to these artisans that they can just as well make profane objects.

There was not only manufacturing, there was also trade : ' If a man selling meat for sacrifices is converted, will you allow him to go on with his trade[36] ? ' The same applied to incense and the other exotic things used for sacrifices to idols. ' How will a christian vendor of incense, when he crosses a temple, have the face to spit on the smoking altars and extinguish them, when it is he who supplies them? ' Nevertheless, distinctions were drawn. The sin of the maker of idols was more serious than that of the vendor of perfumes, for the latter might be used as medicine, and also for christian funerals. Christians, in their economic life, were bound to abstain from all cooperation with idolatry.

Besides the problems arising from idolatry, there were others arising from immoral practices. Certain jobs were automatically ruled out — for example, that of pimp. More difficult was the question of economic

35. *Idol.*, II, 2-3.
36. *Idol.*, XI, 6.

morality. Clement of Alexandria lays down three points : never have two prices; do not take oaths in business matters; tell the truth[37]. In this he was only repeating Plato's doctrine[38]. It was natural morality which here again Christianity insisted upon. Tertullian saw the difficulty clearly; profit seemed to him immoral. He forbade loans with interest and deferred payments. Apollonius took the same attitude (*HE*, V, 19, 11), but at the same time trade is based on profit[39]. How can a christian share in the economic life of his time without being an accomplice to the moral lapses involved in it?

We find the same point of view in the sphere of civic service; the position of christians was specially critical on this point, for they were still accused of being bad citizens. It is certain that here again they were faced with the problem of idolatry : the soldier had to be present at sacrifices to the gods; the wreath of laurel awarded to him had a religious meaning; the office of magistrate entailed rites of worship, but more than anything, emperor-worship seemed to be the basis of civic life. Christians could not take part in these practices; was that a reason for them to stay out of public life? Tertullian remarks first of all that in many matters, which did not raise problems of conscience, the christians are the best citizens. They pay their taxes scrupulously, and what they refuse for the upkeep of temples is much less than what the treasury loses through frauds and false tax declarations on the part of pagans[40].

Christianity implied a civic morality, but, even apart from idolatry, was there not something incompatible in service of the state and service of Christ? The most difficult problem here was that of military service. The *Apostolic Tradition* considers that a catechumen who wants to become a soldier must be dismissed, but it says that soldiers may be baptised without leaving the colours. We know of many christian soldiers and martyrs at this period. What emerges from the writings of Tertullian and Origen is that the christian who serves in a spiritual army must not espouse the cause of this earthly life. But christians deemed it necessary that there should be soldiers to defend the Empire. Military service in itself was in no way immoral. The answer to the pagans' calumnies was to show that, far from being useless to the state, christians were the best citizens. In this way they were integrated into the Roman city, just as they had inherited Roman culture.

The present period is of great interest to the historian of christian civilisation, for although this civilisation was to triumph with Constantine,

37. *Ped.*, III, 11, 78, 4.   39. *Idol.*, XI, 1.
38. *Leg.*, XI, 917, b-c.   40. *Apol.*, XLII, 9.

its development was taking place during the time of Clement, Tertullian and Origen. It is then that Christianity came up against problems in the various spheres of human life. Christians took part in all kinds of work, but they were less and less willing to accept what seemed to them contrary to their religious faith and moral laws; hence their attempt to reject idolatrous and immoral elements and increasingly endow their work with the christian spirit. What occurred was not an unhallowing or secularisation but a steeping of family and social habits in the christian spirit while respecting their rightful qualities : the Roman law relating to the family, the Roman theory of property and Roman patriotism were retained, but instead of the old idolatry, it was now the christian spirit which inspired them.

CHAPTER XIII

ORIGEN, MANES, CYPRIAN

THE beginning of the third century was a turning-point in the history of Christianity. The last ties with Judaeo-Christianity were broken, and henceforward it was to be engaged in the Hellenistic and Roman world; but this world was varied. The middle of the third century was a period of remarkable creativity. We find movements appearing which were to continue in the Christianity of the following centuries. Three great events characterise this period: in the Greek world there was a philosophical revival, represented by Plotinus among the pagans and Origen among the christians, and the influence of these two thinkers was felt in succeeding centuries; in the Latin world Christianity underwent an extraordinary expansion, both territorial and cultural, and became differentiated from eastern Christianity; finally, the Judaeo-Christian ascetical movements stirred up various doctrines in eastern Syria, the most important being Manichaeism.

1. Origen and Plotinus

In the first half of the third century a new intellectual movement appeared in Alexandria: Neo-Platonism, which marked the end of classical thought. Its chief exponent was Plotinus, but he had a christian counterpart in Origen, whose influence extended to all later Greek theology. With him something new arose in the history of Christianity; in fact he embodied several different trends. By birth and education he belonged to the catechetical christian tradition, and his work was one of the most important formulations of that tradition. Through Alexandria he was in touch with Alexandrian and Palestinian Jewish Gnosis, which played a more important part in his work than has generally been recognised. He represents a transition from Middle Platonism to Neo-Platonism, by way of Ammonius Saccas, who was his teacher as well as having been Plotinus's teacher. These are the component parts we must first of all try to define. Then we shall be able to see the end-result and, finally, Origen's place in the third century.

We find much information about Origen in Eusebius, who was one of his successors in the didascalion of Caesarea in Palestine. He was born in 185 into a christian family[1]; we have said something about his education; he was a youth when the persecution of Severus broke out, and his father was one of its victims, in 208. It was in this Church of the martyrs that his christian sensibility was formed and he was to remain stamped by these heroic days. At the age of seventeen he found himself responsible for his mother and young brothers. A charitable lady made it possible for him to continue his studies, and in this way he was able to obtain the post of teacher of literature. At that time there was a crisis of catechists in the Church of Alexandria and certain candidates for baptism came to him; Bishop Demetrius asked him to give up his profession and devote himself to catechesis. He sold his secular books and gave all his time to the study of Scripture and teaching catechumens; the latter were specially persecuted and Origen helped them.

But his experience as a catechist brought him up against a new problem; his audience was composed of ' heretics, men trained in Greek studies and philosophers ' (*HE*, VI, 19, 12). He realised that in order to be able to take part in discussions with them, he would have to master their teaching : ' I did that in imitation of Pantaenus, who, before our time, steeped himself in the Greeks ' (VI, 19, 13). To do so, he had to get rid of the burden of elementary catechesis; this he entrusted to Heraclas, while he himself resumed his studies. Until then he had not studied philosophy, his studies had been purely literary, and he was going to complete them. This philosophy was contemporary philosophy. Origen studied text-books where the philosophical opinions of various schools were listed, and he was drawn towards Middle Platonism. His thought shows clear links with Maximus of Tyre, Albinus and Plutarch.

But Origen did not only study books. He was the pupil of a man who played a decisive role in the intellectual life of his day : Ammonius Saccas. On this point we have the explicit evidence of Porphyry, as recorded by Eusebius (*HE*, VI, 19, 3). Now Ammonius Saccas was also Plotinus's teacher, some years later. We should like to know who this Ammonius was, but unfortunately our information about his teaching is confined to two references, one in Nemesius, the other in Photius. From these the most diverse pictures have been built up : Heinemann

1. See J. Daniélou, *Origène*, Paris 1958, p. 2-40.

considers him a great Platonist, Seeberg and Benz an Indian missionary who had settled in Alexandria, Dörrie a Pythagorean wonder-worker and ecstatic, Langerbeck an avant-garde christian theologian. He does seem to have been a christian — Prophyry's information on this point seems correct — but he had strayed from Christianity.

Can we at least say something about the relations between Origen and Plotinus? Porphyry several times mentions Origen and Plotinus together, for example, in his *Life of Plotinus* he writes : ' Herennius, Origen and Plotinus agreed to keep secret the teaching of Ammonius ' (III). Further on, he says that Origen came to attend one of Plotinus's courses in Rome (XIV). But is this Origen the same as ours? Cadiou and Hanson say Yes, but the identity is now universally rejected. Dodds, Puech, Dörrie, Langerbeck and Weber agree in thinking that Porphyry is speaking of two different persons, both disciples of Ammonius[2]. So we cannot be sure that our Origen ever met Plotinus. He was, moreover, Plotinus's senior by more than twenty years and his thought is totally independent of Plotinus's, although it represents a parallel development. It is this comparison which reveals something of the influence of the master they had in common.

This philosophical training allowed Origen to carry out the project which Pantaenus and Clement had realised before him : a kind of university, the didascalion, where all human knowledge would be used to attain greater understanding of the word of God. He taught there from 212 until 231. This was also the period when he wrote his early works, which reflected his theological and exegetical teaching. The didascalion also published books. His friend Ambrose provided for the upkeep of seven tachygraphers who took turns to write at Origen's dictation, copyists and young women trained in calligraphy to make copies (*HE*, VI, 23, 1). Finally Origen visited Palestine where his friend, Bishop Alexander of Jerusalem, invited him to comment on Scripture in the christian assembly (*HE*, VI, 19, 15). Origen then delivered his first homilies. During a second stay, in 230, he was ordained priest by the Bishop of Caesarea, Theoctistus.

In 231, this decision called down on Origen a condemnation by the Bishop of Alexandria, Demetrius. Origen was declared unworthy to teach and driven from Alexandria. He retired to Caesarea, where the Bishop, Theoctistus, was his friend, and he made this town an intellectual centre of great importance. It was there that his pupils included two Cappadocians : Gregory, future Bishop of Neo-Caesarea,

2. See E. R. Dodds, ' Numenius and Ammonius ', in ' Les Sources de Plotin ', *Entretiens sur l'Antiquité classique*, V, Geneva (1960), p. 1-33; K. O. Weber, ' Origenes der Neuplatoniker ', Munich 1962.

and his brother, probably attracted by Alexander, who had been Bishop in Cappadocia before becoming Bishop of Jerusalem. Henceforward he not only taught but preached in the assembly. Most of his sermons have been lost, for until the age of sixty he forbade the tachygraphers to record them (*HE*, VI, 26, 1). At this period his influence became wider. He had already visited the Bishop of Rome, Zephyrinus, before 217. In 232, he went to Athens on urgent ecclesiastical business (*HE*, VI, 23, 4). About this time Julia Mammaea, the niece of Julia Domna, Septimus Severus's wife and mother of Alexander Severus, bade him come to Antioch in order to discuss with him ' the glory of the Saviour ' (VI, 21, 3).

In 235 Alexander Severus died, and was succeeded by Maximinus. A persecution then broke out; Ambrose, Origen's friend, was threatened. To him Origen addressed his *Exhortation to Martyrdom*. He himself seems to have fled to Cappadocia, staying with Firmilian, Bishop of Caesarea in Cappadocia (*HE*, VI, 37, 1). Returning from Caesarea to Palestine, he was several times called to Arabia for discussions with bishops[3]. Eusebius mentions two of these debates, one about 240, the other about 248; we shall speak of them later. About 215 the governor of Arabia, resident at Bostra, had asked Bishop Demetrius to send him Origen. This link with Arabia is a continuation of Pantaenus's; Arabia was a mission of the Judaeo-Christian Church of Alexandria.

Origen's extensive correspondence would be precious in understanding the world at that time. Eusebius speaks of his correspondence with the Emperor Philip the Arabian (*HE*, VI, 26, 3) and of his letter to Pope Fabian (*HE*, VI, 36, 4). Another letter of apology quoted by Eusebius (*HE*, VI, 19, 12-14) was probably addressed to Alexander of Jerusalem[4]. We possess an exchange of letters with Julius Africanus, who had settled in Emmaüs and whom therefore he may have known personally. Another letter replied to the *Panegyric* of Gregory the Wonder-worker. Origen's career ended shortly after the middle of the century. In 247, at the time of the persecution of Decius, he was arrested and tortured. Pamphilus tells us that he died at Tyre, in the reign of Gallus, in 252-253, which coincides with Porphyry's statement that in his youth he met Origen. Porphyry was a Syrian and probably aged about twenty in 252.

Origen's writings are extensive and important, being mainly works of exegesis. There are extant several great commentaries, a number of *Homilies* and fragments. There is wide variety : the treatise *De Principiis*,

3. C. Kretschmar, ' Origenes und die Araber ', *Zeitsch. Theol. Kirch.*, 50 (1953), p. 258-280.
4. On Origen's correspondence see P. Nautin, *Lettres et écrivains chrétiens des II* et *III* siècles*, p. 233-265.

which is a theological summa, the *Against Celsus*, the masterpiece of early apologetic, the *Treatise on Prayer*, and the *Exhortation to Martyrdom*. The *Stromata*, the *Treatise on the Resurrection* and many exegetical works have been lost. Much of what exists is only in Latin translation by Rufinus and Jerome. Two works on Easter, recently discovered in Tura, have not yet been published. Finally, there are parts of the *Hexapla*, where in six columns Origen gives Greek translations of the bible, the Hebrew text and the transliteration of the Hebrew into Greek letters.

These works reveal Origen's greatness. His learning was remarkable; he founded biblical criticism with the *Hexapla*. Curiosity led him to study Hebrew etymology and to identify places. He visited Palestine, excavated grottoes on the banks of the Jordan and questioned the Rabbis. As an apologist, he took part in discussions with the paganism and philosophy of his day, showing astonishing boldness and understanding; he welcomed all the Greek values, but he accurately stigmatised the weaknesses of paganism, and he brought out Christianity's originality, universality and historical character with hitherto unequalled profundity. As a preacher he showed an understanding of human nature, a freedom of expression and a spiritual sense which make his *Homilies* masterpieces. In them he is revealed as a man of God. He is one of the founders of christian spirituality and his influence on monastic theory is great. Athanasius, Gregory of Nyssa and Evagrius were later to be his disciples.

No less important but more debatable are his contributions to theology and exegesis. As a theologian he built up a system of genius, unique of its kind, a synthesis of many earlier traditions. Its core was the Church's tradition, the Faith held in common. But this Faith was continued, in Origen, by a Gnosis, the sources of which were chiefly Jewish : a speculation about the mysteries of holy time and holy space, about the heavenly peoples and successive worlds[5]. Finally, Origen organises these categories, which for the Jews were somewhat visionary, into a logical system, inspired both by Platonism as regards its idealism and by Stoicism as regards its evolutionary character. H. Jonas has clearly shown that this systematisation, where inner coherence is the criterion of truth, links Origen with Valentinus, his forerunner, and Plotinus, his successor[6]. With them he constitutes a milestone in the history of thought.

Origen's system operates at two levels, like the Gnostic systems. The upper world includes God, ὁ θέος (ho Theos), the Father, transcendent and incomprehensible. He eternally engenders the Son who is his image,

5. J. Daniélou, *Message évangélique et culture hellénistique*, p. 427-461. (See n. 26, p. 93).
6. *Gnosis und spätantike Geist*, II, 1, Göttingen 1954, p. 171-223.

but an inferior image, both one and many, incomprehensible and comprehensible[7]. In the third place there are the spiritual creatures, the λογικοί (logicoi), pure spirits, all equal at the beginning and sharing in the Logos. In a second period of time all these spirits fall through sin, letting love grow tepid within them. As a result God joins them to bodies more or less heavy. They organise themselves into a universe, ranging from the lowest devils to the highest angels, with men in the middle[8]. In a third period of time the Word of God, by means of a model economy, leads all free wills to be converted to God and so to be restored to their initial state as pure spirits.

Into this synthesis the magnificent genius of Origen inserted certain excellent ideas; he made notable advances in trinitarian theology[9]; his doctrine of redemption was based on the liberation of man, a prisoner of Satan; he stressed the reality of Christ's soul. Later theologians owe him much; as a synthesis, we must concede with Endre von Ivanka that it introduced the facts of Christianity into a framework whereby restoration to the pristine state renders void its real historicity, the decisive characteristic of Christianity, and ends by diluting Christ's action into a kind of cosmic process[10]. Precisely for that reason his work aroused a very sharp reaction during his lifetime and his theses advancing his system were condemned.

His exegesis raises analogous problems. It contains excellent parts, borrowed from earlier typology, from Justin and Melito, which he developed admirably. No one has shown better than he has the progress of the history of salvation from one Testament to the other. He brought out the spiritual content of typology, by showing that it could be legitimately applied to the christian soul, but he also substituted for the conception of the bible as evidence for the history of salvation that of the bible as an immense allegory, all the words of which are full of mysterious meanings. This conception, bookish and literary, influenced by the Platonists' exegesis of Homer, does not deny its historical meaning but prefers to substitute a Gnostic allegory.

2. Beryllus, Bardesanes, Manes

The Jewish world of the third century witnessed Semitic Christianity in full flower, from Transjordan to Babylonia, all around the Fertile

7. See J. Daniélou, *Origène*, p. 250-258.
8. See H. Cornélis, ' Les fondements cosmologiques de l'eschatologie d'Origène ', *RSPT*, 43 (1959), p. 32-80, 201-247.
9. See A. Orbe, *Hacia la primera teología de la procesión del Verbo*, Rome 1958, p. 387-449.
10. ' Der geistige Ort von Peri archon zwischen dem Neuplatonismus, der Gnosis und der christlichen Rechtgläubigkeit ', *Scholastik*, 35 (1960), p. 481-503.

Crescent. We have seen that Christianity was planted in Transjordan very early on. In the third century the most important centre was Bostra, in Auranitis. Politically, it reached its acme under the Severi, at a time when Christianity was flourishing. The Emperor Philip, probably a christian, was an Arabian. Between about 240 and 254 the Bishop of Bostra was Beryllus; Eusebius says he was bishop of the Arabs of Bostra and ranks him among the ecclesiastical writers (*HE*, VI, 20, 2). He corresponded with Alexander of Jerusalem and perhaps with Origen. He was accused of professing a heretical theology; Nautin has clearly shown that in fact his formulation was merely old-fashioned[11]. A synod met at Bostra, in which Origen took part, and at the end of it Beryllus corrected his faulty formulations (*HE*, VI, 1-3).

Some years later, about 248, another synod met in Arabia, which Origen also attended. Beryllus, who is not mentioned, was perhaps dead at that time. The question debated was whether the soul survives the death of the body (*HE*, VI, 37). At Tura there have been found *Acts* of a synod held in Arabia to judge Bishop Heraclides, which Origen attended : it discussed the same errors as those which had been raised in the two synods mentioned by Eusebius[12]. The important point is the clearly Semitic character of the doctrine concerning the mortality of the soul. It is not so much orthodoxy and heterodoxy as the Greek spirit and the Semitic spirit which clash in these synods.

Eusebius mentions, after Beryllus, a certain Hippolytus, whose see he cannot specify. Now, we have the *Quaestiones et Responsiones* by Hippolytus of Bostra. L. M. Froidevaux has shown that the context of this treatise corresponds with the discussions between Dionysius of Alexandria and Dionysius of Rome about 260[13]. So it is quite possible that the Hippolytus mentioned by Eusebius is this Bishop of Bostra, whose episcopal see was evidently not given in the document Eusebius used. He is not the same as Hippolytus of Rome whom we have discussed above and who lived earlier; this Hippolytus was probably Origen's pupil in Caesarea. It is probably he whom Jerome describes as speaking in Origen's presence. All this would be new evidence of Origen's very close links with Arabia. Hippolytus's successor, Maximus, took part in the synods of Antioch in 264 and 268 against Paul of Samosata (*HE*, VII, 28, 1 and 30, 2).

---

11. *Op. cit.*, p. 134-137; 209-219.
12. See ' Entretiens d'Origène avec Héraclide ', Introduction by J. Scherer, *Sources chrétiennes*, 67, Paris 1960, p. 14-46.
13. ' Les " Questions " et Réponses sur la Sainte Trinité ", attribuées à Hippolyte, évêque de Bostra ', *RSR*, 50 (1962), p. 32-74. See also P. Nautin, *op. cit.*, p. 206.

188 PART ONE : TO THE END OF THE THIRD CENTURY

There is precious information about the Bostra community in the *Didascalia Apostolorum*. The work belongs to the middle of the third century; our version is in Syriac, although the original was probably in Greek. It certainly belongs to a Syrian community, perhaps to a community in eastern Syria, but most of the evidence suggests that it comes from Bostra. That is the view of Harnack, Schneider and Kretschmar[14]. Certain features are clearly Semitic. The deaconesses are compared to the Holy Spirit, which suggests a *milieu* where 'spirit' is feminine, and the references to Judaism are numerous. The author warns against the traditions of the mishnah; he refers to the Jewish festivals, which he knows well; he refers repeatedly to the Old Testament; widows have an important place in the community, as in the Church of Jerusalem.

Another part of the world where we find an Aramaean Christianity in the third century is eastern Coele-Syria, that is to say the right bank of the Euphrates. On the whole, the towns of Syria spoke Greek and the countryside Aramaean, but western Syria was more under the influence of Antioch, while eastern Syria was under the influence of Edessa. We have two sources of information for Christianity in this region in the third century. The first is literary; it is an *Apology* in Syriac, addressed probably to Caracalla (211-217) and falsely attributed to Melito. It was published for the first time by Ernest Renan in the *Spicilegium Solesmnese* (II, xxxvii-liii). Its precise references to the town and region of Manbej (Hierapolis) leave little doubt as to its place of origin. So the work is one of the earliest examples of Christian Syriac literature[15].

The second piece of evidence is not literary but archaeological: the church and baptistery of Dura Europos. The town lies on the Euphrates, in Syria, but on the frontier of Osroene. For long occupied by the Parthians, it was conquered by Trajan in 116. A *mithraeum* has been found there with frescoes representing Zoroaster and Ostanes, and a synagogue with remarkable frescoes, showing Parthian influence. We have already mentioned the christian church, the earliest so far discovered; it dates from the second century, and confirms a statement in the *Chronicle of Edessa* that a church existed in Edessa at that time. Osroene was therefore the first country to put up buildings exclusively devoted to worship. The themes of the frescoes in the baptistery and church, as well as their style, show the originality of Christianity in this region, quite different from what we find in Alexandria and Rome at the same date.

14. G. Kretschmar, ' Origenes und die Araber ', *ZTK*, 50 (1953), p. 260-264.
15. See I. Ortis de Urbina, *Patrologia Syriaca*, Rome 1958, p. 39.

But the chief centre of Aramaean Christianity at this period was Osroene. We have mentioned that the region was evangelised as early as the end of the first century. Nothing is known of its history in the second century; but at the end of that period Christianity there appears to have been very flourishing. The facts are these. The churches of Osroene took part in the paschal controversy (*HE*, V, 23, 4). The epitaph of Abercius, at the end of the second century, records that Abercius, after having visited Syria, crossed the Euphrates and visited a town, which may be Nisibis. Everywhere he met Christian assemblies. The *Chronicle of Edessa*, which dates from the sixth century, but uses the town archives, records that a flood took place in 202 and the sanctuary of the christian church was destroyed : this is important evidence for the existence at Edessa of a house consecrated for worship, which implies a community of some size. The *Doctrine of Addai*, a fifth-century recasting of documents known to Eusebius of Caesarea, names the Bishop of Edessa, Palout, who was consecrated by Serpion, Bishop of Antioch (182-209)[16].

Did Osroene at this period have a christian king, Abgar IX (179-214)? This person is mentioned by the *Chronicle of Edessa*, but the latter does not say that he was christian. Julius Africanus, who lived at the Court of Abgar before 216, says that Abgar was a ἱερὸς ἀνήρ (consecrated man). But the meaning of the term is uncertain. The *Book of the Laws of the Lands*, written before 250 by a disciple of Bardesanes, says explicitly that King Abgar became a Christian; at least this is what the Syriac text says, but the Greek text, preserved by Eusebius, says nothing of the sort. So the matter remains in doubt. The memory of a King Abgar converted to Christianity appears in the apocryphon quoted by Eusebius, the *Letter of King Abgar to Jesus*. This King Abgar was certainly not a contemporary of Jesus. Some have concluded that the King is Abgar IX, whose conversion was anticipated by legend. All this amounts only to a number of pointers, not to certainty[17].

We arrive on firmer ground with Bardesanes[18]. Born in 154 in Edessa of parents from Arbel, Bardesanes was brought up at the court of Abgar. Julius Africanus tells us that he was a skilful archer; he wrote equally well in Greek and Syriac. Of his numerous writings only a few fragments remain; Eusebius tells us that he wrote against Marcion.

---

16. See I. Ortis de Urbina, ' Le origine del cristianesimo in Edessa ', *Gregorianum*, 15 (1934), p. 82-91; W. Bauer, *Rechtgläubigkeit und Ketzerei in ältesten Christentum*, Tübingen 1934, p. 6-48; H. E. W. Turner, *The Pattern of the Christian Truth*, London 1954, p. 39-46.

17. See P. E. Kahle, *The Cairo Geniza*, 2nd ed., Oxford 1959, p. 276-280.

18. See P. Nau, ' Scriptorum Testimonia de Bardesanis vita, scriptis, doctrina ', in *Patr. Syr.*, II, Paris 1907, p. 492-527.

Above all, he wrote a large number of hymns; this we are told by Ephraem, who lived in Edessa in the following century and who himself wrote hymns to replace those of Bardesanes. In fact, he considered the latter as a heretic. The doctrinal position of Bardesanes is difficult to define; he fought against heresy, but he was accused of being a disciple of Valentinus and practising astrology. How should we interpret these accusations? Bardesanes certainly professed a Judaeo-Christian Gnosis. Was this Gnosis really dualist, or merely an old-fashioned way of thinking? I am inclined to favour the latter interpretation.

In fact, if we study the doctrines attributed to Bardesanes, they appear different from Gnosticism. He believed in a rather odd cosmology. God created first of all the different elements, separating one from another and assigning each a place, but the elements became mixed up and produced confusion; God then created this world of ours by mixing light and darkness; after six thousand years the elements will be restored to their pristine purity; our bodies belong to the second world and are ruled by the stars; hence physical evils; they will not rise again. We can well understand that this doctrine was censured by Ephraem. It betrays a certain dualism, which may be due to Iranian influences, but it also recalls the Essenes' teaching, as found in the *Rule of the Community*. So Bardesanes may have been influenced by the Judaeo-Christians.

If we no longer possess Bardesanes' writings, we do have a dialogue written by one of his disciples, Philip, which gives us information about his teaching, the *Book of the Laws of the Lands*. This treatise is quoted by Eusebius[19] and is a defence of freedom. Among the arguments put forward, Bardesanes insists on the fact that, in one and the same climate, there are different laws; it is not the planets which determine people's laws, but the free will of their first law-givers; then comes a curious picture of the nations, a scrutiny of the habits of the Seri, the Brahmins, another Indian sect, the Persians, the Geti, the Bactrians, the Britons and the Chaldaeans. The distinction which Bardesanes makes between two categories of Brahmins is interesting. In fact Porphyry tells us that Bardesanes was given information about India by some Indian envoys to Emesa, at the time of Elagabalus (218-222)[20].

This brings us to the question of Syrian Christianity's influence in India. We should bear in mind facts recorded by other christian writers of the same period. Clement of Alexandria distinguishes the Brahmins from the Sarmanians — and also mentions Buddha. Hippolytus

19. *Praep. Ev.*, 5; *PG*, XII, 461 A.
20. Ap. Stob., *Anth.*, I, 4, 56.

(13) ORIGEN, MANES, CYPRIAN 191

of Rome has a passage about the Brahmins which M. Filliozat has shown to be well-informed[21]. Whether Ammonius Saccas, the teacher of Origen and Plotinus, had links with India remains an unsolved question. Christianity turned eastwards at the beginning of the third century; Osroene seems to have been the chief centre, opening out towards Persia and India.

The Christianity of Osroene at this time exercised an influence in two very different spheres : art and ascesis. In the sphere of art, we have mentioned that the first Christian churches appeared in Osroene. The frescoes that decorate them, although inspired by Greek work, have their own characteristics : a more hieratic style and a tendency to narrative. They probably owe this to the influence of Jewish art, which was specially flourishing in this region. They also owe it to Parthian art and the Mithraic tradition[22]. More important is Edessa's influence in the sphere of music. This brings us back to Bardesanes. According to Ephraem, he composed hymns *(madrase)*. These *madrase* were a kind of lyrical lesson with a refrain. His son, Harmonius, composed Greek hymns, the refrains of which were sung as choruses. This seems to have been the beginning of sung responsories, which developed in the Church of Antioch in the fourth century. Bardesanes has an important place in the history of liturgical music[23].

In the sphere of ascesis, Osroene also played an important part at the beginning of the third century. We have mentioned that Syriac Christianity from the very beginning showed marked ascetical tendencies. These continued into the third century; several documents of that period show this. The *Acts of Thomas* tell us that converts renounced marriage. The Church was largely composed of ascetics, and it is they who made up the hard core of the community, who received spiritual gifts and proclaimed the Gospel[24]. The *Tract on Virginity*, falsely attributed to Clement of Rome, is of the same kind. It assumes the existence of those ' spiritual marriages ' where ascetics of both sexes lived under the same roof, a practice which gave rise to abuses; we shall see that in the case of Paul of Samosata. It lasted into the fourth century in Syria, where Chrysostom struggled against it, and appeared in Asia in the

21. *Les relations extérieures de l'Inde*, I, Pondicherry 1956, p. 31-60.
22. See C. Schneider, *Geistesgeschichte des antiken Christentums*, II, Munich 1954, p. 120-121 ;M. I. Rostovtzeff, ' Dura and the Problem of Parthian Art ', *Yale Classical Studies*, 5 (1935), p. 155-304.
23. I have drawn on the unpublished thesis of J. Gélineau, *Antiphona. Recherches sur les formes liturgiques de la psalmodie dans les églises syriaques aux IVe et Ve siècles*, Paris 1960.
24. See A. Vööbus, *Celibacy. A Requirement for Admission to Baptism in the Early Christian Church*, Stockholm 1951, p. 20-34; *History of Asceticism in the Syrian Orient*, I, p. 64-90.

Gospel of Philip, which dates from the beginning of the third century, as the summit of christian initiation[25].

Beyond the Tigris, in Adiabene, Christianity was also growing fast. In the second century it had produced Tatian, who, having returned home after his stay in Rome, had written, perhaps in Syriac, his *Harmony of the Gospels*, which had a great influence on Syriac Christianity. The *Chronicle of Arbela* says that in 224, when the Sassanid dynasty came to power in Persia, there were more than twenty bishoprics in the region bordering the Tigris. The Bishop of Arbela, the eighth according to the *Chronicle*, was then Hairan. Further away still, the *Book of the Laws of the Lands* tells us that there were christians in Parthia, Media and Bactriana. In 240, when Manes went to India, he seems to have met christian communities. If we bear in mind that at the end of the second century, according to the *Chronicle of Arbela*, there was still only one bishop in Adiabene, we realise the extraordinary expansion at the beginning of the third century[26].

Here in the first half of the third century there arose a religion which met with astonishing success : Manichaeism. Fifty years ago our information about it came from its opponents : Cyril of Jerusalem, Augustine and Hegemonius. Today we have actual Manichaean writings. Some were discovered at Turfan in Chinese Turkestan; they are written in Parthian or Persian; they include precious information about the life of Manes and his missions. The others were discovered in 1931 in Fayum in Egypt; they are written in Coptic and contain works essential for an understanding of the Manichaean doctrine : *Homilies*, *Kephalaia* and *Psalms*. Inscriptions and other writings have been found since. We are in a position therefore to form a fairly accurate picture of Manichaeism[27].

The founder of the movement, Manes, was born on 14 April 216, in North Babylonia. His family seems to have been related to the Arsacids. It is important to note, as H. C. Puech has done, that his life was contemporary with the collapse of the Parthian Arsacid dynasty and of the accession of the Persian Sassanid dynasty. The latter gradually re-established traditional Mazdaism and restored the power of the Magi. Manes, on the other hand, professed the religious syncretism which characterised the Parthian period. As a result of a vision, his father, Palek, was converted to an ascetical ideal, and gave up meat, wine and

25. R. M. Grant, ' The Mystery of Marriage in the Gospel of Philip ', *Vig. Christ*, 15 (1961), p. 129-141.
26. See A. Harnack, *Die Mission und Ausbreitung des Christentums in den ersten drei Jahrhunderten*, p. 683-693; P. Kahle, *The Cairo Geniza*, p. 274-276.
27. See H. Ch. Puech, *Le Manichéisme*, Paris 1949, p. 26-29.

a b   a b

8

9

CHRISTIANA TEMPORA : I. Use of Christian symbols

PLATE 19

A SEQUENCE OF COINS SHOWING GROWTH IN THE USE OF CHRISTIAN SYMBOLS

For the significance of coins in the transition of the Roman Empire to Christianity, see chs 16, § 2, and 25.

a = OBVERSE (*Portrait*)
b = REVERSE (*Inscription & Figure*)
c = *Metal, Mint, and Issue date*

1 a Diocletian
  b 'Iovi Conservatori' — Jupiter
  c Gold 284-305

2 a Constantine the Great
  b 'Soli Invicto Comito' Sol
  c Bronze, London 307-313

3 a Constantine the Great
  b 'Spes Public' — Labarum surmounted by Chi-rho planted on serpent
  c Bronze, Constantinople 324-330

4 a Constantine the Great
  b 'Gloria Exercitus' Two soldiers, and standard bearing the Chi-rho
  c Bronze, Arles 335-337

5 a Magnantius
  b 'Salus DD NN Augg et Caess' Chi-rho between Alpha and Omega
  c Bronze, Amiens 351-353

6 a Vetranio
  b 'Hoc Signo Victor eris' Victory crowning Emperor who holds Labarum inscribed with Chi-rho
  c Bronze, Siscia 350

7 a Julian
  b 'Securitas Reipub' Bull of Apis
  c Bronze, Constantinople 361-363

8 a Flacilla, wife of Theodosius I
  b Chi-rho within a wreath
  c Silver, Constantinople 383-388

9 a Honorius (on the cuirass there is a Chi-rho)
  b 'Concordia Augg' Constantinople seated
  c Gold, Constantinople 395-408

By permission of the Warburg Institute, London. Photo : Otto Fein.

CHRISTIANA TEMPORA : II. Mithraism

PLATE 20

Above : MITHRAS THE BULL-SLAYER; FROM THE SITE OF THE WALL-
BROOK MITHRAEUM, LONDON, LATE 2ND OR 3RD CENTURY
Below : MITHRAS THE BULL-SLAYER; FROM OSTIA

By permission of Soprintendenza alle Antichita, Rome.

The context in which the Christian Church
grew and finally triumphed was that of the
'new religious consciousness' (cf. ch. 15, § 2).
Probably the best example of this phenomenon
is the widespread influence of Mithraism
in the Roman Empire. These two radically
different presentations of the same theme
show the breadth of its appeal. *Above,*
in the centre, Mithras, dressed as is usual
in Phrygian cap, short long-sleeved tunic,
cloak and trousers, has just plunged his
dagger into the bull's shoulder. This sacrificial
action of the god was supposed to bring life
out of death, light out of darkness, and so
forth. The meaning of the action is here
emphasised by the inclusion of Cautes on the
left, holding a torch upwards — symbol of
life and light, and on the right Cautopates,
holding a torch reversed — symbol of death
and darkness, understood not as the end,
however, but as the means of entry into
immortality. The inscription helps to place
the object sociologically. It reads : 'Ulpianus
Silvanus, Veteran of the second Augustan
Legion, paid his vow : he was initiated at
Orange.' *Left:* no comment needs to be
made on the very sophisticated, almost
genteel, Hellenistic Mithras from Ostia.

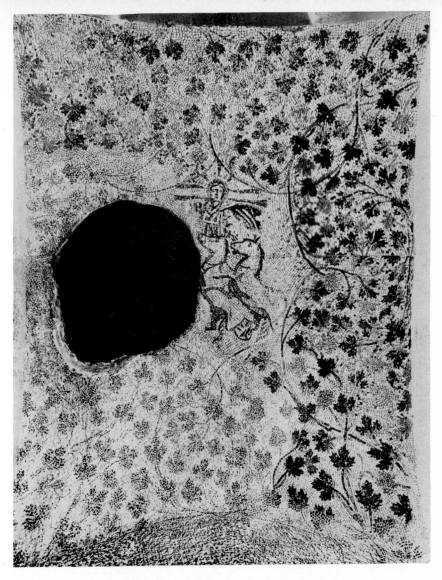

CHRISTIANA TEMPORA: III. The Sun-God

PLATE 21. CHRIST-HELIOS; MOSAIC FROM MAUSOLEUM UNDER ST PETER'S, ROME, LATE 3RD OR EARLY 4TH CENTURY

Within the context referred to under Plate 20, the attitude of Christians towards paganism varied from open, physical hostility (cf. the smashed Mithraeums in Ostia), to subtle, peaceful assimilation. This illustration and the next are examples of the latter process. In this mosaic Christ has assumed the attributes of the Sun-God. He is depicted with cloak flying out behind, holding a globe in his left hand and driving a chariot pulled by a team of horses. It is possible that the nimbus is deliberately constructed in the form of a cross. The vine which frames the central portrait may also be an assimilation of the life-giving vine of Dionysius with the True Vine of Christ. (For a pagan portrayal of the Sun-God, see the top left hand corner of the Wallbrook Mithras in Plate 20a. For a discussion of the relation between Christianity and the religion of the Sun-God, see ch. 24.)

PLATE 22. CHRIST-ORPHEUS; MOSAIC FROM VILLA IN JENAH, NEAR BEIRUT, LATE 5TH OR EARLY 6TH CENTURY

The scene of Orpheus playing his lyre among a group of wild animals was common in Roman art. In this picture the lyre has been replaced by a staff, and this fact, along with its proximity to other Christian mosaics, permits the identification of the central figure as Christ the Good Shepherd. But the basic pattern is still that of Orpheus-pictures, and the figures of Christ and Orpheus are probably consciously merged together. This merging of the two figures has many parallels, among them the passage in Eusebius, *De laudibus Constantani*, § 14, where the comparison between the Logos and Orpheus is carried much further than a mere likeness between the Shepherd among his flock and Orpheus among the animals. Christ's manhood is understood by Eusebius as an 'instrument' (ὄργανον) through which he offers salvation to all, 'just as the μουσικος ἀνηρ [i.e. Orpheus] revealed wisdom through his Lyre'.

By permission of M. Chehab, Beirut.

marriage. He joined a Baptist sect called the Mughtasila, which has aroused the speculations of scholars. Obviously it calls to mind the Sabaeans and the Baptists of Transjordan, ancestors of the Mandaeans. The Mandaeans, in their turn, were influenced by Manichaeism. So again we discover this Baptist movement, which existed both in Transjordanian Syria and in Mesopotamian Syria, and which expressed itself in Jewish, Christian, Mandaean and Manichaean dress.

At first Manes belonged to this Baptist sect, but during his youth in Babylonia he doubtless also came in touch with all shades of religion practised there, from which he borrowed. There was, of course, the traditional religion of Iran, Mazdaism, but Manes also met Brahmins and Buddhists. His first mission was to take him to India. He also met Jews, of whom there were many in Babylonia. Finally, he was in touch with christians. This is an important confirmation of the vitality of Christianity at this period in Babylonia and notably in the region of Seleucia-Ctesiphon, where Manes lived. Among these christians there were certainly some Marcionites : we know that Marcionism had spread in Osroene and Babylonia, and that it had been attacked by Bardesanes; there were also christians of the Great Church, Judaeo-Christian in their attitude, that is to say, with the characteristics of eastern Christianity : asceticism, a strong feeling for liturgy, and gnosis.

In 240 Manes received the revelation which lies at the root of his mission. He believed that this mission was a continuation of that of Zoroaster, Buddha and Jesus, and that he was the supreme revealer, in whom total truth was made manifest. His first mission took him to India, that is to say, Beluchistan; he converted the king of that country. On his return he went to Gundeshapuhr, in Susiana, the capital of the Sassanid Kings, where he was received by Shapuhr I, to whom he explained his doctrine and who allowed him to spread it. He accompanied Shapuhr in a campaign against the Roman Empire, probably that of 242-244 against Gordian III. In that case, by a curious coincidence, he would have found himself opposite the Neo-Platonist, Plotinus, who accompanied Gordian III. But Manes met opposition from the Magi. He was put to death in 277 under Bahram I, the second successor of Shapuhr I.

Manes considered himself the revealer of a new religion : in this sense he was clearly opposed to Christianity. The basis of his system is a dualist Gnosticism, inspired both by Judaeo-Christian Gnosticism and Iranian Zoroastrianism. He borrowed points from the various religions he knew : and this syncretism is an essential part of his message, since he considered himself the heir of all religions, but it is certain that in many respects he was inspired by Syriac Christianity. Similarities have been pointed out between his dualist cosmology and that of Bardesanes. Jesus and the paraclete play an important part in his gnosis : the Passion of Jesus loses its historic significance and takes on a mythical character, but it remains none the less at the heart of his theology of salvation[28]. The Manichaean Church was divided into those who are perfect, the ascetics, who alone make up the Church in the strict sense, and those who are imperfect, the listeners or catechumens : this recalls the organisation of the communities of Osroene and Adiabene.

Manichaeism is in one sense foreign to Christianity and so is really a new religion. It spread very widely, as far as China and North Africa, and continued well into the Middle Ages. But at the same time this new religion can be considered a development of the original Syriac Christianity, whose tendencies it carries to their furthest extreme : a cosmological dualism, which results in a complete condemnation of the material world; and moral Encratism, which forbids marriage and the use of certain food. Manichaean monasticism developed in parallel with Christian monasticism. The latter gradually became aware of its latent exaggerations as it observed in Manichaeism the fruit of those exaggerations. In any case, the middle of the third century witnessed a prodigious expansion in eastern Christianity.

3. Cornelius and Cyprian

The middle of the third century was the period when the Latin west expanded greatly and asserted its originality. The Church spread in Gaul, Spain, northern Italy and Illyria. Gaul, which until the beginning of the third century had only one bishopric — at Lyons — acquired several others in the middle of the century, according to St Cyprian[29] : Arles, Toulouse, Narbonne, Vienne, Paris, Reims and Trèves became episcopal sees[30]. In Spain St Cyprian names the bishops of Astorga, Merida and Saragossa. In north Italy Milan, Aquileia and Ravenna were episcopal sees. But the two main centres of Christianity were still Carthage and Rome, and it was around these two centres that the number of Christians increased and became quite considerable.

The Bishops of Rome, after Callistus (218-223), were Urban (223-230), Pontian (230-235), Anterus (235-236), Fabian (236-250) and Cornelius (251-253). In the Catacomb of Callistus Rome still possesses the vault

---

28. See G. Messina, *Cristianesimo, Buddhismo, Manicheismo*, Rome 1947, p. 233-238.
29. *Epist.*, 1-5.
30. See E. Griffe, *La Gaule chrétienne à l'époque romaine*, I, Paris 1947, p. 57-88.

where, from 235 onwards, the Bishops of Rome were buried, and here one can read the inscriptions of Pontian, Anterus and Fabian; it is noteworthy that all these bishops, except Anterus, were born in Rome. If Greek still seems to have been the official language of the liturgy, the use of Latin was growing. It was at this period that a number of Greek works were translated into Latin, like the *Adversus Haereses* of St Irenaeus[31]. We possess letters written in Latin by Pope Cornelius. Rome at this period also produces its first great writer in Latin, Novatian.

A precious letter from Pope Cornelius, preserved by Eusebius, reveals the importance of the Roman clergy at this time. Cornelius writes that they include forty-six priests, seven deacons, seven subdeacons, forty-two acolytes, fifty-six exorcists, lectors and doorkeepers (*HE*, VI, 34, 1). This passage shows us that Rome already possessed the seven orders which continued to be found there afterwards; it calls for certain comments. The deacons, seven in number, seem to be connected with the institution of the seven diaconates, among which the administration of the town was divided, and which the Liberian Catalogue links with Pope Fabian. The subdeacons appear for the first time; it seems that this is an institution destined to relieve the deacons of part of their burden. We may also point out the mention of the acolytes and doorkeepers, both lacking in Hippolytus's *Apostolic Tradition*. The lectors were mostly youths who read in the assembly. So Rome at this period already had a complete organisation of the hierarchy of orders.

Peninsular Italy also acquired more bishops. The Roman Council of 251, which condemned Novatian, was attended by sixty bishops. These bishoprics were grouped round Rome, which thus constituted a patriarchate[32]. The same organisation is found at this period in the east where the bishops of Antioch and Alexandria also exercised a pre-eminence in their dioceses. It was expressed concretely by the meeting of local Councils. For Rome we know of the Councils of 251 and 260, the latter concerned with the question of Dionysius of Alexandria. These Councils communicated their decisions to the other Churches. A whole organisation of the universal Church clearly appears in the middle of the third century. The Roman Synod and the Bishop of Rome personally appear as enjoying quite a special authority, which Cyprian in particular recognises.

The second great centre was Carthage. In many respects the Church of Africa revealed its special characteristics more markedly than the

---

31. See S. Lundström, *Uebersetzungtechnische Untersuchungen auf dem Gebeite der christlichen Latinität*, Lund 1955, p. 5-7.
32. See N. Marot, ' Les Conciles romains des IIe et IIIe siècles ', in *L'Église et les églises*, Chevetogne 1954, p. 212-214.

Church of Rome; it represented a more homogeneous, less cosmopolitan body of people; as we have seen, at the beginning of the century it produced a great Latin writer in Tertullian; it grew in an extraordinary way during the first half of the third century and a Council which met about 220 in Carthage under Bishop Agrippinus was attended by seventy bishops from proconsular Africa and Numidia; another convoked by Bishop Donatus about 240 was attended by ninety; and the same number attended the Council convoked by Cyprian in 256. It is not impossible that this growth of Christianity was partly linked at Carthage with political factors and that it was an expression of African particularism, and its opposition to the authority of the Emperor, as Frend, in particular, has stressed[33]. Christianity certainly favoured nationalism. We find the same thing in Egypt. Later, the extreme expressions of this tendency were African Donatism and the Melitian schism in Egypt.

In the middle of the third century, the Church in Africa produced an exceptional figure in Caecilius Cyprianus, Bishop of Carthage. Cyprian was first of all a great writer. Born of Carthaginian parents, he started his career as a rhetorician; he has left a number of books. Less original than Tertullian, yet in style and vocabulary he is both more classical and more dependent on Scripture. Two of his works are specially important; one is the treatise *On the Unity of the Church*, the first work of ecclesiology, and one which was to have an immense influence; the other is the collection of *Testimonia ad Quirinum*, which gathered together passages from the bible used in catechesis and is one of the outstanding examples of the literary genre known as *Testimonia*. But Cyprian was not only a great writer; Bishop of Carthage in 248 and therefore metropolitan of Africa, he played a leading role in the life of the African Church and of the Latin west in general.

If the problems of Syrian Christianity were primarily ascetical and those of Alexandrian Christianity primarily theological, the problems of Latin Christianity at this period were mainly concerned with the organisation of the Church. Three great questions were raised : one concerning the discipline of penance, the second about baptism, the third about the episcopate. Latent difficulties came to light and demanded a solution. We have already seen the presence of diverse traditions in the Churches of Rome and Carthage. Ever since the beginning the Roman Church had been composed of diverse communities. We have considered the conflict between Hippolytus and Callistus. This conflict continued with the schism of Novatian. The ideal of a Church of prophets,

33. *The Donatist Church*, Oxford 1952, p. 106-107.

confessors and virgins was opposed by the notion of a great Christian people.

The community of Carthage was more homogeneous. It did not have the complexities of the Roman community, but it too had its problems. In discussing Tertullian we have seen its affinities with Asiatic groups. True, Tertullian went to extremes in adhering to Montanism. But the fact remains that African views were closer to those of the Asiatics than to the Roman tradition. It was not by chance that the only work translated from Greek into Latin at Carthage in the first half of the third century was a homily by Melito *Against the Jews*[34]. In the conflicts between Cyprian and Cornelius on the question whether baptism could be administered more than once, Firmilian of Caesarea gave Cyprian his unconditional support. But if, as André Mandouze as clearly shown, Cyprian was on the same side as Novatian in matters like Anabaptism, he nonetheless defended the authority of the episcopate against the claims of the 'confessors'. He condemned the imprudent quest for martyrdom, he allowed mitigation of the rigours of penance and he remained in communion with the legitimate bishop of Rome[35].

Such was the background to the grave problems facing the Latin west in the middle of the third century. The first concerned the discipline of penance. At the beginning of 250 the Emperor Decius ordered all citizens to take part in a general sacrifice to the immortal gods; it was a manifestation of national unity which was not demanded only of the christians, but it put the latter in a dilemma. They were ordered to burn a few grains of incense in front of idols, in exchange for which they would receive a certificate. Often only the certificate was asked for by the authorities, without any further action. Many christians obeyed, including two bishops in Africa. Once the storm had passed, the question arose of the attitude to be adopted towards the *lapsi*.

In this way the problem of the discipline of penance arose once more as a critical matter. In Carthage a number of priests reconciled the *lapsi*, at the request of 'confessors', without demanding a period of repentance. Over against the doctrine Cyprian developed his own theory; he did not debar the 'confessors' from playing the role of intercessors, he also admitted that the *lapsi* could be reconciled, but he insisted on the necessity of a severe and prolonged penance. As long as their new conversion remained uncertain, they were not to be reconciled, except *in articulo mortis;* he did not exclude the possibility of reconciliation taking place more than once. So Cyprian seems to

34. See E. Peterson, 'Ps-Cyprian Adversus Judaeos und Melito von Sardes', *Vig. Christ.*, 6 (1952), p. 42-43.
35. 'Encore le donatisme', *Ant. Class.*, 29 (1960), p. 96-97.

have been much more demanding than the priests he attacks, but he was less strict than Tertullian. Tertullian considered that there were certain sins, apostasy in particular, which the Church could not absolve; he also explicitly ruled out any repetition of penance.

In fact Cyprian's position appears as the traditional position of the Church. It had been held in the past by Dionysius of Corinth and the bishops of Rome. Cyprian's position did not differ from that of Callistus, whom Hippolytus had treated as lax, nor from that of Hermas, which Tertullian had rejected. But it was also held by Clement of Alexandria and Origen. The characteristic of this doctrine held in common seems to be that reconciliation was in principle unlimited, but entailed very heavy obligations. There must be no doubt that the intention to carry out the duties of a christian life had been adequately guaranteed in order to avoid any danger of another lapse. Now the sin had shown that this intention had in the first place been inadequate, so the Church had to be more exacting for penance than for baptism[36]. Penance was compared to baptism.

Cyprian told the other Churches about his ruling. Rome in 250 had no bishop; Fabian had been martyred at the beginning of the persecution of Decius and not yet replaced. But we have the reply of the Church of Rome; it was written by Novatian, ' in the name of the priests and deacons residing in Rome '. As we have seen, Novatian at that time was one of the outstanding members of the Roman clergy. His letter is very prudent; he says that he agrees with Cyprian in principle, but he adds that the Church of Rome is waiting for the meeting of its next synod and the election of its bishop before taking a final decision on the question of the *lapsi*, except in regard to cases *in articulo mortis*, where those who have given adequate signs of repentance can certainly be reconciled.

But in 251 Cornelius was elected Bishop of Rome. Novatian then set himself up against Cornelius and had himself ordained bishop. He revealed his attitude towards the *lapsi;* he considered that no reconciliation should be granted them. It was virtually a renewal of the conflict between Hippolytus and Callistus, and by that we find that the same two trends had continued at Rome. Novatian sent envoys to Africa, Alexandria and Antioch; in Gaul he won over Marcian of Arles[37]; in Antioch he was supported by Fabius, but on his side Cornelius convoked a Council in Rome which condemned Novatian (*HE*, VI, 43, 1). A synodal letter was sent to the bishops of Italy, to Cyprian and to Fabius. Cornelius

---

36. See K. Rahner, ' Die Busslehre des hl. Cyprianum von Karthago ', *ZKT*, 74 (1952), p. 257-276; 381-438.
37. *Epist.*, LXVIII, 2-3.

also sent a personal letter to Fabius of Antioch, of which we have long extracts (*HE*, VI, 43, 3-4). We do not possess his letter to Dionysius of Alexandria (*HE*, VI, 46, 3)[38]. Cyprian expressed his total agreement with the Bishop of Rome. And inversely, his opponent Novatus, although opposed to strict demands, joined forces with Novatian : both represented the party of ' confessors '.

So this first dispute was not in any way a battle between Rome and Carthage; it was the expression once again of two theories of the Church. For Novatian, the Church was a small group of the spiritually-minded, in inevitable conflict with the earthly city : a Church of prophets and martyrs. On the other side was the bishops' view; for them the Church was a people which must gather together all men, and must therefore take account of the different levels implied by the arrival of a great many people within the Church. There was a place for an élite of spiritually-minded members; monasticism would satisfy their needs, but there was also room for the immense crowd of ordinary Christians. In this there was no relaxing of the Gospel's demands; this attitude was the traditional attitude of the Church. Cyprian and Cornelius were its great witnesses in the third century and thus prepared the way for the unfolding of the Constantinian Church, whereas the sects of ' pure people ', as Eusebius calls the disciples of Novatian (*HE*, VI, 3, 11), gradually withered away.

The second conflict in the west was quite different. This time divergent traditions clashed. The question at issue was the validity of baptism administered by heretics. The African Church contested the validity of such baptism; that was Tertullian's view in his *De Baptismo* (15). About the year 200 an African Council convoked by Agrippinus, Bishop of Carthage, had also decided that such baptism was not valid. Cyprian shared this opinion. In 251, discussing the schism of Felicissimus, he affirmed it in the *De Unitate Ecclesiae*. When the schism of Novatian spread in Africa, the problem arose again. It seems to have been the custom in Mauritania to consider baptism of heretics valid; this is shown notably by the treatise *De Rebaptismate*. Cyprian contested the legitimacy of this practice (*Epist.*, LXIX, 1; LXXI, 3). The Councils convoked in Carthage by Cyprian in 355 and 356 confirmed this view.

The Bishop of Rome, Stephen, adopted a vigorous stand against Cyprian. He considered his view an innovation and asserted that according to tradition heretics who are converted have only to be reconciled by a laying-on of hands, but do not have to receive baptism.

38. On this correspondence see P. Nautin, *Lettres et écrivains chrétiens des II*e *et III*e *siècles*, p. 143-167.

This amounted to saying that, even when administered by a heretic, baptism was valid. The question was certainly complex. The heretics included very varied groups, ranging from simple schismatics, like the disciples of Novatian, to Gnostics. So it was possible to be uneasy about the validity of certain of these baptisms. But Stephen was certainly correct in laying down the principle that in cases where baptism had been administered under the required conditions, the fact that the person who administered it was a schismatic did not prevent the baptism from being effective, and so it could not be administered a second time. This principle was to remain that of the Church, and Stephen claimed to bear witness to tradition.

In fact the opposition was not only between Rome and Carthage; the problem had also arisen in the east. Dionysius of Alexandria shared Rome's view. Thanks to Eusebius, we have important passages from the letters he wrote on this subject. He says that it was traditional practice in his Church not to rebaptise converted heretics; he went as far as to extend this principle to Montanism, for which St Basil later reproached him; he tells us that a member of the Alexandrian community, converted from heresy, listening to the answers of those about to receive baptism, declared that ' the baptism he had received from the heretics was not that kind of baptism, but was full of impiety and blasphemies ' (*HE*, VII, 9, 2). But Dionysius hesitated to rebaptise him, saying that the communion he had with the Church and the eucharist that he had received were sufficient. Dionysius seems to go too far towards endorsing the validity of the baptism of heretics.

Inversely, Cyprian found support among the Asiatics. The bishops of Phrygia had debated the question with regard to the baptism of the Montanists. Synods held in Iconium and Synnad, about 230, had decided that baptism by heretics was not valid (*HE*, VII, 7, 5). Dionysius of Alexandria did not dare condemn their tradition, and they were probably right as far as the Montanists were concerned, just as Stephen was right to take the opposite position with regard to the Roman schismatics. But on both sides the necessary distinctions were not made and the two attitudes were by and large opposed. The fact is that when Stephen condemned the Carthaginian practice in 256, Firmilian, Bishop of Caesarea in Cappadocia, a disciple of Origen, sided with Cyprian and wrote an extremely violent letter to the Bishop of Rome.

If we compare the two conflicts in which the west engaged in the middle of the third century, it is striking to find that Cyprian's attitude to Rome was different in each case. In the conflict about the *lapsi*, he sided with the Bishop of Rome against the African as well as the Roman schismatics; in the clash over a second administration of baptism, he was opposed to Stephen. This brings us to a final question : Cyprian's ecclesiology. It is clear that there are, on this point, two poles to his work. On the one hand, he is one of the great upholders of the unity of the Church, based on the unity of the episcopal body in communion with the Bishop of Rome. His treatise *De Unitate Ecclesiae* declares : ' The episcopal dignity is one : each bishop possesses a part without a division of the whole ', and the *Primatus Petri* is affirmed in the first edition of the book. In the matter of Novatian, and in that of Marcian, he had recourse to the Bishop of Rome.

On the other hand, Cyprian, as we have seen, held a very pronounced theology of the local episcopate. The bishop is the principle of unity in the community; he is sovereign in his province, and in particular he is the guardian of tradition, as received from his predecessors; Cyprian here appeared as the champion of episcopalism, and it is this right of the local episcopate which he defended in his controversy with Stephen. So he stressed each of the two aspects in turn. We have concrete proof of this in the fact that the second edition of the *De Unitate Ecclesiae* modified the passage on Peter's primacy and replaced it by a more general statement of the Church's oneness, as M. Bévenot has shown[39].

It is clear that Cyprian's thought contains an ambiguity on this point; or, more exactly, he stands at the junction of two movements, to both of which he bears witness, but whose reconciliation he does not foresee. He is attached to the unity of the universal Church and in particular to the primacy of Rome, but he is also well aware of the rights of the local episcopate. Stephen on his side appears fully aware of his right to intervene in the affairs of other Churches, and Cyprian also recognises this right since he asks Stephen to intervene in the case of Marcian of Arles. This ambiguity explains why Cyprian, at the time of the Donatist schism in the fourth century, was claimed as an ally both by the Donatists, on the one hand, and by Augustine on the other. Even today, J. P. Brisson has tried to show that he was the ancestor of African particularism[40]. But André Mandouze has shown that this is to simplify the problem of the Bishop of Carthage in an inadmissible way[41].

If, over and above particular questions, we try to discover the significance of the controversy, we realise its importance. It concerns the principle and modalities of the primacy of Rome. The primacy

39. *The Tradition of Manuscripts. A Study in the Tradition of St Cyprian's Treatises*, Oxford 1961, p. 99-101; 140-141.
40. *Autonomisme et Christianisme dans l'Afrique romaine de Septime-Sévère à l'invasion vandale*, Paris 1958, p. 207.
41. *Art. cit.*, p. 106-107.

itself is not in dispute — Cyprian is one of its great upholders — what is in dispute is its extent. What Cyprian declines to accept is intervention in a field which seems to him to depend on the prerogatives of the local Church; he is sure that the violence of Stephen's condemnation reveals a tendency on the part of the Bishop of Rome to abuse his authority. To the extent that he defends the legitimacy of various liturgical traditions, Cyprian was within his rights in protesting against Rome's tendency to centralise. But to the extent that dogma was involved, Stephen was acting lawfully in asserting his right to intervene. As the future will show, he was right. Deeper insight made it possible to solve the problem. But the dangers of particularism, on the one hand, and of authoritarianism on the other can already be foreseen in this great debate.

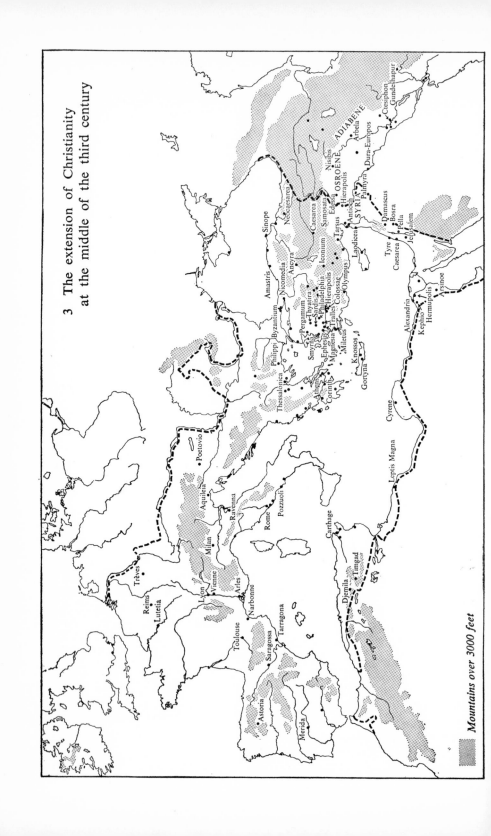

3 The extension of Christianity at the middle of the third century

Mountains over 3000 feet

CHAPTER XIV

THE END
OF THE THIRD CENTURY

THE second half of the third century was a period of transition in every field. Politically, anarchy set in after the dynasty of the Severi, the old Roman institutions crumbled and a new type of regime prepared to emerge. The Graeco-Roman civilisation, which, since the time of Alexander, had been supreme in a large part of the inhabited world was threatened everywhere by large-scale movements among the nations. The Goths on the Danube, the Persians in the east battered its frontiers; movements of independence emerged in Egypt, Africa and Gaul. The Church suffered from these events, but at the same time its prestige grew; it became the greatest spiritual force of the empire; it was ready to take over where ancient paganism left off, and to inspire the new civilisation which was coming to birth.

1. From Decius to Aurelian

The last of the Severi, Alexander, had been assassinated in 235. It was then that a period of disorder set in, when power belonged to the military leaders, who tried to maintain order in the empire. Several of them persecuted the christians, whom they considered a force working against unity. Maximinus, who succeeded Alexander, was a brave but short-sighted general; he attacked the outstanding members of Roman society, and among the christians he attacked the bishops (*HE*, VI, 28). Pope Pontian was exiled. After the short dynasty of the Gordians, Philip the Arabian again applied a policy of toleration. We have mentioned that he corresponded with Origen; it is possible that he was a christian. During his reign a violent persecution was launched against the christians of Alexandria, but it stemmed from a local pogrom unrelated to imperial policy (*HE*, VI, 40).

With his successor, Decius, the first of the Illyrian emperors, the first persecution decreed by the Roman government broke out. In 250, in order to strengthen Roman unity on a basis of religion, he ordered all citizens to take part in a general sacrifice. This persecution was the one we have mentioned in discussing Cyprian; many Christians yielded and sacrificed; others obtained a certificate, *libellus*, after which they were no longer bothered; but there were many martyrs, including Pope Fabian (20 January 250). Dionysius of Alexandria and Cyprian of Carthage fled to escape capture; Origen was imprisoned and tortured. A letter from Dionysius of Alexandria to Fabius of Antioch is of outstanding importance for an understanding of the persecution in Alexandria (VI, 41-42).

In 251, Decius suspended the persecution. It was then that Fabian's successor was probably appointed, after the see of Rome had been vacant for one year. Cornelius was elected in preference to Novatian. Then the question of the *lapsi* was raised. Decius was killed in the marshes of Abrittos, while making war against the Goths. Vibius Trebonianus Gallus had himself proclaimed emperor and associated his son Veldum-mianus Volusianus with himself. In 252 the persecution flared up again; Pope Cornelius had to go into exile; he died in exile in 253; his successor Lucius was also exiled. Dionysius of Alexandria tells us of this resumption of persecution in Egypt (*HE*, VII, 1). M. Aemilianus crushed Gallus in Nesia but was himself conquered and killed by Valerian.

Valerian reigned from 253 to 260. At first christians had an easier time, but things changed in 257. Dionysius attributes this change to the influence of the Minister of Finance, Macrianus, on the emperor. Macrianus had two reasons to hate the christians; first, he was an important member of Egyptian pagan confraternities: Dionysius says he was ' archisynagogue of the magicians of Egypt ' (*HE*, VII, 10, 4). This was something new. Septimus Severus and Decius had persecuted the christians in the name of the traditional religion of the empire. What appears with Macrianus is a pagan mysticism driven by passionate hatred of Christianity; he was a contemporary of Porphyry, also a initiate of theurgy, who attacked the christians in a famous work; Hierocles is another example, a little later. It is this pagan mysticism which was revived later by Julian, and which was the last form of pagan opposition to Christianity.

But these ideological reasons are not the only ones. A Magus of Egypt, Macrianus was also Minister of Finance. Now, under Valerian, the financial position of the empire was very serious; military expenditure was considerable; the treasury was obliged to resort to inflation and the percentage of precious metal in the currency became progressively lower, which led to devaluation. The government compelled the acceptance of depreciated currency, but real wealth was still lacking. As H. Grégoire puts it, Macrianus was the first politician to use anto-christian feeling to fill the treasury[1]. This is also proof of the importance of Church property, and the fact that some of the moneyed aristocracy belonged to the Church. We may note, incidentally, that the persecution was directed against Church dignitaries and high-ranking lay people.

A first edict was issued in 257, forbidding christian worship and gatherings in cemeteries, and obliging members of the hierarchy to sacrifice; for the first time christian worship had been forbidden. A second edict, in 258, ordered the immediate execution of members of the clergy who had not sacrificed and the confiscation of property belonging to christians of the upper classes; this persecution and that of Decius are the bloodiest on record. In Egypt, Dionysius of Alexandria was imprisoned in Kephro, and many christians martyred (*HE*, VII, 11). Eusebius also mentions martyrs in Palestine and Carthage. Cyprian, arrested as a result of the first edict, was executed as a result of the second; the authentic records of his trial are in existence. In Rome, Sixtus II was martyred with his deacons[2]. In Spain, Bishop Fructuosus of Tarragona was put to death with two deacons.

In 260 Valerian was made prisoner by Shapur II and put to death. His son, Gallien, associated with Valerian since 253, remained sole emperor. The sons of Macrianus proclaimed themselves emperors, but they were killed by the army, one in the east, the other on the Danube. Gallien succeeded in restoring order in the empire and guarding the frontiers against barbarian pressure; in 260 he promulgated an edict tolerating Christianity; the gist of this edict can be gathered from a letter of Dionysius of Alexandria, who refers to its promulgation in Egypt in 262. This rescript authorised worship in churches, which had to be restored to christians. Another rescript authorised christians to take possession of their cemeteries again. These rescripts of Gallien are very important; they did not yet make Christianity a *religio licita*, but they amounted to *de facto* recognition. Church property was also recognised implicitly.

Gallien's policy was continued by his successors, Claudius (268-270) and Aurelian (270-275). The latter tried to encourage solar monotheism, the final expression of emperor-worship, but he was tolerant of christians. During his reign an incident occurred which shows that the State recognised the Church's authority. The Bishop of Antioch, Paul of

1. H. Grégoire, *op. cit.*, p. 48.
2. See Cyprian, *Épist.*, LXXX, I, 1.

Samosata, having been removed from office by ecclesiastical authority, refused to leave the episcopal residence. The case was submitted to Aurelian, when he captured Antioch from Queen Zenobia. Aurelian decided that the house belonged to those ' who were in communion with the bishops of the christian doctrine in Rome and in Italy '.

That was to recognise a legitimate ecclesiastical authority. It also shows that the criterion of this legitimacy was communion with the Roman Church. No example shows more clearly how, on the threshold of the fourth century, the Church had become something which the State could not ignore. Constantine only ratified legally a situation which was already in existence at this period. The blood of martyrs had made a christian people possible.

2. The Church in the East

At the end of the third century, the Church was solidly rooted in the west, but it had scarcely passed beyond the great towns, except at Rome and Carthage, and it was only beginning to have a cultural influence and to use Latin. In the east, on the other hand, the Church which had already been established for two centuries underwent a remarkable expansion. Asia, Cappadocia, Syria, Palestine and Egypt were largely christian. Christianity, moreover, had established a theological and literary tradition; Origen had given christian thought an extraordinary lustre; we find influential men in all the Churches. Eusebius is a very precious primary source for this period, and thanks to him we get a clear picture of christian society.

Alexandria had a great bishop in the middle of the third century : Dionysius. He succeeded Heraclas at the head of the catechetical school about 231, when Heraclas became bishop, and on the latter's death in 248 he succeeded him in the see of Alexandria, which he occupied until 264. We have already mentioned that he fled the persecution of Decius, was arrested under Valerian and was in touch with Stephen over the matter of rebaptism. A great bishop, he was also an accomplished writer. The fragments of his work which, thanks to Eusebius, have come down to us are important from several points of view. In the first place they reveal some of the intellectual movements of the day; Eusebius has preserved some fragments of his treatise *On Nature*, where he refutes the Epicureans. Side by side with that we may mention that the African Arnobus also attacked Epicureanism a little later[3]. This shows the vitality of that philosophy at the end of the third century.

3. See H. Hagendahl, *Latin Fathers and the Classics*, Göteborg 1958.

A second treatise by Dionysius, *On Promises*, is more interesting. Eusebius has described the circumstances which gave rise to it. The Bishop of Arsinoe, Nepos, had published a book, *Refutation of the Allegorists*, in which he defended Millenarianism. For that he drew support fiom the *Apocalypse*. Millenarianism had been professed by the majority of christian writers before Origen. Later, a little after Nepos, it was professed by Methodius of Olympus, also an opponent of Origen, and in the fourth century by Apollinarius of Laodicea. We may wonder whether, in Nepos's day, the revival of Millenarianist hopes was not linked to the idea of the imminent end of the world, suggested by the violent persecutions of Decius and Valerian. That was true a little later of Commodian, at the time of Diocletian's persecution[4]. The *Apocalypse*, written for Christians persecuted under Nero and Domitian, once more became vitally important.

Dionysius, a disciple of Origen (*HE*, CI, 29, 4), was probably not predisposed to accept a very material conception of the eschatological promises proposed by Nepos. The latter having died meanwhile, Dionysius called for discussions at Arsinoe, during which he studied and refuted the disciples of Nepos, who swung over to his views. In his treatise, Dionysius first of all explains his reasons for refuting Millenarianism; the second part is a discussion of the Johannine authenticity of the *Apocalypse*. It has been preserved by Eusebius (*HE*, VII, 25); it recalls Origen's discussion of the authenticity of the *Epistle to the Hebrews*, and shows that Dionysius had received excellent training; it concludes that the *Apocalypse* is not by St John.

The most important part of Dionysius's work known to us through Eusebius is his correspondence. First of all, there is an early group, the *Paschal Letters*. Eusebius tells us that 'Dionysius wrote festal letters in which he raises his voice to make solemn pronouncements about the feast of Easter' (*HE*, VII, 20). The object of these letters was to announce the date of the feast of Easter; they were a kind of Lenten pastoral letter. Those by Dionysius are the first examples we possess. The practice was continued in Alexandria. We possess *Paschal Letters* by Athanasius, Peter of Alexandria and Cyril of Alexandria.

Besides the *Paschal Letters*, there are extracts from Dionysius's correspondence with Rome, which shows Dionysius's link with his Church. The *Letter to Fabian* (*HE*, VI, 41, 42 & 44) is a historical document of the first importance for the persecution of Alexandria in 248, and it also discusses the question of the reconciliation of the *lapsi*. Then comes a letter which Eusebius entiles ' *Diaconal Letter*

4. See J. Gagé, ' Commodien et le mouvement millénariste du IIIe siècle ', *RHPR*, 4 (1961), 355-379.

(diaconike) by Hippolytus' *(HE,* VI, 45, 5); the word *diaconike* is found only here. J. M. Hanssens thinks that a contrast is intended with an autograph letter *(idia)*, and that it was addressed by Hippolytus, acting as an intermediary. But who is this Hippolytus? Hanssens thinks that he is the Roman priest, Callistus's opponent[5]. Hippolytus would then have been an intermediary between Alexandria and Rome, which would be an argument for his Egyptian birth, but it seems improbable that he was an Egyptian. So here we have another Hippolytus, a deacon of Alexandria, sent on a mission to Rome. The Novatian episode occasioned a letter addressed to Cornelius, two others addressed to the Romans *On Peace and on Penance,* a letter to the Roman confessors supporting Novatian, and another to the same confessors after their submission *(HE,* VI, 46, 5). To these we must add the *Letter to Novatian,* (VI, 4, 5)[6]. Dionysius again wrote to Stephen (VI, 4 & 5, 1-2), to Sixtus *(HE,* VII, 5, 3-6; VII, 9), and to Dionysius (VII, 7, 6 & 8); and finally to the Roman priest, Philemon *(HE,* VII, 7).

The interest of Dionysius's correspondence is that it reflects the great problems of the Church at that time : persecutions, theological controversies and problems of Church discipline; but it also expresses concern for communion between various local Churches, and especially with the Church of Rome. It provides excellent evidence for the collegial structure of the Church before the time of the oecumenical Councils. Finally, it shows Dionysius as a man remarkable for the refinement of his culture, his spirit of gentleness and peace, and the prudence of his actions. We find him playing the part of mediator between Rome and Antioch; mediation was to remain a tradition in the Egyptian Church in succeeding centuries. Dionysius died in 264, at the time of the Council of Antioch. His last letter was addressed to the members of the Council *(HE,* VII, 27, 2).

Dionysius was not the only remarkable man in Alexandria at the end of the third century. We know little about his two immediate successors in the episcopal see, Maximus and Theonas; on the other hand, he had outstanding successors at the Didascalion. We know Theognostus only through Photius, who summarised his *Hypotoses;* he specialised in the problem of matter, and Photius praises his style. Pierius was head of the Catechetical school from 282 onwards, under Theonas; Eusebius praises his austere life and his knowledge of philosophy; Jerome mentions his *Homily on Hosea,* given during the Paschal Vigil[7].

5. *La liturgie d'Hippolyte,* p. 294-295, 299-300.
6. See P. Nautin, *Lettres et écrivains chrétiens du IIe et IIIe siècles,* p. 157-165.
7. *Vir. ill.,* 76.

Not only Alexandria but Palestine too could boast of outstanding men. Origen had taught in Caesarea during the second half of his life and founded a library there. Eusebius, Bishop of Caesarea fifty years later, may have had access to these documents and met the heirs of Origen's thought. About 260 the bishop was Theotechus, who, according to Eusebius, was a disciple of Origen (VII, 14). Under his successor, Agapius, Eusebius knew a certain Pamphilus in Caesarea. Pamphilus had been born in Phoenicia and educated in Alexandria by Pierius; he settled in Caesarea, where he was ordained priest by Agapius; he opened a theological school to continue Origen's tradition; above all, he compiled a large library, where Eusebius and later Jerome found the documents which made it possible for them to preserve for us writings of the first Christian centuries. Pamphilus wrote an *Apology* for Origen, the first volume of which was translated by Rufinus.

As for Syria, Christians in Laodicea seem to have been in close touch with Alexandria. About 260 the bishop there was Eusebius. Eusebius of Caesarea says that he was born in Alexandria (*HE*, VII, 32, 5); he was deacon of that town (*HE*, VII, 11, 16) and under Valerian showed outstanding zeal in looking after imprisoned Christians (*HE*, VII, 11, 24). He came to Antioch for the Council of 264; during his visit the people of Laodicea asked him to become their bishop in place of Socrates, who had just died (*HE*, VII, 32, 5). His successor, Anatolius, was also an Alexandrian (*HE*, VII, 32, 6). At Alexandria he had won a great reputation for his skill in arithmetic, geometry, physics, dialectic and rhetoric (*HE*, VII, 32, 6). This is a precious piece of evidence for the revival of Aristotelianism at that time. This revival is also to be found in the pagan Porphyry, at Tyre, and Lucian, at Antioch. Eusebius gives us an important passage by Anatolius on the question of the date of Easter (*HE*, VII, 32, 14-19). Earlier, he had been coadjutor-bishop of Caesarea (*HE*, VII, 14-21).

Origen's influence is again seen in the bishops of Cappadocia and Pontus at this period. Firmilian became Bishop of Caesarea about 230; Eusebius tells us that ' he was so attached to Origen that he invited him to visit his country ' (*HE*, VI, 27). This stay probably took place at the time when Origen was driven out of Alexandria, about 230. Firmilian then came to Caesarea to complete his education (*HE*, VI, 27); he supported Novatian (*HE*, VII, 5, 4), and invited Dionysius of Alexandria to the Council of Antioch in 252 (*HE*, VI, 46, 3). A very stern letter of his is extant addressed to Cyprian against Cornelius, but he ended by adopting the Roman point of view (*HE*, VII, 5, 2). He was present at the Council of Antioch in 264 (*HE*, VI, 28, 1) and died at Tarsus in 268, while travelling to a new synod concerning Paul of Samosata, towards whom he had already adopted a critical position.

Another of Origen's disciples was Bishop of Neo-Caesarea, in Pontus, at that time. Gregory, also known as Theodore (VI, 33), had been a pupil of Origen in Caesarea. His *Thanksgiving to Origen* is extant, a precious source of information about his master in Caesarea. Phedim, Bishop of Amasya in Pontus, consecrated him shortly after 238 as Bishop of Neo-Caesarea; he was the great apostle of Pontus and among his notable converts were the grandparents of Basil and Gregory of Nyssa — the latter wrote a eulogy about him — and it is through him that the Cappadocians came to know Origen's ideas. He attended the Council of Antioch in 264 (*HE*, VII, 28, 1) and died shortly afterwards. Gregory of Nyssa has preserved a very interesting Creed by him; he was a contemporary of Dionysius of Alexandria and Firmilian of Caesarea. This generation of bishops, educated in Origen's school, founded many churches; they are probably one of the most remarkable groups in the history of Christianity.

While Alexandria was influencing Palestine, Phoenicia, Cappadocia and Pontus, Antioch was beginning to emerge as a centre of inventive Christian culture. During the first half of the third century almost nothing is known about the Church in Antioch, but at the end of the century we find curious figures appearing there : Dorotheus, Malchion and Lucian. Dorotheus, a great Hebrew scholar as well as a master of Greek studies, was put in charge of the Tyrian purple dye works by Aurelian (*HE*, VII, 32, 2-4). At the same time Malchion, a priest of Antioch, was put in charge of the rhetoric course in the Antioch schools; in this post he was a forerunner of Libanius (*HE*, VII, 29, 2). Lucian, also a priest of Antioch, was an eminent theologian (*HE*, IX, 6, 3). Like Dorotheus, he seems to have known both Hebrew and secular Greek studies. Among his pupils the first Arians were recruited, who called themselves ' Collucianists '; he was martyred under Diocletian (*HE*, VIII, 13, 2)[8].

These men have certain features in common, typical of the school of Antioch. Whereas the Alexandrians continued the tradition of Hellenistic Judaism and its mystical Platonism, the Antiochians were more matter-of-fact. They were in touch with the Aramaean world of the east, and closer to Rabbinic Judaism; many of them knew Hebrew, and this makes their exegesis more scientific; they had also studied Jewish exegesis. Moreover, pagan Antioch was more literary than philosophical; the christians of Antioch followed a Greek course of studies — grammar,

8. See G. Bardy, *Recherches sur Lucien d'Antioche et son école*, Paris 1936.

dialectic and geometry — which they used in their exegesis. They were especially well-trained dialecticians : Malchion is an example; they also had a taste for rhetoric, but they mistrusted philosophical speculation. Whereas Alexandria remained a great centre of speculative theology and allegorical exegesis, Antioch developed in the direction of pastoral theology and scientific exegesis.

But besides these scholars Antioch produced a very curious man of quite another sort at the end of the third century. In 260, at the death of Valerian, the situation in Syria was dramatic; Shapur threatened the country; Quietus, one of the sons of Macrianus, had himself proclaimed emperor in Emesa and refused to recognise Gallien. It was then that the Prince of Palmyra, Odenathus, took the title of king; he defeated Shapur at Ctesiphon, routed Quietus at Emesa and established his rule in Egypt and Asia. The Bishop of Antioch, Demetrian, had been led captive by Shapur in 260; he was replaced by Paul, who was born in Samosata. Paul was related to the Palmyrean dynasty and was probably elected with the support of Odenathus and, above all, of his wife Zenobia. To his episcopal duties he added those of ducenary (*HE*, VII, 30, 8), that is to say, Minister of Finance. Eusebius reproaches him with having made money out of this post. He shows him putting on the airs of a satrap and taking a bodyguard, erecting a throne in his church and conducting religious ceremonies with worldly pomp. In fact, Paul represents the arrival at Antioch of east Syrian practices.

Paul was also accused of holding heterodox opinions, which we shall discuss later; he was condemned by two Antiochene Synods, in 264 and 268, but thanks to the support of Zenobia, widowed in 267, he managed to remain in the episcopal house. At that time the court of Zenobia was a brilliant centre, counting among its members not only Paul but the rhetor Longinus. But in 272 Aurelian seized Palmyra; the Palmyran kingdom crumbled and Paul disappears from history. Primarily, he stood for Semitic Christianity's resistance to Romanisation. He was also a representative of a period when the temporal power of the Church was growing and the bishops tempted to abuse their new privileges. About this time, in his *De Lapsis*, Cyprian was attacking bishops who became stewards of great landowners.

There remains one last area about which, surprisingly enough, Eusebius tells us nothing : Asia, or rather the western coast of Asia Minor. A very lively centre for the development of Christianity in the second century, Asia seems to have led an isolated existence during the third. Eusebius does not name any bishop of Smyrna, Ephesus or Miletus. Under Decius we hear only about the martyrdom of Pionius at Smyrna in Pergamum. But there is one outstanding representative of Asia at the end of the century : Methodius, Bishop of Olympus in Lycia[9]. Some of his writings are extant; his most famous book, the *Banquet of the Ten Virgins*, shows him to be the heir of the great second-century Asiatics. He is a refined writer, influenced by Plato and Homer[10], an ascetic who glorifies virginity, and also a Millenarianist, who speculates about the end of time; his point of view tallies with that of Nepos, in Egypt, and it is not surprising that he appears as a great opponent of Origen in his treatise *On the Resurrection*, and that Eusebius is silent about him.

3. Theological Discussions

The end of the third century is an important period in the history of the dogma of the Trinity. There was opposition between various imperfect attempts to express the original data in the bible and the Church's tradition. At this period there emerged the conflicts which Councils of later centuries were to resolve. It is difficult to define exact frontiers between the various attitudes; each assumed forms that were more or less orthodox. According to the region, bishops were more aware of this or that danger. So the end of the third century forms an introduction to a situation which we shall find throughout the latter part of the fourth century. It is an indispensable preamble to the great controversies of the later period.

We have seen these trinitarian discussions appear in Rome during the pontificates of Victor, Zephyrinus and Callistus. Epigonus, a disciple of Noetus of Smyrna, had taught Monarchianism; his theology so stressed the unicity of the Divine subsistence as to deny that the Son is a proper substance. His disciple Cleomenes seems to have professed a more orthodox doctrine, for Zephyrinus and Callistus were favourable to him. Hippolytus, our source for this period, was hostile to him but tells us nothing about his doctrine. There is probably an echo of it in the teaching which Hippolytus attributes to Callistus. It is against this background that Sabellius appears; he was a Cyrenean from the Pentapolis (*HE*, VII, 6), came to Rome under Zephyrinus and was a disciple of Cleomenes; according to Hippolytus, he was at first encouraged by Callistus, at that time still a deacon. This is quite possible, for we know that Callistus sympathised with Monarchianism, but once elected Pope, in 217, Callistus condemned Sabellius. Hippolytus considered this a piece of intrigue but we cannot be certain. With Sabellius Monarchianism became sharply heterodox. Unfortunately, none of his own views have survived.

9. See P. Nautin, *op. cit.*, p. 257-258.
10. See V. Buckheit, *Studien zu Methodios von Olympes*, Berlin 1958.

The problem became troublesome again forty years later. In 257 the doctrines of Sabellius became influential in Cyrenaica. By this time Sabellius was dead, but it would seem that after his condemnation by Rome he returned to his own country and founded a school there. The inhabitants of Cyrenaica were divided in their views. Some bishops were won over by the Sabellians and no longer dared speak of the Son. Both sides sent documents to Dionysius of Alexandria (*HE*, VII, 6). Dionysius wrote a memorandum on the matter, a copy of which he sent to the priest Philemon in Rome, and he also wrote to Ammon, Bishop of Berenice in Cyrenaica, on the same subject (VII, 26) and to the other bishops of the region. These first letters did not succeed in convincing the Sabellian bishops. Dionysius then sent a new letter to Ammon and Eupator, explaining in greater detail the distinction between the Father and the Son, whom the Sabellians confused[11]. The people of Cyrenaica then appealed to the Bishop of Rome, at that time Dionysius, who had just succeeded Sixtus, and with whom Dionysius of Alexandria had been in correspondence when he was only a priest (*HE*, VII, 7, 6).

This appeal is interesting for the history of the primacy of Rome in doctrinal matters, but it was also a clever piece of strategy, for the Roman theological tradition regarding the Trinity was Monarchian in tendency, that is to say it stressed the unity of the Divine substance. If Callistus had condemned Sabellius, he had also been favourable to Cleomenes; furthermore, he had been in conflict with Hippolytus. Hippolytus, in the tradition of Justin, held that the one God had uttered the Logos from himself, the same Logos who was in him invisibly, and had conferred on him his own subsistence with a view to creation. So the Logos has a subsistence distinct from the Father's, but he acquired this subsistence by a free act of God. In Alexandria Origen had held a similar doctrine, speaking of the free generation of the Logos, and insisting on his inferiority to the Father. He seems to have been in difficulty with Pope Fabian and to have tried to justify himself. Now Dionysius of Alexandria was a disciple of Origen. It was the same conflict flaring up again between two equally inadequate expressions of the dogma of the Trinity.

Athanasius tells us how the bishops of Cyrenaica criticised Dionysius of Alexandria; he separated and estranged the Son from the Father; he asserted that the Son did not exist before being engendered and so that there was a time when he did not exist, therefore he was not eternal; he arrived afterwards. This meant that the Son is a creation *(poiema)* and a product *(geneton);* in essence he is foreign to the Father, as the

11. Athanasius, *Sent. Dionys.*, 5.

vine is to the vine-dresser or the ship to the shipwright. Finally, said Dionysius, they accuse me falsely of saying that Christ is not consubstantial *(homoousios)* with God. There is no doubt that these charges, if they hardened Dionysius's views, brought out certain weak points, as Basil was later to admit. Dionysius of Rome convoked a Synod in Rome, which condemned the arraigned propositions. He addressed a letter to the Cyrenaeans about the way to refute Sabellianism in which he did not name the Bishop of Alexandria, but he sent the bishop a personal letter. It was to this letter that Dionysius replied with a *Refutation and Apology*, important parts of which have been preserved by Eusebius and Athanasius.

The *Apology* of Dionysius of Alexandria perfected those formulas in his doctrine capable of misinterpretation. He continued to say that there were three hypostases, but denied that they were separate. He asked his critics to interpret certain comparisons in the light of others, such as that of the spring and the river, the root and the plant. He agreed to reject the term *homoousios* because it was not in Scripture, but he accused his critics of having passed over in silence other passages where he asserted practically the same doctrine. He explained the significance he gave the term *poiema* for the Word and clearly asserted that there never had been a time when the Word was not. In short, Dionysius of Alexandria said that basically he was in full agreement with the Bishop of Rome, but he maintained his own vocabulary and perspective. The importance of this debate is obvious. The two bishops condemned certain errors, some Monarchian, others Subordinationist. On the other hand, differences about the Trinity between the Roman and Alexandrian theological schools became more pronounced. Certain questions had not been cleared up. Arianism was later to raise them again, thus leading to new and more exact formulations.

A conflict parallel to that between the Bishops of Cyrenaica and Dionysius of Alexandria developed in Antioch[12]; its result was different. We have spoken of Paul of Samosata, who succeeded Bishop Demetrian at the head of the Church in 260; his nomination coincided with Queen Zenobia's influence in the east; he too came from Samosata on the Euphrates, and he was typically eastern, practising the customs of eastern Syria. He was criticised for the custom of *virgines subintroductae*, which went back to the very early Syrian Church (*HE*, VII, 30, 11). For the singing of psalms he introduced the practice of having a choir of virgins alternating with a men's choir (*HE*, VII, 30, 10), an east Syrian

---

12. See C. Bardy, *Paul de Samosate*, Paris 1929; C. Downey, *A History of Antioch in Syria*, Princeton 1961, p. 338.

custom. He condemned hymns in honour of Christ as an innovation, and attacked Origen (*HE*, VII, 30, 9).

His nomination evidently aroused opposition in the more Hellenised circles of Antioch, influenced by Greek philosophy. We have seen that the leaders of this group were Lucian and Malchion. They aimed their attack at Paul's theology. Eusebius accused him of having professed the same heresy as Artemon (*HE*, V, 28, 1; VII, 30, 16-17). This heresy was active in Rome in the middle of the third century and continued the Adoptionism of Theodotus of Byzantium. But it seems that this attack was a mere piece of polemic, and that there was no link between Artemon's doctrine and Paul's. Paul's doctrine was evidently closer to that of Beryllus of Bostra : it stressed both the unity of God and the humanity of Christ; it did not have a detailed theology of the generation of the Word, and it easily led to charges of Modalism and Adoptionism. These attacks took the form of convocation of a Synod, which the whole crowd of Origenists attended. This synod was probably preceded by skirmishes, but the historians do not mention them. Perhaps they can help to explain one of the riddles of the third-century Church : the riddle of Lucian.

Eusebius refers only to his learning and his martyrdom, but it is certain that he ran into doctrinal difficulties. The Arians considered him as their ancestor. It is probable that while Dionysius of Alexandria was struggling against the Modalism of Sabellius, Lucian was doing likewise against Paul's Modalism, but like Dionysius he probably went too far in the other direction and like Dionysius was probably denounced to Rome. Now Eusebius tells us of a letter from Dionysius of Alexandria to Dionysius of Rome ' on the subject of Lucian ' (*HE*, VII, 9, 6). This letter was written after the accession of Dionysius of Rome and before the death of Dionysius of Alexandria : that is, between 260 and 264, precisely the years preceding the Synod of Antioch. Lucian was evidently condemned by the Bishop of Antioch, Paul; and the latter tried to get this sentence ratified by Dionysius of Rome, who was hostile to Origenist theology. The Synod of Antioch marked the Origenists' counter-offensive against Paul, who was deposed and succeeded by Domnus (268-271), and later Timaeus. But in fact Paul continued to discharge his duties until Aurelian's victory over Zenobia in 272. Lucian, therefore, was excluded from the Church under the three bishops, Paul, Domnus and Timaeus. At least, this is the interpretation that can be placed on a passage in Alexander of Jerusalem[13], trying to discredit Lucian as an ancestor of Arianism.

13. *Epist. ad Alex. Byz.*, 5.

The Council which gathered in Antioch in 264 included the most outstanding bishops of the east : Firmilian of Caesarea, Gregory the Wonderworker and Theotechus of Caesarea. Dionysius of Alexandria, who was ill, wrote to excuse himself and give his opinion (*HE*, VII, 37, 2; 38, 1). The Council seems to have held several sessions; Paul's ideas were discussed. During the last session, in 268, Malchion, the priest of Antioch, fully unmasked Paul's heresy, having doubtless obtained shorthand reports of Paul's statements outside the Council meetings[14]. Paul was solemnly condemned. Eusebius has preserved long passages from the Synodal letter, which was addressed to the Bishop of Rome, Dionysius, to Maximus, Bishop of Alexandria, and to the other provinces[15].

During the debates leading up to Paul's condemnation and in reaction against him, the Antioch Fathers adopted two positions which were later to give rise to difficulties. The first concerns the word *homoousios*, applied to the Trinity. We have seen that Dionysius put it aside as non-scriptural. At Antioch it was considered an expression of Paul's Modalism and was rejected. That explains why the eastern Fathers were so reticent about it when the west wanted to impose it at Nicaea[16]. On the other hand, at the Christological level it seems clear that Malchion and the Fathers of the Council, wishing to show that Christ was really God, compared his union with his human nature to the union that exists between a soul and a body. The Word had the same place in Christ as the soul has in us, and so the Word was united to a body and not to a human soul. This seems to be the source of the theory which Apollinarius of Laodicea was to defend at Antioch a century later. It is true, then, that the great theological controversies which filled the fourth century were already taking shape in the second part of the third.

4. Ecclesiastical Organisation

For the Church the end of the third century was a period of expansion which had repercussions at the levels of organisation, economics and civil life. Until the middle of the third century, the bishop could group local communities around him. But the great increase in the number of christians in the towns, and the spreading of the Gospel in the country made this centralisation more and more impossible. The solution

---

14. See M. Richard, ' Malchion et Paul de Samosate ', *ETL*, 35 (1959), p. 326-329.
15. See H. de Riedmatton, *Les Actes du Procès de Paul de Samosate*, Fribourg 1952, p. 46-67.
16. See G. Kretschmar, *Studien zur frühchrislichen Trinitäts theologie*, Tübingen 1956, p. 17-18.

seems to have varied with the region. In large towns more districts were created, especially in the suburbs, and a priest was put in charge of them. In this way the Roman *tituli* were formed, probably at this time. The same thing happened in Alexandria.

The problem of the countryside was much more difficult. Sometimes small groups of christians lived far from a town. Several solutions were adopted. In Africa and central Italy, more bishoprics were created. Several hundred bishops attended the African Councils at the beginning of the fourth century, which implies that small market towns had their bishops. Likewise, around Rome, many small towns had their bishops. In Asia Minor at this period chorepiscopi are found : bishops of villages, considered inferior in rank, who disappeared at the end of the fourth century. They appeared at the beginning of the third (*HE*, V, 16, 17). But the usual solution which later became general, was to do as in the towns and increase the number of ' parishes ', with priests in charge, under the bishop of the nearest town. This happened notably in Gaul.

A certain hierarchy of bishoprics appeared or became more marked at this period. As we have seen, as early as the second century the bishop of a metropolis of a civil province had pre-eminence over the other bishops of his province, convoked the local Council and collected opinions. Sometimes, rather, this pre-eminence belonged to the oldest, to the primate, of the bishops in the province. But what characterises our period is the appearance of a higher unit, corresponding not to a province but to a ' diocese ', an institution which first appeared in Egypt. The Bishop of Alexandria was the Patriarch of the diocese of Egypt, which included several provinces. It would seem that something similar took place in the diocese of the east, where the Bishop of Antioch enjoyed pre-eminence, and in the diocese of Africa, where it was the Bishop of Carthage.

While the Church was growing in numbers, it reached new groups. Most important was the conversion of many members of the ruling classes, which we have already mentioned. In this sense it is untrue to say that the ruling classes turned towards Christianity only when the empire was officially christian, for political reasons. This trend was already evident in the second half of the third century. Eusebius notes that under the emperors who succeeded Valerian, under Gallien, Claudius, Aurelian, Tacitus, Probus and Carus, some christians were provincial governors (VIII, 1, 2), and he adds that there were many christians in the imperial household and even in the family of the emperors (VIII, 1, 3). Inscriptions show us christians occupying posts in the municipal curias. Anatolius, Bishop of Laodicea, had previously been a member of the Alexandrian senate and his predecessor, Eusebius, was a rich Alexandrian (*HE*, VII, 32, 5-10). Astyrius was a senator (VII, 16, 1) and Domnus held a high command in the army (VII, 15, 2). Dorotheus was put in charge of the purple dye works in Tyre by the emperor (*HE*, VII, 38, 3). Gregory and Athenodorus, the apostles of the Pontus, seem to have belonged to a senatorial family. This is also true of the ancestors of St Basil and St Gregory of Nyssa, Basil and Macrina, who were converted by Gregory.

The part played by christians in municipal functions raised problems, for the magistrates were usually obliged to take part in acts of worship. Eusebius tells us that the emperors dispensed christian provincial governors from these acts (VIII, 1, 1), but that was something exceptional. The usual procedure is clear from the canons of the Council of Elvira; the fifty-sixth stipulates that the duumvirs, who presided over civic government, had to abstain from coming to Church during their term of office. This implies that the acceptance of municipal posts was possible. Other canons absolutely forbid acceptance of the office of flamen. However secularised the municipal priesthood, its holders had to take part in sacrifices. Even the honorary flamen, who only wore the crown, his insignia of office, was admitted to communion only after two years' penance.

The paradox of these situations is evident. The vital forces of the empire were largely christian; pagan worship was often purely formal, but the fact remained that the official life of the empire demanded acts of pagan worship. So those christians who were appointed magistrates found themselves in a difficult position, which could hardly last. The framework no longer corresponded to reality. By loosing the empire's ties with paganism, Constantine was not a revolutionary; he was merely recognising *de jure* a *de facto* situation.

PART TWO

THE GREAT PERSECUTION
TO THE EMERGENCE OF MEDIEVAL
CHRISTIANITY

BY

HENRI MARROU

CHAPTER XV

CHRISTIANITY ON THE EVE
OF THE GREAT PERSECUTION

THIS history has now reached a decisive stage. The next ten or twenty years will bring two dramatic changes of fortune. With the persecution of Diocletian in 303-304 and the following years, the pagan Empire makes a last attempt, more violent than ever before, to wipe out the christian religion; thereafter during the period 306/312-324, Constantine's steady rise to power until he is at last sole master of the Empire, soon leads to a complete change of status for Christianity. Instead of being persecuted, it now emerges as a religion in accordance with law, privileged and presently to become the State religion; instead of being encysted in society like an unwanted foreign body, it becomes a directive principle, a vital centre within the Empire which, with the conversion of its ruler, has now become christian.

When the first edict of persecution, decreed by Diocletian and his colleagues in the tetrarchy, was posted in the imperial residence of Nicomedia on the Asiatic shore of the Sea of Marmara on 23 February 303, it was pulled down and torn to pieces by a hothead. This action, which naturally cost the man his life, shows how much surprise and scandal was caused by such an unexpected imperial decree.

Since the short but severe persecutions of Decius (250-251) and Valerian (257-260), the christian Church had been left more or less in peace by the civil authorities. Although its legal position had never been completely clarified and Christianity was, in principle, practically a forbidden religion, we now find what can be called *de facto* recognition. Christian communities can show themselves openly and enjoy their property in peace. They have their own cemeteries either underground (catacombs) or open-air *(areae)* and have had them in Rome since the time of Pope Callistus (217-222); they have churches or at least houses for worship and prayer, though it is difficult to be specific about the architectural style, and in Nicomedia one of these was built opposite the imperial palace. The pagan Porphyry and the christian historian Eusebius of Caesarea both record that on the eve of the persecution the increased number of christians made it necessary to build new and larger churches.

1. The Minor Peace of the Church[1]

There is justification, then, for speaking of a first ' minor peace of the Church ', thanks to which it was possible for christian missionary work to develop freely and make great progress both superficially by geographic expansion and in depth through the penetration of society.

Born at a point very near the eastern border of the Roman Empire, the gospel had quickly spread from Palestine beyond the frontier. In fact the christian religion had attained its earliest spectacular successes eastwards beyond the Euphrates, and the small vassal Kingdom of Edessa or Osroene had been the first State to become officially christian with the conversion of its King Abgar IX (179-216).

During the third century Christianity had reached Adiabene, east of the Tigris, and spread across Mesopotamia in what is now Iraq. But for christian propaganda this Semitic country, politically a part of the Iranian Empire, presented great difficulties. These often extended to open persecution which began with the accession of the Sassanid dynasty (224). From then onwards this powerful empire, continually a rival, a challenge and a model for Rome, linked its destiny with Mazdaism, the national religion of Zoroaster, and Christianity, already suspect because it came from the hereditary Roman enemy, ran up against the uneasy suspicions of a State religion which was also a rival religion. For Mazdaism was similarly universal in its aims and actuated by a like missionary impulse, a powerful creed led by a strictly hierarchical clergy under the authority of a Priest of Priests, *Mobadham-Mobadh*, who was ready to invoke the help of the State to silence dissident or rival voices, whether they were heretic Mazdaites, Manichaeans or christians.

At the time of the victorious war waged by the great King Shapur against the Emperor Valerian, christians from Syria were deported to Fars, formerly Elam, and so helped to spread the gospel as far east as the heart of the Iranian Empire. But the difficulties mentioned above explain why at the end of the third century the christian Church composed of these eastern Syrians was still only sketchily organized around the

1. The phrase is Walter Pater's. In *Marius the Epicurean*, ch. 22, he applies it to the age of Marcus Aurelius, but it is even more applicable to the third century.

the sacrifice of Abraham, the Arrest of St Peter, Christ giving the Law to SS Peter and Paul, Christ taken to Pilate, Christ before Pilate.

Lower Row : Job, Adam and Eve, the Entry into Jerusalem, Daniel in the Lions' Den, St Paul going to martyrdom.

There is something very genteel and elegant about the scenes on this sarcophagus, as befits the sarcophagus of a Prefect of the City of Rome. Notice the contrast of the central panel with the same scene in the S. Constanza mosaic in Plate 18; and apart from this treatment of the figure of Christ, note also how refined and intelligent Pilate is made to appear in the act of making his great decision. The background of the sarcophagus is conservative Rome. (For aspects of the conversion of the Roman aristocracy, cf. ch. 22, § 3.)

Photo : Leonard von Matt.

CHRISTIANA TEMPORA : V. The Christian Aristocracy (i)

PLATE 23. SARCOPHAGUS OF JUNIUS BASSUS, PREFECT OF THE CITY OF ROME, DIED 25TH AUGUST 359; CRYPT OF ST PETER'S, ROME

CHRISTIANA TEMPORA : VI. The Christian Aristocracy (ii)

PLATE 24. HUNTING SCENE FROM MAUSOLEUM; CENTCELLES, SPAIN, MID-4TH CENTURY

The most recent hypothesis about this building is that it is the mausoleum of Constans (died 350), son of Constantine the Great. The immediate significance of this full-blooded picture of a hunting scene is that it serves as a healthy reminder of other dimensions in the life of the Christian aristocracy. In the same mausoleum we find familiar biblical motifs — eg. the three young men in the fiery furnace,

Jonah, Daniel etc. — juxtaposed with this scene just as, presumably, the new faith and the traditional pastimes of their class were juxtaposed in the lives of many Christian aristocrats. (For evidence in support of the hypothesis mentioned above, see T. Hauschile und H. Schlunk: 'Vorbericht über die Arbeiten in Centcelles', *Madrider Mitteilungen*, 2, 1961.)

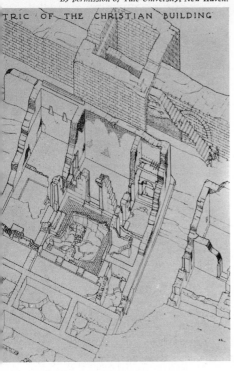

CHRISTIAN ARCHITECTURE: I.

PLATE 25.

Left : SKETCH OF THE HOUSE CHURCH AT DURA-EUROPOS

The baptistry, in which wall paintings have survived (cf. Plate 7), is in the top right hand corner of this sketch. (Cf. ch. 12, § 2.)

Scale   30 feet

Below : FACADE OF 3RD CENTURY HOUSE FACING THE PALATINE, ROME; LATER CON-VERTED INTO THE CHURCH OF ST ANASTASIUS

Archaeological work on the Church of St Anastasius has shown that it is a complex structure stemming from several different generations. This facade was built on to an existing house in the 3rd century and is an interesting example of Roman architecture in the imperial epoch. The lower portion of the house is no longer visible, but the top storey was later incorporated into the basilica. (Cf. ch. 13, § 2)

Photo : Rivista di Archeologia Cristiana.

CHRISTIAN ARCHITECTURE : II

PLATE 26. S. SABINA, ROME; VIEW OF THE INTERIOR LOOKING TOWARDS THE ALTAR, 422-432

The basilica of S. Sabina was built during the time of Pope Celestinus (422-432). According to tradition, it was built on the site of an ancient House Church. Of all those surviving in Rome, it best preserves the character and stamp of the early Christian basilica. Note the contrast of light and shade in the windowless side aisles, and the more open central nave. Most of the later medieval additions were removed during the restoration of 1914-19, but the floor is medieval, the roof modern and the barrier towards the altar is a modern restoration based on a 9th century structure. In early Christian times there was a barrier between the third pair of columns at the altar end.

Photo : Alinari.

episcopal see of the twin ' royal towns ' of Seleucia-Ctesiphon between Babylon and Baghdad; for many years to come they continued to look west and to lean doctrinally, canonically and spiritually on the churches of the Roman Empire.

Geographically, Christianity belongs first and foremost to the Mediterranean.   Round about the year 300 it has practically covered the whole Roman Empire and penetrated its most distant provinces; at the Council of Arles in 314 three bishops from Britain are present, including those of London and York.   But christian communities are far from being evenly distributed throughout, and the network of organised churches still seems to contain many gaps in the Latin, Western part of the Roman Empire.   Thus, at the Council of Elvira (Granada) held either in 300 or 309 at about the time of the great persecution, thirty-three Spanish churches are known to have been represented, nineteen by their bishops, fourteen by simple priests, either as delegates of absent bishops or because the churches in question were still incompletely organised.   But a glance at map no. 4 (p. 222) shows that nearly all these churches are grouped in a single region corresponding to present-day Andalusia; there are only five in other parts of the Iberian peninsula.   Similarly in Gaul where the gospel seems about that time to have made less progress, there were sixteen Gaulish churches present at the Council of Arles, of which twelve were represented by their bishops.   But half of these are clustered in the south-east in present-day Provence, and in the rest of Gaul only a few of the most important towns seem at this date to possess a fully developed christian community.   Only in the peninsula of Italy roughly from Ravenna to Naples, and in Roman Africa, that is to say north-east of the Magreb, do the christian communities appear more numerous.   In a Roman Synod of 250-251 sixty Italian bishops sat round Pope Cornelius; and about the same date (256-257) eighty-seven African bishops attended a Synod presided over by the Bishop of Carthage, St Cyprian.

On the whole, Christianity still mainly recruits its members in the eastern provinces from Cyrenaica to the Balkans where Greek is the language of cultivated people.   The most vigorous cells are in Egypt, in Palestine, in Syria pre-eminently, and in Asia Minor.   In Egypt, the ecclesiastical metropolis of Alexandria, largest city of the Empire after Rome, imposes its great authority on the multitude of small churches, and under its powerful impulse they seed themselves across the flat country from the Delta to the Thebaid.   Ever since the time of Paul, Antioch, the capital of Syria, had always played a leading role in christian life and history on account of its importance as third city of the Empire and its central position at the very heart of the East.

Finally, Asia Minor still remains at this period the bulwark of Christianity, the christian country *par excellence*, the region with the greatest number of faithful both proportionately and absolutely. During the early Empire this region bordering the Aegean and classified for administrative purposes as part of Asia had been the most flourishing and thickly populated part of the Roman world; without any doubt it was only there (with the exception of certain districts of Egypt) that most of the population were already christian and certain small villages were entirely christian.

Progress is no less remarkable from a sociological viewpoint. The new faith has gradually percolated through the various strata of the Roman population. It is no longer only or chiefly the religion of those groups scorned or downtrodden by the highly aristocratic system of imperial society : children, women, slaves, the poor. About 177-180 Celsus could speak sarcastically of a religion of wool-carders, cobblers and laundry-men. The picture now is very different; about 270 Porphyry speaks of rich noble ladies who, in obedience to the Gospel's counsel of perfection, have given all their goods to the Church or the poor. In 303, when persecution comes, Christianity has taken a hold among the working class, among magistrates and provincial governors, and in the Palace where high officials such as the chamberlains Dorotheus and Gorgonius will later be numbered among the first martyrs; and even if none of the imperial family are actually christians, it is rumoured that Diocletian's wife and daughter, Prisca and Valeria, have been more or less drawn to the new faith.

From the spiritual point of view, of course, this progress was not wholly beneficial. The calm enjoyed by the Church deprived it of the sieve of martyrdom and on the whole lowered the quality of recruits; there is evidence of contamination, compromise, and some infiltration from the surrounding paganism, and we are no longer aware of the early fervour of the Church of the Saints. In Spain, the disciplinary canons adopted by the council of Elvira reveal very curious signs of this : the faithful had to be warned against superstitions of pagan origin, games of chance, usury; and a scale of penances had to be fixed against bigamy, abortion, and adultery for which the period was five years — very little if one thinks of the scandal previously caused when Pope Callistus showed mercy on this class of sinners by allowing them to be reconciled without waiting for the point of death.

The extent to which christians and pagans mingled and merged in their ordinary day-to-day activities is especially striking; christians had to be reminded of the ban on mixed marriages and christian women were criticised for lending their best clothes to pagan neighbours to wear for festivals of the gods. Worse still were christians who went up to the Capitol and took part in sacrifices; for this ten years' penance was prescribed.

This merging was most important of all in the case of magistrates. In the Roman world municipal office and pagan priesthood, which involved heavy expenses, had become obligatory for whoever possessed the requisite personal fortune; the same was beginning to be true in certain cases of military service, causing many difficulties of conscience, for example, for sons of veterans. The performance of these functions normally entailed participation in pagan worship and in games considered religious, as well as shocking, by christians. A whole range of practical solutions was in fact applied or could be envisaged. With the connivance of the higher authorities the christian magistrate could purely and simply abstain from the sacrifices or else, possibly at a price, find someone to substitute for him; he could replace gladiator fights and also, if possible, chariot races, by useful public works — or else do as everyone else did and behave practically as a pagan.

There was a rude awakening on the day of persecution. But we cannot understand what that persecution was like, its spasmodic, irregular virulence and finally its failure, unless we set the problem of Christianity in the general framework of the political and religious evolution of the whole Roman world.

2. The Late Empire : a Totalitarian State and a New Religious Consciousness

In the third century the Empire had undergone a terrible crisis in which it almost foundered (235-285); a crisis abroad : Sassanid rivalry, pressure of Germanic invasions on the Rhine and Danube frontiers; a crisis within : instability of power, civil war, economic failure, anarchy. ' The Emperors of the fourth century, and above all Diocletian [aimed] to save the Roman Empire and they succeeded. To this end they used, with the best intentions, the means familiar to them, violence and compulsion. They never asked whether it was worthwhile to save the Roman Empire in order to make it a vast prison for scores of millions of men '[2]. So writes a liberal historian and his judgment is very severe. One must emphasise on the other hand just how prodigiously effective was the solution imposed by Diocletian's revolution. It needs to be remembered that what we called the Late Roman Empire or the end of antiquity coincides with the first Byzantine era and that the regime

2. M. Rostovtsev, *The Social and Economic History of the Roman World;* 2nd (posthum.) ed., Oxford 1957, I, p. 531-532.

inaugurated by Diocletian was prolonged by a continuous, homogeneous evolution right up to the capture of Constantinople by the Turks in 1453.

It is quite true that in order to overcome the dangers which threatened in the Roman world it had to accept a very severe discipline. The new Empire seems to us a veritable totalitarian state — in the most modern sense of the word, trying to subordinate to its authority all the energy of its subjects by absorbing and unifying them. The authority of the sovereign, bent on absolute power, is exercised through cunningly hierarchic administrative machinery. Obtrusive bureaucracy and increased military expenditure lead to high and soon to crippling taxes and a strictly regulated economy which tends to over-centralise. Like every totalitarian regime, the Late Empire is a police state whose heavy threats hang over everyone : to unleash repressive measures there is no need to be accused of plotting; one day's delay in paying taxes may lead to prison, torture, death in frightful pain. Finally, and most important, the new ideal extols the charismatic quality of the Leader : the prince is held to possess qualities which make him in some sense divine and raise him above common humanity. Since Augustus, the structure of imperial power has always contained a religious ingredient; with the new regime this is accentuated and even becomes different in kind.

This transformation of the structure of the state took place in a profoundly new religious climate. Towards the end of the third century there occurred another revolution, this time at the spiritual level, and the ancient world entered what we can call with Spengler[3] the second, or new, religious consciousness. This was a phase when, after the relative unbelief and dulling of religious fervour which had characterised the Hellenistic period (and the beginning of the Early Empire), Mediterranean man once more discovered a deep sense of the Holy again, which became the dominant central element in his conception of the world and of life. But compared to the first religious consciousness of the ancient polytheism rooted in the old Indo-European heritage, this second manifestation is quite new in character.

Classical paganism expressed its awareness of the Holy by the neutral notion of the Divine (τὸ θεῖον), whereas in this new phase religious consciousness is haunted by the idea of God (ὁ θεός), an Absolute, a Transcendent with a personal character, the beginning and end of all things, the object of adoration and love. It is superfluous to point out the oriental, Semitic — especially Jewish — and later christian influences

3. We borrow the word (p. 382) and the conception (p. 383 ff.) from O. Spengler, *Der Untergang des Abendlandes*, Vol. II, Munich 1922, although he does not use the former to refer to the latter.

which led to the triumph of this new religious mentality. But if the birth and progress of Christianity quite naturally have a place in the history of this mentality, it was neither obvious nor inevitable round about the year 300 that Christianity was going to canalise and absorb all its resources.

The new religious ideal was also expressed under many other rival forms. Among these forms were various oriental religions widely practised in Roman society, such as that of Mithra which combined elements of Iranian and Mesopotamian origin : almost everywhere in the Roman world archaeologists have found a great number (eighteen in Ostia alone) of the little underground sanctuaries where groups of initiates gathered, chiefly people connected with the army. Traditional polytheism which for so many centuries had been practically emptied of its original content, now found a new life by lending itself to reinterpretation in accordance with the prevailing mood. We notice how one deity is assimilated to another playing an equivalent role : Athena is also Hecate of Hades, the Moon, queen of heaven, Minerva or even the Latins' Ceres, the Egyptian Isis; or how deities are graded in a strict hierarchy : the Sun, a visible god, is intermediary between men and the supreme God of which he is the perceptible image.

It is in this religious context that we must place the imperial ideology of the Late Empire. The comparative history of religions bears witness that the holy nature almost universally attributed to the Sovereign is in direct relation with the more or less exalted idea that people have of divinity itself. To treat a King, a man of flesh and blood, as a ' god ', does not require a very high notion of godhead. The growth of worship of the Sovereign in the Hellenistic monarchies and later in the Early Roman Empire seems linked to a certain impoverishment of the word ' god ', a lessening of the distinction, so sharp in early paganism, between the human and the divine. The atmosphere has become very different by the fourth century : as God is conceived to be more and more radically transcendent, so the religious attributes which the Emperor, as God's reflection, is believed to possess raise him all the higher above common humanity. This will be seen clearly when, from the time of Constantine and especially of his sons, the Emperor and with him the Empire become christian : the person and power of the Emperor will be no less holy, and this feature will be much more pronounced than in the time of the Emperors of pagan Rome, even when their names were Caligula, Domitian or Commodus. The latter could believe themselves ' god ', but they identified themselves only with the godlings of the polytheist pantheon; the former, while remaining men, reflect the fearful majesty of the God of Abraham, Isaac and Jacob.

For the time being, however, paganism still remains the official religion of the Empire. However revolutionary Diocletian's action may appear in certain spheres, at the religious level he remains an old Roman very much attached to the traditional religion : it is in language and forms borrowed from this ancient source that he expresses the ideal of sovereignty as conceived by the new way of thinking. Diocletian himself, his co-regent taken in 285/6, the second Augustus Maximianus, the two Caesars, joint Emperors and future successors who reign with them from the year 293, all these most holy, most sacred Emperors are invested with their authority by the Supreme God, the Most High Jupiter Exsuperantissimus[4] and receive with that authority on the day of their investiture a character of holiness. Not that they are ' gods ' strictly speaking; they prefer to call themselves god-born, *diis geniti*. They are not assimilated, as they would have been in former times, to Jupiter or Hercules but use the derived surnames *Jovius* and *Herculius :* this derivation expresses the Emperor's state of dependence on his heavenly patron and protector.

4. The noun is traditional, but the epithet is an expression of the second phase of religious consciousness.

CHAPTER XVI

THE LAST PERSECUTION
AND THE PEACE
OF THE CHURCH

IT SEEMS likely that a clash between the pagan Empire and the christian religion was inevitable on account of Diocletian's attachment to the religious traditions of ancient Rome and the passionate ideal of cohesion or unity expressed by all his political actions. Consider the preambles of the edict promulgated on 31 March 297 against the Manichaeans, a religion suspected, as Christianity had once been, of criminal practices, *maleficia*, and which, furthermore, could cause special disquiet because of its Iranian origins or links. The edict brought against it a charge which could equally well be applied to Christianity, namely, the fact that it was a new religion which broke with the tradition of the Roman nation : ' it is criminal to throw doubts on what has been established from ancient times... '[1].

However, during the first twenty years of Diocletian's reign christians had not been seriously molested : between 284 and 303 we know of only a few isolated cases of soldiers being martyred. Moreover, these cases present certain difficulties of interpretation. Are they conscientious objectors faithful to the ideal of non-violence held by the earliest Christians, and victims of the new system of conscription which makes military service compulsory? Or are they reacting against the recent development of Emperor-worship, the religious character of which, formerly rather vague, becomes more accentuated and demands of soldiers a positive participation in pagan rites? Such incidents perhaps led to a first restrictive measure against the christians, their expulsion from the army (or at least from the active list) referred to in certain passages of Eusebius (302?), a foretaste of the great persecution.

1. *Mosaicarum et Romanarum legum collatio*, 15, 2, ed. E. Seckel-R. Kuebler (*Jurisprudentia anteiustiniana.*, vol. II, 2), p. 382.

1. The Edicts of Persecution and their Application

This persecution, though systematic and extensive, came with startling suddenness; in less than one year (23 February 303 — January/ February 304) four successive edicts made clear its severity. The first amounted in all essentials to the banning of christian worship : the confiscation of books and sacred vessels, the destruction of churches. In addition, christians were already excluded from public functions and subject to a number of legal disqualifications. But the Emperor was soon led to attack certain persons more directly : the second edict ordered the arrest of ' heads of churches ' (by that was meant all members of the clergy, including those of low rank); this was a provisional measure which led naturally to the third edict : the release of those imprisoned if they consented to make libations and sacrifice. Since the time of Trajan that had been the test for detecting christians and exonerating apostates. The resistance encountered explains the fourth edict : as in the time of Decius, it was made obligatory for all the inhabitants of the Empire to sacrifice to the gods, under threat of the worst torments — often a cruel death, or deportation to the mines which was not much better than the extermination camps conceived by our own barbarous era.

As always, it is difficult to decide what were Diocletian's exact motives in commiting himself to such a policy. We may suppose that he was subject to pressure from fanatical pagans : the historians of the period, Lactantius and Eusebius, emphasise the role of Caesar Galerius. But after the first step, the logic of a totalitarian system is sufficient to explain the crescendo of the persecution : every order coming from the Emperor, however arbitrary or futile, is, as it were, ballasted with all the majesty of the supreme power, any resistance threatens that majesty and must be broken as though it were treason and impiety. Very characteristic evidence of this state of mind is contained in the special account of how the police swooped on the church of Cirta (Constantine, in North Africa) in accordance with the first edict of persecution, on 19 May 303. Not without delays and attempts at concealment, the Subdeacon Silvanus consented to hand over to the magistrate a small case and a lamp, both made of silver, whereupon he heard the municipal secretary reply drily, ' If you had not found them, it would have been death for you ', *mortuus fueras, si non illa invenisses*[2].

Because of its severity and because of its after-effects, which were sometimes lasting, the persecution of Diocletian profoundly affected the life of the Church. The violence and duration of this crisis varied

---

2. *Gesta apud Zenophilum*, ed. C. Ziusa (Optatus of Milevis, *Appendix*), p. 187.

widely according to regions.   In Gaul and Britain, which were subject
to the authority of Caesar Constantius Chlorus, father of the future
Emperor Constantine, only the first edict concerning sacred buildings
was enforced and, it would seem, rather slackly.   In the provinces
directly under Augustus Maximianus persecution was sharp but short-
lived and lasted less than two years in all.   The same was true of Italy,
where the Church of Rome was for nearly four years unable to name
a successor to Pope Marcellinus who died during the persecution but
not as a result of it. Oppression was short-lived also in Africa for which
there is particularly full evidence.   About Spain and the provinces of
the Upper Danube little is known with certainty.   Nor is it certain that
the most severe of the four edicts was ever promulgated, or at least
systematically applied : the first was quite sufficient to ensure victims,
provided that a magistrate enforced it with severity or enthusiastic
christians took the opportunity of expressing their zeal.

We are told that the Sicilian martyr Euplius of Catania had himself
arrested by parading before the Governor's office waving a book
containing the Gospels.   There were doubtless all manner of different
cases between these voluntary martyrs, on the one hand, and, on the
other, the weaker brethren who cautiously took refuge in apostasy — not
to mention cunning persons like the Bishop of Carthage, Mensurius, who
later boasted of having ' handed over ' on the day when his house was
searched, *dies traditionis*, a few books written by heretics, instead of the
Holy Scriptures which had been demanded.

In the East, on the other hand, the persecution was much more
severe and lasted until Spring 313 with, admittedly, a period of
abatement.   Successive rulers in Egypt, Syria and Asia Minor were
more and more hostile to Christianity.   Diocletian, who abdicated
in 305, was succeeded as Augustus by the pagan Galerius, and the new
Caesar who assisted him, Maximinus Daia, was still more fanatical.
With him, in his last years, the persecution was to become more
systematic and have recourse to propaganda methods which appear very
modern : the organisation of ' spontaneous ' demonstrations and the
required reading in schools of the apocryphal *Acts* of Pilate, which
contain blasphemies against Jesus.

As in the West, attitudes varied widely.   Some easy-going pagans,
in order to get rid of their Christian prisoners, freed certain of them who
would undertake to perform sacrifice, while those who were recalcitrant
were merely ordered not to speak of their obduracy.   Some Christians
showed themselves prudent or lukewarm and had recourse to flight or
else, as had happened in the time of Decius, obtained false certificates
declaring that they had sacrificed.   As always, there were many apostates;

but there were also martyrs, and these were treated with all the sadistic cruelty of this era of renewed barbarism which readily practised refinements of torture : the very detailed picture given by Eusebius of Caesarea, himself an eyewitness, in his *Martyrs of Palestine*, leaves us in no doubt about the savagery of the executioners and the courage of the victims. There has been much discussion about the number of martyrs; clearly this persecution does not bear comparison with the millions of victims claimed by modern techniques of genocide, but on the other hand the number must not be limited simply to the total of those cases recorded in narrative sources, and chosen because they were specially memorable.

Despite its violence, the persecution finally lost momentum. Six days before his death the Emperor Galerius was obliged to recognise that this policy had failed, and at Nicomedia on 30 April 311 he promulgated an edict of toleration. This was doubtless drawn up with rather bad grace, for it deplores the obstinacy and madness of those christians who, in large numbers, have refused to return to the religion of ancient Rome. It was applied with even worse grace by his successor Maximinus Daia who, less than six months later, renewed the persecution more severely than ever but only for a short time. At the end of 312 he had to return to more or less complete toleration and subsequently to re-establish religious peace, but he did so in face of threats and later under the blows dealt him by his colleagues and rivals in the West Constantine and Licinius.

This is not the moment to describe in detail the complicated events which took place elsewhere in the Empire during the years 306-312. The system of succession ingeniously perfected by Diocletian worked only once (305) and soon broke down. At one moment, in the beginning of 310, the Empire had no less than seven Emperors, of whom the majority were considered usurpers by their rivals : Constantine, who was proclaimed in 306 after the death of his father Constantius; his father-in-law Maximianus, who had twice taken up the purple which he had abdicated in 305; his son, Maxentius, *de facto* master of Italy but not, at least for the moment, of Africa, where Domitius Alexander was in revolt; Licinius in Illyria (present-day Yugoslavia), who alone was able to hold out until 324 either in alliance with or in opposition to Constantine; Galerius in the Balkans and Asia Minor; Maximinus Daia in the Balkans and Syria and Egypt.

We need only remember that in contrast to the last two, all the ' Western ' Emperors adopted on the whole a pacific attitude towards Christianity and ended by being favourable towards it. Galerius's very cautious edict of toleration in 311 was met by a much more liberal gesture on the part of Maxentius; not content with having formally granted complete freedom to the christians under his rule in Italy and in Africa which he had recaptured, he ordered their property, confiscated during the persecution, to be returned to them.

2. Constantine's religious attitude and policy

It was left to Constantine to go much further : his reign (306-338) witnessed perhaps the most important change in the history of the Church before those of modern times. The historian would like to be able to link the sweeping political decisions taken by this Emperor with his inner development and personal convictions. Unfortunately it is easier to formulate hypotheses on this subject than to establish precise and undisputed facts.

That Constantine was first a pagan — though an enlightened and tolerant pagan like his father — and was later converted to Christianity there can be no doubt at all. That he waited until he was on the point of dying before asking for and receiving baptism corresponds to a custom frequent at that period, and can be explained by the harsh necessities involved in being Emperor : if we list only his most startling crimes, Constantine was responsible in turn for the death of his father-in-law, three brothers-in-law, his eldest son and his wife. This raises the problem of the date at which he accepted the christian faith. Was it a progressive development? Or a sudden conversion? Can we say precisely when or at least before what date?

Must we believe that as early as the decisive battle of the Milvian Bridge, where Maxentius was killed (12 October 312) Constantine's army displayed a christian motif on its shields? The anecdote, which was gradually embroidered into legend, was being told in Christian circles at court as early as 318-320, that is, six or eight years after the battle. But it is difficult for us to extricate from this historical evidence the kernel of truth, enveloped as it is in layers of rhetoric, by a taste for the marvellous, by idealisation of the Emperor and an attempt to bring him into the orbit of Christianity.

It is more prudent to give up this attempt to isolate something which falls to pieces as we handle it : more important to history than the intimate convictions of Constantine is his policy, and it is this that we can in fact grasp. On 15 June 313, on the day after his victory over Maximinus Daia laid open the provinces of Asia, his colleague and temporary ally, Licinius, issued a decree in specially friendly terms granting christians complete and entire freedom of worship and the immediate restitution of all confiscated goods. In the course of this decree he referred expressly to a decision taken jointly with Constantine at the beginning of the year, during their interview at Milan on the occasion of the marriage of Licinius with Constantine's half-sister, Constantia.

Licinius himself was to remain a pagan and at the end of his reign, on the eve of his definite break with and elimination by Constantine, he was to switch to a policy of pinpricks if not open persecution of christians suspected of showing too much sympathy for his rival.

In fact there can be no doubt that as soon as he won his victory over Maxentius, Constantine showed active sympathy towards Christianity. We see the proof of this as early as the opening months of this same year 313 in his new provinces of Africa where to the already generous measures taken by Licinius he added favours which benefited the clergy of the ' Very Holy Catholic Church ', including tax exemptions and the distribution of money.

This policy was to continue and become increasingly marked, save for certain changes of tone, until the end of the reign. In principle toleration and freedom of worship are the official doctrine, but a balance must be kept between paganism and Christianity. The first christian symbols appear on the coinage, that wonderful instrument of propaganda, in 315; the last pagan representations disappear in 323. The Catholic Church receives a privileged legal status : sentences passed by the episcopal tribunal, even in purely civil cases, are recognised as valid by the State; churches are granted the right to succeed to property, a measure which allows them to increase their heritage.

Places of worship multiply. It is doubtless at this period that the architectural form of the basilica comes into common use : a rectangular ground plan divided into naves by rows of columns with an apse at the end. Soon there are more than forty in Rome. The generosity of the Emperor and his family (the Empress Mother, St Helena, and Constantine's sisters are all christians) permits the construction and adornment of magnificent buildings. At Rome the buildings included the basilica of the Vatican where the adjoining palace, later the residence of the Pope, seems to have been at the Pope's disposal as early as 314, though it did not yet belong to him; and the basilicas of St Peter, of the Apostles (today St Sebastian) on the Via Appia, of St Agnes, and many others. Jerusalem had a magnificent group of buildings at the Holy Sepulchre; while the new capital, Constantinople (dedicated in 330), could boast several christian churches including that of the Twelve Apostles where Constantine was later to prepare his own tomb, besides new or restored pagan temples.

Christian inspiration extends to the legislation and even the vocabulary of imperial constitutions. Christians for the first time rise to the highest posts : the Consulate in 323, the Prefecture of Rome in 325, the Prefecture of the Praetorium in 329. At the same time the first restrictive measures against pagan practices appear; in 318 private sacrifices, magic and reading of entrails in private houses are forbidden. Finally — and this is important, for it concerns the future — Constantine has his children educated as christians. Certainly he is quite justified in considering himself the first christian Emperor. There is nevertheless quite a large degree of idealisation in the image of him presented by Byzantine tradition, as the very holy Emperor considered in some sense to be the equal of the Apostles *(isapostolos)*. Legend began its work in the generation after his death with the *Life of Constantine*, published under the name of Eusebius but doubtless revised by one of his successors in the see of Caesarea. It was, however, his sons and heirs, more than Constantine himself, who strove to make this ideal a reality. It is especially noticeable in the case of the youngest and last of them, the Emperor Constantius II who, like his father before him, was to succeed in bringing the whole Roman world under his authority in the final years of his reign (353-361).

The history of Christianity has now entered quite a new phase, for the Church has truly found peace. All the barriers, legal or material, which formerly prevented the spread of the gospel have been lifted; henceforward it can make free and steadily more effective progress. In all parts of the Roman Empire conversions multiply, reaching the masses and circles formerly hostile; everywhere new episcopal sees are founded; there is intense theological activity. The imperial policy which in so many ways tends to favour the new religion, and even the Emperor's own example which is particularly effective in this notably monarchical regime — everything suggests that the whole Roman Empire will become christian.

This progress is stopped and reversed for a few months only during the reign of the Emperor Julian the Apostate (361-363) who succeeds Constantine's nephew Constantius. Having lapsed into paganism, Julian quite naturally tries to make the Empire do likewise. His paganism, moreover, is very original and very different from that of ancient Rome; it is marked by the philosophic influence of Neo-Platonism and especially by irrational elements of the occult and theurgy, which Neo-Platonism tends more and more to patronise.

This is only an episode without serious consequences. Julian's successors are once more christian Emperors and display increasing fervour and conviction. Even if Valentinian at his accession in 364 proclaims a new freedom of conscience for all men, this prudent policy only marks a pause, an attempt at stabilisation after the winding up of

Julian's scheme. After that, his brother and co-regent Valens, his son Gratian, and even more their successor Theodosius the Great (379-395) continue the development started under Constantine and Constantius. More and more the Empire tends to become a christian Empire; Christianity in its orthodox form becomes almost the State religion; heretics are persecuted (381), paganism finally banned, and temples are closed or destroyed (391).

CHAPTER XVII

THE CHURCH
IN THE FIRST HALF
OF THE FOURTH CENTURY

PEOPLE were naturally dazzled by this great turn in the tide of history. In the first flush of enthusiasm they imagined that the Empire, christian from now on, was going to be something like an image of the Kingdom of God upon earth. But in fact problems were soon to arise. In order to measure the difficulties involved in solving them, a glance must be taken at the structure of christian society and at the mentality of the period. The structure has two poles: on the one hand, strictly ecclesiastical institutions; on the other hand, the Emperor.

1. Ecclesiastical Institutions

By the years 300-330, with nearly three centuries of history behind it, the Church had had time to develop its organisation. With the exception of monasticism, which was still only in its beginnings, all its fundamental institutions were already in place and had reached a stage of development close to maturity.

The Roman Empire has been defined as a mosaic of cities each with a certain autonomy. In the same way the whole of the Catholic — that is to say Universal — Church seems to have been divided into a series of local communities each under the authority of a bishop. The episcopal church was the basic unit of the whole group of institutions.

There was a clearly marked distinction between the mass of the faithful and the clergy, who were arranged in a strict hierarchy : bishop, priests, deacons, subdeacons. The frontier was rather blurred, at least to our eyes, between the lowest ranks of minor clerics and simple employees of the Church. Below the doorkeepers were the gravediggers *(fossores, copiatae)*, who for quite some time were included among the clerics. On the other hand, bodies *(ordines)* of widows, of consecrated virgins and of deaconesses had a status which set them apart from simple lay people. Finally, the dividing-line between clergy and laity did not prevent the most cultivated, the richest and most generous lay people from exercising a sometimes important influence on the administration, government and even the life of the Church. The intervention of intriguing ladies, especially rich benefactors, in episcopal elections was often deplored. For in principle it was still the christian people who elected their bishop, and in fact this sometimes did still happen, although most often the election was in the hands of the local clergy (notably in Rome), or of the provincial or regional bishops.

If, in geographical terms, the basic unit was the local church or the urban church (a christian community was often, but not always, coterminous with the boundaries of a city), the unity of the Church was not lost in this multiplicity. From the fourth century onwards a plan of coordination was sketched which opened the way to a more complex and hierarchical structure. The bishops of a single Roman province (notice the influence of the secular administrative framework), or of a larger region, tended to gather around and under the authority of a metropolitan, who was usually the bishop of the principal city and church.

This institution, still in its infancy, varied from region to region. In Egypt, for example, where the bishops were very numerous and towns few, the bishoprics were unified and very closely controlled by the often domineering authority of the see of Alexandria. Latin Africa also possessed a certain unity, but on a much larger scale : the Bishop of Carthage enjoyed a certain pre-eminence there, but the various provinces retained their autonomy. For example, in Numidia the bishops recognised as their head or primate not the titular of a particular see but their *Senex*, the bishop who had held office longest.

Although divided into ten provinces for civil government, peninsular Italy (south of the line Siena-Arezzo) was treated as a single ecclesiastical whole, all its bishops being equally subject to the direct authority of the Roman see, which served them all as a metropolis.

The influence of the *Cathedra Petri* was doubtless exercised well beyond these limits and already reached to all parts of the Church. But if no other see disputed its right to be honoured above all others and if it had special authority on doctrinal matters, its disciplinary power for settling appeals was not yet evident in practice. Many generations were to pass before it was recognised as one of the organs necessary for the normal functioning of the ecclesiastical institution.

2. The Christian Emperor

The dividing-line between the temporal and the spiritual, the profane and the sacred, was not yet clearly established in the case of the institutions of the Church and those of the Empire. Gradually, sometimes dramatically, it came to be defined in the very depths of the highly complex personality of the Christian Emperor.

The Emperor was first of all the leader and the person responsible for the terrestrial city, the State, the Roman Fatherland, which was threatened by danger and must if possible be saved. The price of safety we have already pointed out. As danger increased from generation to generation, preservation of the Empire demanded increasingly strenuous efforts at every level — demographic, military and financial; hence a growing harshness, more and more severity and terror. The conscript who mutilated himself in order to escape military service was, under Constantine, forced to join one of the auxiliary corps; from the time of Valentinian he was condemned to be slowly burned alive — a barbarous penalty introduced under Diocletian. From the time of Theodosius not only were soldiers branded with a red-hot iron like convicts, but also workers in State factories.

Despite such acts of violence, the Empire could not take entire possession of its subjects' souls, for in an era so deeply concerned with religion man considered himself not only a citizen in a State, at the service of a terrestrial fatherland, but also and perhaps primarily a ' citizen of heaven ', a member of a spiritual society in the framework of which he could find an answer to the problem he considered fundamental : that of his relations with God.

Now the Emperor himself, in his very capacity as Emperor, was no stranger to this sphere of spiritual realities. At this period religious problems occupied too large a place in the thoughts and daily life of his subjects for a policy of separation of Church and State in the modern manner even to have been conceivable. There was an intimate mingling between the two; as we shall see later, the interested parties themselves were the first to ask the Emperor and his departments to intervene in their religious quarrels.

We must not interpret this as a simple act of policing designed to suppress any grounds for disorder and to re-establish the peace necessary for the sound working of society. The Emperor's interest in religious questions was much more direct and more profound than that; he too was filled with the new religious spirit. We have already pointed out that in becoming a christian the Emperor lost no part of his sacred character, quite the contrary.

The imperial power, unifying under its authority the whole Roman world, that is the whole civilised world, appeared like an earthly image of the divine monarchy. A visible manifestation of God on earth, a veritable theophany, the ' very pious ' Emperor ' well-loved of God ', felt himself responsible before heaven for the salvation of his subjects, no longer only for their temporal welfare. He felt called upon to guide the human race towards the true religion which he proclaimed and taught. His court theologians went so far as to attribute to him a sort of episcopal power over the whole Empire : that was only an image, a panegyrist's phrase, which must not be pressed too far. But we should remember that the Christian Emperor of the fourth century had too wide a conception of his duties towards the Church merely to act as its ' secular arm ', in the sense which the Western Middle Ages were one day to conceive that term.

For example, the Emperor was not content merely to facilitate the holding of councils and to lend his authority for carrying our their decisions. He himself took the initiative in summoning councils and laid before them the dogmatic or disciplinary problems which they were to handle. He followed their discussions and helped to establish a majority or unanimity. He had to make up his own mind about the strictly ecclesiastical problems at stake, and this led him to play a part in their elaboration — often a disastrous part. In this context let us not be overhasty in using the word Caesaropapism, which is based on notions foreign to the thought of the age. Let us simply say that, being a christian, the Emperor thought of himself quite naturally as the leader of the christian people : as a new Moses, a new David, at the head of the true Israel, that of the New Covenant.

What has just been said is the definition of an ideal; its practice very soon raised unmanageable difficulties. Such an ideal of coordination between the earthly city and the city of God, of cooperation between strictly ecclesiastical institutions and those of a State which desired to be christian, presupposed that the Church and the Emperor were in firm agreement on the essential point : that is to say, on the articles of their faith. The moment he ceased to be orthodox, the very holy and very pious Emperor became a mere tyrant, a persecutor, a precursor of Antichrist, a tool of Satan.

Now, with the peace of Constantine the Church entered a period of violent theological debate, when the very definition of dogma was put in doubt. As a result serious questions arose concerning the canonical validity of the nomination or deposition of bishops and also concerning excommunication. Who was to lay down the law? Who was to define truth? We must remember that those responsible for the organisation of the Church were not yet ready to formulate the desired answer with sufficient precision and authority to compel recognition by all the faithful of goodwill. Quite naturally the Emperors were led to take sides, but their authority encountered resistance and was repulsed more than once by convictions rising from too deep a part of the religious soul to submit to an outside authority.

Since Gibbon and Hegel the Late Empire has too often been described as a disturbed period which witnessed the rule of weakness, meanness and lack of character. True, there was no lack of servility and too often, as we shall see, large sections of Christian opinion, beginning with the episcopate, submissively followed, even in its variations, the theological line adopted or supported at court. But the fourth century was also a century of strong personalities, men of steel who knew how to withstand the powerful forces of the day and oppose violence with the firmness of their faith. We need only mention Athanasius of Alexandria who spent seventeen and a half years of his episcopacy in exile, undergoing five successive periods of exile under four Emperors.

It was a period of proud men, but also of headstrong wills and obstinate schisms; not all the opposing views, seen in retrospect and from the standpoint of theology, appear to have been equally justified. But it is necessary to indicate their existence so that the reader may realise that the bi-polar structure of the Christian Empire was something more than a division of powers between churchmen and statesmen. It was much more complex and much more serious than that : a veritable ' schism in the soul ', as Professor Arnold Toynbee would say. Beneath the level of institutions this schism reached down to individual consciences, which were often torn between two contradictory but equally exacting loyalties.

3. Schisms Resulting From Persecution : Donatism

The first problem within the Church, which the Emperor Constantine had to attend to only a few months after his victory over Maxentius, allows us to watch the clash of these tendencies. It was a question of the African schism of the Donatists, the most serious of the local crises raised by the sequels to the persecution of Diocletian. Its starting-point was strictly limited : at this stage the problem in Africa had not yet developed into the more general question of whether more or less severe penance should be demanded of apostates seeking readmission.

It invariably happens that when persecution comes the weaker brethren give way, even though they repent once the danger has passed. This had happened in the time of St Cyprian after the persecution of

Decius. It happened again after the very serious persecution which began in 304-305. In Egypt, for example, as early as 306 Bishop Melitius of Lycopolis clashed with the leader of the Egyptian episcopate, the future martyr Peter of Alexandria who was at that time in prison and whose attitude towards the *lapsi* he considered too indulgent. Melitius in his turn was arrested, then deported to the mines of Phaeno in Palestine. But he continued the controversy, held many ordinations and after his return organized a schismatic hierarchy in Egypt, ' the Church of the Martyrs ', over against the Catholic hierarchy. This led to very serious consequences which complicated, and sometimes merged with, those of Arianism.

Donatism, when it emerged, proved even more serious than the Melitian schism. For the time being it was not a question of the *lapsi* but only of the fate of those bishops who consented to the *traditio* called for by Diocletian's first edict, those who were in fact *traditores*, having betrayed the faith by handing over the holy books to magistrates searching the churches. The provincial Council of Numidia held at Cirta on 5 March 305 had already shown how bitterly the African bishops conducted purges against one another; as often happens, those most eager to accuse others were not always blameless themselves.

The starting-point of the whole affair was the election of the archdeacon Caecilian to the see of Carthage in 312. This aroused the opposition of a local party, somewhat severe in outlook, which was supported by the Numidian episcopacy. In very precise terms the opposition party contested the validity of Caecilian's episcopal conse-cration, on the grounds that one of the three bishops who had preceded him in the see, Felix of Apthungi, was guilty of *traditio*. In opposition to Caecilian another bishop was elected, and he was soon succeeded by the great Donatus, who came from his first see of *Casae Nigrae*. Donatus, an energetic and efficient man, was the true organiser of the schismatic Church to which history has given his name.

The Donatists in effect considered the crime of *traditio* so serious that the simple fact of being in communion with one of the guilty persons (and, with the passing of time, of being in communion with the heirs of those who had formerly been in communion with those guilty persons) was enough to contract the same guilt, to become in turn a *traditor*, an apostate unworthy of the name of christian. All the sacraments given or received by the *traditores* were considered null and void; the Donatists re-baptised all the Catholics who either freely or under duress joined their ranks. That is why the schism gradually spread. Not only in Carthage but in a large number of the numerous episcopal sees of Africa, bishop confronted bishop and two parallel hierarchies opposed

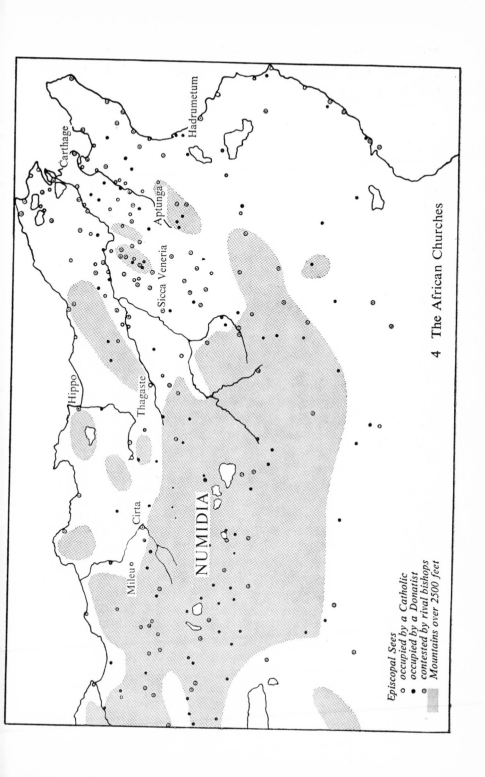

Episcopal Sees
○ occupied by a Catholic
● occupied by a Donatist
◉ contested by rival bishops
Mountains over 2500 feet

4 The African Churches

Hadrumetum

Carthage

Aptunga

Sicca Veneria

Hippo

Thagaste

NUMIDIA

Cirta

Mileu

each other, 'the Church of the Saints' against that of the *traditores*, Donatist against Catholic.

Since Constantine had expressly stipulated that only Catholics should benefit from grants and exemptions bestowed on the clergy, the Donatists — and this is an important point — took the initiative in laying their difference with Caecilian before the Emperor on 15 April 313. Their claims were declared groundless by the three successive courts before which their case was brought : a Roman Synod held in the Lateran palace with the Pope presiding (15 February 314), a Council of Gaulish bishops (Arles, 1 July 314), and the tribunal of the Emperor himself sitting at Milan (10 November 316). This tribunal made use of information obtained by very searching inquiries on the part of imperial representatives in Africa. Their official reports have come down to us, revealing the atmosphere of police terror which characterised the regime.

To end the matter Constantine, having heard the case, decided to throw the weight of the secular authority into the scales. In the spring of 317 he promulgated a very severe law against the schismatics, who had to hand over their churches. A chain reaction followed. Sure of themselves and obstinate in their convictions, the Donatists refused to hand over their churches and resisted the authorities; the army intervened and took repressive measures. Violent disturbances broke out; victims were at once treated as martyrs; finally, the obstinacy of the schismatics forced the authorities to accept the situation and grant them an edict of toleration (5 May 321).

With this the party of Donatus spread, grew strong and asserted itself intransigently. The same process was repeated throughout the century, with the same ultimately sterile alternation of repression and toleration. In 347 Constantius again persecuted the Donatists; Julian, on the other hand, favoured them (361/2), finding it expedient to let the christians tear one another to pieces; and Gratian once more confiscated their churches (376/7). The final episode took place in 411. After having changed his policy five times, the Emperor Honorius held a great conference, where the two parties met for the last time, and where St Augustine, among the Catholics, was called upon to play a leading role. Once more the Donatists were dismissed and outlawed, but it was too late : in 429 the Vandals arrived, and their invasion sounded the death-knell of Roman Africa.

Christian Africa exhausted its strength in this affair : we are painfully aware to what extent its missionary expansion was checked by internal strife. We may marvel at the extent of the blaze touched off by such a small spark, at such an unleashing of fanaticism and violence.

As always, the historian would like to discover behind the circumstances which occasioned it the deep causes of the movement.

The causes have sometimes been sought at the political level. Was Donatism the expression of national resistance against colonial domination by Rome? To tell the truth, Berber nationalism is scarcely to be found in the documents which survive, and if some strictly Berber recruits appeared in the Donatist ranks we ought to regard that as a factor of purely social significance. It would appear that the schism was recruited especially from the poorest classes of society, and in consequence the least deeply Romanised.

Their shock troops, those who beat up and often murdered Catholics, notably the clergy, were composed of gangs of ‘ circumcellions ’ — vagabonds without house or fixed abode — and perhaps also of agricultural labourers, a proletariat which was the victim of economic developments and the agrarian policy. In everything they did there was a revolutionary element; we find them using threats to enforce their demands, abolishing debts, terrorising landowners and defending the humble. One day a party of ‘ circumcellions ’ met a rich lord comfortably sitting in his carriage while a slave ran in front of the horses; they stopped him, made the slave sit in the master’s place and forced the master to run with the horses[1].

But the strictly religious aspect of the movement must not be ignored. In a period of intense religious consciousness it was normal that the political and social complexes should express themselves and unfold in religious terms. There developed a doctrinal atmosphere and a spirituality characteristic of Donatism, the pathological features of which may be deplored by theologian and psychologist alike. The schismatic Church considered itself a ‘ Church of Saints ’, making no sort of compromise with the century in which it lived, either with the Emperor who persecuted its members or the body of the universal Church which was compromised with the *traditores*.

Their consciences were clear and, like all sects, they felt convinced that they were in the right, and everyone else in the wrong. They believed they were soldiers of Christ fighting for a good cause : their Church was also the Church of the martyrs.

The enthusiastic and superstitious veneration which accompanied the cult of their mementos and relics, together with the glorification and defence of martyrs, led the Donatists to accept martyrdom with joy, even to seek it out and provoke it. Sure that they would share the fate of the glorious victims of Diocletian, the more fanatical took every

1. Optatus of Milevis, *Contra Parmenianum*, III, 4, p. 81 Ziwsa.

advantage of clashes with the police, or with their Catholic adversaries; they themselves provoked incidents and sometimes even went to the point of suicide. We find cases of collective suicide either by jumping into a ravine or lighting a pyre, which foreshadowed similar excesses practised by some of the ' schismatics ', the *Raskolniki*, of the Russian Orthodox Church in the seventeenth century.

We end with a feeling of weariness as we read through the long, unbearably monotonous controversies sustained by the Catholic doctors, Optatus of Milevis (c. 365-385) and St Augustine (especially between 394 and 420), *à propos* of this Caecilian Affair, if we may so call the Donatist quarrel, with allusion to the Dreyfus Affair, for in both cases there was a sharply contested historical fact as a result of which uncontrollable passions were unleashed. The Caecilian Affair gave rise to few doctrinal definitions, although, it is true, the Latin Church was led to define more accurately its doctrine of the validity of the sacraments *ex opere operato* (however personally unworthy the person administering them may be) and especially to rethink and develop its theology of unity, which is an essential feature of the Church, *unam sanctam*. But meanwhile in the Eastern countries there had arisen another controversy, this time in the highest degree doctrinal : Arianism.

CHAPTER XVIII

ARIUS AND THE COUNCIL
OF NICAEA

AFTER the defeat and surrender of Licinius in the autumn of 324 Constantine found the christians of the East as violently divided as he had found those of Africa in 313. The same drama was staged. The Emperor ordered Hosius of Cordova, his expert in ecclesiastical affairs, to hold an enquiry into the troubles at Alexandria and in Asia Minor, just as he had ordered him to go on an earlier mission to discover the facts about Donatism at Carthage. Because the problem proved so complex once again he had to summon a Council.

For some years or possibly only some months (318, or possibly only in July 323) a certain Arius, a priest of the Church of Alexandria and perhaps a deserter from the Melitian schism, had shown violent opposition to his bishop, Alexander. This time the issue was important, being nothing less than the theology of the Trinity. We have seen that the problems raised by this theology had already excited passionate discussions during earlier generations in the Church of Alexandria as in the rest of the Christian world; notably in the last years of the episcopate of Dionysius (260-264/5).

In its early stages Arianism took the form of a discussion within the Church of Alexandria between proponents of two opposed theological tendencies. Both of these tendencies belonged to its tradition and, paradoxically, seem to have been found in turn in the thought of the aforesaid Dionysius. Arius, as we know from other sources, had been the pupil or at least considered himself the disciple of the martyr Lucian, a priest of Antioch, but he would seem to have adopted the Subordinationist tendency first shown by Dionysius of Alexandria in his polemic against the Sabellians of Cyrenaica, (for which Dionysius had been severely censured by the Bishop of Rome, also called Dionysius). As a result Arius had shifted his position and finally been led to affirm the opposite point of view : namely, complete substantial equality between the Father and the Logos.

A heresy often starts out as the vehement assertion of an authentic but partial aspect of revelation which, developed unilaterally, soon becomes deformed and compromises the balance of theology as a whole. Arius seems to have been dominated by an obsession. Within the Trinity he was determined to safeguard the originality and privileges of the Father, ' the only one to be *agennetos*, that is to say not engendered, but also (no precise distinction was made between the two participles derived from *gennao* and *gignomai*) not " become ", not having entered into being; the Father alone is eternal, he alone is without beginning, in short he alone is true God '. For — and this is the essential point — ' he is absolutely alone in being *arkhé* ', the principle of all beings. This emphasis led Arius to devalue the Logos to a corresponding degree. The Logos, he declared, ' is not eternal, nor coeternal with the Father, nor uncreated like the Father (literally, not-engendered, not-become, like the Father) for it is from the Father that he has received life and being '[1].

Hence arose formulas which orthodoxy considered blasphemous, such as ' he was not before he came to be engendered '. Arius probably did not go so far as to declare expressly what his adversaries claimed that he said : ' There was a time when the Word did not exist. ' He was trying to express an ontological superiority rather than a chronological priority but in vain did he increase his precautions, saying that the generation of the Word took place ' before all time, before all the ages ' and pointing out that even if the Word had been ' created ' (Pro 8 : 22, the most important verse for the Arians) he was a perfect divine creature not comparable to other created beings. The Subordinationist tendency in Arius was indisputable : Arianism was not an invention of his enemies.

Reaction was not long in coming. In the Church of Egypt, so firmly kept in hand by the Bishop of Alexandria, no one could attack the theology professed by its head and remain unscathed. Alexander of Alexandria called a Council of nearly a hundred bishops from Egypt and Libya, which anathematised the errors of Arius and excommunicated him together with his partisans, who comprised a small group of five other priests, six deacons and only two bishops, belonging to the western dependencies of Egypt : Theonas of Marmarica and Secundus of Ptolemais in Cyrenaica.

---

1. Letter of Arius to Alexander of Alexandria (Athanasius, *De Synodis*, 16, Epiphanius, *Panarion*, 69, 7; Hilary, *De Trinitate*, IV, 11-12 : VI, 4), ed. Opitz; *Urkunden*, no. 6.

The matter was not confined to Egypt. Arius, who did not accept this condemnation, had already sought support in Palestine (as Origen had formerly done in like circumstances) from the erudite Eusebius of Caesarea, Origen's apologist and heir. Arius had also sought assistance in the rest of the East and in Asia Minor from those who, like himself, had been pupils and disciples of Lucian of Antioch. We still possess the letter in which he called for help from one of these 'Sylloukianists', Eusebius of Nicomedia. This Eusebius was an influential person if ever there was one — the very type of an ambitious, turbulent prelate in the Late Empire (he had just had himself transferred from his first see, Beirut, to that of the imperial residence; he was to end his days, after a second move, in the new capital Constantinople, which had been founded meanwhile). On their initiative provincial synods of Bithynia and Palestine soon opposed the decision taken by the Council at Alexandria and rehabilitated Arius.

This action, in turn, encountered hostility close at hand. Macarius of Jerusalem took a stand against the bishop of Caesarea; the friends whom Arius found in Phoenicia and Cilicia were opposed by the bishops of Tripoli and especially by the bishops of Antioch, where about 323/4 the great Eustathius succeeded Philogonius. The Bithynian party grouped around the other Eusebius was answered in Galatia by Marcellus of Ancyra (the present-day Ankara), whose behaviour soon became suspect. Meanwhile Alexander did not remain idle; he communicated and defended his position in encyclical or personal letters addressed to the bishops of the Greek countries and to Sylvester of Rome. The commotion spread. Faced with a situation quickly become so complex, Constantine, understandably enough, was more or less forced to consider calling a great Council.

Since Constantine was now master of the whole Empire, an Empire which Roman pride, ignoring the existence of its Sassanid rival, gladly identified with the civilised universe, the Council would be a world Council — the first ecumenical Council in history. Nevertheless the three hundred or so bishops who came together at Nicaea, near Nicomedia, on 20 May 325 were not drawn in equal numbers from the various provinces. Although the Emperor had given every help to the bishops, in particular granting them the exceptional privilege of *evectio*, the right to use the imperial post, material difficulties explain the evident disproportion. More than a hundred of the bishops came from Asia Minor, about thirty from Syria-Phoenicia, less than twenty from Palestine and Egypt. The Latin West was hardly represented at all : the three or four bishops who attended could have been at the imperial court for some personal reason, as for example Hosius of Cordova.

Pope Sylvester delegated two Roman priests to attend in his place. His absence was perhaps only accidental, but it created a precedent : as a result in later ecumenical councils the see of Rome was regularly represented by legates.

We can picture the different theological tendencies in the Council like an open fan. At the extreme left lay the small hard core of the first Arians, supported by their Sylloukianist friends, grouped around Eusebius of Nicomedia. Next came a sort of left centre, whose spokesman was Eusebius of Caesarea, grouping the moderate Subordinationists in the tradition of Origen with those who could be called conservatives. The conservatives were composed of uncertain or timid theologians (a similar tendency will be found more than once in later councils) more concerned for unity than for precise definitions and hence hostile to all new formulas; they tried to hold on to traditional teaching expressed in strictly biblical terms. Further to the right were those who had discovered the danger of Arianism : Alexander of Alexandria (accompanied by his deacon and future successor, Athanasius) and Hosius of Cordova, who seems to have played a specially active role. They were supported by an extreme right wing, whose backing they seemed to consider free from danger : Eustathius of Antioch and especially Marcellus of Ancyra. The latter in particular was all the more violently anti-Arian in that his passionate, one-sided devotion to the principle of divine ' monarchy ' led him to veer into the diametrically opposite heresy. His enemies seem to have been correct in attributing to him an acknowledged or implicit Modalism, the old error of Sabellius.

This analysis does not bring out the relative importance of the different parties. In fact, a powerful majority easily took shape to disapprove of the errors of Arius. Disregarding the protests of the ' conservatives ', the Council took as its basis the profession of faith proposed by Eusebius of Caesarea, but added to his rather vague text certain very precise definitions. Not content with proclaiming the Son ' God of God, Light of Light ', they expressly stated that he is true God of true God, engendered and not created, consubstantial with his Father, *homoousios*.

The adoption of this word, in defence of which severe battles were later to be fought, marks a memorable date in the doctrinal history of Christianity. By thus inserting in the profession of faith a new term which originated no longer in Scripture but in man's reason, the Council of Nicaea recognized as fruitful the purely theological attempt at elucidating revelation, and used its authority to sanction the progress made in rendering explicit the contents of faith. With this Council the Church resolutely entered on the path which would eventually lead, in modern times, to such solemn 'definitions' as the dogmas of the Immaculate Conception, Papal infallibility and the Assumption of the Blessed Virgin Mary.

Despite the fact that he was probably not a competent theologian, and whether he acted by persuasion or intimidation, the Emperor Constantine certainly helped to bring the debates to a successful and speedy conclusion. In any case, when the result was declared, he supported it with the whole weight of his authority. Two bishops only, the two first associates of Arius already mentioned, refused to accept the term 'consubstantial' and the anathemas which accompanied it. They and Arius himself were sent into exile. Three months later in autumn 325 Eusebius of Nicomedia and two of his neighbours who wished to withdraw their signature were also exiled. The Emperor could well be satisfied, for the problem now seemed solved. But in fact it was far from solved : the dispute soon flared up again.

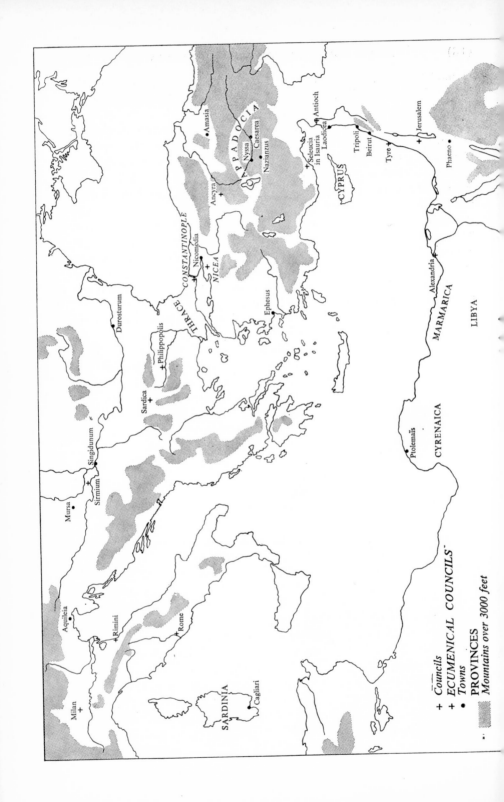

Councils

+ ECUMENICAL COUNCILS

• Towns

PROVINCES

Mountains over 3000 feet

CHAPTER XIX

THE VICISSITUDES
OF THE ARIAN CRISIS

MANY of the Eastern bishops had accepted the idea of 'consubstantial' only with some hesitation and reserve. It seems to have been a term in normal use in the West (Tertullian speaks in Latin of unity of substance) and had been officially used in Egypt since Pope Dionysius's warning shot to Dionysius of Alexandria. But elsewhere it gave rise to many objections. It was criticised as being too material in character, not to say materialist, for in common parlance the term *homoousios* was used of two objects, two coins, for example, made of the same metal. The word was also criticised because it had been used by heretics — by the Gnostics, for example — and perhaps more recently by Paul of Samosata, as a result of which application of the word to the Trinity had been solemnly condemned.

The discussions which soon became very lively in ecclesiastical circles after the council of Nicaea did nothing to weaken these prejudices.

The defenders of *homoousios*, who were already viewed by many with suspicion, helped to make the term seem alarming. Marcellus of Ancyra criticised the proposals put forward by a propagandist named Asterius who, if not an outright Arian, at least had tendencies in that direction; whereupon Eusebius of Caesarea, scandalized by Marcellus's line of argument which he considered tainted with Sabellianism, at once replied with a whole long treatise. But Eustathius of Antioch in his turn accused Eusebius of corrupting the faith of Nicaea. Eusebius protested that he was acting in good faith and hurled back at Eustathius the charge of being a Sabellian. Everywhere there was nothing but partisan lawsuits and mutual accusations; yet the confusion was only just beginning.

It is extremely difficult to condense in a clear, precise manner the story of the developments of the Arian crisis during the troubled period from 325 to 381. History has a polyphonic structure and it is important to be able to grasp and combine all its different aspects simultaneously. We are dealing both with time and with space : generation follows generation and problems change. We shall find an almost continuous opposition between the Latin West (including Egypt) peacefully established on the definition of Nicaea, and the Greek East, much more unsure of itself and extremely sensitive to the Sabellian danger which the West was to discover only twenty years later. We are dealing with ideas and with men : personal questions often complicated doctrinal problems, and this period, as we have already pointed out, was rich in strong personalities. On 8 June 328 when Athanasius mounted the throne of Alexandria, *homoousios* gained a tireless champion but his very energy and, it must be admitted, the violence of his character made Athanasius many enemies and often put him in difficult situations. Finally, we are dealing with what we have called the bi-polar structure of christian society. On the one hand, the bishops discussed and the Councils tried to define, but on the other hand there was the Emperor, who intervened to support one group, to exile or depose others. When there was a new Emperor, or when the Emperor changed his mind, the life of the Church was immediately affected.

For example, less than three years after the Council of Nicaea Constantine had completely swung round, perhaps under the influence of his half-sister Constantia, the widow of Licinius. The Arians and Arius himself were recalled from exile, rehabilitated and considered orthodox on the strength of confessions of faith which were more or less vague and more or less sincere. Eusebius of Nicomedia returned to favour; as for Eusebius of Caesarea, he had never lost favour. With certain exceptions Constantine supported the opponents of the definition of Nicaea until the end of his reign.

In order to make the account as clear as possible, we will organise it in terms of the history of ideas, of the development of doctrine. From this point of view four phases can be distinguished in the development of the crisis.

1. The Anti-Nicaean Reaction in the East.

After the anathemas of Nicaea, rejecting the most extreme of the formulas put forward by Arius or attributed to him, and after the submission of Arius, which the Emperor considered adequate, many Eastern bishops believed that there no longer remained any problem in this quarter of the theological horizon. On the other hand the reality and seriousness of the Sabellian heresy, which was being so actively proclaimed by Marcellus of Ancyra, seemed to them to demand constant

CHRISTIAN ARCHITECTURE: III

PLATE 27. S. VITALE, RAVENNA, 547. 1. VIEW FROM THE SOUTH (SEE ALSO PLATES 28, 29, 30)

If there is one church which, more than any other, can perhaps serve to illustrate the essentials of the early Byzantine epoch within the compass of a few photographs, is S. Vitale. This plate and the three which follow it demonstrate three important points: the unity of conception behind the architecture, one solution of the problem of providing a central point, and the fact that mosaics in Byzantine churches are not mere decoration but an organic part of the building.

Details about the date and building of S. Vitale are given in the caption to Plate 17. In style and shape the church draws upon traditions of both eccelsiastical and secular architecture. It has strong similarities, for instance, to the audience hall of an imperial palace, and ecclesiastically it is related to another Byzantine church, that of SS. Sergius and Bacchus in Constantinople (527), which is a particularly good example of a different attempt to focus a church on a central point.

Photo : Hirmer Fotoarchiv, Munich.

(continued on Plate 28)

PLATE 28. S. VITALE, RAVENNA, 547. 2. THE AMBULATORIUM FROM THE GREAT ENTRANCE,
LOOKING TOWARDS THE SOUTHEAST

(continued from Plate 27)

Plates 27, 28, 29 show how the building of S. Vitale was dominated by this problem, and how its structure is dictated by the central point around which the whole building revolves. In the sophisticated atmosphere of the early Byzantine epoch, such problems were consciously posed and consciously solved, and the technical knowledge and skills involved in the construction of S. Vitale were noticed and praised by contemporaries. So, for example, Agnellus said of the church

that it surpassed other churches not only as a building, but as a work of mechanic (*Liber Pontificalis*, 24, 8).

The same three pictures also show another important element in any building or work of art regarded as beautiful by Byzantine critics : the rhythm of the building. 'We have come to recognize that beauty is that which irradiates symmetry, rather than symmetry itself, and it is that which truly calls out love' (Plotinus, *Ennead* VI, 7, 22)

By permission of F. W. Deichmann (Frühchristliche Bauten und Mosaiken von Ravenna, Verlag Bruno Grimm, Baden-Bade
Photo : Deutsches Archäologisches Institut, Madrid.

Photo : Hirmer Fotoarchiv, Munich.

CHRISTIAN ARCHITECTURE : V

PLATE 29. S. VITALE, RAVENNA, 547. 3. VIEW THROUGH THE CENTRE OF THE
CHURCH TOWARDS THE APSE

By permission of F. W. Deichmann (Frühchristliche Bauten und Mosaiken von Ravenna, *Verlag Bruno Grimm Baden–Baden*)
Photo : *Deutsches Archäologisches Institut, Madrid.*

CHRISTIAN ARCHITECTURE : VI

PLATE 30

S. VITALE, RAVENNA, 547. 4. Mosaic ON THE NORTH WALL OF THE PRESBYTERIUM

Left : Abraham and the three men at the Oak of Memre.
Right : Abraham about to sacrifice Isaac.

It is for its mosaics, however, that S. Vitale is most famous. A careful inspection of this picture will give some idea of how they arise out of the rhythm of the whole building; note particularly such details as the hands of Sarah, or the gesture of Abraham on the right of the picture, or the relation of Abraham's clothing to the lamb at his feet. The picture is also an example of how the mosaics in S. Vitale define and enhance its purpose as a place of worship and as a place, above all, in which the sacrifice of the eucharist is re-enacted. This mosaic has special relevance to the eucharistic theme, both in its position overlooking the altar and in its subject. The meeting of Abraham with the three men at the Oak of Memre (Genesis 18) was interpreted by the early Church as a meeting with the triune God. The mosaic therefore points beyond the historical incident to the inner life of the Godhead; but, besides this, by its portrayal of the meal and by its proximity to the altar it reminds the worshippers that through the eucharist they are invited to participate in the life of the Godhead.

vigilance, inasmuch as it showed the ambiguity of ' consubstantial '. It was understandable that a common anti-Sabellian front should have been established, grouping together very varied points of view, and this front soon became powerful.

It was led first by Eusebius of Caesarea (what interests us most today is his precious historical writing, but his role as a theologian is also worthy of attention), then, after his return from exile, by the great Eusebius of Nicomedia, the real head of the party, a man of action well able to conduct an intrigue and strongly entrenched at court.

This coalition, which from the very beginning probably represented a majority, soon launched a counter-attack and undertook systematically to eliminate from the whole of the East those who considered that orthodoxy had been defined by the formula of Nicaea. As a result a good dozen episcopal sees from Palestine to Thrace saw their titular deposed and replaced, sometimes not without difficulty, in a series of synods between 326 and 335. It is sometimes difficult to date these events : for example, the deposition of Eustathius and of Marcellus. It was at the violent and rowdy Council of Tyre-Jerusalem, held from July to September 335, that this policy finally triumphed through the deposition of Athanasius of Alexandria, a sentence soon confirmed by the Emperor's order of exile.

It is remarkable that the proceedings which were brought in consequence rested less on theological points than on strictly personal, moral or political accusations and calumnies. Eustathius was accused of adultery on the evidence of a prostitute and — more serious — of having spread offensive rumours about the origins of the Empress Mother Helena. Athanasius was reproached with his violence towards recalcitrant Melitians and although there was a kernel of truth in this, it was expressly exaggerated. In the hope of making Constantine punish him severely, it was decided to add that Athanasius had boasted of being able to prevent the transport of corn for the capital on its way from Alexandria to Constantinople. These allegations, whether true or false (in any case they were believed to be true), salved the conscience of the victorious party. When the Church of Rome came to consider the affair (338-339) and wanted to bring the deposition of its Nicaean friends before the court, the Eastern bishops refused to allow the sentences to be questioned, for in their opinion they had been pronounced quite regularly.

2. The Common Front Against Sabellianism

The victory of the anti-Sabellian front was therefore complete in the East and for more than twenty years was not seriously questioned.

True, the situation was never absolutely stable and was more than once disturbed by political events such as the death of Constantine in 338 which resulted in a temporary amnesty, and developments in the relations, often tense but occasionally conciliatory as in the years 342 to 346, between the young princes who shared the Empire. The Nicaean West was ruled by Constans, himself a Nicaean; the East by Constans II who, if he sometimes shifted his position in a search for balance, almost always remained under the influence of Arianising theologians.

After the reconquest of the Latin provinces from the usurper Magnentius, who had murdered Constans, the Empire was reunited (351-353) and adopted the doctrinal views henceforth officially held in the East. Councils submissively enacted the imperial will; Arles in 353, Milan in 355, Béziers in 356. Only a few strong men resisted this state of bondage and dared to proclaim their loyalty to Nicaea. They were promptly exiled: for example Lucifer of Cagliari, Hilary of Poitiers, Pope Liberius, and in his old age Hosius of Cordova.

Arius died in 335, Eusebius of Caesarea in 340, Eusebius of Nicomedia at the end of 341; and a new generation came on stage. We find new representatives of the Subordinationist heresy, particularly in Illyricum : Ursacius of Singidunum and Valens of Mursa, who exercised a great influence on Constantius' thought especially after 351. A new representative of Sabellianism appeared in the person of Photinus of Sirmium, whom the Westerners condemned in 345, either because they were more clearsighted or because they had a freer hand with him than with his master Marcellus of Ancyra.

What characterised this second phase was a vain attempt at stabilising doctrine. Over against the West which stood by Nicaea, the Easterners multiplied their attempts to replace the Nicene creed with a definition which appeared to them more satisfactory. In ten years (341-351) at least seven different formulas were successively envisaged : so many attempts to solve the problem show clearly that the difficulties were felt to be insurmountable. Strictly speaking, these formulas were not positively Arian. The first of the four connected with the Council of Encaenia (the ' dedication ' of the great basilica of Antioch in 341) began with the significant phrase : ' We are not in tow behind Arius '[1]. The formulas did not directly oppose the orthodoxy defined at Nicaea but, following the line taken by the conservatives in 325, avoided defining the degree of resemblance between God and the Logos. They were precise only in condemning the Sabellian errors.

1. 1st formula of the Council of Encaenia, in Athanasius, *De Synodis*, 22; Socrates, *History of the Church*, X, 5.

Despite the number of formulas scarcely any progress was made. From this point of view the detailed exposition *(ekthesis macrostiche)* adopted by another Council of Antioch in 345 was particularly remarkable. It ran to about 1400 words but in vain did it heap up images and anathemas; it went round and round the problem without ever tackling it directly.

Formulas of virulent Arianism were more and more energetically rejected : ' The Son drawn from nothingness ', ' there was a time when the Son was not ' — but it is doubtful whether these formulas had ever been held. On the other hand the Nicaean party was attacked by means of obvious exaggerations : it was accused of tritheism, that is to say belief in several non-engendered persons. Such a formula could be interpreted as orthodox, for it proclaimed the Son inseparable from the Father, were it not for the fact that it said nothing about the technical term ' consubstantial ', *homoousios;* indeed it deliberately refused to adopt the term. That meant tolerating or covering up many kinds of Subordinationism.

3.   The Anomoean Bid and the Victory of Homoeism

Dogmatic ambiguity could not continue indefinitely. The danger of the one-sided attitude which had prevailed in the East so far became apparent at last. The common front against Sabellianism was forced to splinter in face of the rise, at the other end of the doctrinal fan, of a kind of neo-Arianism more radical than that held by Arius himself : the Anomoeism of Aetius and his disciple Eunomius.

The doctrine first appeared about 350, when Aetius was imprudently made a deacon, an appointment which caused scandal at Antioch. Aetius combined the views of the old Sylloukianists, his teachers, with a sound, markedly Aristotelian philosophical training and an almost excessive taste for dialectical argument at which he was a master. He took up a reckless stand lacking in subtlety and identified the divine essence with the notion of the non-engendered clearly appropriate to the Father. He drew the conclusion that the Son, far from being consubstantial with him or even similar to him, was in fact totally different (ἀνόμοιος *anomoios*), whence the name of Anomoeism. Such an extreme position — and Eunomius made no attempt to moderate it — provoked a shock and the formation of a third party. This third party was soon divided into several groups by the expansion or rather by the progress of theological analysis. They all agreed to reject the *anomoios*, but how far did the resemblance between the groups go? The right wing did not hesitate to move very far forward : it held that the Word is like the Father in all things, that it is without alteration and, in particular, as regards substance, that it is of a like substance with the Father (ὁμοιούσιος *homoiousios*). But this entailed moving dangerously close to the 'consubstantial' of Nicaea, indeed to within an iota of it. These Homoiousians were led by Basil of Ancyra, the man who had been chosen about 335 to replace Marcellus : he had gone a long way since then! From the Homoiousians, at intervals, different groups detached themselves. These groups shrank from a point of view which was becoming more and more close to Nicaean orthodoxy; they were always more or less Subordinationist and clung to the vague formula : the Son is like the Father *(homoios)*, whence their name Homoeans. Their leader was Acacius, a pupil and successor of Eusebius of Caesarea.

At least during the agitated and confused period of the last years of the reign of Constantius (357-361), we find the Councils once more multiplying formulas, notably at the imperial residence in Sirmium on the Danube frontier. Formulas followed formulas and one tendency opposed another. The reason was not merely that the parties clashed on the theological plane, but also, and primarily, because the Emperor was still hesitant. In the divided East the Emperor had to take sides : the whole problem was to know which theology he would favour.

For two years the needle fluctuated. The formula of the Council of Sirmium in 357 was markedly Subordinationist because the group led by Ursatius and Valens was still in the lead. At Sirmium in 358, on the other hand, Basil of Ancyra was victorious (it was his formula, on the whole capable of an orthodox interpretation, which Pope Liberius, broken by years of exile, agreed to sign). The ' dated Credo ', prepared the following year (22 May 359) again at Sirmium, marked yet another step forward.

But the wind was going to change. The different tendencies clashed violently for a last time during the following months in the double Council of Rimini (for the Westerners) and Seleucia in Isauria (for the East). But the decision was finally taken by the Emperor : Constantius threw in his lot with the Homoeism of Acacius. A Council opened at Constantinople on 1 January 360 and solemnly proclaimed what henceforth must be considered the official faith of the Empire : by persuasion or force the bishops were brought round, while the diehards as always were deposed or exiled.

This important landmark put an end to the period of doctrinal elaboration. The Homoean creed of 360 defines what we can call historic Arianism as henceforth professed by communities or nations hostile to Catholic orthodoxy and to the Nicene creed.

For the time being confusion soon returned with the arrival of Julian the Apostate. He adopted a policy of clever, treacherous toleration, as we have seen in our discussion of Donatism. In fact, his general amnesty allowed the parties dismantled by Constantius to recuperate their strength : for example, the Anomoeans, who had been severely persecuted since 358, and those who remained orthodox. With the other Nicaean bishops who like him had returned from exile, Athanasius summoned the Council of Confessors which, on moderate lines, tried to clear up the difficulties resulting from a period of uncertainty and confusion.

The situation was sometimes very complex. For example, at Antioch the crisis caused by the deposition of Eustathius lasted eighty-five years (from 327/330 to 412/415). In 362 it reached its greatest complexity : at that time there were no less than five rival Christian communities in Antioch. First, we find the strict Nicaeans faithful to the memory of Eustathius. At that time they formed a separate Church, their leader Paulinus having been consecrated bishop by Lucifer of Cagliari, an extremist of the Nicaean party who, hostile to all compromise, broke with Rome and ended up as a schismatic.

Then came Meletius, suspected of Arianism by the former group : during the winter of 360 he was transferred to Antioch by the victorious Homoeans. But he was a Homoean of the right, so lukewarm towards the imperial theology that he was hardly installed before Constantius sent him into exile; soon we shall find him again in the ranks of the neo-orthodox party.

The official bishop was the man who replaced Meletius. His name was Euzoios, and he was a genuine Arian from the very beginning : as a mere deacon he had been excommunicated with Arius by Alexander of Alexandria. However, that was not enough to make him acceptable to the pure Anomoeans. From Constantinople the leaders of the party, Aetius and Eunomius, sent Antioch their great man, the wonder-working Theophilus the Indian, with orders to bring Euzoios round to their way of thinking and, if he could not, to replace him by someone else.

From the year 362 we find signs of another tendency inspired by the neighbouring bishop, Apollinaris of Laodicea, who, though strictly Nicaean in regard to the Trinity, unfortunately developed a much less sound doctrine concerning christology. Fifteen years later, about 376/7, this viewpoint was proclaimed by yet another bishop in Antioch, a certain Vitalis, who disputed the rights of the three other bishops.

Here we find the polyphonic structure of history : doctrinal problems rise up in turn like voices in a fugue. The Arian question had not yet been resolved before other debates began, in logical relation with the first. A discussion of the full divinity of the Son necessarily led to a consideration of the question of the Holy Spirit. This happened in Egypt about 360, as we know from St Athanasius's reply, and in the years 370-380 in Asia Minor. There the Pneumatomachian heresy was spreading through the ranks of the Homoiousians, introducing another cause of strife among them (the great Basil of Caesarea fought against the Pneumatomachian error). Similarly, it seems to have been Basil's polemic against the truncated christology of the Arians which led Apollinaris to formulate his system. Apollinaris declared that in the Incarnation the divine Word plays the role of vital principle normally played in an ordinary man by the spirit or soul — a theory which orthodox Christians claimed mutilated Christ's humanity and left it imperfect.

4. From Valens to Theodosius

But Arianism was not yet beaten. Fortunately the reign of Julian was too short (361/363) for the pagan reaction to cause more than superficial havoc. The reign of Valentinian (364-375) was a period of reconstruction and stabilisation. Valentinian was by personal conviction a Christian and Nicaean but not very much inclined to take part in theological debates; he seems to have been chiefly preoccupied with gathering all the strength of the Empire against the barbarians. In religious matters he adopted a peaceful, tolerant attitude. In the Latin provinces where, save in Illyricum, Nicaean orthodoxy had a powerful majority, he did not disturb the few Homoean bishops imposed by Constantius.

In the East, on the other hand, his brother Valens, who at the end of a month became his associate (364-378), emerged as an Emperor who was also a theologian, like Constantius and for the same reasons. Like Constantius, he adopted the modified Arianism of the Homoeans as defined at Constantinople in 360, and made life difficult not only for the Anomoeans but also for the Homoiousians and the partisans of Nicaea. Once more there followed a campaign of intimidation, deposition and exile of bishops. Athanasius, now an old man, was driven from Alexandria for the fifth time.

In the following table we recapitulate his troubled career, which is typical of a whole era. Although exceptional, this career was not unique; that of Paul of Constantinople, another Nicaean many times deposed, was almost as complex (334/6-343/50).

ATHANASIUS : born in 295.

> took part in the Council of Nicaea as Alexander's deacon in 325,

consecrated Bishop of Alexandria 8 June 328.

1st exile : under Constantine, 11 July 335 — 22 November 337; lived at Trèves.

2nd exile : under Constantius, 16 April 339 — 21 October 346; lived at Rome.

3rd exile : under the same, 9 February 356 — 21 February 362; in the Egyptian desert.

4th exile : under Julian, 24 October 362 — 5 September 363; in the Egyptian desert.

5th exile : under Valens, 5 October 365 — 31 January 366; in the Egyptian desert.

died 2 May 373.

Athanasius died full of years and crowned with glory, but another generation had already taken over his work. Other men than he had led and would continue to lead the great battle against Anomoeism. The problems had changed, and so too had the men. The decisive event during the reign of Valens was the growth of a new party which can be called neo-orthodox; it went out to meet the Nicaeans and ended by fusing with them.

Its recruits were not drawn primarily from among the Homoiousians for the notion of *homoiousios* was perhaps contradictory in itself, as the recently converted Roman philosopher Marius Victorinus objected in 358, and was in any case a dead end. The party emerged from the Homoean right wing (who declared the Son to be completely like the Father in all things) and numbered men like Mecenus of Antioch and the three great Cappadocian Doctors, Basil of Caesarea, a leader and man of action, his friend Gregory of Nazianzus, a humanist and exquisite writer, and his brother Gregory of Nyssa, a bold philosopher and mystic.

We can say that the fullness of the Catholic faith has preserved the precious heritage of the Nicaeans, who were vigilant against any sign of Subordinationism, and the equally precious heritage of those neo-orthodox theologians who transmitted anything of value in the Eastern anti-Sabellian reaction. The reserved attitude so long shown in the East towards the Nicaeans no longer had any good reason to continue, since the latter had kept Marcellus of Acyra at a distance and vigorously anathematised Photinus of Sirmium. What remained to be done was to convince them in their turn that the new theology was harmless. These neo-orthodox christians were viewed with some suspicion by those whom the Latins of the Nicaean faith considered their surest friends : by Paulinus of Antioch, the rival of Meletius, and by Peter of Alexandria, the successor of Athanasius, who did not scruple to treat them all as Arians, in view of their compromising origins.

Above all, it was necessary to overcome the obstacles that stood in the way of mutual understanding. These included the difference of language (from now on the Latins began to have a rather poor knowledge of Greek, while the Greeks had never used Latin very much), the difference of intellectual climate, and the difference of theological tradition. With the progress of research a vocabulary quickly grew and within each group words borrowed from common parlance or from philosophy gradually took on a definite theological meaning.

The problem was to bring about the meeting of the two formulas evolved by the two different parties to sum up the doctrine of the Trinity : one *ousia*, three *hypostases*, held by the Cappadocians, and *una substantia, tres personae*, held by the Latins. The former appeared to the latter tainted with Arianism, if not with tritheism, while the latter savoured of Sabellianism in the opinion of the former. Two letters written to Pope Damasus (376-377) by St Jerome, then living alone in a Syrian desert within the province of Antioch, give us an idea of the perplexing situation. Was it necessary, he asked, to profess three *hypostases?* Surely *hypostasis* was synonymous with *ousia*, substance, nature? On the other hand, with which of the three Nicaean bishops should he be in communion, since all three declared themselves to be in communion with Rome[2]?

St Basil had the merit of working tirelessly to overcome this mutual misunderstanding and promote the indispensable work of reuniting the Churches. He was installed in the metropolitan see of Caesarea of Cappadocia in 370, and we find him in the following year negotiating first with Athanasius, then directly with Pope Damasus. These negotiations were long, difficult and full of disappointments. Basil died on 1 January 379 without having attained his goal. But the situation had ripened and before the end of the year a Council of 153 bishops from the East, among them all the leading figures of the neo-orthodox movement, gathered at Antioch, accepted the faith of Damasus and fell into line with the Western Church.

The extent and effectiveness of this movement were, moreover, increased as a result of a change of Emperor. Valens had just relaxed his pressure in favour of Homoeism when he died in the disaster of Adrianople while vainly trying to stem the Gothic invasion (30 May 378). On the following 19 January his successor in the East was proclaimed : the Spanish-born general Theodosius, who was a fervent christian and, being a good Westerner, a convinced Nicaean. Theodosius changed the direction of religious policy. On 28 February 380 he promulgated

2. Jerome, *Letters* 15 and 16.

an edict at Thessalonica imposing on his subjects Catholic orthodoxy, defined by reference to the see of Peter, its titular Damasus and his ally the Bishop of Alexandria.

As always, the imperial will was expressed in visible changes. For example, he had hardly arrived at Constantinople when Theodosius drove the Arian Demophilus from the episcopal see and installed in his place a man who had hitherto been merely the leader of the small orthodox community in the capital, Gregory of Nazianzus. Gregory, however, did not remain there long. Temperamentally he was hypersensitive and uneasy in mind; he could not stand the strain of the first intrigues against him during the Council summoned by Theodosius to help in re-establishing orthodoxy. That was the second ecumenical Council, which met in Constantinople in 381.

Orthodoxy and the general movement rallying round it were not, however, affected. In 381 before and after the Council, and again at the end of a final conference, where representatives of the different opinions met once again, as well as in 383, 384 and 391, Theodosius decreed a whole series of new edicts which expressed his determination to support with the full weight of his authority the religious unity which had been re-established to the advantage of the faith of Nicaea.

During this time despite many political disturbances the Western Church made comparable progress thanks to its energetic leaders, Pope Damasus (366-384) and the Bishop of Milan, St Ambrose (374-397). Various usurpers rose up against the sons and successors of Valentinian. Theodosius had to intervene to help or avenge his colleagues; for a few months at the end of his reign he reunited the whole Empire under his authority (8 September 394 — 17 January 395).

In these Latin countries the main task facing orthodoxy was to crush the bastion of Arianism established in Illyricum since the exile of Arius to that region, and especially since the time of Ursacius and Valens. Despite the protection afforded it by the Empress Mother Justina, who was Regent for her young son Valentinian II at the court of Sirmium, and later at Milan (373/383-387), the bastion was gradually dismantled. This was largely due to the perseverance of St Ambrose at the Council which he summoned and to the influence he exercised (chiefly from 376 to 383) on Gratian, the elder of the two Emperors of the West. Finally, the intervention of Theodosius proved decisive. It was with Theodosius that Justina and her son sought refuge during the dangerous days when Maximus usurped power. In the campaign of 388 Theodosius reconquered the West for them and for himself; he then repealed the measures of toleration decreed by Valentinian II in favour of the Arians.

Henceforward, in the West as in the East, Arianism (to keep the name traditionally applied to the Homoean sect) was definitively conquered. Roman subjects throughout the Empire could profess it only by breaking the law and keeping their beliefs a secret. Similarly, still more severe legislation was passed against pagan survivals and the last political twitching of paganism was crushed. At the end of the reign of Theodosius Christianity, or rather orthodox Catholicism, became the official religion of the whole Roman world.

So the long crisis resulting from the condemnation of Arius came to an end. The importance of his role in the development of christian theological thinking and the formulation of dogma must not be underestimated. The historian must also point out the place which this crisis held in the thought and daily life of christians at that period.

We must not imagine that the professional theologians, the bishops and the Councils were the only ones to concern themselves with it. This doctrinal problem excited the masses. As a propaganda measure Arius summed up his theology in a popular song which was, we are told, sung by sailors, millers and travellers. The orthodox Doctors more than once felt obliged to protest against the abuse of discussions bearing on such a holy mystery as the inner structure of God's being, discussions where, all too clearly, the Greeks brought to a christian context that love of subtle, excited argument which the long rivalry of philosophic schools had enabled them to indulge in pagan times. Not without irony Gregory of Nyssa mentions the money-changer who, if asked the exchange rate, replied with a dissertation on the engendered and non-engendered; you go to the baker's shop : the Father, he tells you, is greater than the Son; at the hot baths you ask whether your bath is ready : you are told that the Son came from nothingness [3].

At a more serious level Gregory of Nazianzus reminded the Anomoeans, who were unduly proud of their syllogisms, that it was not given to everyone to discuss God but only to those who had shown their capacity for it by advancing far enough in the way of perfection [4]. But these popular feelings were deep; in February 386 when the Empress Justina demanded that one of the basilicas of Milan should be handed over for Arian worship, St Ambrose made a public appeal, and had the disputed building occupied day and night by his faithful flock, whose enthusiasm he skillfully kept at high pitch. It was on this occasion, we are told by St Augustine, who was then in Milan and on the point

3. Gregory of Nyssa, *On the Divinity of the Son and the Holy Spirit*, *PG*, Vol. 46, col. 557 B.
4. Gregory of Nazianzus, *Discourse* 27 (*Theol.*, I), 3, *PG*, Vol. 36, col. 13 C-15 A.

of being converted, that St Ambrose introduced into the Latin Church the Eastern practice of having hymns and psalms sung by the congregation [5].

5. Augustine, *Confessions*, IX, 7 (15).

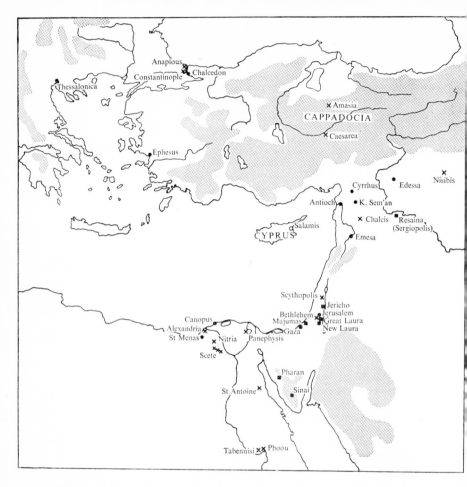

× *Monastic sites in the 4th and 5th centuries*
■ *Monastic sites in the 6th century*
● *Centres of pilgrimage*
   Mountains over 3000 feet

6   Eastern Monasticism

CHAPTER XX

THE ORIGINS
AND FIRST DEVELOPMENTS
OF MONASTICISM

HOWEVER impassioned these debates and however serious their repercussions, we must not imagine that throughout the whole of the fourth century the christian Church allowed itself to be totally absorbed by the problem of the theology of the Trinity. In fact during these very years 310-410 we witness many other signs of the Church's vitality. First of all, there was the emergence and speedy growth of a new institution : monasticism.

Here we must retrace our steps and return to the time of Diocletian. If the notion of holy virginity goes back to the very origins of Christianity, monasticism was an original institution which must not be confused with the former (to be more precise, we must not identify the former with the latter). Monasticism now arrived to take over, as it were, from persecution, both ideologically and chronologically.

As long as the threat of persecution remained, martyrdom, the highest grace, was normally held to be the final stage in the spiritual ascent of a christian soul called to perfection. When peace came to the Church Christianity was welcomed in the world and installed itself comfortably there — sometimes rather too comfortably. We have only to think of those court bishops, too easily dazzled by the Emperor's favour and rather inclined to invest the new christian Empire with a lustre borrowed from the splendours of the eschatological city of God! The flood of often superficial or selfish conversions both in the masses and among the élite was bound to bring about a relaxation of spiritual tension within the Church.

In these conditions it is understandable that flight from the world appeared to be the most favourable if not the necessary condition for attaining perfection. The idea was later to be expressed in Irish monastic circles of the sixth century by the curious distinction between red martyrdom — the bloody martyrdom of persecution — and white or green martyrdoms, which were attained by a life of renunciation and mortification.

Solitude, asceticism, contemplation; Christian monasticism turned to its own use these ideals which are among the most deeply rooted in the very structure of human nature. In the comparative history of religions we can find the equivalent of monasticism in the most varied civilizations : in India, Central Asia, China, perhaps even in pre-Columbian America; on the other hand it had so far remained curiously absent from the classical countries of the Mediterranean. Our monasticism is separated by a gap from its Jewish antecedents, the Essenes of Qumran and the Therapeutae of Alexandria, who were described or idealised by Philo. The links which scholars have tried to establish, when analysed, are found to be inconsistent, apart from a very few features borrowed by both Jews and Christians from Ptolemaic Egypt.

Monasticism appeared in Egypt at the end of the third century; its first representatives were hermits or anchorites. The kind of life which they adopted was not in itself a novelty. The anachoresis, literally ' going up to the desert ', perhaps we might translate it as ' taking to the bush ', had been a common practice in Egypt at this time among all those with good reason to get away from society : criminals, bandits, people who could not pay their debts, people hounded by the Treasury for not paying their taxes, asocial people of all kinds. During persecution Christians also fled to the desert — for example, the grandparents of St Basil in Cappadocia. But the monk chose the desert for reasons of a spiritual nature.

1.   St Antony, Father of Monks

Monasticism first appears in history with St Antony, the ' father of monks ', who died in 356 aged more than a hundred (people live to a great age in the desert). History and literary history are often inseparable : we cannot separate St Antony the man from the biography written by the great St Athanasius. It probably dates from sometime in the 360s, was soon translated twice into Latin, and exercised a considerable influence, doing much to spread the new ideal and to stimulate vocations. St Augustine read it at a decisive moment of his conversion, and in his *Confessions* describes the shattering effect the book had on him and on some of his contemporaries.

This monograph, which is both a narrative and a portrait, shows that St Antony was an Egyptian peasant of humble birth and practically illiterate. In contrast to the pride of newly converted intellectuals, who brought to Christianity the aristocratic tradition of their pagan masters, monasticism reaffirmed, as Franciscanism was later to do in the thirteenth century, the pre-eminence of simple people, which is one of the essential aspects of the Gospel message.

Born a christian and brought up piously, Antony was converted to a life of perfection at the age of eighteen or twenty on the day when he entered a church and heard a reading of the passage where the Lord says to the rich young man : ' If you want to be perfect, go and sell all you possess, give to the poor, and come and follow me '. The monk was first and foremost a christian who took the counsels of the Gospel seriously and followed them literally.

Having broken all his ties with the world, Antony gave himself up to a solitary life. His long career can be divided into three stages, each of which was a search for more complete isolation. First, he established himself in the immediate neighbourhood of the village where he was born in order to be able to profit from the advice of an old man more experienced than he. This point is essential : the hermit's life was a hard school and could not be learned without a master. Later, for nearly twenty years he lived in a small abandoned fort, one of those forts with which the Romans had marked out the tracks between the Nile and the Red Sea, and finally settled even deeper in the desert.

The life he led appears first of all to have been an increasingly rigorous life of penance and asceticism. Essentially quite different from the asceticism of the Platonists or Gnostics, christian asceticism originated in the following empirical observation dear to the Fathers of the Church — we find it in almost identical terms in the works of Clement of Alexandria and St Augustine : ' The man who lets himself do everything that is allowed will very soon become slack and do what is not allowed '. Naturally everything depended on the context of the civilisation. The first Egyptian monks, rough Coptic peasants, were used to so low a standard of living that their eagerness to repress concupiscence often led them to disconcerting excesses in such matters as privation of comfort, food or sleep. One way or another the problem was to try and master the passions completely, to attain what the theoretical thinker of the desert, Evagrius the Pontic, tried to express by the unfortunately ambiguous word *apatheia*, tranquillity (or apathy).

This asceticism was not limited to the inner, psychological life. The hermit went out into the desert to confront the forces of evil and, specifically, the Devil, with his temptations and attacks; hence the place taken up in the *Life of Antony* by those descriptions of devilry which, having captured the imagination of Brueghel, have very often scandalised modern readers, but whose deep theological significance must be sought beneath the turns and twists of the story.

The hermit worked with his hands, kept vigil and prayed. 'Pray unceasingly', St Paul had said; 'Watch and pray', Christ had recommended in the Gospel. The monk, as always, took these counsels very seriously. He would have liked to be able to realise them literally, and in the end attain a life like that of the angels *(isangelikos)*. Hence the part played in his life by reading, or rather reciting, the psalms and chapters of Holy Scripture which were usually learned by heart. Passages were ceaselessly repeated and meditated. Prayer was prolonged and became contemplation, which in turn opened the way to even higher experiebces. Except in cases of deviation or excess, christian asceticism was not an end in itself but rather prepared and orientated the whole personality for mystical experience : it was a means to that end.

In the eyes of pagans of the fourth century, to say nothing of modern pagans, the monk seemed to be a kind of madman suffering from misanthropy, oblivious of the fact that man is made for society and civilisation : those are the very words used by Julian the Apostate[1]. But no, the monk remained a man and took all humanity with him to the desert; he remained a christian and felt himself bound up with the whole Church.

It is a remarkable fact that St Antony left the desert and went to Alexandria only twice in his life, the first time during the persecution of Diocletian to bolster the courage of confessors by exposing himself to possible martyrdom; the second time at the height of the Arian dispute to lend the episcopacy the support of his personal prestige and to help it defend orthodoxy. This link between the prophet and the priest needs to be emphasised. It found its symbolic expression in the fact that Athanasius himself, bishop and doctor, felt obliged to become the historian of St Antony and the propagandist of monasticism.

Similarly, we need to emphasise the fact that the monks and particularly St Antony played an important role in the Church's life. St Antony retired to the desert in order to attain an objective which may seem purely personal : his own perfection and sanctity. But this sanctity which God confirmed by granting special graces had its own special influence and acted on other Christians as a pole of attraction and a ferment. Paradoxically, or rather by a strange reversal of roles, the hermit attracted a crowd of visitors who came to ask for the help of his prayers, the curing of diseases, both physical and spiritual, for advice or simply for a good example. We shall find this again when

1. *Letter* 89 b, p. 155, 17 Bidez.

we come to discuss pilgrimages. Some returned, edified and comforted, to their daily routine. Others, deeply affected by his example, installed themselves beside him, placed themselves under his direction and tried in their turn to imitate his way of life.

So, even during the lifetime of St Antony and more and more after his death, monasticism spread throughout the whole Christian world, enriching the body of the Church with a new kind of vocation to sanctity. Naturally as it progressed it took several different forms. Even within the fourth century we can distinguish four varieties of the monastic institution, each of which corresponds to a stage in its development :

(a) The Grouping of Anchorites

This is the oldest and most rudimentary form of organization. Disciples who had come to the desert to be trained by a holy old man built cells in the neighbourhood of his cell. Their number could become more or less great. Between solitude and life in common every possible variation is found. As a rule each monk lived, worked and meditated alone in his cell; all came together for prayer in common, either daily at fixed times (what was later to become the monastic office was sketched out at a very early date) or once a week for the solemn liturgy of Saturday or Sunday, or in the case of those judged worthy and capable of a more complete eremitical life, more rarely still.

That was the system outlined during the lifetime of St Antony, when, despite himself, his spiritual children twice got the better of his desire for solitude. From Middle Egypt, where St Antony was born and had lived, it spread throughout Egypt, to the South in the Thebaid, to the North in the borders of the Delta — abandoned country and something of a wilderness — and in the regions nearby. The most famous group, which has lasted right up to modern times, was that in the desert of Scete at Wadi Natrun, west of the Delta.

Scete was founded in the 330s, was made famous by the great Macarius, and harboured that very curious person Evagrius the Pontic from 382 to his death in 399. Evagrius had been St Basil's lector in Caesarea and deacon to St Gregory of Nazianzus, whom he followed to Constantinople. In Constantinople he delivered the sermons which made him famous, but despite this twofold patronage he was a theologian of doubtful orthodoxy. A disciple of Origen, he lovingly developed to the point of heresy the most questionable of his master's tendencies, thereby justifying the posthumous condemnations which were to fall on Origenism at the end of the fourth century and later in the sixth. On the other hand his spiritual doctrine, enriched by all the experience gathered from great hermits, was extremely valuable and was later to exercise a deep influence. Intellectuals were rare in the desert : the role of Evagrius was to systematise the teaching of the monks and to make of it a body of doctrine.

The wisdom of the monks of Egypt has also been handed down to us in a more direct manner in racy collections of apophthegms, where a whole spirituality is summed up in an anecdote of a few lines, or a phrase or even three words — such as this motto of the holy abbot Arsenius, so expressive in the original Greek : ' flee, be silent, be calm '². Another source is the long accounts which travellers have left of the conversations they had with some of the great hermits. The three most famous are first the *History of the Monks*, written about 400, an anonymous work describing a journey made in 394/5 which was widely read in the enlarged Latin translation of Rufinus of Aquileia; secondly, the *History dedicated to Lausus* by the Galatian bishop, Palladius (419/420; he stayed at Scete between 388 and 399); and thirdly the *Institutes* and *Conferences* which the Rumanian-born monk John Cassian wrote in Marseilles during the 420s towards the end of his life. They describe his memories of a long stay in Lower Egypt some twenty or thirty years earlier. All these works very clearly reflect the teaching of Evagrius at Scete, the first two openly, the third — that of Cassian — with prudent discretion.

(b) Pachomian Cenobitism

However well adapted it might be to the Egyptian temperament, such an organisation was still too weak and involved many dangers, both spiritual (by favouring individualism) and material (when the number of monks increased beyond bounds). With St Pachomius there appeared another kind of monasticism which, by reaction, put the accent on life in common, *koinos bios* — cenobitism. In 323, having trained himself in eremitical life for seven years, Pachomius founded his first community in an abandoned village at Tabennisi in Upper Egypt.

This community soon grew and received from its founder a well-knit structure : to begin with, a rule — the first monastic rule, strictly speaking — with 194 articles defining precisely the rhythm of the monk's daily life, work, prayer in common and discipline. Surrounded by an enclosure, the Pachomian monastery comprised a chapel and outbuildings and a series of houses grouping a score of monks under the authority of a provost assisted by a deputy. Three or four houses made up a tribe, the whole owing obedience to the superior who, with his assistant, looked after the spiritual direction of the community and the smooth working of the general services. These included a bakery, kitchen,

2. *Apophtegmes*, Arsenius, 1-2, *PG*, vol. 65, col. 88 BC.

infirmary, etc. To staff them the different houses every week delegated the requisite number of monks.

This first monastery proved a success and St Pachomius was soon led to create a second of the same sort at Pboou, another abandoned village of the neighbourhood. Other foundations followed. At his death in 346 St Pachomius had founded nine convents for men and two for women, the first women's convent having been established about 340 near Tabennisi by his sister Mary. Under his successors expansion continued throughout all Egypt. At the end of the century we even find a Pachomian monastery installed at the gates of Alexandria, at Canopus : this was the famous monastery of Penance, Metanoia.

The sum total of these convents formed a congregation under the authority of a superior general installed at Tabennisi and later at Pboou. It was he who appointed the heads of each monastery. At a chapter-general they gathered round him twice a year : at Easter and on 13 August. Then they had to give a detailed account of the working of their monastery to the chief bursar, who helped the superior in the handling of business affecting the congregation as a whole.

The importance of the economic side of this institution did in fact increase with the number of monks. The Pachomian monasteries eventually counted their monks by thousands, perhaps by tens of thousands. For Egyptian agriculture they represented a by no means negligible supply of seasonal labour : whole crowds would leave the monastery at harvest time and spread through the valley of the Nile where, in a few days, they earned enough to support the community for the whole year and also provide what was needed for works of charity.

If the work of St Pachomius himself seems inspired by remarkable prudence and moderation, such an increase in numbers was certainly the reason why other monastic organisers were eventually led to increase the severity of his rule and to make discipline even stricter. Sometimes they went to excess : notably the fiery Shenoute, who was head of the White Monastery, in Upper Egypt, from the year 388 onwards.

(c) The Basilian Community

Throughout Christian antiquity Egypt never ceased to appear the chosen land of monasticism, but monasticism was not confined to Egypt. Difficult though it is to date with certainty the first stages of its development, we soon see the new institution expanding more and more throughout the East. Monasticism appeared in Palestine at the beginning of the century with St Hilarion of Gaza. About 335 a monastery was founded by St Epiphanius, who became Bishop of Salamis in Cyprus in 367. Until his death in 403 Epiphanius played the thankless but doubtless necessary role of heresy-hunter.

Monasticism also appeared in Syria, especially in the more or less desert regions near Antioch. It appeared in Asia Minor, where the pioneer was Eustathius. Promoted about 356 to be Bishop of Sebaste in Roman Armenia, Eustathius was a complex person who became involved in the Trinitarian disputes of the period, not to mention those aroused by his zealous ascetical propaganda, which was considered by some indiscreet. Rather late the movement ended by reaching Constantinople itself. In 382 the Syrian, Isaac, founded a first monastery there, that of Dalmatius, so called from the name of its second abbot.

Decisive progress was made by St Basil. About 357, soon after his baptism, he embraced the monastic life and, after a fact-finding journey which took him as far as Egypt, settled in his family property of Annesi in the mountains of Pontus. He tried to group around him certain friends, including St Gregory of Nazianzus; but he could not keep Gregory for long, since he was psychologically too restless to settle in one place. Nevertheless, St Basil gradually grouped around him a veritable community which was to serve as a model for many others.

The monastic career of St Basil was short, because he was ordained priest for Caesarea of Cappadocia and in 365 settled there for good, becoming metropolitan in 370. But his role in monastic history was none the less considerable, thanks to his work as organiser and legislator. The monastic regulations which he drew up, and whose influence was to be so great, were in fact based on quite a new conception of monasticism.

Henceforth the accent is deliberately put on living in community, conceived as the normal framework of the growth of the spiritual life. Anchoritism rather disappeared from the horizon. The heroic examples of the Old Testament so dear to the early anchorites — the calling of Abraham, the ascent of Elijah — were replaced in St Basil's writings by a picture of the early Christians of Jerusalem as described for us by the *Acts of the Apostles*. Hence the stress put on obedience, the duty of giving up one's own will and confidently abandoning oneself to the hands of a superior.

(d) St Jerome and Ascetical Propaganda in Roman Circles

Monasticism also reached the West. During his exile in Trèves and later in Rome St Athanasius began to make known the existence of monasticism; but it is above all the name of St Jerome which deserves to be stressed here. After three years' training in the desert of Chalcis near Antioch (375-377) he came to settle in Rome beside Pope Damasus. There his propaganda for the ascetical ideal met with great success, notably among a certain number of ladies, widows or virgins belonging to the highest senatorial aristocracy.

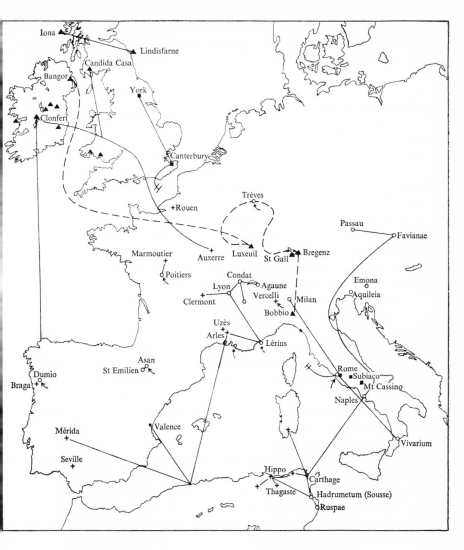

Iona ▲
Lindisfarne ▲
Candida Casa ▲
Bangor ▲
York ▲
Clonfert ▲
▲
▲
Canterbury ▲
ᚼ
+Rouen
Trèves
Passau ○
○ Favianae
Marmoutier
Auxerre +
Luxeuil ▲
St Gall ▲ ▲ Bregenz
Poitiers ○
Emona
Condat ○
Lyon ○
Agaune ○
Vercelli ○
Aquileia ○
Clermont +
○ Milan
Bobbio ▲
Uzès
Arles +
Lérins ○
Rome ■
Subiaco ■
Mt Cassino ■
Asan
St Emilien ○○
Dumio ○
Braga +
Naples ○
Mérida +
Valence ▲
Vivarium ○
Seville +
Hippo +
Carthage
Thagaste +
Hadrumetum (Sousse)
Ruspae ○

Character of monasteries   ↖ Centres of Eastern influence
   ○ Eastern   === Filiations and influential links
   + Episcopal
   ▲ Celtic
   ■ Benedictine

7   Western Monasticism

This success did not fail to arouse opposition. Like every innovation in the life of the Church, monasticism, when it first appeared in Rome, was subjected to much criticism. Storms and discussions arose in which St Jerome's zest as a controversialist was displayed on more than one occasion, much to the profit of christian theology in the spheres of Mariology, marriage and virginity.

St Jerome had to leave Rome in 385 and was soon followed by several of the christian ladies who had placed themselves under his spiritual direction. After making the usual pilgrimage to Syria and Egypt, St Jerome settled in Bethlehem at the monastery which the ladies founded under the direction of one of their number, St Paula, who was later succeeded by her daughter Eustochium. Another great Roman lady, St Melania the elder, settled quite near, at Jerusalem. She, too, had founded a convent of enclosed Latin nuns, whose almoner was Rufinus Aquileia, an old friend of St Jerome and almost his compatriot. Later, unfortunately, he was to quarrel with St Jerome over the Origenist dispute aroused by the trouble-maker Epiphanius (393-402).

(e) Episcopal Monasteries of the West

Meanwhile monasticism continued to spread in Italy : in Milan it flourished around St Ambrose. It spread also in Africa, in Spain and in Gaul : about 360 St Martin settled at Ligugé near Poitiers. This first Latin monasticism was directly fed from Eastern sources. Pilgrimages and visits were made to the asceteria of Egypt. Biographies of monks, apophthegms and rules were translated : St Jerome translated that of Pachomius, Rufinus those of Basil. The monastery of Lérins, founded by St Honoratus about 400 on the coast of Provence, is a good example of these communities, which were still very much like their Egyptian models. It was largely for this kind of monastery that John Cassian, himself the founder of two monasteries in Marseilles, wrote his memories of Egypt.

Something very different and much more original appears for the first time with Eusebius, Bishop of Vercelli in Piedmont from about 345. An ardent defender of Nicaean orthodoxy, Eusebius was later, in 355, exiled for his opinions by the Emperor Constantius. Exile gave him an opportunity to visit the East, where he became particularly friendly with Evagrius of Antioch, the second translator of the *Life of St Antony*. Eusebius was a bishop but he also wanted to be a monk; he grouped the members of his clergy round him in order to lead an ascetical form of life in community.

Other bishops in their turn imitated Eusebius : for example, St Augustine in Africa. Augustine had embraced the monastic life at the time when he asked to be baptised, but the first community he grouped around him on his return to his native town of Tagaste in 388 was still more original and produced no successors. It was a monastery of intellectuals where scientific and philosophical studies went hand in hand with the religious life, thus realising on the christian plane the dream of a community of thinkers which Plotinus had once toyed with.

In 391, when he was called to become a member of the clergy of Hippo, St Augustine doubtless renounced this splendid dream of a life of solitude and peaceful meditation, but not his ascetical vocation. As a priest he grouped around him a certain number of clerics. When he became bishop some years later in 395, he turned his house into an episcopal monastery, imposing on all his clergy monastic renunciation and notably the vow of poverty. Some of his sermons show how carefully he ensured that this vow should be strictly observed.

A slightly different yet strikingly analogous case is that of St Martin. When he was uprooted from a solitary life to become bishop of Tours in 370/1 he did not abandon the communal existence he had led at Ligugé. He too gathered a community under his direction, not, like the preceding bishops, actually in the episcopal town, but at least very near it, at Marmoutiers. Like the community of Hippo, which produced a dozen bishops, it was a centre of ecclesiastical training and influenced the whole district. His achievement was not unique, for St Paulinus of Nola did much the same in Campania, and St Victricius of Rouen in Northern Gaul, but it had important consequences for the future. It opened the way for communities of canons regular and that inter-penetration — so characteristic of the Western Church — between the life of the secular clergy and the demands of the monastic state.

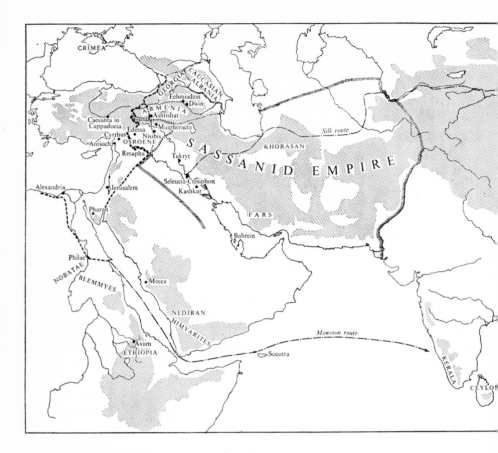

Frontiers between the Roman and Sassanid empires

 ------. *in 284*

 •|•|•|• *in 297*

 .... *in 363*

 ▨ *Mountains over 3000 feet*

8   Expansion outside the Roman World

CHAPTER XXI

THE EXPANSION
OF CHRISTIANITY
OUTSIDE THE ROMAN WORLD

HOWEVER rich and varied its developments, monasticism remained an institution whose influence was chiefly felt *within* the Church. But the Church had not forgotten its duties to the world outside or its vocation to be a universal religion : in fact the years from 310 to 410 witnessed great progress in the movement to evangelise the world. We must beware of an anachronism : there is no question yet of an officially organised mission, directed from above by hierarchical authority; for that we must wait until 596, when St Gregory the Great sent a mission to the Anglo-Saxons. In the fourth century this movement was much more spontaneous and its most spectacular successes were due to personal initiative in very special circumstances.

In this connection it is well to re-read and ponder a splendid passage by Eusebius of Caesarea. In his *History of the Church* he inserts it in his account of the very beginning of the second century, but it should be seen, rather, as an idealised picture of the missionary movement in general, as Eusebius imagined it on the strength of what was taking place before his eyes, in his own day, during the first third of the fourth century. ' At that time many christians felt their souls struck by the divine Word with a violent love for perfection. They began by fulfilling Our Saviour's counsel and distributed their goods to the poor; then, leaving their country, they undertook the mission of evangelists, intending to preach to those who as yet had not heard the word of faith and to bring them the books of the divine Gospel; they were content to lay the foundations of the faith in some foreign country, then they established other pastors and handed over to them the task of caring for those whom they had just converted. After that they departed once more for other countries and other nations with the grace and help of God. . ."[1].

First we must record the progress made outside the Roman Empire.

1. In the Sassanid Empire

We have already met the first of these foreign Churches, that of the Eastern Syrians of Sassanid Mesopotamia, which we found solidly rooted at the beginning of the fourth century. It grew during the century despite more and more unfavourable political conditions. Viewed with suspicion by their Iranian ruler because they disrupted the religious unity of his subjects by adopting a religion of foreign origin, these christians became still more suspect when peace came to the Church and the Emperor was converted, making Christianity in some sense the official religion of the Roman Empire. We have the text of a letter from Constantine to his colleague beyond the Euphrates, the King of Kings, recommending the christians to his goodwill[2]. The authenticity of this text has not been proved; it is not even certain that Constantine took any such action; but there was no need for him to do so to make these christian communities appear in the eyes of the Sassanid Sovereign a fifth column in the heart of Persian territory, taking orders from Rome.

Now this century saw the long reign of Shapur II (309-379), one of the greatest kings of the dynasty, a typically Sassanid ruler, a fierce enemy of Rome and a firm believer in national Mazdaism. During the whole second part of his reign, from the year 339/340 onwards, he launched a violent, bitter persecution against the christian minority. He systematically strove to dismantle the structure of the Church, reserving his attacks especially for members of the clergy and men and women who had taken a vow of virginity. Three successive titulars of the episcopal see of Seleucia-Ctesiphon suffered martyrdom, as a result of which this central see remained vacant for nearly forty years (c. 348-388).

Cruelly decimated, the Persian Church struggled to survive by seeking help from the other Syrian-language communities, long established and flourishing in the districts of Upper Mesopotamia under the authority of Rome (since 297 and the victories of Galerius, the frontier of the Empire had been moved forward beyond the Tigris). We must emphasise the especially fruitful role played by the School

---

1. Eusebius, *HE*, III, 37, 2-3.
2. Ps.(?)-Eusebius, *Life of Constantine*, IV, 9-13; cf. Sozomenus, *History of the Church*, II, 15; Theodoret, *History of the Church*, I, 25.

of Persians installed first at Nisibis, then forced back to Edessa in the year 363, after Julian the Apostate's disastrous defeat; a school famous chiefly for the teaching of the great Doctor St Ephraem (306-373). The school was original in that it combined the features of an ecclesiastical seminary with those of a christian university. In the Roman Empire Christianity had, as it were, been grafted on to the vigorous tree of classical culture and made use of secular schools, Greek or Latin, — the only ones which existed; in Semitic Mesopotamia for the first time we find a type of higher education organised to serve the needs of the life of the Church. Lessons were given in the vernacular, thus favouring the growth of a national culture.

When the persecution ended, a bishop of this frontier region named Maruthas of Maijpherkat directed the reconstruction of the Persian Church. Maruthas was a member of several Roman embassies to the court of the fourth successor of Shapur II, Yezdegerd I (399-420). He was warmly welcomed by the king who, doubtless preoccupied with his struggle against the encroachments of the Mazdean clergy, bravely adopted a policy of toleration towards his christian subjects. For example, at Seleucia in 410, Maruthas was able to hold a council of about forty bishops, who solemnly adopted the dogmatic disciplinary decisions of the Council of Nicaea, thus strengthening links with the Church of the ' Western Fathers '. Moreover, he re-established order and a hierarchy in the whole Persian Church : one church to a parish, one bishop to a diocese, one metropolitan to a province; at the head of them all the ' great metropolitan and chief bishop ', his see being Seleucia-Ctesiphon (only a little later, about 421-456, did he receive the title of Catholicos). Reconstructed in this way, the Church of the Persian Empire was able to prepare to withstand the new persecutions in store for it in the fifth century and, meanwhile, to pursue its missionary activity. In 410 bishops are found installed as far afield as the Bahrein Islands in the Persian Gulf and Khorassan in the direction of Central Asia. As is well known, this movement eventually swept across the immense continent of Asia and finally reached China in the seventh century.

2. Armenia

From the beginning of the fourth century a second foreign Church began to develop north of the former : that of Armenia. An apple of discord between the two great empires, Rome and Iran, throughout the centuries Armenia passed back and forward under the influence and even under the protection, now of one, now of the other. Its conversion to Christianity deserves to be noticed in some detail for it offers several characteristic features which we shall find elsewhere. It is the work of a single man — a great man — St Gregory the Illuminator.

Of noble birth and related to the former royal family, Gregory was exiled, baptised and educated as a christian in a Roman town, at Caesarea in Cappadocia, where he later returned to be ordained. He went back to Armenia and succeeded in converting King Tiridates (the exact date is unknown, but lies between 280 and 290). From the King and the aristocracy the new religion quickly spread throughout the whole nation. The pagan clergy, hostile at first, were converted *en masse*, but managed to retain the rich estates they owned. The Armenian Church was also organized around a central see, occupied, quite naturally, by St Gregory, and after him by his dynasty, for this Church had not adopted celibacy, even for bishops.

Such a rapid conversion could not be effected without checks; there were some revivals of paganism and conflicts between the King and the Catholicos on moral and political grounds. If the adoption of Christianity could appear to Tiridates as a means of keeping his distance from the Sassanids, at other times fears were expressed that he was thereby too closely dependent on the Emperor of Constantinople, also a christian. But as the fourth century passed, the more deeply did Christianity become rooted in the Armenian people. This progress was due in particular to the perseverance of the great bishops Nerses (364-374) and Shanak (390-420/439), who brought to fulfilment the work begun by their ancestor St Gregory.

In 365 at his residence in Ashtishat, Bishop Nevses held a first national council, which gave this young Church the disciplinary rules it needed. Under Bishop Shanak, in the early years of the fifth century, the erudite Mesrob provided the Armenian language with a new alphabet and turned it into a language of culture — a national culture, but first and foremost a christian culture. He translated Holy Scripture, the Patristic commentaries and treatises, and above all the liturgy into Armenian. Henceforward the Armenian nation and its Church were knit together so closely as to resist all attacks down the ages. We see this clearly after 450, when the Persian King Yezdegerd hoped to emulate his great predecessors Shapur I and II by working for the expansion of Mazdaism and tried in vain to convert Armenia to that religion.

3. The Countries of the Caucasus

In these Eastern Churches we have seen how the spread of the Gospel was linked to a growth of culture and the fostering of a national language and mentality. When, in its progress north-east of Armenia,

Christianity reached the Albania of the Caucasus (today Azerbaijan), it was Mesrob once again who immediately worked out a new alphabet so that the language could be written and used to serve the Church.

We find the same features in another centre of Christianity which grew up independently of Armenia, this time to the north-west, at the heart of a people whom the ancient writers called the Iberi : present-day Georgia. Like Armenia, it was continually in dispute, the Romans (297-370) and the Iranians (363, 378) in turn taking it under their influence or protection.

This time conversion was the work of a woman. It is not certain that history has correctly handed down her name; she is venerated as St Nino, probably meaning ' the nun ', or simply as Christiana, ' the christian woman '. She was a slave, carried off in some barbarian raid on Roman territory, who attracted the attention of the royal family of Georgia by her piety and the cures she obtained by her prayers. King Miriam was converted probably during the 330s and the conversion of the whole nation followed. Constantinople was asked for a bishop and priests, a Church was organised and soon became autonomous. Here again a special alphabet, Khutsuri, was either created anew or adapted from an earlier alphabet; it was used to write the Georgian language, and a national Christian literature was created, beginning naturally with the translation of the holy books and liturgical texts.

4. The Arab Countries

We may remember that the Gospel had already made some progress among the Arab tribes leading a nomadic life on the desert fringe of the Roman Empire, and more or less within the orbit of Roman rule. Often the reputation of some holy monk living alone in the neighbourhood led to the conversion of this or that tribe. The conversion of the Saracens, for example, was brought about by the efforts of Queen Maria and their bishop, the monk Moses, for whom, about the year 374, the see of Pharan in the Sinai peninsula was created. But these conversions were still few and did not give birth to true national Churches.

The diffusion of Christianity was still more sporadic in Arabia proper. The Roman merchants who visited the ports of the Red Sea were often able to make a few proselytes. In the decade beginning 350 the Emperor Constantius sent an embassy to the court of the King of the Himyarites in what is now Upper Yemen to ask the King to be favourable to christian missions. Although received in a friendly manner, the embassy does not seem to have borne much fruit.

It would be interesting to know more about the personality of Theophilus the Indian, the ambassador chosen by Constantius. Theophilus was a curious person born in some distant island which unfortunately cannot be located with accuracy; perhaps it was one of the islands in the Red Sea, or in the Indian Ocean. He had been sent at an early age as a hostage to the court of the Emperor Constantius, was educated in the Roman Empire, converted to Christianity, raised to the diaconate by Eusebius of Nicomedia and later to the episcopacy by members of his party; he had embraced the most virulent form of Arianism, that of the Anomoeans; and this sect held him in great honour, venerating him as a wonder-worker. On the occasion of his mission to Southern Arabia he probably visited the island where he had been born and other regions bordering on the Indian Ocean, where he seems to have found christians practising their religion more or less strictly; but about this it is very difficult to be explicit.

5. Ethiopia

Meanwhile, south of the Red Sea, there had already emerged another Church, another christian nation, that of Abyssinia; it was one of the most paradoxical and fruitful successes of the apostolate of the fourth century. Two young men from Tyre in Phoenicia named Frumentius and Aidesius, who had accompanied their tutor on a voyage of discovery, were the sole survivors of their expedition, which was massacred by natives of the Somali coast. Made slaves, they arrived at the court of the ruler of Ethiopia, whose capital at that time was Axum. They soon rose to occupy important positions; the first was the King's secretary, the second his cupbearer. Their rise continued after the death of the King; the Queen entrusted to them the education of her son or sons. They took advantage of their position to spread the christian faith and later obtained permission from their pupil, King Ezana, to return to their own country. Frumentius duly left and informed the Bishop of Alexandria, who was then St Athanasius, that the kingdom of Axum offered good prospects for spreading the Gospel and urged him to send a bishop there. Athanasius could not find a better candidate than Frumentius himself (this episode in Athanasius's career is difficult to date, but occurred sometime between 328 and 356).

We may suppose that once he returned to Axum as bishop, Frumentius met with increased success, but more or less total darkness surrounds the history of the early growth of the Abyssinian Church. It seems that King Ezana went further than merely showing Christianity a kindly toleration and that he was finally converted; but it is possible that some of his successors reverted to paganism and it is only late in the fifth century that we can definitely establish that the Ethiopian people were officially converted.

As early as the first half of the fourth century the national language, Ge'ez, adopted a form of writing derived from a south-Arabian alphabet. It is an extremely exact form of writing : Ethiopian is the only Semitic language which normally takes note of vowels. However, it was only after several generations, as in Armenia, that the work of translation and editing was accomplished. This gave the Ethiopian Church, like the other Eastern Churches, its own version of the scriptures, and a christian liturgy and literature.

Ordained by St Athanasius, Frumentius had solidly established his Church in the strictest Nicaean orthodoxy. Later the Emperor Constantius tried in vain to bring it over to the Arianising trend, which he was then leading to victory in the Empire; diplomatic negotiation with this in view was perhaps one of the purposes of Theophilus the Indian's mission to the country, which can then be dated to the year 356/7. Arianism was to meet with more success elsewhere.

6. The Germanic Peoples and Wulfila

The migrations which resulted in the great invasions had led a group of Germanic tribes, the Goths, to settle in the plains bordering on the Black Sea, between the Danube and the Dnieper. Sometime in the third century the Gospel began to be spread among them from the christian bases of the Crimea or of Dobrogea. But here again the most decisive results were due to the initiative of a single man, Wulfila, whose life presents many features in common with those of the great missionaries mentioned above.

He was the grandson of Christiana from Cappadocia who had been carried off by the Goths during their raid on Asia Minor in 257/8 and led captive beyond the Danube. After two generations Wulfila (his Germanic name is characteristic; he was perhaps of mixed blood) had a perfect knowedge of the language and customs of the Gothic people, yet had not forgotten Greek and Latin or Christianity. He performed the ecclesiastical functions of lector and had doubtless already begun his apostolate when an embassy sent to the Roman Empire gave him the opportunity of making contact with the authorities of the Church. But the embassy arrived under Constantius, in 341, at the time of the Council of Encaenia, when the anti-Nicaean reaction was triumphing in the East; Wulfila was made bishop by Eusebius of Nicomedia. and quite naturally adopted the theological outlook then prevailing. He seems to have died, in 383, before he was able to be retrieved for orthodoxy under the influence of Theodosius, so that Wulfila and the Church founded by him always professed Arianism in the sense defined by the Homoean Council of Constantinople in 360, at which Wulfila had been present.

When he returned to the country of the Goths Wulfila established a zealous and fruitful mission; he adopted methods similar to those employed almost everywhere. In place of the runic characters which the Germanic people already possessed but used very little, chiefly for magic, Wulfila substituted a more precise language which he used for writing his translation of most of the holy books. His Gothic Bible is an outstanding landmark in the development of the German language and large parts of it still survive.

Wulfila ended his career in the former Roman province of Mesia, south of the Danube. He retired there either to escape one of the persecutions directed — as it turned out, in vain — at checking the progress of the christian religion among the Goths, or to accompany the installation of a group of Goths in Roman territory. It is common knowledge that the Visigoths, followed later by the Ostrogoths, were driven forward by the increasing pressure of the Huns in their rear and irrupted into Roman territory. They settled to the north in the Balkans and later in Illyria, before advancing further west.

It will be remembered that Arianism had put down deep roots in Illyricum since the time of Arius himself, and of Ursacius and Valens; it seems likely that the Churches established as a result of Wulfila's preaching found there the intellectual framework required for building up a doctrinal tradition.

Little, in fact, remains of a christian literature in the Germanic language, only some fragments of a commentary on St John and of a liturgical calendar. On the other hand the works by Arian bishops writing in Latin are of considerable interest. These bishops included disciples or successors of Wulfila like Auxentius of Durostorum, Palladius of Ratiaria (two towns on the Danube frontier) and Maximinus, who had the honour of debating with St Ambrose at Milan and later, in Africa, with St Augustine.

The movement of conversion steadily spread and Christianity, once again in its Homoean form, became in some sense the national religion of most of the Germanic peoples, not only those who paid more or less short visits to the crucible of the Lower Danube plains but also those who always remained quite far from this principal centre, such as the Vandals, one of whose branches, that of the Silingii, had settled in the country which still bears their name, Silesia, before setting off in the direction of the Rhine frontier.

By permission of the French Archaeological Institute, Beirut.

CHRISTIAN ARCHITECTURE : VII

PLATE 31   QALAT SEM'AN, SYRIA, GENERAL VIEW OF THE RUINS, LATE 5TH CENTURY

Because the church is built round the pillar of S. Simeon the Elder (cf. ch. 32), and was the object of many pilgrimages, it may be classed as a marturion or basilica built round the physical remains of a martyr (cf. ch. 24, 4). In this picture of the ruins the apse is at the left end, and in the centre between the apse and the three-aisled exedrae is the octagonal shaped section containing the base of the pillar. The significant feature of the building is that its structure is dictated by a central point which is a pillar instead of the physical remains of the saint.

CHRISTIAN ARCHITECTURE: VIII

PLATE 32. CHAPEL OF LA TRINITÉ, LÉRINS, (?) 6TH CENTURY

Right - General view.

Below - The front of the chapel.

By no means all Christian churches were as magnificent as S. Vitale, but even this little chapel on an island off the south coast of Gaul — 'the nearest thing the western monks could find to a desert' — shows the influence of developments in the larger churches. The ground plan of the church is basically cruciform and it therefore stands in the tradition of pagan mausolea and early marturia, but the shape of the cupola and the type of internal decoration show the more immediate influence of Byzantium.

By permission of Direction des Antiquités, Marseille.

CHRISTIAN DEVOTION : I. The Mother of God - Theotokos

PLATE 33   ADORATION OF THE SHEPHERDS AND THE MAGI; AN AMPULLA
FROM MONZA, ITALY, 6TH CENTURY

This ampulla is one of several brought to Italy by pilgrims to the Holy Places in the 6th century and preserved at Monza and Bobbio. They are flat, silver bottles intended originally to contain oil and probably in most cases worn round the neck of the pilgrim. A contemporary writer says that the pilgrims took the ampullae and touched the 'wood of Life' with them. The contact was thought to give the oil atropaic and prophylactic qualities. This particular example shows the Mother of God enthroned, with the child on her knees. Above her are two angels; with one hand they point at the great star over her head, but their heads are turned towards the shepherds and Magi on either side of the throne. The Magi, a perfectly arranged group, each dressed in short cloak, Persian trousers and a Phrygian cap, present their gifts on the left of the picture. Over on the right, the shepherds, in some disarray because of their surprise, adopt a variety of gestures. The first shepherd, standing up, points at the star, and turns his head towards his companions. The second shepherd can

only look in amazement at the star, whereas the other (perhaps overcome?) is seated. Below this picture there is an inscription in Greek which reads, 'Emmanuel — God is with us'. Below the inscription is a scene with sheep and goats. On the circumference of the ampulla there is a formula which occurs several times in the series : 'Oil of the wood of Life, of the holy places of Christ', and on the neck of the bottle, as on every ampulla, there is a cross. Two further interrelated points need to be made : first, in the posture of the Virgin and the arrangement of the picture as a whole, there is a clear affinity with the imperial portrait of Theodosius I (Plate 16); secondly, although made in Palestine, this ampulla cannot be cited as an example of any Palestinian style; the strongest influence is imperial, which is not surprising in view of the long imperial connection with the Holy Places from Constantine to Justinian I. (For a very different way of commemorating a holy event or place, see Plate 38 which is Palestinian.)

CHRISTIAN DEVOTION: II. Saints

PLATE 34. SS. SERGIUS AND BACCHUS: ICON DISCOVERED AT MOUNT SINAI, NOW IN KIEV MUSEUM (FORMERLY ECCLESIASTICAL ACADEMY), 6TH CENTURY (SEE CH. 34)

Both saints were officers who died in the reign of Diocletian and they are here depicted as high ranking officers with golden bulla round their necks. The sanctuary of Sergius in particular, in the desert city of Resafe, was famous throughout the Christian world. The portraiture owes a great deal to a tradition of Egyptian funerary paintings but there are also echoes of Imperial portraiture (cf. Plate 17). Note also the small *clipeus* of Christ; for its significance, see note to Plate 40.

By permission of Collection Hautes Etudes, Paris.

Of all the peoples who were successively to invade and conquer the western provinces of the Roman Empire only the Franks and a part of the Lombards had so far been untouched by Christianity. The heretical nature of the trinitarian beliefs of these Germanic Churches must not make us forget the sincerity and depth of their Christian life. In fact these peoples were so attached to their national religion that, as we shall see, great difficulties and struggles arose with their Catholic subjects in the kingdoms they established in the former territory of the Empire.

We can now measure the extent of Christianity in the course of the fourth century. From the Rhine to the Caucasus, from the Caspian to Ethiopia an immense arc of Churches and new Christian communities was unfolded beyond the Mediterranean countries, and a trail was blazed for spreading the Gospel throughout the world.

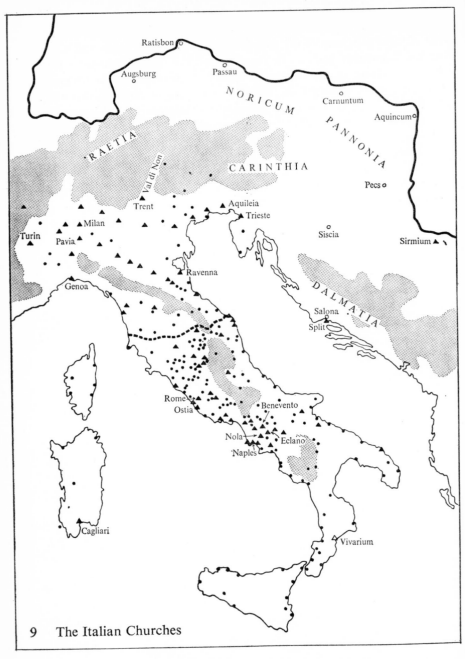

9   The Italian Churches

▲ *Episcopal sees existing at the end of the 4th century*

● *Episcopal sees created during the 5th and 6th centuries*

- - - *Border between Annonairian Italy (to the north)*
          and Suburbicairian Italy (to the south)

    Mountains over 3000 feet

CHAPTER XXII

THE PROGRESS
OF CHRISTIANITY
WITHIN THE EMPIRE

PROGRESS was no less remarkable within the Roman Empire. A feeling of triumphant happiness is evident throughout the fourth century from Lactantius to St Augustine. On all fronts paganism was in retreat and the faith of Christ was becoming, in fact practically had become, the religion of the whole Roman world. Soon there would remain only a handful of die-hards; in order to convince them of their error a rather premature theology of history went so far as to base an argument on this unexpected, miraculous success of the Gospel. The christians of this period had, as we should say today, the feeling of moving in the direction of history.

The decisive turning-point was the conversion of the Emperor himself. From the reign of Constantine and his sons to that of Theodosius the Emperor expressed his goodwill by building and endowing churches, granting immunity and other privileges to the clergy and placing more and more legal restrictions on paganism. More important still for Christianity was the personal example given by the all-powerful ruler placed by Providence at the top of the earthly hierarchy. The totalitarian tendency of the Late Empire now profited christians. Society, threatened with disintegration, felt a strong need for unity, and this tended to take the form of religious unity. The factors which under Diocletian militated in favour of the gods of ancient Rome now swung round to the service of the new religion.

1. The Latin West

About 400-410 the Church was at last deeply rooted in all the provinces of the Empire. Progress was particularly striking in the

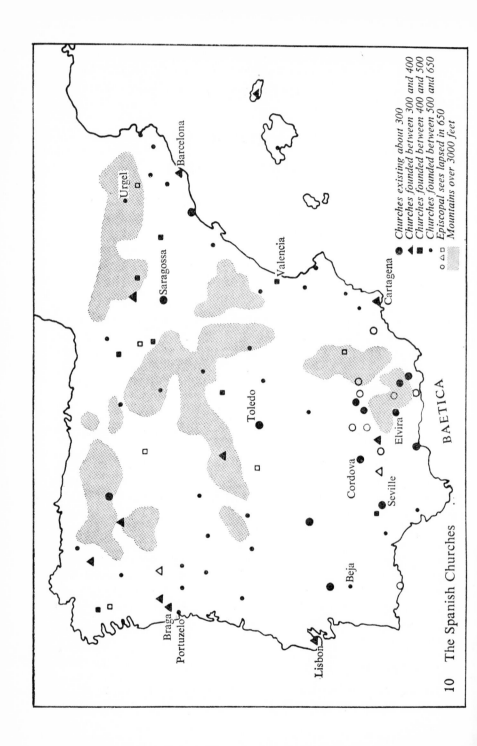

Churches existing about 300
Churches founded between 300 and 400
Churches founded between 400 and 500
Churches founded between 500 and 650
Episcopal sees lapsed in 650
Mountains over 3000 feet

Urgel

Barcelona

Saragossa

Valencia

Cartagena

Toledo

Cordova

Elvira

Seville

Beja

Braga
Portuzelo

Lisbon

BAETICA

10   The Spanish Churches

Latin West, where, as we have seen, so much still remained to be done at the beginning of the fourth century. About 300 North Italy, for example, still had only five or six bishops : Ravenna, Aquileia, Milan, etc., whereas in 400 they numbered about fifty, that is to say there were bishops in practically all the urban centres of any importance.

Similarly in Gaul : in 314 there were twenty-two episcopal sees; by the end of the century there were seventy, and, as in Italy, this network was now spread out evenly across the whole country.

We are not in a position to give precise figures for Spain, but there too the Church spread from Andalusia to cover the whole peninsula. The number of Spanish bishops who played a part in the trinitarian disputes of the period bears witness to the vitality of Christianity in that country. We meet them at all points of the theological horizon; Potamius, first Bishop of Lisbon, belonged to the Arianising left, while Gregory of Elvira, who incidentally was an original preacher, belonged to the extreme Luciferian right. Others were Hosius of Cordova and his deacon Chalcidius, translator and commentator of Plato's *Timaeus;* at the end of the century there was Pacianus of Barcelona, the theologian of Penance.

Since heresy, a by-product of theological progress, is always a sure sign of vigour, it is characteristic that Spain should have produced an original heresy : Priscillianism. It is difficult to define to-day — it may have been neo-Gnosticism, illuminism or a form of asceticism — but there can be no doubt about its importance, to judge by the violent reactions it aroused. Its leader, Priscillian, was condemned by the Councils of Saragossa (380) and Bordeaux (384), sentenced to death by the usurper Maximus and executed at Trèves in 385, the first heretic to die at the hands of the secular power.

The christian tide came in to the very frontiers of the Empire. The birthplace of St Patrick, the future apostle of Ireland, seems to have been what is now Cumberland, a little south of Hadrian's Wall. The date of his birth was about 389. He came of a Romano-British family which had been christian for at least two generations (his father was a deacon, his grandfather a priest).

On the continent of Europe literary works and monuments bear witness to the presence and vitality of Christianity at the mouths of the Rhine and Danube, the two rivers which marked the frontier of the Empire from the end of the third century. One example is Xanten, where the martyr St Victor was venerated from the end of the fourth century; for that reason the old name *Colonia Traiana* was changed to its modern form of Xanten, *ad Sanctos;* other Christian towns were Bonn, Cologne, Mainz, Worms and Speyer. Further back, on the

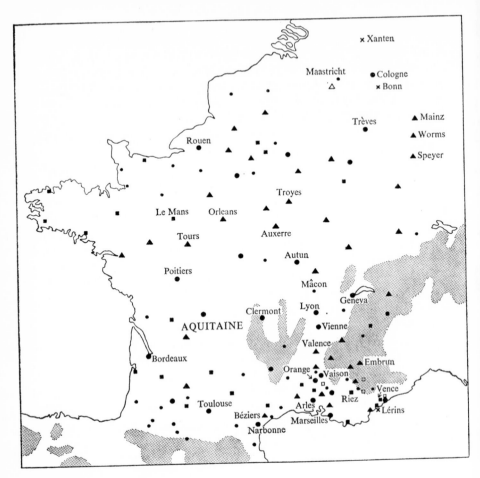

Xanten

Maastricht   Cologne
             Bonn

Rouen   Trèves   Mainz
                         Worms
                         Speyer

Troyes

Le Mans Orleans

Tours   Auxerre

Poitiers Autun

          Mâcon

Clermont Lyon   Geneva

AQUITAINE Vienne

          Valence

Bordeaux Orange Vaison Embrun

          Arles   Riez   Vence

Toulouse Béziers   Lérins

          Marseilles

          Narbonne

Episcopal sees

● *existing at the beginning of the 4th century*

▲ *created during the 4th century*

■ *created during the 5th century*

• *created during the 6th century*

△ □ *lapsed by the 6th century*

░ *Mountains over 3000 feet*

11   The Churches of Gaul

Moselle, Trèves, the imperial residence from Constantine to Maximus, was the ecclesiastical centre of these Rhine countries.

On the Danube Christianity flourished at Regensburg, Passau, Lorch, *Carnuntum*, east of Vienna, and at *Aquincum* (present-day Budapest) as far as the towns of the province of Scythia Minor (Dobrudja). These Scythian towns were Latin in the interior, Greek on the coast. Both from the religious and administrative point of view Sirmium on the Savus was the Danubian equivalent of Trèves and Milan.

So far we have discussed only the Latin West, where the work of spreading the Gospel had most ground to make up. But progress was no less notable in the Greek East. Everywhere the network of episcopal sees grew tighter, conversions increased and Christianity reached the mass of the people; while provinces which formerly played a very limited role not only in the life of the Church but in that of the civilised world now assumed importance. For example, in the heart of Asia Minor, where during the second half of the fourth century the province of Cappadocia produced a group of outstanding bishops who rank among the Church's greatest theologians.

Nevertheless, the conversion of the population of the Roman Empire in its entirety was still far from being complete about the years 400-410. In all parts of the Empire we still find a more or less numerous minority of pagans strongly resisting the new religion. Here our analysis must switch from geography to sociology. This remnant of paganism was chiefly made up of two classes, on the one hand the peasants, on the other the cultivated aristocracy.

2. The Conversion of the Countryside

The urban masses were not all converted. Towards the end of the century, thanks to the increasingly strong support granted them by imperial legislation, the christians succeeded in getting possession of pagan sanctuaries still in use and often destroyed them, but they did so not without difficulty or violence. We have an example of this in the famous Serapeum of Alexandria in 389, while the temple of the local god Marnas and seven other temples were destroyed by Bishop Porphyrius of Gaza in 402. Phoenicia remained a stronghold of paganism: St John Chrysostom sent a mission there which aroused sharp reactions about 406. Similarly in the West, where the temple of Juno Caelestis at Carthage was destroyed in 399. The Church's objective was clear : to put an end to the last, still popular, pagan rites and complete the work of christianisation.

In the countryside this work was still much less far advanced than in the towns. The mass of people dwelling in the country had played only a very small part in the flowering of classical culture, which had been chiefly restricted to the cities.   Their religious life had continued to draw most of its nourishment from an old heritage of ancestral beliefs rooted very far in the past, perhaps even in the neolithic period.   Their worship of the forces of nature had taken the form of festivals and traditional rites, often associated with places where men sensed the presence of something holy such as a mountain, a grove or tree, or a holy spring.

Under Greek or Roman influence these rites had usually put on masks borrowed from the official polytheism, but under the names of Saturn (in Africa) or Mercury (in Gaul), of Artemis or of Cybele, it was always this same old religion which survived.   With Hellenistic decadence and the flowering of a new religious awareness classical paganism was in a sense emptied of its substance, and this old heritage alone preserved some vitality.   In fact it was the chief enemy of the missionaries whom we find at work in the last decades of the fourth century, when the movement of evangelisation, for long confined to the towns, finally spread to the countryside.

Everywhere we meet the same problems and see the same methods applied, so that an account of the missionaries' exploits would end by becoming a piece of conventional hagiography.   Everywhere they ' overthrow the statues of the gods, cut down the sacred groves, burn temples and sanctuaries, build' — often on the same site — ' a church or chapel, consecrate an altar there and proceed to baptise crowds of people. . . '[1].

The best known of these missionaries in Gaul is St Martin, Bishop of Tours (370/2-397).   His fame, like that of St Antony, is largely the result of a successful book : the biography written by Sulpicius Severus between 397 and 403/4.   It shows St Martin spreading the Gospel in the rural districts of his diocese, despite the often obstinate resistance of the villagers.   More than once in order to obtain the destruction of an idol he had to strengthen the effect of his preaching by his fame and powers as a wonder-worker.   When the village was converted, he had to extend and consolidate the results : St Martin is credited with having created six rural parishes, chiefly on the edge of his diocese.

Contrary to what we find in Egypt, in Africa and in Southern Italy, the dioceses of Gaul and those of Upper Italy were too extensive for the episcopal church in the town to be able to continue satisfying the liturgical needs of all the christians.   As the countryside became christian, so rural parishes appeared and grew, but the network was slow in

1. *Life* of Saints Julius and Julianus of Orta (BHL-4558).

becoming established (in the same diocese of Tours, the successors of St Martin had to continue his efforts for three generations) and the canonical autonomy of the parish was also slow to emerge. These parishes usually sprang up in the small towns or other regional centres or centres of administration, commerce or religion. More than once the christian church replaced the pagan sanctuary so smoothly that the adoption of Christianity did not interrupt the continuity of life in the district.

But St Martin is not an isolated example : we possess evidence of very similar activity among many other bishops of the same period, for example St Victricius of Rouen, the apostle of the former country of the Morins and Nervians (present-day Flanders), and St Simplicius of Autun. Outside Gaul, we find St Vigilius of Trent in the Julian Alps : in 397 a mission composed of three clerics which he had sent into the Valley of Nona suffered martyrdom at the hands of fanatical mountain-dwellers.

The same problems and methods are found in Greek countries where, though the Gospel had been spread further and earlier than in the West, there still remained plenty to do. Well advanced though it appeared to be about 400-410, nowhere was the work anything like finished, and it had to be continued in the following century.

In the same years, 380-390, we find a parallel to St Martin at the other end of the Roman world : the monk Jonas. Like St Martin, Jonas was a former soldier. He was born in Armenia and founded the monastery of Halmyrissus, west of Constantinople. We read in the Life of his disciple St Hypatius : ' As soon as he learned that a tree or similar object was receiving worship he went with the monks who were his disciples and cut down the tree, which he then burned; and so the people gradually became christians. In fact the lord Jonas, who had been the spiritual father of Hypatius, had civilised Thrace in this way and made its inhabitants christian '².

3. The Aristocracy and the Educated Class

At the other end of the social scale we find those families owning large estates from which the Empire had long recruited most of its high officials. Even when they were of relatively recent origin (many emerged from the social disturbances of the third century), they felt themselves interdependent and laid a claim to the heritage of all the historic past of Rome. For example, the maternal family of St Paula, one of the spiritual children of St Jerome, claimed descent from the Scipios and

2. *Life* of Saint Hypatius of Rufinianae, p. 103, ed. Bonn.

Gracchi. The old national religion, paganism, was part of Rome's historic past. They clung to it with a piety all the more fervent as the heritage appeared increasingly threatened and emptied of its substance by the march of history.

This was particularly true of the senatorial circles of ancient Rome. Abandoned by the Emperors, they no longer played a part as administrators except at a municipal or, at most, a regional level. Throughout the fourth century we find in these circles a muted opposition to the policy of the christian Emperors. It made itself heard in 379 when the young Emperor Gratian gave up the title of Pontifex Maximus which all his predecessors since Augustus had assumed, and thus openly demonstrated the separation of paganism from the State. The pagan senators protested against the removal of the altar of Victory which adorned and made holy their meeting-hall (382; the matter was later raised again in 384, 389, 392 and 402/3). We are well acquainted with this senatorial world of the 380s; in the next generation it was described in the *Saturnales* of Macrobius, another witness to the long pagan resistance.

Precisely because we know them well, so that we can even trace their family trees, we are able to watch Christianity gradually penetrate into the aristocratic families which had been hostile to it for so long. For it was now their turn to be converted. Let us take as an example the noble family of the Caeionii Albini; belonging or related to it were the holy nuns directed by St Jerome or his friend Rufinus : St Marcella and St Paula and the Saints Melania. The first conversions, in the middle of the century, were conversions of ladies : Marcella and her sister Asella. The men mostly remained pagan and in fact their uncle married a priestess of Isis; but a cousin, the senator Pammachius, later became a christian and, furthermore, a monk. In the next generation the men agreed to marry christian ladies and in this way the new religion was soon well acclimatised. From 400 onwards it became dominant : only the eldest sons, heads of a branch of the family, clung for a time to the ancestral tradition. But all their followers, parents, allies and friends were now christian and they themselves in later life or on their deathbed ended by asking to be baptised.

The resistance of the pagan senators of Rome was also to some extent intellectual, for culture was part of the traditions of the aristocracy. A group of cultivated senators, often led by writers, welcomed and inspired the last pagan Latin authors : Praetextatus, Symmachus, Nicomachus Flavian, Rutilius Namatianus, the grammarian Donatus, the historian Ammianus Marcellinus and the mysterious forgers of the *Historia Augusta* (unless they belong to the next generation).

Similarly, in Greek countries paganism maintained one of its last strongholds in intellectual circles. This was true of the neo-Platonist philosophers : the pupils and successors of Jamblicus, who died in 330, moved steadily closer to the pagan religion, even in its least rational forms. It was also true of the teachers of sophistry, professors of rhetoric and orators like Himerius at Athens, Themistius at Constantinople, where he won the highest honours, and Libanius at Antioch (they died respectively in 386, 388 and 393).

However, even this group, so obstinately hostile, began to be influenced by the Gospel. At Athens, the most active university city of the day, the colleague and rival of Himerius was a convinced christian, Prohaeresius. About 355 their Latin equivalent in Rome, the famous rhetor Marius Victorinus, was converted in his old age, remaining energetic enough to launch out on a new career as a theologian in the service of his faith. Thirty years later in the autumn of 386 another famous teacher, like Marius Victorinus of African birth, held the municipal chair of rhetoric in Milan and was converted by his example : his name is St Augustine.

The fact that the slowly slackening link between paganism and classical culture was an organic one is clearly shown by the remarkable case of the Emperor Julian. We know the negative reasons which made him abandon Christianity. He had escaped from the massacre of 338, when he had seen his father, uncle and cousins perish. Christianity was the religion professed by the assassins of those near and dear to him, the religion of his persecutors and gaolers. The churchmen whom he had seen most often were either court prelates like Eusebius of Nicomedia, his distant relation and first tutor, or abstract theologians like the Anomoean Aetius, to whom his half-brother, the Caesar Gallus, had entrusted him.

But if we try to find the positive reasons that led him to paganism, there is no doubt that long before he came in touch with neo-Platonism and the mirage of its charlatans, he was attracted by the splendours of classical literature. These had been revealed to him by his tutor, the christian eunuch Mardonius, during his six years' exile in the fortress of Macellum. The apostasy of Julian is the first example in the history of Christianity (many others were to follow right down to modern times) of a neo-pagan renaissance, stemming from the rediscovery of the literature and arts of antiquity. Christianity, the religion of the fishermen of Galilee, was for Julian a barbarous religion, and as such to be scorned, whereas paganism had been a noble religion as far back as Homeric times.

CHAPTER XXIII

THE GOLDEN AGE
OF THE CHURCH FATHERS

AMONG all the hostile measures decreed by Julian the one which christians most bitterly resented was the education law of 17 June 362 forbidding them to teach the classics and scornfully sending back ' the Galileans to their churches to annotate Matthew and Luke '[1]. As we see in Ammianus, even pagan opinion considered the law too harsh; in fact this sort of radical opposition between ' Hellenism ' and Christianity no longer corresponded to reality and had already begun to disappear. The christian Church had grown more aware of the value of the humanities — though still aware of their dangers — and had first tolerated, then fully accepted, traditional education and teaching.

The attitude adopted by Julian was, at this date, something of an anachronism and, in the strict sense of the word, reactionary. There was no longer any opposition between the intellectual élite and christian faith; christian noblemen, professors and educated people appear to have been no less cultured than their pagan colleagues. Indeed, the basic training and mental equipment which they received from their classical education helped to serve the new religious ideal and, by means of unexpected transpositions and applications, received new life from it. Whereas the culture of educated pagans, with the partial exception of philosophy, usually tended to harden and grow decadent, the fourth century revealed the flowering of a christian culture, traditional in its materials, original in its synthesis.

The life of the spirit, cut off from the deep springs of its being, was wilting and indulging in purely formal refinements. Religious inspiration brought it a new vigour which appeared under unexpected forms. The study and meditation of Holy Scripture took the place

1. Julian, *Letter* 61 c (42), p. 423 D.

of Homer and Virgil as the basis of education; the sermon replaced the public lecture as the dominant literary form; the splendours of the liturgy satisfied the needs which had given birth to the theatre; even romantic feeling found an outlet in the legendary flowering of the *Apocrypha* and of hagiography.

Biblical exegesis inherited the techniques minutely perfected by the school of grammarians in order to explain the classical poets. Similarly, the sermon inherited from rhetoric, controversy from dialectic, and theology from the whole arsenal of philosophy. This was no pure and simple transfer : original creation was also involved. If Marius Victorinus, to take him as an example once more, skilfully put to use his profound knowledge of Neo-Platonism and in particular of Porphyrius in the elaboration of his trinitarian theology in order to defend the Nicaean dogma, he did so by making a whole series of transpositions which turned it into an original kind of Neo-Platonism quite different from that of his pagan masters and rivals. He truly created that christian Neo-Platonism in Latin which St Ambrose and above all St Augustine were later to exploit in all its riches and show to be so fruitful.

We must go still further. Over against paganism, which had become impoverished by the usury of time or compromised by its flirtations with occultism, it was Christianity which was active and in the ascendent. Christianity was the leading principle of the *Zeitgeist*, of the cultural atmosphere of the century. We must also stress the invariable link between sociology and culture. Statistically speaking Christianity was in the lead; it is scarcely surprising therefore that the new ideal of christian culture should have brought together the majority of the best minds of the age.

The second half of the fourth century witnessed the flowering of what can be called the golden age of the Church Fathers. That was the period of the greatest writers and thinkers of Christian antiquity, both in the Greek East and in the Latin West, of nearly all the *maiores doctores* whom we venerate in both Churches. Nothing is more telling than to bring together their names and their dates (see table on p. 303). Born, most of them, in the years 330-350, that is in the two generations which followed the peace of the Church, they make a coherent cluster; all were contemporaries and many had direct relations one with another or exercised mutual influence, so that they form a very characteristic group. They are easily distinguishable from their predecessors; the preceding generation, for example, that of Athanasius and Hilary, appear by contrast more as specialist theologians, limited by their very technicalities. They are also easily distinguishable from their successors, beginning with the generation of Cyril and Theodoret, whom we shall

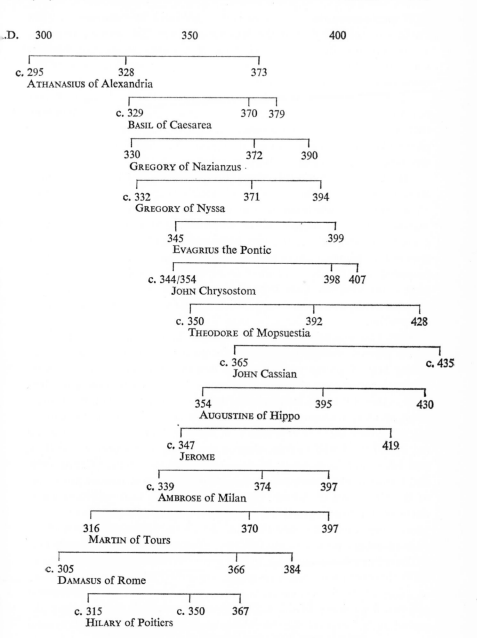

A.D.   300   350   400

c. 295   328   373
ATHANASIUS of Alexandria

        c. 329   370   379
        BASIL of Caesarea

            330   372   390
            GREGORY of Nazianzus

            c. 332   371   394
            GREGORY of Nyssa

                345   399
                EVAGRIUS the Pontic

                c. 344/354   398   407
                JOHN Chrysostom

                    c. 350   392   428
                    THEODORE of Mopsuestia

                        c. 365   c. 435
                        JOHN Cassian

                    354   395   430
                    AUGUSTINE of Hippo

                c. 347   419
                JEROME

            c. 339   374   397
            AMBROSE of Milan

        316   370   397
        MARTIN of Tours

    c. 305   366   384
    DAMASUS of Rome

        c. 315   c. 350   367
        HILARY of Poitiers

(The date of accession to the episcopacy is given midway)

THE FOURTH CENTURY FATHERS

meet much later; they too seem rather specialist by comparison. The Fathers of the fourth and the beginning of the fifth century represent a specially precious moment of balance between an ancient heritage still scarcely touched by decadence and perfectly assimilated, and on the other hand christian inspiration which had reached full maturity.

They were all great and powerful personalities. Each was very much of an individual, but their lives have so many features in common that we can risk sketching a composite picture, an ideal type of Father of the Church. On the way we shall point out exceptions and so avoid any disadvantages in this composite method.

(a) Evidently as a result of the progress made by Christianity within Roman society, the Fathers of the Church belonged by birth to the élite of society and sometimes to the very highest families. St Ambrose was the son of a prefect of the praetorium, St John Chrysostom of a master of the militia, the two highest civil and military posts in the imperial hierarchy. A notable exception here is St Augustine, who belonged to a family of *curiales* or municipal notables crushed by the pitiless taxes of the Late Empire, a class that has been described, in modern terms, as a lower bourgeoisie on the way to becoming part of the proletariat.

(b) This exception is very revealing. The ambition and devotion of his parents and the protection of a patron made it possible for this young boy of genius to receive the first-rate education given to boys of the upper classes. St Augustine was thus able to become a teacher, which opened the way to his rise in the social scale : this cultural upstart owed his start to culture. Henceforward he takes his place in the general category; born into the aristocracy or, more often, into a good provincial family, all the Fathers of the Church studied long and deeply. St Basil and his friend St Gregory of Nazianzus left their native Cappadocia, and for many years attended courses given by the most famous professors of the University of Athens. St Jerome, born in Dalmatia somewhere north of Trieste, attended the grammarian Donatus's lessons in Rome, while Chrysostom attended those of the rhetor Libanius in Antioch — pagan teachers, no doubt, but famous. Though Julian the Apostate may not have liked it, higher studies at this period were quite unbiassed, the students choosing their teacher no matter what their religion or his might be.

This education was essentially literary and its crown was the patient and obstinate study of the technique of oratory : we have reached the period of the ' Second Sophistry ' which witnessed the apogee of classical rhetoric. All the Fathers of the Church were great writers, especially if they are judged by the ideal of their period; in any case all brought to the service of their thought an incomparable mastery of language.

Since there are no exceptions, let us take a look at the various types. St Jerome, a specialist in sacred philology and Biblical Studies, learned Greek better than the majority of his Latin contemporaries, St Augustine for example (if St Ambrose had a thorough knowledge of Greek, that was his privilege as an aristocrat); much rarer, St Jerome also knew Hebrew. All the educated people at this period had a more or less thorough knowledge of philosophy but only St Gregory of Nyssa among the Greeks was a genuine philosopher both by temperament and training. Among the Latins St Augustine was certainly a philosopher by temperament but he lacked a basic training in philosophy such as Gregory enjoyed; as a philosopher St Augustine was self-taught.

(c) All the Fathers of the Church found the christian faith, as it were, installed in their cradle, either because their whole family had been converted, sometimes several generations back, as was the case with St Basil and his brothers, or at least because their mothers were christian. The part played by these holy christian women in their sons' spiritual training and growth was often considerable. Everyone knows the part played by St Monica in the life of St Augustine, but there are many other examples : the mother of St Ambrose, and the mother of St John Chrysostom — Anthousa. Widowed at twenty, Anthousa did not remarry — this aroused the astonished admiration of a pagan like Libanius — in order to devote herself entirely to the education of her son. St Macrina, the elder sister of St Basil, likewise devoted herself to her young brother Gregory of Nyssa : she remained a virgin and ended her days in a convent.

(d) Having finished their studies, the majority began a career in the world, usually that of teacher, as befitted good pupils : for example Basil, the two Gregorys and St Augustine. The fortunes of Gregory of Nyssa and Theodore of Mopsuestia are curious : after having tried the ecclesiastical or religious life they returned to the world; Gregory of Nyssa, the future theologian of Virginity, even married. Special cases are those of St Martin who, being the son of a veteran, was obliged to enter the army, and of St Ambrose, whose birth led him to high posts in the administration : at the time of his election as bishop he was *consularis*, that is to say civil governor, of the province of Liguria whose capital was Milan, where the Emperor resided.

(e) Another exception was St Augustine, whose brilliant teaching career — in thirteen years it took him from Tagaste, his home town, to Carthage, Rome and Milan — lasted as long as the successive inner struggles which gradually led him through hundreds of doctrinal difficulties to the faith of his childhood. With these exceptions, the first phase of their life did not last very long, and was interrupted by a conversion, in Pascal's sense of the word — when they heard and followed the call to perfection. It is then, often about the age of thirty, that we find them receiving the baptism which so far they had postponed, following the usual practice of the time, because the responsibilities implicit in baptism were taken very seriously.

For men of the fourth century perfection of life was to be found in the desert : all the Fathers of the Church were monks for a certain time and practised an often strict asceticism, either close to, or as disciples of, some master of the spiritual life. As we have seen, several played an important part in the history of monasticism.

The only exception to this general rule, but it is a remarkable exception, is St Ambrose. As a good Roman magistrate, he came to re-establish order in the stormy assembly whose duty it was to fill the vacant see of Milan. He controlled the crowd with so much authority that he was unanimously acclaimed bishop. Once the Emperor had authorised his appointment, he was baptised and eight days later consecrated, despite canon law, which laid down that the episcopacy should not be held by a neophyte. The case of Gregory of Nyssa is also somewhat exceptional : as a married man he did not begin by being a monk and became one only on the death of his wife, by which time he had already been a bishop for thirteen years.

(f) Trained in solitude, for which all their life they remained nostalgic, they soon returned to society, usually at the end of three or five years, and, answering the Church's call, agreed to consecrate themselves entirely to its service.

This is true even of St Jerome, who did not rise to be a bishop but remained a simple monk all his life. He, too, first tried the life of a hermit for a short spell (374-376) in the desert of Chalcis near Antioch; then he left it in order to go and finish his education at Antioch, Alexandria and Constantinople. He returned to Rome, where he played an important part in the life of Pope Damasus before retiring definitively, as we have seen, to his monastery of Bethlehem (385-414). Ordained priest about 379 by Pantinus of Antioch, he never considered himself attached to a particular Church; perhaps this was an intellectual's reflex action, an attempt to preserve his freedom to study. It may be so, but these very studies — translations, commentaries, polemics — show that he was bent on filling the needs of the universal Church; in his own vocation also he obeyed the same call.

If there is a real exception, it is Evagrius the Pontic, whose life was the very reverse of the notion we have outlined. As we have seen, he began in the secular clergy and ended up in the desert of Scete where his restless soul was cloistered in strict retirement; he obstinately refused to leave in order to accept a bishopric. But it is doubtful whether we can count this professedly heretical adventurer of the mind among the Fathers of the Church.

The Fathers of the Church in the strict sense of the word did not withdraw from the world; they became bishops and proved themselves great bishops, faithfully attached to the Church which had chosen them. That was true even of Gregory of Nazianzus, despite his complicated career which, moreover, betrays a certain psychological instability. Although he was made bishop of an obscure small Cappadocian town, Sasima, by his friend and Metropolitan Basil, and had earlier occupied the see of Constantinople for some time (379-381), he well deserves the surname which history has given him, for it was at Nazianzus that he fulfilled his episcopal duties for the longest time, as coadjutor, then as successor (374), to his own father, Gregory the Elder.

Finally, their chief work was done during the period when they were bishops, although the majority of them began by serving quite a long apprenticeship as priests. Perhaps St John Chrysostom should be considered an exception. His episcopate was short and troubled (398-404, the end of his life being spent in exile); he, too, held the difficult see of Constantinople. The twelve years spent as priest in the Church of Antioch were much more fruitful; there he won his fame as a magnificent preacher (386-397).

(g) Later on we shall try to describe the hard task of being a bishop; but in the traditional notion of Fathers of the Church it is intellectual achievement which, together with holiness, occupies the most important place. These bishops were first of all writers, orators (at this time the spoken word still retained its traditional predominance over the written word) and religious thinkers.

Their work was considerable and took the form of a series of very characteristic literary writings : first and foremost, sermons, which were always rich in doctrine and contained Biblical quotations and explanations; exegesis in the strict sense, which provided both a scientific and a spiritual commentary on the holy books; and theology. In this still remote period, swept by so many storms, theology usually took the form of a controversy. There were few doctrinal treatises not in fact inspired by the necessity of refuting some mischievous heretic and which were not written ' against ' someone. The Fathers also left a varied correspondence in which spiritual direction occupies an important place : for them the inner life was never something merely theoretical, even in a treatise *ex professo* very far removed from practice.

This short list is enough to reveal the main lines and originality of the christian culture, the *Doctrina Christiana*, whose charter

St Augustine drew up in a text-book with that title begun in 397 and taken up again and completed thirty years later. It was a religious culture, completely organised around the faith and spiritual life. Henceforth the Church offered this culture to the élite of the faithful, to clergy and laity, to monks and people in the world. Let us make no mistake : if the Fathers of the Church who laid its foundations and rendered it illustrious were churchmen (in the modern sense), this culture nonetheless compelled recognition from all christians capable of becoming interested in spiritual matters. Nothing is more foreign to the ideal of the new religious consciousness, which was the driving force of civilisation in the fourth century, than the medieval notion of a strictly clerical religious culture or the modern distinction at the heart of our culture between the domain of strictly lay values and a domain reserved for what is sacred.

CHAPTER XXIV

CHRISTIAN LIFE AT THE END OF THE FOURTH CENTURY

WE have now come to the end of this great fourth century, so decisive for our history, and it is worthwhile to pause in order to try and answer the general question : what did it mean to be a christian at that period? Let us place ourselves near the year 400 : what particular forms had christian life then assumed? How did the influence of Christianity appear in daily life, personal or collective, and more generally, in the civilization of men of that period?

1. The Organisation of the Church

To be a christian is first and foremost to occupy a place in an original, highly structural society, the Church. In the course of the century which we have seen unfold the Church developed its organisation and defined its inner discipline.

In this respect we must emphasise the influential part played by an original institution : the Councils. So far we have chiefly spoken of their role in doctrinal disputes : but they were no less important in making rules for the Church. Even the assemblies which had been summoned in order to solve a particular problem raised by a schism or heresy, from the time of the Councils of Arles (314) and Nicaea (325) to that of Constantinople (381), even these assemblies concerned themselves with problems of organisation. Each promulgated a certain number of rulings or canons concerning, for example, recruitment of the clergy, Church hierarchy, administration of the sacraments, reconciliation of heretics, etc. The rules thus laid down were gradually collected and served as a basis for the working-out of what has become canon law.

The provincial and especially the regional Councils of which we find an increasing number about the end of the century were also concerned to give practical solutions to such problems. At the same time they solved doctrinal and disciplinary questions of local interest, such as the stamping out of Arianism in Illyricum or the Priscillianist affair in Spain. Canonical work was done at the Councils of Valence in Gaul (374), of Rome, or rather of the Vatican, in 386 (the first expressly stated to have been held *ad sancti apostoli Petri reliquias*), of Hippo (393) and of Carthage (397). It was at the Council of 393 that St Augustine, recently ordained priest, preached his maiden sermon, *De fide et symbolo*, before the assembly. The African Church, strongly organised around the see of Carthage, held its ' plenary council ' in that city almost every year. A similar Council of suburbican Italy (the southern two-thirds of the peninsula) was held by the Pope in Rome.

But these institutions remained rather fluid and the intervention of a strong personality was sufficient to modify their normal working considerably. For example, the powerful influence of St Ambrose is seen throughout his episcopacy (373-397) in a series of Synods relating not only to North Italy and Aquileia, but also to Gaul (Council of Turin, 398), to Illyricum and even to the Latin provinces of the Lower Danube, Moesia or Dacia.

At this level, the part played by St Ambrose slightly eclipsed the very important role of his contemporary Pope Damasus (366-384). On the other hand we find the latter's successor, Pope Siricius (384-399), exercising not only an occasional jurisdiction in appeal cases but a true disciplinary authority, legislative in form. This authority was exercised over the Italian bishops within his immediate competence and also throughout the whole of the christian West. We find him writing letters to a Spanish bishop in 385, and to the African and Gaulish episcopacy; these letters laid down authoritatively the exact course to be followed. They were true ' decretals ', the first to survive of an abundant series which was later to prove one of the major sources of our canon law.

Once the doctrinal problem raised by Arianism had been resolved (this happened, at the theological level, when the bishops of the East accepted the faith of Damasus at Antioch in 379), Rome scarcely intervened in the government of the Greek-speaking Churches, which tended to conduct their own administration autonomously.

At the end of the fourth century we find great regional regroupings taking shape, thus preparing the way for future patriarchates. The third canon of the Council of Constantinople (381) claimed for the bishop of that city the primacy of honour second only to that of Rome. This was a claim heavy with threats for the future; for the present, the new Rome still played a rather secondary role, even politically. It had been Arian under Constantius and Valens, and under Theodosius and his sons it appointed two great bishops, St Gregory of Nazianzus (379-381) and St John Chrysostom (398-403/4). However, it failed to keep them, for the court, like the capital, was much too worldly to submit to the rule of saints. But at the level of ecclesiastical administration Constantinople already exerted an influence beyond its own domain, European Thrace, as far as Asia Minor, to the detriment of the metropolitan Churches of Ephesus and Caesarea in Cappadocia.

In Syria (the ' East ', according to official terminology) Antioch remained the pole of attraction, an active centre, impetuous and sometimes stormy. In Palestine Jerusalem, the holy city, vied with Caesarea. Egypt was firmly kept in hand by the powerful Bishop of Alexandria; strong because of his traditional alliance with Rome and accustomed to be master in his own diocese, he tended to intervene outside rather too much. It is unfortunate to find the Alexandrians, Timothy and Theophilus, coming in turn to aggravate the difficulties of the two holy bishops of Constantinople and helping to depose them.

2. The Liturgy and the Sacraments

But Christianity is essentially a community organised to pay worship to the true God in the spirit and truth of the new covenant. The religious life of the christian, at the end of the fourth century no less than today, was centred on his participation in this official worship, on the liturgy and the Eucharistic sacrifice. The liturgy had almost everywhere become a daily event, celebrated with more solemnity on Sunday (in Egypt, on Saturday or Sunday) and on feast days.

The Church's year was beginning to take shape. Its calendar was organised round two poles : the first of course being Easter, although Greek East and Latin West did not yet calculate the date according to the same principles. The feast of feasts extended in one direction towards Pentecost, and, in the other, was preceded by a season of penance, Lent. During the fourth century Lenten discipline was laid down, with local variations, chiefly as regards the length of the fast.

The second pole, that of the winter feasts devoted to the mystery of the Incarnation, had a more complex origin. The Churches of the East had fixed 6 January as a somewhat ideological feast celebrating the appearance and manifestation of God on earth : Epiphany, Theophany. Commemoration of the Nativity on 25 December emerged in Rome some time before 336. It would seem that Christianity, in triumphing, adopted and changed the significance of the pagan feast of the anniversary of the Unconquered Sun, this feast stemming from a religion which the Emperor Aurelian had tried to impose on the Empire in 274. Christians seem to have argued that Christ, after all, was the true Sun of Justice. Towards the end of the fourth century the different Churches borrowed each other's feast-days, which came to stand side by side in their calendars.

Among other names the Eucharistic liturgy was called in Greek *synaxis*, the 'assembling' of the faithful at the altar. The general rule was that christians should attend divine worship and go to Communion; but too often when great numbers came to church there was a decline in fervour, while the congregation tended to become passive and irregular in its attendance. The sermons of St John Chrysostom and St Ambrose show that in their day, at Antioch and Milan, certain christians went to Communion only on great feasts, or even once a year at Easter. In Spain, a Council of Toledo in 400 was obliged to threaten the excommunication of christians who were so lukewarm as to stay away from church for three or four successive Sundays.

Also about the end of the fourth century the different liturgical families, among which the christian world was eventually to be divided, began to take shape and their rites to be fixed. One example is the Roman liturgy. It is generally admitted that in the 370's, under Pope Damasus, at a time when Latin had definitively replaced Greek, the text of the canon of the Mass was formulated in all essentials, just as we know it today.

These liturgies show great diversity, not only in the Eastern Churches but also in the Latin West, where we find both an African liturgy and a Gallican liturgy (at this period little is known about Spain). Although strongly influenced by Rome the liturgy of North Italy also had its own special characteristics, as we see in the Ambrosian liturgy kept by the Church of Milan.

At this still remote period these various rites were doubtless not yet as markedly different as they were to become later. They had features in common which in some were to grow, and in others die out : for example, in the prayer of consecration the account of its institution, the anamnesis *(Unde et memores. . .)* and the epiclesis *(Supplices te rogamus. . . ,* and *Quam oblationem. . .).*

But the characteristics special to each family were already sufficiently pronounced to strike the modern archaeologist, for they were translated into the plan and layout of the basilicas. Because the Latin Mass was said facing the people, the altar, generally at the level of the nave, is found in front of the raised choir, at the end of which sat the bishop surrounded by his clergy, who were seated on a semi-circular bench running round the concave apse. At Antioch, on the other hand, and in all Northern Syria, the altar was near the end of the apse, the celebrant turning his back to the congregation. During the whole first part of the Mass, the clergy were gathered on a curious platform shaped like a horse-shoe, which was situated in the middle of the central nave and also served as an ambo for the lectors and the preacher.

Although congregations may sometimes have been very large, as we see by the size of the great basilicas, worship was still a celebration of mysteries : the essential part of the holy rites was celebrated behind closed doors in the presence of qualified initiates. In all the liturgies a special rite emphasised the division of the ceremony into two parts : the preparatory part of the Mass and the strictly Eucharistic part which began with the solemn dialogue of the preface. At that point members of the community who were unworthy to take part in the celebration were sent away : the catechumens and also, depending on the place, the penitents and the energumens (those who were possessed or mad : the christian Church was charitable to these unfortunate people).

Here we touch on the second aspect of the strictly religious life of the christian : the reception of the sacraments. Baptism, as a general rule, was administered to adults and, as we have seen in our discussion of the Fathers of the Church, often coincided with a decisive step in the spiritual life. Understandably, it was preceded by a period of serious probation and preparation, including an inquiry and careful scrutiny, special rites (exorcism, etc.), and in particular by a short but intense doctrinal training which continued in the days following the adminis-tration of baptism. We possess sermons addressed to catechumens or those newly baptised by Cyril of Jerusalem, Theodore of Mopsuestia, St Ambrose, St Augustine, St John Chrysostom and other great bishops of the fourth century : they give us a good idea of the serious regard in which this training was held.

The ceremony took place during the night before Easter, sometimes also at Pentecost, and in the East (as well as in places subject to Eastern influence) also at the Epiphany or at Christmas. A special building, the baptistery, was set aside for it. But we must not be deceived by the pool of water in the middle; baptism was administered by pouring water over the head, not by total immersion. Confirmation, administered nearby, followed immediately.

The sacrament of penance was still an impressive affair. Penance was public and reconciliation was granted only after a long period of expiation, indeed the Councils were much concerned about laying down the length of this period and relating it to the seriousness of the offence; it lasted several years, sometimes to the moments before death. The reconciliation of sinners was the object of a solemn ceremony, held at Rome on Holy Thursday. Once this sacrament had been received, it could not be received again; the baptised Christian had a vocation to sanctity!

The fourth century also witnessed the development (although not yet general or obligatory) of the solemn blessing of bride and bridegroom as soon as they had been married. This blessing was accompanied by rites derived from pagan customs : for example at Rome a veil was placed on the head of the married couple, *velatio conjugalis*. These same rites reappear in the consecration and blessing of virgins, the transposition being quite natural : the consecrated virgins were considered as *sponsae Christi*.

3. Forms of Devotion

We shall say nothing of the other sacraments. Beside these official expressions of christian worship, a large part was also played by devotional movements arising from private initiative, movements which the Church as an institution tried to win over, to control and, finally, to integrate.

Private devotions were often inspired by monasticism. When a christian living in the world wanted to lead a more intense religious life, quite naturally he looked to the monks to define the kind of life which, in all due proportion, he would try to imitate. It was, moreover, this kind of ascetical life which the Church prescribed for its public sinners during their period of expiation. It can be summed up in three words : fasting, prayer, alms.

The link with monasticism is found very early. The celebration of the divine office at canonical hours was originally a strictly monastic practice but it steadily spread : for example, at Jerusalem about 400 we find pious laymen and women coming to join monks and virgins at the sanctuary of the Anastasis in order to sing matins in their company under the direction of some cleric. Fasting was accompanied by a whole series of other austerities relating to sleep, clothes, comfort and property : as a symbol of the whole we may take the fact that some christians gave up using hot baths, the characteristic luxury of the Roman *dolce vita*.

4. The Cult of Martyrs

Even more important because of the role they played in the religious life of the period, and certainly more spectacular, were the movements arising from popular devotion. This was an obvious result of the conversion of the masses who, when they joined the Church, brought with them a sensibility moulded by old traditions, and a special psychology with its demands and its limitations. The Church of the fourth century, already very 'catholic' in the modern sense of the word, showed itself very comprehensive. While watchful for possible deviations and excesses, it gave a warm welcome to any forms of piety which showed the need for a more concrete religion, for tangible assurance, for intercessors who were close and easily accessible, and for devotions sometimes quite new, sometimes faithful to ancestral practices.

The most important was the truly abundant growth of the cult of martyrs. True, this had been known and in some sense officially recognised by the christian Church since the end of the second century, but from the time of the end of the great persecutions and with the coming of peace under Constantine the veneration and enthusiasm aroused by the 'witnesses' of Christ did not cease to grow and assert itself forcefully. If the historian based his judgment only on the most visible external evidence, these signs of the cult of martyrs could well seem to be the major phenomenon of the religious life of the fourth century.

The motives behind this veneration were of course specifically christian : belief in the help of saints who, because they are already in the presence of God, are able to intercede for us. The faithful expected saints to grant favours which were not all of an eschatological or even a spiritual nature : hence so many accounts of miraculous cures and other signs of their power as wonder-workers. Similarly, the honour paid to their remains was addressed to what was left of flesh sanctified by the spirit, proof positive of the victorious power of Christ. This flesh, moreover, had been promised resurrection (which explains why christians, in agreement with the majority of people in the Roman world, always rejected cremation and preferred burial, out of respect for the body).

But the ways in which such beliefs were expressed largely stemmed from traditional practices. The pagans honoured their dead and specially those who they believed had become heroes (originally this privileged status in after-life was reserved for very exceptional figures, but under the Empire it spread very widely). Particular attention was given to the burial-place, which was often marked with a monument, and to banquets celebrated near the tomb on the day of the funeral and on the same day in every following year. This last practice was held to have symbolic value because it foreshadowed the heavenly banquet, but it also gave rise to rather crude superstitions, such as feeding the dead : so that we find Christians hesitating over what attitude to adopt to the practice.

The custom of the funeral banquet or *refrigerium* in honour of the dead, especially of martyrs, had been accepted by the Church as a lesser evil in order that it might replace pagan feasts of the same kind; but we find the Fathers of the Church at the end of the fourth century striving to check the abuses which resulted from it. St Augustine tells us that St Ambrose had forbidden this practice at Milan; and he himself suppressed it at Hippo as soon as he became a priest in 392. Side by side with the *refrigerium* and finally replacing it we find the celebration of the Eucharistic sacrifice for the feast of the martyr, which was fixed as the anniversary of his *depositio*.

Across the whole christian world archaeologists have found numerous monuments erected on the tombs of martyrs. They vary greatly, being sometimes perhaps a simple table *(mensa)* or a room arranged for the commemorative banquet; others, more sumptuous, adopted one of the architectural forms created by the pagans for their mausoleums.

In North Syria sarcophagi or reliquaries are often found in a chapel side by side with the sanctuary of the basilicas, at the end of one of the side-aisles. Finally, to answer the ever-growing needs of popular devotion, some of these *martyria* assumed the proportions of very large churches. For example, the ruins have been found near Antioch of a vast building with four naves in the shape of a cross around a square sanctuary; dating, as its mosaics prove, from the year 397, it was doubtless consecrated to St Babylas, a martyr specially venerated at Antioch. Again, on the Vatican at Rome an immense basilica with five naves dedicated to St Peter was built by the Emperors Constantine and Constantius, in order to house the marble reliquary which held the remains of the mysterious monument raised in the time of Pope Zephyrinus, about the year 200, in honour of the Prince of the Apostles.

All these great *martyria*-churches were built in the suburbs, usually in the neighbourhood of a cemetery. At first the strictly urban basilicas, located *intra muros*, did not possess the bodies of saints, for the old Roman law forbidding burial within the city was scrupulously observed, at least until the end of the century.

Veneration of martyrs appears in the sphere of literature with the proliferation of hagiographical writing — acts, passions, collections of miracles — which were more or less historically true (the fictional element was later often to become excessive), as well as sermons and panegyrics given during the liturgy celebrated in their honour.

However, it was the actual relics of the martyrs which were the object of special attention, precisely because they made possible direct contact with the saint. Hence, for example, the practice of burial *ad sanctos* : christians tried to find a grave as near as possible to the place where the remains of a venerated martyr lay buried, in the conviction (naively expressed on the epitaphs) that the saint would welcome the dead person placed under his protection and would be his advocate before the Lord on the day of Judgment. Under the very ground, or in the immediate surroundings of the *martyria*, archaeologists have found an incredible number of Christian tombs, huddled one against the next, often piled up in several layers.

The Fathers of the Church consulted one another rather uneasily about this type of devotion and tried to spiritualise it : for example, St Augustine wrote his treatise *De cura pro mortuis gerenda* at the request of St Paulinus of Nola, who saw this practice growing in his own church around the tomb of the martyr St Felix.

But the passionate attachment to relics gave rise to many other abuses. The need to possess them soon led to many transfers or translations : for example, a recently founded town like Constantinople received the presumed relics of St Timothy in 356 and those of St Andrew and St Luke in 357. A region like Gaul, having suffered little from persecution, had few martyrs, and had to import relics; for example, in the years 380 or 390 St Victricius ordered relics of Saints John the Baptist, Andrew, Thomas, etc. from Italy for his cathedral of Rouen. This was true also of regions such as the Danube, where the population had moved before the threat of invasion.

Another characteristic phenomenon was the finding or discovery of relics hitherto forgotten or unknown, the discovery usually being provoked or guaranteed by some happening judged miraculous, by a dream or by a vision. For example, the relics of St Gervase and St Protase were discovered by St Ambrose in 386 at Milan, at the height of his struggle against the Arian Empress Justina; they were solemnly transferred by him and placed under the altar of a basilica outside the city.

Discoveries and translations increased in number despite the strong opposition of imperial legislation (for example, by Theodosius in this same year, 386). The whole body of the martyr was not always transferred, but only a part, a fragment or even some symbolic relics : a piece of material that had touched the saint's body, scented oil introduced into the reliquary and carefully collected again by means of an ingenious system of apertures, or even a little dust scraped from the tomb. The above-mentioned law of Theodosius leaves us in no doubt about the abuses which sometimes arose : he was obliged to forbid all traffic or commerce in relics[1]. These abuses grew worse

1. *Code of Theodosius*, IX, 17, 7.

with the increase in private devotion and the desire among zealous or superstitious Christians to possess some precious relic.

5. Pilgrimages

The fourth century also witnessed another typical devotion : pilgrimages. Crowds, often from very far afield, travelled to sanctuaries consecrated to famous martyrs. These included St Menas in Egypt; west of the Delta, the Seven brothers Maccabee; St Babylas in Antioch; St John in Ephesus; St Demetrius in Thessalonica; in Illyricum St Anastasia at Sirmium, St Quirinus at Siscia (before their transfer to Rome), etc. The sanctuaries of the holy places of Palestine were also visited : they were a special kind of *martyria* and the first to become important, as early as the 330s. Eusebius and the buildings of Constantine bear witness to that importance : for example, at Jerusalem the dome of the Anastasis above the tomb of Christ, the neighbouring basilica on the site of Calvary, that of the Eleona on the Mount of Olives, and the sanctuary of the Ascension; at Bethlehem the basilica of the Nativity, etc. Pilgrims also visited a whole series of *martyria* consecrated to the memory of the Old Testament, that of Abraham at Mamre, that of Job at Carneas and, of course, those of Moses on Mount Nebo and, much further away, on Mount Sinai.

These pilgrimages were very important in themselves and they have left important evidence : for example, an itinerary from Bordeaux to Jerusalem dated 333, and the picturesque travel diary of the nun Etheria who was born in Galicia or in Aquitania about 400 (the precise date is perhaps 395, more probably 411 or 417). Her diary is full of precious details about the liturgy celebrated at Jerusalem, a liturgy which, precisely because of pilgrimages, was going to be diffused throughout the Church.

Pilgrimage is a complex activity containing elements of varying value, among them piety and a legitimate devotion to the historic roots of the christian faith; it also has an ascetical, if not a penitential side, given the difficulties and length of the journeys. Mixed up with these are more profane elements, such as curiosity, sight-seeing, sometimes a little psychological or sociological instability. We can understand why some of the Fathers of the Church, St Gregory of Nyssa for example, viewed this form of devotion with reservations similar to those made a millennium later in the *Imitation of Christ*.

A last category of pilgrims visited holy persons already venerated during their lifetime. In our discussion of monasticism we have mentioned how the great hermits, notably St Antony, drew crowds of people who came to follow their example or to ask for advice, prayers

or miracles.   After their death the places they had made famous, and
above all their tombs, continued to draw pilgrims in the same way as the
Holy Places or the relics of the martyrs.   An example is the tomb of
St Martin of Tours, who died in 397.   To distinguish them from martyrs
in the strict sense these saints, ascetics and wonder-workers were given
the title of confessor, which originally meant those who during a
persecution had suffered for their faith — either imprisonment, relegation
or torture — without actually being put to death.

CHRISTIAN DEVOTION: III. The Cult of the Martyrs

PLATE 35. IVORY PYX; PROBABLY FROM CONSTANTINOPLE, 6TH CENTURY, BRITISH MUSEUM, LONDON

The shrine of St Menas, discovered south of Alexandria in 1907, was one of the most important in the life of the early Church. From the evidence of excavations it had by the 8th century become the centre of a fairly large oasis town, while ampullae discovered all over the Christian world show that pilgrims to the shrine came from many different areas. For such a famous martyr, the evidence about his actual martyrdom is very confused, but it is probable that he was an Egyptian officer who was martyred in Kotyaion in Phrygia during the reign of Diocletian. On this ivory pyx we see, above, St Menas wearing only a loin cloth, being dragged before a Roman official who is seated as judge at a table; an angel is also shown assisting the saint. Below is the sanctuary of St Menas; the saint is portrayed as an orante beneath an arch which represents his shrine. On either side worshippers approach the shrine.

CHRISTIAN DEVOTION: IV. The Cross

PLATE 36. THE CRUCIFIXION; SCENE FROM THE RABBULA GOSPELS, ZAGBA, EASTERN SYRIA, 586

Although the Cross took an important place in the devotion of the early Church, actual representation of the crucifixion is very rare; this is one of the earliest as well as one of the finest examples. Some of the hesitancy to portray the crucified Lord can be detected even here, since the Christ is given a long robe as a sign of respect in contrast to the two robbers. In the crucifixion scenes on the Monza ampullae (cf. Plate 33), the central cross is decorated but entirely empty and only the head of the triumphant Christ is shown over it, while the other two crosses carry the two robbers portrayed of course with little sympathy or respect. Note that the picture telescopes two events : Christ is offered the hyssop at the same time as Longinus plunges his spear into his side. Note also that Christ is bearded (cf. Plates 7 and 23), but that he is by no means an old man (cf. Plate 45).

CHAPTER XXV

CHRISTIANA TEMPORA

WE must now try to discover how far the christian's faith exercised an influence beyond the strictly religious sphere. Several times St Augustine makes use of the expression *Christiana tempora*, ' the Christian epoch ', to describe, in contrast to the pagan centuries, the period of history following the conversion of Constantine. Is the expression justified? In what sense and just how far can one say that the civilisation of the Roman world of the fourth century was a christian civilisation?

There can be no doubt that the State at that period thought like a christian and wanted to be christian. This was a consequence of the monolithic structure of the absolute monarchy. From the moment when the omnipotent sovereign declared himself a christian, the Empire, quite naturally so to speak, became christian with him. In a way this was expressed officially : from 315 onwards the coinage bears the monogram of Christ engraved on Constantine's helmet; in the years 326-330 there appears the *labarum*, the triumphal standard, the square banner of the Roman cavalry adorned with portraits of the reigning sovereigns, the staff of which is topped with the same monogram surrounded with a crown of laurels (whence the name *Laureatum* which when transposed into Greek becomes *Labarum*).

This was not a merely theoretical concept : from Constantine and Constantius to Gratian and Theodosius (due allowance made for the reaction attempted by Julian and the neutral period under Valentinian), we have seen the Empire progressively loosen its links with paganism and end by proclaiming Christianity, in its Catholic form, the State religion.

Once detached from paganism, the State merged closely with the Church : one result of this was Book XVI of the Code of Theodosius, which was compiled in the years 429-439. In Book XVI, devoted to religious questions, there are about a hundred and fifty decisions in

defence of orthodoxy, even attempts at defining what it was. The
Emperor intervened in ecclesiastical discipline even on points of detail;
in 390 a constitution of Theodosius forbade women to come to church
if, ' contrary to human and divine law ', they dared to cut their hair,
and provided for sanctions against the bishops who let them come to
church[1]. This policy of intervention was accompanied, we have seen,
by a whole series of different privileges and favours for the benefit of the
Church and its clergy.

1. Christian Influence on Legislation

The respect and favours granted to the christian religion by the
imperial government did not reflect a mere pose, either hypocritical
or self-seeking. The government made a real effort to infuse the
structure of the institutions, even the very life of the Roman world,
with the christian spirit. The christian calendar came to regulate the
rhythm of social life : in 325 Sunday became an official holiday. Pagan
festivals doubtless continued, for the people loved them, especially in
Rome and in the large towns, because of the spectacles and other
amusements with which they were celebrated, but attempts were made
to eliminate their religious character, and finally they lost all official
recognition. The list of holidays, as laid down by a constitution of 389,
comprises the christian feasts, and also 1 January, the birthdays of the
Emperors and the feasts marking the foundation of the two capitals.

It is well known that the christian Emperors undertook a great
work of legislation which profoundly changed the shape of Roman law.
To what extent did Christianity influence this legislation? By turns
its influence has been overestimated and underestimated. The facts are
often difficult to interpret; for example, in 320 when Constantine abolished
the legal restrictions on unmarried men and women, formerly imposed
by Augustus as part of his policy for increasing the birth rate, can we
be sure that he did so in order to honour the christian ideal of holy
virginity? The influence of the moral code of the Gospel and of
ecclesiastical discipline is more surely evident in the constitutions relating
to marriage. Married men were forbidden to keep a concubine, adultery
and rape were treated severely and obstacles put in the way of divorce,
which had become much too easy.

Measures were likewise taken to make the slave's lot easier, though,
it is true, these measures continued an already clearly marked tendency
under Stoic influence in the law of the Early Empire. It was forbidden

1. *Code of Theodosius*, XVI, 2, 27.

to separate the members of a family of slaves, and emancipation was made easier : notably, it could be performed in a church, by simple declaration in the presence of the bishop.

More original and very worthy of notice are the efforts made to introduce a little humanity into the atrocious prison conditions. Under this heading the Code of Theodosius lists seven laws dating from 320 to 409; the first forbids gaolers to let their prisoners die of hunger; the last orders prisoners to be taken to the bath-house once a week, on Sunday : for this, religious motives are expressly given. The clergy, both bishops and priests, are allowed to look after these poor unfortunates.

2. The Extent to which Morality became Christian

But these are measures on points of detail which do not adequately solve the problem : Was civilisation at that time christian? That is a difficult question which demands a complex and qualified answer.

(a) It was no easy task in a few years or a few generations to christianise a civilisation which had been born and grown to maturity in the midst of paganism. Age-old reflexes, especially among the masses, were not so easily changed : only a few chosen spirits were capable of recognising the practical implications of the new religious ideal which they had just glimpsed or adopted.

As a test, let us take the two practices characteristic of pagan society which the apologists of the second century forcibly attacked : the exposure of new-born infants and fights between gladiators. On the subject of the first the legislation enacted by the christian Emperors was contradictory and confused. There were certainly some measures making it easier for a child who had been rescued and raised in slavery to recover his freedom. In 374 infanticide was forbidden, but it does not appear as though the abandoning of a child was in itself ever forbidden, despite the fact that this practice was an expression of contempt for the human person. Gladiator fights were first banned in 325, but for a long time the law remained purely theoretical, despite christian propaganda : only about 434-438 was it fully applied. Fights in the amphitheatre continued, but were limited to displays not between man and man but only between man and wild animals. Gradually, however, interest shifted from the shedding of blood to the skill of the protagonist : his acrobatics.

(b) Christianity, having been adopted by the head of the State and by the masses, was now obliged to take responsibility for the earthly city. We must not jump to the conclusion that the Church had become worldly; it was simply that christians of the fourth century could not refuse the tasks imposed on them by the very success of the Gospel in the Roman world.

As long as they had been only a weak minority, suspect and barely tolerated, they had been able to live as it were encysted in the social organism, leaving to others — the pagan majority, the pagan State — the task of grappling with and solving the difficult problems raised by the needs of mankind.

For example, there was the problem of war. In the time of Tertullian and Origen the christian could obey the Decalogue literally (' Thou shalt not kill ') and follow the spirit of the Gospel by giving himself entirely to his vocation — in some way a priestly vocation : ' by incessant prayers ', writes Tertullian, ' let us ask for all the Emperors a calm reign, a safe palace, brave troops, a faithful senate, a loyal people, a peaceful world '[2]. At that period there had been plenty of volunteers to strengthen the army which ensured peace on the frontiers. But now the military situation, the population figures and the religion of the Late Empire no longer made such an attitude possible; moreover the attitude itself was rather ambiguous inasmuch as christians enjoyed the Roman peace without paying for it.

Very early on the Church had to face up to its new responsibilities. In 314 the third canon of the Council of Arles made provision for the excommunication of soldiers who desert, ' since the State has stopped its persecutions ' (at least if we take the obscure and much-disputed phrase *in pace*, ' in time of peace ', to have a religious connotation). Not that the Church had resigned itself to sacrificing the Gospel ideal of non-violence : the attitude of its most authoritative doctors showed that clearly enough, and they were all bishops fully aware of their pastoral duties. Again, in the 370s St Basil urged soldiers with blood on their hands to undergo three years of penance.

Similarly, a little later St Ambrose approved the action of magistrates who abstained from the sacraments after having pronounced sentence of death, though he did not go so far as to oblige them to abstain. The severity of penal law in force at that time involved as many violent measures in the civil service as in the army; in fact both wore the same uniform and were called by the same name : ' militia '.

Here we find the beginnings of opposition between the demands of the earthly city and the city of God. The contradiction even appeared in imperial policy. On the one hand we find the clergy in 313 benefiting from a great number of exemptions of every kind : exemption from

2. Tertullian, *Apologetic*, 30, 4.

taxes, from civic duties, etc.; on the other hand, the complex, rigid structure of the social system, on which the smooth working of the State depended, could not allow holy orders to become a means of shirking civic duties.

In 329 Constantine forbade the clergy to belong to the *curiales*, those dignitaries who were collectively responsible for the payment of municipal taxes to the State. But this meant drying up an important source of priests. The lawmakers had to come back to this matter : from 361 to 399 we find a good dozen laws on the subject which in various ways applied concessions, restrictions or an amnesty.

If it had only been a question of the *curiales*, the damage would have been slight. But many other social groups with a duty to the State were forbidden to take holy orders : in 361 Treasury employees, in 365 the bakers, in 398 workers in the purple-dye works, in 408 the pork-butchers.

(c) Finally we must take account of the inertia in any civilisation, for a civilisation grows according to an inner logic, causes and effects being linked in such a way that forces from outside can exercise only a limited influence, at least directly. Once in existence the totalitarian regime inaugurated by Diocletian inevitably gave rise under his successors to coercion, tyranny, terror and cruelty — despite the moral exhortations which the Christian Church ceaselessly addressed to its leaders and representatives : appeals to clemency, mercy and humanity.

The letters of the great bishops of the fourth century show how they continually intervened with the authorities to help the weak and the victims of an oppressive regime. Sometimes they pleaded for individuals, sometimes for groups : for example, in 387 Bishop Flavian asked Theodosius to pardon his town of Antioch after the uprising in which statues of the Emperor had been profaned. In a similar case in 390 St Ambrose was unable to prevent the savage repressive measures ordered by the same Emperor at Thessalonica — 7000 people were gathered in the circus and pitilessly massacred. But he dared to demand, and in fact obtained, public penance from the guilty man. True, the penance was mitigated and the sanction only one of principle, but for the first time an Emperor agreed to recognise the superiority of God's law and to submit to the spiritual authority of the Church.

But if christian influence had a beneficial effect in a certain number of particular cases, it could not reach the root causes of such excesses, nor check the consequences implicit in the very principle of the established regime. We have already alluded to the increasing barbarism of the penal laws and even of the administration of the Late Empire; nothing is more characteristic than the more and more frequent use of torture.

To its honour, at the end of the Republic Roman law gave up torture almost completely though it always remained in use for slaves. It was reintroduced surreptitiously under the Empire in cases of high treason, but once the principle had been admitted it did not cease to spread.

It was logical for a monarchy of Eastern pattern — a police state — always to fear conspiracy. At the slightest breath of suspicion torture was applied to those presumed guilty, to possible accomplices and finally to simple witnesses — in the hope of obtaining the scantiest clue. Where were the limits of high treason to be drawn? It could be argued that someone behind with his taxes, a man who owed money to the Treasury, threatened the security of the State.

Finally we have to reckon with arbitrary decisions. The representatives of the absolute power were themselves omnipotent — at least for as long as the Emperor trusted them. When they fell into disgrace they became mere traitors, and with them their kin, their friends and their protégés.

Christians could only deplore this odious system. The case is quoted of certain poor wretches unjustly condemned whom the christian people venerated after their death almost as martyrs, like the ' suffering saints ' dear to Russian piety. St Augustine has a fine passage in the *City of God* on the absurdity of torture, an unfailing source of miscarriages of justice and unjustified suffering. But this passage forms part of his pessimistic picture of the misfortunes inherent in man's estate : like war, famine, sickness, it seems to him both intolerable and inevitable. Here we see how a moralist and theologian is strictly limited by the context of his civilisation, and as it were imprisoned by the attitude it imposes on him.

The same may be said of the Church's intervention in economic and social matters. It showed a distrust of business people, who were suspected of making an illicit profit, and severity towards money-lenders. Councils and theologians of the fourth century agreed in condemning loans with interest, but this attitude, because of the decline of the monetary economy, did not have the importance it was later to assume.

The Church was also relatively powerless in face of the growth of the pre- or quasi-feudal structures which accompanied the increase of large properties. It could only protest against abuses committed by the ' powerful ', those great lords who exacted excessive privileges from the State and oppressed the peasants on their domains. If the status of slaves in the country tended to rise and become what the Middle Ages was later to describe as serfage, the fate of the *coloni* or free peasants grew steadily worse; between the two classes there was only a difference of degree.

We find bishops adopting the same policy of intervention and moral pressure towards the ' masters ' as towards the administrative and judicial authorities. But here too this appeal to pity and kindness could only remedy particular excesses without hoping to reform the whole system. The State itself tried in vain to do so, instituting ' defenders of the people ' (368) appointed to protect the humble against iniquities from the powerful; but this office soon degenerated and was eventually taken over by the very men it was designed to oppose (409). We must wait for the year 400 to see a Spanish council threaten with excommunication any lord who robbed a cleric or a poor person.

3. Growth of Charitable Institutions

From what has been said it may perhaps be concluded that the influence of Christianity on Roman society of the fourth century was marginal. It is quite true that the conversion of that society to Christianity was not accompanied all at once by a general flowering of the Gospel ideal. Let us look at things from the collective, even statistical, point of view, with the eyes of a historian of civilisation. At this tragic period, ' this time of troubles ' (to use one of Professor Arnold Toynbee's fundamental concepts), we find a hardening of sensibility, an increasing savagery in personal behaviour and in institutions; by one of those paradoxes of which history is full, the Roman world had succeeded in overcoming the challenge of the barbarian threat only by letting itself become in certain ways barbarian.

But our picture is still incomplete. Christianity had also introduced to civilisation new preoccupations, which gave rise to original institutions. In future centuries these were to develop enormously but even now they were important; for instance, the notion of charity in the social meaning of the word, the feeling of solidarity and responsibility of man towards his brethren, however disinherited, towards the poor, the homeless, tramps or travellers, the sick in body and mind.

The pagan world had not felt this religious respect for the human person considered as having absolute value, as an object of the merciful love of God, Creator and Saviour. The generosity of a patron towards his dependents was something quite different; so too were the ' bread and circuses ' given to the people of the capital, a dividend levied on the yield from conquests by the heirs of those who had conquered the Empire. In this respect the fourth century well deserves to be called a christian epoch : it showed ample signs of charity.

Almsgiving was recognised as one of the essential duties of Christianity and reached the proportions of a public service, because of the enormous wealth of the artistocracy from which part of the christian élite was recruited. On the death of his wife Paulina in 397 the Senator Pammachius, one of the friends of St Jerome, summoned all the poor of Rome to a feast in the basilica of St Peter's on the Vatican; they filled the immense basilica, overflowing into the atrium and even into the square. St Paulinus of Nola, who recorded the incident, was well aware of the reversal effected in social values : he called beggars ' patrons of our souls ', *patronos animarum nostrarum :* it was the rich now who appeared as dependents.

As always, the bishops played a leading role. Doubtless helped by gifts from the Emperor, they took the initiative in organising works of charity on an institutional basis. From 372 onwards, in a suburb of his episcopal town, Caesarea in Cappadocia, St Basil began erecting a group of buildings : church, monastery, hostel and hospital, with the necessary qualified staff, doctors and male nurses, destined to shelter travellers, poor people and the sick, especially lepers. ' Houses for the poor ', *ptokhotrophia*, such as this, were not an isolated phenomenon. At the same period we find several others : for example, at Amasya in Pontus and in other towns of the East.

The Church of Alexandria, as usual, did things on a grand scale. It had its own group of male nurses — *parabolani* — at the orders of the bishop; their large numbers (more than five hundred in 416/18) and unruly behaviour eventually worried the imperial authorities. The West followed suit : we find the same Pammachius founding a hostel-inn, *xenodochium*, at the Port of Rome, beside Ostia, where so many pilgrims and travellers disembarked. In Rome another great Roman lady, Fabiola, who also belonged to the group of ascetics directed by St Jerome, founded the first hospital, *nosokomion*, devoted to the service of the sick.

Here we touch on the origin of institutions such as public assistance and social security which are now secularised and an essential feature of every civilised State. The historian of civilisation is bound to stress that they owe their origin to Christianity, that they were born, grew up and for many centuries yet were to live under the Church's protection. They give the fourth century its real value. Rather than be astonished at the slowness with which it was able to bring men round to its spiritual ideal, we should be grateful that it began the slow work of christianising the social institutions which were to flourish long afterwards in the medieval city.

CHAPTER XXVI

THE GULF GROWS WIDER BETWEEN CHRISTIANS OF EAST AND WEST

So far we have been able to study the history of Christianity more or less as a single whole, without having to take much account of regional differences. Apart from the young missionary Churches in barbarian countries (as we have seen, the role they played was quite small), the main historical events have taken place within the framework of the Roman Empire and reflected the Empire's solid unity at the political, economic, social and cultural levels.

During the fourth century, however, disturbing symptoms of disintegration had already begun to appear. More and more often the administration and even the government were divided between several rulers each controlling a particular part of the Empire. From the abdication of Diocletian to the death of Theodosius, that is, for almost a century (305-395), the Roman world was united under the authority of a single head only for twenty-two years and a few months. True, the old Roman idea of joint rule safeguarded the unity of the Empire as a legal entity : the laws decreed by each Emperor were theoretically decreed in the name of all; but behind this façade of unanimity autonomous and sometimes divergent policies were at work. For example, in religion we have seen how Constans and his brother Constantius, Valentinian and his brother Valens, the former in the Latin West, the latter in the East, adopted totally different attitudes to the problems raised by Arianism. With the sons of Theodosius or rather with their ministers, Stilicho in Italy, Rufinus and Eutropius at Constantinople, from 395 to 408 the two halves of the Empire appear not only separated but antagonistic, and even in open conflict. After their time unity was never again re-established, except in a quite provisional manner (for four months in 423) or as a convenient fiction.

We must not allow this constitutional façade to hide the true political drama which unfolded during the fifth century, in the course of which the separation became radical : each of the two halves of the *orbis Romanus* reacted quite differently when confronted by that important event, the Germanic invasions.   We might have expected the Eastern Empire, struck so early and so severely (the Emperor Valens perished in the disaster of Adrianople in 378), to have succumbed to the Germanic attacks.   Far from it.   We know that this Empire, traditionally called Byzantine, with its capital at Constantinople, succeeded in holding its own and surviving until 1453, even though it continually had to fight on two fronts, in Europe and in Asia.

We can date the beginning of this movement towards the restoration of nationalism to the years 400-401 : at home it was then that the party opposed to the influence of barbarian mercenaries gained the upper hand; while abroad a clever but selfish policy succeeded in diverting towards Italy and the West the threat of Alaric's Visigoths who had up till then laid waste the Balkan peninsula and Greece.   The lesson was not lost and at the end of the century the Eastern Empire used similar methods to get rid of Theodoric's Ostrogoths, who, in their turn, marched off to conquer Italy (488-493).

Meanwhile, as is well known, the Western Empire collapsed under barbarian attacks.   On 31 December 406 the Rhine frontier was smashed in, just as the Danube frontier had been a generation earlier; Gaul and with it all the Latin countries watched waves of successive invasions break over them.   Contemporaries were painfully shocked by the capture and plundering of Rome itself by Alaric in 410, an event considered symbolic; but this was only one episode in a long series of ordeals the result of which was to replace Roman power everywhere by the domination of the invaders, and to shatter the unity of empire into a number of practically independent kingdoms.

True, until 476 the Western Empire still nominally possessed a titular ruler, but he was usually a mere puppet in the hands of a barbarian protector, commander-in-chief of the army and sole master of the country. And if, at this or a later period, certain of these Germanic kings recognised the nominal sovereignty of the Emperor of Ravenna or of Constantinople and governed in his name, this was only a means of ensuring the legitimacy of their position and increasing their prestige without in fact alienating their real power.   In 486 when the last regions of Gaul to remain nominally Roman fell to Frankish forces all the West was in fact lost to the Empire.   In the sixth century the tenacious efforts of Justinian succeeded in reconquering only Vandal Africa, a very small part of Spain and peninsular Italy : this reconquest was difficult and also precarious; hardly was it completed (562) when the threat of a new invasion, that of the Lombards, loomed across the frontiers of Italy (568).

The country which suffered the greatest upheaval as a result of the invasions was that between the Danube and the Adriatic : Illyricum, which throughout the third and fourth centuries had been a stronghold of Rome, a seed-bed of soldiers and Emperors. Unfortunately its geographical position made it an essential starting-point or thoroughfare for the invaders; and so it witnessed in turn the arrival, meeting and sometimes the retreat of Germans, Turks and Slavs, Visigoths, Ostrogoths, Huns, Skiri, Rugians, Gepidae, Heruli, Lombards, Bulgars, Anti, Sclaveni, Avars... This country had played the part of a bridge linking East and West : under repeated blows it collapsed from 380 onwards; only its two outermost piers held; in the centre Roman influence withdrew to the Dalmatian coast. The deepening of this physical gulf between the two halves of the Mediterranean world coincided with another macroscopic event : the break-up of that cultural unity which linked the Greek and Latin countries within the same imperial civilisation.

The historian of civilisations, recognising the fact that only a small number of civilisations have been truly original, stresses the unity of Hellenistic and Roman culture, *die hellenistisch-römische Kultur*, at the end of the Republic and during the first centuries of the Empire : the culture expressed in Latin countries appears as a side branch which developed late on the vigorous trunk of Hellenism. In the time of Cicero a cultivated man was one who knew Greek; but the flowering and subsequent fame of a Latin literature naturally brought about a decline in Greek just as in modern times Latin has everywhere given way to national literatures. This decline was already evident at the end of the first century, as we see from Quintilian; at the beginning of the fifth the emancipation of Latin culture was an accepted fact, thanks partly to another new event : the exhaustion of the Empire, overpowered by barbarian threats, resulting in a decline in the general standard of Western culture.

As was only natural, this retreat of Hellenism did not take place everywhere in the same way. Certain social or cultural circles put up a stiffer or longer defence : the aristocracy, the world of medicine, above all philosophy. Among these bodies of resistance was Christianity, an Oriental religion with an élite of professional theologians. But here again we find an increasing differentiation : the point of cleavage can be placed symbolically between St Ambrose and St Augustine. The former died in 397, having always united the Roman fatherland

and the christian faith in a single loyalty and a single hope for the future.   It is significant to find him towards the end of his life writing to Fritigil, Queen of the Marcomanni, trying to attract both her and her subjects into the orbit of Rome, while at the same time answering her request for instruction in the christian religion.   A member of one of the great families of Rome, he profited from the traditional education still given there : as an aristocrat he had a thorough knowledge of Greek, which allowed him, when he had to improvise as a theologian, to assimilate easily not only the classic masters, Philo and Origen, but the most recent works of his Eastern contemporaries : his *De Spiritu Sancto* (381) drew freely from works on the same subject by Didymus of Alexandria, St Basil (375) and St Gregory of Nazianzus (380).

A difference of social class further separated him from St Augustine, his junior by fifteen years.   Of much lower birth, the latter received a narrower, more utilitarian education; he did not learn much Greek and never came to know it well; this shortcoming was a sign of the times and did not prevent him, as we have seen, from enjoying a brilliant career as a teacher of rhetoric.   But the historical background had rapidly changed.   St Augustine died in 430 in his episcopal town of Hippo, besieged by the Vandals; the first fall of Rome in 410 had led him to meditate on the radically ephemeral nature of all earthly States and to formulate in his *City of God* (413-427) the principles of a christian theology of history.   A pure Latin, largely self-taught, despite or perhaps because of this handicap, St Augustine was, in a sense, thrown back on originality.

In fact, with the help of his genius, it was he who in his *De Trinitate* (399-419) worked out the first strictly Western theology of this great mystery, though Tertullian and Hilary of Poitiers may be called his forerunners in this field.   In the history of culture, the work of St Augustine appears as the continuation and fulfilment of that begun by the first masterpieces of Cicero and Virgil : with him, and very largely thanks to him, the Latin Church acquired doctrinal autonomy, and the West its maturity.

From that time onwards the links between Greeks and Latins grew looser and looser.   The Greeks had never shown much curiosity about people whom they still considered barbarians; the only notable exceptions came from three severely restricted circles : the army, the law and the imperial Court of Constantinople; but during the fifth and sixth centuries these too were steadily reabsorbed by Hellenism. On the Latins' side relations with the East were the result of particular circumstances (for example, the ' Scythian ' monks, who originally came from Latin Dobruja and settled in Constantinople), exceptional vocations (such as that of the last philosophers like Claudianus Mamertus in Gaul in the fifth century and of Boethius in Italy in the sixth), or of men specialising in cultural relations. Between St Ambrose and St Augustine, St Jerome is a typical example of the latter group : a Latin, educated in the East, who settled for good in Bethlehem in 386, chiefly engaged — his polemical writings apart — on translation and adaptation.

Under these conditions it is hardly surprising that each of the two halves of the Church gradually began to lead its own way of life. But there was no question yet of a definitive break, although there were many temporary quarrels. For example, communion was broken between the sees of Rome and Constantinople for eleven consecutive years as a result of the irregular deposition of St John Chrysostom (404-415), and for thirty-five years because of the policy of appeasement towards the Monophysites adopted by the Emperors Zeno and Anastasius (484-519).

As in politics and cultural matters the first symptoms of this growing apart can be seen well before the fifth century. During the long Arian crisis we have seen how very different — taken as a whole — were the reactions of the East on the one hand and of Rome and the West (with Athanasius's Egypt) on the other, the former more aware of the Sabellian danger, the latter of the Subordinationist heresy. From the Council of Tyre (335) to the Synod of Antioch (379) opposition remained almost constant, sometimes going as far as schism, for example at the time of the Council of Sardica in 343, when a fruitless attempt was made to collect all the bishops of the Empire : the Greek bishops refused to sit with their Western colleagues and went away to hold a counter-synod at Philippopolis.

Yet East and West were still often in touch during the fourth century; the Arian crisis was itself the occasion of a kind of mingling. Many fruitful meetings took place through Councils, embassies and, not least, through the large number of exiles : it was because it harboured Arius that Illyricum became a centre of Arianism. At Trèves and at Rome Athanasius tightened his links with the West and made known there the new monastic ideal. In the opposite direction many Latin bishops found themselves in the East and took the unexpected opportunity of learning, thinking and working there : Hilary of Poitiers, Eusebius of Vercelli, Lucifer of Cagliari.

Moreover, different though their attitudes might be, it was one and the same problem of the Trinity which at that time passionately interested both Greeks and Latins. In the fifth and sixth centuries, on the other hand, the great theological disputes which shook and sometimes split the Church were peculiar to each of the two cultures.

The Christological problems and the heresies arising therefrom, Apollinarianism, Nestorianism, Monophysitism, were in essence specifically Eastern concerns; Pelagianism, on the other hand, was the first Western heresy (if one excludes Priscillianism) : the Greeks never really raised the problem which divided St Augustine from Pelagius and Julian of Eclana, the problem which was later to obsess and as it were mould the Western psyche.

Naturally such sweeping statements need to be toned down : personal and perhaps doctrinal relations did exist between the champions of Pelagianism and of Nestorianism; recognition of the growing influence of the Papacy obliged Latin theologians to study problems debated in the East; the authority of Rome sometimes intervened at a decisive moment, as with St Leo at the time of the Council of Chalcedon (451); finally Justinian's reconquest put Rome and Carthage under the authority of the Emperor of Constantinople, and this authority was freely exercised in the sphere of religion, whence arose new contacts, though these were sometimes occasioned by disputes. In a more general way thanks to the links we have mentioned there was never a total interruption in religious or cultural relations between the Latin West and the Greek East.

But all these facts, though very interesting to the historian, modify only slightly the general picture we first sketched. It remains quite true that the two halves of the Christian world became increasingly differentiated during these two centuries : the Roman unity characteristic of Antiquity was replaced by a division, pregnant with important consequences, between Byzantine East and the Latin Middle Ages. Not only did theologians work at different tasks but the whole way of Christian life became different : ecclesiastical institutions, liturgy, the monastic ideal, popular devotions, the place of Christianity in daily life : in every sphere differences appeared. It is therefore appropriate to discuss East and West separately.

CHAPTER XXVII

THE FIRST
CHRISTOLOGICAL DISPUTES:
FROM APOLLINARIUS
TO NESTORIUS

DURING the fifth and sixth centuries the christian East turned from the trinitarian problem raised by Arianism — that of the structure *ad intra* of the Divine reality — to the strictly Christological problem. How was it, they asked, that what comes from God and what is human are united in the Incarnate Word to make up the unique Lord Jesus Christ? The two questions were only gradually distinguished : chronologically they overlap and at the beginning are found mixed up. The beginning of these long disputes relating to the economy of the Incarnation may be dated to the quarrels which broke out even within the Nicaean ranks in 362 — we mentioned them then — at the time when the Council of Confessors met around Athanasius in Alexandria. But in order to grasp the root of the problem we must go back even further. The Arians had their own Christology; the Anomoeans, and before them the first disciples of Arius, had envisaged the Divine Word as a vital principle analogous to the soul in man, and they held this vital principle responsible for the weaknesses which beset Jesus in the Gospel narrative : for example, he was hungry, thirsty, sat down tired at the Woman of Samaria's well, wept over the tomb of Lazarus and trembled at the prospect of death. These incidents provided experimental proof, so to speak, of the inferiority of the Logos, as defined by the Arians, by comparison with God and his essentially unchangeable nature. But the trouble with this Arian doctrine was that it gave Christ an incomplete and mutilated humanity, a body without a soul or, at most, a soul deprived of reason.

Nicaean orthodoxy was not slow to raise objections, notably those put forward by Eustathius of Antioch. Nevertheless, there can be no doubt about the Arian ancestry of Apollinarius of Laodicea, with whom there now begins a long series of Christological heresies and the chain reactions arising from them. Apollinarius was a well-educated man and a strong supporter of Nicaea — this fact is remarkable for Syria, if not totally Arian, was at least extremely reserved towards the *homoousios*. He was also a faithful ally of Athanasius, a champion of christian civilisation against Julian the Apostate and a famous exegetist, whose pupil St Jerome was proud to have been. He was influenced, doubtless without knowing it, by the categories of his Arian opponents. He, too, pictured the Incarnation in the following terms : the Word, evidently defined as being strictly consubstantial with God, is united to an incomplete humanity; in the composite being of Jesus Christ it plays either the role of the soul in the body or that of the spirit in the body and vegetative or animal soul, depending on whether reference is made to the trichotomy of I Thess 5 : 23, or to the words implying dichotomy which St Paul more often uses.

But the centre of the problem has shifted. The arguments relate no longer to the apologetic exegesis of the human passions of Christ but directly to the study of man as an animal. For Apollinarius, a human being cannot be free from sin because of the weakness and tyranny of the flesh; man's freedom implies at least the possibility of sin. In order for Christ to have been sinless a Divine soul or spirit would have had to come into Him and guide the flesh He assumed in order to become like unto us. The problem, for Apollinarius, was to free Christ from that painful duality which is ours, torn as we are between the contrary inclinations of the flesh and the spirit. Hence his characteristic insistence on the unity of the man-God; Apollinarius is the author of the formula which was to play such an important role in later controversies : ' Unique is the nature [the concrete reality] of the Divine Word which was made incarnate '[1]. This refusal to divide or separate the two elements which were combined in the Incarnation led him explicitly to profess — sometimes in paradoxical fashion — not only ' the communication of idioms ', but the holiness and adorable character of the body of Christ.

The ideas of Apollinarius found supporters; we know of a whole group of his disciples including several bishops. The active figure was that same Vitalis whom we have already met at Antioch, one of the four or five rival bishops contesting that unhappy Church, and one of three, with Melitius and Paulinus, who quoted as their authority

---

1. Pseudo-Athanasius (Apollinarius) *Ad Jovianum,* p. 251 : 1-3 Lietzmann.

the faith of Nicaea and communion with Damasus. As often happens, the supporters of Apollinarius subsequently divided into several groups, some more moderate, others pushing the logic of the system to extremes; as, for example, Polemon, who openly professed Synousiasm, that is to say the perfect consubstantiality of the Logos and of his flesh made divine.

Orthodoxy reacted very strongly against what it was bound to consider a heresy. The Synod of the Confessors in 362 was doubtless too preoccupied with the urgent problem raised by Arianism not to try and appease as far as possible the nascent differences within the Nicaean party; nevertheless, despite the reserve and deliberate vagueness of its pronouncements, we find there, at least implicitly, the great argument which was continually used against Apollinarianism : only that can be saved (in man) which has been assumed (by Christ).

The conflict entered its sharpest phase in 374. Epiphanius of Salamis, a professional heresy-hunter, came to hold an enquiry at Antioch and was soon given the facts. Having been abused by Vitalis, Pope Damasus solemnly condemned the errors of Apollinarius in a Roman Synod held in 377; the same condemnation followed in Alexandria (378), in Antioch (379) and in Constantinople at the great Council of 381; by the laws of 383/4 and 388 the Emperor Theodosius put the secular arm at the service of the repression of this heresy.

Apollinarianism persisted into the decade beginning 420, but it led an underground life; if it managed to circulate and find a public for books by leaders of the sect, it did so by pretending that they were written by the most respected writers : Gregory the Wonder-Worker, Pope Julius of Rome and St Athanasius himself. These impudent forgeries later brought harm to many, starting with the great St Cyril of Alexandria.

The reaction against Apollinarianism was not limited to disciplinary measures; it was the occasion of an intense doctrinal activity. Among the leading opponents of the heresy were the great Cappadocian doctors, Gregory of Nyssa, Gregory of Nazianzus, and the latter's cousin Amphilocius of Iconium. Polemical writing spread to Egypt also, as we see in the treatise of a disciple of Athanasius; but the chief repercussions were in Antioch.

It would seem, in fact, that Diodorus of Tarsus was concerned to attack the errors of Apollinarianism when he formulated what has come to be called in perhaps too general a phrase the Antiochene Christology, a point of view characteristic of Syrian theology at the beginning of the fifth century, but which, it must be emphasised, did not appear there before his lifetime (exactly when in his long career it is unfortunately difficult to say). Before becoming Bishop of Tarsus in Cilicia (from 376 to his death some time before 394) he had lived at Antioch where, first as a simple layman, then as a priest, he was one of the founders of resistance to the Arian bishops appointed by the Emperor Constantius : Leontius (344-357/8) and Euzoios (361-376). He belonged to the minority who remained loyal to Bishop Melitius during his long exile and therefore to one of the first hard cores of the neo-Orthodox party.

Against the Arians Diodorus stoutly defended the full divinity of the Word; in opposition to Apollinarius, on the other hand, he upheld the total humanity which the Word assumed in the Incarnation. This led him to draw a sharp distinction in Jesus Christ between the Son of God and the son of Mary — and, through her, the son of David. To draw a distinction does not necessarily mean to separate, but there was a danger of separation and Diodorus himself seems to have sensed it, for having drawn the distinction he felt the need of adding forcibly : ' but there are not two sons '[2], without being able to explain this unity in a very satisfactory manner.

The same approach to the Christological problem is to be found in Diodorus's pupils and successors. In fact Diodorus seems to have been virtually the head of a school. He was very erudite, a prolific writer and an excellent apologist : Julian the Apostate considered Diodorus his most gifted opponent. Thanks to his work as an exegetist the exegetic school of Antioch came into being, a school characterised by its emphasis on literal meaning and its reserve towards spiritual adaptation. Diodorus was an ascetic and a teacher of asceticism no less than a theologian. The most famous of his disciples, St John Chrysostom, was a catechist who usually avoided the thorny question of Christology; his formulas, balanced in masterly fashion, more than once anticipated later definitions by nearly half a century.

From the Christological point of view the true successor of Diodorus was Theodore of Mopsuestia. He, too, was first a priest of Antioch, then a bishop in Cilicia (392-428). His long intellectual and pastoral career, unlike that of his co-disciple and friend Chrysostom, passed without any storms : posthumously, however, his destiny was unusually tormented. Having died in the peace of the Church, respected for his learning and books, particularly for his works of exegesis, he was later held responsible for the blasphemies condemned in the person of his disciple Nestorius and solemnly anathematised a hundred and twenty-five years after his death (553). As a result of these disputes most of his writings have been lost or handed down in suspicious circumstances,

---

2. *Adversus Synousiastas*, fragm. 30-31, p. 271. Brière (*Revue de l'Orient chrétien*, 3e série, X (30), 1946).

and the echo of these past controversies is found today in the judgments of modern scholars, who remain very divided in their opinions of Theodore.

Taking account only of what seem to be his authentic works, we may say that Theodore follows in the steps of his master Diodorus and like him is especially concerned to resist the truncated Christology of the Arians and Apollinarianists : hence his insistence on the distinction of the two natures, divine and human, of the incarnate Word. The difficulty which then arises and which, even more than Diodorus, he was concerned to surmount is to know how these two components — the two *quids* — can make a single someone *(quis)*. Theodore took good care not to speak of two Lords or two Sons; the term to which he usually had recourse to formulate his answer, a term which later theologians decided they could not retain, was that of ' conjunction ' which he often qualified (perhaps dimly aware of the insufficiency and ambiguity of the term) with epithets of praise : an ' exact ' conjunction, ' marvellous and sublime ', ' ineffable and eternally indissoluble '[3]. As used in common parlance, the word in fact chiefly suggested the uniting of two different things, for example the uniting of man and woman who in marriage form one flesh, rather than the unity which results therefrom. Theodore, nevertheless, took care to safeguard what is called the communication of idioms and attributed to the man the titles of the Son of God, though not the weaknesses of man to the Divine Word. But since his fundamental concern was to ensure the full humanity of Christ — to make Christ assume everything which had to be saved — he was led by force of circumstances to meditate less on the mystery of God who lowered himself to our level than to throw light on man raised up, on the honours he receives, on his splendid destiny.

It is understandable that as dogma became better elaborated, so fears began to be felt about such a formula. Did it sufficiently respect the unique character of the Incarnation? Did it not draw too close a comparison between the Incarnation and the presence of God in the Christian soul through sanctification by sacramental grace? The catechesis of Theodore did in fact work out a whole spirituality of baptism and the Eucharist. Hence the suspicion later aroused by Theodore's favourite expressions, images which nevertheless were based on the very words of the Gospel : the ' dwelling ' of the Word among us (Jn 1 : 14) in the ' temple ' of his humanity (Jn 2 : 21).

Did this ' conjunction ', however close, avoid the danger of dividing Christ? In the case of Theodore the question certainly has to be faced

3. *Catechetical Homilies* V, 6, p. 107 Tonneau-Devreesse; VIII, p. 205 : VIII, 10, p. 199, 201.

and historians still debate the matter; the answer emerges clearly when we look at the verbal excesses of his disciple Nestorius.

Nestorius began as a monk near Antioch, then became a priest and famous preacher in that town before being summoned by the Emperor Theodosius II to the still disputed see of the capital city, Constantinople. As soon as he was enthroned (10 April 428), Nestorius gave free rein to his violent and headstrong character and to his rather blundering zeal : for example, he considered it opportune to intercede for the condemned Pelagians with Pope Celestine.   He immediately waged war on the heretics who swarmed in the capital, demanding that the imperial authorities intervene and himself taking the lead with energetic measures against them.   Naturally he aroused many enemies ready to seize on his blunders.

These were not wanting: the sermons which he ordered to be preached, or preached himself, brutally and almost aggressively expounded the most daring conclusions of the Antiochene theologians on the distinction of the two natures, denying that we can say with accuracy that the Word suffered during the Passion and, above all, refusing the Blessed Virgin Mary the title of ' Mother of God ' *(Theotokos)*.   Nestorius considered the title incorrect since she gave birth to a man, or at least dangerous and likely to help in masking Arian or Apollinarianist errors; he made as it were a scarecrow of this title, which was regularly used in Christian devotions and is attested in Egypt as early as the end of the third century.   He is also said to have refused to call the Infant Jesus — a baby of two or three months — by the name of God.   But his attack on the word Theotokos provoked the greatest scandal and brought about a crisis : it was not the last time that Mariology served as a touchstone to test the health of a theology and reveal the appearance of a germ of heresy.

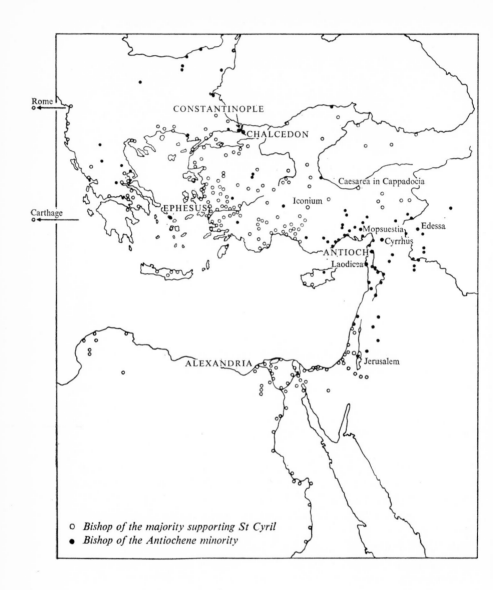

○ *Bishop of the majority supporting St Cyril*
● *Bishop of the Antiochene minority*

Labels on map: Rome, Carthage, CONSTANTINOPLE, CHALCEDON, EPHESUS, Iconium, Caesarea in Cappadocia, Mopsuestia, Edessa, Cyrrhus, ANTIOCH, Laodicea, ALEXANDRIA, Jerusalem

12   The Council of Ephesus

CHAPTER XXVIII

FROM THE COUNCIL OF EPHESUS (431) TO THE COUNCIL OF CHALCEDON (451)

SUCH excesses of language immediately provoked widespread and indignant reactions : at Constantinople among both clergy and laity alike, for in Byzantium everyone took a passionate interest in theology; at Rome, however badly informed it might be — at one point a letter from Nestorius had to wait several months for a reply because no one able to translate it could be found; and in Egypt, especially at Alexandria where the bishop, St Cyrial, became a fierce opponent of the unhappy Nestorius. There was traditional hostility between the sees of Alexandria and Constantinople, and doubtless too St Cyril was giving expression to his fiery, dominating temperament; but the opposition was rooted deeper than that, at the level of theology.

It would be artificial to maintain, as has too often been done, that Alexandria and Antioch represent two parallel doctrinal traditions persisting through the generations and centuries. In fact, it was the Christological problem which gave birth to the School of Antioch with Diodorus and Theodore of Mopsuestia; and it is with Cyril that a strictly Alexandrian theology appears. The opposition between them is none the less radical for being more recent.

The Nestorian affair gave St Cyril the opportunity of developing his thought, but he had already worked out its essential points. It centres entirely around one main intuition : for him the subject of the Incarnation is the second person of the Trinity, and this theocentric Christology develops from a consideration of the Divine Word which for us and our salvation humbled itself to man's estate. His first reaction to

Nestorianism was quite naturally expressed in these words : ' for if our Lord Jesus Christ is God, how can it be that the Holy Virgin who gave birth to Him is not the Mother of God, Theotokos '[1]? The primary, fundamental fact is the divinity of Christ; with St Cyril this is a deep emotion amounting almost to an obsession, but it is also what Christian faith and devotion have always considered essential. We can understand why the Church has continued to regard St Cyril as the Doctor *par excellence* of the Incarnation, despite his plain-spokenness and the stiffness of his formulas which with the rapid growth of theological thought were soon to become archaic and ambiguous.

To elaborate his doctrine St Cyril made use of the materials furnished by the ecclesiastical traditions that were accessible to him, starting with the work of his great predecessor St Athanasius. But this was nearly a century old and provided little direct help in the problems facing St Cyril about 430. That this Alexandrian, or rather Cyrillian, Christology possesses new, not to say improvised, features is clear from the fact that St Cyril, taking up any available weapons without much critical sense, was led to use the Apollinarianist apocrypha which circulated under the names of Athanasius himself or other equally respected writers. Believing Athanasius to be the author, Cyril used the formula forged by Apollinarius : μία φύσις. . . This seemed to him to express wonderfully well the sense of ' unity of being ' given by him to a term which if translated by ' nature ' would entail falling into the Monophysite heresy. By ' unity of being ' Cyril meant the unity of person of the incarnate Word, but this latter notion was clearly distinguished only from the sixth century onwards. If St Cyril is the first to use the famous expression ' hypostatic union ' (ἕνωσις ὑποστατική) it is simply with the meaning of ' real, true ' union and not in the technical sense it later assumed of union ' according to the person '. It remains true that this theme of the indissoluble unity between God and man in the Incarnation plays a very characteristic and important role in St Cyril's thought.

With this in mind the promptness and violence of his reaction to Nestorius is understandable. St Cyril hastened to put the monks of Egypt on their guard and wrote his opponent long letters which are both diplomatic notes and dogmatic treatises. He wrote to the court of Constantinople, trying to enlighten and win the support of the Emperor and the princesses who exercised so much influence on the mind and heart of the weak Theodosius II, his eldest sister Pulcheria and his wife Eudocia. As in the Arian crisis in the time of St Athanasius, the

1. *Epist. ad monachos Aegypti*, 4, p. 11, 28-29 Schwartz (*Acta Concil. Oecum.*, I, 1, 1).

Rome-Alexandria axis was in full swing; Pope Celestine received from Cyril a full account of the affair, prudently translated into Latin; in a Roman Synod (11 August 430) he condemned Nestorius, threatened him with deposition if he did not retract, and gave St Cyril himself orders to carry out this sentence.

Cyril was not a man to hesitate. Interpreting in broad terms the mission entrusted to him, he drew up a long document which the docile Egyptian bishops at once ratified, expounding his own Christological doctrine in terms of great technical precision and ending by condensing it into twelve propositions or anathemas. All these formulas today belong to the theological patrimony of the Church but more than a century had to pass before they were definitively integrated; by then the debates which had meanwhile arisen made it possible to add to them the necessary corollaries, interpretations, limitations and accompaniments.

In the autumn of 430 they were still merely a private opinion yielding matter for dispute, especially in the eyes of the representatives of the School of Antioch, who were antagonised by their abrupt and aggressive form and saw in them only ambiguity and dangers. The formulas were also fiercely criticised not only by Nestorius but also by the best theologians of this circle, Andrew of Samosata and Theodoret of Cyrrhus.

Having been given formal notice not only to retract in accordance with the decision of Rome but to accept without further ado the theology of the opposite school, it is understandable that Nestorius should have become obdurate and protested (30 Nov. - 6 Dec. 430). He did so amid general agitation. Letters were exchanged thick and fast; from Rome, from Alexandria, from Constantinople letters were sent to the principal bishops; lobbying and intrigues increased at the Imperial court. The idea of settling the matter by a council was soon accepted and as early as 19 November Theodosius II summoned for the following year at Ephesus what became the third Ecumenical Council.

The skilful manœuvering and sometimes rather ruthless energy of St Cyril disappointed any hopes which the friends of Nestorius may have expected from this gathering. In face of the delaying tactics of the Syrian and Cilician bishops grouped around John of Antioch, who were doubtless in no great hurry to take part in the trial of a representative of their point of view, Cyril precipitated matters and opened the Council on 22 June 431. Nestorius, who refused to appear, was condemned and deposed. Cyril had not waited either for the Eastern representatives or for the Roman legates, who arrived at Ephesus, the former five days, the latter more than two weeks afterwards; but when they did arrive the Pope's legates confirmed (11 July) a decision so much in harmony with the judgment made eleven months earlier in Rome. Meanwhile the group of Eastern representatives had protested and, assembled in a counter-synod, had replied by claiming to depose Cyril himself and his ally Memnon, Bishop of Ephesus; at which the majority in support of Cyril, now numbering nearly two hundred bishops, countered by excommunicating John of Antioch and the thirty-four supporters remaining to him.

Confusion continued to grow owing to the intervention in various directions of the imperial civil servants at the Council, then of the Emperor himself who inevitably took up the matter and to whom, moreover, both sides appealed. A paradoxical situation arose : for some weeks Nestorius on the one hand and St Cyril and Memnon on the other were all considered as deposed, put under arrest and kept hidden. As negotiations were continued the intrigues redoubled and were accompanied, as was normal at that time, by attempts to bribe influential people at court. Christians in general, especially the monks, felt involved in these dogmatic debates and cared about them passionately, even more so than during the period of Arianism. It was a sign of the times that the common people became agitated and sometimes even rioted.

If Theodosius II ended by seeming to lean towards the majority party, he nevertheless refused to condemn that of the Eastern bishops and he dismissed the Council on a severe note, deploring that it had failed in its task of reconciliation (October 431).

Those under arrest were set free and went back to their sees, except only Nestorius who, still deposed, was replaced and withdrew to a convent near Antioch. His presence in such a place could not fail to arouse new waves of excitement; four years later he was sent to the depths of the Egyptian desert, and about 450 ended his life in this painful exile.

Supported by similar conciliatory action on the part of the new Pope Sixtus III, the Emperor soon renewed his efforts for peace. Through the intermediary of a trusted civil servant negotiations were opened between the heads of the two parties, John of Antioch and Cyril of Alexandria, but they proved long and difficult. It is much to the credit of these two great bishops that they forgot their differences and the violent quarrels of Ephesus and persevered until they reached final agreement. This was sealed in April 433 by an exchange of letters in which each made use of a single profession of faith; that of St Cyril, justly famous, begins significantly with the words : ' Let the heavens rejoice and the earth tremble with gladness ' (Ps 96 : 11), ' the wall which separates us is now demolished ' (Eph 2 : 14)[2]. The agreement rested

2. *Laetentur Coeli*, 1, p. 15. Schwartz (*Acta Concil. Oecum.*, I, 1, 4).

on mutual concessions. Antioch, on the one hand, accepted the condemnation of Nestorius and of his pernicious doctrine (for good reason no further details were given); on the other hand, St Cyril renounced his plan of imposing his own ideas and contented himself with accepting the text of a *Credo* drawn up by Antioch and declaring on his own responsibility that it expressed the faith of the Church.

This *Credo*, with the exception of one phrase added in conclusion, which corrected on an important point one of the most debated of Cyril's anathemas, was the same profession of faith addressed to the Emperor Theodosius in the month of August, 431 by the counter-synod of Eastern bishops. Its text has sometimes been called the 'creed of Ephesus' and the description would seem to be justified. Far better than the minutes of the tumultuous sessions of the Council proper, it bears witness to the ground gained in the working out of the dogma. At the doctrinal level it condenses the contribution of this serious crisis. Although drawn up by Eastern bishops, this profession of faith is not strictly Antiochene in inspiration and it represents a remarkable effort of synthesis between the two rival theologies; the ambiguous 'conjunction' has been replaced by the peculiarly Cyrillian term 'union' (ἕνωσις, *unitio*), but qualified by the epithet 'without confusion' (ἀσύγχυτος) which safeguards the distinction of the two notions[3].

Like every compromise solution, that which took place in 433 left the extremists on both sides unsatisfied. Cyril had to reassure those of his supporters who were uneasy at such concessions. His explanations show, moreover, that if in the interests of peace he knew the importance of not demanding too much from the other side, he himself remained just as closely attached to the doctrine expressed by his anathemas. On his side, John of Antioch had to use diplomacy and patience in order to obtain the support of his friends; he was obliged, moreover, to exile a few diehards. It is worth bearing in mind one incident in these troubled proceedings : in 435 the second successor of Nestorius in the see of Constantinople, Proclus, replied to a memorandum presented by three Armenian priests. In the course of a long exposition of faith he proposed a new Christological formula which was destined to play an important role in later disputes. 'We confess', he said, 'the Incarnation of the Divine Word, one [of the persons] of the Trinity' (τὸν ἕνα τῆς Τριάδος, *unum de Trinitate*)[4]. This was a less reserved formula than those of the creed of 433. Cleverly touched up by the Monophysites who replaced the word 'incarnate' by 'crucified', it served as grist to their propaganda mill; later we shall find it retrieved by orthodoxy.

3. *Acta Concil. Oecum.*, I, 1, 4, p. 15, 5 (= Denzinger[31], 5003).
4. *Tomus ad Armen.*, 21, p. 192, 7. Schwartz (*Acta Concil. Oecum.*, IV, 2).

Some years passed during which a new generation came to office. In 440 St Leo succeeded Sixtus III at Rome, John of Antioch died about 441-2, St Cyril died in 444 and his successor Dioscorus unfortunately inherited only his defects in exaggerated form; at Constantinople Flavian succeeded Proclus in 445. Of those who had taken part in the Nestorian crisis, only the great Theodoret survived, until 457-8 or even perhaps 466-8; the Emperor Theodosius II died in 450 and the energetic Pulcheria then came to the throne of the Eastern Empire with Marcian as her colleague.

The Christological disputes again broke out in 447 and 448, when opposition began to appear against the ideas professed by Eutyches, an old monk of Constantinople who was another survivor of the generation of Ephesus, belonging this time to the anti-Nestorian party. Eutyches was archimandrite or superior of a monastery numbering more than three hundred monks, he enjoyed a strong position at court and he was in touch with all those supporters of St Cyril's theology throughout the East who could not resign themselves to the union of 433. We can easily understand why Theodoret was the first to attack him in the three books of his *Eranistes* (447).

With Eutyches appears the heresy called Monophysite. The tendency which it embodies is diametrically opposed to Nestorianism, and can be defined as an excessive emphasis on what comes from God in the Incarnation, to the prejudice of the strictly human element. When due allowance has been made for the clumsiness and exaggerations inherent in polemical writing and for tendentious interpretations, it is a much more difficult matter to discover at what moment this tendency was pushed too far and led Eutyches into formal heresy. The chief charge against him is that he declared Jesus Christ to have been formed ' from two natures ' (ἐκ δύο φύσεων); if, argued his opponents, there are really two natures before the union, only one remains in the union; whence a literal and thereby excessive interpretation of the Apollinarian and Cyrillian formula : ' unique is the nature of the Word Incarnate '. Eutyches seems to have felt considerable repugnance to accepting the second part of the perfectly balanced formula of the creed of Ephesus : ' consubstantial with us in humanity '.

Eutyches was denounced to the Bishop of Constantinople by the same Eusebius who in 428 had been the first to attack Nestorius, and who had meanwhile become Bishop of Dorylaeum. The Church always has bloodhounds of orthodoxy like Eusebius; a similar role was played by Epiphanius of Salamis in the previous century. Eutyches was condemned on 22 November 448 by a Synod summoned in Constantinople and at once appealed against this decision. Supported by Dioscorus of Alexandria and by his protector the eunuch Chrysaphius, at that time all-powerful with the Eastern Emperor, he persuaded Theodosius II to call (30 March 449) a new ecumenical council which appropriately was also held at Ephesus.

At this point Pope St Leo intervened. That was an event of great importance, for it seems that Rome had learned a lesson from its embarrassing position after the Nestorian affair when it had been reduced to using intermediaries whose competence and impartiality were open to doubt. Moreover the strong personality of so great a pope as St Leo (440-461) was also a significant factor. Not content, as custom decreed, to designate legates to represent him, he went to the heart of the matter in a letter addressed to the Bishop of Constantinople, the famous *Tome to Flavian* (13 June 449), a document conceived with a deep knowledge of the problem and formulated with clarity and precision. Two years later the text was used to draw up the definition which the Church has retained as the most perfect expression of the Christological dogma.

The solution of the problem was delayed by the painful episode of the ' Robber Council ' of Ephesus. The proposed council had been carefully prepared by the friends of Eutyches; Theodoret, for example, had been forbidden to attend and Dioscorus chosen to preside. The latter, inspired by the prompt methods which St Cyril had used and giving free rein to his impetuous nature, conjured away the Pope's document, intimidated the majority, and silenced those who protested. As a result he obtained the rehabilitation of Eutyches, the deposition of his enemies, Flavian, Eusebius, Theodoret, and with the latter some of the chief representatives of the school of Antioch, all considered Nestorians (August 449).

In vain did the victims appeal; in vain was such violence attacked by the Pope, by the Gaulish and Italian bishops whom he alerted, and by the Western Court of Valentinian III who was both cousin and son-in-law of Theodosius II. The Emperor at Constantinople remained unbending. His unexpected death (28 July 450) resulted in one of those dramatic *coups* so frequent under totalitarian regimes : Chrysaphius was removed from office and soon executed, Marcian and Pulcheria protested their loyalty to the Pope, while the bishops became docile and hastened to toe the new line. At the express desire of the sovereign a new ecumenical council was held at Chalcedon, near Constantinople, from 8 October to 1 November 451.

More than five hundred bishops took part representing all the provinces of the Eastern Empire from Egypt to Illyria, a tumultuous crowd which was controlled with difficulty by the senior civil servants in charge of regulating the debates. It was easy to annul the acts of the ' Robber Council ' of Ephesus; with due solemnity Flavian was posthumously rehabilitated, while Dioscorus, who remained obstinately Monophysite, was in his turn deposed.   Not until the end of the Council was the case of Theodoret settled; he ended by reluctantly making a formal condemnation of his co-disciple Nestorius, something he had always refused to do even after 443.

For there were still two opposed parties.   The Council of Chalcedon was a revenge for the Robber Council of 449, and not a revenge for the Council of Ephesus of 431, as the Monophysites later claimed it to be. Doubtless Leo's *Tome* was read and approved but it was also proclaimed to be in substantial agreement with the thought of St Cyril whose memory was solemnly acclaimed.   Only with difficulty was a decision taken to formulate a new creed, and approval finally given to its formula, which had been drafted in commission.

In essence it made use of the same basic terms as the *Tome to Flavian*, though it supplemented and elaborated them.   It confessed ' one single Christ, Son, Lord, Monogenic, without confusion, without change, without division, without separation, the difference of natures being in no way suppressed by the union, but rather the properties of each being safeguarded and reunited in a single person (πρόσωπον) and a single hypostasis '[5].

This creed was proclaimed on 25 October 451 at a formal session in the presence of the Emperor; he and the Empress were hailed as ' the torches of the orthodox faith ' : ' through you peace reigns everywhere!   Marcian the new Constantine, Pulcheria the new Helen[6] '! Such hyperboles were current coin at that period; the sequel was destined cruelly to belie their forced enthusiasm.

5. *Actio* V, 34 : *Acta Concil. Oecum.*, II, 1, 2, p. 325-326 (= Denzinger[31], 148).
6. *Actio* VI, 11 : *Ibid.*, p. 351.

SIRMIUM
Viminacium
Tomi
Ratiaria
Serdica
Marcianopolis
Scupi
Stobi
Adrianople CONSTANTINOPLE
THESSALONICA
Heraclea
Nicomedia Gangra Neocaesarea
Cyzicus Amasia
Ancyra Sebaste
Nicopolis
Sardis Eucarpia CAESAREA IN CAPPADOCIA
Corinth
Ephesus Iconium Tyana Ami
Aphrodisias Laodicea Antioch
in Pisidia
Side Tarsus Hierapolis Edessa
Myra Seleucia
Rhodes in Isauria ANTIOCH
CYPRUS Salamis
Tyre Bostra
Cyrene Caesarea
in Palestine
Marmarica JERUSALEM
ALEXANDRIA

.—.— *Ecclesiastical boundaries defined at the council of Constantinople (381)*
----   *Ecclesiastical boundaries defined at the council of Chalcedon (451)*
.... *Limits of use of Latin and Greek*
▒▒▒   *Mountains over 3000 feet*

13   Metropolitan Sees and Patriarchates of the Eastern Church

PLATE 37.   SIMEON STYLITES; PART OF A RELIQUARY IN BEATEN SILVER, PARTLY GILDED,
PROBABLY FROM HAMA IN SYRIA, 6TH CENTURY, LOUVRE, PARIS

This curious portrait of a curious saint shows him sitting
on his pillar, wearing a cloak and menaced by the serpent
who of course symbolises evil and temptation. (For the
story of St Simeon cf. ch. 32 and the note on plate 27.)

PLATE 38. BASKET OF LOAVES AND TWO FISHES; DETAIL OF MOSAIC FROM THE TRANSEPT BEHIND THE ALTAR, CHURCH OF THE MIRACLE OF THE BREAD AND THE FISH, ET TABGHA (HEPTAGEGON), ISRAEL, 5TH CENTURY

The church to which this mosaic belongs stands on what was believed to be the site of the miracle of the loaves and fishes, and this very restrained mosaic shows simply two fish and a basket of bread in which the four visible loaves bear the sign of the Cross. A comparison of this 'memorial' of a Holy Place with an example of those other 'memorials' of Holy Places, the Monza ampullae (Plate 33), shows a radically different treatment, and it is probable that this mosaic is executed in a genuinely Palestinian style of which the most famous example is the map mosaic from Madaba.

By permission of the Israel Embassy, London.

CHAPTER XXIX

THE ANTI-CHALCEDONIAN
OPPOSITION

FAR from putting an end to the problem raised by Eutyches, the Council of Chalcedon in fact proved the start of a long crisis which filled the end of the fifth century, the whole of the sixth century and lasted well beyond that. It was still going on when the Arab invasion burst on Eastern Christendom and the lacerations it caused in the very body of the Church are not yet healed, for a considerable part of the Eastern Churches today remain separated precisely because they still refuse to accept as valid the decisions taken in 451.

The unconditional support of the Imperial authority was insufficient to make the decisions acceptable even for the time being in all circles of the Church in the Eastern Empire. During the Council's sessions the insolent attitude of the delegation representing the monks of Constantinople, and the shocked feelings of the Egyptian bishops had already provided a foretaste of what was later to become a violent anti-Chalcedonian reaction, and a glimpse of the direction from which it would come.

The reaction appeared first in Egypt. We recall the strong unity of the Egyptian Church. Loyal to its tradition, it supported Dioscorus almost unanimously, despite his condemnation. Marcian deported him to the depths of Paphlagonia and imposed an orthodox successor by the use of violence — the army had to be called in and fierce street fighting took place — but all in vain : the mass of the people remained loyal to their deposed patriarch. When he died in 454 his supporters succeeded in getting one of their number appointed bishop, Timothy 'the Cat' (Αἴλουρος), while the other unfortunate candidate was soon assassinated. Timothy in turn was exiled but the new orthodox patriarch imposed by the Emperor did not enjoy a much more secure position than the old.   At the first opportunity — when the usurper Basiliscus disputed the throne with Zeno — Timothy again took possession of his see.   When he died in 477 another of the leaders of the same party succeeded him, Peter 'the Stammerer' (Μογγός), and his authority was finally recognised (482-489).

True, at Alexandria there still remained a small group of Chalcedonians; incidentally, Arius also had rallied some supporters in that city against Alexander and Athanasius.   The Chalcedonians asserted themselves in 482 when their leader, John Talaia, was consecrated bishop by his supporters and attempted to resist Peter Mongus.   But Talaia got no support from the Emperor and could not hold out; he had to flee and eventually escaped to Rome.   The anti-Chalcedonian opposition became so to speak the national religion of the Egyptian people.   Its authority was accepted in the interior of the country by the masses who, little affected by Greek influences, still used the old Coptic language.   Even in Alexandria Chalcedonian orthodoxy recruited most of its supporters from a Greek-speaking élite which ended by appearing almost foreign, and from circles near to the government, at least while the latter remained firmly attached to the doctrinal principles defined by the Council of 451.

Without meeting such general support everywhere, the opposition was not limited to Egypt alone.   It appeared likewise in Palestine, for example, where as an aftermath to Chalcedon the orthodox Patriarch Juvenal of Jerusalem was driven out and replaced by an unqualified priest; he regained his see only after the army had intervened and fought pitched battles against the hostile crowd of monks (453).   Brief though his sojourn was, the usurper had time to ordain bishops of his choice and install them almost everywhere.   These included Peter the Iberian, who was the son of one of the first Christian Kings of Georgia.   He had been brought up as a hostage in Constantinople, and after living as a monk first in Jerusalem, then near Gaza, he was consecrated Bishop of Maiouma.   He was driven out and fled to Egypt; we find him leaving the desert in order to consecrate Timothy Aelurus.   Until his death in 488 Peter continued to be one of the active figures in a party which had many active members.

The same tendency appears even in Syria, in the region around Antioch, which in the decade beginning 430 had been almost unanimous in its opposition to the theology of St Cyril.   Things had certainly changed : Nestorianism — to give this creed its traditional, though incorrect name — was so to speak drained away; doubtless it continued to exist, but only on the fringes, and finally beyond the very frontiers of the Empire.

True, the Syrian East did not rally to the opposite viewpoint in a completely unanimous way. Chalcedonians and Monophysites confronted one another and there were occasional mishaps and violence. This confused situation emerges clearly in the tormented career of Peter the Fuller, the first Patriarch of Antioch favourable to Monophysitism. From 464/5 to his death in 490 Peter the Fuller occupied the episcopal see on four different occasions, was thrice driven out and thrice reinstalled by means of intrigues supported by brawls; one of his orthodox competitors was savagely assassinated by angry Monophysites.

Although it found a larger audience in Syria than in Egypt, Chalcedonian orthodoxy in Syria often appeared to be a party which drew its strength from the support of the central government. It was the party of the ' Imperials ' — *Basilics* in Greek, *Melchites* in Syriac, and the latter name, of course, has been retained. Monophysitism was more deeply rooted in the country. One of the chief bishops installed by Peter the Fuller was Philoxenus or, better, Aksenaya, Metropolitan of Mabbug from 485 until his exile in 518/9. With Peter's help and even after Peter's death he played a leading role in the party of resistance. It is remarkable that he was a pure Syrian and wrote all his books in Syriac : books important both for their dogma and for their spirituality. It is understandable that modern historians should sometimes wonder, as in the case of the African Donatists, whether opposition to the council did not serve to express the rancour and rebellion of all those with complaints against the imperial power, and particularly the nationalist feelings of those Copts and Syrians hostile to Hellenism.

From the purely religious point of view it is certain that a theology suffers as well as gains from the protection accorded it by an oppressive power with its army and police. The Chalcedonian, Melchite Church depended too closely on such a power not to appear quite often as an over-official Church, too tied to the world, in some sense part of the civil service. The bishops on the whole were too inclined to follow the fluctuations of the religious policy adopted in the Palace of Constantinople. Five, or perhaps, seven hundred of them hastened to sign the *Encyclical* whereby Basiliscus anathematised the Council of Chalcedon (475); however, they all very quickly declared themselves Catholics in the time of Marcian and Leo; nearly all changed their views again when the usurper was beaten and orthodoxy returned to power with Zeno.

With the generation of St Cyril and Theodoret the golden age of the Church Fathers came to an end. We must wait a long time — until the seventh century and St Maximus the Confessor — before we again find among Catholics the equivalent of these great Doctors, spiritual writers and saints. In the fifth and sixth centuries the unfortunate fact remains that most of the great men and the strong personalities emerged among the Monophysites : for example, Peter the Iberian, Peter the Fuller and Philoxenus. Later we shall meet Severus of Antioch and James Baradaeus. These were all ' first-class men; to oppose them the Chalcedonians had no one of equal stature '[1].

Whatever one's opinion of their theology, Monophysites were often intensely religious and remarkable for their piety no less than for their liturgical and spiritual activity. We happen to have records of the liturgical changes on which Peter the Fuller based his propaganda : to the hymn of the *Trisagion* (Holy God, strong God, immortal God...) he added the incisive ' who was crucified for us ' (σταυρωθεὶς δι' ἡμῶν), which became the typical party slogan. Peter the Fuller was also responsible for a happier and more lasting change : it was he who introduced the Credo into solemn Mass — unless this was done by the Patriarch Timothy of Constantinople (511-518), who also held Mono-physite views. There was a polemical reason for this innovation. To return to the creed of Nicaea-Constantinople was to ignore and thereby reject the more recent Creed of Chalcedon. It is also interesting to observe the efforts made by the Monophysites to strengthen Christianity among the Arab tribes of the desert of Syria : they made it easier for these nomads to receive the Eucharist and to take part in the liturgy despite the absence of churches and indeed of regular altars.

This movement naturally attracted the most zealous souls, and won especial success in monastic circles : these always provided the Monophysites with a number of eager and resolute supporters. At certain moments the situation seemed to crystallize into the opposition of two parties : one Catholic — that of the bishops, and one anti-Chalcedonian — that of the monks. However, we must not make too much of this; with the exception once again of Egypt, Monophysitism was never unanimously accepted, even by the monks. In Palestine we find that certain monasteries remained loyal to orthodoxy : for example, that of St Euthymius in the years after 450, and at the beginning of the sixth century that of St Sabbas. At Constantinople the Chalcedonian tradition found tireless supporters in the community of the Acoemetae ('Ακοίμητοι, ' those who take no rest ', a reference to their practice of the *laus perennis*).

What we have just said is sufficient to show the considerable body of opinion supporting resistance to the dogmatic decisions taken in 451. In vain did the Emperors in turn try to break it : as we have seen, they put all the authority and strength they could muster at the service of

---

1. Ch. Moeller, in A. Grillemeier — H. Bacht, *Das Konzil von Chalkedon*, Würzburg 1959, vol. I, p. 645.

orthodoxy, not hesitating to exercise violence in order to impose orthodox bishops on those who proved recalcitrant, and to reinstate them when they had been driven out of their see.

Such a policy of vigorous intervention, practised, as we have seen, by the Emperor Marcian, was continued or resumed by his successors. These included Leo, Zeno (at least until 482), Justin I and Justinian. Justinian's intervention was marked by the nuances and sudden changes which we shall mention later in discussing his long reign, from 525 to 565. Justin II also intervened after 571. This repressive action was doubtless slowed down or checked by an influential opposition at the very centre of government : for example, the all-powerful General Aspar, an Alan, under Leo, and Justinian's wife, the Empress Theodora, who exercised a very effective influence in opposition to her husband's distinctly Monophysite views.

On the other hand it was natural that the Emperors, when faced with an obstinate and ultimately indomitable resistance, should sometimes have vacillated. Abruptly changing their attitude, they tried by turns a substitute policy, involving reconciliation with the opposition and, more exactly, reunion. This policy seemed likely to succeed because the doctrinal gap separating the orthodox and their opponents did not seem to be unbridgeably wide.

In October 457 the Emperor Leo considered it his duty if not to take up anew the Council of Chalcedon, at least to consult the bishops on the Council's decions. The bishops almost unanimously replied that they favoured loyalty to the Council. The first marked change of attitude took place under Zeno the Isaurian. After having worked to re-establish orthodoxy in the first years which followed his consolidation of power (476), in 482 Zeno promulgated an edict of union, *Henoticon*, under the influence of the Patriarch of Constantinople, Acacius, who himself had wavered considerably. The *Henoticon* condemned Eutyches as well as Nestorius and revered the memory of St Cyril and his twelve propositions. It mentioned the Council of 451 only in an indirect and pejorative manner : at the end of a rather vague statement of dogma it anathematised those who ' at Chalcedon or elsewhere ' might have held different views. It concluded with an appeal to unity around the Nicene Creed considered as the one official definition of faith. For thirty-six years Zeno and his successor Anastasius (491-518) tried to rally all the Empire round this ambiguous formula of union. The *Henoticon* was received with more or less open repugnance by the most convinced Monophysites — those in Alexandria, and in the monasteries of Egypt or Palestine — and appeared inadmissible to the most zealous Chalcedonians. The Chalcedonians were widely diffused : there was

John Talaia in Egypt, the Acoemetae in Constantinople and the Patriarch Calandion in Antioch; Calandion however was involved in a plot and deposed in 484, which led to the return of Peter the Fuller. Finally and most important, as might have been expected, Rome in the person of the energetic Felix III upheld the doctrine defined by St Leo, nad solemnly condemned both the *Henoticon* and Acacius. Thence arose a schism, one of the most important to separate Constantinople and Rome before 1054; it lasted thirty-four years (484-519) until the re-establishment of orthodoxy after the accession of the Emperor Justin.

True, the great majority of the Eastern bishops as always hastened to obey the imperial will, but the unity so obtained was purely formal. At the doctrinal level the very ambiguity of the edict of union, which was susceptible of different interpretations, encouraged the growth of the most diverse points of view.

This diversity emerged clearly during the reign of Anastasius. Anastasius was a great Emperor, whose home and foreign policy were happier than his religious policy. He himself was distinctly favourable to the Monophysites and became more and more openly so as time passed. For example, the successors of Acacius of Constantinople, while refusing to condemn the memory of their predecessor and while accepting the *Henoticon*, nonetheless remained at heart attached to the doctrine of the Council of Chalcedon; thereupon Anastasius deposed them one after the other, in 496 and in 511. Likewise in Syria and in Palestine the sees of Antioch and Jerusalem passed into the hands of titulars who, always under cover of the *Henoticon*, showed themselves to be closer to orthodoxy than their predecessors. They were opposed by the zealous Philoxenus of Mabbug. Philoxenus was one of the few survivors of the previous generation, for most of the players in the first act of this drama — Acacius and the three Peters, the Iberian, the Fuller and the Stammerer — died between 488 and 490. After many vicissitudes Philoxenus finally triumphed : in 512 the Patriarch of Antioch was deposed and replaced by the learned monk Severus. In 515 Severus caused a definitely anti-Chalcedonian interpretation of the *Henoticon* to prevail at the Synod of Tyre, in reaction against the moderate tendency which had until then flourished unchecked.

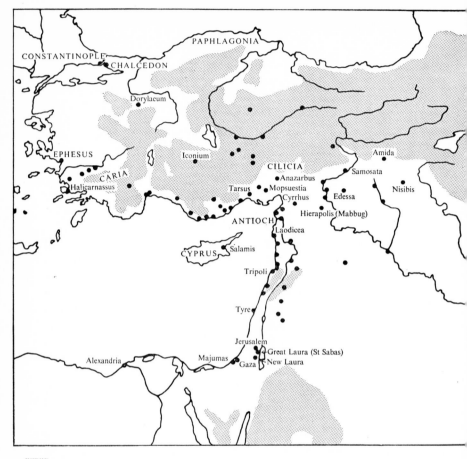

Mountains over 3000 feet

14   The spread of Monophysitism in the East

CHAPTER XXX

MONOPHYSITES
AND NEO-CHALCEDONIANS

SEVERUS of Antioch was a man of action, a tireless controversialist and a logical thinker. In the course of a long career abounding in contradictory episodes he showed himself to be the driving force of the anti-Chalcedonian opposition, notably in Syria-Palestine. Before he became bishop he appeared as spokesman at the head of a delegation of Palestinian monks at the Court of Anastasius, where he stayed from 508 to 511. Deposed by Justin, he fled to Egypt, where he exerted widespread influence : in the course of ten fruitful years of exile (518-527/8) he wrote many of his books. We find him again at Constantinople between 531/2 and 536, protected by Theodora, who was the defender of the Monophysite cause at the court of Justinian : condemned again, he ended his life an exile in Egypt (536-538). Severus of Antioch not only restored the situation of his party thanks to his energetic action in Syria; he likewise gave it doctrinal equipment and determined its theology : we can say that the Monophysitism of history, the doctrine which has lasted until modern times, is Severian Monophysitism.

We must now define the dogmatic content of this term which, although traditionally applied to the anti-Chalcedonian opposition, is very largely inappropriate. The doctrinal stand taken by Severus and the bulk of the party, either during his lifetime or after his death, is in fact very far from being the plain and outright heresy which the term may suggest. His views were subtle and are therefore sometimes difficult to grasp; their negative aspect is most readily apparent. Severus and his followers rejected with horror Leo's *Tome*, the definition of Chalcedon and their statements about the two natures, considering them tainted with Nestorianism, and even comparing them outright to Nestorianism. The positive aspect found its chief expression in a passionate, literal and total devotion to the teaching of St Cyril : the

Severians were obstinately attached to his vocabulary and continued to identify the ' nature ' (φύσις) with the hypostasis and with the person. At a deeper level — and here once again we detect a markedly spiritual note — their thought grew out of contemplation of the eternal Word; it was always on Him, on his divinity, that they meditated when they passed from the Trinity to the Incarnation, from the Son of God to Jesus Christ.   His unity was exalted above everything else, the two natures being distinguished only by virtue of a logical, not a real distinction.

But Severus of Antioch did not go as far as to tolerate the excesses of Eutyches, whom he considered as much a heretic as Nestorius.   It is typical of him that he should have attacked, in turn, a Chalcedonian like John the Grammarian and Neo-Eutychians like Sergius or Julian of Halicarnassus.   Henceforward heresy, if heresy there was, became merely an attitude, dangerous in itself although carefully controlled, its material content limited to a residual minimum.   Not without astonishment and regret the historian finds that in these long, bitter disputes which rent the Church, heresy as such counted for less than men's passionate attachment to their own will, than party spirit and obstinacy in schism.

In Egypt things were more complex.   The anti-Chalcedonian tendency — which for short we shall continue to call ' Monophysite ' — gained an almost total victory; from 482 to 537 the imperial power even gave up imposing a Chalcedonian patriarch there.   No longer under the necessity of fighting an external enemy, the party crumbled in Alexandria at least with the multiplication of rival doctrines; that was one of the aspects of the very brilliant cultural flowering which took place in Alexandria in the sixth century, and which was marked, at the philosophical level, by a renewal of Aristotelianism, especially in the fields of dialectic and logic.   The wholly new proficiency so gained was turned to theological use in this great town, a powerful centre of Hellenism installed on the fringe of the Coptic country.   In these passionate discussions, which were pushed to the extreme limit of subtlety, we again find the tradition of debate characteristic of Hellenistic philosophies.   The Monophysite party disintegrated into a series of sects and sub-sects; a score of them have been catalogued.

First of all, there were intransigent groups of those Dioscorians who did not recognise a legitimate patriarch since 454, Timothy Aelurus being disqualified in their view for having reconciled some Chalcedonian clerics.   They were known as the Acephali and subdivided into three grouplets by inner schisms.   They would not pardon Peter the Stammerer and his successors for having accepted the *Henoticon :* they formed a kind of little Church which continued even after the death of its last priest. At the doctrinal level they started out by being Eutychian; from 517/8 onwards the extremist tendency was embodied in the School of Julian of Halicarnassus, whose supporters were dubbed by their opponents Aphthartodocetae, because they believed that the body of the incarnate Word was incorruptible, or Phantasiasts, since this body was only an ideal form, a ' phantom '. This party split into two opposed wings. One wing adopted the moderate opinion of Severus of Antioch that the body of Christ was preserved from corruption by the power of the Word. The other wing was truly neo-Eutychian and held that the body of the Lord was not only incorruptible in itself but strictly ' increased ', hence their name of Actistetae.

The Severians themselves were scornfully described by their opponents as Pthartolaters, those who adored what was corruptible. The Severians gave rise to the School of Agnoetae : according to the Agnoetae, Christ in his humanity was ' ignorant ' of certain things. It is worth pointing out that from Arius to the Modernists the problem of Christ's human knowledge has continued to puzzle many thinkers.

A more noteworthy feature of these discussion groups was that interest ebbed from the strictly Christological problem back to the problem of the Trinity, which one might have thought had been exhausted. A single ' nature ' in the Incarnate Word, well and good; but then (given the ambiguity of this word among the Cyrillians) must one not distinguish at the very heart of the Trinity three natures, three essences, since there are three hypostases there? That view was to become the heresy stigmatised as tritheism; it appeared about 557 and became important during the decade beginning 560 through the fame of that remarkable man John Philoponus. Philoponus was a nickname meaning the ' Indefatigable ', unless we are to believe that ' Philoponus ' was a member of the confraternity of pious laymen of that name who ' spent ' themselves in the service of the Church. He was a learned man, bursting with energy; about 570 he wrote a treatise on the manner of the resurrection (he claimed that it involved the destruction of matter); this treatise aroused lively discussions and provoked a schism within his own sect. Criticism of tritheism, on the other hand, gave rise to the clumsy heresy of the Tetradites. The Tetradites held that the Divine nature is juxtaposed with those of the three persons, so that the Three become Four.

Such divisions sometimes weakened Monophysitism. About 556 we find four rival patriarchs disputing the throne of Alexandria, not to speak of a fifth titular, the Chalcedonian reinstated by Justinian. Anarchy reigned in Alexandria and the attempt to dispel it, from 575 onwards, led to a quarrel between the two Monophysite Churches of Egypt and Syria. Discord still persisted at the end of the century, but from another point of view this multiplication of doctrines appears as a sign of the party's vitality, its wealth of men and ideas.

Under these circumstances we can understand why theologians and politicians on the Catholic side pondered ways and means to end the schism. Unity imposed from without, as attempted by the *Henoticon*, had merely made confusion worse confounded; only at the dogmatic level could a solution be sought. Hence a tendency to draw as close as possible to the position fiercely held by the dissenters, to move forward to meet them.

As we have seen with Severus of Antioch, the distance which separated the Monophysites from orthodoxy properly understood was usually very small indeed.

This new attitude has sometimes been called by the slightly ambiguous name of Neo-Chalcedonianism; it was rather a Post-Chalcedonianism, a backward movement of the theological balancing-pole; an attempt, in fact, to make acceptable a ' revised and corrected ' edition of the Council[1] (such oscillations are almost the rule in the doctrinal history of the Church). After the blow struck in 451 surely, went the argument, it was right to make clear that in no sense did it amount to a revenge for the victims of the Council of Ephesus.

In fact we find that all those Catholic controversialists opposed to Severus of Antioch were no less concerned to burn their bridges with the Nestorians than was Severus to dissociate himself from Eutyches. Leontius of Byzantium is a good example. He, moreover, made by no means negligible progress in defining the concept of hypostasis. He defined it as ' that which exists by itself ' (τὸ καθ' ἑαυτό) and he applied this definition to the theology of the incarnate Word. The new tendency was expressed in this way : while firmly upholding the authority of the Council of Chalcedon and its definition, it swallowed increasingly strong doses of St Cyril's teaching, spirituality and terminology, for example the twelve anathemas.

1) The powerful impression made by Severus of Antioch during his first stay in Constantinople (509-511), if it did not give rise to the movement, seems at least to have contributed to its progress. Paradoxically it emerged immediately after the Emperor Justin came to the throne in 518 and once again imposed a policy favourable to the Chalcedonians. It was led by a curious group of Scythian monks established at Constantinople who thought they had found a panacea in the ' Theopaschite ' formula *Unus de Trinitate...* ' One of the Trinity suffered for us in the flesh '. This formula had been renewed

---

1. Liberatus of Carthage, *Breviarium,* 22, p. 208 Schwartz (*Acta Conc. Oecum.,* IV, ii).

or rather adapted by Proclus. In order to make it prevail with the Catholic authorities the Scythian monks acted in a zealous but sometimes muddle-headed way. In 520 Pope Hormisdas finally got rid of them; they returned to Constantinople, where they quarrelled more bitterly than before with the rival monastery of the Acoemetae, the recognised defenders of the Chalcedonian faith. Insults were hurled back and forth; treated as Eutychians by the Acoemetae, the Scythian monks replied by accusing the Acoemetae of pernicious Nestorianism.

2) In 532/3 the new Emperor, Justinian, yielding in his turn to the attractive policy of union, and influenced also by Theodora, held a quarrelsome conference between representatives of the orthodox and the Severians. The intransigence of the latter practically wrecked it but the Emperor came away from the conference convinced of the necessity of making yet another step towards the opposite camp. On 15 March 533 he enacted a profession of faith drawn up in a way that would give the greatest possible satisfaction to Monophysite susceptibilities. He passed over in silence Chalcedon and the two natures and, in order to express the Christological dogma, used the formula set aside thirteen years earlier : *Unus de Trinitate....* The following year he obtained from Pope John II acceptance of this Theopaschite formula and condemnation of the Acoemetae who persisted in rejecting it (25 March 534); significantly, these two decisions were given a prominent place in the second edition of the *Justinian Code* promulgated in this same year 534[2]. In a contemporary document addressed to the Roman Senators Pope John II quotes among the authorities invoked to support his action the most important of the twelve anathemas of St Cyril : ' anathema to him who does not confess that the Word suffered in the flesh... '. For the first time this long disputed document was officially and explicitly approved by the Church of Rome.

3) Justinian was soon obliged to recognise that his will to appeasement always ran up against the obstinacy of the Monophysite party; he resumed with greater brutality the policy of repression by the police, without however losing hope of bringing the rebels to reason. Urged on not only by the Empress but by Origenist monks from Palestine anxious to re-establish their good name after their recent condemnation, he decided on a new approach in order to make clear in a still more solemn manner the gulf separating the Chalcedonian position from detested Nestorianism. The Monophysites argued now, as they had done at the time of the conference in 532/3, from the fact that the Council of Chalcedon had re-established the good name of three of the victims

2. *Codex Justinian.*, I, i. 6 and 7.

of the ' Robber Council ' of Ephesus : the great Theodore of Mopsuestia, who was a forerunner of Nestorius, the latter's friend Theodoret and finally their disciple Ibas of Edessa. Ibas was the most vulnerable because he had written a *Letter to Mari* in which he bluntly expressed strong criticism of St Cyril and his anathemas.

In 543/4 Justinian published a new dogmatic edict condemning what has come to be called the *Three Chapters*, that is to say a collection of texts attributed, sometimes with scanty justification, to the above-mentioned three authors. As he simultaneously proclaimed his loyalty to Chalcedon, this new move produced no effect on the Monophysites whom he was trying to reconcile; on the contrary it plunged the Church into a confused and painful crisis.

The condemnation of the *Three Chapters* was accepted by the Eastern patriarch, though with rather ill grace, but it ran up against strong opposition from the West. Because Western theologians ran no risk of yielding to Monophysite temptations, they were all the more constant in their loyalty to the dogma defined by St Leo and the Council of Chalcedon.

Justinian decided to ensure the support of Pope Vigilius. He had the Pope seized and in January 547 brought to Constantinople, where he was confined. He was to remain there for more than seven years under inhuman pressure from the imperial court which used now persuasion, now threats. The unhappy Vigilius was a sick old man. He resisted for a long time, yielded with his *Judicatum* of 11 April 548, negotiated again, broke with the Emperor in August 551, took refuge at Chalcedon and solemnly retracted in his Encyclical of 5 February 552. He was brought back to Constantinople and ended by yielding again, but the formula he worked out in the *Constitutum* of 14 May 553 was not judged explicit enough; he had to bend even farther to the imperial will and published a formula which finally satisfied the Emperor, the *Constitutum* of 23 February 554.

To satisfy Justinian, Vigilius was obliged not only to declare materially heretical a group of texts which had been manipulated in such a way as to give an impression of Nestorianism but also to anathematise retrospectively Theodore of Mopsuestia as a person, though he had died in the peace of the Church more than one hundred and twenty years earlier. Meanwhile, to support his demands, the Emperor had published a second doctrinal edict (June 551) and convoked and assembled a Council in Constantinople — the fifth Ecumenical Council (5 May - 2 June 553).

Theologians still debate the precise implication to be attached to the documents signed by Vigilius and the authority possessed by the various decisions of the fifth Council. From 26 May onwards, at Justinian's request, the Council considered Vigilius as deposed. However, the Council did not go so far as to excommunicate him or break with the apostolic see; it drew a too convenient distinction between the latter and the person of the Pope who occupied it, *inter sedem et sedentem.*

Whether sincere or forced, total or partial, approval was in fact given to the fifth Council by Pope Vigilius and then after his death (June 555) by his successor, the same Pelagius who until his accession had proved himself an eloquent and courageous defender of the *Three Chapters.* This approval immediately produced serious disruptions within the Latin Churches. We shall discuss them presently. In the East, at the doctrinal level, the contribution of the affair of the *Three Chapters* was, all told, rather meagre. The Nestorian danger, against which it was claimed so many precautions were taken, was not the most immediate threat to Greek theology. The rather too exclusive nature of the approval granted to the tradition stemming from St Cyril set Eastern thought on a road soon found to be bristling with traps. If too much stress was laid on the divinity of the incarnate Word, the full humanity of the latter was in danger of being undervalued, if not of losing its integrity. This was shown by the new heresies which appeared at the beginning of the seventh century — Monoergism and Monothelism — and by the fierce battles they aroused.

At the legal level Justinian's immense efforts, pursued with such obstinacy, proved to be absolutely sterile : from the moment when the Monophysites were not granted express condemnation of the Council of Chalcedon (and they firmly decided not to be content with less), all hope of reuniting them to the Catholic Church was lost. Justinian soon realised this and renewed his policy of persecution and police terror towards them.

When his long reign ended (527-565), the old Emperor, an impenitent theologian, had just embarked on a new venture. He claimed to impose on the Church (though of course protesting his attachment to Chalcedon) the most disputed doctrine of the Monophysite extremists : the incorruptibility of the human body of Christ, Aphthartodocetism. His death cut short this plan, which would certainly have complicated ecclesiastical matters still further. He left his successors at grips with the still unsolved Monophysite problem. They did not make a better showing than he. Justin II again tried a policy of appeasement and promulgated an edict of union, *Henoticon*, which was renewed by Zeno in 567. Finally, as the Monophysites' resistance stiffened, they were again persecuted (571-578). The relative mildness of Tiberius II (578-582) and the open tolerance of Maurice (582-602) did not obtain better results.

Meanwhile, to be exact in the decade starting 540, the situation of the Monophysite party changed profoundly. For a long time it had seemed to be a kind of attitude within the Church : through a change in circumstances Monophysites might for a time occupy an episcopal see, direct such and such a monastery, or find a majority in some given region; but now we are dealing with a real Church, separated. Unity is broken.

The violent repressive measures taken by Justin and later by Justinian, if they did not wipe out the Monophysites completely, at least dealt them severe blows. Their leaders, deposed or exiled, disappeared one after the other; ordination of priests carried out hastily and almost in secret could not suffice to fill the gaps in their ranks caused by death : for lack of bishops and priests the party was threatened with extinction. It was saved thanks to the energetic but patient action of one man, James Baradaeus, whose Syriac sobriquet means ' the ragged '.

In 542/3 at the request of the sovereign of the Ghassanid Arabs, who was a sincere Christian but a Monophysite, and of Theodora, James Baradaeus was consecrated bishop by the Patriarch of Alexandria, Theodosius, who had been deposed in 537 but was still resident in Constantinople under the protection of the Empress. James Baradaeus set himself the task of reviving his greatly diminished party. Disguised as a beggar (hence his sobriquet), he travelled throughout the East from Asia Minor to Egypt, evading the police and ordaining many priests. He hurried to Alexandria, called a Synod of the bishops there and managed to snatch Egyptian Monophysitism from the anarchy in which it was engulfed.

At the end of a dozen years he took the decisive step of giving the dissident party a complete autonomous hierarchy, regularly instituted; he had two of his companions consecrated in Egypt so that the three of them could validly consecrate metropolitans and bishops. In 560 he eventually succeeded in installing at Antioch a Monophysite patriarch; this patriarch resumed the tradition interrupted since the time of the great Severus, who had died in 538 but been deposed in 518. James Baradaeus likewise consecrated a second successor three years later. Tradition holds that besides these two patriarchs he consecrated twenty-seven bishops, twelve of them in Egypt, and a hundred thousand priests — but we must make allowances for oriental exaggeration. He continued his work unflaggingly; on the eve of his death in 578 he was still trying to reconcile the two separated branches of Egypt and Syria. Even if he failed to complete his work at every level, he laid the foundations of an autonomous Monophysite Church, having cut all bridges with Catholic orthodoxy. In his memory it is quite rightly known even today as the Jacobite Church.

CHAPTER XXXI

THE FATE OF THE CHURCHES OUTSIDE THE EMPIRE

THE result of these upheavals was no less grave for the Churches outside the Roman Empire, from Ethiopia to the Caucasus : before the end of the fifth century they too became ' separated Churches '.

1. The Persian Church becomes Nestorian

In 410, as we have seen, the Church of the Eastern Syrians, recruited largely in the Semitic provinces of the Sassanid Empire, was bipolar in structure : the centre of the hierarchy at Seleucia-Ctesiphon, the intellectual centre at the school of Edessa, in Roman territory. Just like Antioch, the see of Edessa was torn by the Christological disputes which came to a head in Syria in the first half of the fifth century : St Cyril's theology was one moment supported, the next moment attacked. Rabbula strongly favoured St Cyril, especially in the final years of his episcopate, which lasted from 415 to 435/6, but he was succeeded by the high-spirited Hiba (or Ibas), one of the future victims of the affair of the *Three Chapters*, and already exiled by Rabbula for his hostile attitude when in charge of the Persian school.

From 437 to 457 under the direction of Narsai the school itself remained firmly attached to the ' Antiochene ' or ' Nestorian ' tradition. But gradually the opposite tradition triumphed in Syria : even the pure Chalcedonians, we have seen, declared themselves more and more loyal to the teaching of St Cyril. This finally made their opponents' position impossible. In 457 those responsible for the school crossed the frontier and settled at Nisibis (a Persian town since 363), where classes were resumed. The school of Edessa was closed by the Emperor Zeno in 489 : a decision which may have owed something to the action of Philoxenus of Mabbug, himself a former pupil of the school, whose role in the growth of the Monophysite party we have noted.

The school of Nisibis was finally reorganised, still under the direction
of Narsai, who died only in 502 at about the age of a hundred, and
it was protected by the local Bishop, Barsumas, also a firm supporter
of the same anti-Cyrillian theology. The school of Nisibis had a wide
influence among Sassanid Christians and contributed to the triumph
in that region of the Nestorian Christology, which was finally officially
accepted by a general Synod of the Churches of the Persian Empire
held in 486 at Seleucia.

We must here repeat what we said in our discussion of the
' Monophysitism ' of Severus : the term ' Nestorian ' has to be treated
as a traditional label used in history, with a meaning which cannot
always be guaranteed.   In fact, apart from their refusal to join in
condemning Nestorius the man, the heresy of these Persian Churches
is difficult to discover.   We must leave to theologians the task of
appraising possible shortcomings or dangers in their formulation of the
distinction of the two natures in the Incarnate Word; for us it is enough
to note that they were strictly faithful to the teaching of Theodore of
Mopsuestia, considered a master to be followed in every matter,
particularly as the best interpreter of Scripture.   Indeed, his Syriac
surname means ' Interpreter '.

Here again what comes to light is less an explicitly professed heresy
than a will to schism.   A will which seems to have been quite conscious :
some sources, admittedly Monophysite and therefore hostile, assert that
Barsumas had obligingly explained to the Sassanid ruler, the Shahinshah
Peroz (457/9-484), that it would be to his political advantage to cut
off christians under his rule from the Churches of the Roman Empire,
his hereditary enemy.   He used this as an argument to obtain help from
the secular arm in his struggle with the Monophysites, who, as we have
seen, were strongly entrenched among the Arab tribes of the Syrian
desert and had made some progress in Upper Mesopotamia.

But these tactical precautions were insufficient to disarm the ingrained
hostility of Mazdaism, the only true national religion of the Sassanid
State.   Hence many persecutions (there had already been persecutions
in 420, 421/2 and 445-7); the threat of these continually weighed on the
Church of the Eastern Syrians, which was very rich in martyrs.   It
enjoyed real tolerance only during the short periods when the evolution
of foreign policy obliged the king to conciliate the Roman Empire :
for example, under Bahram V after the victories of Ardabur, the general
of Theodosius II (422), or at the beginning of the reign of Khosrov II,
who owed his throne to the support of the Emperor Maurice.   Persecution
revived, however, as soon as relations worsened between the two rival
countries, as in the time of Khosrov I and Justinian (540-545), or of

Khosrov II and Heraclius (602 and the following years; the see of the Catholicos was again to remain vacant for many years : from 609 to 628). The Persian Church suffered likewise from troubles within its ranks such as disputes over elections, schisms and anarchy. Fortunately it enjoyed a period of vigour under the catholicate of a great reformer, Mar Aba (540-552) who overcame many difficulties and managed to restore order and discipline. In spite of so many obstacles Christianity succeeded not only in maintaining its strength but in making progress within Sassanid society, finding converts among the ruling class, and even in the royal family and Mazdaean priesthood.

Missionary work continued to make progress in the mountains of Kurdistan where even today the last Nestorian communities — the Assyrians — are to be found; it also extended towards Central Asia and India. The Hephtalite Huns, living on the banks of the Amu Darya, asked Mar Aba to send them a bishop in 549. The Alexandrian traveller, Cosmas, who voyaged in the Indian Ocean during the years 520-525 (whence his surname Indicopleustes) tells of a Church organised in the Island of Socotra and of a colony of christians of Persian origin as far off as Ceylon. The Syro-Malabar Church, which still flourishes today in Kerala (South India), perhaps owes its origin to Nestorian missionaries; or to groups of emigrants driven out by persecution. The tradition which links this Church to the memory of the apostle St Thomas may simply express its distant descent from the Church of Edessa.

As time went on, the Nestorian Church became isolated from the rest of Christianity. In 420, continuing the work of the Council of 410, the Persian Church had again been forced to observe the discipline laid down by the fourth-century Councils in Greek countries, whereas in 424 it proclaimed its canonical independence of the Western Churches. Contacts, when resumed, were merely on a personal basis : thus we find certain representatives of the Eastern Syrians at the Court of Constantinople in the years 525-532/3. The Nestorian Church henceforth developed according to its own rhythm. In 484 Barsumas made it lawful for bishops to marry; that was a concession to national custom. Evidently the Persian Church considered it enough to resist on essential points the pressure exercised by the dominant religion, by opposing, for example, the incestuous unions extolled by Mazdaism. Defence of Christian teaching on this point was later one of the main concerns of Mar Aba. In theology and especially in Christology the Church's position hardened; when one of the masters in the school of Nisibis, a certain Henana, urged the adoption of a slightly different doctrine nearer to Catholic orthodoxy, he was excommunicated in 585 and his supporters pitilessly persecuted.

Moreover, the ardent proselytism of the Monophysites, from Philoxenus of Mabbug to James Baradaeus, extended also to Persian territory. Despite all their efforts, the Nestorians never managed to eliminate these rivals, who here, as in the Roman East, ended by organising themselves as a separate Church with their own network of bishops and monasteries, especially numerous in Northern Mesopotamia. This parallel hierarchy was unified under the authority of a supreme see, established by Baradaeus himself in 559 at Takryt on the Tigris : in the seventh century its titular received the title of *maphriana*.

2. Armenia and the countries of the Caucasus torn between Monophysitism and Chalcedonianism

The attitude taken by the Armenian Church and its neighbours was even more complex. We must make a clear distinction both of time and place. During the second half of the fifth century all the strength of Armenian Christianity was spent in obstinate and ultimately successful resistance to Sassanid oppression and Mazdaean persecution. It virtually stood aside from the Christological disputes : the only incident worthy of notice being its approach to Proclus of Constantinople in 435.

Beginning in 505/6, the Armenian episcopate became increasingly hostile to Nestorianism and to everything resembling it. This happened partly under the influence of the anti-Chalcedonian movement which was triumphing in Constantinople, partly under cover of the *Henoticon* during the reign of Anastasius, but chiefly as a result of the still active propaganda of Monophysites from Mesopotamia and later from Syria. Despite some converts in the opposite direction this movement gathered strength. Towards the middle of the sixth century the Council of Chalcedon was expressly condemned, along with the *Tome* of Leo and the interpolated phrase ' Crucified for us ' introduced into the Trisagion. From that moment onward Monophysitism became an integral part of the patrimony of this national Church.

This appeared clearly when the Emperor Maurice, having obtained from Khosrov II the Western part of Armenia in 562, tried to bring that region back in its entirety to Chalcedonian orthodoxy. He obtained the adherence only of the twenty-one bishops directly under his authority and thus provoked a schism, the first in the history of this closely united Church of Armenia (591/2-610/1). His overtures were rejected by all the other bishops, grouped round the Catholicos of Dvin, whose scornful reply is typical of the man : ' I will not cross the frontier to eat cake and drink tepid water ' — an allusion to the special Byzantine Eucharistic rites[1]. Evidently the Armenians used any argument, whether from Christology or the liturgy, to assert their individuality with regard to Constantinople!

Georgia had fallen under the Sassanid yoke, like Armenia but half a century later (499). In ecclesiastical affairs its Church, like that of the Albanians (or Aghouanghks), had associated itself with, and was partly dependent upon, that of Armenia. This special relationship was ratified at the Council of Dvin in 505/6.

When Georgia, with Byzantine help, recovered its independence in the reign of the Emperor Maurice, its Catholicos Kvirion took the opportunity of detaching himself from Armenia, both in canonical and theological matters. Moving closer to Byzantium in religion, as his king was doing in politics, he rallied Chalcedonian orthodoxy. In 608/9 he was solemnly excommunicated on the same grounds as the Greeks by the Armenian Catholicos, to whom, however, the christian community of Albania in the Caucasus (no longer in existence today) remained loyal. But for Armenia this was not a final choice.

We must not reduce the history of these Eastern Churches to mere debates about Christology, at the risk of overlooking their remarkable riches. Mainly during the fifth century there took place a cultural development, whose beginnings we have noted. The inventor of the Armenian alphabet, Mesrob, died as late as about 440. Armenian became a literary language and the ' Holy Translators ' began work on the Bible, the Fathers, and the canonical collections. Presently they also translated the disciplinary rules formulated in the national Council. A special liturgy was created and, finally, a native literature flourished. Before the middle of the fifth century a masterpiece appeared : a work of apologetics by Bishop Eznik of Kolb, directed especially against Mazdaism. History had an important place in this rich Armenian civilization, which expressed both the national genius and an authentic christian spirit. Music flourished also, and at a later date architecture : at the beginning of the seventh century Armenians built those beautiful domed churches which are perhaps a distant source of Romanesque art.

3.   The Church of Ethiopia grows within the framework of Monophysitism

Much the same may be said of the Church founded by St Frumentius : the fifth and sixth centuries were a glorious period when civilisation took root, expanded and flowered. But here the growth seems to have

1. ' Narratio de rebus Armeniae ', *PG* 132, c. 1248 B-1249 A.

been a little slower : for example, the translation of the Bible into Ge'ez was perhaps begun only during the second half of the fifth century, and finished only in the seventh. At the same time the basic monastic and theological texts were translated, while a national liturgy and christian art took shape.

The Ethiopian Church depended closely on that of Egypt, in fact not until 1951 did the *abuna*, the head of the Abyssinian Church, cease to be a Coptic dignitary appointed by Alexandria. It is therefore scarcely surprising that the Ethiopian Church drifted into Monophysitism. The basic book in its theological library was a patristic anthology known under the name of *Qerlos*, which, significantly enough, claimed to be sponsored by St Cyril and opens with three anti-Nestorian tracts by him. The Egyptian influence, however, was not the only one at work. The Ethiopian Church venerated the memory of the ' Nine Saints ' who came from the Roman Empire to Ethiopia and ' rectified the faith ' there. Apparently they were a group of Syrian monks, doubtless Monophysites, who sought refuge in Ethiopia at a critical moment of the Catholic persecution; but they may equally well have been Monophysite proselytes. They arrived possibly at the end of the fifth century.

Diplomatic relations with the court of Constantinople were opened sometime after 525 by the Ethiopian rulers, who had finally been converted to Christianity, and these might have led to a change of attitude favourable to orthodoxy, had not the Emperor Justinian's efforts in this direction been immediately thwarted by the enterprising Theodora, chief protector of the Monophysites.

4. Progress of Monophysite Christianity in Nubia and Southern Arabia

The same rivalry between opposed influences is to be found in the conversion of the more or less nomadic peoples of Nubia, between Abyssinia and Egypt (in what we now call the Sudan). These peoples — Blemmyers, Alodes, Nobades — were bellicose and feared by their two neighbours. For a long time they remained pagan. In their case, even after the general closing of the temples, the Christian Emperors had had to tolerate the cult of Isis in the famous sanctuary of Philae above the first cataract of the Nile. About 535 Justinian decided to end this tolerance. Shortly afterwards two missions, one Catholic, the other Monophysite, were sent to try and convert the Nobades. Theodora succeeded in intercepting the mission supported by Justinian : only the second was able to accomplish its task, and the christian community founded by it received its bishop from the Monophysite patriarch,

Theodosius of Alexandria, who had been relegated to Constantinople but was still active. The majority of the other peoples of Nubia were also converted to Christianity in the same way.

In the country of the Himyarites, present-day Yemen, Christianity continually met difficulties due as much to South Arabian paganism as to Judaism, which was making many converts there. On the other hand it was helped by the diplomatic activity of Justinian, always anxious to remove Sassanid influence from his frontier and from the shores of the Red Sea, and also by the progressive seizure of this region by the Ethiopians. Having reached its highest point, the Abyssinian Kingdom of Axum was in fact expanding first its commercial, then its political activity in Arabia. An initial expedition seems to date from the end of the fifth century. After a revolt led by a sheikh converted to Judaism, in the course of which many christians were massacred, the Negus sent a powerful army against the Himyarites and re-established the Ethiopian protectorate (525/6). Despite a number of vicissitudes, this lasted until the conquest of Yemen by the Persians in 570.

Thanks to the Ethiopian protectorate, the christian religion grew until it counted quite an important minority of the population, notably in the region of Najran, where it got the worse of an encounter with rising Islam (Mubhala, ' challenge by ordeal ', 631). The strength and weakness of this Arab Christianity, Monophysite in its origins and links, are reflected significantly in the distorted picture given by the Koran. The Muslim tradition held that the Prophet would be born in ' the year of the Elephant ', the year of an unsuccessful expedition against Mecca and the sanctuary of the Kasbah by the christian Abyssinian, Abraha, at that time ruler of Yemen. According to tradition the date was 570, but the event, if it really happened, took place thirty years earlier.

CHAPTER XXXII

EASTERN MONASTICISM
IN THE FIFTH AND
SIXTH CENTURIES

This remarkable growth of the Churches outside the Empire was everywhere accompanied by a flowering of monasticism. That is true of Ethiopia, where the *Life of St Antony* and the *Rule* of St Pachomius were among the first books to be translated; and of Sassanid Mesopotamia, thanks especially to the work of that great organiser Abraham of Kashkar (491/501-586). It is true of Armenia, where the monasteries, beginning with that of Echmiadzin, were active spiritual and cultural centres; it is true finally of Georgia, where monasticism was specially developed by the 'Thirteen Fathers' from Syria, the equivalent of the 'Nine Saints' of Ethiopia (about 550).

The growth of monasticism was still more remarkable within the Roman Empire, where we have already seen it so deeply rooted in the fourth century. Monks were to be found everywhere in the Eastern provinces, from Egypt, where they originated and which still remained an active centre, as far as Thrace, where monasteries were established late. In 518 Constantinople and its immediate surroundings counted at least sixty-seven monasteries for men, not to mention communities for women. Their numbers increased, as we can see from their interventions in Christological disputes. They sent delegations of dozens, even hundreds to the great Councils or to the Court : two hundred monks accompanied Severus of Antioch when he travelled for the first time from Palestine to Constantinople in 508. By thousands they took part in the riots which shattered the towns divided by theological factions and which sometimes caused bloodshed : for example, at Jerusalem in 453; at Antioch in the time of Peter the Fuller (471 and the years following) to say nothing of Alexandria, which was always turbulent.

From the time of Eutyches they played a role of the first importance in the Monophysite affair and its long sequels : we have noted the bitter conflicts in Constantinople between the Acoemetae and the Scythian monks.

During these two centuries the centres of monasticism which perhaps deserve special notice are those of Palestine and Syria. The narratives and collections of anecdotes which had been written about the Fathers of the Egyptian desert during the fourth century were now succeeded by two books : the *Historia philotheos*, compiled by the great Theodoret of Cyrrhus between 437 and 449 and dealing with Antioch and the neighbouring regions, and the *Spiritual Meadow* of John Moschus (615-619), which was more particularly concerned with the monks living between Jerusalem and the Dead Sea. There were also biographies of these monks by Cyril of Scythopolis, who lived in the middle of the sixth century.

These collections resembled the earlier ones both in content and character, for in Syro-Palestinian monasticism we witness a continual replenishing of the original tradition. As in Egypt, the ideal offered as a model to generous souls was still that of the recluse, the hero of asceticism; we still find the same mighty feats, the same striving after extremes.

The most typical example is that of the stylite saints : particularly of the first and greatest, St Simeon the elder. Born in Cilicia about 390, he began his monastic career in a community numbering about a hundred monks. In his search for a still more austere life he became a hermit and shut himself up for three years in a little cell where he spent the whole of Lent without eating. Then he isolated himself for five years in an enclosure on top of a hill, attached to an iron chain, until a bishop pointed out to him that his will made this material bond useless. He spent the next two years on a pedestal, then on three columns each higher than the last and finally on a great column more than fifty feet high, on the capital of which he spent the last thirty years of his life (429-459).

A strange ascension whereby the saint seems to rise higher and higher above the world in order to get closer to God; but that was his means of isolating himself further from man, for the heroic nature of his achievement naturally attracted the curiosity, admiration and piety of crowds of people. From all parts they came to ask his prayers, intercession, miracles, judgment and advice; indeed, the balance and sanity of his spiritual direction clearly reveal the authentic saint under the eccentric trappings of his personality. St Simeon's column later became the goal of very popular pilgrimages and remained so after his death, when it was enclosed by the great cross-shaped basilica whose impressive remains can still be admired at Kalaat Sagnan.

Simeon the Great had imitators and rivals such as Daniel the Stylite, who paid him two visits. Like Simeon, Daniel was first a cenobite and recluse, then lived on several different columns in turn at Anaplous on the Bosphorus from 460 to 493, giving advice to the Emperor, the Empress and other important people. Another imitator was Simeon the Younger, from Antioch, a stylite from the age of seven until his death in 592 at the age of seventy-five : he, too, was a spiritual director and wonder-worker.

That is not the only kind of extraordinary feat we find. We hear of recluses in grottoes, tombs, a hollow tree, even in a suspended cage; there were men who remained standing still for days and weeks until they were exhausted, and *boskoi* or Browsers who fed only on grass and roots.

Besides these anchorites we also meet monks living in communities — and these formed the majority. The communities varied greatly : there was no single rule and each monastery followed the regime established by its founder. But we can distinguish two main types : the *Coenobion*, the rule of which was fully communal, as with St Pachomius or St Basil, and the Laura, more like the original type at Scete, where after a period of probation those monks deemed worthy of it led a solitary life, spending the first five days of the week in their cell or hermitage and gathering on Saturday and Sunday to celebrate the liturgy.

The most famous of these foundations were those of St Euthymius the Great (377-473), who came from the frontiers of Armenia to Palestine. He founded several Lauras in the ravines of the desert of Judah about 405/6, including that which retained his name and whose church was consecrated by the Patriarch Juvenal of Jerusalem in 428/9. He influenced the nomad Arabs who had established their *douars* or *paremboles* west of the Jordan, as well as members of high society in Jerusalem, like the Empress Eudocia, widow of Theodosius II. His disciple St Sabbas (439-532), who came from Cappadocia, also spent his monastic life in Palestine, where he founded the Great Laura (473), which still stands even today and, as a result of a split in the community, the New Laura (507). In 493 the Patriarch of Jerusalem named him archimandrite, or general superior, of all the Lauras in his diocese. St Sabbas also exercised an influence beyond the limits of strictly monastic circles. Twice towards the end of his life, in 521 and 531, we find him at the Court of Constantinople, using his prestige to obtain from the imperial government various measures to help the people, in particular a reduction of taxes.

This influence was also used to help orthodoxy. St Sabbas, and St Euthymius before him, were strongly attached to the Council of Chalcedon and doubtless thanks to them Palestine, and particularly its monks, was less generally contaminated by heresy or the Monophysite schism than the rest of the East from Syria to Egypt. Mixed up like this with all the great theological disputes which disturbed the Church during their day, the Eastern monks also had their own problems, difficulties and heresies.

The most significant — for its speculative errors were closely linked to the ascetical and mystical life — was that of the Messalians or Euchites. These two words, the first Syriac, the second Greek, have the same meaning : ' the men of prayer '. Messalianism had already been attacked about 390 by Amphilochius of Iconium, a minor star in the Cappadocian constellation, and condemned at the Council of Ephesus. It was rampant throughout the fifth century and even later, as much in the Eastern provinces of the Roman Empire as among the Nestorians of the Sassanid Kingdom. Among the chief teachers of the sect was one Simeon, who came from Mesopotamia.

The heresy took as its starting-point a painful empirical fact : even after baptism, man is aware of evil tendencies which impel him to sin. Lacking the West's classic distinction between original sin and concupiscence, the Messalians interpreted the existence of concupiscence as showing that in the soul dwelled a devil. To drive out the devil, to conquer the passions once and for all and to attain blessed *apatheia*, man must have recourse to rigorous asceticism and above all to prayer, the constant uninterrupted prayer recommended by St Paul (1 Ths 5 : 17). The Messalians claimed that just as evil makes itself felt in concupiscence, so the presence of the Holy Spirit, which penetrates the soul, sets it aflame, purifies it and makes it divine, is also felt in a physical way and accompanied by luminous phenomena and ecstasies. Hence the pejorative names, ' enthusiasts ' and ' chorentes ' (dancers), applied to them by their opponents. Many other charges were also made : of laziness, of moral laxity, even of orgies, — but in this charge-sheet it is difficult to differentiate those points which are deviations typical of any false mysticism and those which are calumnies logically deduced *a priori* from the Messalians' first principles.

In a prudently sweetened form Messalian ideas and practices spread widely throughout the East. It was falsely claimed that they were endorsed by sound men such as the great Macarius, one of the heroes of Scete in the fourth century. Their influence was particularly strong on the growth of Hesychasm. Hesychasm began to emerge during the seventh century at Mount Sinai with St John Climacus, who died about 649, and developed much later on Mount Athos. Indeed, we may ask whether all mysticism was not in grave danger of slipping from ontology into psychology and ending up as mere sensory illusion.

Another spiritual adventure was the Origenist crisis under Justinian. Severe censure had been passed on the dangerous ideas of Evagrius the Pontic immediately after his death in 399 — for Evagrius even more than Origen was the target during the great debate led so forcefully by Epiphanius of Salamis, St Jerome and Theophilus of Alexandria in 397 and the following years, especially from 400 to 402. Despite this censure, monastic circles greatly esteemed Evagrius's strictly ascetical work, which is indeed precious, a real *summa* containing in condensed form all the spirituality of the Desert Fathers. It was inevitable that despite all precautions (these were not lacking, as we see from apophthegms and anecdotes) curiosity and interest should sooner or later be aroused in the author's other works, for example in his *Gnostic Chapters*. This book expressed in esoteric form a wild gnosis which had developed from the time of Origen on the verge of orthodoxy if not actually outside authentic Christianity; among its assumptions were the pre-cosmic fall of rational creatures, and a distinction between the Word and Christ.

At the beginning of the sixth century Evagrian Origenism emerged in striking fashion in the communities founded by St Sabbas in Palestine. In 518 the superior of the New Laura had to expel four of his monks who supported this suspect doctrine; one of their friends, Leontius of Byzantium, belonged to the escort which accompanied St Sabbas to Constantinople in 531. Dismissed by his master, Leontius remained in the capital, where we find him playing a part in the anti-Monophysite intrigues and arguments. Tension increased after the death of St Sabbas in 532 and led to riots. Attacked in the Great Laura, Origenism triumphed in the New, for in 536 one of the heads of the movement, Theodore Askidas, also went to Constantinople where he became one of the most influential theological advisers of Justinian and one of the men who inspired his ' neo-Chalcedonian ' policy. But for the moment he could not prevent his enemies getting the upper hand at court with the Roman deacon and future Pope, Pelagius, and finally with the Emperor. In January 543 the latter promulgated a first edict condemning ten Origenist propositions.

Though approved by the Pope and all the bishops, this condemnation was not accepted by the Origenists in Palestine, where restlessness increased. The party had successes and setbacks; as often happens, with the continuation of controversy it split into two (547). The extremists were called *Isochrists* (they believed that at the final apocatastasis divinised souls will become equals of Christ) and the moderate *Protoctists* (they at least upheld the privileges of Christ's primacy); the latter ended by embracing orthodoxy in 552.

Justinian had to intervene once again. Without waiting for the official opening of what was going to be the fifth ecumenical Council he made the bishops already present in Constantinople approve fifteen new anathemas aimed directly at the teaching of Evagrius (March/April 553). The following year the Origenists lost their stronghold, the New Laura, and were expelled from Palestine.

If we overemphasise these difficulties within monasticism, we shall risk missing the essential point : the influence of the monks on christians as a whole. Once again the monks were everywhere; here is what archaeological research has brought to light in North Syria : ' The convents of the Antiochene in the fifth and sixth centuries were farming communities established on the main roads, playing a large part economically in the peasants' lives by means of their church and the building with a portico which was typical of the community and which, in the opinion of G. Tchalenko, served as a meeting-place, workshop, refectory and alms house (ξενοδοχεῖον), both church and building being freely open to the faithful '[1]. But this physical presence among the people was not the thing that mattered most. Nor, even, was the increase in the people's welfare which resulted. The monks took part in public welfare schemes, whose appearance in the fourth century we have noted. The fifth and sixth centuries produced the quite new institutions known as *diaconiae*, which were originally part of a monastery's charitable work, later a more or less autonomous body, and finally a monastic community specialising in a particular social service.

Still more precious was their purely religious role. In the midst of a christian or would-be christian society threatened by the spirit of the world and tepidness, the monk was there to show the Gospel ideal in all its strictness and its refusal to make any compromise; he was there to bear witness to the call to perfection, the narrow way, the folly of the Cross. But this ideal was also fulness of spiritual life, enthusiasm, effusion of the Spirit. This last point is perhaps the most striking feature of Eastern monasticism : the monk was a ' pneumatic ' a ' pneumatophor ', he bore witness to the presence of the Spirit by the charismata granted to him, and that was the highest function which he had to fulfil in the body of the Church.

1. M. Rodinson, 'De l'archéologie à la sociologie historique, notes méthodologiques sur le dernier ouvrage de G. Tchalenko ', (*Villages antiques de la Syrie du Nord,* Paris 1955-1958), *Syria,* 1961, p. 186.

CHAPTER XXXIII

THE EASTERN EMPIRE
AS A CHRISTIAN EMPIRE

To end the present section we must again try to sum up briefly the original features of Christianity as practised by the men of this place and time, the countries of the East in the fifth and sixth centuries. These two centuries witnessed the apogee of the first Byzantine period, the between Diocletian and Heraclius, in contrast to the two other periods, between Diocletian and Heraceius, in contrast to the two other periods, Middle and Late Byzantine *(Mittel-* and *Spabyzantinisch)*, the seventh to eleventh, and twelfth to fifteenth centuries. The most striking feature of this period in the East is its continuity with preceding centuries. Here there is no break between Antiquity and the Middle Ages; the latter prolong the former. The fifth and sixth centuries continue the work of the fourth; more than ever the Empire, which still calls itself Roman, appears as a christian Empire.

Abroad it claimed to be the born protector of Christ's religion. For example, in the treaty which Khosrov I agreed to sign in 532, Justinian added a clause guaranteeing religious freedom to christian subjects of the Sassanid King of Kings, as Constantine himself had perhaps done. The missionary activity which we have noted in the south of the Empire had its equivalent on the northern frontier. During the same year 528 the King of the Heruli, a Germanic people established south of the Danube, and the King of the Crimean Huns came to be baptised in Constantinople. Justinian himself, who was already associated with the throne, stood godfather to them.

1. J. R. Palanque, 'La vie et l'œuvre d'Ernest Stein', in E. Stein, *Histoire du Bas-Empire*, Vol. II, Paris-Brussels, p. xi, referring to E. Stein, 'Untersuchungen zur Spätbyzantinische Verfassungs- und Wirtschaftsgeschichte', *Mitteilungen zur Osmanischen Geschichte*, Vol. II (1925), p. 1-62.

There were missions also within the Empire. As we have seen, much remained to be done before the conversion of people living in the countryside was complete, even in those provinces where Christianity had been longest established and most fully developed, for example in those of Asia Minor, Asia in the strict sense, Caria, Lydia and Ph rygia About 542 the same Justinian ordered the monk John of Amida, future Monophysite Archbishop of Ephesus, to preach the Gospel there This mission met with great success : some 70,000 p agans were baptised ninety-six churches built and twelve monasteries founded. The support and generosity of the Emperor played their part : each of the new converts received a small gold coin, while the Treasury paid for more than half of the cost of constructing and endowing churches. To this we must add the severity of the laws, which were increasingly harsh towards pagans, Manichaeans and heretics of every kind, and towards Samaritans and Jews. Since the time of Constantine, the latter were subject to restrictions which contrast with the favourable treatment they had enjoyed in the pagan Empire.

These violent measures were enforced with particular vigilance at the other end of the social ladder, among the aristocratic and cultura. élite which comprised the second core of pagan resistance. In Constantinople important lawsuits were brought against the Manichaeans in 527, and against the pagans in 529 and 545/6. As usual they were conducted with cruelty which included imprisonment, torture and burning. The lawsuits involved very high civil servants, even some in the Emperor's suite, men and women of the highest rank and intellectuals such as teachers, lawyers and doctors. Similar lawsuits were brought not only in the capital but in Asia and Syria in 562 and later still. To this policy may be linked the closing in 529 of the Neo-Platonist school of Athens, which had become a hotbed of paganism and occult beliefs.

Nevertheless, this survival of old creeds in intellectual circles is less striking than the progress made there by the new faith. In this respect Alexandria rather than Athens deserves to be chosen for study. True, neither Egypt nor its metropolis were wholly christian — indeed there were still pagans in Egypt in the seventh and even in the eighth centuries — but Christianity was making definite progress. Despite some violence, such as the lynching of the pagan woman philosopher Hypatia in 415l and that of a christian student about 485/7, the philosophical studies which flourished at Alexandria developed in an atmosphere of religious neutrality. Until the beginning of the sixth century the teachers in its school were pagan, but from the beginning of the fifth century their opinions were such that they could be followed by christian pupils. Gradually they turned their teaching into channels more acceptable

THE SPAN OF CHRISTIANITY: II.
Armenia

PLATE 39

CHURCH OF ODZOUN, ARMENIA; LATE 6TH OR 7TH CENTURY

Odzoun was not an important place, but its church is an interesting example of early Armenian architecture. It shows a fusion of the basilica with the cupola, and it is even possible that there may have been an original basilica on to which the cupola was added. The cupola itself, built on to an octagonal base, dates the church at the end of the 6th or the beginning of the 7th century. On the vexed question of the relation of the Armenian cupola churches to the Byzantine churches, especially of the 6th century, it is important to recognize a great deal more independence in the development of the architectural idea in each area than, for example, Strzygowski was prepared to accept when he tried to trace to Armenia the origins of the cupola (*Orient oder Rom*). A general feature of Armenian churches which distinguishes them from churches further West, is the lack of light and contact with the outside world and the absence of magnificent internal decorations. These features express a fundamental element in the Armenian Church's attitude towards the world, and even today the same idea is expressed in the Armenian Liturgy: 'Guard the Doors, the Doors.' With the greatest vigilance and with all possible care...'

By permission of Collection Hautes Etudes, Paris.

THE SPAN OF CHRISTIANITY: III. Egypt

PLATE 40. St Menas and Christ; wooden icon from Bawit, Egypt, 6th century, Louvre, Paris

Quite apart from being a very good example of Coptic art, this icon also provides a most important insight into the significance of icons in the lives of 6th century Christians. The inscription on the left and the dress of the saint make it probable that this St Menas is not the national saint (cf. Plate 35), but an abbot venerated as a saint, probably an abbot of the monastery to which the icon belonged. The icon encompasses the frontier between two worlds; the saint, with his halo and fixed stance, is already in heaven, but this representation of him guarantees his presence among his people (cf. Plate 17). In this particular icon however, an additional guarantee is given by virtue of the fact that Christ has his right hand on the shoulder of the abbot in a gesture which is extraordinarily tender and alive and which clearly signifies Christ's protection, but which also, in the context of an icon made for the abbot's people, almost certainly signifies Christ's presentation of the saint to his people as an effective mediator and intercessor on their behalf. (Perhaps the *clipeus* of Christ in the icon of SS. Sergius and Bacchus should also be interpreted in the same way, cf. Plate 34.)

Photo : Georg Gerster.

THE SPAN OF CHRISTIANITY: IV. Nubia

PLATE 41. The Hermit Onophorus; fresco in basilica at Faras

Faras, in ancient times Pachoras, must have been a town
of some importance in the Nubian kingdom both as an
episcopal see and as the centre of the Anchorites.
Onophorus, who is shown here in a string garment, died
at the end of the 4th or the beginning of the 5th century. He is thought to have been a son of an Ethiopian
hereditary prince and he has been venerated in Italy, Spain,
France and Germany since the time of the Crusades.

THE SPAN OF CHRISTIANITY: V. Ethiopia

PLATE 42. A PAGAN AND CHRISTIAN COIN FROM THE REIGN OF THE EMPEROR EZANA
OF ETHIOPIA, 4TH CENTURY

These coins illustrate the transition from paganism to
Christianity, which took place in the long reign of the great
4th century Emperor Ezana.   The inscriptions are normally
in Greek and it is interesting to note that Ethiopian coins of
the 3rd and 4th centuries are, for the most part, almost
identical in type and weight with the coins of the same
period in the Roman Empire.   This may reflect, in pagan
times, a conscious object of Ethiopian imperial policy, to keep
in step with the Roman Empire.   It may therefore be no
coincidence that Frumentius and Aedisius became important
in the court at Axum in the reign of Constantine the Great.
The coin above carries the Mohammedan star and crescent,
the coin below bears the Christian cross.

By permission of Dr Jean Doresse, Paris.

to the christians and finally, in the decisive year 529, a true christian, that same John Philoponus whom we have met in the history of Nestorianism, took charge of the movement, claimed to be head of the school and fought the pagan views of Athenian Neo-Platonism put forward by Proclus.

With him the whole school of Alexandria became christian; but in the course of the two previous generations it had already educated remarkable representatives of christian thought like Aeneas of Gaza, who was writing about 490. These men were genuine philosophers who dared to confront the difficult problems resulting from the encounter between the christian faith and the Neo-Platonist system : problems such as the soul's origin, the resurrection of the body, the creation or eternity of the world. A secondary yet active centre, Gaza, produced other representatives of this attitude. It is doubtless in the same Palestinian group, fed by Greek culture and Platonism, that we must look for the mysterious author who dared to adopt the illustrious name of Dionysius the Areopagite and who, thanks to that, was later to exert such a great influence during the Middle Ages in the East and especially in the West, where his work penetrated during Carolingian times.

Everything is out of the ordinary in this learned, profound and often obscure thinker who dared to swallow huge doses of Proclus's Neo-Platonism and bravely to explore the most formidable arcana of mystical theology. Yet he can serve to illustrate a very widespread phenomenon : the high level of religious speculation during this first Byzantine period. The unending arguments occasioned by the Monophysite quarrel give us an opportunity to verify the fact. Theology in the fifth and sixth centuries had become highly technical, reflecting the vitality of contemporary culture : that was a natural result of the great number of converts from the intellectual and social élite of the period.

True, the movement was already well under way in the fourth century but, as it gathered strength, new features developed; vitality implies growth, and growth change. Two changes in particular deserve to be singled out :

1) The resources of Aristotelian logic were set to work. The growth of Neo-Platonism had been accompanied by a return to Aristotle and especially to the *Organon* : Porphyrius was the author of the *Introduction to the Categories*, which in future was to serve as a basic textbook of elementary philosophy. The School of Alexandria produced the majority of our *Commentaria in Aristotelem Graeca* : among the contributors were John Philoponus and his christian pupils, Stephen, David and Elias. Theologians had occasionally used this precious and formidable arsenal even in the previous century, as we have seen with the Anomoeans :

in the fifth and sixth centuries this became normal practice with the Monophysites and with their Chalcedonian or Neo-Chalcedonian opponents.

2) The argument from authority remained decisive. But besides the authority of scripture we now have that of qualified representatives of the Church's tradition — often taking first place. We can sum up in this way : in the theological disputes of the first four centuries discussion was based on verses from Scripture, whereas the Byzantines argued with quotations from the Fathers. The collections of Biblical *testimonia* were succeeded by dogmatic anthologies which grouped quotations from authorised writers by subject-matter. We find the same thing in exegesis : *Chains* were produced linking to a verse from Holy Scripture brief passages from commentaries by the most famous Fathers of the Church.

This practice has often been adversely criticised. The disadvantages of the method are obvious : quotations were cut short and sometimes falsified, and attributed to this or that author on doubtful evidence or even with deliberate intent to deceive. Critics of the method argue as if the truly creative period of Christian thought had ended with St Cyril, 'seal of the Fathers' (σφραγὶς τῶν πατέρων)[2], as if the golden age of the Church Fathers was followed by a scholasticism without originality. That is a mistaken view which does scant justice to the Byzantine theologians' refined technique and considerable progress in the analysis of such difficult concepts as nature, hypostasis and person. Moreover, we must bear in mind the problem posed by doctrinal and cultural tradition : the Byzantines could not help being *epigoni*, successors; the method of the digest and summary was forced upon them just as it is forced upon us, upon every civilisation rooted in a past whose accumulated and doubtless increasing heritage it wants to enjoy. Their theologians had to build up Patristic records just as they built up voluminous records of acts and other conciliar documents, which E. Schwartz, continuing the work of seventeenth- and eighteenth- century scholars, collected in his *Acta Conciliorum Oecumenicorum*.

We must speak therefore of richness and ripeness rather than of decadence; that is how christian thought and culture appear during this first Byzantine period. The old tradition was still vigorous and endured. In the fifth and sixth centuries we again find the typical features already displayed by christian society in the previous century. On the one hand the classical education inherited from paganism continued to provide the intellectual and social élite with a sound humanist training.

2. Anastasius the Sinaite, *Viae dux adversus Acephalos*, 7, *PG*, vol. 89, c. 113 D.

With the single exception of the monasteries, there were still no purely christian schools. In 425 the Emperor Theodosius II created a State University at Constantinople and organised the curriculum on the most traditional lines : profane literature both Greek and Latin, grammar and rhetoric, philosophy and law.

Educated Byzantines were in every way worthy of their predecessors in the Hellenistic period or under the Early Empire. The daringly original architects of the new St Sophia, Isidore of Miletus and Anthemius of Tralles, knew, edited and wrote commentaries on the work of the great Greek mathematicians, Archimedes and Euclid. Anthemius, moreover, was the pupil of Ammonius at Alexandria, like John Philophonus and the Latin Boethius.

The princess Juliana Anicia (died 528), who was a descendant of the glorious Theodosian dynasty, owned a magnificent specially illuminated manuscript of the famous treatise on medicine by Dioscorides of Anazarbus. The *Anthology* records the text of the beautiful inscriptions in hexameters celebrating the lavish decorations with which she endowed the churches of St Polyeuctus in Constantinople and St Euphemia in Chalcedon. Finally, about 512 we find the same Juliana among the leaders of the movement of the Chalcedonian resistance which, even at the court of the Emperor Anastasius, opposed the latter's pro-Monophysite policy.

The second characteristic feature is that this Byzantine élite put its own culture, curiosity and richness of character in the service of Christianity. We do not always find in the East the gulf which we later find in the West between clergy and laity. As in the fourth century, religious questions passionately interested both, and both took part in them with equal enthusiasm and often with equal competence. It was a lawyer, Eusebius, who first denounced the blasphemies of Nestorius; it was a senior civil servant, Count Irenaeus, who most ably defended him, and the fact that both later became bishops, one of Dorylaeum, the other of Tyre, does not alter my point.

Only within this cultural context can we duly appreciate the role played by the Emperors Theodosius II and Marcian at the time of the councils of Ephesus and Chalcedon, and the initiative taken by Zeno, Justin, Justinian and his successors to settle Monophysite and other questions. Before acting as Emperors, they behaved as representatives of the christian élite which felt immensely concerned by these grave problems, these attacks on the Church's health and peace.

Let us take the greatest and best known of them, Justinian. We cannot say that his action resulted merely from the influence of his successive ecclesiastical advisers; he was, in fact, himself an amateur theologian. Several of his dogmatic treatises have come down to us, and they lack neither originality nor merit; we find, for example, the application of the subtle idea, 'compound hypostasis' (σύνθετος ὑπόστασις), still with reference to the Incarnation. They represent a by no means negligible stage in the development of Neo-Chalcedonianism.

Justinian and his peers were of course also Emperors, christian Emperors; and the religious character of the sovereign was increasingly emphasised. In the time of Leo (459) it began to be customary for the Emperor to be crowned in public by the Patriarch; starting with Zenonis, wife of the usurper Basiliscus (475), the Empress was also crowned in this manner. The ceremony was accompanied by a profession of the orthodox faith; this was demanded for the first time in 491 from Anastasius, whose attachment to Chalcedonian orthodoxy the Patriarch had good reason to doubt.

Justinian's great legislative work, the *Corpus Iuris Civilis*, in which he gathered the fruits of Rome's legal genius, opens with an invocation : ' In the name of Our Lord Jesus Christ ' and the first heading of the Code, Book I, is devoted to an official definition *Of the most high Trinity and of the Catholic faith.*

The Byzantine Emperor of the fifth or sixth centuries was indeed the heir of Constantine, Constantius and Theodosius. He still had the same monarchical and pastoral ideal, which was a transposition into christian terms of Diocletian's absolutism. Master of the world, the Emperor felt responsible before God for the spiritual even more than for the temporal welfare of his subjects. If something set him apart from his fourth-century predecessors, it was the increased competence with which he intervened in religious matters; in doing this he gave the impression not of invading a basically foreign domain but rather of trying to fulfil better the duties incumbent upon him.

It is not enough to say that in every piece of legislation the Emperor tried to express the Gospel spirit — as far, at least, as this proved conceivable (in fact the Byzantines did not succeed any better than their predecessors in making the penal code or the tax system less inhuman). The Emperor's solicitude extended to the strictly ecclesiastical sphere. He supervised and laid down rules for the administration of Church property, monastic estates and charitable institutions, which continued to grow. Better still, he decreed precise instructions concerning the conditions necessary for taking holy orders, concerning episcopal elections, monastic life and religious discipline. In the Byzantine Church what corresponds to our canon law is contained in texts from two sources : imperial laws (νόμοι) and conciliar canons or other Church documents : hence the term *Nomocanon* which serves to designate the collections in which they are contained.   If the word came into use only in the ninth century, the texts themselves appeared at the end of the sixth in the form of the two first mixed collections, that ' of the fourteen titles ' (between 577 and 582), and that ' of the fifty titles ', compiled in the reign of the Emperor Maurice (582-602).

Finally, the Emperor intervened with great authority not only, as we have seen, at the dogmatic level, but in the administration and daily life of the Church.   He nominated and, if necessary, deposed bishops and patriarchs.   This is clearly seen at Constantinople : under the Emperor Anastasius, Euphemius was dismissed in 495 and Macedonius in 511 for showing too much favour to Chalcedonianism. Anthimus, on the other hand, was deposed under Justinian in 536 for not showing enough.   At the end of his reign the old Emperor deposed Eutychius, who refused to be a party to his final theological about-turn (565); he was reinstalled in 577 by the future Tiberius II, at that time Caesar and Regent of the Empire.

We may speak then not of confusion but of a close association and intermingling between the two domains, the spiritual and the temporal, which the West has taught us to differentiate.   For if, as we have seen, the Emperor interfered in the Church's intimate life, on the other hand he demanded, as a natural right, that the Church should help in making his own institutions work well : bishops were officially ordered to play a role in municipal administration.   At first the bishops' influence was mainly moral — protecting the weak and denouncing abuses — but it gradually became more widespread.   A constitution dated 530 ended by placing the bishops ' at the head of all financial administration in the towns, including food supplies and public works '[3].

3. E. Stein, *Histoire du Bas-Empire*, II, p. 400.

CHAPTER XXXIV

THE BYZANTINE CHURCH AND BYZANTINE PIETY

THE progress of Christianity in the Empire was of course accompanied by a growth of the Church's institutional framework. We have mentioned the importance which monasticism acquired; the clergy also grew considerably in numbers. Take an important example : in Constantinople the personnel of the Cathedral of St Sophia and of its outlying buildings increased to the point where in 535 the Emperor was forced to limit their numbers to four hundred and twenty-five : sixty priests, one hundred deacons, ninety subdeacons, one hundred and ten lectors, forty deaconesses, and twenty-five cantors. In the large towns and places of popular pilgrimage there were numerous sanctuaries. Within each episcopal province a thick network of country churches had been established, the equivalent of our parishes : Theodoret counted eight hundred of them in his diocese of Cyrrhus.

At first they had been served by *chorepiscopi,* who more or less ranked as bishops. As the *chorepiscopi* tended to infringe the privileges of the head of the diocese, they were gradually replaced during the fifth and sixth centuries by simple priests, the *periodentes* or ' visitors ', whose very name emphasises their subordinate role.

The most original institution to grow up in the Eastern Church during the two centuries we are studying was that of the patriarchs, a rank in the hierarchy above bishops and metropolitans. It was Egypt which had set the example of an episcopal see exercising authority throughout an extensive region. Alexandria was only too inclined to extend its rights further, and it was in order to prevent her encroachments that the ecumenical Council of Constantinople in 381 divided the East into four provinces : Egypt, the East (from Sinai to Cilicia), Pontus and Asia (respectively, the interior and the West of Asia Minor).

In order to satisfy the claims made in 431 at the council of Ephesus, the Council of Chalcedon in 451 confirmed that the Church of Cyprus formed no part of either of these two last-mentioned provinces; it also took the provinces of Palestine from Antioch and placed them under the authority of Jerusalem. Finally, the jurisdiction of Constantinople had extended considerably and in future was to cover all Asia Minor, where it replaced the jurisdiction of Ephesus and Caesarea of Cappadocia. The whole of the christian world was thenceforth divided into five patriarchates : Rome, Constantinople, Alexandria, Antioch and Jerusalem. The word patriarchate and the idea it expressed were made official in legislation drawn up by Justinian. The whole of the West, as it stood in 314, that is to say including Macedonia and Greece, depended on the see of Rome, which exercised authority over the Eastern provinces — the vicariate of Thessalonica — through the intermediary of the metropolitan of Thessalonica.

This new organisation reflected the increasing importance of Constantinople in the life of the Empire and consequently of the Church. The role played in the Church by the Emperor was the reason why, despite all the measures taken to discourage such journeys, a number of bishops and high ecclesiastical dignitaries found it expedient to go to court and stay there for longer or shorter periods. These guests even comprised a kind of ' permanent council ' (σύνοδος ἐνδημοῦσα), on which the sovereign relied in order to work out his decisions on religious matters and get them ratified.

The strict symmetry established by Constantine himself between the old Rome and his new Rome provided an apt argument for transforming the existing situation into a legal privilege. Returning to the ' primacy of honour ' recognised by the Council of 381, the 28th Canon of Chalcedon stipulated that the imperial city, which in civil matters enjoyed the same privileges as the former capital, should have the same power as Rome in Church matters, though remaining ' second to her '[1]. We can understand why this 28th canon at once aroused protests first from the Roman delegates, then from Pope St Leo, and has never been recognised either by him or by his successors. Quite rightly, for two other canons of the same Council had stipulated hat Constantinople could play the role of a higher court of appeal in e. clesiastical matters relating to all the East : its patriarch exercising in the East an authority comparable to that of the apostolic see in the West. This tended to impose on the Church a kind of diarchy, the primacy of honour still accorded to Rome gradually becoming

1. *Actio* XVII, 8, p. 448, 7-9. Schwartz (*Acta Concil. Oecum.*, II, 1, 3).

drained of all actual content, particularly from the jurisdictional point of view.

This was still only a tendency. It still occasionally happened that members of the Eastern clergy condemned in Constantinople appealed to the Pope, and the latter's judgement in the last resort settled the matter once and for all. A case of this kind occurred under Gregory the Great in the years 593-596. But the latent conflict finally broke out in 587 when the Patriarch John the Faster, flaunting the doubtless vague but heavily pretentious title of ecumenical, that is to say universal, Patriarch, which had already been assumed by several of his predecessors, claimed authority in the case of the Patriarch of Antioch and the right to judge him before his own tribunal. Pope Pelagius II protested energetically. So at a later date did his successor St Gregory, when he repeatedly, but more or less unsuccessfully, intervened with both the Patriarch and the Emperor, as well as with their successors (595, 597, 598, 599, 603).

Constantinople kept more and more aloof from Rome. Taking advantage of the presence of St Andrew's relics, which had been brought to the city by the Emperor Constantius in 357, Constantinople worked out the legend of a pretended apostolic origin, with the idea of establishing perfect equality with Rome, if not even a vague supremacy over the Western city : according to the narrative in Jn 1 : 40-41, even before St Peter, the apostle St Andrew was ' the first called ', *protokletos.* In the East the ascendancy of Constantinople was secured all the more easily since the other Orthodox Patriarchs had been weakened by the results of the Christological disputes and the growth of separated Churches. Over against the Patriarch in the capital little if any weight could be brought to bear by the unhappy Melchite Patriarch of Alexandria, who owed his position in an enemy country to the support of the imperial police.

As time passed, like two brothers who grow up apart and become used to leading separate lives, the two Churches of East and West tended to become increasingly different. The fact is evident in all spheres of christian life, starting with the liturgy. As an example let us take the strictly Byzantine liturgy, which during the Middle Ages finally supplanted the other Greek-language rites, the various liturgical families being thenceforth represented only in the Eastern languages of the dissident Churches.

During the fifth and especially during the sixth centuries we find the gradual introduction of a whole series of innovations which, as they accumulated, gradually shaped its Eastern appearance. In 535/6 the solemn entrance of the celebrants began to be accompanied by the singing of the *Monogenes*; this was introduced by Justinian, who is sometimes said to have written it.   Shortly before the Council of Chalcedon in 451 the readings, at last reduced to two — Epistle and Gospel — were preceded by the triple acclamation of the *Trisagion :* ' Holy God, strong God, immortal God '.   This was the *Trisagion* which Peter the Fuller later amplified, giving it a Monophysite flavour.   The Roman liturgy uses it in a bilingual form in the adoration of the Cross on Good Friday.   A few moments earlier on the same day came the public prayer of the faithful, with various entreaties for the Church, its hierarchy, each category of christians, etc.   Such a prayer became rare in the Latin countries, but has remained an integral part of the Eastern liturgy.   It takes the form of a litany; the intentions are recited by the deacon, while the people reply with a *Kyrie eleison.*

In 574 the magnificent Cherubic hymn was adopted — ' we who mystically represent the cherubim. . . ' — despite the reserve shown by the patriarch Eutychius, who considered praise of the King of Glory premature, coming as it did before the consecration.   The Cherubic hymn accompanied what is known today as the great entrance — the procession escorting the chalice and bread, which had been prepared in a sacristy, *prothesis*, located at the left of the sanctuary.   But in the sixth century this preparation had not yet assumed the importance of the long ceremonies which today comprise the *proskomide.*

Then came the Eucharistic prayer in the true sense, the *anaphora*, our canon.   In 565 the Emperor Justinian in vain attempted to check the growing tendency to pronounce the words in a voice so low that the people could not hear them — a sure sign of a development towards a still more hieratic kind of ceremony.   Although the main lines of this prayer of consecration had been laid down a long time before, it too evolved.   The importance of the recital of the institution tended to fade before the *epiklesis*, the prayer addressed to the Holy Spirit asking Him to come and change the bread and wine of the oblation into the body and blood of Christ.

Before the *Pater* a new prayer of intercession for the dead and the living was inserted : the wording of these *diptychs* has often been a cause of conflict.   Rome agreed to re-establish communion with Constantinople in 495 only after the insertion of the commemoration of St John Chrysostom, whom she considered to have been unjustly deposed in 404.

But such an analysis, part by part, is insufficient to make the reader aware of the special atmosphere of the Eastern liturgy, whose particular features and general characteristics became more marked with the passing of time.   Let us note three of them.

1) We have already pointed out the tendency to hieraticism, the sense of the holy, respect pushed to the point of awe of the holiness of the mysteries. Constantinople was always to keep the dismissal at the end of the Mass of the Catechumens : ' Catechumens, outside! ', though this had become almost pointless since it was now the general practice to administer baptism to children. This was yet another way of stressing an essential feature which in earliest times had been very pronounced : that a mysterious celebration was taking place reserved for initiates who were fully worthy. Again, when the consecrated bread and wine were shown before the Communion, the signal was given : ' The holy things for the holy! ' (Τὰ ἅγια τοῖς ἁγίοις). As yet there was no iconostasis shutting off the naves from the sanctuary, but the curtains which hung from an entablature supported by columns were drawn at certain moments. Those at St Sophia were sumptuous and memorable; on one side Christ was shown blessing Justinian, on the other the Virgin with Theodora.

2) Another characteristic not opposed but complementary to the first was the dramatic community spirit of the celebration, in which the people played their part. Hence the irreplaceable role of the deacon, who served as intermediary between the celebrants and the people. He directed their prayer, called upon them to answer, roused their attention and indicated the important moments of the ceremony, for example, with the beautiful words : ' Wisdom, stand up! ' (Σοφία ὀρθοί) before the reading of the Gospel.

3) Finally — and this is far removed from the severe sobriety of the Roman rite — we find a steady increase in the Byzantines' taste for pomp, display and splendour, which accompanied the growth of ceremonial at the court of Constantinople. This was a characteristic feature inherited from the Late Empire and it became increasingly pronounced.

Sumptuousness was certainly increased in the large sanctuaries by the impressive nature of the architecture. The fifth and sixth centuries were a period of great artistic achievement in the East. Long narrow basilicas were, it is true, still being built, with tribunes or *gynaeceas* reserved for women above the side-aisles, but under the influence of the *martyria*, churches built in honour of the martyrs, which had drawn on the style of circular or polygonal mausoleums displayed by classical funerary architecture, more and more often churches were built around a central point, which led to the posing and solution of the difficult problem of the cupola. The most magnificent illustration of the way the problem was solved is the new St Sophia, built from 532 to 537, the great cupola of which collapsed in 558 and was reconstructed in 562, thus permitting the aged Emperor Justinian to celebrate its dedication a second time.

These great churches were decorated with increasing luxury : marble, pavements, mosaics on the walls and vaults. All the arts contributed to this flowering of the Byzantine liturgy, which made a deep impression on those barbarians permitted to watch it : to them it seemed more than a mere image or foretaste of the eternal liturgy of heaven!

Because we do not possess any Byzantine musical notation, we can no longer realise the importance of the part played by music, but we have the words of Byzantine lyric poetry (lyric in the true sense, that is, written to be sung) and of Byzantine liturgical and paraliturgical poetry, which was very popular from the sixth century onwards. The flourishing of these arts is linked with the name of St Romanos ' Melodus ', who was both a poet and a composer. He was born in Syria and seems to have lived in Constantinople in the first half of the century. His verse canticles or *Kontakia* display the same florid style found in Byzantine homilies, with their wealth of images and their prolixity, which is slightly disconcerting to Western taste. We can judge their worth by the *acathistus* hymn (' he who sings standing up ') which was composed in honour of the Virgin Mary. It is an acknowledged jewel in this rich collection, but its author and date are difficult to determine : it has been attributed to Romanos but that is only one hypothesis among many.

Besides its intrinsic value, this religious literature has great historic interest; it is the best means of getting in touch with Byzantine devotion, of discovering its intense feeling and riches. We should have a false idea of the Eastern Church's inner life if our knowledge of its history were limited to the theological disputes, sometimes so dry and technical.

Byzantine devotion developed in the fifth and sixth centuries along lines traced out by the previous century. We find the same veneration of martyrs and now, more generally, of saints, the same trust in their intercession and miraculous powers, the same attachment to their relics, the same fondness for pilgrimages to places hallowed by their presence or the memory of venerable figures.

In the East a number of sensational discoveries of relics occurred during the first half of the fifth century. Often the circumstances were considered miraculous and the relics aroused much curiosity and veneration. For example, at the beginning of the century the relics of St Menas were found west of Alexandria on the edge of the desert and soon attracted crowds of pilgrims. A vast basilica was built to house them by the Emperor Arcadius, who died in 408, and decorated by Zeno (474-491), who also enlarged it with dependent buildings.

In 415 the relics of the protomartyr St Stephen were found near Jerusalem. St Stephen immediately became famous throughout Christendom, and pieces of his relics were sent as far as Numidia and Spain.

In 452 the skull of St John the Baptist was supposed to have been discovered in a monastery of Emesa. In the years following the Council of Ephesus devotion to Saints Cosmas and Damian, which had hitherto been merely local, became widespread. Their tomb was preserved in Theodoret's own diocese and they were later to become the healing saints *par excellence* throughout the East, doctors who treated patients without asking a fee, *anargyres.* The martyr saint, Sergius of Rosapha, became popular in the diocese of Hierapolis. His sanctuary was in the middle of the desert, but that did not prevent it from drawing a crowd of pilgrims from great distances. Homage sometimes came to it from unexpected sources, for example from the King of Kings Khosrov II, who was a Mazdaean. Again, at the beginning of the fifth century Thessalonica received the relics of a martyr of Sirmium, St Demetrius, who became the acknowledged protector of the great city, was endowed with a magnificent sanctuary in 412/3 and received eager marks of attention.

The holy places of Palestine continued to exercise the same appeal and of all relics the most precious and sought after was still that of the true cross, fragments of which continued to travel throughout Christendom : the capital received some several times. Constantinople also gathered in its numerous churches an incomparable collection of precious relics, the enumeration of which is somewhat disconcerting for our modern critical sense but which no one at that time doubted were authentic : Moses's staff, a trumpet from Jericho, the Woman of Samaria's well. Since the reign of the Emperor Leo (457-474) the convent of Blakhernes boasted of possessing an outstanding relic, the Blessed Virgin Mary's funeral veil or *Maphorion.*

This is the place to notice the following very important fact : veneration of the Mother of Christ has now come to assume a supereminent place among that accorded to martyrs and saints. The Council of Ephesus proved the devotion of christian people and of the Church as a whole to the Theotokos. Since then the movement has grown unceasingly, appearing in many ways : in the veneration of her relics, in the building of sanctuaries and in liturgical feasts.

As regards the latter, Jerusalem and Palestine of course led the way, but Constantinople and the whole of the Eastern Empire adopted their innovations one after the other. In 534 Justinian made the Purification a general feast, though Byzantines prefer to call it *Hypapanti,* the ' meeting ' of the old man Simeon with the child Jesus, and consider it a feast of our Lord rather than of His mother. The dedication of the Church of St Mary the New in Jerusalem in 543 later became the feast of the Presentation of the Virgin, a product not of the canonical but of the apocryphal Gospels. The feast of her Nativity was also celebrated although we cannot say exactly when it was introduced; at the end of the century the Emperor Maurice extended to the whole Empire the feast of the Dormition, whose date, 15 August, we still observe.

These liturgical developments were accompanied by the writing of many books. The peak here was reached in the seventh and eighth centuries, but the movement was well under way at the end of the sixth. Hymns and homilies to the Virgin were not only pious but showed a deep awareness of dogma; their enthusiasm, warmth and bold imagery are singularly attractive. In this form — that is to say in the form of poetry, rather than of speculative theology in the strict sense — Mariology appeared in the East several centuries in advance of the Latin West : not until the twelfth century did the latter catch up and eventually take the lead from the Greek East.

Devotion to the Virgin and to saints, martyrs or confessors was expressed in concrete terms by many traditional or new practices. These included the transfer and distribution of relics, even if that meant breaking them up. Thanks to the Empress Pulcheria the church of Daphni acquired the whole of St Stephen's right hand, but the church of Hippo in Africa could boast of receiving only a simple pinch of dust, *exiguus pulvis*. When relics in the strict sense were lacking, pilgrims liked to take back with them something hallowed by contact with the venerated remains : a piece of material, a small flask of clay or silver containing oil from lamps lit in the *martyrion*, or better still perfumed oil which, by an ingenious device, was poured into the reliquary and recovered after it had flowed round the bones.

Of all these forms of Eastern piety the most significant, in terms of the future, was the cult of holy images or icons, which is first attested during the fifth century and which became suddenly popular in the last half of the sixth, from the time of Justin II (565-578). Ever since its origins, or at least since the earliest remaining evidence which dates from the decade beginning 230, Christian art had inherited a tradition of religious iconography from the Hellenised synagogue and represented types or scenes from Holy Scripture on the walls of its monuments. These representations were decorative and helped to teach the faithful; they also helped to make the monuments holy.

What now appears is a more concrete and direct type of representation. We must not go so far as to speak of idolatry, like the iconoclasts of the eighth century. The prayer, faith and hope of the faithful were always addressed beyond the symbol to the person or mystery represented, but the image itself became an object of veneration; it was considered to possess its own power of intercession, even miraculous properties.

Curiously enough, this kind of devotion was not in itself of christian origin; it evolved from the marks of respect paid to the official portraits of the reigning Emperors during the Late Empire. These portraits were considered a true substitute for the sovereign's presence : their reception was accompanied by solemn processions, like those to welcome a visiting Emperor, *adventus Augusti*. The images of the Emperors were the object of a veritable cult and all the usages, or rather rites, concerning the icons had already been practised towards the images; they were treated with respectful homage which went as far as prostration, draperies, incense and candles.

It is noteworthy that the first christian images known to have been surrounded with the marks of a cult were portraits of persons venerated while still alive. Chrysostom says that before his time, in the decade beginning 360, Melitius of Antioch had been venerated in this way because his exile by Constantius, who hated orthodoxy, made of him a confessor of the faith. The same veneration was later accorded to the two Saints Simeon, the Stylites. As regards artistic technique the icons of martyrs stem directly from Egyptian funerary portraits. The resemblance is striking in the case of the icon showing the bust of Saints Sergius and Bacchus found at Sinai and today in Kiev — one of the oldest portable icons in existence — together with the magnificent Madonna in the Church of S. Maria Nuova on the Roman forum.

The first signs of this cult, as of every novelty, are difficult to discern. It became general, as already mentioned, in the decade beginning 570 : and it was then that miraculous images appeared in increasing numbers, ' not made by human hands ' (ἀχειροποίητος). These were considered a source of supernatural protection in cities, palaces and presently in the army, which adopted them as palladia. One of the most famous is the image of Christ on which the city of Edessa counted to repel its Sassanid enemies; indeed it played this role in the siege of 544, according to stories current in the last years of the sixth century. Another famous image is the one which came from Camouliana in Asia Minor and was venerated in that region during the decade beginning 560; it was later carried solemnly to Constantinople. It was perhaps before the end of the sixth century when this image of Christ was set up above the great bronze door of the Imperial Palace. When it was destroyed in 727 on the orders of Leo III the Isaurian, this event marked the beginning of the iconoclast crisis. It was certainly Tiberius II (578-582) who commissioned the mosaics of the Saviour in majesty which decorated the apse of the reception chamber of the chrysotriklinos or triple golden throne.

For a long time now no one had shown the reserve which greeted the first images at the end of the fourth century, whether on the part of a finicky champion of orthodoxy like Epiphanius of Salamis or from a Westerner like St Augustine. In 388 Augustine had placed the *picturarum adoratores* among those groups of christians who were more superstitious than enlightened. It had now become normal in the East for a devout workman or a monk to possess a holy icon in his workshop or cell, and to protect it with a curtain, to have a lamp or candle burning in front of it and to treat it with scrupulous respect. We have well and truly entered the strictly Byzantine period : the East appears resolutely set out on its own road, a road so different in very many ways from that which the West has meanwhile chosen to follow. We must now leave the East and return to the West.

CHAPTER XXXV

PELAGIANISM

THE years 410-412 mark a turning-point both in the history of the African Church and in the life and thought of St Augustine. The conference of 411 had been brought to a happy conclusion and thanks to the unreserved support of the secular arm, the old Donatist enemy was apparently beaten once and for all, when there appeared a new heresy — Pelagianism. It was in Africa that it met its first and most outright opposition, and the ensuing battles gradually occupied all the working hours of the great Doctor until the time of his death (430), which coincided, as already noted, with the collapse of Roman Africa before the attacks of the Vandals.

The invasion of Alaric and the capture of Rome (410) had grave moral consequences for Africa — those agonising problems which St Augustine tried to solve in his *City of God;* but they also brought the arrival of streams of refugees, rich and poor, in a hurry to put the sea between them and the barbarians. Among these displaced persons was a monk, Pelagius, born in Britain (the first writer and thinker produced by that country), but long resident at Rome (390/400); there, a little like St Jerome at an earlier date, he acquired a reputation and even fame in Church circles and among the Christian nobility by his exemplary life, his propaganda for the ascetic ideal, his authority as a director of consciences and master of the spiritual life.

But it would seem that the originality of his thought had already aroused some suspicion, to judge by St Augustine's reserve when Pelagius, on his arrival, tried to establish relations with him. He did not linger in Africa and during that same year 411 he left for Palestine, thus following the example of many other Italian refugees. He left behind in Carthage one of his staunchest disciples, Caelestius, whose indiscreet propaganda soon aroused counter-measures. Towards the end of that same year Caelestius was led before a council at Carthage presided over by the head of the African bishops, Aurelius. ' Condemned but not convinced '[1], he left to continue the same discussion in Sicily and later in Asia Minor, while St Augustine began to draw up the first of his innumerable refutations against the Pelagian heresy — fifteen treatises, amounting in all to thirty-five books, excluding letters and sermons.

Pelagius and Augustine differed on almost every point. Pelagius found an occasion of scandal in the very formulas whereby the flashing pen of St Augustine had summed up that theocentric spirituality which was the fruit of a convert's meditation, of a repentant and grateful sinner : ' give what you command and command what you will ', *da quod iubes et iube quod vis*[2]. Augustine, on his side, found even more to admonish : the commentary of Pelagius on the Epistles of St Paul is still extant; it shows an astonishing misunderstanding of the most obvious meaning of those same texts which St Augustine most liked to comment upon : Pelagius minimises to excess the scope of the dogmatic passages while he exaggerates the Apostle's moral teaching, always so prudent and moderate. By temperament Pelagius was not much of a theologian, still less of a mystic; he seems to have been primarily a moralist. He preached an ideal of perfection based on the Gospel counsels : ' become irreproachable and pure, children of God without stain. . . '[3] — a strict ideal made up of self-denial which, failing to come to fruition as mysticism, somehow turns in on itself and results in puritanism. This puritanism is neo-Jewish in certain respects, so much does it stress obedience to God's law; it takes scant account of the fact that in matters of morality the Gospel has improved on the old law. Pelagius was an ascetic, skilled in asceticism, conscious — perhaps too conscious — of the progress he had attained, and he insisted above all on the need for struggle and effort. In theory he taught men to become morally perfect, but he ended by becoming more interested in means than in the end, by working out a doctrine based less on God than on man and the road he has to follow : hence he appears as human, all too human.

But the serious thing was that this practical morality explicitly formulated its own theory : by a paradox which is merely apparent, this strict asceticism was based on a theology of excessive optimism. Such ' perfectionism ', calling man to practise self-denial, led Pelagius to emphasise, above all, man's responsibility and the role played by free will, to label as dangerous anything which could seem to obstruct free will or limit its play, so that in the last analysis Pelagius reduced to a

1. St Augustine, *Epist.* 157, 3 (22).
2. St Augustine, *Confessions* X, 20 (40), 31 (45), 37 (60), and for Pelagius's reaction : *De dono perseverantiae*, 20 (53).
3. Phil 2 : 24, a verse quoted and commented on by Pelagius, *Epist. ad Demetriadem*, 15-17, *PL*, vol. 33, c. 1109-1110.

minimum the notion of original sin, even if he did not make it completely meaningless. (It is true that he envisaged original sin in the over-simple and almost materialist form of Traducianism, a viewpoint which still attracted St Augustine but which he and the Church with him later abandoned.)

Hence his embarrassment towards the practice, universally admitted if not in general use, of baptising children. That is one of the first obstacles upon which we find Caelestius stumbling, and this liturgical argument was to remain until the end St Augustine's decisive weapon against the Pelagians. The latter likewise emptied of their specific content the words election, predestination (which they reduced to the foreseeing of merit) and even grace itself. When, pressed by his opponents, Pelagius consented to re-introduce this term, so essential to the christian tradition, he gave it quite a new and very special meaning : the first and greatest grace, for him, is nature itself and, more exactly, the splendid attribute with which the Creator has endowed man, namely freedom, the free will whose greatness he never stopped praising. Thanks to it, if we apply ourselves and make the best use of it, it is possible for us to practise virtue, attain holiness and, at least as an ideal, not to know sin ' *impeccantia* '.

That was to depart in striking fashion from St Paul. It was felt to mutilate the Church's traditional teaching so as to make it unrecognisable and to dilute if not totally abandon the scandal and mystery of the Cross. Much more than a redeemer, Pelagius shows Christ to be the author of certain teaching, a model to be imitated. True, his doctrine has a religious and christian framework : the notions of creation and final end play an essential part in his thought; he insists on the Judgment and promised rewards; but as conceived by him holiness is strikingly like the ideal of the Stoic sage. At any rate there are curious coincidences, due to the very logic of the two systems, both very closely-knit : for example, the idea that there are no slight faults, that every infraction of the moral law, however minute, is extremely serious.

In these circumstances we can understand the scandal felt by St Augustine and his colleagues in the African episcopate when they learned that in December 415 Pelagius had succeeded in having himself declared innocent by a Palestinian provincial council gathered in Diospolis. He had known how to turn to his advantage the inexperience of Easterners for whom these problems were quite new and strange, and the prejudice shown against his Latin adversaries there, St Jerome and a young Spanish priest, Orosius, a disciple of St Augustine recently arrived from Africa. It must also be said that he used some duplicity and mental reservations in his denials.

At once St Augustine snatched up his pen; provincial councils in Carthage and Mileve (summer of 416) renewed the condemnation made five years earlier and alerted Pope Innocent who ratified their decision, while leaving the door open should those who were guilty want to repent. Cleverly profiting from a change of Pope (March 417) Caelestius returned to Rome and obtained from the new Pope Zosimus at least a temporary re-establishment of his good name as well as that of Pelagius, and an order that their case should be heard over again.

This caused great agitation among the Africans, who brought pressure to bear on the Pope, the Italian bishops and Imperial court circles in Ravenna. Their efforts were crowned with success. A plenary council of all Africa solemnly renewed the condemnation of the Pelagians (May 418); at the same time the Emperor Honorius decided to treat them with all the harshness reserved for heresy; and finally Pope Zosimus, better informed, overcame his first hesitations and solemnly admonished their errors. The same attitude was maintained in the years following by the imperial government and the successors of Zosimus, Popes Boniface (418-422) and Celestine (422). The purely doctrinal phase of the Pelagian affair had ended.

But the crisis was not over. Pelagius said nothing, Caelestius was exiled to the East, but Pelagianism kept close links notably with the Italian bishops. In the forefront was the young bishop of Eclanum in Campania, Julian. A formidable dialectician and of a pugnacious turn of mind, Julian now stepped forward to defend the condemned heresy; fiercely and with obstinate persistence he counter-attacked St Augustine himself. For twelve years we find them launching and answering charges, arguing and making rejoinders. Death carried away St Augustine while he was busy (in his *Opus imperfectum*) refuting with scrupulous care, phrase by phrase, the eight books of Julian's *ad Florum*.

Driven from Italy in his turn, Julian of Eclanum first sought exile in Cilicia with Theodore of Mopsuestia; in 429 we find him at Constantinople, accompanied by Caelestius and Florus, asking the protection of Nestorius, a move which was soon shown to be imprudent, for Pelagianism was solemnly censured after the condemnation of Nestorius in a final session of the Council of Ephesus (431). The commotion caused by Pelagius reached right to the other end of the Roman world, to Britain, and in 429, also, a mission directed by St Germanus of Auxerre went to re-establish orthodoxy there. Even in Italy we find Pelagianism making its last open appearance in 439, when Julian of Eclanum tried in vain to have himself readmitted to the Church by Pope Sixtus III. The Pelagian group was able to continue in existence longer still, but clandestinely; and, as often with defeated heresies, the writings of Pelagius and Julian were distributed under cover of false names, such as Pope Sixtus, St Jerome and even, paradoxically, St Augustine.

Polemic was the keynote of the treatises drawn up by Julian of Eclanum in this second phase. He scarcely ever tried to defend or llustrate Pelagian teaching with new arguments, and limited himself either to monotonous praise of the Creator's goodness and the privileges conferred by him on his creatures, or to answering Augustine's attacks. For that, all arguments were good : Julian behaved less as a theologian than as a barrister and a good pupil in rhetoric.

Overwhelmingly prolix, disputing each foot of ground, clever to parry attacks, he did not hesitate to use arguments *ad hominem*, burrowing into his opponent's private life and earlier writings. Did not St Augustine formerly write three books in praise of free will? Does he not admit in his *Confessions*, among other crimes, that he used to be a Manichaean for nine years and longer? Manichaean he has remained — and that explains why he is haunted by sin, corruption, concupiscence. And so forth.

All was fair in war, taught the Pelagian school; and they used another weapon drawn from the arsenal of rhetoric : logical deduction of extreme and if possible absurd consequences from the propositions put forward by an opponent. Does not original sin contracted at birth imply a condemnation of christian marriage? If the absolute, universal necessity of baptism be admitted, does not that entail eternal damnation for so many small children without personal sin, as well as for the innumerable mass of unbelievers who remain in invincible ignorance? If predestination and the small number of elect be admitted, what becomes of the goodness of God, his justice, the effectiveness of the redemptive sacrifice? Yet it is written that ' God wants to save all men ' (1 Tim 2 : 4)!

The interest of such quibbles would be slight were they not the first link in a chain reaction, destined to continue for several generations, of which the Christological disputes in the East, from Apollinarius to Eutyches, have already provided a first example. The dialectic of the chain reaction developed in this way :

(1) Himself the almost too perfect heir of classical rhetoric, St Augustine felt obliged to accept the challenge offered him by Julian and to leave no argument without a reply. This led to the continuous strengthening of his own position. He was often provided with an opportunity for adding to his own teaching elements of decisive import-ance and great richness : for example, concerning the notion of freedom, placing above freedom of indifference the *libertas non peccandi*, a capacity for sinning no longer whereby redeemed mankind participates in true

freedom, that which God naturally possesses. This was a bold conception which resolves, by transcending it, the opposition between grace and free will.

However, there is no doubt that the aged Bishop of Hippo, driven back on the defensive, was too often led by his implacable opponent's pressure to tighten his guard, harden his thought and use formulas which perhaps went beyond his deep conviction and certainly beyond the authentic faith professed by the Church. If the Church has continued to venerate him as the Doctor of Grace, it is also quite true that she has always kept well on the safe side of certain exaggerations contained in these anti-Pelagian works; there exists in these at least the beginning of danger and of the error into which so many readers of the books have fallen, from Gottschalk to Jansenius, by way of Wycliffe, Luther and Baius.

(2) A reaction at once set in : typically, it came from monastic circles, from professionals of the ascetic life easily disturbed by any doctrine which seemed to them capable of encouraging slackness or tepidness. It appeared with the greatest stir in Southern Gaul : even in Africa St Augustine had had to calm the anxiety caused by his opinions among the monks of Hadrumetum (today Susa in Tunisia). The two works which he wrote for that purpose aggravated rather than calmed the disapproval which likewise appeared among the monks living in Marseilles around John Cassian, among those of Lérins and among the bishops of Provence who had once been monks themselves or were influenced by monks.

At that time (428) John Cassian was busy recording the second series of his talks with the Desert Fathers, which he was going to dedicate to the two monks of Lérins, Honoratus and Eucherius, future bishops of Arles and Lyons. He set out his counter-propositions on the vexed question of grace and free will, placing them in his *Conlatio XIX* in the mouth of the abbot Cheremon of Panephysis in the Delta of Egypt. This was a mere literary device : in reality he was tilting at St Augustine.

Cassian, however, did not rest content with putting forward the traditional doctrine of those Eastern circles where he had been brought up, — God and man, grace and free will co-operating intimately, and in a way that is mysterious to us, in the work of salvation; like St Augustine, he allowed himself to be drawn on to Pelagius's ground and to become absorbed by this new problem which in future was to typify Western speculation. He too tried to solve the mystery of personal salvation by viewing it psychologically.

With him the central difficulty became that of ' the beginning of good will ', *initium bonae voluntatis*. His explanations on this point were rather awkward : the first step seems to be attributed now to God, now to man. But in the latter case, as grace cannot fail to come and reward and strengthen and develop this first gesture, was he not in the last analysis giving man instead of God all the credit for salvation? This point defines the heresy usually called Semi-Pelagianism, a rather unhappy term popularised in the seventeenth century : it is uselessly pejorative and suggests a direct link with Pelagius, whereas the doctrine is in fact Anti-Augustinianism.

(3) At any rate this was enough to anger the many loyal supporters of the great African Doctor; one of them, the most enthusiastic and intransigent, was living in a district hostile to Marseilles : Prosper of Aquitaine, a simple layman leading the monastic life. From 428/9 to 434/5, he spent himself untiringly to defend the man whom he called ' his admirable, his incomparable master ', *ineffabiliter mirabilis, incomparabiliter honorandus, praestantissimus patronus*[4]. He hastened to warn him of this new opposition, himself undertook to reply both in prose and in verse, took the ' lecturer '-abbot to task, thundered against those who denied grace, those ungrateful people, *ingrati*, refuted one by one the objections put forward in Genoa, Lérins and elsewhere, and even hurried to Rome in the hope of obtaining the decisive support of the apostolic see (431). In fact he obtained from Pope Celestine only a moderate declaration couched in the prudent terms typical of Rome in the form of a letter addressed to the Gaulish bishops. This letter praised St Augustine in the highest terms, as one of the most reliable Doctors, *inter magistros optimos*, called for peace and openly chided innovators who attacked the traditional faith. But no one at that time was making innovations unless it were the Augustinians, led by controversy to tighten their system still further.

(4) To their passionate defence they added a further hardening of the position already taken by St Augustine in his last books, a position in itself somewhat exaggerated. Hence a still more marked reserve on the part of their opponents, who considered this attitude as an aggravated heresy — Predestinationism. Starting from St Augustine's emphasis on the mystery of election and the importance of final perseverance, it was quite enough to accuse his supporters of believing, for example, that those not among the predestined can multiply their efforts and good works but all in vain, for God will choose to withhold his grace and thus prevent them from persevering in goodness. They made other extravagant charges in this vein.

The opposition to Augustinianism, conducted in perfectly good faith, continued strong, notably in Lérins and all south-east Gaul where

4. Ap. Augustine, *Epist.*, 225.

the influence of this monastery was felt. The progress of the reaction can be measured some forty years later in the person of Faustus of Riez, promoted bishop of this little episcopal town (between 455 and 462) after having long been a monk and later abbot of Lérins. About 473-475 we find him clashing with an Augustinian of strict observance, the priest Lucidus, at once accusing him of Predestinationism, refuting and convincing him, then having the said ' heresy ' condemned in Councils held successively at Arles and Lyons.

Faustus died, much venerated, having been friendly with all the most important Gallo-Roman bishops. But he too cannot escape criticism. One must certainly bear in mind the progressive deterioration of the cultural level in the West which was more and more becoming barbarian territory (Provence itself fell to the Visigoths in 477 and Faustus was immediately exiled by their King, Euric); Lérins, moreover, boasted an ascetical rather than an intellectual tradition. There is in Faustus a kind of naïve fundamentalism, for example in his notion of a material soul (Scripture likens it to blood). This lack of a solid training is doubtless the reason why Faustus somewhat simplified his theology, and that was very dangerous in a problem as delicate as that of the relationship between nature and grace. Without perhaps realising the implication of his statement, we find him, in his turn, praising the magnificent gifts conferred by the Creator on man made in his image and likeness : free will, that ' first grace '; the natural law; the salvation of Gentiles, for did not Scripture itself bear witness to the possibility of their salvation in certain rare but startling instances[5]? Here Faustus was slipping into a Semi-, if not a Neo-Pelagianism.

(5) Rome had been anxious about this new danger from a very early stage and in 496 Pope Gelasius called upon Bishop Honoratus to make his profession of faith. Some years later, about 519, the anti-Predestinationism of the Provençals was called in question at Constantinople by the Scythian monks whom we have already met in the Monophysite crisis, criticised by the African bishops who — faithful if not very competent disciples of St Augustine — had been driven to Sardinia by the Vandal persecution, and refuted by the most qualified among them, Fulgentius of Ruspe.

The situation in Provence was set to rights at the beginning of the sixth century by that great bishop, Caesarius of Arles. St Caesarius had been educated at Lérins, he was familiar with Faustus' work and even more familiar with that of St Augustine, his master and model as pastor and preacher. In 529 under the inspiration and direction of Caesarius

5. Faustus of Riez, *De gratia*, II, 9, p. 80; I, 12-15 Engelbrecht.

the second Council of Orange solemnly condemned the tendency to Semi-Pelagianism mentioned in sections (3) and (4) above. Their condemnation was couched in terms of a relatively reserved Augustinianism. The canons of this council, which were carefully drawn up, later enjoyed great authority and were, for instance, used by the Council of Trent against the Lutherans' excessive Paulinism.

CHAPTER XXXVI

THE EFFECTS
OF THE BARBARIAN INVASIONS

WHILE these long controversies were taking place, there occurred that great historical change which gave rise to the medieval and modern West : the Roman Empire was replaced by a collection of kingdoms founded by Germanic conquerors, and this great migration of peoples, *Völkerwanderung*, resulted in important social and political changes which conditioned the rise of the nations of Europe as we know them today. All this was accompanied by many ordeals, much suffering and considerable ruin : the countryside was laid waste, depopulated and colonised anew by the invaders, towns captured and recaptured. Among capitals, Trèves was four times taken and plundered between 405 and 440 before finally falling to the Franks about 464/5. Sirmium changed hands seven times. The first occasion was in 427, when the West, which was finally cut off from this distant region, yielded it to the Emperor of Constantinople. Finally, Sirmium was destroyed by the Avars in 582. It is easy to imagine the disastrous results of such catastrophes for the religious life. A clear distinction must be drawn between the different regions and circumstances :

(1) On the edge of the Empire, because Christianity was perhaps less deeply rooted but chiefly because the invasions did more damage there, we witness a temporary withdrawal or an almost complete obliteration of the Church : detailed archaeological research has uncovered some survivals of Christianity in these barbarised regions, but they are tiny almost imperceptible vestiges : a few embers under the ashes.

That is true of the former Pannonia, the plain between the Danube and the Drava, the crucible where so many elements were later to be melted before producing in the tenth century the Hungarian nation. Further West, south of the Danube and astride the Rhine, it is true also of the former provinces of Noricum and Rhaetia which were colonised by the Bavarians and Alamanni. All these countries were brought back to Christianity only as the result of new missionary activity which bore fruit especially in the seventh century onwards. A similar obliteration took place beside the North Sea, in the Flemish plain which, to tell the truth, had been little touched by the Gospel, and in Great Britain where on what was later the soil of England the Celts, more or less Romanised but already largely christian, retreated or were steadily submerged under the tide of Anglo-Saxon invaders.

A rare document, the *Life of St Severinus*, written in 511 by his disciple Eugippius, gives us a glimpse of events on the line of the Danube between Regensburg or Passau and Vienna in the years 453-488; it draws a striking picture of insecurity in this frontier district, of the difficult life led by the christian and Roman population on the right bank of the river. Had this Germanic world proved a little more stable, somehow or other they would have succeeded in adjusting themselves to the uncomfortable proximity of the barbarians, who at that time were Rugians — East Germans who had been swept on with Attila's hordes and settled in this region after the disruption of that short-lived empire.

Hardly had they succeeded in working out a *modus vivendi*, a kind of protectorate, with the Rugians when new enemies appeared : the Alamanni who had settled in Rhaetia and who, themselves pressed closely by the Thuringians, tried to spread East beyond the Isar, and later the Inn. The Romans withdrew, evacuating one after the other their towns and villages, and sought shelter with their protectors. But the latter were also at a low ebb, racked by dynastic rivalry, and checked in their attempt to expand southwards.

Italy at that time was in the hands of a German general, Odoacer, — the same who in 476 had just brought to an end the fiction of a Western Roman Empire. He reacted vigorously, practically annihilated the Rugians and ordered the transfer *en masse* of the Roman refugees to Italy, with all their possessions. The monks of the convent founded by St Severinus did not fail to take with them their most treasured possession, the relics of their founder : they finally settled at the gates of Naples.

This is not an isolated case. During the fifth and sixth centuries we find many similar translations of relics typical of the crumbling of Christian Illyricum, of the at least partial depopulation of the region, of the disorganisation and finally the disappearance of its churches. In 412/3 Sirmium allowed the relics of St Demetrius to go to Thessalonica, and at some time during 453/8 those of St Anastasia to Constantinople. From Sirmium again or that neighbourhood there arrived in Aquileia the remains of St Hermogenes (or Hermagoras) and his companions, and in Rome those of St Pollio of Cybalae; Rome also welcomed the Four Crowned Martyrs from the Region of Pécs and St Quirinus from Sabaria in southern Pannonia. The exodus continued. The tide of barbarians reached or threatened the Dalmatian coast and on the destruction of Salona, the metropolis, by the Avars about 614 its inhabitants fled to the islands or behind the walls of the nearby palace of Diocletian at Split. Pope John IV (640-642) ordered the relics of the martyrs of Salona and even those of St Maurus of Parenzo in Istria to be carried to Rome and sheltered in the beautiful oratory of St Venantius on the Lateran Hill.

(2) The situation was different in the regions standing back from the aforementioned areas : Carinthia, for example, the left bank of the Rhine, North-East Gaul (between what is now North Wallonia in Belgium and the Seine), a part of Normandy, and Brittany. Here the settling of a new Celt or Germanic population (it was then that Armorica became Brittany with the influx of refugees from the British Isles) and the ravages of invasion certainly disorganised the Church's life for a longer or shorter period, witness the gaps in many lists of bishops until just before the sixth century. But christian life, difficult and perhaps curtailed, was not interrupted : at a number of places — Strasbourg, Trèves or Mainz, and at Xanten — archaeology proves this continuity by showing that the same sites, churches or cemeteries, were frequented from Roman to Carolingian times throughout the whole Frankish period. In decline they might be : but the towns survived and with them some Roman oases, cells of people able to maintain the traditions of the Imperial period, including the most precious of all — Christianity. This survival in such a difficult historical context clearly shows what solid results had been obtained by fourth-century missionaries.

Because this was to have important consequences, it is necessary to stress the leading role played by churchmen throughout the disturbed period of invasion. When the Roman Empire grew weak and crumbled bit by bit, dragging down with it most of the institutions on which the old civilisation was based, the Church alone or almost alone survived, and it was to the Church that christians gradually grew accustomed to turn for support — and even survival.

The biography of St Severinus already mentioned attributes to its hero a very complex role. Because of his prestige as a holy man and wonder-worker, he was the acknowledged leader of the Romans of Noricum and the lack of all secular authority meant that this role quickly extended beyond the purely religious sphere. Doubtless he worked to strengthen faith and devotion, preached charity and developed monasticism, but he was also led to impose order and discipline, even to direct police operations and still more often to negotiate with the barbarian leaders who, though they might be pagans or heretics, were also aware of his influence.

The case of St Severinus is exceptional only because he was a monk, which at that time meant a layman : but even that is not without parallels, for example St Geneviève of Paris (422-502). St Severinus's complex role was almost everywhere the normal role of the bishops and many times we find them organising resistance and mediating with the invader; as, for example, St Aignan at Orleans, St Loup at Troyes, Pope St Leo the Great himself, at the time of Attila's raids on Gaul (451) and Italy (452).

Paradoxically, it even happened that a man of God became a warrior chief. If we are to believe the biography of St Germanus of Auxerre, the most striking among the Gaulish bishops in the first half of the fifth century (418-448), he placed himself, during his anti-Pelagian mission in Great Britain, at the head of Britons threatened by a combined raid of Saxons and Celts from Scotland and won a victory by his skilful strategy and the religious enthusiasm with which he inspired his troops (Battle of the Alleluia, Easter 429?).

Later, after the barbarians had conquered and the first bitterness had passed, the bishops again played a mediating role with the Germanic kings who now ruled their countries. They protected the code of the law and defended the people, just as we have seen them do during the fourth century when faced by harshness on the part of the Imperial administration.

(3) What I have just said is true also of the other regions of the West, where the upheavals seem to have been less extensive, the invasions less complex and therefore less disastrous, the demographic changes less radical, the barbarians themselves more orderly, so that Roman civilisation was able to lead a waning but tenacious life for several generations. The towns carried on with a minimum of municipal institutions, and so too did a certain number of aristocratic families. These families retained the style of life they had led in the Low Empire, with the tradition of culture typical of their class, — and finally, most important, they retained Christianity, for it had become an integral part of this Roman heritage.

We find this happening in Italy (and in Provence, which for long had shared Italy's destiny), where the Imperial régime lasted until 476. The Ostrogoth conquerors (489-493) respectfully conserved the Roman legacy : their King, the great Theodoric (died 526), had been educated in Constantinople as a hostage and granted high honours by the Emperor, and the Ostrogoths themselves had been in contact with Roman civilisation (even if these contacts were often a result of war) during their

stay in the Danube provinces.   They had been settled there, theoretically
as allies, as early as 455.

A similar but earlier period of probation (about 380-400) had
likewise removed some of their uncouth ways from the Visigoths who,
having laid Italy waste, established their rule in South Gaul (413/8-507)
and later in Spain, which they first entered in 456 and which they
conquered first in the name of the Empire and presently on their own
account, exchanging Toulouse for Barcelona and then for Toledo as their
capital city.

An analogous fact explains the relative gentleness of Burgundian
rule.   Before settling in *Sapaudia* (443) and spreading around Geneva
and Lyon, the Burgundians had been confined, since 407, on the Rhine
in the region of Mainz and Worms.   Finally, the Vandals seem to have
left unconquered the whole Western part of Roman Africa, from Cirta
(Constantine) to the Atlantic.   This region reverted to barbarism, but
Christianity did not disappear.   Some inscriptions prove its survival
until the Arab invasion, but in this ' forgotten Africa '[1] it led a very
tenuous life, as in the worst hit regions we have been considering.   On
the other hand in the countries under their rule from 442 onwards — the
most Romanised districts — the Vandals respected Roman civilisation,
gradually became Romanised themselves and imposed order not too
unworthy of the imperial past.

Such a situation was not altogether beneficial to the Church.   To the
extent that the Germanic peoples had felt the influence of the Roman
world, they had also been touched by Christianity; in fact, all these
peoples, with the sole exception of the Franks and the late comers to the
Danubian countries (for example, a part of the Lombards), were already
christian when they took possession of the Latin countries.   But, as we
know, their Christianity had been received from Wulfila and was in fact
Arianism as defined by the Councils of Rimini and Seleucia at the end
of the reign of the Emperor Constantius.   This faith, professed with
sincerity and fervour, was to cause many difficulties between the new
rulers and the Catholic populations who had fallen under their power.

The clash was most violent in Africa; it has been called an
' implacable struggle '[2].   Not only religion was at stake; in Europe
as in Africa the Vandal Kingdom was almost continually at war with the
Empire (Genseric took Rome on 2 June 455 and plundered it despite
the pleas of Pope St Leo, who was less successful with Genseric than he

1. C. Courtois, *Les Vandales et l'Afrique*, Paris 1955, p. 325.
2. C. Courtois, *op. cit.*, p. 289.

had been with Attila).   In the eyes of their Arian masters Catholics seemed likely to treat with the enemy, and in fact when they were persecuted they did ask for Roman help.   Statesmen capable of working out a coherent and deliberate policy, such as Genseric (c. 428-477), his son and successor Huneric, and the fourth Vandal King, Thrasamund, conscientiously tried to apply the same policy of religious unity, as a guarantee of national unity, which we have seen adopted by the Christian Emperors. Convinced Arians, they tried to rally their people to Arianism : hence the persecutions which raged for many years, though there were some periods of abatement, notably under the third King, Gunthamund (485-496).   These persecutions were very cleverly carried out and accompanied by a campaign of conversion and moral pressure.   Attempts were made to paralyse Catholicism by confiscating its churches, exiling the bishops and preventing the appointment of new ones.   One of Genseric's first actions after taking Carthage (439) was to drive out its bishop, Quodvultdeus, and the see of the capital remained empty for twenty-four years (456/7-480/1).

This policy finally failed, and increased rather than diminished Catholic hostility to the Vandals.   The tolerant attitude of the next to last King, Hilderic, did not succeed in wiping out the memory of the evils endured under his predecessors, and the Byzantine troops sent to Africa under Belisarius's command by the Emperor Justinian were welcomed as liberators (533).

The bishops had done their best to lead or support the resistance of the Catholics during this difficult period.   In the front rank of these theologians and controversialists was Fulgentius, Bishop of Ruspe (died 523).   He played a leading part not only in Africa : during his long years of exile (502-515, 517-523), he settled at Cagliari in Sardinia where he founded a monastery (he had been a monk before becoming a bishop), encouraged the work of spiritual guidance, corresponded with the Scythian monks, and intervened (as we have seen) in the semi-Pelagian dispute, upholding as best he could the strictest Augustinian tradition. His case is not an isolated one : there were other exiles or refugees, bishops or monks, who likewise did useful work in the countries that harboured them : Campania, Provence, Spain.   All this is greatly to the honour of the African Church, but such an exodus, coming on top of the effects of persecution and the return to barbarism, also played a part in weakening the Church.   It was a greatly diminished Christianity which Justinian and his successors later tried to revive.

Elsewhere in the West Germanic Arianism did not raise such serious problems.   The shock there was less brutal, perhaps because for generations people had been accustomed to see barbarians serving as

PLATE 43.   THE RUINS OF THE GREAT BASILICA, HIPPO REGIUS, 4th CENTURY

This is almost certainly the episcopal church of St Augustine. Built probably in the second half of the 4th century, it was, as the ruins show, a three-aisled basilica with, Augustine says, a raised apse in which there were seats for the clergy and an episcopal chair. The altar was not in the apse itself but further out towards the people. Augustine, in Sermon 219, talked of the magnificence and great size of the cathedral, and its dimensions (138 feet long, 65 feet wide) make it one of the largest discovered in North Africa. The basilica stands in what appears to have been an *Insula Christiana* in which were other smaller church buildings such as the library, the baptistry and a house for the clergy. To the right of the church and connected with it at the far end, a large house has been discovered; probably the house of *clarissimi et egregii iuvenis Juliani*, described by Augustine in *Ep.* 99, 3, and which in about 408 he tried fairly hard to acquire for the Church. The bishop need not have worried, because, as has often happened since in similar cases, Julianus, who died without heirs, left the house to the Church.

Photo : Service des Antiquités de l'Algérie.

THE SPAN OF CHRISTIANITY: VII. North Africa (ii)

PLATE 44

Above : CHRISTIAN SARCOPHAGUS FROM DELLYS, 4TH CENTURY
Below : CARVED STONE FROM CHAPEL AT HENCHIR TENTILIA, THEVESTE, 4TH CENTURY

The sarcophagus shows some of the miracles of Christ, the denial of Peter (far right) and Christ giving the Law, and is firmly in the tradition of Roman sarcophagi, both pagan and Christian. The panel showing Christ giving the Law, for example, is very similar to the central panel of the Junius Bassus sarcophagus (Plate 23). The stone from Henchir Tentilla, on the other hand, is radically different. It is not the most beautiful example of the 'revival of Berber art' in the 4th century, but it is a significant one because it and other stones in the same chapel have clearly been reshaped and redecorated with new patterns by Berber craftsmen; there is another one, for instance, where the portrait of a man and his wife in Roman costume has been broken up and the inscription erased, while fine geometrical patterns have been added on the three remaining sides. Such a contrast in styles, on that stone and in these two pictures, is perhaps not completely irrelevant to the struggle within the 4th century African Church.

Above : Photo : Service des Antiquités de l'Algérie.
Right : Photo : Dr W. H. C. Frend, Cambridge.

THE SPAN OF CHRISTIANITY : VIII. Vienna and Arles

PLATE 45. CHRIST GIVING THE LAW; DETAIL FROM
SARCOPHAGUS OF GEMINUS, ARLES, EARLY
5TH CENTURY

This detail shows only Christ. He is bearded, and his head is topped by a cross and latinised Rho symbol. With his right hand he blesses and with his left he gives the Law. The sarcophagus is shown here largely because the portrait of Christ is so different from any of the other interpretations shown in this book. It is interesting also as another example of a sarcophagus of a high ranking Roman. Geminus was Administrator of the Treasury of the Five Provinces and therefore a very important official. Until 395 he was based on Vienna but after this date he moved to Arles, where he died at the beginning of the 5th century.

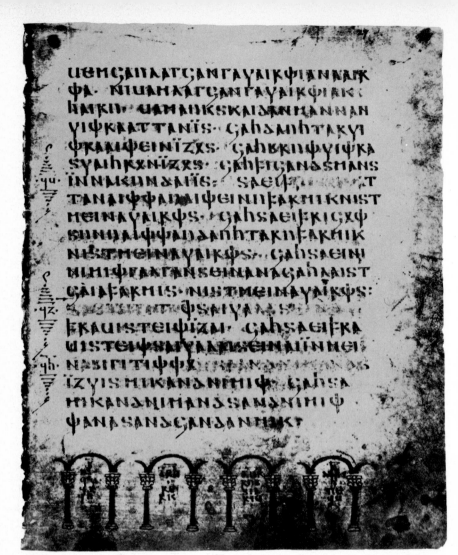

By permission of the University Library, Upsala.

THE SPAN OF CHRISTIANITY: IX. The Germanic lands

PLATE 46. THE 'CODEX ARGENTEUS' OF BISHOP WULFILLA

Wulfilla (311-383), Bishop of the Goths, who came from Cappadocia, translated the entire bible into Gothic from a Greek text edited in Constantinople. This bible, known as the *Codex Argenteus*, is one of the oldest literary remains of the Germanic lands and is a landmark in the development of the German language. The folio shown here is no. 27, Matthew 10.34-40. A copy in silver ink on purple parchment exists in the Upsala University library in Sweden. (Cf. G. W. S. Friedrichsen, *The Gothic Version of the Gospels*, Oxford 1926.)

mercenaries in the Imperial army, and eventually forming its core; others had been settled in the countryside, provided with land in virtue of a contract, or convenient fiction, whereby they became ' allies ', *foederati*. As a result a transition took place between the two régimes : for long the Germanic population was considered rather as a foreign army of occupation, forced upon Latin or Romanised provincials. These two elements of the population were divided by language, customs (dress and food) and law (different laws were applied by Romans and barbarians within the same kingdom); many centuries would pass before the two groups merged and gave birth to the peoples of modern Europe. The difference of creed, though doubtless strongly felt, was only one more obstacle to this merging.

True, there were points of friction, for example with the Visigoths of Aquitania and Spain. The behaviour towards Catholics of their King, Euric (466-484), recalls in some ways that of his Vandal colleagues. Hardly had he gained possession of some new province than he would exile the leading bishops. The fate suffered by Faustus of Riez after the annexation of Provence (477) was shared by Simplicius of Bourges and Sidonius Apollinaris of Clermont after the conquest of Auvergne (475). King Euric seems also to have opposed the replacement of bishops who had died, and this policy here as in Africa eventually threatened the Church with extinction.

Political advantage is sufficient to explain such acts of harshness. The bishops had often been the heart of resistance; some belonged to great aristocratic families closely linked with the Empire, and this was notably true of Sidonius Apollinaris. But when we consider the Kingdom of Toulouse or that of Toledo, we find unease and temporary difficulties rather than persecution.

Most of the Visigothic Kings were tolerant towards their Catholic subjects : for example, Amalaric authorised the meeting of a general council (Toledo, 527). The only noteworthy crisis occurred late, under Leovigild (567-586). Leovigild's eldest son Mennengild, appointed regent in Andalusia, became a Catholic as a result of the influence of his wife, a Frankish princess, and of the great bishop, Leander of Seville. He rebelled against his father, and was soon defeated and executed. An Arian reaction quite naturally followed and a Council of Arian bishops (580) tried skilfully but without much success to obtain the support of the Catholic bishops.

But the second son and successor of Leovigild, Recared, also became a Catholic shortly after his accession (587), and with him a large number of the Gothic lords and bishops. Arianism, it is true, did not disappear all at once; it even stirred under Viteric (603-610) but thenceforth it was doomed. The third Council of Toledo met solemnly in 589 and with it began a new period in the history of the Visigothic Kingdom, characterised by a close medieval-style collaboration between Church and State. This collaboration was made particularly clear at the time of great national councils, of which fifteen more met between 633 and 702 in Toledo, the ecclesiastical as well as the political capital.

Meanwhile the Suevi had also become converts to the Catholic Church. They had entered Spain with the Vandals and been forced back by the Visigoths into the north-eastern part of the Iberian peninsula. Pagans on their arrival, it seems that they had had a Catholic King, Rechiarius (448-457), and then passed to Arianism. Their final conversion occurred about 556 under King Charriaric, largely thanks to a great apostle, St Martin of Braga, who had first settled in Galicia as a monk, later becoming Bishop of Dumium (556) and finally Metropolitan of Braga (c. 570/1-579). The kingdom of the Suevi was annexed to the Visigothic State in 585.

The same tolerance was shown in Gaul by the Burgundians. Perhaps they too had been touched by Catholicism when they first settled on the Rhine, but they had passed to Arianism when we find them in the second half of the fifth century living in the region of the Rhône. The bishops of that country, chief among them St Avitus of Vienne (c. 494-518), exercised much influence on the royal family : under Gondebad (died 516) several princesses were already Catholics, while his son and successor, Sigismund, was also converted. His tragic death at the hands of his enemies, the Franks, deeply affected his people. They venerated as a martyr this pious King who was also, like all the barbarian kings, violent and cruel : he had murdered his own son.

A niece of king Gondebad, St Clotilde, had married the King of the Franks, Clovis. Under her influence and that of the Bishop of Reims, St Remi, Clovis asked for and received baptism shortly before or after 500. As usual, a large number of his suite and people did the same. Passing directly from paganism to Catholicism, the Franks and their dynasty thereby won the attachment of the Gallo-Roman subjects in northern Gaul and of those southern provinces which they were gradually going to conquer : Aquitania, won from the Visigoths in 507, the Burgundian Kingdom in 532/4, Provence, won from the Ostrogoths in 536.

In Italy the presence of Germanic elements, whether mercenaries, invaders or protectors, did not seriously change the religious situation. As long as the Empire lasted, it remained faithful to its traditional policy : Catholicism was the State religion.

The Italian Churches had no more to suffer after 476, under the reign of Odoacer and from 489-493 onwards under the domination of the Ostrogoths. A significant feature of the wise rule of their great King Theodoric (died 526) was his tolerance towards Catholics and his respectful relations with the Papacy. The conflict which had raged since 484 between the Byzantine Church and the Latin Church over Acacius and the *Henoticon* reassured him in the sphere of politics. When communion between Rome and Constantinople was re-established (519), things changed and part of the Roman aristocracy which had tended to hold aloof from their Ostrogothic masters looked kindly towards the Emperor of the East. This, rather than a sudden outbreak of Arian persecution, is the probable explanation of the disgrace (523) and execution (524) of the great philosopher Boethius, who had entered the service of Theodoric late in life as master of the household (522).

The Ostrogothic King doubtless felt a solidarity with Arianism, which had become as it were the national religion of Germanic people in the service of the Empire. Pope John I died (526) in the prison where Theodoric had put him after the failure of the mission to Constantinople undertaken at his orders — a strange mission for a pope, because its purpose was to intervene on behalf of the Arians, who were being severely treated by the Emperor Justinian. But there were only a few painful incidents of this kind; and tempers cooled after the death of Theodoric in that same year 526. It should be noted that Cassiodorus, that other typical representative of the Italian *intelligentsia* of the period, agreed to succeed Boethius as master of the household; later from 533 to 538 he occupied the highest post in the magistracy, the prefecture of the praetorium : Justinian's reconquest had already begun (535).

CHAPTER XXXVII

THE END
OF THE PATRISTIC PERIOD
IN THE WEST

IN all the regions where the tide of invasions had not too drastically shaken the administrative, economic and social structure of the Roman world, life went on as before when the storm passed. Within this essentially unchanged framework the Church's life in particular continued along the patterns laid down in the fourth century. That is true for what remained of Illyricum — Dalmatia — for that part of Africa under Vandal rule, and in a certain measure also for the edge of the Iberian peninsula (the Visigoths were established chiefly in the central *meseta*, in old Castille); it is still more true for Gaul south of the Loire, and finally for Italy.

Roman life continued, though somewhat diminished : we have entered a period of decadence, though we must not exaggerate the extent or the speed of disintegration. The splendour of the monuments in Ravenna is there to show us even today that the old civilisation was still vital in Italy during the fifth and sixth centuries, still artistically creative. Ravenna was the imperial residence from 402/4. It was made famous by the stay of the Regent Galla Placidia (423-450). It became capital of Italy under King Theodoric and his successors (493-535), then from 540 came under Byzantine rule. The city allows us to trace the continuity of a tradition in flower for more than a century, roughly from the middle of the fifth to the middle of the sixth century. There was no break yet with previous generations; as in the East, it was still the same Christian antiquity, the same *Spätantike*.

Even at Rome, despite the ruins heaped up by so many disasters, lootings (410, 455, 472), surrenders and sieges (536, 537-8, 545-6, 547, 550, 552), we come to the same conclusion if we study what remains of the churches founded, reconstructed or decorated at that time. The fifth and sixth centuries witnessed the creation of the most beautiful monumental mosaics, from the triumphal arch of St Mary Major, dedicated soon after the Council of Ephesus by Pope Sixtus III (432-440), to the apse of SS Cosmas and Damian, dedicated by Pope Felix IV (526-530), who transformed into a church a group of old pagan buildings beside the Sacred Way.

Life went on; the Church was still faced with the same old tasks, the first being to finish making the Gospel known throughout the West. In the fifth century there were still pagans to convert not only in distant parts of the provinces but in the great cities and even in Rome. We find them stirring during periods of crisis; at the time of Alaric's invasion (408-410) they wanted to revive sacrifices, declaring that the misfortunes of the Roman fatherland stemmed from abandonment of the ancestral religion. This argument was considered serious enough for St Augustine to combat it with his monumental *City of God* (413-427). About 495 Pope Gelasius again had to protest against the celebration of the Lupercalia; there was even talk of re-opening the temple of Janus at the time of the siege of 537-8.

But the centre of pagan resistance was crumbling. As we have seen, Christianity had already spread among the great senatorial families by the end of the fourth century, and by the beginning of the sixth most of this cultural and social élite had been converted. The *tutor* and father-in-law of Boethius, like him a christian, was the great-grandson of the great Symmachus, who in his day had been leader of the pagan party and the enemy of St Ambrose. In the person of Boethius himself we can appreciate the high quality of the Christianity professed by these last Romans; it was a learned religion fed with philosophy, faithful to the classical tradition but orthodox in its faith, perfectly familiar with the Church's current theological and canonical problems.

The same situation is found in the provinces. A kind of common front seems to have been formed by Christianity and culture in general against the mounting tide of barbarism. Very typical is the career of an educated man like Sidonius Apollinaris. Born in Lyons about 430, he was an aristocrat, son and grandson of prefects of the praetorium, and son-in-law of one of the last Emperors of the West, Avitus (455/6). He rose to become prefect of Rome in 468. Brought up a christian, though in early life he was rather tepid, he took orders and ended his life as Bishop of the city of the Arverni, in the part of the country where he had an estate and most enjoyed living (471 - c. 486). He witnessed in turn the fall of Lyons to the Burgundians in 470/4 and of Auvergne to the Visigoths in 475. Amid these storms, service of the Church was the only means Sidonius could find of remaining faithful to the various traditions which, to the very end, he chose to uphold. So we do not find in the West any equivalent of the obstinate resistance shown for example by the last Neo-Platonists of the School of Athens.

The problems which still remained to be solved were substantially the same for the élite and for the urban and rural masses. Here and there the Church had to fight vestiges of paganism — traditional customs rather than conscious statements of belief, well on the way to becoming mere superstitions. The latter threatened to survive by contaminating christians, and warnings against such practices play a large part in sermons of the time. For example, in a Christmas sermon during the 440s Pope St Leo admonished the faithful for turning round like pagans to address a deep bow to the rising sun before coming into St Peter's.

Not that the Church's attitude in this respect was uniformly negative. She had adapted to her own use certain old traditions, having first made the changes necessary to fit them for Christian devotion. For example, the old Roman processions of the *ambarvalia* had their christian equivalent in the triduum of Rogations organised in his diocese of Vienne by Bishop St Mamertus (died c. 470) — the eldest brother of the philosopher Claudianus Marmetus who was one of the last representatives of Greek culture in the West.

This work of spreading the Gospel and deepening Christianity which marked the fifth and sixth centuries was inspired by great bishops who, like the Fathers of the fourth century, were both spiritual leaders and Doctors. At Rome a typical example is the man who came to be known, with good reason, as St Leo the Great (440-461). If his correspondence reveals him as a Pope intervening with authority both in the East and in the West in order to lay down the law in matters of faith and discipline, his sermons show him as a bishop, concerned to instruct his people. He gave short, sober and condensed sermons, chiefly doctrinal, the theology reduced to its essential elements. We may note his concern as a teacher to trim them to the capacity or needs of his audience, and also the way they reflect the historical context : the period of germination and creation is over, and dogma appears stabilised. St Leo expressed himself in a very simple style, using a clear, harmonious language rich in well-turned concise phrases. His language is woven of liturgical reminiscences and with masterful discretion uses the best-tried techniques of classical rhetoric, such as antithesis, parallelism, assonance and variations of rhythm. Every reader today is still struck by the richness of the material and the effective style; the historian notices, in addition, the merits of this deliberate sobriety. A half-tone style, it represents a remarkable reaction, greatly to St Leo's credit, against intemperate rhetoric, undue preciosity, and the artificial, too erudite language affected by educated people of that time which was one of the most characteristic features of the decade.

Among other bishops we find the same importance given to preaching and instruction in doctrine, the same tendency also to simplify things, even in theology (a far cry from the refinements and subtleties we have met in the East). We might point to Italian bishops of the previous generation like Maximus of Turia (died before 423) or contemporaries like Peter Chrysologus of Ravenna (c. 432/440-450). Later examples in other countries are Caesarius of Arles (503-542) in Gaul, and Martin of Braga (561-580) in Galicia. The two last-mentioned bishops were great organisers; they summoned and took the lead in councils, and tried to solve the problems raised by the growth of Church institutions, a growth which ran parallel with progress in spreading the Gospel.

They also tried their best to spread the Gospel message by word of mouth, to raise the level of religious life and to fight the superstitious practices through which paganism survived. This difficult struggle was to last for centuries with varying success. Certain of these practices were finally suppressed, for example, masquerades in animal dress which accompanied pagan festivals on New Year's Day (despite Islam, vestiges of them survive today in North Africa). Others survived at the level of folklore : certain Continental countries have kept the custom of exchanging gifts and good wishes on January 1st, though this is a pagan custom which was attacked by christian preachers. Alone among the languages of Western Europe, Portuguese adopted the Church's usage, which was general in Greek countries, of calling the days of the week by the number of their place in the week, instead of giving them the names of the astral divinities of the astrological week : day of the Moon, day of Mars, etc.

The network of bishoprics grew tighter : for example, the part of Gaul bordering the Mediterranean (the two provinces of Narbonensis, the South of the Viennoise and the Alpes Maritimes), which counted a score of episcopal sees at the end of the fourth century, increased their number by a dozen more in the fifth, and by almost as many again in the sixth. The Iberian peninsula at this time had sixty-nine in all.

In the countryside also where, as we have seen, so much remained to be done, rapid progress was made in spreading the Gospel : hence the necessity for founding rural churches. Many were built in former pagan centres and in former villages or new settlements which arose within the great estates, already almost medieval in structure. This was an innovation in striking contrast to the traditional structure of the Church which had originally been concentrated in urban centres, tightly grouped round a bishop.

As in the East, the country parish did not immediately attain its final status. Numerous regional councils allow us to follow its gradual growth; for example in Southern Gaul the Councils of Riez in 439, Vaison in 442, Agde in 506, Arles in 524 and Vaison in 529. The same happened in Spain from the first Council of Toledo in 400 to the third in 589. The number of these parishes gradually became considerable. Galicia is one of the rare places where records have survived : in 569 the diocese of Braga numbered twenty-nine parishes, and the neighbouring diocese, Portucale, twenty-four.

The priest serving a country church at first received only strictly limited canonical powers and financial support. For a long time yet attempts were made to gather all the faithful in the episcopal, or at least in the principal, church for the most important feasts.

The North and Centre of Italy had an original, more complex organisation, the *pieve*, which marked an intermediate stage between bishopric and parish : the country churches of a district formed a kind of community under the authority of the principal church, which was the only one where baptism might be administered.

At a higher level the bishops were grouped by province under the authority of the metropolitan. This principle was not questioned even if the extent of jurisdiction sometimes was, either as a result of personal ambition or because changes of civil administration tended to be mirrored in ecclesiastical geography. For example, in Southern Gaul the authority of the see of Arles, where the prefecture of the praetorium of Trèves had withdrawn at the end of the fourth century, asserted its authority against the former metropolis, Vienne. The hierarchical situation of the bishops in this region was regulated in principle by the Council of Turin (398) but was repeatedly challenged during the fifth century. As a result there were bitter disputes, which led to the intervention of several Popes from Zosimus (417-418) to Hilary (461-468).

The whole Latin Church was centred round the see of Rome. The links may seem to us rather loose if we compare them to present-day centralisation, or even to what we find in Eastern patriarchates of the fifth and sixth centuries; and yet during this period we witness a very marked progress in the recognition of Roman primacy all along the line — in dogma, discipline and jurisdiction.

This progress was made despite unfavourable conditions and was due to the action of great popes, who were very conscious of their authority and concerned to have it recognised and respected. From Innocent I (401-417) to St Gregory the Great (590-604) there were too many of them to list here, but we must at least mention the names of St Leo (440-441) and Gelasius (492-496). Despite his relatively short reign there are extant some 150 letters or fragments of letters by Gelasius. These popes were attentive to all the needs of the Church and did not hesitate to intervene repeatedly, often in considerable detail. A letter dated 428 from Pope Celestine to the Bishop of Provence condemned the practice of wearing a special dress, doubtless of monastic origin, which had been introduced by bishops from Lérins. This is the first evidence we have relating to ecclesiastical dress. Up till then, as the Pope wished, the clergy were distinguished from the faithful ' only by their learning, virtues, orthodoxy and not by their clothes ', *doctrina non veste, conversatione non habita, mentis puritate non cultu*[1].

There is no need to stress once more the often decisive role played by Rome in the Christological and Pelagian disputes. From the point of view of jurisdiction, it was an unquestioned principle that recourse to the apostolic see was a final appeal. But in fact the very natural tendency of regional Churches to settle their own internal difficulties meant that such appeals were few and far between. One sometimes gets the impression that the Roman curia was only too pleased to grasp the opportunity of exercising its rights, and tended to listen with a favourable ear to whoever came to plead before it and to send him away absolved without listening to the other side. This often led to protests and a renewal of proceedings : the case of an African priest, Apiarius of Sicca Veneria, excommunicated for misconduct by his bishop, dragged on from 417/8 to 426 and occupied the attention of Popes Innocent, Boniface and Celestine.

The exercise of this authority, on the other hand, became increasingly difficult because of political upheavals. After the invasion of 406 relations between the Papacy and North Gaul were practically broken; even with the provinces of the South-East, which had remained Roman and politically united to Italy, communications were not very easy. We see this clearly in a serious matter like the Monophysite crisis. On 5 May 450 St Leo took care to send the bishops of Provence a copy of his famous *Tome to Flavian*. The reply of the Council of Arles arrived at Rome too late for the Roman legates to take account of it, as the Pope would have wished, at the Council of Chalcedon : St Leo's acknowledgement is dated 27 January 452. Curiously, in this reply he ordered the Gaulish bishops to tell the bishops of Spain about the good results obtained by

1. Celestine, *Epist.*, 4. (Jaffé-Waltenbach 369), 1 (2), *PL*, vol. 50, c. 431 B.

the Council, as if he could not tell them directly. In these letters we find that communications depended on the visit *ad limina* of this or that prelate, in this case the metropolitan of Embrun who had come to Rome over a jurisdictional question. It was a bishop of Grenoble who brought this same *Tome to Flavian* to Milan.

Some attempts were made to remedy this state of affairs. Following the example of the vicariate of Thessalonica, which the Pope used in order to exercise his authority indirectly on the Greek provinces of his patriarchate (the institution was finally perfected under Innocent in 412), attempts were sometimes made to appoint a more or less permanent delegate able to serve as a relay between Rome and the different ecclesiastical provinces of a region.

In Mediterranean Gaul this privilege was requested for Arles. It was granted in 417 by Pope Zosimus to the intriguer Patroclus. The primacy of Arles was eclipsed from 419 onwards and the energetic St Leo firmly opposed the initiative taken by St Hilary outside his own province. The vicariate was re-established about 462, again in 514 to the benefit of St Caesarius, and a last time under St Gregory the Great, but it did not take root, partly because of political upheavals in Southern Gaul, which was disputed by Visigoths, Ostrogoths, Burgundians and Franks. When Gaul was united under the Merovingians, the Bishop of Lyons took first place *de facto* in 570 and received the title of primate in 585, but he did not exercise the functions of a vicar of the Pope in the strict sense.

In Spain, likewise, we find a vicariate conferred on the Bishop of Seville by Popes Simplicius (468-483), Felix (483-492) and Hormisdas (514-523). The latter laid down that the vicar's jurisdiction should extend to the provinces of Boetica and Lusitania. He seems to have entrusted like functions to a bishop of Tarraconensis. But there too it was a question of temporary concessions; the future did not lie in that direction. Instead, Spain chose to have a national Church united around the see of Toledo. The latter was at first a simple suffragan of Cartagena, but in 527 it became metropolitan; after the conversion of King Recared in 587 the occupant of the see of Toledo became *de facto* primate of all Spain, though the title appeared only in 647.

The fifth and sixth centuries reveal monasticism in full growth; here too it was the tradition established in the previous century which continued without much change. The centres already established sent off colonies : Lérins was the first to do so, in the region of Vienne-Lyons, and thence into the Jura and the Valais. Condate, today Saint-Claude, was founded in 450 and Agaune, today Saint-Maurice, in 515. New centres appeared : for example, in Spain, where Asan in Aragon was founded by St Emilian and made famous by St Victorian, who died in 558, while Dumio and Braga in Galicia were founded in the 550's by St Martin.

St Martin of Braga was a Pannonian by birth, like his namesake and patron St Martin of Tours, and he became aware of his religious and apostolic vocation during a stay in Palestine. Like Provençal monasticism, Spanish monasticism was directly inspired by the first monks of the East; St Martin ordered and in part undertook the translation of the *Apophthegms* of the Desert Fathers. Other influences were also at work, particularly those brought by refugees from Africa. In 569 there arrived in the Valence region an abbot Donatus accompanied by seventy monks and a cargo of books, and in the following years an abbot named Nanctus who settled at Merida. Through him the influence of St Augustine's rule was probably introduced to Spain.

But that is insufficient to explain something which now becomes general : the contribution of monasticism to the recruitment of bishops. Here historical circumstances played their part. Increasing moral barbarism and a general decline in culture made the choice of good bishops more difficult : mistrust on both sides was overcome and more and more monks were appointed : Lérins for example was a seedbed of bishops during these two centuries. Its founder, St Honoratus, ended his career at the see of Arles (427-430), preceded or followed by three of his disciples; others continued the tradition, among them the great St Caesarius (503-542). The influence of Lérins extended throughout south-east Gaul : about the middle of the fifth century we find St Eucherius at Lyons, one of his sons, Salonius, at Geneva, and the other, Veranus, at Vence. The same thing appears in Africa and Spain. Rome, which was always conservative, followed later; we must wait until the end of the sixth century to find a former monk as Pope — but what a Pope! — St Gregory the Great (590-604).

When they became bishops, these monks did not abandon their ideal : they remained monks at heart and in fact — even in their dress. Though we have little evidence on the subject, they doubtless grouped around them a certain number of their clerics to lead a community life : certainly they spread monasticism as founders or legislators.

This flowering took place in a rather anarchic atmosphere. As in the East, each monastery adopted the organisation or the spirit defined by its founder; hence the typical profusion of *Rules*, a score of which are extant. Not everything in them is, of course, original. Some were translations or adaptations of Eastern rules, and the others copied a great deal. In certain cases borrowings and applications are clearly evident : for example, St Caesarius's two *Rules*, one for men, the other for women, were derived from St Augustine and doubtless also from the tradition of Lérins. They inspired the series of rules set out by Aurelian of Arles, called the *Regula Tarnantensis* and the *Regula Ferreoli*, to say nothing of their influence on Spain and Italy.

In this rather confused context the most famous and fruitful of these rules was written — that which we owe to St Benedict of Nursia, who was a monk at Subiaco, then at Monte Cassino, where he wrote his rule probably about 540. Its relationship with other texts and in particular with the mysterious *Regula Magistri* still remains a subject for much discussion, but whatever the extent of its dependence, there can be no doubt about its originality and its merits : sobriety and precision, a sense of moderation, wise balance, and insistence on stability, on obedience and on the communal life. It is traditional to venerate St Benedict as the Father of Western monasticism. He deserves the title, but it must be accompanied by two qualifications :

(1) Although the Benedictine *Rule* was immediately made known in Italy, its spread was soon checked by upheavals arising from the Lombard invasion. Monte Cassino itself was devastated in 577 and its monks had to flee to the Lateran. It reached Gaul only in the seventh century, and Spain perhaps even later. It was only in the Carolingian period, thanks notably to the reforms of St Benedict of Ariane (who died in 821) that this *Rule* came into general use and took its place as one of the characteristic features of Western monasticism.

(2) The *Rule* doubtless seems to be very Western in spirit, if only because it expresses a legacy of Roman legal tradition, but St Benedict himself was a very Eastern sort of saint. He was a pneumatic and charismatic wonder-worker in the tradition inaugurated by St Antony. We must not forget that his *Rule* was intended only as a way of life for beginners, and that his sixty-third and final chapter opens up wider horizons beyond this simple ' beginning of monastic life ', *initium conversationis*. He advises whoever aspires to the perfect life to go to school with the old Fathers and sends his followers back to the *Conferences* and *Institutions* of John Cassian, to the *Lives* of the Desert Fathers and to the *Rules* of St Basil.

In the last analysis, and this holds good not only for St Benedict but for all monasticism in Mediterranean countries in the fifth and sixth centuries, we are still in the presence of the monastic ideal inherited from antiquity. It can be defined primarily as flight from the world, and chief among the world's false values which it renounces is intellectual culture or rather the very decadent culture of contemporary educated circles. Only in the seventh and eighth centuries do we find the beginning of learned, civilising monasticism, which became such a feature of the medieval West.

We find the same continuity in the sphere of devotion and the religious life. The cult of martyrs and saints developed along lines laid down in the fourth century, and as in the East a prominent place was given to the Virgin Mary. In Rome at the beginning of the fifth century it was not yet the custom to distinguish the various churches by the name of a saint; they were always called by the name of a generous benefactor. That was even so for the twenty-fifth titular church, or urban parish, founded under Pope Innocent : that of St Vitalis, which was first known under the name of *titulus Vestinae*. A change took place some thirty years later, after the Council of Ephesus. When Sixtus III decorated the basilica which he had renovated on the Esquiline, he did not hesitate formally to dedicate his new buildings to the *Theotokos : Virgo Maria, tibi Xystus nova tecta dicavi* [2]. The practice became general and at the end of the sixth century the founders of the old titular charches were all provided with the epithet ' saint ' : the *titulus sabinae* became St Sabina, that founded in 336 by Pope Mark during his brief pontificate became St Mark.

This cult of the saints still took the form of veneration of their relics, with the inevitable abuses resulting from a passionate desire to possess or acquire them, and of pilgrimages to the sanctuaries where these mementoes were kept.

Christians from the West, as we have seen, continued to frequent the sanctuaries of the East. Rome and its catacombs received many pilgrims; the cathedral of Monza in Lombardy possessed a collection of ampullas which had once contained oil from lamps burning in front of the *memoriae* of various Roman martyrs, and each ampulla was identified by a label stating its origin. A devout priest had given them to Theodolinda, Queen of the Lombards in 590-604.

As happened still at the beginning of the nineteenth century, simple christians buried in the catacombs were doubtless sometimes mistaken for real martyrs. This cult, also, was influenced by the general decline of culture. In order to satisfy the curiosity of the devout and of pilgrims a legendary literature began to grow up at this time, providing imaginary biographies for saints of whom in fact only the name and what may be called the hagiographic co-ordinates were known, that is to say the site of the tomb and the date of commemoration.

We have much other evidence for this lack of historical sense, of seriousness and sometimes of commonsense. For example, at the time of the schism provoked by the disputed election of St Symmachus, a complex affair which developed from 498 to 507, his supporters did not

---

2. *ICUR*, vol. II, p. 71, no. 42 (Diehl 796), 1.

hesitate to forge documents in order to put up a better defence for him. The problem was whether the Pope, who had been accused of various crimes or misdeeds — these charges seem to have been calumnies — could be brought before a tribunal of bishops. The better to prove that such procedure was inadmissible, the authors of the Symmachian apocrypha alleged that the problem had been raised and solved during earlier pontificates; hence, for example, the *Constititum Silvestri*, the protocol of a purely imaginary Council held at Rome under Constantine in the presence of the Emperor, recently baptised and miraculously cured of leprosy by the Pope himself.

But we must not linger too long on the disconcerting signs of a culture in decline. We must give credit to this same period and *milieu* for a great work, admirable from every point of view : the development of the Roman liturgy. It was during the fifth and sixth centuries that the liturgy came to maturity; in Carolingian times it was to spread throughout the West and, apart from a few local survivals in Milan, Lyons and Toledo, to become the liturgy of the whole Latin Church.

True, such a wide extension had not occurred nor was it even foreseeable at the end of the sixth century. Despite the efforts of the Popes, who would have liked the various Churches to fall into line with Roman usage, there remained great diversity of liturgical tradition. Moreover, all the traditions were vigorous. Africa had its own tradition and so had Spain, but the usual epithet, ' Mozarabic ', is an anachronism; ' Visigothic ' would be a better name. Both Gaul and Northern Italy, including the central provinces, also had their own liturgies. A letter from Pope Innocent to the Bishop of Gubbio — barely 75 miles north of Rome — shows that at the beginning of the fifth century Umbria had not yet adopted the rites in use in the capital. There seems to have been no exact uniformity even in Rome, where a distinction must be drawn between the Papal liturgy and that of the priestly ' titles '. We are still in a creative period; varied traditions are still growing up.

Let us look at a single ceremony : the Eucharistic sacrifice. Our Roman missal, of course, reveals a complex stratification, for each period has left traces there. The contribution of the clergy of the Carolingian Empire is specially notable; it has even been called a Romano-Frankish liturgy. Nevertheless, its main features and a good part of its final form go back to fifth- and sixth-century Rome.

During these centuries the arrangement and text of the central part of the Ordinary, the Canon, were definitively settled. True, work was already well under way : it was only a question of putting the final touches to the text. All the great Popes of this period, St Leo, Gelasius, Symmachus, Vigilius and St Gregory, contributed to it, touching it up or introducing a new clause.   We can say that by 600 the work was complete and centuries to come would change no more than a few words.

The Latin Mass had taken shape.   In contrast to practice in the Eastern Churches, which usually have a choice of several liturgies, the Canon was made constant and fixed, apart from the *Communicantes* and *Hanc igitur*, which were special for certain great feasts, and a certain choice of Prefaces.   Similarly, the Proper was organised : texts were chosen to be read and prayers composed.   The oldest Roman lectionary extant shows how the pericopes, Epistles and Gospels were divided up during the liturgical year, as it stood in the seventh century.   The choice was substantially the same as today, but with more variety.   Allusions in the texts, particularly in the homilies of St Leo, suggest that the tradition was often laid down much earlier.   For the prayers we have clearer evidence.   We possess several old sacramentaries, the first of which, the *Leonianum*, is a compilation dating from shortly after 550. There again analysis suggests the hand of several fifth- and sixth-century Popes, such as St Leo, Gelasius, etc.   The Leonine reveals the abundant riches of this creative period, which were much curtailed by later generations.   The Leonine contains no less than 267 different Prefaces; among later sacramentaries, the Gelasian (end of the seventh century) contains only 53, and the Gregorian fourteen; the missal today, the form of which was finally settled after the thirteenth century, contains, as we know, even fewer.   Many of these prayers — 175 have been counted in the Leonine — continued through the centuries to the present day without notable change.   Moreover, the style of these old prayers has served as a model or norm for later ones; the Roman missal, therefore, took on its definitive features at this period.

As well as its historical importance we must also stress the intrinsic value, both cultural and religious, of this great work.   Historians of the Latin language and literature are not accustomed to do so, but they ought to consider the Roman liturgy as the last and by no means the least masterpiece of classical civilization.

Liturgical Latin is an original variety of literary Latin and as such a learned and stylised language; it would be naive to see in it a direct echo of daily speech at the time.   Liturgical Latin is also a hieratic language, wherein Roman gravity expresses what is holy, holy in a very Roman sense, that is to say with the accent on authority and law.   It is a learned language which shows the influence of Hellenistic rhetoric as popularised by the schools in its Ciceronian fulness, in its antithetical balance of parallel phrases, and in its rhythm, the whole being nearly always handled soberly.   Yet it is so faithful to the genius of the Latin language that when we pray we are in fact using the style of the oldest prayers of the ancestral religion practised by peasants in Latium. It is, finally, a language which possesses a rich and varied range. There is the style of the Prefaces, which have a somewhat oratorical and lyrical rhythm and contain much highly compressed theology; their style shows signs of the improvisation which was for long a feature of this solemn moment in the liturgy. The style of the Prefaces presents a contrast with the more measured, almost lapidary style of the rest of the Canon, and an even more striking contrast with the style of the prayers : these have been carefully composed, often in a literary style, with phrases that are more complex and more tightly woven — in short, more learned.

But the liturgy is not a mere collection of texts. The solemn Latin Mass also achieves admirable success in quite another way : as a ceremony addressed to a crowd of people, a ceremony in which the whole congregation participates. The Romans had been incomparable manipulators of crowds and from this point of view the liturgy is rooted in the most authentic imperial tradition — that of the profane ceremonies. These ceremonies, incidentally, also contained sacred elements, for the new religious consciousness considered nothing wholly profane. The ceremonies have been somewhat improperly called the imperial ' liturgy ' — indeed during the Late Empire the sovereign held his solemn audiences in a basilica; and there was also a ' liturgy ' of the hippodrome, with special processions. The Church profited from this technique. The Mass moves to the rhythm of three solemn processions, those of the Introit, Offertory and Communion, accompanied and accentuated by the singing of psalms, which are today reduced to anthems.

Finally, a comparison with the Eastern liturgies brings out the originality of the Roman Mass at the purely religious level : it is sober simple and dignified, yet manages to attain grandeur. A sense of the holy is no less present, but it is expressed in a different way, by austerity and reserve — an attitude stemming from Rome's aristocratic tradition. This feature steadily increased as the gulf between clergy and laity grew more marked at the canonical, social and cultural levels.

The liturgy shows how carefully the historian must handle the ambiguous concept of decadence. He cannot pass a purely and simply negative judgement on this confused period, which has been too readily defined as that of the Dark Ages in Western Europe.

CHAPTER XXXVIII

MEDIEVAL CHRISTIANITY EMERGES

IT is as difficult to decide exactly when a great cultural period ends as it is to decide exactly when it begins : the old tradition, even reduced to a flickering flame, takes a long time to put out. The conditions under which there occurred ' the upsurge of intellectual life in the Visigothic Church ' at the end of the sixth century lead one to believe that ' the literary tradition had survived the terrible century that followed the invasion of 410 '[1]. In Southern Gaul some Roman schools continued in existence until quite late in the fifth century; and when they disappeared the Gallo-Roman aristocracy, by means of family tradition, remained educated for several generations. The Church was only too happy to recruit bishops from this educated class. Classical culture and its educational institutions survived even better in Ostrogothic Italy and in Vandal Africa, until the Byzantine reconquest.

It would serve no useful purpose to over-estimate the level of this culture. There were many rhetors who used a bombastic style and artificial language, *sermo scholasticus :* one example is Ennodius, Bishop of Pavia, who died in 521. But side by side with the rhetors were a few more reliable and more profound thinkers, well aware of the future problems of Christian culture. In Claudianus Mamertus, a priest of Vienne who died about 474, Gaul produced a true philosopher and a christian Neo-Platonist, widely read in Porphyry. Claudianus Mamertus was better equipped than his opponent, the naïve Faustus of Riez, to handle the metaphysical complexity of a problem like that of the nature of the soul. Faustus, incidentally, was trained at Lérins, which produced holy men rather than theologians. At Naples there was Eugippius, who wrote the life of St Severinus and edited St Augustine; he died about 533. At Rome there was Dionysius Exiguus, a Scythian from the Dobruja who flourished about 500-545. He was a canonist,

---

1. J. Fontaine, *Isidore de Séville et la culture classique dans l'Espagne wisigothique,* Paris 1959, I, p. 9.

translator and computer of calendars : someone still able to keep in touch with the Greek world.

The great name of Boethius has already been mentioned. He also was a genuine philosopher who — unusual for a Latin — had received a regular philosophical training, perhaps in Alexandria. By his text-books, translations and commentaries he tried to bring about a renaissance of philosophical studies, which he hoped to ' naturalise ' once and for all in the West, thus completing the work begun by Cicero.

More directly concerned with the immediate needs of the christian faith was the foundation in 535 by Pope Agapitus and his friend Cassio-dorus of a centre of advanced religious studies in Rome. The latter was inspired by a similar ideal when, on retiring from public life to his Calabrian monastery of Vivarium, he set up there a workshop of editors and translators and wrote encyclopaedic works. These men worked for posterity : *scribantur haec in generatione altera.* The disasters of the period prevented their plans from coming to immediate fruition, but we know how much medieval culture owed to the works of these pioneers, which were piously collected, transmitted and studied over the years.

When Justinian became master of the Western provinces which he had reconquered, he set about restoring the schools. Relations were of course established with the capital, Constantinople, sometimes to the advantage of religious culture in Christian Africa and Southern Spain. About 542 the quaestor Junilius, a senior civil servant of African birth serving in Constantinople , there translated into Latin a textbook of exegesis in use in the Nestorian school of Nisibis; and there too, about 583, Leander of Seville met the future Pope St Gregory, who was staying in the city as apocrisiary, the equivalent of a nuncio today.

These contacts interested Italy also, but little advantage seems to have been taken of them, for Italy had been bled white by twenty years of war (535-555), due to the fierce resistance put up by the Ostrogoths against the advancing Byzantines. Rome in particular had suffered so much from the war that she was virtually buried under ruins. After taking the city on 17 December 546 and fearing he could not hold it, King Totila decided to deport the whole population to Campania. For forty days Rome remained virtually a desert : an astonishing incident which symbol-ically divides in two the eternal city's long career.

The Byzantines had hardly restored order when the Lombards, one of the most barbarous Germanic peoples, advanced to invade Italy (568). They quickly gained possession of the Northern plain and filtered into the peninsula. They could not drive Byzantium, a sea power, from its strongpoints : the islands of Venetia, Ravenna, Genoa and Naples; but they settled in the impregnable mountain chain of the Appenines.

In 570-571 they were in Spoleto and Benevento, threatening Rome; chronic war raged with its train of suffering : plunder, raids, famine and epidemics.

Reunion with the Eastern Empire was not always beneficial to the Latin Churches : they found themselves mixed up in theological disputes for which they were ill prepared. We have seen the reluctance of Popes Vigilius and Pelagius to let themselves be persuaded by Justinian to condemn the *Three Chapters*. They had even more difficulty in getting their decision accepted by Western bishops and theologians, who were unfamiliar with the subtleties of Neo-Chalcedonianism and judged things in a rough and ready way. They considered the new tendency defined by the council of 553 as a revenge by the Monophysites for their defeat in 451.

Except in Rome, protests were almost general; they were voiced in Africa, where controversialists energetically put forward the opposition case, in Illyricum, and in Dalmatia. All northern Italy seceded under the the metropolitans of Milan and Aquileia; indeed the latter profited from this to assume the title of patriarch in 558. The same attitude of refusal, without however going as far as schism, was shown by Spain and Gaul, which lay even further off and were worse informed : Bishop Nicetius of Trèves paradoxically accused Justinian of holding Christ to be a man pure and simple, *purum hominem*[2].

According to his well-tried method Justinian on his own authority imprisoned, exiled, deposed or won over the recalcitrant. But thanks to the Lombard advance some escaped the heavy hand of the imperial authority. Milan again established relations with Rome in 570/3, not that all resistance had disappeared there : Queen Theodolinda, though a Catholic, remained attached to the *Three Chapters*. The Patriarch of Aquileia, on the other hand, fled to Grado in 568 and obstinately remained in schism. St Gregory's perseverance succeeded in detaching a certain number of Istrian and Venetian bishops from their obedience to the Patriarch, but the dispute dragged on, coming to an end only in 607; the last holders of the see were reconciled only under Pope Sergius (687-701).

The complexity of the historical situation becomes strikingly clear in the rich and attractive figure of St Gregory (590-604). The epithet ' Great ' given to him by posterity certainly seems well deserved on several counts, corresponding to the very different aspects of his work. First of all, we have a great pope in the line of his predecessors in the fifth and sixth centuries, steering Peter's ship with the energy and authoritative

2. *Epist. Austrasicae* (*MGH*, Epist. III), 7, p. 118, 1. 35.

spirit of a magistrate in classical Rome : before becoming a monk and being recruited to the service of the Church by his predecessor Pelagius II, Gregory had followed an administrative career. In 573 we find him Prefect of the City and his verse epitaph recalled that he later became ' consul of God ', *Dei consul factus*[3]. His correspondence, 850 letters of which are extant, shows us how firmly he directed his Church — clergy, monasteries and works of charity . He kept watch on the bishops of peninsular Italy who depended directly on his authority, and he exercised his rights over the metropolitans of other regions in the West with whom the political situation of the time allowed him to keep or re-establish contact. Communications had not improved since the time of St Leo : an event as important as the conversion of King Recared in 587, with all its implications, including the conversion of the Spanish Visigoths to Catholicism, took three or four years to come to the Pope's knowledge. Only in 599 was direct communication established between St Gregory and the King of Toledo. Everywhere St Gregory was careful to maintain and exercise his rights; we have seen him contesting the claims of the Patriarch of Constantinople.

Like his predecessors, he had a very exalted notion of his duties as a bishop. He worked out their theory in his *Pastoral Treatise*, which was translated into Greek at Antioch by 609, and into Anglo-Saxon by King Alfred in the ninth century. St Gregory continued the Patristic tradition by his work as preacher, commentator on Scripture and hagiographer : it is through his *Dialogues* that certain already half-legendary echoes of St Benedict's life have reached us. He wrote one original work : his *Moralia*, a meditation in thirty-five ' books ' on the text of *Job*. The *Moralia* is disconcerting if we turn to it for the equivalent of present-day exegesis; it is in fact a textbook of the spiritual life, an introduction to contemplation. Between the time of St Augustine and that of St Bernard, St Gregory, a theologian of the mystical life, emerges as one of the greatest masters of Western spirituality. We can understand why writers in the Middle Ages, when his spirituality was widely practised, accorded him a place beside and equal to St Ambrose, St Jerome and St Augustine as one of the four great doctors of the Latin Church. The title *egregii doctores* appeared about 800 and has been official since the time of Boniface VIII.

Only in our own day are we beginning to recognise the truth of this judgment. For a long time people found it difficult to rank St Gregory so high. They were too aware of what seems to be a reflection of his age, of that unhappy period when Italy, in her turn, was sinking into

3. *ICUR*, II, p. 52, no. 1 (Diehl 990), 15.

barbarism. The culture was impoverished and suffering from sclerosis. True, St Gregory wrote essentially correct classical Latin, very different from the spoken language which St Benedict used in his *Rule;* his style is easy and virtually transparent, but his mental equipment is strictly limited. He approached the study of *Job* without troubling to know what had been written before on that subject by Hilary, Ambrose, Augustine, Julian of Eclanum and others, without mentioning Eastern writers — but St Gregory, who lived several years in Constantinople, did not learn Greek.

In this restricted world problems become simple and disappear. ' Who wrote the book of *Job?* ' Moses, or one of the prophets, or Job himself? What good can come of asking, since in any case it is the Holy Spirit who inspired the book[4]. In matters of dogma, St Gregory, like St Leo, is very faithful to the Augustinian tradition. But these three men, Augustine, Leo and Gregory, are landmarks in a movement which must be called decadence : from one to the next shades of thought are lost, difficulties no longer appreciated and a calm dogmatism emerges. With Gregory it is no longer a question of working out a theology or even of defending the faith; heresy has been conquered, men are now in peaceful possession of the truth; it is only a matter of living by it — if possible to the point of perfection. In Gregory's work there is a tragic contrast between the greatness and originality of the thought and the mediocre quality of the instruments at its service.

The political situation at the time of St Gregory was extremely difficult. He would have liked nothing better than to behave as an obedient and devoted subject of the ' very pious ' Emperor of Constantinople; in fact he never ceased to consider himself as such. But the weakness and final disappearance of the Imperial power in Italy obliged the Pope, like the bishops elsewhere, to assume a role which that power was clearly incapable of filling. The Lombard threat loomed larger, but the Byzantine governor, who was hardly able to defend Ravenna, could neither overcome the enemy nor decide to treat with him. The Pope was obliged to organise the defence of Rome himself and, in despair, to make terms with the Lombards : Rome was provisionally saved but at the cost of a heavy tribute, a new burden on the Church's treasury.

The civil administration was likewise failing and the civil servants were paid as irregularly as the soldiers. Again the Pope had to remind them of their duty, take care that provisions of corn arrived from Sicily (famine, like plague, was a permanent threat to Rome), and ensure the working of public welfare services, of poor relief, of the ransom of

4. *Moralia in Job,* I, praef., 1-2.

prisoners captured by the Lombards. Legally Rome continued to depend on the Empire, for the Duke representing the Empire disappeared only about 752-757; in fact it was the Pope who more and more found himself obliged to exercise the administrative and governmental responsibilities there. Thus began the growth of what was later to become the constitution of the Papal State. We have entered the strictly medieval period of Rome's history. Faced by the barbarians, the Church was the only organised force still able to embody the terrestrial city; it was the Church that steered ' the abandoned ship, pilotless, in a great storm ' *(nave senza nocchiere en gran tempesta)*. In a specially striking way Rome illustrates a general phenomenon, common to the whole West. If the institutional void was not as complete elsewhere, at every level the crudely organised kingdoms founded by the barbarians had to take the place of that complex structure, the Roman Empire. Each time the secular institutions were found wanting, the Church was led to take their place. Hence the appearance of a new system, that of Sacral Christianity, where the Church took on itself a role of director or administrator in society as though assuming the place and duties of a priest-king. For many centuries this was to characterise the civilisation of Western Europe

The system appeared, for example, in the sphere of education. The Patristic period has shown what a close symbiosis had grown up between Christianity and classical culture; as long as something of the latter survived, the Church continued to profit from it We have seen the Gaulish bishops willingly recruited from senatorial families, the last to have kept alive a love of learning. But after the disappearance of teaching institutions, when this tradition itself grew dangerously weak and threatened to die, the Church had to act. Taking the place of the waning temporal power, it assumed responsibility for education, without which the recruitment of a competent clergy would have become endangered, and with it the christian life itself.

Here, almost in reverse, we again find the widespread phenomenon we observed when discussing the birth of Churches outside the Empire. Christianity was a learned religion; it could not dispense with a certain level of culture, of knowledge and of literature. In the East we have seen it civilising the barbarians, from Ethiopia to the Caucasus : it could not without great danger allow the West to become barbarian.

Up until now the Church had taken charge only of the professional training of its clergy, their education in the strict sense being carried out by the school and the family. While still children, those who wished to become clerics entered the ranks of the episcopal clergy as lectors. Only the monasteries, which were concerned to keep all contact with the outside world to a minimum, taught their young oblates to read.

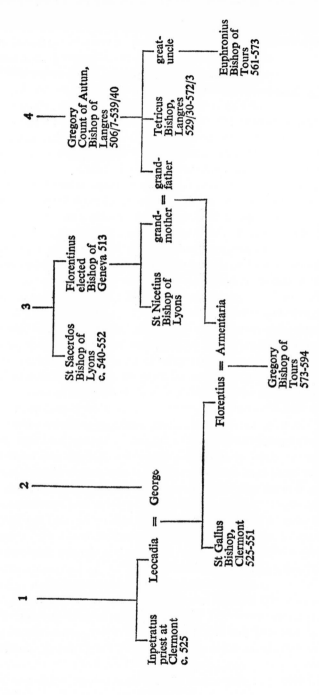

SOME SIXTH CENTURY SENATORIAL FAMILIES OF AUVERGNE AND BURGUNDY

1

Inpetratus
priest at
Clermont
c. 525

Leocadia = George

St Gallus
Bishop,
Clermont
525-551

Florentius = Armentaria

Gregory
Bishop of
Tours
573-594

2

3

St Sacerdos
Bishop of
Lyons
c. 540-552

Florentinus
elected
Bishop of
Geneva 513

St Nicetius
Bishop of
Lyons

grand-
mother
=
grand-
father

4

Gregory
Count of Autun,
Bishop of
Langres
506/7-539/40

Tetricus
Bishop,
Langres
529/30-572/3

great-
uncle

Euphronius
Bishop of
Tours
561-573

Now, however, the bishop himself had to provide his clergy with a minimum of knowledge, without which they could not carry out their duties properly. Hence the appearance at the beginning of the sixth century of the episcopal school — the nucleus from which our our universities were later to develop. We find it in existence in Provence during the bishopric of St Caesarius (503-542). In Spain, a council of Toledo in 527 organised the episcopal school with care : the young tonsured clerics were to live in community in the episcopal house and take lessons from a specially appointed teacher; at eighteen they were to choose between marriage and taking major Orders.

The institution became general. A good many Churchmen of the sixth century about whom we have biographical information were brought up from childhood in *litteris ecclesiasticis* near some learned and holy bishop. That was true of the future Gregory of Tours, who was born in 538, educated by his uncle Gallus, Bishop of Auvergne, then by his great-uncle, St Nicetius of Lyons, himself the son and nephew of bishops. A glance at his family tree shows how, partly because of ordination late in life, the last senatorial families changed into priestly families (see genealogical table on p. 441).

According to circumstances this new institution grew up and developed in certain places more quickly than in others. A curious letter from St Gregory the Great to Bishop St Didier of Vienne reproaches the latter bitterly for undertaking the teaching of grammar. The meaning of the text is disputed. It may mean that Didier tended to lay too much stress on profane literature, but another explanation is plausible. This letter may reflect a lag between the cultural situation in Rome where, even in 599, something still remained of a cultural tradition, and that in the Rhône Valley, plunged in darkness, where the bishops may well have had to take in hand even the most elementary education of his clergy.

Likewise, the multiplication of rural parishes made it still more urgent to educate a larger number of priests, at a time when civilisation as a whole was becoming steadily more barbarised. The solution adopted for the episcopal churches had to be made general : hence the emergence of the priestly school. In Provence again, still under the inspiration of St Caesarius, the second Council of Vaison in 529 laid down that all priests in charge of a parish should give a christian education to young children provisionally admitted as lectors ' to prepare from among their number worthy successors '[5]. This is a justly famous passage, which can be called the birth certificate of our free country school (unknown to antiquity), both in its more general form as our primary school and,

5. *Concilia aevi merovingici* (*MGH, Leges* III. *Concilia*, vol. I). p. 56. can. 1.

as we shall see later, as our christian school. The priestly school may have been in existence even earlier, because the Council of Vaison refers to some kind of education already general in Italy, and even in Gaul there may perhaps have been a few priestly schools before 529. This type of school spread rapidly because it answered a widespread need. Throughout the sixth century Councils took care to bar from the priesthood illiterate candidates, or even priests already ordained who could not learn to read; Orléans in 533 and Narbonne in 589.

We cannot overstress the importance of these educational innovations. By making general a kind of education which so far had existed only within the cloisters, these schools, episcopal or parish, effected a synthesis between the schoolmaster and the spiritual director, a synthesis unknown to antiquity and still unknown to Byzantium. In this way arose the type of christian education to which the Church has remained firmly attached right down to the present day.

For the time being the important historical fact is that this christian school, which filled a need in the Dark Ages, was for long centuries the only school known to the West. Hence the characteristic ambiguity of the word ' cleric ' in the Middle Ages : *clericus* means successively, and nearly always at the same time, a member of the clergy and an educated man. With education all culture too became ' clerical ' — or almost all, the exception being the training of notaries to draw up the written acts of civil law. It became not only christian, but Church culture. This it was to remain for centuries, until the appearance of a courtly literature.

In the second half of the sixth century, when the aristocracy of Germanic origin began to lead a more refined kind of life than their barbarian predecessors, it is to this new clerical kind of culture that we find them turning. Take the case of one of Clovis's grandsons, King Chilperic of Neustria (561-584). He evidently wished to play the role of restorer of classical culture or, more exactly, to pose as an imitator of that famous model, the *basileus* of Constantinople, for the Byzantine mirage continued to attract the Latins throughout the first half of the Middle Ages. But his culture was that of the new age. He tried writing Latin poetry, but it was religious poetry, imitated from Sedulius as we can see in a hymn to St Medard which is still extant. He undertook apologetics, tried to convert a Jew, and even dabbled in the theology of the Trinity, not without scandalising his bishops, who were frightened of his clumsy incompetence.

But the bishops were scarcely able to do better, apart from remaining orthodox. The intellectual level of the clergy of Frankish Gaul was extremely low. At the Council of Macon in 585 one of the bishops claimed that the word *homo* could not be applied to a woman : he was refuted by the quotation of verses or expressions from Scripture where the word ' man ' is applied to both sexes. This anecdote is famous and has often been unjustly distorted; in fact these Merovingian bishops did not go so far as to doubt whether women have souls. It shows us how people were beginning to reflect on the basis of elementary grammar — all that remained of this lowly culture of barbarian times. We know the part which grammar was later to play in the growth of medieval thought; here we witness the first unsteady steps of a new technique.

The stamp of the Church is found not only in intellectual culture but in all spheres. It sets this Western Christianity apart from the Christianity of the Late Empire and of the Byzantine world, which, as we have seen, continued the Late Empire. We are dealing in the West with quite another working-out of the Christian ideal in its application to the institutions of the terrestrial city. We can speak of a bi-polar structure. Intimately linked and sometimes intermixed though these two principles might be, there was always the Church on one side, and over against it the Emperor, the heir of a continuous tradition since Augustus and Diocletian. With the Emperor went a whole system of temporal values which, even when they became Christian, retained their own structure, — for example, at the cultural level, knowledge of Homer and the classics.

In the West the new civilisation rose and organised itself around the Church in answer to the Church's needs, as these appeared at the end of the period of barbarian anarchy. This is clearly evident in the correspondence of St Gregory the Great. One is struck by the different tone the Pope uses on the one hand to address the Emperor Maurice, or his successor Phocas, and on the other hand to write to the Merovingian prince, Childebert II, or to his mother Brunehaut. To the former he is humble and deferential, to the latter his tone is much more peremptory. He admonishes and makes suggestions which are virtual orders. He lays down a programme for them to follow, ordering them to lend a hand in spreading the Gospel and imposing Church discipline.

At this stage there clearly emerges the doctrine of the ministerial function of the sovereign, *ministerium regis.* Power is given to him so that his terrestrial kingdom may be placed at the service of the Kingdom of Heaven. The formulas used by St Gregory are so clear that in the eleventh century his distant successor Gregory VII, in his struggle with the Emperor Henry IV, was able to take advantage of a certain clause in a privilege of 602 threatening with deposition and excommunication anyone, even a King, who ventured to contravene it.

Hence the role played by the bishops in Frankish society and, after the conversion of Recared, in the Visigothic State. We find them in the King's suite as advisers, and not merely on Church matters. We find them in their own city, side by side with, and often over against, the Court. As in the Late Empire, they were the natural champions of the people against the rapacity of those in power. But the public services of the barbarian state were reduced to a minimum and, like St Gregory in Rome, the bishops often had to undertake and control welfare schemes and even public works.

But the maintenance of civilisation, though intimately linked with the work of Christianity, was only a subordinate, if not accessory, aspect of the Church's principal task. Then as now that task was to spread the Gospel, to convert, and to make good christians. It had much to do, even in regions where movements of population had not uprooted or shaken it. Under the impact of the invasions the old legacy of ancestral paganism had often reappeared in the countryside, where the work of conversion, as we have seen, was still barely established and even incomplete. The Germanic conquerors, moreover, brought with them other beliefs and superstitious practices, whose vitality is shown both in books and in the funeral customs revealed by excavations in their cemeteries.

Among the duties which St Gregory pointed out to Brunehaut, Regent of Austrasia, was the duty to fight against idolatry, against the worship of sacred trees and against the sacrifice of animals. For, says the Pope, ' numerous Christians frequent the churches without however giving up the worship of spirits '[6]. The frequent Councils which met in Central Gaul during the sixth century returned ceaselessly to this problem, It was solved only much later, when pagan rites slowly fell into ruins in the course of generations, finally becoming clandestine witchcraft or being watered down into folk-customs, performed subconsciously.

The Church had difficulty in planting the moral ideas of the Gospel in a society which had grown so barbarous. The *Historia Francorum* of Gregory of Tours sketches a striking picture of its brutal and savage behaviour : a train of violence, crime and the unleashing of elemental passions. A bad example was set from above, for numerous crimes were committed in the royal families. Blood stained the hands of the rival queens, Fredegunde, the wife of Chilperic of Neustria, and her sister-in-law Brunehaut, whom the former's son later put to death in terrible fashion as the ' murderer of ten kings '.

Humanity and gentleness fled to the cloister. We have an example in St Radegund, a Thuringian prisoner who became the wife of the

6. *Epist.*, VIII, 4 (*MGH, Epist.*, II, p. 7).

violent King Clotaire I. She withdrew from court and in Poitiers founded the monastery of the Holy Cross, named after the precious relic sent to her by the Emperor Justin II. She spent the rest of her days there in a calm atmosphere. Her very austere piety was softened by humanism and even urbanity : for example, she welcomed Fortunatus, one of the last court poets of Italy. She died in 587.

But even in this oasis of peace old passions were still at work. Witness the scandal caused by two granddaughters of the same Clotaire — Chrodielda and Basina, who were both nuns at the Holy Cross, though, it is true, the latter had been sent there forcibly by her stepmother Fredegunde. They rebelled, left the cloister, organised an armed attack and imprisoned the abbess. When the authorities discovered and tried to arrest her, Chrodielda replied proudly : ' I am a queen, a king's daughter, cousin of another king : watch out for his vengeance[7] '!

The clergy itself, starting with the bishops, were contaminated by secular influence : too much glory, wealth and power surrounded the episcopal office for ambition and greed not to arise. The Pope and Councils continually attacked simony and the ordination of ill-educated laymen. The kings all too often rewarded their supporters with the grant of a bishopric — for example Bodegiselus, Chilperi's majordomo, was installed by royal favour in the see of Le Mans. He was a greedy, cruel man who, moreover, received bad advice from his wife; on one occasion he retorted : ' Because I have become a cleric, is that a reason why I should not avenge my wrongs[8] '?

Fortunately at this difficult period the Church also numbered many saints. Many were spontaneously canonised by the people, thus affording a glimpse of the people's religious sensitivity and deepest feelings. For example, it was the people's protest against the general cruelty of the age which was shown in the veneration accorded the innocent victims of an undeserved death — the equivalent of the ' suffering saints ', *svatie stratoterptsi*, in the Russian Church. This popular veneration was inspired by a truly evangelical mercy and devotion. We have mentioned the case of the Burgundian King, St Sigismund. There were many others, for example St Praetextatus, Bishop of Rouen, who in 586 was a victim of Fredegunde's malice, and St Didier of Vienne (he who was scolded as a grammarian), who perished as a result of intrigues fomented against him by the hatred of Brunehaut with the connivance, it must be admitted, of his colleague, Bishop St Aregius of Lyons. The modern reader's first impression will doubtless be that these good

7. Gregory of Tours *Historia Francorum,* X, 15.
8 Id , *Ibid.,* VIII, 39.

people often canonised easily : but that practice expressed astonished admiration on the part of simple souls when confronted with virtue which, in their eyes, contrasting as it did with the surrounding disorder, could only be explained by the working of the Spirit. The age scarcely favoured the blossoming forth of average goodness; the texts, at least, reveal only opposed extremes : criminals and saints.

Among the saints were monks and also hermits like St Vulfilaicus, who was a Lombard by birth. At Carignan in North Gaul he tried to imitate the feats of the Eastern stylites, an excess from which he was promptly dissuaded by the ecclesiastical authorities. Vulfilaicus died about 544. But it is the bishop, above all, who is the typical saint of this period. It is the bishop who spreads the Gospel in person, a model of virtue, usually a wonder-worker who heals the sick and exorcises devils; he also practises charity, performs many good works and protects the weak; he is a severe counsellor of princes, an apostle of peace — in short, a man of God.

It was a period of robust, rather simple faith, little encumbered by critical scruples. We know that charlatans abused the general credulity and taste for wonders, and the passionate desire to possess relics. The cult of the saints and the veneration of their tombs and their remains were accompanied by some superstitious features. Their sanctuaries were greatly venerated : indeed this was the period when the highly developed right of asylum was generally respected. It was not always respected, of course, but those who infringed it were conscious of guilt and the threat of God's curse. When the soldiers of Theodoric I, who was at war with his brother Childebert, had plundered the basilica of St Julian of Brioude, the unhappy perpetrators of this crime felt themselves to be possessed, as it were, by a devil and tormented by the holy martyr.

The feeling which seems to dominate is that of reverential fear inspired by the sovereign power of God and his saints. The threat of punishment, in this world or the next, was the major argument used to strengthen a bishop's other arguments when he tried to make a prince perform his duties. Devotion had assumed a less communal, more individual aspect. Preoccupation with personal salvation had become obsessive. The powerful, in particular, whose conscience was often ill at ease, were anxious to make atonement by alms, pious bequests, donations to churches and foundations. Brunehaut, for example, founded at Autun a church dedicated to St Martin, a convent of enclosed nuns and a hospice or hospital. Much trust was placed in the communion of saints and in the ability to be helped by others' merits and by the prayers of the Church. It was easier to have a Mass said for one's intention than to receive Communion oneself.

An awareness of the presence of something holy, in which the *tremendum* counted for more than the *fascinans*, penetrated daily life and even institutions.   Hence the growth of new practices foreign to Roman law and later codified in the collections of national laws which were beginning to be drawn up : the *Gombette Law* among the Burgundians and the *Salic Law* among the Franks began to be codified at the beginning of the sixth century.   The majority of these collections, such as the Laws of the Ripuarian Franks, of the Alemanni, of the Thuringians and of the Bavarians, were drawn up only in later centuries.

Among these customs we find a widespread use of the oath.   The accused or defendant could, as the phrase went, ' purge himself ' by an oath, and this presupposed a civilisation where the name of God was not lightly invoked.   True, perjury was not unknown, hence the custom whereby co-swearers also took an oath to confirm that taken by the first person.   Finally there was the direct appeal to God's judgment, one form of which was ordeal by plunging one's hand into boiling water or grasping red-hot iron, and another form the legal duel : it was unthinkable that God should abandon a man who had a just cause and openly championed the law.   This practice took root despite protests from churchmen who were heirs of the old tradition.   St Avitus, Archbishop of Vienna (c. 494-518), protested among the Burgundians, and Cassiodorus, writing in the name of King Theodoric, in Illyricum.   But the current proved too strong.   It is well known how greatly these practices influenced medieval law and Western customs, and to what an extent the duel, the last echo of this appeal to God's judgment, worried moralists of later centuries.

Tradition attributes this wooden reading desk to St Radegund, daughter of a Thuringian king and unwilling wife of King Clotaire I. In 544 she fled to the cloister and later became abbess of a monastery in Poitiers. There is no literary evidence to support the tradition, but the decoration suggests at least that the desk comes from the right period, for it shows clear signs of the oriental influence which is known to have been strong on the Merovingian art of this time of which there are several other examples in Poitiers alone. Thus, in Syrian churches of the same period the lintels sometimes carry a decoration of crosses and doves surrounding a lamb (which represents Christ), and use is also made of the pattern in which the figure of Christ is framed by the angel, the eagle, the lion and the ox, the four figures taken over by the Church from the vision of Ezekiel as symbols of the four Evangelists. The desk is the first instance in France where the four symbols appear together in this particular arrangement and the pattern later had an important history in medieval art.

By permission of Archives Photographiques, Paris

PLATE 48

Above : THE CROWN OF PETRIE; IRELAND
        6TH OR 7TH CENTURY

Below : THE PILLAR OF REASK; IRELAND
        6TH OR 7TH CENTURY

The Crown of Petrie was probably original
part of a votive crown with a series of conic
points, made to be hung in a church.
design, with its bold, beautifully execute
curves sweeping delicately into bird-hea
terminations, draws on a strong native tr
dition of abstract art. The same may be sa
of the Pillar of Reask, although here t
connection with the pagan past may be ev
stronger. In the conversion of Ireland, o
cultural tradition did not replace anoth
but the new religion took over the old si
and the old ways. Thus Christian symb
were carved on many stones or rocks venera
by the pagans, and this may be the case w
the Pillar of Reask.

By permission of the Irish Cultural Relations Commi
Dublin.

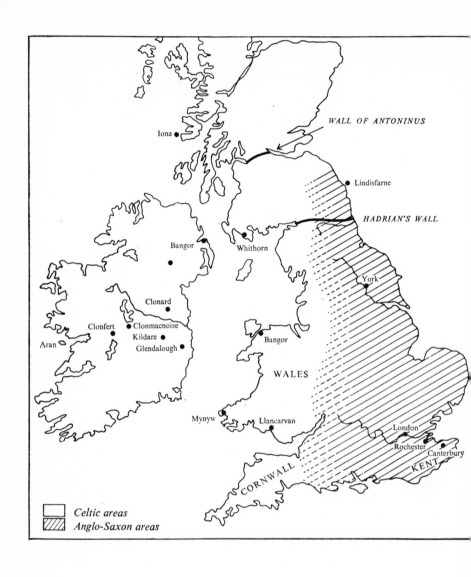

WALL OF ANTONINUS

Iona •

Lindisfarne •

HADRIAN'S WALL

Whithorn •

Bangor •

York •

Clonard •

Clonfert •   • Clonmacnoise
Kildare •
Aran   Glendalough •

Bangor •

WALES

Mynyw •   • Llancarvan

London •
Rochester •
Canterbury •

CORNWALL

KENT

☐ *Celtic areas*
▨ *Anglo-Saxon areas*

15   Britain and Ireland

CHAPTER XXXIX

TOWARDS THE CONVERSION
OF NORTHERN EUROPE

As often happens in the history of civilisation, the change from antiquity to the Middle Ages was accompanied by a shift in the centres of culture. While Italy was about to succumb to the ravages of the Lombard invasion and Southern Gaul, in its turn, was about to witness the final extinction of the Roman tradition that had for long tenaciously survived there, new life appeared elsewhere. The first renaissance took place in Spain. The destruction of the Suabian Kingdom in 585 and the conversion of King Recared in 587 completed the political and religious unification of the Iberian peninsula. Already a certain stability had been created and this, linked with stimulating contributions from Byzantium and Africa, made possible a renewal of ecclesiastical studies in the monasteries and in the episcopacy.

This renewal appeared in mid-sixth century with Justus of Urgel, who wrote a commentary on the *Song of Songs*, and Apringius of Beja, who wrote a commentary on the *Apocalypse*. A little later, in the years 580-600, came Eutropius of Valencia, Licinianus of Cartagena and Leander of Seville (584-608). Leander's most endearing claim to fame is that he educated his young brother and successor, Isidore, who died in 636. Isidore's encyclopaedic work, which was both a collection of materials garnered from the inheritance of ancient learning and a first attempt at organising facts in the hope of achieving a new synthesis, remained throughout the Middle Ages one of the basic textbooks of Western civilisation.

After the Franks' victory over the Visigoths at Vouillé in 507 Aquitania was annexed to the Frankish Kingdom. This benefited North Gaul, which, as we have seen, had suffered so cruelly from invasions. The South helped to reconstruct the northern and eastern provinces, and in particular helped to reorganise their churches. From Nantes to Maestricht the movement was to grow in the seventh century, but it began in the previous century.   Under Bishop St Nicetius, himself perhaps born in Limoges, the Church of Trèves received clergy from Auvergne and called in Italian artisans.   About the year 500 missions were preached and monasteries founded in the Rhine district from Lake Constance to the Moselle.   The leaders here were St Goar and St Fridolin; both came from Aquitania and St Fridolin had been abbot of a monastery in Poitiers.

Another movement grew up centred on Aquileia which resulted about 580 in the restoration of the episcopal sees of the Valley of the Drav in Carinthia.   In that region missionaries encountered priests ordained by Gaulish bishops.   This gave rise to a conflict of jurisdiction which had to be settled by Pope St Gregory, indirect evidence of the Frankish clergy's missionary activity within Germany.   Their work was unexpectedly continued by missionaries from the British Isles; but this makes it necessary to go back a few years.

We left Britain violently disturbed by the Anglo-Saxon invasion. Between 457 and 604 all mention of the town of London disappears from surviving documents.   In the east of the country Christianity practically disappeared before the tide of pagan conquerors.   On the other hand the departure of Britons for western districts seems to have favoured the spread of Christianity.   Whereas the veneer of Roman civilisation peeled off quite quickly as Celtic characteristics reasserted themselves, in Cornwall and Wales the christian religion not only survived but spread.   In those regions the geographical distribution of christian inscriptions from the fifth to the seventh centuries suggests that there were many christian sites besides those founded in the Roman period.   Certainly a new epoch was opening for the history of this part of the country and its Church.   As far as we can judge from the not always reliable nature of the relevant documents concerning the saints who made the Church famous, notably in the sixth century, it was a Church of a very different type from that of the Roman period, a mainly monastic Church with striking Celtic features.   Among its saints were St Illtyd, who died about 527-537, and his disciples and successors, St Gildas, who died in 570, St David of Menevia, the most popular Welsh saint and the patron of Wales who died about 601, and St Samson. St Samson, who died about 565/573, was Bishop-Abbot of Dol in Brittany, where immigrants from the British Isles brought their christian faith and their own traditions in devotional practices and ecclesiastical organisation.

Britain, of course, produced St Patrick, the apostle of Ireland. The beginnings of Christianity in Ireland, which had escaped the Roman domination, are wrapped in obscurity, but the decisive role played in its conversion by St Patrick is not disputed. He belonged, as we have seen, to an old Christian family, and at the age of nearly sixteen was carried off by pirates from Ireland. He spent six years in slavery there and escaped to the Continent, where he completed his religious training probably at Auxerre under St Amator and his successor St Germanus. Returning home, he felt called by God to spread the Gospel in Ireland; thenceforth he devoted himself to that work, for which he was consecrated bishop. His apostolate must be dated probably from 432 to 461. It is difficult to reconstruct the phases and changes whereby the country became christian. Christianity had to overcome the resistance of the Druid class, upholders of a cultural tradition which, though unwritten, was none the less original and rich.

This tradition and the vigorous national character expressed thereby, joined to the relative isolation in which Irish Christianity developed, explain why, when the latter emerged into full daylight during the sixth century, it showed very special features. These distinguish the Church in Ireland from all the rest of the Latin West: we can truly speak of a Celtic Church.

This Church had its own usages, some of which later provoked violent conflicts: a special form of tonsure, for example, and the use of an old system of calculating the date of Easter. But the important point is the extraordinary success of the monastic ideal. Monasticism grew prodigiously in Ireland. As once before in Egypt, we find a swarm of hermitages and of convents for monks and enclosed nuns, whose numbers sometimes ran into several thousand. A still more remarkable fact is this: whereas in the rest of the Christian world the episcopal church was the basic unit of religious organisation, in Ireland and also to a large extent in the other Celtic countries it was the monastery almost exclusively which filled this role. Its jurisdiction spread to the neighbouring countryside. Its abbot may well have been a consecrated bishop; if not, for the liturgy he called in one or more monastic bishops living under his authority.

In this unusual framework took place a remarkable flowering of culture. As in the Eastern Churches outside the Roman Empire, the planting of Christianity gave rise in Ireland to a culture and a literature. The culture was first and foremost Latin: as happened throughout the remainder of the West, even the Germanic West, Latin remained the only liturgical language in Celtic countries. Gaelic already possessed its letters patent of nobility and even an alphabet, the *ogham*, but the alphabet was hardly used except to record short inscriptions. During the christian period the Latin alphabet was used and in the seventh century there appeared the first great works of Irish Christian literature. Only in the following century are there signs of a profane literature inspired by local traditions, the Druids having survived in the corporations of poets, *filid*, and of bards. Parallel with this Irish literature there also grew up a christian literature written in Latin.

To be a monk it was necessary to have some knowledge at least of this learned language, if only to read and recite the psalter. The important thing to note is that in Ireland by contrast with Roman countries Latin was learned as a language wholly foreign to the native tongue. Hence recourse was had to a new and effective educational method : students passed directly from the alphabet to reading some verses of the psalms, using a technique which recalls the archaic manner in which the Koran is taught and our own modern technique of reading by whole sentences.

It would be an error to over-estimate the standard of this teaching and culture which were first evolved to meet the most urgent needs of the religious life. But they did provide a starting-point, a seed from which there steadily grew a much wider curiosity based on more extensive knowledge; to such a point that at the end of the period under consideration Ireland appears as a centre of civilisation influencing the almost completely barbarised European continent. Ireland was one of the main centres to nourish the Carolingian renaissance and through that the whole cultural growth of the medieval and modern West.

Insula doctorum, but first and foremost *insula sanctorum :* Ireland is proud of having produced a splendid body of saints, particularly in the fifth and sixth centuries. Spirituality bloomed in an unusual atmosphere, which ensures the Celtic Church a place apart in the company of christian nations. To mention some of the saints by name : St Enda, who settled in the Isle of Arran about 520, his contemporaries St Finnian of Clonard and St Brigid of Kildare, and also St Finnian of Moville, St Brendan of Clonfert, St Ciaran of Clonmacnoise and St Coemgen of Glendalough, all of whom belonged to monasteries founded in the decade beginning 540. As for Celtic spirituality, it was based on a fiery temperament which tended to go to extremes, and it showed unusual zeal for the penitential life, for mortification and for asceticism. Despite the difference of climate and surroundings, we find in Ireland the same charismatic atmosphere, the same feasts, sometimes the same excesses we have sometimes encountered among the early Desert Fathers in Egypt and in the East. Also, a fairly large number of the practices we find in Ireland, such as poverty, austere dwellings and limitation of sleep and food, had their equivalent in Eastern monasticism. The Irish sometimes practised an absolute fast and sometimes fasted 'against someone', to make right or their own will triumph over an enemy. They went without baths, even as a measure of cleanliness; on the other hand they would remain immersed for a long time in an icy pond. In their various mortifications they showed contempt and even defiance of nature; they withdrew into isolation, kept silence and in every detail obeyed their master or abbot. All this made for a rather tense atmosphere (the peaks of asceticism were considered as the real equivalent of martyrdom) with something fierce about it, tempered only by the tendency to fantasy and wonders so characteristic of the Celtic genius.

Without claiming to make an exhaustive inventory, we can mention here two at least of the practices characteristic of Irish spirituality, because of their deep influence on Latin Christianity as a whole. First, the sacrament of penance was considered as a private affair, which could be repeated many times. In other countries this attitude to penance had not gone beyond the embryonic stage, and in Spain it was again denounced as scandalous by the great Council of Toledo in 589. But it developed considerably in the monasteries of Ireland. Frequent, even daily confession of sins was part of the usual ascetical way of life. It was not only what monks even today know as the 'Chapter of Faults' and 'manifestation of conscience' to the Superior, but the association of the Superior in the sacrament of penance in the true sense. That is the innovation which became widespread; it even affected lay people, who came to ask the abbot or priests how to expiate their sins.

This practice is reflected in the curious literature of penitential books which originated in Ireland. In almost legal fashion they fix a scale of penances varying with the seriousness of the sins, the degree of will and the state in life of the sinner, a monk and cleric being more severely treated than a simple layman. For example, in addition to other mortifications and pious works a fast of bread and water for several years was imposed as penance in cases of murder and adultery, and for a certain number of days in the case of lesser sins. A curious system of compensation permitted a sinner to substitute for a long penalty one which was shorter but more severe. One year of bread and water, for example, could be replaced by three days and three nights without sleep, during which prayers and psalms had to be recited without interruption in the sanctuary or 'purgatory' of a saint — for example, that of St Patrick in an island of Lough Deig.

Today these practices strike most people as very severe, but the Continent discovered and adopted such a form of penance with relief and gratitude because it answered a deeply felt pastoral need. A later development is well known. Latin Catholicism became the heir of one of the most typical aspects of devotion in ancient Ireland : frequent confession and the intimate association of the sacrament of penance with spiritual guidance.

One of the ascetical practices most dear to the Celtic monks was voluntary exile, what they called *peregrinari pro Christo*, or *pro amore Dei* : to leave one's family and country in order to go and live in unknown, more or less hostile surroundings and to place this exile at Christ's service, that is to say, to work at spreading the Gospel among foreigners. Even allowing for merely human motives such as a taste for adventure and a certain psychological restlessness, this practice still remains a highly fruitful religious ideal. It was astonishingly popular and the name ' *Scotti* ', which had first been applied by the Romano-Britons to the pirates who infested the Irish Sea, became on the Continent a synonym for ' wandering missionaries of island origin '.

This spiritual expansion took place in Britain on the one hand, in Gaul and Germany on the other. The Irish monks first worked to convert the Picts, the Celtic tribes of present-day Scotland, who had scarcely been touched by missionaries from Roman Brittany. The foundation by St Ninian of the monastery of *Candida Casa* (Whithorn in Galloway) beyond Hadrian's Wall is well attested, but the traditional date (397) seems too early; it is more likely to have been about 500. The monastery's influence and even its duration are matters of dispute.

On the other hand we know that St Columba, after founding several monasteries in Ireland, left his native island in 583/5 to go and reconstruct that of I or Iona, on a small island off the west coast of Scotland. This soon became very prosperous and a missionary centre for all the North of Britain, even for the Orkneys. Finally it turned its influence in the other direction towards the Anglo-Saxons themselves, whom the Britons were too busy fighting to try to convert. It was a monk of Iona, St Aidan, who about 655 went to found the monastery of Lindisfarne on an island off Northumberland; he did so at the request of King Oswald, who had been converted during a period of exile among christian Celts. Lindisfarne became a second ' holy island ', whence the Gospel was spread among the country's Germanic conquerors.

This missionary activity was not the only one at work in Britain. In 597 a group of missionaries who had been sent direct from Rome by St Gregory the Great, landed in Kent. St Gregory was not the first Pope to strive for the conversion of these northern islands. The chronicle of Prosper of Aquitaine, who must have been well informed since he was writing in Rome, says that in 431 Pope Celestine had ordained his deacon Palladius as the first bishop destined for Ireland. We hear nothing more about this Palladius, and for that reason, but apparently on insufficient evidence, he has been identified with St Patrick.   It is not known whether he completed his mission; in any case it left no visible traces.

The mission dispatched by St Gregory was much more fruitful. It sent not only to the Celts but also to the Anglo-Saxons a team of missionaries directed by a monk from the convent which St Gregory had founded in his own family house of the Coelius.   This monk was St Augustine, later to become the first Archbishop of Canterbury. The missionaries found their path well prepared, thanks to the influence of a Catholic Frankish princess, Queen Bertha, who was the wife of Ethelbert, King of Kent and a great-grand-daughter of Clovis.   Ethelbert was at once converted and received baptism in that same year 597, with a large number of his subjects.   The movement became fairly widespread and in 604 St Augustine was able to create two bishoprics suffragan to Canterbury, in London and in Rochester.   But that was only a first step; the base was later to be strengthened by a new mission which Pope Vitalian organised in 668/9.

The two groups of missionaries, Celtic and Roman, were prevented by the language barrier from coordinating their efforts.   But by 600, as a result of this two-fold movement which finally converged, the conversion of the Anglo-Saxons was well on the way to being achieved.

Meanwhile, influences crossed yet again when the *Scotti* arrived on the Continent to try to strengthen and complete the work of spreading the Gospel.   The great name to remember here is that of St Columbanus. He left St Comgall's monastery in Bangor and travelled to Gaul with twelve companions in 590/1.   He settled in King Gontran's Burgundy, where he founded the three neighbouring monasteries of Annegray, Luxeuil and Fontaine; the second in particular grew very important. By his personal influence, and with the help of his *Rules* and his *Penitential Rule* which are very Irish in their austerity and strictness, St Columbanus exercised a great influence on the monks who came to live under his direction and on the crowds who hurried to him in order to make their peace with God.

After twenty years he incurred the anger of the King and of the terrible Brunehaut, the King's grandmother, for upholding too steadfastly the demands of christian morality.   He was sent into exile, but at the very moment when he was about to embark at Nantes for the British Isles he managed to escape.   Crossing Neustria, which was ruled by Clotaire II, and Austrasia, ruled by Theodebert, he reached the countries of the Moselle and Rhine, and everywhere aroused a surge of enthusiasm and of vocations to the religious life, which, notably in Brie east of Paris, later gave rise to new monasteries.   He himself founded one in Bregenz at the end of Lake Constance.   He also distributed his disciples *en route :* St Gall for instance, having accompanied him from Bangor, departed to go and found the abbey which has kept his name.   St Columbanus intended not only to revive and stimulate the faith of the Christian populations among whom he travelled; he was also concerned to preach the Gospel among the many Germanic pagans, notably the Alemanni of present-day Alsace and Switzerland, who had hitherto barely been touched by missionaries from the Merovingian courts.   The preaching of St Columbanus and his disciples, together with similar efforts on the part of others, did much towards the conversion of this people even though it was completed only much later.

Christ's pilgrim to the end, St Columbanus left Bregenz, crossed the Alps, and in the Ligurian Appenines founded the monastery of Bobbio, a Catholic citadel over against the Arianism of the Lombards. There he died in 615.

This first volume takes leave of the reader at a moment when the expansion of a movement is in full swing.   The conversion of the Germanic peoples on the borders of the Roman countries has begun with the Anglo-Saxons and the Alemanni, and during the generations and the centuries to come, the expansion will continue.   In the end, the conversion of the North will give Western Europe its definitive form and this will shift the axis of Latin Christianity.

We have seen how, in the early period, the christian religion established itself preponderantly in the mediterranean countries.   In the Middle Ages, the area of Western Christianity will move northwards and come to coincide essentially with the continent of Europe.   The Arab conquest of the Magreb and later of Spain no doubt intensified this movement, but it had begun as early as the Vandal invasion, with the breaking away of Roman Africa and the steady disintegration of its Church.   In the early period, it seemed that the impetus behind the history of Christianity was often in the dialogue — sometimes in the opposition — between the Eastern Churches and the Latin Church. This first kind of dialectical tension will be replaced by new types of dialogue; from the conversion of Northern Europe after the invasions, from the Germanic and Celtic influences spread by the missionary *Scotti,* and from the divergence of Greeks and Latins to separate paths, from all these things will arise a dialogue between Celt and Continental, between Germanic peoples and Romans.   These new types of dialogue are a radical characteristic of medieval Christianity and differentiate it clearly from the Christianity of antiquity.

BIBLIOGRAPHY

AND

LIST OF ABBREVIATIONS

LIST OF ABBREVIATIONS

PERIODICALS

ACO	Acta Conciliorum Oecumenicorum
An. Boll.	Analecta Bollandiana
ATR	Anglican Theological Review
BLE	Bulletin de Littérature Ecclésiastique
BZ	Byzantinische Zeitschrift
EE	Estudios Ecclesiasticos
EL	Ephemerides Liturgicae
ET	Evangelische Theologie
ETL	Ephemerides Theologicae Lovanienses
HTR	Harvard Theological Review
ICUR	Inscriptiones Christianae Urbis Romae
JBL	Journal of Biblical Literature
JEH	Journal of Ecclesiastical History
JJS	Journal of Jewish Studies
JTS	Journal of Theological Studies
MSR	Mélanges de Science Religieuse
NRT	Nouvelle Revue Théologique
NTS	New Testament Studies
OCP	Orientalia Christiana Periodica
RB	Revue Biblique
REG	Revue des Etudes Grecques
REJ	Revue des Etudes Juives
RH	Revue Historique
RHE	Revue d'Histoire Ecclésiastique
RHPR	Revue d'Histoire et de Philosophie Religieuse
RHR	Revue d'Histoire des Religions
ROC	Revue de l'Orient Chrétien
RQ	Römische Quartalschrift
RQH	Revue des Questions Historiques
RSPT	Revue des Sciences Philosophiques et Théologiques
RSR	Recherches de Science Religieuse
Rev SR	Revue des Sciences Religieuses
Riv AC	Rivista di Archeologia Cristiana
RTAM	Recherches de Théologie Ancienne et Médiévale
SJT	Scottish Journal of Theology
SKG	Schriften der Königsberger Gelehrtengesellschaft
ST	Studia Theologica
TQ	Theologische Quartalschrift
TS	Theological Studies
TZ	Theologische Zeitschrift
VC	Vigiliae Christianae

VD	Verbum Domini
VS	Vie Spirituelle
VT	Vetus Testamentum
ZKG	Zeitschrift für Kirchengeschichte
ZKT	Zeitschrift für Katholische Theologie
ZNTW	Zeitschrift für Neutestamentliche Wissenschaft
ZRGG	Zeitschrift für Religions- und Geistesgeschichte
ZTK	Zeitschrift für Theologie und Kirche

SERIES

ACW	Ancient Christian Writers
BHL	Bibliotheca Hagiographica Latina Antiquae et Mediae Aetatis
CIG	Corpus Inscriptionorum Graecarum
CIL	Corpus Inscriptionorum Latinarum
CSCO	Corpus Scriptorum Christianorum Orientalium
CSEL	Corpus Scriptorum Ecclesiasticorum Latinorum
GCS	Griechische Christliche Schriftsteller
HE	Historia Ecclesiastica (Eusebius)
MGH	Monumenta Germaniae Historica
PG	Patrologia Graeca
PL	Patrologia Latina
PO	Patrologia Orientale
PS	Patrologia Syriaca
SC	Sources Chrétiennes
TS	Texts and Studies
TU	Texte und Untersuchungen

LEXICONS

DACL	Dictionnaire d'Archéologie Chrétienne et de Liturgie
DTC	Dictionnaire de Théologie Catholique
EB	Encyclopaedia Biblica
RAC	Reallexikon für Antike und Christentum
TWNT	Theologisches Wörterbuch zum Neuen Testament

DEAD SEA SCROLLS

CDC	The Damascus Fragment
DSD	The Manual of Discipline (Rule of the Community)
DSH	The Habakkuk Commentary
DST	The Psalms of Thanksgiving
DSW	The War between the Sons of Light and the Sons of Darkness

BIBLIOGRAPHY TO PART I

GENERAL

I. SOURCES

The main source is

EUSEBIUS, *History of the Church*.
A critical edition by Edward Schwartz was published in *GCS*, Leipzig 1903-1909.
A critical study of the documents used by Eusebius is to be found in
P. NAUTIN, *Lettres et écrivains chrétiens des IIe et IIIe siècles*, Paris 1961.

All the texts of the **pagan writers on Christianity** in the first three centuries are to be found in

W. DEN BOER, *Scriptorum paganorum I-IV Saec. de Christianis Testimonia*, Leiden 1948.
I have not used the *Historia Augusta*, the authenticity of which is disputed.
The earliest **Christian papyri** have been collected by
C. WESSELY, *Patr. Or.*, 18, 1924, 99-210.
Christian inscriptions are to be found in general collections, such as *CIG* and *CIL*.
For Latin Christian inscriptions see
E. DUHL, *Inscriptiones latinae christianae*, 3 vol., Berlin 1925-1931.
A. SELVAGNI, *Inscriptiones christianae urbis Romae*, III, 1957.

The writings of the New Testament have been edited critically, notably by Nestlé and Merk.

The **Judaeo-Christian apocrypha in the Old Testament** have been translated by
CHARLES, *Apocrypha and Pseudepigraphia of the O.T.*, II, Oxford 1913.
For the **New Testament Apocrypha,** see the English translation by M. R. JAMES, Oxford 1924. The Greek text of the apocryphal *Acts of the Apostles* has been edited by LIPSIUS-BONNET, Leipzig 1891-1903.
For **Coptic works of Gnosticism,** the published texts are
Gospel of Mary, Apocryphon of John, Wisdom of Jesus Christ, edited by W. R. C. TILL, Berlin 1955.
Gospel of Truth, edited by MICHEL MALININE, H.-CH. PUECH, G. QUISPEL, Zürich 1956.
Gospel of Thomas, edited by A. GUILLAUMONT, H.-CH. PUECH, G. QUISPEL, W. TILL, YASSAH 'ABD AL LASIH, Leiden & London 1959.
There is a German translation of the *Hypostasis of the Archons* and of the *Gospe of Philip* by
H. SCHENKE, *Koptisch-gnostische Schriften aus den Papyrus-Codices von Nag Hammadi*, Hamburg 1960. *The Gospel of Philip* has been translated into English by C. J. DE CATANZARO in *J.T.S.*, N.S. 13 (1962) 35-72.
A selection of Gnostic texts in English has been made by
R. M. GRANT : *Gnosticism*, New York 1961.
For **Greek and Latin Christian writers,** refer to the Berlin *Corpus*, the Venice *Corpus*, the *Corpus Christianorum*, Christian source-books and Migne's Patrologies.

For a useful selection of **texts bearing on the early history of Christianity,** see

C. Kirch, *Enchiridion fontium historiae ecclesiasticae antiquae*, 8th ed., Freiburg 1960.

J. Stevenson, *A New Eusebius : Documents illustrative of the History of the Church to A.D.337*, London 1957.

II. GENERAL STUDIES

Among the numerous **histories of the early Church,** we may note

A. von Harnack, *The Mission and Expansion of Christianity in the first three centuries*, 2nd ed., London 1908. (still the main work)

H. Duchesne, *Histoire ancienne de l'Eglise*, 3 vol., Paris 1906-1910. (still useful)

H. Litzmann, *Geschichte des alten Kirche*, I, Leipzig 1932. (more concerned with intellectual movements)

P. Carrington, *The Early Christian Church*, 2 vol., Cambridge 1957.

For the **history of doctrine,** we may note

A. von Harnack, *Lehrbuch der Dogmengeschichte*, 3 vol., Tübingen 1909.

M. Werner, *Die Entstehung des christlichen Dogmas*, Berne 1941. (debatable)

H. E. W. Turner, *The Pattern of Christian Thought.* (very balanced)

J. N. D. Kelly, *Early Christian Doctrine*, Edinburg 1958.

J. Daniélou, *The development of Christian doctrine up to the Council of Nicaea*, I : *The Theology of Jewish Christianity*, London & Chicago 1964; II : *The Gospel and Hellenic Christianity*, London & Chicago (about to be published).

On the **relations between Christianity and ancient culture,** see

Hatch, *The Influence of Greek Ideas and Usages upon the Christian Church*, London 1890.

C. Schneider, *Geistesgeschichte des antiken Christentums*, 2 vol., Munich 1954. (contains much precious information, but the ideas behind it are mistaken)

III. REFERENCE BOOKS

Several dictionaries contain important articles, notably

Dictionnaire d'archéologie chrétienne et de liturgie (DACL).

Realexicon für Antike und Christentum (RAC).

Theologische Wörterbuch des Neuen Testaments (TWNT).

Patristic Greek Lexicon (PGL).

Atlas of the Early Christian World, by F. van der Meer & C. Mohrmann contains the most important maps for the early history of the Church and excellent notes.

The *Patrologies* by Quasten and Altaner are useful and contain valuable bibliographies.

The *Bibliographia patristica*, directed by W. Schneemelcher, publishes an annual bibliography of works concerning the history of the early Church.

Bulletins about the history of Christian origins are published in the *Theologische Rundschau*, and *Recherches de Science Religieuse* (J. Daniélou).

CHAPTER 1

On the **Acts of the Apostles** as a historical source

J. Dupont, *Les problèmes du Livre des Actes d'après les travaux récents*, Louvain 1950. (a good general view)

F. J. FOAKES JACKSON & KIRSOPP LAKE, *The Beginnings of Christianity*, 5 vol., London 1920-1923. (still fundamental)

E. GRÄSSER, ' Die Apostelgeschichte in der Forschung der Gegenwart ', *Theol. Rund.*, 26 (1960), 93-167.

E. HAENCHEN, *Die Apostelgeschichte*, Göttingen 1956.

W. L. KNOX, *The Acts of the Apostles*, Cambridge 1948.

W. G. KÜMMEL, ' Das Urchristentum ', *Theol. Rund.*, N.F., 14 (1942) 81-95; 153-173; 17 (1948) 3-50; 103-142; 18 (1950) 1-53.

E. TROCMÉ, *Le Livre des Actes et l'histoire*, Paris 1957.

On the community of Jerusalem

L. CERFAUX, in *Recueil Lucien Cerfaux*, II, Gembloux 1954, p. 63-315.

P. GAECHTER, *Petrus und seine Zeit*, Innsbruck 1957.

On the relations between Christianity and the Jewish sects, particularly the Sadocite-Essenes

I. ABRAHAMS, *Studies in Pharisaism and the Gospels*, 2 vol., Cambridge 1917 & 1924.

M. BLACK, *The Scrolls and Christian Origins*, London 1961.

H. BRAUN, *Spätjudisch-häretischer und frühchristlicher Radikalismus*, 2 vol., Tübingen 1957.

O. CULLMANN, *Dieu et César*, Paris 1956.

J. DANIÉLOU, *Les manuscrits de la mer Morte et les origines du Christianisme*, Paris 1956.

D. DAUBE, *The New Testament and Rabbinic Judaism*, London 1956.

W. D. DAVIES, *Paul and Rabbinic Judaism*, London 1948.

H. KOSMALA, *Hebräer, Essener, Christen*, Leiden 1959.

M. SIMON, *Les sectes juives au temps de Jésus*, Paris 1960. K. STENDAHL (ed.), *The Scrolls and the New Testament*, London 1938.

On the origins of the hierarchy

P. BENOÎT, *Exégèse et Théologie*, II, Paris 1961, 232-317.

H. VON CAMPENHAUSEN, *Kirchliches Amt und Geistliche Vollmacht in den ersten drei Jahrhunderten*, Tübingen 1953.

J. COLSON, *Les fonctions diaconales aux premiers siècles de l'Eglise*, Paris 1961.

K. E. KIRK (ed.), *The Apostolic Ministry*, London.

CHAPTER 2

On Christianity in Transjordan

K. RUDOLF, *Die Mandäer*, 2 vol., Göttingen 1960 & 1962.

J. THOMAS, *Le mouvement baptiste en Palestine et en Syrie*, Gembloux 1935.

On Christianity in Galilee

L. F. ELLIOT-BINNS, *Galilean Christianity*, Chicago 1956.

H. LOHMEYER, *Galiläa und Jerusalem*, Göttingen 1936.

On Christianity in Samaria

O. CULLMANN, ' La Samarie et les origines de la mission chrétienne ', *An Et Rel.* 1953-1954, 10.

Mc L. WILSON, ' Simon, Dositheus and the Dead Sea Scrolls ', *ZRGG*, 9 (1957) 21-40.

On Christianity in Egypt

L. W. BANNARD, ' St. Stephen and Early Alexandrian Christianity ', *NTS* 7 (1961) 31-45.

H.-I. BELL, *Jews and Christians in Egypt*, London 1924.

J. L. PLUMLEY, ' Early Christianity in Egypt ', *Pal Ex Quat* 89 (1957) 70-81.

C. SPICQ, ' L'Epître aux Hébreux, Apollos, Jean-Baptiste, les Hellénistes et Qumran ', *Rev. Quar.*, 3 (1959) 365-391.

CHAPTER 3

On the **Judaeo-Christian** community and the **crisis of Judaism**

S. G. F. BRANDON, *The Fall of Jerusalem and the Christian Church*, London 1951.

G. DIX, *Greek and Jew*, Westminster 1953.

L. GOPPELT, *Christentum und Judentum in ersten und zweiten Jahrhunderten*, Gütersloh 1954.

B. REICKE, *Diakonie, Festfreude und Zelos*, Upsala 1951.

H. J. SCHOEPS, *Theologie und Geschichte des Judenchristentums*, Tübingen 1949. Id., *Aus Frühchristicher Zeit*, Tübingen 1950.

M. SIMON, *Verus Israël*, Paris 1948.

On St Paul in History

R. BULTMANN, ' Zur Geschichte der Paulus Forschung ', *Theol. Rund.*, N.F. 6 (1934) 229-246; 8 (1936) 1-22.

J. DUPONT, ' Pierre et Paul à Antioche et à Jérusalem ', *R.S.R.* 45 (1957) 42-60; 225-240.

B. M. METZGER, *Index to Periodical literature of the Apostle Paul*, Leiden 1960.

J. MUNCK, *Paul und die Heilsgeschichte*, Copenhagen 1954.

The Synoptic Gospels

M. DIBELIUS, *Die Formgeschichte des Evangeliums*, Tübingen 1919.

X LÉON-DUFOUR, ' Formgeschichte et Redaktionsgeschichte des Evangiles Synoptiques '. *RSR*, 46 (1958) 237-270.

H. RIESENFELD, *The Gospel Tradition and its Beginnings*, London 1957.

K. L. SCHMIDT, *Le problème du christianisme primitif*, Paris 1938.

CHAPTER 4

On St John and Asiatic Christianity

F. H. BRAUN, *Jean le théologien et son Evangile dans l'Eglise ancienne*, Paris 1959.

S. GIET, *L'Apocalypse et l'histoire*, Paris 1957.

S. E. JOHNSON, ' Early Christianity in Asia Minor ', *JBL* 77 (1958) 1-17.

P. H. MENOUD, *L'Evangile de Jean d'après les recherches récentes*, Paris 1947.

On the origins of Christianity in Osroene

A. ADAM, *Die Psalmen des Thomas und das Perlenlied als Zeugnisse vorchristlicher Gnosis*, 1959.

W. BAUER, *Rechtgläubigkeit und Ketzerei im ältesten Christentum*, Tübingen 1954: 6-49.

J. DORESSE, *Un recueil inédit de paroles de Jésus*, Paris 1958, 41-47.

P. E. KAHLE, *The Cairo Geniza*, 2nd ed., Oxford 1959.

E. KIRSTEN, ' Edessa ', *RAC*, IV, 1959, 552-597.

H. E. W. TURNER, *The Pattern of the Christian Church*, London 1954, 40-46.

A. VÖÖBUS, ' History of Asceticism in the Syrian Orient ', I, *The Origin of Asceticism*, Louvain 1958.

On the **origins of Christianity in Rome**
J. CARCOPINO, *De Pythagore aux Apôtres*, Paris 1956, 225-377.
O. CULLMANN, *Saint Pierre*, Paris 1952.
E. KIRSCHBAUM, *Die Gräber der Apostelfürsten*, Frankfurt 1957.
H.-I. MARROU, ' Fouilles du Vatican ', *DACL*. 15, Paris 1953, 3292-3346.
J. TOYNBEE and J. W. PERKINS, *The Shrine of Peter and the Vatican Excavations,* London 1958.

CHAPTER 5

On the **origins of Gnosticism**
R. M. GRANT, *Gnosticism and Early Christianity*, New York 1959 (The most important book on the origins of specifically Gnostic dualism).
M. FRIEDLÄNDER, *Der Vorschristliche jüdische Gnosticismus*, Göttingen 1898 (a precursor).
G. QUISPEL, ' Christliche Gnosis und Jüdische Heterodoxie', *Evang. Theol.*, 14 (1954) 1-11.
G. SCHOLEM, *Major Trends im Jewish Mysticism*, London 1955.

On **Ebionism**
O. CULLMANN, *Le problème littéraire et historique des romans pseudo-clémentins,* Paris 1930.
H. J. SCHOEPS, *Urgemeinde, Judenchristentum, Gnosis*, Tübingen 1956.
G. STRECKER, *Das Judenschristentum in den Pseudo-Klementinen*, Berlin 1958.

On **Elkesaism**
G. STRECKER, ' Elksai ', *RAC*, IV (1959) 1171-1186.

The **Apocryphon of John**
J. DORESSE, *The Secret Books of the Gnostics*, London 1961.
S. GIVERSEN, ' Johannes ' apokryfon og Genesis ', *Dansk. Theol. Tids.*, 1957 (65-80).
H.-CH. PUECH, ' Gnosticisme ', *Enc. fr.*, XIX, 1942, 4-13.
W. TILL, ' The Gnostic Apocryphon of John ', *JEH*, 3, (1952) 14-22.

Basilides
J. H. WASZINCK, ' Basilides ', *RAC*, I (1950) 1217-1225.

CHAPTER 6

General Studies
M. BLACK, *An Aramaic Approach to the Gospels and Acts*, Oxford 1954.
J. DANIÉLOU, *The Theology of Jewish Christianity*, London & Chicago 1964.
E. PETERSON, *Frünkirche, Judentum und Gnosis*, Freiburg 1959.
E. TESTA, *II Simbolisme dei Giudeo-Cristiani*, Jerusalem 1962.
C. C. TORREY, ' The Aramaic Period of the Nascent Christian Church ', *ZNTW,* 44 (1952), 205-223.

On **Judaeo-Christian Catechesis**
L. W. BANNARD, ' The Epistle of Barnabas and the Tannaitic Catechism ', *Angl. Theol. Rev.*, 41 (1959) 177-190.
P. CARRINGTON, *The Primitive Christian Catechism*, Cambridge 1950.

468 THE CHRISTIAN CENTURIES : VOLUME I

G. SCHILLE, ' Das Evangelium des Mathäus als Catechismus ', *NTS,* 4 (1958), 101-114.
' Katechese und Taufliturgie ', *ZNTW,* 59 (1960), 113-131.
' Zur Urchristichen Tauflehre, Stilistischen Beichbachtungen am Barnabasbrief ', *ZNTW,* 57 (1958) 31-32.

A. SEEBERG, *Der Katechismus der Urchristenheit,* Leipzig 1903.

E. G. SELWYN, *The first Epistle of Peter,* 2nd ed. London 1947.

On the *Testimonia* of the Old Testament

L. CERFAUX, ' Un chapitre du Livre des Testimonia ', *Rec. Luc. Cerf.,* II, Gembloux 1954, 219-226.

J. DANIÉLOU, ' Un Testimonium sur la vigne dans Bar. XI, 1 ', *RSR* (1962).

C. H. DODD, *According to the Scripture,* London 1952.

E. EARLE ELLIS, *Paul's Use of the Old Testament,* Edinburgh 1957.

J. RENDEL HARRIS, *Testimonies,* 2 vol., Cambridge 1916-1920.

R. A. KRAFT, ' Barnabas's Isaiah Text and the Testimony Book Hypothesis ', *JBL,* 79 (1960) 336-350.

P. PRIGENT, *L'Epître de Barnabé I, XVI et ses sources,* Paris 1961.

K. STENDAHL, *The School of St. Matthew,* Upsala 1954.

On the **Judaeo-Christian evangelical tradition**

W. BAUER, *Das Leben Jesus im Zeitalter des Neutestamentlichen Apokryphen,* Tübingen 1909.

E. HENNECKE and W. SCHNEEMELCHER, *Neutestamantliche Apokryphen I,* Evangelien, 3rd ed., Tübingen 1959.

H. KÖSTER, *Synoptische Überlieferung bei den Apostolischen Vätern,* Berlin 1957.

E. MASSAUX, *Influence de l'évangile de saint Mathieu sur la littérature chrétienne avant Irénée,* Louvain 1950.

K. L. SCHMIDT, *Le problème du christianisme primitif,* Paris 1938.

R. MCL. WILSON, *Studies in the Gospel of Thomas,* London 1960.

The **Origins of typology**

J. DANIÉLOU, *Sacramentum futuri,* London 1958.

R. M. GRANT, *The Letter and the Spirit,* London 1957.

R. P. H. HANSON, *Allegory and Event,* London 1950.

Theology and Apocalyptic ideas

J. BARBEL, *Christos Angelos,* Bonn 1941.

W. BIEDER, *Die Vorstellung von den Höllenfahrt J.-C.,* Zürich 1949.

H. BIETENHARD, *Die himmlischen Welt im Urchristentum und Spätjudentum,* Tübingen 1951.

———— *Das Tausendjährige Reich,* 2nd ed., Zürich 1955.

H. SCHLIER, *Religionsgeschichtliche Untersuchungen zu den Ignatiusbriefen,* Giessen 1929.

On **Judaeo-Christian worship**

A. ADAM, ' Erwägungen zur Herkunft der Didache ', *ZKG,* 68 (1957) 1-48.

J. P. AUDET, *La Didaché, Instruction des Apôtres,* Paris 1958.

———— ' Esquisse du genre littéraire de la Bénédiction juive et de l'Eucharistie chrétienne ', *RB,* 65 (1958) 371-400.

———— ' Jésus et le calendrier sacerdotal ancien ', *Sc. Eccl.,* 10 (1958) 361-383.

A. BENOÎT, *Le baptême au second siècle,* Paris 1951.

J. H. BERNARD, *The Odes of Solomon,* Cambridge 1912.

F.-M. BOISMARD, ' Une liturgie baptismale dans la Prima Petri ', *RB,* 65 (1958) 182-208; 66 (1957) 161-183.

O. CULLMANN, *Le culte dans l'Eglise primitive*, Paris 1943.
——— *Les sacrements dans l'Evangile johannique*, Paris 1945.
J. VON GOUDOEVER, *Biblical Calendars*, Leiden 1959.
B. LOHSE, *Das Passafest der Quartodecimaner*, Gütersloh 1953.
W. O. E. OESTERLEY, *The Jewish Background of the Christian Liturgy*, Oxford 1925.
E. SEGELBERG, *Masbùthà*, Upsala 1958.

CHAPTER 7

On the first persecutions

W. H. C. FREND, ' The Persecutions. Some Links between Judaism and the Early Church ', *JEH*, 9 (1958) 141-158.
H. GRÉGOIRE, *Les persécutions dans l'Empire romain*, Brussells 1951.
J. MOREAU, *Les persécutions du christianisme dans l'Empire romain*, Paris 1956.
H. LAST, ' Christenverfolgung (jüridisch) ', *RAC*, II, Stuttgart 1954, 1208-1229.
C. SAUMAGNE, ' Les incendiaires de Rome (ann. 64 P.C.) et les lois pénales des Romains ', *RH*, 80 (1962) 337-361.
A.-N. SHERWIN-WHITE, ' The Early Persecutions and the Roman Law Again ', *JTS*, NS, 3 (1952), 199-213.
M. SORDI, ' I rescritti di Trajano e di Adriano sui cristiani ', *Riv. Stor. Ch. Ital.*, 14 (1960) 344-370.
J. VOGT, ' Christenverfolgung (historisch) ', *RAC*, II, Stuttgart 1954, 1159-1183.
A. WLOSOK, ' Die Rechtsgrundlagen der Christenverfolgungen der ersten zwei Jahrhunderten ', *Gymn.*, 66 (1959) 14-32.

On the pagan reaction

C. ANDRESEN, *Logos und Nomos. Die Polemik des Kelsos wider das Christentum*, Berlin 1955.
P. DE LABRIOLLE, *La réaction païenne*, Paris 1934.

On the Apologists

J. GEFFCKEN, *Zwei griechische Apologeten*, Leipzig 1907.
R. M. GRANT, ' The Chronology of the Greek Apologists ', *VC*, 9 (1955) 22-23.
V. MONACHINO, ' Intento pratico e propagandistico nell' apologia greca del secondo secolo ', *Greg.*, 32 (1951) 5-49; 187-222.
N. PELLEGRINO, *Studi sull'Antica apologetica*, Rome 1947.

On the Apologists' Greek Philosophy and Rhetoric

C. ANDRESEN, ' Justin und der mittlere Platonismus ', *ZNTW*, 44 (1952-1953) 157-195.
J. DANIÉLOU, *The Gospel and Hellenic Christianity*, London & Chicago 1964.
M. ELZE, *Tatian und seine Theologie*, Göttingen 1960.
M. SPANNEUT, *Le Stoïcisme des Pères de l'Eglise de Clément de Rome à Clément d'Alexandrie*, Paris 1957.

CHAPTER 8

On Marcion

E. C. BLACKMAN, *Marcion and his influence*, London 1948.
A. VON HARNACK, *Marcion, Das Evangelium vom fremden Gott*, Leipzig 1924.

On Valentinus and his School

W. FOERSTER, *Von Valentin zu Herakleon*, Giessen 1928.

H. Jonas, *Gnosis und Spätantike Geist*, 2 vol., Göttingen 1954.

A. Orbe, *Estudios valentinianos*, 4 vol., Rome 1955-1961.

E. Peterson, ' Valentino ', *Enc. Gatt.*, XII, Vatican 1954, 979-980.

H.-Ch. Puech and G. Quispel, ' Le quatrième écrit du Codex Jung ', *VC*, 9 (1955) 65-102.

F. M. M. Sagnard, *La gnose valentinienne et le témoignage de saint Irénée*, Paris 1947.

The Question of the ' Gospel of Truth '

H.-Ch. Puech and G. Quispel, ' Les écrits gnostiques du Codex Jung ', *VC*, 8 (1954) 1-51.

H.-M. Schenke, *Die Herkunft des sogenannten ' Evangelium Veritatis '*, Göttingen 1959.

E. Segelberg, ' Evangelium Veritatis ', *Orient. Suec.*, 25, 8 (1959) 1-42.

W. C. Van Unnik, *Het Kortgeleden Ontdetkte ' Evangelie de Waarhud ' en het Nieuwe Testament*, Amsterdam 1954.

On **Montanism**

K. Aland, *Kirchengeschichtliche Entwürfe*, Gütersloh 1960, 105-149.

P. de Labriolle, *La crise montaniste*, Paris 1913.

On **Tatian**

F. Bolgiani, ' La tradizione eresiologica sull'encratismo ', *Att : Ac. Sc. Torin.*, 91 (1956-1957) 1-77.

R. M. Grant, ' The Heresy of Tatian ', *JTS*, NS, 5 (1954) 62-68.

On the **Paschal controversy**

B. Lohse, *Das Passafest der Quartadecimaner*, Gütersloh 1953.

M. Richard, ' La question pascale au second siècle ', *Or. Syr.*, 6 (1961) 179-213.

On the **Roman Schools** at the end of the **Second Century**

G. Hardy, ' Les écoles romaines au second siècle ', *RHE*, 28 (1932) 501-532.

G. La Piana, ' The Roman Church at the End of the Second Century ', *HTR*, 12 (1925) 201-277.

On the **Bishops**

P. Nautin, *Lettres et écrivains chrétiens aux II e et III e siècles*, Paris 1962.

On **Irenaeus**

A. Benoît, *Saint Irénée, Introduction à l'étude de sa théologie*, Paris 1960.

CHAPTER 9

On **Encratism**

F. Bolgiani, ' La tradizione eresiologica sull' encratismo ', *Att. Acad. Scienz. Torin.*, 91 (1956-1957) 1-77.

E. Holland, ' La circoncision, le baptême et l'autorité du décret apostolique ', *Stud. Theol.*, 9 (1955), 1-39.

E. Peterson, *Frühkirche, Judentum und Gnosis*, Freiburg 1959.

G. Quispel, ' Das Thomas Evangelium und das Alte Testament', *Neotestamentica et Patristica* (Freudesgabe Oscar Cullmann), Leiden 1962, p. 243-249.

A. Vööbus, *Celibacy. A Requirement for Admission to Christian Baptism in the Early Syrian Church*, Stockholm 1951.

On **martyrdom**

H. von Campenhausen, *Die Idee des Martyriums in der alten Kirche*, Göttingen 1936.

M. Pellegrino, ' Le sens ecclésial du martyre ', *Rev SR*, 35 (1961) 152-175.
E. Peterson, *Theologische Traktate*, Munich 1951, p. 167-224.

CHAPTER 10

The origins of the School of Alexandria

G. Bardy, 'Aux origines de l'Ecole d'Alexandrie ', *RSR*, 27 (1954) 65-90; 'Pour l'histoire de l'Ecole d'Alexandrie ', *Vivre et Penser*, 2 (1942) 60-109.
W. Bousset, *Jüdisch-christlicher Schulbetrieb in Alexandria und Roma*, Göttingen 1915.
J. Pépin, *Mythe et Allégorie*, Paris 1958.

Clement of Alexandria

P. J. C. Gussen, *Het Leven in Alexandrie*, Assen 1955.
G. Lazzati, *Introduzione allo studio di Clementi Alessandrino*, Milan 1939.
J. Meifort, *Der Platonismus bei Clemens Alexandrinus*, Tübingen 1928.
J. Munck, *Untersuchungen über Klemens von Alexandria*, Stuttgart 1933.
E. F. Osborn, *The Philosophy of Clement of Alexandria*, Cambridge 1957.
F. Quatember, *Die christliche Lebenshaltung des Klemens von Alexandrien nach seinem Pädogogus*, Vienna 1946.

CHAPTER 11

On the Edict of Severus

I. Schmidt, ' Ein Beitrag zur Chronologie der Schriften Tertullians und der Prokon-sulten von Afrika ', *Rhein. Mur.*, 46 (1891) 77-98.
A. Quacquarelli, *Q. S. F. Tertulliani Ad Scapulam*, Rome 1951.

The question of Hippolytus

A. Amore, ' La personalità dello scrittore Ippolito ', *Ant.*, 36 (1961) 3-28.
J. M. Hanssens, *La Liturgie d'Hippolyte*, Rome 1959.
P. Nautin, *Hippolyte et Josippe*, Paris 1947.
M. Richard, ' Comput et chronographie chez saint Hippolyte ', *MSR*, 7 (1950) 237-268; 8 (1951) 19-50; ' Encore le problème d'Hippolyte ', *MSR*, 10 (1953) 13-52.

On the origins of African Christianity

J. Mesnage, *Le christianisme en Afrique*, 3 vol., Paris 1915.
C. Mohrmann, *Etudes sur le latin des chrétiens*, Rome 1958.
P. Monceaux, *Histoire littéraire de l'Afrique chrétienne*, I, Paris 1901.
A. M. Schneider, ' Africa ', *RAC*, I, 1950, 173-179.

On Tertullian

C. Guignebert, *Tertullien. Etude sur ses sentiments à l'égard de l'Empire et de la société civile*, Paris 1901.
S. Otto, ' *Natura'* und '*Dispositio'*. *Untersuchunq zur Naturbegriffe und zur Denkform Tertullians*, Munich 1960. See *RSR*, 49 (1961) 592-594.
J. H. Waszink, *Tertulliani De Anima*, Amsterdam 1947.

CHAPTER 12

On the **Catechumenate**

B. CAPELLE, ' L'introduction du catéchuménat à Rome au début du IIIᵉ siècle ', *RTAM*, 5 (1933) 129-154.

J. DANIÉLOU, *Bible et Liturgie*, 2nd ed., Notre Dame 1956 - London 1960.

A. G. MARTIMORT, ' L'iconographie des catacombes et la catéchèse antique ', *Riv. AC*, 25 (1949) 3-12.

On **reconciliation**

B. POSCHMANN, *Busse und letzte Ölung*, Freiburg 1951.

K. RAHNER, ' La doctrine d'Origène sur la pénitence ', *RSR*, 38 (1950) 47-97; 252-286; 422-456; ' Die Busslehre des Hl. Cyprianus von Carthago ', *ZKT*, 74 (1952) 257-276; 381-438.

On the **ministry of women**

J. DANIÉLOU, ' Le ministère des femmes dans l'Eglise ancienne ', *Mais.-Dieu*, 61 (1960) 70-97.

KALKSBACH, ' Diakonisse ', *RAC*, III (1957) 917-928.

On the place of **worship**

J. R. LAUTIN, ' Le lieu du culte chrétien ', *Studi sulla chiesa antica e sull'Umanesimo*, Rome 1954.

F. S. DÖLGER, ' " Unsere Taube Haus ". Die Lage des christlichen Kultes bei Tertullian ', *Antike und Christentum*, 2 (1930) 41-56.

G. P. KIRSCH, ' La " Domus Ecclesiae cristiana " del III Secolo a Dura Europos ', *Studi Paolo Ubaldi*, Milan 1947, 73-82.

On the **Catacombs**

A. AMORE, ' Note di toponomastica cimiteriale romana ', *Riv. AC*, 32 (1956) 59-87.

A. P. FÉVRIER, ' Etudes sur les catacombes romaines ', *Cah. Arch.*, 10 (1959) 31-45; 11 (1960) 1-14.

L. HERTLING and E. KIRSCHBAUM, *The Roman Catacombs and their Martyrs*, Milwaukee 1956 - London 1960.

P. STYGER, *Die römischen Katacomben*, Berlin 1933.

M. DE VISSHER, ' Le régime juridique des plus anciens cimetières chrétiens à Rome ', *An. Bol.*, 69 (1951) 38-54.

On the themes of **Christian Art**

L. DE BRUYNE, ' La décoration des baptistères paléo-chrétiens ', *Mel. Mohlberg*, I, 1948, 189-220.

J. DANIÉLOU, ' Daniel ', *RAC*, III (1957) 575-585; ' David ' *RAC*, III (1957) 594-603.

J. HOOYMAN, ' Die Noe-Darstellung in der Früchristlichen Kunst ', *VC*, 12 (1958) 113-136.

J. QUASTEN, *Das Bild des Guten Hirten in den altchristlichen Baptisterien*, Pisciculi, Münster 1959, 220-244.

L. RÉAU, *Iconographie de l'art chrétien*, 4 vol., Paris 1954-57.

P. WILPERT, *La Fede della Chiesa nascente*, Vatican 1938.

On **Christians and Military Service**

H. VON CAMPENHAUSEN, *Der Kriegsdienst der Christen*, Festschrift K. Jaspers, Munich 1954, p. 255-264.

J. Danélou, *La non-violence dans l'Ecriture et la tradition*, Action chrétienne et non-violence, Paris 1955, 9-32.
J.-M. Hornus, *Evangile et Labarum*, Geneva 1960.   (contains an exhaustive bibliography)

CHAPTER 13

On Origen and his sources

R. Cadiou, *La jeunesse d'Origène*, Paris 1936.
Crouzel, ' Origène et Plotin élèves d'Ammonius Saccas ', *BLE*, 57, 4 (1956) 193-214.
J. Danélou, *Origène*, Paris 1948.
E. R. Dodds, *Numenius and Ammonius. The sources of Plotinus*, Geneva 1960.
Hanson, *Origen's Doctrine of Tradition*, London 1954.
M. Harl, *Origène et la fonction révélatrice du Verbe incarné*, Paris 1958.
A. von Harnack, *Die Kirchengeschichtliche Ertrag des exegetischen Arbeiten des Origenes*, 2 vol., Leipzig 1918-1919.
E. von Ivanka. ' Zur Geistgeschichtlichen Einordnung des Origenismus ', *BZ*, 44 (1951) 291-303.
H. Koch, *Paideusis und Pronoia*, Leipzig 1932.
K. O. Weber, *Origenes der Neuplatoniker*, Munich 1962.

On Edessa

E. Kirsten, ' Edessa ', *RAC*, IV (1959) 552-597.
F. Nau, ' Scriptorum Testimonia de Bardesanis vita, scriptis, doctrina ', *PS*, II, Paris (1907) 492-527.
Ortiz de Urbina, ' Le Origine del Cristianesimo in Edesse ', *Greg*, 15 (1934) 82-91.
H.-Ch. Puech, *Le manichéisme*, Paris 1949.

On the origins of Donatism

J.-P. Brisson, *Autonomisme et christianisme dans l'Afrique Romaine de Septime-Sévère à l'invasion vandale*, Paris 1958.
W. H. C. Frend, *The Donatist Church*, Oxford 1952.
A. Mandouse, ' Encore le Donatisme ', *Ant Class*, 29 (1960) 61-107.

CHAPTER 14

On the persecutions of the Middle of the Third Century

A. Alföldi, ' Zu den Christenverfolgungen in der Mitte des 3 Jh. ', *Klio*, 31 (1938) 323-348.
J. R. Knipfing, ' The Libelli of the Decian Persecution ', *HTR*, 16 (1923) 345-390.

On Paul of Samosata

G. Bardy, *Paul de Samosate*, Paris 1929.
G. Downey, *A History of Antioch in Syria*, Princeton 1961.
G. Kretschmar, *Studien zur frühchristlichen Trinitätstheologie*, Tübingen 1956.
M. Richard, ' Malchion et Paul de Samosate ', *ETL*, 35 (1959) 326-329.
H. de Riedmarten, *Les actes du procès de Paul de Samosate*, Fribourg 1952.

On **Lucian of Antioch**

G. BARDY, *Recherches sur Lucien d'Antioche et son école*, Paris 1936.
A. BUONAIUTI, *Saggi di Storia del Christianesimo*, Vicenza 1957, p. 219-257.
B. M. METZGER, ' Lucian and the Lucianic Version of the Greek Bible ', *NTS* 8 (1962) 189-204.

BIBLIOGRAPHY TO PART II

GENERAL AND CHAPTER 15

Religious history should not be separated from the general history of the ancient world, in which Christianity became increasingly important from the fourth century onwards. The best work, both a synthesis and a text-book, is :

E. STEIN, *Geschichte des spätrömischen Reiches, I : Vom römischen zumbyzantinischen Staat, 284-476*, Vienna 1928.

Stein's book uses, supersedes and presupposes a knowledge of the classic work :

O. SEEK, *Geschichte des Untergangs der antiken Welt*, Berlin 1897-1921.

Another work of synthesis, covering the period 395-565 :

J. B. BURY, *History of the Later Roman Empire from the death of Theodosius I to the death of Justinian*, London 1923.

The basic sources are first and foremost a series of **Histories of the Church :**
For the **period of the tetrarchy** and the **reign of Constantine until 324** :

EUSEBIUS OF CAESAREA, *Historia Ecclesiastica :* the earliest and a model of its kind; there is a critical edition by E. Schwartz; English translation by H. J. Lawlor and J. E. L. Oulton, 1927-1954.

Two other works, in the form in which they have come down to us, are not by the hand of Eusebius alone :

Chronological Tables or *Chronicle*, which have survived in an Armenian translation and with additions which bring them **down to 378/9.** There is a Latin adaptation by St. Jerome, edited by R. HELM, *GCS*, XLVII, Berlin 1956.

Vita Constantini, or rather the funeral eulogy *On the life of the blessed Emperor Constantine*, edited by I. A. HEIKEL, *GCS*, VII, Berlin 1962. There has been much discussion about the authenticity of this work, of quotations in it and documents related to it. There is a bibliography of the subject in the text book by

B. ALTANER, *Patrologie : Leben, Schriften und Lehre der Kirchenväter*, 5th ed., Freiburg 1958, p. 208-9.

In its present form the *Vita* seems to be a posthumous work, edited and doubtless reshaped by one of Eusebius's successors in the see of Caesarea; perhaps by Euzoios, as H. Grégoire believes, or by Acacius.

The Latin translation of Eusebius's *History* by Rufinus of Aquileia is continued in two original Books (X-XI), which bring the narrative **down to 395** (edited by T. MOMMSEN in SCHWARTZ's edition of Eusebius — *GCS*, IX, 11, 111, Berlin 1909, p. 957-1040). Some critics, probably mistakenly, have maintained that in these two books Rufinus of Aquileia is still merely translating, and that the original is by Gelasius of Caesarea, the second successor of Eusebius. There is a bibliography of the question in ALTANER, *Patrologie*, p. 213.

The *History of the Church* by the Eunomian PHILOSTORGIUS covers the **period 300-425;** it is precious in that it shows the Arian point of view. Only part has survived, largely thanks to the long extracts collected by the patriarch Photius (edited by J. BIDEZ, *GCS*, XXI, Berlin 1913).

Next, there are three parallel interdependent *Histories*, still with the same title : SOCRATES THE SCHOLASTIC (i.e. the lawyer), who lived in Constantinople, gives much new information and covers the **period 305-439** (edited by R. HUSSEY, Oxford 1853).

SOZOMEN, also a lawyer in Constantinople, describes events until 439; the surviving part covers the **years 324-425** (edited by J. BIDEZ, *GCS*, L, Berlin 1960).

THEODORET OF CYRRHUS covers the **period 323-428** (edited by L. PERMENTIER, F. SCHNEIDWEILER, *GCS*, XIX, Berlin[2] 1954). The same great theologian has also left a *Summary of the History of Heresies* (*PG* 83, col. 335-556), and a *Monastic History*, (*PG* 82, col. 1283-1496); analysis of extracts in A. J. FESTUGIÈRE, *Antioche païenne et chrétienne*, Paris 1959, p. 245-328, 348-357, 387-401.

The *History of the Church* by GELASIUS OF CYZICUS (c 475) is a compilation made from Eusebius, Gelasius of Caesarea, Socrates and Theodoret; the supplementary information which it contains is rightly suspect.

ZACHARIAS RHETOR (or ' OF GAZA ') wrote a history of the **years 450-491** during his ' Monophysite ' period (he ended up as orthodox Bishop of Mytilene); a Syriac translation has survived in a Chronicle which continues the narrative **until 569/10** (edited by E. W. BROOKS, *CSCO*, 83-84; Script. Syri 38; Latin translation, *ibid.*, 87-88; Script. Syri 41, Louvain 1919-1924).

THEODORE THE LECTOR (of St. Sophia in Constantinople) made a compilation of Socrates, Sozomen and Theodoret in his *Tripartite History*.

CASSIODORUS followed his example in Latin; there is an edition by W. JACOB and R. HANSLIK, *CSEL*, 71, Vienna 1952. He continued the narrative in an original *History* which runs **from 439 to 527**; surviving fragments are published in *PG* 16, I (ed. 1860), Col. 165-228; *Historisches Jahrbuch*, 1903, p. 553-558.

JOHN, (Monophysite) BISHOP OF EPHESUS, wrote a *History of the Church* of which the third part (the **years 571-585**) has come down to us in a Syriac translation edited by E. W. BROOKS, *CSCO*, 105, Script. Syri 54 (Syriac text); *CSCO*, 106, Script. Syri 55 (Latin translation, Louvain 1935-1936).

EVAGRIUS THE SCHOLASTIC wrote about the **period 431-594** (edited by J. BIDEZ and L. PARMENTIER, Louvain 1898).

These general histories are supplemented by **works more limited in scope** :

LIBERATUS OF CARTHAGE, *Brevarium causae Nestorianorum et Eutychianorum* from the time of **Nestorius to 553** (edited by E. SCHWARTZ, *Acta Concil. Oecumen.*, II, v, p. 98-141).

The History of the Patriarchs of the Coptic Church of Alexandria, II (Peter I to Benjamin I, 661), (edited by B. EVETTS; Arabic text and English translation : *Patrologia Orientale*, I, 2 (1905), p. 383-518).

Chronicle of Seert, Nestorian History (edited by A. SCHER; Arabic text and French translation : *Patrologia Orientale* (1908), p. 215-313; 7 (1911), p. 97-203).

Shorter accounts are provided by the Chroniclers : there is a bibliography in ALTANER, *Patrologie*, p. 216-221. Secular histories and books by contemporary writers, particularly by Christian writers, are the other main source : for editions, translations and critical studies of the latter, see B. ALTANER, *Patrologie*.

Modern works : the most detailed is

A. FLICHE and V. MARTIN, *Histoire de l'Eglise.* It is sometimes rather confused, and ecclesiastical politics are unfortunately treated more fully than religious thought, the spiritual life and the liturgy.

Other modern works

J. LEBRETON and J. ZEILLER, *De la fin du IIe siècle à la paix constantinienne*, Paris 1935.

P. DE LABRIOLLE, G. BARDY and J. R. PALANQUE, *De la paix constantinienne à la mort de Théodose*, Paris 1936.

P. DE LABRIOLLE, G. BARDY, L. BRÉHIER and G. DE PLINVAL, *De la mort de Théodose à l'avènement de Grégoire le Grand*, Paris 1937.

L. BRÉHIER and R. AIGRAIN, *Grégoire le Grand, les Etats barbares et la conquête arabe*, Paris 1938.

It is often useful to turn back to

S. LE NAIN DE TILLEMONT, *Mémoires pour servir à l'histoire ecclésiastique des six premiers siècles*, Paris 1698-1712,

and it is a pleasure to reread

L. DUCHESNE, *The Early History of the Christian Church*, English translation, London 1909-22. Duchesne's work is theologically inadequate but his pen is lively and his judgement balanced.

CHAPTER 16

The Persecution of Diocletian

In addition to Eusebius of Caesarea, an important source is :

LACTANTIUS, *De mortibus persecutorum*, edited with notes by J. MOREAU, (*Sources Chrétiennes*, 39), Paris 1954.

Among the many *Acts* and *Legends* of martyrs, patient and critical study is needed in order to decide which are historically true, and which are imaginary; see for example :

B. DE GAIFFIER, ' Palatins et eunuques dans quelques documents hagiographiques ', *An. Boll.*, 75 (1957), p. 17-46.

There is a good synthesis in :

J.ₓVOGT, ' Christenverfolgung ', *RAC*, 2 (1954), col. 1192-1204.

The following article gives useful details about the ways in which persecution and the reaction of Christians varied from region to region :

G. E. M. DE STE CROIX, ' Aspects of the " Great " Persecution ', *HTR*, 47 (1954), 75-113.

Constantine's religious attitude and policy

These questions were passionately debated by an older generation of scholars. It is useful to know the mains lines of research. See :

A. FIGANIOL, ' L'état actuel de la question constantinienne, 1930/49 ', *Historia, Zeitschr. f. alte Gesch.*, I (1950), p. 82-96.

J. VOGT, ' Die Constantinische Frage ', *Xe Cong. Intern. Sc. Stor.*, Roma 1955, *Atti*, 6, p. 733-779;

———— ' Constantinus der Grosse ', *RAC*, 3 (1957), col. 300-379.

K. ALAND, ' Die religiöse Haltung Kaiser Konstantins ', *Studia Patristica I* (Text und. Unters. 63), Berlin 1957, p. 549-600.

The chief documents are conveniently collected in a German translation :
H. D. DÖRRIES, ' Das Selbstzeugnis Kaiser Konstantins ', *Abhandl. d. Akad. d. Wiss. zu Göttingen, Phil.-hist. Kl.*, 3 F., 34 (1954).

CHAPTER 17

The state of Christianity about 290-300

Despite its date, the fundamental work is still :
A. VON HARNACK, *The Mission and Expansion of Christianity in the first three centuries*, 2nd ed., London 1908.
A more recent study is :
K. S. LATOURETTE, *A History of the Expansion of Christianity*, 1-2, London 1947.

Church institutions

A useful textbook, although mainly devoted to the Latin Church :
J. GAUDEMET, *L'Eglise dans l'Empire romain (IVe-Ve siècles)* (Histoire du Droit et des institutions de l'Eglise en Occident, III), Paris 1958.

The Christian Emperor

E. PETERSON, *Der Monotheismus als politisches Problem*, Leipzig 1935. This little book, which was remarkable in its day, paved the way for numerous studies, notably :
H. EGER, ' Kaiser und Kirche in der Geschichtstheologie Eusebs von Caesarea ', *ZNTW*, 33 (1939), p. 97-115.
H. BERKHOF, *Kirche und Kaiser : eine Untersuchung der Entstehung der theokratischen Staatsauffassung um. 4. Jh.*, Zürich 1947.

Donatism

The original documents, preserved thanks to historians and later polemical writers such as Optatus of Milevis and St. Augustine, are analysed in :
P. MONCEAUX, *Histoire littéraire de l'Afrique chrétienne*, 4-6, Paris 1912-1922.
Among the many works devoted to the subject the liveliest is :
W. H. C. FREND, *The Donatist Church, a Movement of Protest in Roman North Africa*, Oxford 1952, but it is curiously biased in favour of the schismatics.

CHAPTERS 18 AND 19

Arianism

Most of the documents relating to the first phase of the crisis have been translated in :
J. STEVENSON, *A new Eusebius : documents illustrative of the History of the Church to A.D. 337*, London 1957.
Among modern histories, an excellent book in its day was :
GWATKIN, *Studies of Arianism*, Cambridge 1882²-1900, but it is now superseded by :
E. SCHWARTZ, *Zur Geschichte des Athanasius* (Gesammelte Schriften, III), Berlin 1959, a collection of articles which appeared in *Nachrichten Gesellsch. Wiss. Göttingen* from 1904 to 1911. Also by the same author :
———— *Zur Geschichte der alten Kirche und ihres Rechts* (Gesamm. Schr. IV), p. 1-110.

The date when the heresy appeared is much debated. Some scholars favour 318, others 323. Among the former :

H. G. OPITZ, ' Die Zeitfolge des Arianischen Streites von den Anfängen bis zum Jahre 328 ' : *Zeitschr. neutest. Wiss.*, 38 (1934), p. 131-159.

W. SCHNEEMELCHER, ' Zur Chronologie des Arianischen Streites ' : *Theol. Liter. Zeit.*, 79, 1954, col. 393-400.

Among the latter :

E. SCHWARTZ, *Zur Geschichte des Athanasius*, p. 167.

W. TELFER, ' When did the Arian controversy begin? ', *JTS*, 47 (1946), p. 129-142; 48 (1949), p. 187-191.

Another question is whether in the year 325 the **Council of Nicaea** was preceded by a **Council of Antioch,** presided over by Ossius and at which Eusebius of Caesarea was severely censured : in support of the theory advanced by E. SCHWARTZ in *Zur Geschichte des Athanasius* (Ges. Schr. III), p. 134-155 (a synodal letter preserved in a Syriac translation), see :

H. CHADWICK, ' Ossius of Cordova and the Presidency of the Council of Antioch, 325 ', *JTS*, NS, 9 (1958), p. 292-304.

On the career of **Paul of Constantinople,** which was so complicated that it is difficult for the historian to piece it together

W. TELFER, ' Paul of Constantinople ', *HTR*, 34 (1950), p. 31-92.

As for

T. E. POLLARD, ' The Origins of Arianism ', *JTS*, (1958).

A. H. WOLFSON, ' Philosophical implications of Arianism and Apollinarism ' : *Dumbarton Oaks Papers*, 12 (1958), p. 5-28.

————— *The Philosophy of the Church Fathers*, I : *Faith, Trinity, Incarnation :* Cambridge, Mass. 1956.

these three are chiefly concerned with the philosophical implications of Arianism; I have attempted a more direct interpretation and linked Arius with the opinions of **Dionysius of Alexandria;** see :

DE GHELLINCK, *Mélanges Mercati*, I (Studi e Testi 121), p. 127-144; and

P. NAUTIN, ' Mélanges P. Peeters I ' (*An. Boll.* 67, 1949), p. 131-141.

The ideas raised by these **Trinitarian disputes** have been admirably analysed by :

G. L. PRESTIGE, *God in Patristic Thought*, London 1936.

There are also many useful suggestions in

A. ORBE, ' Hacia la primera teologia de la procesion del Verbo ' : Estudios Valentinianos, I, 1-2 (*Analecta Gregoriana* 99-100), Rome 1958, p. 465-473, 617-632, 679-698, 727-744.

For the development of the crises **after 342,** a good starting-point is

F. CAVALLERA, *Le schisme d'Antioche*, Paris 1905.

It is difficult to over-estimate the importance of the movement which progressively brought together the first Nicaeans and an increasingly large number of the Eastern bishops who were originally affiliated to the ' Homoeans of the right ' rather than to the ' Homoiousians ' in the strict sense. This movement bore fruit in the great **Cappadocian Doctors** centred around **St. Basil.** Works by liberal Protestant historians include

TH. ZAHN, *Marcellus von Ankyra, ein Beitrag zur Geschichte der Theologie*, Gotha 1867.

F. LOOFS, *Leitfaden zum Studium der Dogmengeschichte*, Halle⁴ 1906, p. 255-261.

A. VON HARNACK, *Lehrbuch der Dogmengeschichte*, Tübingen⁵ 1931, II, p. 263-284.

These are tendentious and wrongly suppose that the Homoiousian heresy finally supplanted strict Nicaean orthodoxy. A good Catholic reply is :

J. LEBON, 'Le sort du " consubstantiel" nicéen ' : *RHE*, 47 (1952), p. 485-529 (St Athanasius); 48 (1953), p. 632-682 (St. Basil).

I have tried to show how the Catholic tradition synthesised the two attitudes. The recently discovered catechetical homilies by **St. John Chrysostom** provide conclusive proof : in the *Credo* of the Church of Antioch (*c.* 390), the formula inherited from the Homoeans of the right — ' like in everything ' is juxtaposed with the ' consubstantial ' of the Nicene Creed

JOHN CHRYSOSTOM, *Huit Catéchèses baptismales inédites*, ed. A. Wenger, (Sources Chrétiennes 50), Paris 1957, I, 21, p. 119.

On the originality of Anomoean doctrine

E. VANDENBUSSCHE, ' La part de la dialectique dans la théologie d'Eunomius " le technologue " ' : *RHE*, 40 (1944-1945), p. 47-72.

J. DANIÉLOU, ' Eunome l'arien et l'exégèse néo-platonicienne du " *Cratyle* " ', *REG*, 69 (1956), p. 412-432.

CHAPTER 20

The origins of monasticism

The main sources have been mentioned in the text : Athanasius, *Historia monachorum*, Palladius, Cassian and the *Apophthegms*, for which the classic work is :

W. BOUSSET, *Apophtegmata, Studien zur Geschichte des ältesten Mönchtums*, Tübingen 1923.

Also :

J. C. GUY, *Recherches sur la traduction grecque des ' Apophtegmata Patrum* ' (Subsidia Hagiographica, 36), Brussells 1962.

On **early monasticism in general,** the most detailed studies are by Protestant historians :

K. ROLL, *Enthusiasmus und Bussgewalt beim griechischen Mönchtum*, Leipzig 1898.

R. REITZENSTEIN, ' *Historia Monachorum* ' und ' *Historia Lausiaca* ', eine Studie zur Geschichte des Mönchtums und der frühchristlichen Begriffe Gnostiker und Pneumatiker (Forschungen z. Rel. Liter. d. A. u. N. Test. 24), Göttingen 1916.

K. HEUSSI, *Der Ursprung des Mönchtums*, Tübingen 1936.

But there is much of value in the following short work :

M. VILLER and K. RAHNER, *Aszese und Mystik in der Väterzeit, ein Abriss*, Freiburg 1939.

See also the valuable collection of writings by :

H. KOCH, *Quellen zur Geschichte der Askese und des Mönchtums in der alten Kirche*, Tübingen 1931.

Recent research on the great figure of **St. Antony** includes :

L. VON HERTLING, ' Studi antoniani negli ultimi trent' anni '; *Antonius Magnus Eremita* (Studia Anselmiana, 38), Rome 1956, p. 13-34.

On the controversial figure of **Evagrius the Pontic :**

G. GUILLAUMONT, *Les ' Kephalaia Gnostica ' d'Evagre le Pontique et l'histoire de l'origénisme chez les Grecs et les Syriens :* (Patristica Sorbonensia, 5), Paris 1962.

A fundamental work is :

P. LADEUSE, *Etude sur le cénobitisme pakhomien pendant le IVe siècle et la première moitié du Ve*, Louvain 1898, but the biography of St. Pachomius needs revising in the light of newly published Coptic sources :

L. TH. LEFORT, *Les Vies coptes de saint Pachome et de ses premiers successeurs*, a French translation (Bibl. du Museon 16), Louvain 1943; see the perhaps over-enthusiastic remarks by :

P. PEETERS, ' Le dossier copte de saint Pachome et ses rapports avec la tradition grecque '; *An. Boll.*, 64 (1946), p. 258-277.

On Shenoute :

J. LEIPOLDT, *Schenute von Atripo und die Entstehung des national-aegyptischen Christentums (TU*, 25¹), Leipzig 1904.

On **St Hilarion** and the **origins of Palestinian monasticism,** we have a partly fictitious *Vita* by St. Jerome, the value of which is difficult to estimate :

E. COLERO, ' St. Jerome's Lives of the Hermits ', *VC*, II (1957), p. 161-178.

For **Constantinople,** see the works translated and with notes by :

A. J. FESTUGIÈRE, *Les moines d'Orient*, II : *Les moines de la région de Constantinople*, Paris 1961.

The **Basilian community :**

D. AMAND, *L'ascèse monastique de saint Basile*, Maredsous 1949.

On St. Jerome's ascetical propaganda :

D. GORCE, *La Lection divina*, I, *Saint Jérôme et la lecture sacrée dans le milieu ascétique romain*, Paris 1925.

Episcopal monasteries :

A. MANRIQUE, *La Vida monastica en San Augustin, Enchiridion historico, Doctrinal y Regla*, El Escorial 1959.

SYMPOSIUM, ' Saint Martin et son temps, Mémorial du XVIe Centenaire des débuts du monachisme en Gaule ', *Studia Anselmiana*, 46, Rome 1961.

CHAPTER 21

On the **Church of Mesopotamia,** there is a good basic work :

J. LABOURT, *Le Christianisme dans l'empire perse sous la dynastie sassanide*, Paris 1904, which can be brought up to date with :

E. TISSERANT, ' Nestorius, II, l'église nestorienne ', *DTC XI*, I (Paris 1931), col. 157-323. It is more difficult to find an accurate, well-documented account of the origins of the **other Eastern Churches;** the following may prove useful :

For **Ethiopia,** an excellent introductory article :

B. VELAT, ' Ethiopie ', in *Dictionnaire de Spiritualité IV*, 2 (1961), 1453-1477.

J. DORESSE, *L'Empire du prêtre Jean*, I, *L'Ethiopie antique*, Paris 1957. A popular account with a detailed biography which includes in the archaeological section :

E. LITTMANN, D. KREANCKER, TH. VON LUPKE, *Deutsche Aksum-Expedition*, Berlin 1913.

For Nubia

U. MONNERET DE VILLARD, 'Storia della Nubia cristiana ' : *Orientalia Christiana Analecta 118,* Rome 1938.

For Armenia

F. TOURNEBIZE, *Histoire politique et religieuse de l'Arménie,* Paris 1910, which is condensed, with slight changes, in the article : 'Arménie ' : *Dict. Hist. et Géogr. Ecclés.,* 4 (1940), col. 290-303.

Armenian historians have done much research since that date; unfortunately their work is difficult for the western reader to come by. The following should be used with caution :

ORMANIAN-POLADIAN, *The Church of Armenia,* London 1955.

See the remarks in :

M. VAN ESBROECK, ' Chronique arménienne ' : *An. Bol.,* 80 (1962), p. 423-441.

For Georgia

M. TAMARATI, *L'Eglise géorgienne,* Rome 1910.

P. PEETERS, ' Les débuts du christianisme en Géorgie d'après les sources hagiographiques ' : *An. Boll.,* 50 (1932), p. 5-58.

For Iberia and the Aghouans

P. PEETERS, ' Jérémie, évêque de l'Ibérie perse (431) ' : *An. Boll.,* 51 (1953), p. 5-33.

For the Germanic peoples converted by Wulfila

J. ZEILLER, *Les origines chrétiennes dans les provinces danubiennes de l'Empire romain,* Paris 1918.

K. D. SCHMIDT, *Die Bekehrung der Germanen zum Christentum,* 3-4, 1935, 1937.

CHAPTER 22

For Italy

F. LANZONI, *Le Diocesi d'Italia dalle origini al principio del secolo VII* (Studi e Testi, 35, 1-2)², Faenza 1927.

F. SAVIO, *Gli antichi vescovi d'Italia dalle origini al 1300 descritti per regioni : Il Piedmonte,* Turin 1898; *La Lombardia,* I, Florence 1913; 2, 1-2, Bergamo 1929-1932.

For Gaul there is a masterly work

L. DUCHESNE, *Fastes épiscopaux de l'ancienne Gaule,* 1-2, Paris² 1907-1910, 3, Paris 1915.

Little is added to Duchesne by the rather confused text-book :

GRIFFE, *La Gaule chrétienne à l'époque romaine,* 1-2, Paris 1947-1957.

For Spain

P. B. GAMA, *Kirchengeschichte von Spanien,* Regensburg 1862-1879.

Z. GARCIA VILLADA, *Historia eclesiastica de España,* Madrid 1926-1936.

On the excavations at Xanten

W. NEUSS, ' Eine altchristliche Märtyrerkirche unter dem Chor der St Viktorkirche in Xanten ', *RQ,* 42 (1934), p. 177-182.

For the Danubian provinces

J. ZEILLER, *Les origines chrétiennes* (listed for ch. 21).

R. NOLL, *Früheschristentum in Oesterreich,* Vienna 1954.

On pagan resistance, at a popular level in the East, see for example the account by :

MARK THE DEACON, *Vie de Porphyre évêque de Gaza*, in the edition translated and with commentary by H. GRÉGOIRE and M. A. KUGENER, Paris 1930.
And among the educated classes :
P. DE LABRIOLLE, *La réaction païenne, étude sur la polémique antichrétienne du Ier au VIe siècle*, Paris 1934.

CHAPTER 23

Extensive bibliographies of the **golden age of the Church Fathers** are to be found in : ALTANER, *Patrologie*, Freiburg ⁵1958.
J. QUASTEN, *Patrology*, 3, *The Golden Age of Greek Patristic Literature, from the Council of Nicaea to the Council of Chalcedon*, Utrecht 1960.
There is space only to mention a monograph or a short introductory book about each of the main figures in the chronological table on p. 303.

Athanasius : the famous work of
J. A. MÖHLER, *Athanasius der Grosse und die Kirche seiner Zeit*, Mainz ²1844 is still worth reading. For modern research see :
F. L. CROSS, *The Study of St Athanasius*, Oxford 1945.

Basil of Caesarea
S. GIET, *Les idées et l'action sociale de saint Basile*, Paris 1941.

Gregory of Nazianzus
P. GALLAY, *La vie de saint Grégoire de Nazianze*, Lyon 1943.
J. PLAGNIEUX, *Saint Grégoire de Nazianze, théologien*, Paris 1952.

Gregory of Nyssa has been a favourite subject for historical research by the present generation; there are many books to choose from :
H. VON BALTHASAR, *Présence et Pensée, essai sur la philosophie religieuse de Grégoire de Nysse*, Paris 1942.
J. DANIÉLOU, *Platonisme et théologie mystique, essai sur la doctrine spirituelle de saint Grégoire de Nysse*, Paris ²1954.

Evagrius the Pontic
A. GUILLAUMONT, *Les 'Kephalaia...* (listed on p. 480).

John Chrysostom
C. BAUR, *St. John Chrysostom and His Time*, London 1960.

Theodore of Mopsuestia
R. DEVREESSE, ' Essai sur Théodore de Mopsueste ', *Studi e Testi*, 141, Vatican 1948, somewhat optimistic and insufficiently detailed in theological matters.

John Cassian
O. CHADWICK, *John Cassian, a Study in primitive Monasticism*, Cambridge 1950. which is supplemented and corrected in the article by :
P. MUNZ, ' John Cassian ', *JEH*, XI (1960), p. 1-22.

On **Augustine** there is an immense bibliography. An introductory study is :
H. I. MARROU and A. M. BONNARDIÈRE, *St. Augustine and His Influence*, London 1957.

Ambrose
F. H. DUDDEN, *The Life and Times of St. Ambrose*, Oxford 1935.

484   THE CHRISTIAN CENTURIES : VOLUME I

Jerome

F. CAVALLERA, *Saint Jérôme, sa vie et son œuvre*, I, 1-2, Louvain 1922; the biography is very complete; the study of Jerome's thought which was to have followed never appeared.

A general sketch :

P. ANTIN, *Essai sur saint Jérôme*, Paris 1951.

Martin

SYMPOSIUM, ' Saint Martin et son temps, Mémorial du XVIe centenaire des débuts du monachisme en Gaule ', *Studia Anselmiana*, 46, Rome 1961.

Damasus

A. FERRUA, *Epigrammata Damasiana*, Vatican 1942; (introduction and notes).

Hilary

A. AINGRAIN, ' Où en est l'étude des œuvres de saint Hilaire? ' *Bull. Soc. des Antiqu. de l'Ouest*, 3e Ser. XI (1936-1938), p. 691-710.

P. GAULTIER, *Saint Hilaire, le premier docteur de l'Eglise latine*, Paris 1960.

CHAPTER 24

For **ecclesiastical institutions**, see

J. GAUDEMET, *L'Eglise dans l'Empire romain*, Paris 1958.

On the **Councils**

K. J. HEFELE and J. HERGENRÖTHER, *Konziliengeschichte*, Frankfurt ²1873-1890.

The **history of the liturgy** raises very complex problems. A good general work is MARTIMORT, *L'Eglise en prière, Introduction à la liturgie*, Paris 1961.

On **the Mass**, the best book is

J. A. JUNGMANN, *The Mass of the Roman Rite*, London 1959. As the title suggests, the book deals mainly with the development of the Roman liturgy; for a wider study, see the rather complicated work by

N. M. D. R. BOULET, *Euchariste ou la Messe dans ses variétés, son histoire et ses origines*, Paris 1953.

On the **cult of the martyrs**

H. DELEHAYE, ' *Sanctus* ', *essai sur le culte des saints dans l'antiquité* (Subs. hagiogr. 17), Brussells 1927.

———— *Les légendes hagiographiques* (Id. 18a), Brussells ⁴1955.

———— *Les origines du culte des martyrs* (Id. 20), Brussells ²1933.

For an **archaeologist's approach** to the subject

A. GRABER, *Martyrium, Recherches sur le culte des reliques et l'art chrétien antique*, Paris 1943-1946.

On **pilgrimages**

B. KÖTTING, *Peregrinatio religiosa, Wallfahrten in der Antiken und des Pilgerwesen in der alten Kirche*, Münster i. W. 1950.

CHAPTER 25

Here again the book by GAUDEMET provides a good introduction.

The **Christian Emperor** : see the works recommended in Chapter 16.

For **Constantine's successors**

J. MOREAU, ' Constantinus II, Constantius II, Constans ' : *Jahrbuch für Antike und Christentum*, 2 (1959), p. 160-184.

J. BIDEZ, *La vie de l'empereur Julien*, Paris 1930.

A. ALFÖLFI, *A conflict of Ideas in the Late Roman Empire : the Clash between the Senate and Valentinian I*, Oxford 1952.

W. ENSSLIN, ' Die Religionspolitik des Kaisers Theodosius d. Gr.' *(Sitz. Ber. Bayer. Akad. Wiss. München, phil.-hist. Kl, 1953, 2)*.

On the thorny question of **Christian influence on Imperial legislation**, see

J. GAUDEMET, *op. cit.*, p. 507-513.

B. BIONDI, *Il diritto romano cristiano*, I, Milan 1952-1953.

On the **Christian attitude to war**, the following book should be used with caution

J. M. HORNUS, *Evangile et Labarum, Etude sur l'attitude du Christianisme primitif devant les problèmes de l'Etat, de la guerre et de la violence*, Geneva 1960.

On the disappearance of **gladiatorial shows**

G. VILLE, ' Les jeux de gladiateurs dans l'Empire chrétien '; *Mélanges d'Archéologie et d'Histoire* (1960) p. 273-335.

CHAPTER 26

The **East-West division** is treated in :

H. I. MARROU, ' La place du haut moyen âge dans l'histoire du Christianisme : Il passagio dall' antichità al medioevo in Occidente, *(Settimane di Studio d. Centro Ital. di Stud. sull'Alto Medioevo, 9)*, Spoleto 1962, p. 595-630.

On the **collapse of Illyricum**

A. ALFÖLDI, *Der Untergang der Römerherrschaft in Pannonien*, (Ungarische Bibliothek, I, 10 & 12), Berlin 1924-1926.

——————— ' Tracce del Cristianesimo nell'epoca delle grandi migrazioni in Ungheria ' : *Quaderni dell'Impero*, III, 2, Rome 1938.

CHAPTER 27

The difficult and extremely complex **Christological questions** discussed in this and the two following chapters have been treated in the following work by scholars from various countries :

A. GRILLMEIER and H. BACHT, *Das Konzil von Chalkedon, Geschichte und Gegenwart*, 1-2, Würzburg 1951-1953, ²1959.

For the **philosophical ideas** utilised by theologians there is no reliable guide, though there are useful pages in the often controversial book by :

H. A. WOLFSON, *The Philosophy of the Church Fathers*, I, Cambridge, Mass. 1956, pp. 364-493, 599-600, ' The Mystery of the Incarnation '.

Fortunately, there is a very reliable first chapter in the book :

A. GRILLMEIER, ' *Die theologische und sprachliche Vorbereitung der christologischen Formel von Chalkedon* ' : I, p. 5-202.

On ' **Arian** ' **Christology** (in reality, the Christology of Asterios the Sophist), *art cit.*, p. 68-77.

The evidence of **Eustathius of Antioch** is in :

M. SPANNEUT, ' Recherches sur les écrits d'Eustache d'Antioche ' : *Mém. et Trav. Fac. Cathol. de Lille*, 55, Lille 1948, p. 100, No. 15.

On **Didymus the Blind**, see

A. GESCHÉ, *La christologie du " Commentaire sur les Psaumes " découvert à Tours,* Gembloux 1962.

For **Apollinaris,** the sources are collected in

H. LIETZMANN, *Apollinaris von Laodicea und seine Schule, Texte und Untersuchungen,* Tübingen 1904. The introduction gives the history of Apollinaris and his school.

For the theological aspect see

M. RICHARD, ' L'introduction du mot " hypostase " dans la théologie de l'Incarnation ' : *Mél. de Sc. Rel.*, 2 (1945), p. 5-32.

H. DE RIEDMATTEN, ' La christologie d'Apollinaire de Laodicée ' : *Studia Patristica 2* (Texte und Unters. 64), Berlin 1957, p. 208-234.

On the reaction of the **Cappadocians**

M. RICHARD, *art. cit.*, p. 12-21 (see above).

And a selection of writings in an English translation

E. R. HARDY and C. C. RICHARDSON, *Christology of the Later Fathers* (The Library of Christian Classics, 4), London 1954.

On **Diodorus of Tarsus**

A. GRILLMEIER, *art. cit.*, p. 136-144 (see this bibliography, p. 485).

With the appearance of the **Christological School of Antioch,** the ground becomes more treacherous : these old disputes are difficult to interpret because theologians today are themselves divided over the same problems; for example, concerning the work of DEODAT DE BASLY OFM., (1863-1937) who was a firm supporter of the formula renewed at Antioch : *Assumptus Homo.* The general tendency of Catholic historians today — though they are not followed by all theologians — is to restore the reputation of the School of Antioch (Diodorus, Theodore of Mopsuestia, Theodoret) which suffered in the eyes of posterity from Monophysite calumnies and the tactics of the Neo-Chalcedonians during the reign of the Emperor Justinian.

Difficulties arise first of all at the level of philology : all too often the writings which are debated today have come down in the form of extracts in collections of anthologies compiled in a polemical spirit. It is difficult to know which of these extracts preserve the true spirit of the authors who were hated by the ' Monophysites ' and praised by later ' Nestorians ', and which have been deliberately distorted. The question arises for Diodorus — see the bibliography in GRILLMEIER; and *a fortiori* for Theodore of Mopsuestia. The views of critics concerning the relative value of the **Greek and Latin anthologies** and of the **Syriac traditions** in

R. DEVREESSE, ' Essai sur Théodore de Mopsueste ', *Studi e Testi, 141,* Vatican 1948,

M. RICHARD, ' La tradition des fragments du traité *de Incarnatione* de Théodore de Mopsueste ' : *Museon*, 46 (1943), p. 55-75.

As a contrast see

F. A. SULLIVAN, ' The Christology of Theodore of Mopsuestia ', *Analecta Gregoriana* 82, Rome 1956.

And the slightly less advanced position taken by

J. MacKenzie, 'Annotations on the Christology of Theodore of Mopsuestia':
Theological Studies 19 (1958), p. 345-373.
On top of all this, there are the theological divergencies. The point of view of those historians who believe it necessary to revise the decision of 553 is put forward with moderation in

E. Amann, 'Théodore de Mopsueste': DTC. 15, I (1946), col. 235-279; Nestorius, I, ibid., XI, I (1931), col. 76-157.

Th. Camelot, ' De Nestorius à Eutychès, l'opposition de deux christologies '.

A. Grillmeier and H. Bacht, Das Konzil von Chalcedon, I, p. 213-229.
On the other hand, the anti-' Nestorian ' viewpoint, that held by Justinian's contemporaries, has recently been defended by

P. Parente, ' Una reabilitazione de Teodore Mopsuestano ': Doctor Communis, 1950, p. 24-29, and especially by his pupil

H. Diepen, ' Sur les notions doctrinales opposées à Apollinaire ': Rev. Thom. 51 (1951), p. 553-572;

————— ' L'Assumptus Homo à Chalcédoine ', ibid., p. 573-608;

————— Douze dialogues de christologie ancienne, Rome 1960;

————— La théologie de l'Emmanuel, les lignes maîtresses d'une Christologie, Bruges 1960. Diepen's defence is energetic but not, apparently, convincing; the publication of his book

————— Les Trois Chapitres au concile de Chalcédoine, Oosterhout 1953, aroused sharp controversy : see for example

M. Richard, ' A propos d'un ouvrage récent sur le concile de Chalcédoine ', MSR, XI (1954), p. 89-92.

J. Daniélou, Review in RSR, 43 (1955), p. 595-597.

H. Diepen, ' Théodoret et le dogme d'Ephèse ', ibid., 44 (1956) p. 243-247.

J. Daniélou, ' Réplique ', ibid., p. 247-248.

CHAPTER 28

On St. Cyril of Alexandria

G. Jouassard, ' Cyrill von Alexandrien ', RAC, 3 (1956), col. 499-516.
But Cyril's complex character, like the interpretation of his thought and its development, has given rise to controversy

J. Liebaert, La doctrine christologique de saint Cyrille d'Alexandrie avant la querelle nestorienne, Lille 1951.

A. Grillmeier, art. cit., p. 165-182 (see this bibliography, p. 485).

P. Galtier, ' L'unio secundum hypostatin chez saint Cyrille ': Gregorianum, 33 (1952), p. 351-398.

G. Jouassard, ' Saint Cyrille d'Alexandrie et le schéma de l'Incarnation " Verbe-Chair " ': RSR, 44 (1956), p. 234-242 (corrects Grillmeier).

H. Diepen, Aux origines de l'anthropologie de saint Cyrille d'Alexandrie, Bruges 1957 (takes a different view from Liebaert and Jouassard).

On the Council of Ephesus

The sources have been collected and critically edited in

E. Schwartz, Acta Conciliorum Oecumenicorum, I (in 5 vol.), Berlin 1922-1930.
Introductory articles

R. Devreesse, ' Les Actes du Concile d'Ephèse ': RSPT, 19 (1929), p. 223-242, 408-431

P. GALTIER, ' Le Centenaire d'Ephèse : Les Actes du Concile, Rome et le Concile ' : *RSR*, 21 (1931) p. 169-197.
On the men who took part in the Council
E. GERLAND and V. LAURENT, *Corpus Notitiarum Episcopatuum Ecclesiae Orientalis Græcæ*, I, *Les Listes conciliaires*, 2, Kadiköy 1936, p. 15-97.
For the **period between Ephesus and Chalcedon**
A. GRILLMEIER, *art. cit.*, Grillmeier-Bacht, I, p. 159-202.
TH. CAMELOT, *art. cit.*, Grillmeier-Bacht, I, p. 229-242.
M. RICHARD, ' Proclus de Constantinople et le Théopaschisme ', *RHE*, 38 (1942), p. 303-331.
W. ELERT, ' Die theopaschitische Formel ' : *Theol. Lit. Zeit.*, 75 (1950) col. 195-206.
On the **Council of Chalcedon**
As with Ephesus, the sources have been collected and carefully edited by
E. SCHWARTZ, *Acta Conciliorum Oecumenicorum*, II (in 6 vol.), Berlin 1932-1938.
Once again, see the collection by
A. GRILLMEIER and H. BACHT, *Das Konzil von Chalkedon*, especially Vol. I, *Der Glaube von Chalkedon*, Würzburg 1951, ²1959.

CHAPTERS 29 AND 30

Again, see GRILLMEIER-BACHT, notably Section IV, ' Der theologische Kampf um Chalkedon ', I, p. 419-768; and ' Chalkedon als geschichtliche Wende ', II, p. 3-314.
In the same work
J. LEBON, ' La christologie du monophysisme sévérien ', II, p. 425-480, which brings up to date his thesis
——— *Le Monophysisme sévérien, étude historique, littéraire et théologique*, Louvain 1909.
See also
R. DRAGUET, *Julien d'Halicarnasse et sa controverse avec Sévère d'Antioche sur l'incorruptibilité du corps du Christ*, Louvain 1924.
On **Egypt**
J. MASPERO, *Histoire des patriarches d'Alexandrie (518-616)*, Paris 1923.
E. HONIGMANN, ' Juvenal und Jerusalem ' : *Dumbarton Oaks Papers* (1950), p. 211-279.
On the **Scythian monks** and ' **Neo-Chalcedonianism** '
CH. MOELLER, ' Le chalcédonisme et le néo-chalcédonisme en Orient de 451 à la fin du VIᵉ siècle ', in GRILLMEIER-BACHT, I, p. 637-720.
For the difficult **problems of literary history** see
F. LOOFS, *Leontius von Byzanz und die gleichnamigen Schriftsteller der griechischen Kirche : TU* 31, 1-2, Leipzig 1887, which lumps the four personnages into one and is sharply criticised by
M. RICHARD, ' Léonce de Jérusalem et Léonce de Byzance ' : *MSR*, I (1944), p. 35-88, which distinguishes them.
For the disputes of the **Three Chapters** and the **Ecumenical Council of 553**
E. AMANN, ' Trois Chapitres (Affaire des) ' : *DTC*, IV, 2 (1950), col. 1868-1924. I have followed this prudent, balanced account of the complex question and consider valid only the first decision of Pope Vigilius, that of the Constitution of 14 May 553. AMANN's conclusions are supported by
CH. MOELLER, *art. cit.*, Grillmeier-Bacht, I, p. 687-690.

The opposite point of view, which considers valid all the decisions taken by the Fifth Council under Justinian's influence, is held by
H. DIEPEN, ' Sur les notions doctrinales opposées à Apollinaire ', *Rev. Thom.*, 51 (1951), p. 553-572. This point of view was taken by the anti-Roman Byzantine lawyers. See
R. DEVREESSE, ' Le cinquième concile et l'œcuménicité byzantine ' : *Mélanges G. Mercati* III (Studi e Testi 123), Rome 1946, p. 1-15.
The publication of a critical edition of the sources was never completed
E. SCHWARTZ, *ACO*, IV, 2, Strasbourg 1914.

On the **Jacobite Church**
A. VAN ROEY, ' Les débuts de l'Eglise jacobite ' : GRILLMEIER-BACHT, II, p. 339-360.
E. HONIGMANN, *Evêques et Evêchés monophysites dans l'Asie antérieure au VIe siècle :* CSCO 127 (Subsidia 2), Louvain 1951.

CHAPTER 31

In addition to the bibliography for Chapter 21, see, for the **Persian Church**
W. DE VRIES, ' Die syrisch-nestorianische Haltung zu Chalkedon ', in GRILLMEIER-BACHT, I, p. 603-635.

For **Armenia** and the **Caucasus**
V. INGLISIAN, ' Chalkedon und die armenische Kirche ', *ibid.*, II, p. 361-417.
G. GARITTE, *La ' Narratio de rebus Armeniae '*, critical edition and commentary : CSCO 132 (Subsidia 4), Louvain 1951.
M. VAN ESBROEK, ' Chronique arménienne ' : *An. Boll.*, 80 (1962) p. 439-440.

For the **Yemen**
R. AIGRAIN, ' Arabie, VII-IX ' : *Dict. Hist. et Géogr. Ecclés.*, III (1922) col. 1233-1260.

CHAPTER 32

The main sources on **Eastern monasticism in the 5th and 6th centuries** are given in the text.
On the biographies of Cyril of Scythopolis
E. SCHWARTZ, ' Kyrillos von Skythopolis, Texte, Bemerkungen ' : *TU* 49, 2, Berlin 1939, with the important reviews by
F. DÖLGER, *BZ*, 40 (1940), p. 474-484.
E. STEIN, *An. Boll.*, 62 (1944), p. 169-186.

Two classics, now somewhat dated
J. PARGOIRE, *L'Eglise byzantine de 527 à 847*, Paris ³1923.
P. VAN CAUWENBERGH, *Etude sur les moines d'Egypte depuis le concile de Chalcédoine (451) jusqu'à l'invasion arabe (640)*, Paris 1914.

See the modern works
A. VÖÖBUS, *History of Asceticism in the Syrian Orient*, I-II: CSCO 184 (Subsidia 14, 17,) Louvain 1958, 1960.
A. J. FESTUGIÈRE, *Les moines d'Orient, II : Les moines de la région de Constantinople*, Paris 1961 (a translation, with notes, of the Lives of Hypatios and Daniel the Stylite).

On the Stylites

H. DELEHAYE, *Les saints stylites* (Subsidia Hagiographica, 14), Brussells 1923.

P. PEETERS, ' Saint Syméon le stylite et ses premiers biographes ' : *An. Boll.*, 61 (1943), p. 29-71.

A. J. FESTUGIÈRE, *Antioche païenne et chrétienne*, Paris 1959, p. 347-401.

For Origenism among the monks of Palestine

A. GUILLAUMONT, *Les ' Kephalia Gnostica ' d'Evagre le Pontique et l'histoire de l'origénisme*, Patristica Sorbonensia 5, Paris 1962.

On Messalianism

H. DÖRRIES, *Symeon von Mesopotamien, die Ueberlieferung des Messalianischen ' Makarius '-Schriften*, TU 55, Leipzig 1941.

E. KLOSTERMANN and H. BERTHOLD, *Neue Homilien des Makarius Symeon*, I, (*Ibid.*, 72), Berlin 1961.

Also the bibliography in ALTANER, *Patrologie*, p. 236.

For its doctrine

I. HAUSSHER, ' L'erreur fondamentale et la logique du Messalianisme ' : *Orientalia Christ. Period. I* (1935), p. 328-368.

For a general understanding of Eastern monasticism, the short but profound article :

C. LIALINE, ' Monachisme oriental et monachisme occidental ', *Irénikon*, 22 (1960), p. 435-459.

See also by way of contrast a Western view

A. J. FESTUGIÈRE, *Les moines d'Orient. I, Culture ou Sainteté*, Paris 1961.

CHAPTER 33

On the Empire under Justinian

E. STEIN, *Histoire du Bas-Empire, II, De la disparition de l'Empire d'Occident à la mort de Justinien (476-565)*, Paris 1949.

On the philosophical movement, a short sketch

H. I. MARROU, *Synesius of Cyrene and Alexandrian Neoplatonism : The Conflict between Paganism and Christianity in the Fourth Century*, London 1963, p. 126-150.

More detailed studies

E. EVRARD, ' Les convictions religieuses de Jean Philopon et la date de son commentaire aux " Météorologiques " ' : *Acad. Roy. de Belgique, Bull. Class. des Lettres*, Ve S., 39 (1953), p. 299-357.

H. D. SAFFREY, ' Le chrétien Jean Philopon et la survivance de l'Ecole d'Alexandrie au VIe siècle ' : *REG*, 67 (1954) p. 512-517.

On Justinian as a theologian

E. SCHWARTZ, *Zur Kirchenpolitik Justinians :* Gesamm. Schriften, IV, p. 276-328.

CH. MOELLER, ' Le chalcédonisme et le néo-chalcédonisme ' in A. GRILLMEIER and H. BACHT, *Das Konzil von Chalkedon*, Würzburg ²1959, I, p. 679-680.

CHAPTER 34

On Byzantium in general :

J. PARGOIRE, *L'Eglise byzantine de 527 à 847*, Paris ³1923, is now out of date. The following are unsatisfactory

L. Bréhier, *Les institutions de l'Empire Byzantin* (Le Monde Byzantin II), Paris 1949, p. 430-579 (Church institutions).
————— *La civilisation byzantine* (Le Monde Byzantin III), Paris 1950, p. 231-570 (Spiritual and intellectual life).
An excellent text-book

H. G. Beck, *Kirche und theologische Literatur im byzantinischen Reich* (Byzantinisches Handbuch in Rahmen des Handbuchs der Altertumswissenschaft, II, I) Munich 1959.

On the **patriarchs and the primacy of Rome,** see the studies in

A. Grillmeier and H. Bacht, *Das Konzil von Chalkedon*, Würzburg ²1959, section V, C : *Chalkedon und die Beziehungen zwischen Rom und Byzanz*, II, p. 433-562.

F. Dvornik, *The Idea of Apostolicity in Byzantium and the Legend of the Apostle Andrew*, Cambridge (Mass.) 1958.

On the Church in **Illyricum**

L. Duchesne, *Autonomies ecclésiastiques, Eglises séparées*, Paris 1896, p. 229-279.

J. Gaudemet, *L'Eglise dans l'Empire romain*, Paris 1958, p. 403-407.

For the **development of the Byzantine liturgy,** see the works mentioned in the bibliography of Chapter 24.

On **Romanos Melodus**

E. Wellecz, *A History of Byzantine music and hymnography*, Oxford 1949.

On the origin of the **cult of icons**

A. Grabar, *L'iconoclasme byzantin, dossier archéologique*, Paris 1957, p. 13-91.

E. Kitzinger, ' The Cult of Images in the age before Iconoclasm ', *Dumbarton Oaks Papers*, 8 (1954), p. 83-150.

CHAPTER 35

A good general study of **Pelagianism**

G. de Plinval, *Pélage, ses écrits, sa vie et sa réforme, étude d'histoire littéraire et religieuse*, Lausanne 1943, and the summary made by the author in

A. Fliche and V. Martin, *Histoire de l'Eglise*, IV, Paris 1937, p. 79-128, 397-419.

On the role of Cassian

O. Chadwick, *John Cassian*, Cambridge 1950, p. 109-138.

Faustus of Riez and Claudianus Mammertus

E. L. Fortin, *Christianisme et culture philosophique au Vᵉ siècle : la querelle de l'âme humaine en Occident*, Paris 1959.

CHAPTER 36

For the **barbarian invasions** in general

P. Courcelle, *Histoire littéraire des grandes invasions germaniques*, Paris 1948.

On **St Severinus and Noricum**

R. Noll, *Das Leben des hl. Severin, lateinisch und deutsch mit Kommentar, Einleitung und Anhang : Denkmäler des frühen Christentums in Oesterreich*, Linz 1947.

On the missions of **St Germain d'Auxerre in Britain**

N. K. Chadwick, *Poetry and Letters in Early Christian Gaul*, London 1955, p. 240-274 (rather hypercritical).

492 THE CHRISTIAN CENTURIES : VOLUME I

On the **Vandal persecution**

CHR. COURTOIS, *Victor de Vita et son œuvre, étude critique*, Algiers 1954. (A pointlessly unfavourable view, not born out by the evidence put forward.)

—————— *Les Vandales et l'Afrique*, Paris 1955, p. 289-323. (biased)

On the **Visigothic monarchy**

E. A. THOMPSON, 'The Conversion of the Visigoths to Catholicism': *Nottingham Mediaeval Studies*, 4 (1960), p. 4-35.

J. N. HILLGARTH, 'La conversion de los Visigodos, notas criticas': *Anal. sacra Tarracon.*, 34 (1961), p. 21-46.

CHAPTER 37

A detailed picture of the **cultural development** at the end of the patristic period in the West.

P. RICHE, *Education et culture dans l'Occident barbare, Vᵉ-VIIIᵉ siècles*, Patristica Sorbonensis, 4, Paris 1962.

Il Passaggio dell'antichità al medioevo in Occidente, Settimane di Studio del Centro Ital. di St. sull'alto medioevo, IX, Spoleto 1962.

On **St Leo**

T. JALLAND, *The Life and Times of Saint Leo the Great*, London 1941.

H. RAHNER, 'Leo der Grosse, der Papst des Konzils', in A. GRILLMEIER and H. BACHT, *Das Konzil von Chalkedon*, I, p. 323-339.

P. GALTIER, 'Saint Cyrille d'Alexandrie et saint Léon le Grand à Chalcédoine', *ibid.*, I, p. 341-418.

P. HOFMANN, 'Der Kampf der Päpste um Konzil und Dogma von Chalkedon, I : Leo der Grosse', *ibid.*, II, p. 15-35.

The **Growth of Bishoprics**

See the studies, by regions, listed in the bibliography to Chapter 21.

The **Problem of Rural Parishes**

P. GAUDEMET, *L'Eglise et l'Empire romain*, Paris 1958, p. 368-377.

Christian Life

H. G. BECK, *The Pastoral Care of Souls in South-East France during the Sixth Century* (Analecta Gregoriana, 51), Rome 1950.

J. P. ALONSO, *La cura pastoral en la España romanovisigoda*, Rome 1955, public. del Ist. Esp. de Est. Eclesiasticos, Monographia, nᵒ 2, Rome 1955.

On **Western Monasticism**

Il monachesimo nell'alto medioevo e la formazione della civiltà occidentale, Settimane di Studio sull'alto medioevo, IV, Spoleto 1957.

'Théologie de la vie monastique, études sur la tradition patristique', *Théologie*, 49, Paris 1961.

On the relationship between '**Regula Magistri**' and the **Benedictine Rule**

G. PENCO, *S. Benedicti Regula, introduzione, testo, apparati, traduzione e commento*, Bibl. di studi super., 39, Florence 1958.

M. D. KNOWLES, *Great Historical Enterprises*, Edinburgh 1963, section on 'Regula Magistri'. For full bibliography see *American Benedictine Review*, X (1959) 86-106.

On the **cult of the saints and the liturgy**, see the bibliography to Chapter 21; for the **religious and literary value** of the Roman liturgy I have followed

CHR. MOHRMANN, *Liturgical Latin, its origins and character*, Washington 1957.

CHAPTER 38

On the **Visigothic renaissance**

J. FONTAINE, *Isidore de Séville et la culture classique dans l'Espagne wisigothique,* Paris 1959.

On the repercussions of the **Three Chapters dispute** in the West

G. BARDY, ' La répercussion des controverses christologiques en Occident entre le concile de Chalcédoine et la mort de l'empereur Anastase (451-518) ', in A. GRILLMEIER and H. BACHTE, *Das Konzil von Chalkedon*, II, p. 771-789.

A. GRILLMEIER, ' Vorbereitung des Mittelalters. Studie über das Verhältnis von Chalkedonismus und Neu-Chalkedonismus in der lateinischen Theologie von Boethius bis zu Gregor d. Gr. ', *ibid.*, II, p. 791-839.

On **St Gregory the Great**

H. DUDDEN, *Gregory the Great, his place in History and in Thought*, London 1905.

C. BUTLER, *Western Mysticism, the Teaching of SS. Augustine, Gregory and Bernard on Contemplation and Contemplative Life*, London ²1927, was the first to do justice to the originality and historical importance of St Gregory's mystical theology. A later book is

M. FRICKEL, ' *Deus totus ubique simul* ', *Untersuchungen zur allgemeinen Gottesgegenwart im Rahmen des Gotteslehre Gregors des Grossen*, Freiburg 1956.

On his **political doctrine and role**

H. X. ARQUILLIÈRE, *L'Augustinisme politique, essai sur la formation des théories politiques du moyen âge*, Paris 1934.

On the Church's **charitable works** and the **institution of the diaconate**

H. I. MARROU, ' L'origine orientale des diaconies romaines ' : *Mélanges d'Archéologie et d'Hist.*, 57 (1940), p. 95-142.

A. P. FRUTAZ, ' Diaconia ' : *Enciclop. Cattol.*, IV (1950), col. 1521-1535.

On the **recruitment of Gaulish bishops** in the sixth century

K. F. STROHEKER, *Der senatorische Adel im spätantiken Gallien*, Tübingen 1948.

On **St Radegunde**

Etudes Mérovingiennes, Actes des Journées de Poitiers, 1-3 Mai 1952, Paris 1953.

On the ' **suffering saints** '

H. I. MARROU, ' Ammien Marcellin et les " Innocents " de Milan : Mélanges J. Lebreton, II ' *RSR* 40, 1952, Paris 1952, p. 179-190.

On **trial by ordeal and duels**

H. LECLERCQ, ' Duel judiciaire ' : *DACL* IV, 2, col. 1660-1670 (1921).

————— ' Ordalie ', *ibid.*, XII, 2 (1936), col. 2377-2390.

On **oaths**

PH. HOFMEISTER, *Die christliche Eidesform, eine liturgische und rechtsgeschichtliche Untersuchung*, Munich 1957.

CHAPTER 39

The **cultural reconquest of Northern Gaul** by the Aquitanians

P. RICHE, *Education et culture dans l'Occident barbare*, Paris 1962, p. 257-258.

Aquileia and the Carinthian churches

G. C. MENIS, *La basilica paleocristiana nelle diocesi settentrionali della metropoli di Aquileia (Studi di Ant. Crist. 24)*, Vatican 1958.

Christianity in Wales during the ' sub-Roman ' period

J. D. LLOYD, *A History of Wales from the earliest times to the Edwardian conquest*, I, London ²1912.

A. W. WADE-EVANS, *Vitae Sanctorum Britanniae et Genealogiae*, Cardiff 1944, of doubtful value because based on later hagiography.

V. E. NASH-WILLIAMS, *The Early Christian Monuments of Wales*, Cardiff 1950, is based on inscriptions, and more reliable.

For **Scotland**

W. D. SIMPSON, *Saint Ninian and the origins of the Christian Church in Scotland*, Edinburgh 1940, uses traditional evidence; for the foundation of Candida Casa he gives a date which is difficult to defend against the objections raised by

P. GROSJEAN, ' Les Pictes apostats dans l'Epître de saint Patrice ' : *An. Boll.*, 76 (1958), p. 354-378, whose conclusions I have followed.

Britain from the Roman to the Anglo-Saxon periods

D. WHITELOCK, *English Historical Documents*, I, c. 500-1042 : London, 1955; and for a short survey :

C. J. GODFREY, *The Church in Anglo-Saxon England*, Cambridge 1962.

R. G. COLLINGWOOD and J. N. L. MYERS, *Roman Britain and the English settlements* (Oxford History of England, I), Oxford 1936.

The apostolate of **St Patrick** : many startling hypotheses (such as the identification of Palladius with Patrick) have now been abandoned. A good discussion — but with a tendency to accept what is merely hypothetical :

L. BIELER, *The Life and Legend of St Patrick, Problems of Modern Scholarship*, Dublin 1949. This return to a traditional point of view is supported by arguments from **philology**

CHR. MOHRMANN, *The Latin of Saint Patrick*, Dublin 1961.

Celtic Christianity

L. GOUGAUD, *Christianity in Celtic Lands*, London 1932 (revised edition of an earlier French work : *Les chrétientés celtiques*, Paris 1911).

For more recent research see

Notes d'hagiographie celtique published by P. GROSJEAN in *An. Boll.* since 1945; notably

P. GROSJEAN, ' Edition et commentaire du " Catalogue sanctorum Hiberniae secundum diversa tempora " ou " De tribus ordinibus sanctorum Hiberniae " ' : *An. Boll.*, 73 (1955), p. 197-213, 289-322.

Early practices of the **Celtic Churches**

L. GOUGAUD, *Devotional and ascetic Practices in the Middle Ages*, London 1927.

————— ' Mulierum consortia, étude sur le syneisaktisme chez les ascètes celtiques ' : *Eriu* IX, 1923, p. 147-156.

The Growth of **Private Confession**

B. POSCHMANN, *Busse und letzte Oelung*, in M. SCHMAUS, J. R. GEISELMANN, K. RAHNER, *Handbuch der Dogmengeschichte*, IV, 3, Freiburg 1951.

C. VOGEL, *La discipline pénitentielle en Gaule des origines à la fin du VIIᵉ siècle*, Paris 1952.

I. LAPORTE, *Le Pénitentiel de saint Colomban, introduction et édition critique*, Monumenta Christiana Selecta, IV, Tournai 1958.

The apostolate of **the Scotti outside Ireland**

L. GOUGAUD, *Les Saints irlandais hors d'Irlande*, Louvain 1936.

On **St Colombanus**

Mélanges colombaniens, Actes du Congrès International de Luxeuil, 20-23 Juillet 1950, Paris 1951.

INDEXES

INDEX OF JEWISH NON-BIBLICAL REFERENCES

501

VI 37
42
IX 4
6
12

IRENAEUS
Adv. Haer.
I 19
23
24
25
26
27
28
30

II 22
III 3
4
IV 1
3
6
17
33
V 20
33

Demonstratio
10

JEROME
De Vir. Illustr.
76

Letters
15, 16

Quest. Gen.
I 1

JUSTIN

I Apology
XV
XVI 1-3
XXVI
XXVI 4
5
7
LVIII
LXI 2
LXV 1
LXVII 2
LXVIII 6
10

Dialogue
XXXVI 5-6

2 99
2 99
58
57
150

63
3 19, 61
8 62
2 62
4 65
1 64
2 56, 57
3 59
1-2 98
2-4 98
60
63
5 63
11 63
59 41
4 41, 59
3 98
1 41
1 41
2 98
4 79
3 135
1 110
4 40, 41

77

210

264 n. 1

78

121
18
60
61
98
88
74
67, 69
74
74
87
87

78

XLVII 1 45
XLVIII 4 56
LI 3 78
LXX 4 20
LXXII 4 79
LXXX 4 17
LXXXI 3-4 122
XC 5 79
XCI 2 79
C 4 78

MARTYRDOM OF PERPETUA
X 6-7 125
9 125
14 125

MARTYRDOM OF POLYCARP
III 1 125
XII 2 125
XVIII 124

METHODIUS
Convivium
IX 1 122

MINUCIUS FELIX
Octavius
IX 1 166
6 87
XXXI 1-2 87

ORIGEN
Contra Celsum
II 17 56
III 51 159

De Oratione
XXVIII 4 163
XXXI 5 166

Hom. Ex.
III 1 165
XII 13 165
XIII 3 164

Hom. Gen.
X 1 165

Hom. Jos.
X 1 165

Hom. Jud.
VI 2 177

Hom. Lev.
IV 3 165
VIII 11 162

POLYCARP
Philippians
IV 34 118

510　　THE CHRISTIAN CENTURIES : VOLUME I

Köster, H., 52 n. 56, 69 n. 2
Kretschmar, G., 49 n. 49, 76 n. 54, 184 n. 3, 188 n. 14, 218 n. 16
Kuebler, R., 231 n. 1

Labriolle, Père de, 88 n. 18
Lactantius, 86, 232, 291
Langerbeck, 183
Laodicaea, 36, 40, 43, 44, 75, 211, 219, 261, 262, 336
Leo the Gt, pope, 334, 348, 349, 350, 358, 361, 366, 372, 392, 414, 415, 423-4, 426-7, 431-2, 438, 439
Leo, emp., 355, 357, 388, 397
Leo III, emp., 400
Leonardi, C., 147 n. 21
Leich, P., 170 n. 22
Lérins, 278, 406, 407, 408, 426, 427, 428, 429, 435
Liberius, pope, 258, 260
Lybia, 250
Licinius, 234, 235, 236, 249, 256
Linus, 51
Lohmeyer, E., 18
Lohse, B., 75 n. 52, 105 n. 33
London, 225, 452
Lösch, S., 23 n. 21
Lot, 21
Lucian of Antioch, 211, 212, 217, 249, 251
Lucian of Samosata, 61, 88, 93, 94
Lucius of Cyrene, 26
Luke, St, 3, 4, 5, 7, 11, 15, 24, 26, 27, 32, 76, 317
Lundberg, P., 70 n. 14, 147 n. 22
Lundström, S., 195 n. 31
Lycaonia, 27, 28, 105
Lydia, 13, 83, 384
Lyons, 89, 101, 103, 110, 111, 194, 406, 408, 415, 422, 423, 427, 428, 431, 446
Lystra, 27, 28, 30, 32

Macarius (St) of Egypt, 380
Macedonia, 26, 32, 33, 36, 51, 392
Magnentius, 258
Magnesia 43, 44
Malchion, 212, 213, 217, 218
Manaen, 12, 26
Mandouze, A., 197 n. 35, 201 n. 41
Manes, 186, 192-4
Marcellinus, pope, 108, 233
Marcellus of Ancyra, 251, 252, 254, 256, 257, 258, 260, 263
Marcian, emp., 348, 349, 350, 353, 355, 387
Marcion, 51, 92, 98, 100, 101, 104, 105, 107, 108, 109, 152, 189
Marcus Aurelius, 87, 88, 89, 91, 92, 93, 108, 109, 137, 141
Mark, St, 12, 26, 33, 51
Mark, pope, 430
Mark the Magus, 40, 99, 100

Marot, N., 110 n. 39, 195 n. 32
Marrou, H. I., 92 n. 25, 139 n. 7, 177 n. 32
Martimont, A.-G., 147 n. 20
Martin (St) of Tours, 278, 279, 296, 303, 305, 319, 428, 447
Mary, Blessed Virgin, 56, 59, 93, 122, 253, 338, 340, 343, 395, 396, 397-8, 430
Mary Magdalene, 45
Mary, mother of St Mark, 12
Mathias, high priest, 8
Maurice, emp., 367, 370, 372, 373, 389, 398, 444
Maxentius, 234, 235, 236, 243
Maximianus, 230, 233, 234
Maximinus, 109, 140, 184, 205
Maximinus Daia, 233, 234, 235
Maximus, 265, 293, 295
Maximus of Tyre, 129, 131, 135, 182
Media, 192
Mediterranean, 21, 225, 289
Meinhold, P., 42 n. 19
Melito, bp of Sardis, 44, 72, 82, 91, 93, 94, 95, 103, 106, 107, 109, 112 n. 43, 129, 148, 152, 169, 170, 186, 188, 197
Menander, 60, 61-2, 64, 65
Mensurius, bp of Carthage, 233
Mesopotamia, 39, 104, 108, 142, 224, 282, 283, 370, 372, 377, 380
Messina, G., 194 n. 28
Methodius, bp of Olympus, 209, 214
Meyer, A., 7 n. 5
Milan, 194, 236, 246, 258, 265, 266, 278, 288, 293, 295, 299, 305, 306, 312, 316, 317, 427, 431, 437
Miletus, 33, 213, 387
Miltiades, pope, 246
Miltiades, apologist, 91, 92, 152
Minucius Felix, 88, 149, 155, 156
Minucius Fundanus, 87
Mithra, 229
Molland, E., 30, 42 n. 19, 124 n. 32
Monica, St, 305
Montanus, 100-3, 104, 135
Monte Cassino, 429
Mohrmann, C., 150 n. 27, 157 n. 40
Moreau, J., 83 nn. 8, 10, 137 n. 1, 141 n. 11, 154 n. 31
Moses, 37, 55, 56, 79, 132, 170, 318, 397, 439
Moses bp of Adiabene, 48
Mycia, 32

Nag Hammadi, 3, 9, 40, 47, 49, 63, 64, 99, 100, 127
Naples, 169, 225, 412, 435, 436
Narcissus, bp of Jerusalem, 46, 109
Nau, F., 189 n. 18
Nautin, P., 98 n. 9, 109 n. 38, 138 n. 2, 139 n. 8, 144 n. 16, 145 n. 19, 163 n. 6, 184 n. 4, 187 nn. 11, 13, 199 n. 38, 210 n. 6, 214 n. 9

Part I : De Licentia Superiorum Ordinis.
Parts I and II : Nihil obstat : Joannes M. T. Barton, S.T.D., L.S.S., Censor Deputatus.
Imprimatur: ✠Georgius L. Craven, Epis. Sebastopolis, Westmonasterii, die 16a Julii,
1963.   The Nihil obstat and Imprimatur are a declaration that a book or pamphlet is
considered to be free from doctrinal or moral error.   It is not implied that those who
have granted the Nihil obstat and Imprimatur agree with the contents, opinions or
statements expressed.

Printed in Belgium by DESCLÉE & Cie, ÉDITEURS, S. A., Tournai — 6.528